THE ROUGH

Tunisia

There are more than two hundred Rough Guide titles
covering destinations from Alaska to Zimbabwe
and subjects from Acoustic Guitar to Travel Health

Forthcoming travel guides include
The Algarve • The Bahamas • Cambodia • Caribbean Islands
Costa Brava • New York Restaurants • South America • Zanzibar

Forthcoming reference guides include
Children's Books • Online Travel • Videogaming • Weather

Rough Guides Online
www.roughguides.com

ROUGH GUIDE

Text editor: David Glen
Series editor: Mark Ellingham
Editorial: Martin Dunford, Jonathan Buckley, Jo Mead, Kate Berens, Ann-Marie Shaw, Helena Smith, Judith Bamber, Orla Duane, Olivia Eccleshall, Ruth Blackmore, Geoff Howard, Claire Saunders, Gavin Thomas, Alexander Mark Rogers, Polly Thomas, Joe Staines, Richard Lim, Duncan Clark, Peter Buckley, Sam Thorne, Lucy Ratcliffe, Clifton Wilkinson, Alison Murchie, Matthew Teller, Andrew Dickson (UK); Andrew Rosenberg, Stephen Timblin, Yuki Takagaki, Richard Koss (US)
Production: Susanne Hillen, Andy Hilliard, Link Hall, Helen Prior, Julia Bovis, Michelle Draycott, Katie

Pringle, ⋯ ⋯ es, Rachel Holmes, Andy Turne⋯
Cartography: ⋯ er, Maxine Repath, Ed Wright, Katie Lloyd-Jones
Picture research: Louise Boulton, Sharon Martins
Online: Kelly Cross, Anja Mutić-Blessing, Jennifer Gold, Audra Epstein, Suzanne Welles (US)
Finance: John Fisher, Gary Singh, Edward Downey, Mark Hall, Tim Bill
Marketing & Publicity: Richard Trillo, Niki Smith, David Wearn, Chloë Roberts, Claire Southern (UK); Simon Carloss, David Wechsler, Kathleen Rushforth (US)
Administration: Tania Hummel, Demelza Dallow, Julie Sanderson

ACKNOWLEDGEMENTS

The editor would like to thank Daniel and Simon for their dedicated work on this book, and Clifton Wilkinson for helping out in the closing stages. Many thanks also to Katie Pringle for typesetting and making it all work, Katie Lloyd-Jones for the maps, Karen Parker for proofreading and to Daniel again for the Arabic place names and the index.

Daniel: Thanks for help to Habib Aljan (Memory of the Earth Museum, Tataouine); Boukhris Amor (ONTT, Douz); Naceur Barka (Hôtel 20 Mars, Douz); Ahmed Barka (Nefzaoua Voyages, Douz); Ali Béchir (Syndicat d'Initiative, Tataouine); Abdellatif Belgacem; Abid Belgacem (Petit Prince, Douz); Habib Belhedi (Association des Amis de la Memoire de la Terre,

Tataouine); Kamel Rouissi (LOVA, Tozeur); Mustapha Sabri (ASNAPED); Mohamed Said (Magasin du Sahara, Tozeur); Arafat Sghaier (Amis du Camping, Kebili); Fathi Taleb and Melita Tilley. Also ONTT London, in particular Jacqui Gilchrist and Sophie Bouallegoa; ONTT Sousse; Syndicat d'Initiative, Matmata; Tunisian Investment and Trade Centre, London; Association de Sauvegarde de l'Île de Jerba; Résidence Karim, Tozeur. Continuing thanks for contributions to past editions to Charles Farr, Adrian Fozzard and Jens Finke.

Simon: Thanks to Arafat, Christine, Emmam, Magdy, Nabil, Omar Abdel Aziz, Rabbi, Sameh and Samir.

PUBLISHING INFORMATION

This sixth edition published November 2001 by Rough Guides Ltd, 62–70 Shorts Gardens, London WC2H 9AH.
Distributed by the Penguin Group:
Penguin Books Ltd, 80 Strand, London WC2R ORL.
Penguin Putnam, Inc. 375 Hudson Street, NY 10014, USA
Penguin Books Australia Ltd, 487 Maroondah Highway, PO Box 257, Ringwood, Victoria 3134, Australia
Penguin Books Canada Ltd, 10 Alcorn Avenue, Toronto, Ontario, Canada M4V 1E4
Penguin Books (NZ) Ltd, 182–190 Wairau Road, Auckland 10, New Zealand
Typeset in Linotron Univers and Century Old Style to an original design by Andrew Oliver.
Printed at Clays Ltd, St Ives PLC
Illustrations in Part One and Part Three by Edward Briant.

THE ROUGH GUIDE TO

Tunisia

written and researched by

Daniel Jacobs and Peter Morris

with additional contributions from

Simon Foster, Linda Cooley, Dee Eltaïef and Dr Carol Higham

We set out to do something different when the first Rough Guide was published in 1982. Mark Ellingham, just out of university, was travelling in Greece. He brought along the popular guides of the day, but found they were all lacking in some way. They were either strong on ruins and museums but went on for pages without mentioning a beach or taverna. Or they were so conscious of the need to save money that they lost sight of Greece's cultural and historical significance. Also, none of the books told him anything about Greece's contemporary life – its politics, its culture, its people, and how they lived.

So with no job in prospect, Mark decided to write his own guidebook, one which aimed to provide practical information that was second to none, detailing the best beaches and the hottest clubs and restaurants, while also giving hard-hitting accounts of every sight, both famous and obscure, and providing up-to-the-minute information on contemporary culture. It was a guide that encouraged independent travellers to find the best of Greece, and was a great success, getting shortlisted for the Thomas Cook travel guide award, and encouraging Mark, along with three friends, to expand the series.

The Rough Guide list grew rapidly and the letters flooded in, indicating a much broader readership than had been anticipated, but one which uniformly appreciated the Rough Guide mix of practical detail and humour, irreverence and enthusiasm. Things haven't changed. The same four friends who began the series are still the caretakers of the Rough Guide mission today: to provide the most reliable, up-to-date and entertaining information to independent-minded travellers of all ages, on all budgets.

We now publish more than 150 titles and have offices in London and New York. The travel guides are written and researched by a dedicated team of more than 100 authors, based in Britain, Europe, the USA and Australia. We have also created a unique series of phrasebooks to accompany the travel series, along with an acclaimed series of music guides, and a best-selling pocket guide to the Internet and World Wide Web. We also publish comprehensive travel information on our website:

www.roughguides.com

THE AUTHORS

Daniel Jacobs has contributed to numerous Rough Guides, including *West Africa*, *Morocco*, *Egypt* and *India*, and is the author of *The Rough Guide to Israel & the Palestinian Territories* and *The Rough Guide to Jerusalem*. He lives in South London.

Simon Foster has previously worked on *The Rough Guide to Egypt*. When he's not updating he leads tours in the Middle East, China and India or helps the lovely inventing folk at What If in London.

Peter Morris wrote the original edition of this book in 1985 and once played a game of football with Glenn Hoddle. He lives in North London.

READERS' LETTERS

Thanks to all the readers who have taken the time and trouble to write in with comments and suggestions:

Frank & Vivienne Adler
Theresa Bennett
Rev & Mrs R.J. Blakeway-Phillips
David Bond
Bernard Bookey
Lee Botsford
Lucy Brown
F. Burke
David A. Callard
Gordon Campbell & Judith Damerell
Neil Campbell
Brian Catlos
Kate Daoud
G. Davers
Mary Drayton
Andrew Emley
Christy Ferguson
Viève Forward
Catherine Gort
Alan Hakim
Justina Hart
Jillian Haynes
Peter Herbert
S. Hillier
Margaret Hoekstra
Terry Homewood
Amanda Hon & Dominic Norman-Taylor
Maggie Hughes & Dermot Dempsey
Veronica Ions
David Jeffcock
Mr A.D. & Mrs P.M.K. Jones
Helen Kirby
Anne Lancashire
Tristam Larder
Dee and Mary Macdonald
Tom McCartney
Karl Middlebrooks
David Miles
Roderick Millard
Sarah Mills
Audrey & Tony Mortlock
Susan Murray
Roo O'Brien
Margarette Oniye
Mr M & Mrs M. Page
Graham Poole
Eric & Gillian Potts
Joe Read
Leatrice Reid
Carmella Ruby
Iain Rutherford
Mark Sedgwick
Ken Shaw
Dennis Simmonds
Eigil Skogstad
Amber Strang
Meryl Sturley
Eric Sundstrøm
Wanda & Barry Syner
Melissa Terras & Dr J. Ross
Emily Thanas
Bill & Carolyn Thomas
Claire Turner
Michael van Balken
Jochem van der Boogert
Chris van Court
René van Havere
Chris Veale
Carly Walton
Ralph Woodward & Clare Selby

CONTENTS

Introduction x

● CHAPTER 4: KAIROUAN AND THE SAHEL 189

● CHAPTER 5: THE TELL 259

● CHAPTER 6: THE JERID 297

● CHAPTER 7: GABÈS AND MATMATA 345

● CHAPTER 8: JERBA AND THE SOUTHEAST COAST 363

● CHAPTER 9: THE KSOUR 393

PART THREE CONTEXTS 423

LIST OF MAPS

MAP SYMBOLS

Road	Mountain range	Internet access
Motorway	Peak	Synagogue
Passenger railway	Marsh	Post office
Freight railway	Oasis	Market
Unsurfaced road	Campground	Fortified wall
Track or trail	Restaurant	Building
Chapter division boundary	Accommodation	Church
International boundary	Petrol	Muslim cemetery
River	Bus & taxi stop	Jewish cemetery
Ferry route	Métro station	Christian cemetery
Ancient site	Hammam	Stadium
Airport	Hospital	Park
Mosque	Tourist office	Beach
Cave	Telephone	Saltpan

INTRODUCTION

Sun, sea and sand are what most people come to Tunisia for, and you can easily pick up a bargain holiday here from Britain, Ireland or mainland Europe, and sun it for a fortnight on the beach at Hammamet, Sousse, Monastlr or Jerba. But if you're a bit more adventurous, there's a land beyond the beach and hotel disco, a land of desert oases, Roman relics, beautiful mosques, and fascinating walled cities. Tunisia may be small, but it's full of sights, and even if you're only here on a package holiday, there's all manner of excursions to be had. The easiest option is to join an organized tour – local travel agencies run them, and many package firms offer their own – but you can also rent a car, or scoot around the place on public transport. Tunisia is friendly, safe and generally hassle-free, but still offers an experience you can genuinely call an adventure.

Tunisia, especially in the north, is recognizably Mediterranean in character and very much moulded by a century of **French colonial rule**. The main language is Arabic, but most people speak French, and the French influence is still strong. As an **Arab country**, it sometimes seems quite Middle Eastern, but sitting on the top of North Africa, it's a far cry from the oil states of the Gulf. Tunisian culture is firmly rooted in the Islamic faith professed by some 99 percent of its residents, but religion sits light, not heavy, on the lives of its citizens. They can drink alcohol if they want to – though most do not – and women have greater equality here than in any other Arab country in the world, largely thanks to Tunisia's modern interpretation of Islam.

But French and Arab are only two of the many influences that have shaped this land. The country's original **Berber** inhabitants, now largely assimilated into the Arab population, are responsible for much of its culture – not least the national dish, couscous. The first cities were built by the **Phoenicians**, a maritime trading nation from Lebanon, whose Carthaginian colonists carved out an empire in their own right, and dared challenge the might of republican Rome, a challenge which ended in their destruction. And the **Romans** left behind more than just ruins: they were the people who established Tunisia's infrastructure, and introduced the olive trees that dominate much of the countryside to this day. Even the **Turks**, whose Ottoman empire was rather a loose confederation of territories, owing often only nominal allegiance to

---

TUNISIA: FACTS AND FIGURES

With an area of 163,610 square kilometres (63,170 square miles), Tunisia is slightly larger than England and Wales, or Florida. The population stands at a little over nine million, of whom some 1.8 million live in Tunis and its suburbs. The official languages are Arabic, spoken by almost everybody, and French, spoken by most school-educated people. A tiny minority speaks Berber. English is not widely spoken, but more and more young people are studying it at school. About 99 percent of the population are Muslims, with small communities of Jews and Christians. On the economic side, Tunisia's main exports are crude oil, textiles and phosphates, and its main trading partners are France, Italy and Germany. Inflation is currently less than ten percent. The head of state, President Zine el Abidine Ben Ali, took office on November 7, 1987. He succeeded the founder of modern Tunisia, Habib Bourguiba, who led the country to independence (March 20, 1956) from French colonial rule. There is an elected National Assembly with a number of legal political parties, though Islamic fundamentalism is outlawed, and no serious opposition is tolerated. At the last presidential election, in October 1999, official figures gave Ben Ali 99.45 percent of the vote.

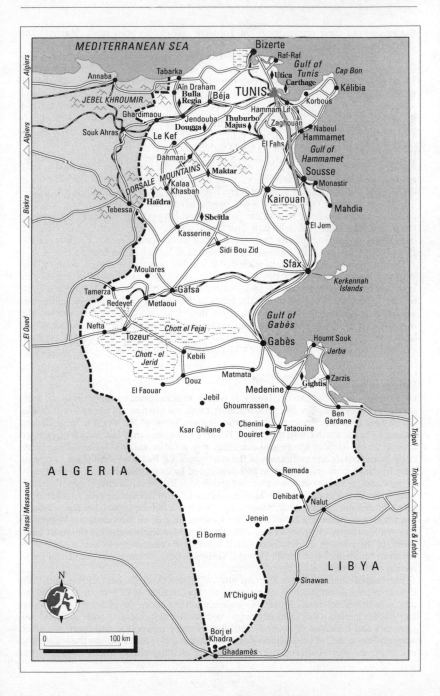

MEDITERRANEAN SEA

Bizerte
Raf-Raf
Gulf of
Tunis
Cap Bon
Utica
Carthage
Kélibia
Tabarka
Annaba
Aïn Draham
Bulla
Regia
Béja
TUNIS
Korbous
JEBEL KHROUMIR
Ghardimaou
Hammam Lif
Zaghouan
Nabeul
Hammamet
Jendouba
Thuburbo
Majus
Souk Ahras
Le Kef
Dougga
El Fahs
Gulf of
Hammamet
Dahmani
Sousse
Monastir
MOUNTAINS
Maktar
DORSALE
Kalaa
Khasbah
Kairouan
Haïdra
Mahdia
Tebessa
Sbeïtla
El Jem
Kasserine
Sidi Bou Zid
Moulares
Sfax
Tamerza
Gafsa
Kerkennah
Islands
Redeyef
Metlaoui
Nefta
Chott el Fejaj
Gulf of
Gabès
Tozeur
Houmt Souk
Chott - el
Jerid
Kebili
Gabès
Jerba
Douz
Matmata
Zarzis
El Faouar
Medenine
Gightis
Jebil
Ghoumrassen
Ben
Gardane
Ksar Ghilane
Chenini
Douiret
Tataouine

ALGERIA

Remada

Dehibat
Nalut

Jenein

El Borma

LIBYA

N

Sinawan

M'Chiguig

0   100 km

Borj el
Khadra
Ghadamès

Algiers
Algiers
Biskra
El Oued
Hassi Messaoud
Tripoli
Tripoli
Khoms & Lebda

the sultan, put their stamp firmly on Tunisian culture, as seen most clearly in the country's architecture.

If the diversity of Tunisia's past cultures and their legacy of monuments comes as a surprise to most first-time visitors, the range of scenery can be even more unexpected. In the north you find shady oak forests reminiscent of the south of France, with the hill station of Aïn Draham even described as "Alpine". The south is plain desert, with colossal dunes, oases and rippling mirages. In fact, the landscape of the desert itself varies a great deal, from the sand *ergs* of the far southwest with their endless dunes – most people's image when they think of desert – to the rocky *hamada* to its north and east. On rugged crags in this *hamada*, Berber villages seem almost to be carved out of the rock they cling to, and indeed they partly are. No less precariously perched are the strange fortified granaries known as *ksour*, where once nomadic tribes kept their food supply, ready to defend it to the death if need be. Also here are the weird salt flats known as chotts, and in particular the Chott el Jerid, inexplicably shown on most maps as a lake. The towns in these desert regions are oases, where you can stroll among the date palms to escape the fierce heat of the Saharan sun. Between the extremes are lush citrus plantations, huge fields with row after row of olive trees, bare steppes with table-top mountains, and rolling hills as green and colourful (in spring) as any English county. Just offshore lie the sandy, palm-scattered islands of Jerba and Kerkennah.

Despite this huge variation in geography, Tunisia is a very compact country, and easy to get around. Even on a two-week holiday, you'll have no problem taking off on a tour that covers coast, mountains and desert alike. The journey from Tunis, the capital on the north coast, to Tataouine, in the heart of the desert, can be made in a little over ten hours by bus or shared taxi and, while most trips are considerably shorter, the majority of journeys in Tunisia leave an impression of real travel in the transformation from one type of landscape and culture to another. All this makes the country very satisfying to explore – an accessible introduction to the Arab world and to the African continent.

Where to go

Of Tunisia's cities, the capital, **Tunis**, is rather a sedate town by Mediterranean standards, and easy to explore, with a fascinating medieval Medina and a very French-influenced new town. Its museum, the Bardo, houses some of the world's finest Roman mosaics. On the north coast, the port of **Bizerte** has a pleasantly laid-back feel, centred around an old harbour where you can relax with a coffee and watch the fishing boats chug in and out. In the mountains of the northwest, **Le Kef** is an ideal place to rest up for a few days, built on a mountain and dominated by its fortified Kasbah. In the centre of the country, **Kairouan** has a more religious feel. Its Great Mosque is Islam's fourth holiest site in the world, and the Medina is chock-full of fascinating religious architecture to check out. Not far away, **Sousse** is now a major holiday resort, but also a vibrant town with a compact and easy-to-explore Medina. Just down the coast, the larger and more industrialized city of **Sfax** has a Medina that most visitors agree is the most interesting in the country, not least because it makes few concessions to tourism and feels far more "authentic" as a result. Beyond, **Gabès** is the gateway to the south, unique in having both an oasis and a beach together.

In terms of monuments, the **Roman sites** of the north are the best known, and, even if your interest is very casual, many are quite spectacular. At El Jem, in the Sahel, an amphitheatre which rivals Rome's Colosseum towers above the plain; at Dougga you can wander around a marvellously preserved Roman city, complete with all the accoutrements and buildings of second- and third-century prosperity; and there are sites, scarcely less grand, at Utica, Bulla Regia, Maktar and Sbeïtla, as well as the legendary, extensive and much-battered Carthage. They're all atmospheric places to visit and at

FILMS SHOT IN TUNISIA

A popular location for desert movie sets, Tunisia has starred on the silver screen as Egypt, Palestine and the planet Tatooine, and many fans make pilgrimages to see where their favourite Hollywood epics were first carved in celluloid. Films shot here include:

• **Jesus of Nazareth** Monastir (see p.211) played the part of Jerusalem in Franco Zeffirelli's six-hour 1977 rendering of the life of Christ, originally made for TV.

• **Star Wars** Matmata and the "Star Wars Canyon" head the list of locations in George Lucas's 1975 cult sci-fi blockbuster – full details in the box on p.319.

• **The Life of Brian** Monastir came back to play Jerusalem once more in Monty Python's controversial 1979 satire on the gospels.

• **Raiders of the Lost Ark** Harrison Ford swashed his buckle down the Star Wars Canyon (see p.319) chasing after religious relics in Steven Spielberg's 1981 piece of Hollywood hokum.

• **The English Patient** Tunisia took on the role of Egypt in Anthony Minghella's 1996 film version of Michael Ondaatje's haunting novel. Onk el Jemal (see p.319) was the main desert set, with the Blackmith's Souk in Sfax (p.247) doubling up as a Cairo bazaar, the British Embassy in Tunis (p.83) as the scene of a Christmas party, and Mahdia (p.228) in the role of Benghazi.

• **The Phantom Menace** Tunisia starred again as the desert planet Tatooine in George Lucas's 1999 *Star Wars* prequel, with locations at Onk el Jemal and Ksar Hadada – again see the box on p.319 for full details.

the smaller sites off the excursion routes, you'll find yourself, as often as not, enjoying them alone.

Islamic Tunisia has a varied architectural legacy, taking in early Arab mosques – most outstandingly at Kairouan, the first Arab capital of North Africa – and the sophisticated **Turkish buildings** of Tunis, as well as the strange **Berber fortresses** of the south. The latter are accompanied by equally weird structures known as *ghorfas*, honeycombed storage and living quarters, and, at Matmata, by underground houses. All reward the small effort it takes to get off the more beaten tracks.

For more hedonistic pleasures, the coast is at its most beautiful – and most commercialized – around **Hammamet**, **Sousse–Monastir** and the island of **Jerba** (connected by causeway to the mainland). Hammamet is a genuinely international resort and its satellites are spreading; but, by Spanish or Greek island standards, developments remain relatively small scale and unusually well planned. Escaping them entirely is not hard either: even within sight of Hammamet, on Cap Bon, there is still wild coastline. **Tabarka**, on the north coast, is a quieter resort, with its Genoese castle, and backdrop of the Khroumerie mountains. For those seeking more splendid isolation, **Raf Raf** offers Tunisia's least-developed stretches of fine sand beach. Along the east coast lies an almost unbroken succession of beaches, starting with the popular purpose-built holiday resort at **Port el Kantaoui**. Next door is the city of **Sousse**, with one of the longest beaches in the country, sharing its airport with the neighbouring resort city of **Monastir**, and in between the beaches of **Skanès**. To the south, **Mahdia**, though marketed as a beach resort, is also a charming and atmospheric old sea dog of a town. The **Kerkennah Islands**, situated just off the coast, are undoubtedly Tunisia's laziest and most laid-back holiday destination, its people mostly engaged in fishing, using traditional methods. Finally, the island of **Jerba**, with several beautiful beaches, offers a fascinating interior, a unique architecture of fortified mosques, and a population more diverse than any other part of the country.

To really appreciate Tunisia however, your time should ideally include a spell in the desert and mountains as well as on the coast. The oases at **Nefta** and **Tozeur** are classically luxuriant, while further south, the *ksour* around **Tataouine** and dunes around Douz give the region an almost expeditionary feel. For the really adventurous, it is also now possible to obtain a permit and explore the remote desert of the far south with a four-wheel-drive vehicle.

All of this ignores one of Tunisia's best facets – its people. While the hassle of some tourist areas (particularly for women) shouldn't be underestimated, visitors are often startled – and exhilarated – by the hospitality which they're shown when away from the major resorts. Few independent travellers leave Tunisia without having been invited, quite spontaneously, to stay with a family. Even during the 1991 Gulf War, when public opinion strongly backed Saddam Hussein, political opposition to the West was always transcended by Tunisians' extraordinary pleasure in meeting visitors, and there was never any hostility shown to tourists as a result. The politics of the wider world rarely hinder personal contact.

When to go

Tunisia follows usual Mediterranean patterns of **climate**. The best time to travel, from a scenic point of view, is **spring**, when the south has not yet reached full heat and the north looks astonishingly fertile – above all, around the orchards and vineyards of Cap Bon. Be warned, though, that March and April are the dampest months of the year in the south and it can bucket down in the north.

Summer has mixed virtues. July and August are much the hottest months of the year – if only slightly more so than in the southern parts of Italy or Greece – and the one time you really do need to lapse into a local way of life, for example resting through the midday hours at a café or taking a siesta at your hotel. Obviously this goes above all for the deep south and the *ksour*. Some of the more exposed beaches of the north coast are only warm enough for swimming from around May until October, and if you wait until **autumn**, you get the best of both worlds, with warm swimming and few crowds, even at the big resorts.

In **winter**, the north and the Tell can get distinctly cold; Aïn Draham, the highest mountain town, commonly has a metre of snow, and in 1985 it even snowed at Bizerte on the Mediterranean coast. Tunis, Cap Bon and Sousse are not so much cold in winter as dull, with sporadic rains. But this is an ideal time for covering the ancient sites at leisure and then migrating south to Jerba's beaches and the Sahara.

AVERAGE TEMPERATURES AND RAINFALL	J	F	M	A	M	J	J	A	S	O	N	D
Tunis												
Min night °C	6	7	8	11	13	17	20	21	19	15	11	7
Max day °C	14	16	18	21	24	29	32	33	31	25	20	16
Rainfall (mm)	64	51	41	36	18	8	3	8	33	51	48	61
Days with rainfall	13	12	11	9	6	5	2	3	7	9	11	14
Gabès												
Min night °C	6	7	9	12	16	19	22	22	21	17	11	7
Max day °C	16	18	21	23	26	28	32	33	31	27	22	17
Rainfall (mm)	23	18	20	10	8	0	0	3	13	31	31	15
Days with rainfall	4	3	4	3	2	0	0	1	3	4	4	4

PART ONE

THE

BASICS

GETTING THERE

Flying is the fastest and the cheapest way to get to Tunisia from most parts of the world. You may well find that a package holiday, or
flight with accommodation, is hardly any more expensive than a flight alone. From the British Isles, surface options such as ferry plus train, bus or car are all feasible – if long-winded – means of getting to the country.

Airfares always depend on the **season**, with the highest being around July and August; fares drop during the "shoulder" seasons – May to June and September to October – and you'll get the best prices during the low season, November to April (excluding Christmas and New Year when prices are hiked up and seats are at a premium).

You can often cut costs by going through a **specialist flight agent** – either a consolidator, who buys up blocks of tickets from the airlines and sells them at a discount, or a **discount agent**, who in addition to dealing with discounted flights

---

ONLINE BOOKING AGENTS AND GENERAL TRAVEL SITES

ⓦ **www.etn.nl/discount.htm** A hub of consolidator and discount agent Web links, maintained by the nonprofit European Travel Network.

ⓦ **www.princeton.edu/Main/air800.html** A list of toll-free numbers for airlines in North America, with links to their websites.

ⓦ **www.flyaow.com** Online air travel info and reservations site.

ⓦ **www.smilinjack.com/airlines.htm** An extensive list of links to airline websites.

ⓦ **www.cheaptickets.com** Discount US flight specialists.

ⓦ **www.cheapflights.com** Flight deals, travel agents, plus links to other travel sites; UK only.

ⓦ **www.lastminute.com** Offers good last-minute holiday package and flight-only deals from the UK.

ⓦ **www.deckchair.com** Bob Geldof's online UK venture, drawing on a wide range of airlines.

ⓦ **www.expedia.com** Discount airfares, all-airline search engine and daily deals.

ⓦ **www.travelocity.com** Destination guides, hot Web fares and best deals for car hire, accommodation & lodging as well as fares. Provides access to the travel agent system SABRE, the most comprehensive central reservations system in the US.

ⓦ **www.hotwire.com** Bookings from the US only. Last-minute savings of up to forty percent on regular published fares. Travellers must be at least 18 and there are no refunds, transfers or changes allowed. Log-in required.

ⓦ **www.priceline.com** Bookings from the US only. Name-your-own-price website that has deals at around forty percent off standard fares. You cannot specify flight times (although you do specify dates) and the tickets are non-refundable, non-transferable and non-changeable.

ⓦ **www.skyauction.com** Bookings from the US only. Auctions tickets and travel packages using a "second bid" scheme. The best strategy is to bid the maximum you're willing to pay, since if you win you'll pay just enough to beat the runner-up regardless of your maximum bid.

ⓦ **www.travelshop.com.au** Australian website offering discounted flights, packages, insurance, online bookings.

ⓦ **www.uniquetravel.com.au** Australian site with a good range of packages and good value flights.

ⓦ **www.gaytravel.com** Gay online travel agent, concentrating mostly on accommodation.

may also offer special student and youth fares and a range of other travel-related services such as travel insurance, rail passes, car rentals, tours and the like. Some agents specialize in **charter flights**, which may be cheaper than anything available on a scheduled flight, but again departure dates are fixed and withdrawal penalties are high. In summer especially, you may even find it cheaper to pick up a bargain last-minute **package deal** from one of the tour operators listed below and then find your own accommodation when you get there.

If Tunisia is only one stop on a longer journey, you might consider buying a **Round-the-World (RTW) ticket**. Some travel agents can sell you an "off-the-shelf" RTW ticket that will touch down in about half a dozen cities; others will assemble one for you, but as Tunis is not commonly included in standard RTW routes this is apt to be more expensive.

BOOKING FLIGHTS ONLINE

Many airlines and discount travel websites offer you the opportunity to book your tickets online, cutting out the costs of agents and middlemen. Good deals can often be found through discount or auction sites, as well as through the airlines' own websites.

FLIGHTS FROM THE UK AND IRELAND

A **scheduled flight** from London to Tunis offers the most flexibility, although open tickets are more expensive than fixed return ones. The full scheduled fare is around £800 – prices quoted here do not include airport departure tax, currently £25 from the UK and around £6 from Tunisia – but you can cut costs greatly by buying an "APEX" ticket. Tunisia's national airline, **Tunisair** flies four times weekly (five in summer) from London Heathrow, with a return fare of around £160 to £225, depending on the season, for an APEX ticket bought at least three days in advance, covering at least one Saturday night, for a maximum stay of one month, with no change of dates. The only other scheduled airline with direct flights from Britain to Tunisia is British Airways franchisee **GB Airways**, whose services are generally a cut above normal BA flights, and far preferable to Tunisair in both reliability and standards of service. GB Airways flies four times weekly from Gatwick, for around £190 to £225 for an APEX ticket with similar conditions.

As for **indirect flights**, the airlines worth considering are Air France via Paris, Air Malta via Malta, or Alitalia via Rome. Air France are the most convenient but not the cheapest, with two daily connecting flights from Paris to Tunis, and fares from £250. Alitalia have return flights via Rome or Milan from £185. Air Malta's return fares start at £190–245 depending on the season, but their flights do not connect very well, so you will probably have to take a stopover in Malta. There is currently a same-day connecting flight once a week, involving a five-hour wait at Malta airport, but this may change in the future.

There are no direct scheduled flights from **regional British airports**, and you either need to take a charter (see below) or a connecting scheduled flight. British Airways fly from most places (the main exception is Birmingham) to London Heathrow, where you can connect with Tunisair to Tunis, or travel to Gatwick for the GB Airways flight. An alternative is Air France from Birmingham, Manchester or Newcastle via Paris. A typical fare on these routes is around £335 return.

CHARTER FLIGHTS

Charter flights are available from most British airports during the summer and from many in winter, too. In theory, charter flights are supposed to be sold in conjunction with accommodation, but it is sometimes possible just to buy the air ticket at a discount through your travel agent, or else simply not use the accommodation. Some package operators, notably Britannia (Thomson), First Choice and Airtours (Aspro), sell deals which are basically flight-only (see below). Charter flights vary in price with the season, from about £130 return from London in low season to about £225 at the end of July or beginning of August.

The very cheapest deals of all are **last-minute charter flights** or packages, usually for one or two weeks and sometimes costing less than £100. These are available a week or two before the departure date and can be found in the windows of travel agents, on Teletext, Ceefax or the internet, or through advertisements in local papers. Their main drawback is that availability is somewhat random, and dates cannot be changed.

Ireland

Ireland has no direct scheduled flights to Tunisia, but Panorama runs weekly **charters** to Monastir from Dublin and Belfast, and in summer from Cork

AIRLINES IN BRITAIN AND IRELAND

Air France in UK ☎0845/0845 111, in Republic of Ireland, ✪www.airfrance.co.uk.
Air Malta in UK ☎0845/607 3710, in Republic of Ireland ☎01/872 1175, ✪www.airmalta.com. Tickets purchased through agents Skylord ☎020/8866 3331 and EZ Travel ☎020/7730 1829.
Alitalia in UK ☎08705/448259, in Republic of Ireland ☎01/677 5171, ✪www.alitalia.it.

British Airways and GB Airways in UK ☎0845/773 3377, in Republic of Ireland ☎0141/222 2345, ✪www.britishairways.com.
Sabena in UK ☎0845/601 0933, in Republic of Ireland ☎01/844 5454, ✪www.sabena.com.
Tunis Air ☎020/7734 7644, ✪www.tunisair.com.tn.

DISCOUNT FLIGHT AGENTS IN BRITAIN

North South Travel ☎ & ☎01245/608 291, ✪www.northsouthtravel.co.uk. Friendly, competitive travel agency, offering discounted fares worldwide – profits are used to support projects in the developing world, especially the promotion of sustainable tourism.
STA Travel ☎0870/160 6070, ✪www.statravel.co.uk. Worldwide specialists in low-cost flights and tours for students and under-26s, though other customers welcome.
Trailfinders ☎020/7628 7628, ✪www.trailfinders.com. One of the

best-informed and most efficient agents for independent travellers.
Travel Bug ☎020/7835 2000, ✪www.flynow.com. Large range of discounted tickets.
Travel Cuts ☎020/7255 2082, ✪www.travel-cuts.co.uk. Canadian company specializing in budget, student and youth travel.
Usit Campus ☎0870/240 1010, ✪www.usit-campus.co.uk. Student/youth travel specialists, offering discount flights.

DISCOUNT FLIGHT AGENTS IN IRELAND

Joe Walsh Tours, ☎01/872 2555 or ☎01/676 3053, ✪www.joewalshtours.ie. General budget fares agent.
Student & Group Travel, ☎01/677 7834. Student specialists.
Trailfinders ☎01/677 7888, ✪www.trailfinders.ie. Competitive fares, plus deals on hotels, insurance, tours and car rental.

USIT Now in the Republic ☎01/602 1777, in Northern Ireland ☎028/9032 7111, ✪www.usit-now.ie. Ireland's main student and youth travel specialists.

and Shannon, too. Airtours and (in summer) Falcon/JWT also run charters from Dublin. These cost around €380/£300 flight-only.

For a scheduled flight to Tunis, you have to pay a tag-on fare and go via mainland Europe, Britain or Malta. **From Dublin**, return fares start at around €510/£400 plus tax, or €380/£300 if you are under 26. BA via London, Sabena via Brussels, Air France via Paris and Alitalia via Rome are all possible carriers. Air Malta via Malta is also a possibility, but there are no same-day connections, so you would need to take a stopover in Malta both going and coming back. **From Belfast**, your choice is with Sabena via Brussels

(currently the cheapest route), or BA via London. Expect to pay £310 to £350 plus tax.

TOUR OPERATORS

Any travel agent will be able to provide details of the many operators that run **package tours** to Tunisia, which often cost little more than a charter flight. Some are straightforward travel-plus-beach-hotel affairs providing a fixed base, whereas others offer archeological discovery tours, trekking or desert expeditions. Almost all the major British operators offer Tunisian holidays, mainly on the Nabeul–Hammamet or Sousse–Monastir coasts.

TUNISIAN HOLIDAY SPECIALISTS

Aspects of Tunisia, ☎020/7836 4999, @aspectsoftunisia.co.uk. Carthage, Tunis, Hammamet, Sousse, Port el Kantaoui, Jerba, Sangho (near Zarzis), Tamerza and Ksar Ghilane, plus fly-drive and desert excursions, and a Roman Tunisia tour, using scheduled fights.

Panorama Tunisia Experience, UK ☎01273/427777, ⓦwww.panoramaholidays.co.uk; Ireland ☎01/630 1700, @club25@iol.ie. The leading specialists in Tunisian holidays, with beach hotels in Gammarth (near Tunis), Hammamet, Sousse, Port el Kantaoui, Mahdia, Kerkennah and Jerba, activities for kids, Sahara excursions, Tunis city breaks and golfing holidays. Charter flights from most British and Irish airports.

Sunnyway, ☎01704/531999, ⓦwww.sunny-way-tunisia.co.uk. Beach holidays in Gammarth, Sidi Bou Saïd, Hammamet, Sousse, Port el Kantaoui, Monastir, Mahdia, Kerkennah and Jerba, with the option of additional nights in Matmata, Douz, Kebili and Tozeur, plus golfing holidays and Tunis city breaks. Scheduled and charter flights out of Heathrow, Gatwick, Luton, Stansted, Birmingham, Belfast, Bristol, Cardiff, East Midlands, Glasgow and Manchester.

PACKAGE HOLIDAY COMPANIES

Airtours (aka **Aspro**), UK ☎0870/241 2567, ⓦwww.airtours.com; Ireland ☎01/603 1600. Hammamet, Sousse, Port el Kantaoui and Monastir; charter flights to Monastir from Gatwick, Luton, Stansted, Dublin, Belfast, Birmingham, Bristol, Cardiff, East Midlands, Glasgow, Leeds/Bradford, Manchester and Teesside.

Cadogan, ☎023/8082 8302, ⓦwww.cadogan-holidays.com. Upmarket firm using scheduled flights and mostly four- and five-star hotels in Hammamet, Sousse, Port el Kantaoui and Monastir. Also offers golfing holidays.

Falcon/JWT, ☎01/605 6555, ⓦwww.jwtholidays.ie. Beach holidays in Hammamet, Sousse and Port el Kantaoui on charter flights from Dublin.

First Choice, ☎0870/750 0001, ⓦwww.firstchoice.co.uk. Hammamet, Sousse, Port el Kantaoui and Monastir. Charter flights to Monastir from Gatwick, Birmingham and Manchester.

Portland Direct, ☎0990/002200, ⓦwww.portland-holidays.co.uk. Holidays in Hammamet, Port el Kantaoui and Sousse, available only directly from the operator (the idea is that they cut prices by cutting out travel agents). Charter flights from Gatwick, Luton, Birmingham, Bristol, East Midlands, Glasgow and Manchester.

Thomson, ☎0990/502555, ⓦwww.thomson-holidays.com. Hammamet, Sousse, Port el Kantaoui and Monastir. Charter flights (trading as Britannia for flight-only deals) from Gatwick, Luton, Birmingham, Glasgow and Manchester.

SPECIALIST TOUR OPERATORS

Andante Travels, ☎01722/713800, ⓦwww.andantetravels.co.uk. Good-value one- and two-week archeological tours with expert guide lecturers.

Dragoman Overland Expeditions, ☎01728/861133, ⓦwww.dragoman.co.uk. Overland tours to Tunisia, Libya and West Africa, or Tunisia, Libya and Egypt, the second of which can be extended to Jordan, Syria and Turkey, or south to East Africa.

Encounter Overland, ☎020/7370 6845, ⓦwww.encounter-overland.com. A 28-day overland trip through Tunisia and Libya, or a 42-day trip through Tunisia, Libya and Egypt.

Explore Worldwide, UK ☎01252/319448, ⓦwww.explore.co.uk; Ireland ☎01/677 9479. Fifteen-day overland adventure holiday including a three-day camel trek.

Holt's Tours, ☎01304/612248, ⓦwww.battle-tours.co.uk. A firm specializing in military history trips, who do a very occasional tour of World War Two battlefields in Tunisia.

Martin Randall Travel, ☎020/8742 3355, @info@martinrandall.co.uk. Annual eight-day escorted Roman archeology tour with guest lecturer.

Mercian Travel, ☎01562/883795, ⓦwww.merciantravel.co.uk. Bridge and bowling holidays in Port el Kantaoui.

TLC Tunisia, ☎01252/728147. Stress-busting "health weeks", with an introduction to aromatherapy, yoga or shiatsu relaxation techniques at an adults-only beach hotel with health spa at Skanes near Monastir.

If your trip is geared around specific interests, packages can work out much cheaper than the same arrangements made on arrival. A package will include flights, accommodation and often transfers to and from your hotel, or a rental car. A complete list of package operators is available from the **Tunisian National Tourist Office**, 77a Wigmore St, London W1U 1QF (☎020/7224-5561).

OVERLAND FROM BRITAIN

You won't save any money by **going overland** between London and Tunis but the routes are obviously worth considering if you want to take in something of France and/or Italy on the way. And if you're under 26 there are bargains to be had on rail tickets.

The route through Italy is probably the most popular. By train it takes around thirty hours from London to **Genoa** and fifty hours to **Trápani**, from where ferries leave for Tunis. An alternative route is to travel to **Marseille** (around twenty hours) for the longer ferry crossing from France. These times can be reduced by several hours if you take the Eurostar via the Channel Tunnel as far as **Paris** – and, depending on special offers and advance booking, it may not work out much more. **Driving** you have the choice of ferry or tunnel (Eurotunnel) to get you across the channel and, to cross the Med, car ferries from Marseille, Genoa, Trápani (Sicily) and Naples.

At one time there were several operators covering the "North African loop" of Morocco–Algeria–Tunisia, but northern Algeria is now so dangerous and unstable that no overland trips currently pass through it, nor are likely to in the near future. For up-to-date information, contact an Africa specialist agent such as Africa Travel Centre (☎020/7387 1211) or STA Travel's Africa Desk (see p.5), or an overland tour operator such as Dragoman, Encounter or Explore (see opposite).

BY RAIL FROM THE UK AND IRELAND

Train tickets for the London–Marseille run start at £130 return if you are over 26, with no cheaper one-way tickets. Under-26s can get a one-way ticket for £65, or a return for £120. These tickets must be booked at least a week in advance.

USEFUL BUS AND RAIL COMPANIES
Eurolines ☎0870/514 3219,
✆ www.eurolines.co.uk.
Eurostar ☎0870/160 6600,
✆ www.eurostar.com.
Eurotunnel ☎0870/535 3535,
✆ www.eurotunnel.com.
European Rail ☎020/7387 0444, ☎7837 0888 (phone and fax bookings only).
International Rail ☎01962/773646.
Trainseurope ☎01354/660222 or ☎020/8699 3654, ✆ www.trainseurope.co.uk

Lowest fares to Genoa are £123 one-way, or £176 return for over-26s, £87.50/£112.50 for under-26s. To Trápani, the cheapest tickets are £155/€286 for over-26s, £127/€225 for over-26s. These fares are for rail-sea-rail tickets, crossing the Channel by ferry, and are available from Trainseurope and International Rail. The same firms sell tickets via the Channel Tunnel, which will save about six hours on your journey and cost anything from £20 to £60 more.

BY BUS

Buses from London to Marseille, Genoa or Rome take about the same time as trains but can cost substantially less. Eurolines, for example, run buses to Marseille for £62 single/£95 return. There are slight reductions for under-25s. You may find other offers in the travel pages of magazines mentioned on p.4 under "Flights from the UK and Ireland".

BY CAR

If you're **driving** to Tunisia and want to see some of Italy, you could travel via Turin, Rome and Naples across to Sicily on the Reggio–Messina ferry, and over to Tunis by ferry from there. A more expensive but somewhat more relaxed option is to cross the Med on the ferry from Genoa or Marseille. With all these crossings, you'll need to book in advance if you're taking a car.

Crossing the **Channel** from Britain to Europe, the fastest, though not the cheapest, way is through the Channel Tunnel with Eurotunnel; it's best to book ahead if you can, though you shouldn't have to wait too long if you just turn up at the port. The alternative cross-Channel options for most travellers are the ferry or hovercraft links from Dover to Calais or Boulogne, Ramsgate to Dunkerque, or Newhaven to Dieppe.

BY FERRY

There are **ferries** to Tunisia from Trápani (Sicily), as well as from Naples and La Spezia (summer only), Genoa, Marseille and Cagliari (Sardinia). In the past there have been ferries from Malta, but curently there are none. Most services arrive in Tunisia at La Goulette, the port for Tunis (see p.108).

The **Trápani–Tunis** ferry crossing is the shortest, with one service a week run by Tirrenia Navigazione, and another run by Linee Lauro. The Tirrenia boat actually starts in Cagliari and can also be picked up there. In midsummer, especially, you'll need to be prepared for a harassed and frantic time buying tickets in Trápani. Booking

ahead is advisable, and essential if taking a car across any time between mid-June and mid-September. You would also be well advised to get a full return ticket in advance, especially if you're planning to return during the last two weeks of August, when the boats are packed with returning migrant workers. There is also a weekly service from **Naples**, operated by Linee Lauro, and a summer service run by the same firm from La Spezia.

Ferries from Genoa and Marseille are in some respects more convenient and certainly pleasanter than those from Trápani, where passengers (mostly Tunisians working in Europe) are often treated more like cattle than customers. Car drivers, however, will need to make reservations three or four months in advance for summer crossings on the Marseille and Genoa routes.

FERRY COMPANIES

Compagnie Tunisienne de la Navigation (CTN or Cotunav): c/o Southern Ferries, 179 Piccadilly, London W1V 9DB ☎020/7491 4968; c/o Tirrenia, Via Milano 51, Genoa ☎010/258041; c/o SNCM, 61 bd des Dames, Marseille ☎04/9156 3010; 122 rue de Yougoslavie, Tunis ☎01/321300, ✉tunisia .ferries@ctn.com.tn; av Habib Bougatfa, La Goulette ☎01/735111.

Linee Lauro: c/o Viamare Travel, Graphic House, 2 Sumatra Rd, London NW6 1PU ☎020/7431 4560, ✇www.viamare.com; Piazza Municipio 88, Naples ☎081/551-3352,

✇www.forti.it/LineeLauro/Inglese/index.html; Stazione Marittima, Trápani ☎0329/24073; c/o Carthage Tours, 59 av Bourguiba, Tunis ☎01/347015.

Tirrenia Navigazione: c/o SMS Travel, 40–42 Kenway Rd, London SW5 0RA ☎020/7 373-6548; 1 Via Campidano, Cagliari ☎070/66065; Corso Italia 48, Trápani ☎0923/21896; 2 Rione Sirignano, PO Box 438, 80121 Naples ☎081/720 1111; Catala Marinai d'Italia, Porto, Palermo ☎091/333300; c/o CTN, 122 rue de Yougoslavie, Tunis ☎01/321300.

FERRY ROUTES AND PRICES

Cheapest single fares

From	To	Operator	Frequency	Time	Passenger	Car	M/bike
Trápani	La Goulette	Tirrenia	1 weekly	10hr	£31.60	£56	£25
Trápani	La Goulette	Lauro	1–2 weekly	8–12hr	£21	£51	£21
Cagliari	La Goulette	Tirrenia	1 weekly	21hr	£38.60	£62	£25.40
Genoa	La Goulette	CTN	1–5 weekly	27hr	£76.70	£153.40	£63.20
La Spezia	La Goulette	Lauro	1 weekly June–Sept	24hr	£41	£89	£41
Naples	La Goulette	Lauro	1–2 weekly	19hr	£41	£82	£34
Marseille	La Goulette*	CTN	2–11 weekly	24hr	£102.60	£226.80	£92.90

*plus occasional extra services to Bizerte, Sousse and Sfax.
Note that fares vary with season as well as standard of accommodation; car and motorbike prices quoted are in addition to foot-passenger prices; prices quoted do not include port taxes.

Both of these are operated by Compagnie Tunisienne de la Navigation (CTN or Cotunav), Tunisia's national line, which runs one weekly ferry in winter rising to as many as three out of Genoa and five out of Marseille in summer, supplemented by SNCM Ferryterranée boats. The Marseille service occasionally departs from Nice or Toulon instead, and occasionally serves Bizerte or Sfax instead of Tunis.

The quarterly *OAG Cruise and Ferry Guide*, available for £50 from OAG, 6 Church St, Dunstable, Beds LU5 4HB (☎ 0000/731 0163), or at many public reference libraries and travel agents, should carry current information on these ferries, as should Thomas Cook's monthly *European Timetables* (the red volume), also available in public libraries or from any branch of Thomas Cook. Latest information, however, is best checked with the operators, or on the websites of their agents (Viamare for Linee Lauro, or SNCM for CTN).

BY YACHT

If you have a private boat, there are marinas at Monastir, Port el Kantaoui, Sidi Bou Said and Tabarka, a small one at Bizerte, and marinas under construction at Hammamet and Houmt Souk (Jerba). Although these are the only places with facilities for pleasure boats, there are a total of 26 ports along the coast where you are allowed to drop anchor.

FLIGHTS FROM THE USA AND CANADA

There are no direct flights to Tunisia from the US or Canada. Instead, you will have to fly to a European gateway city, and take a connecting service to Tunisia. Several European airlines serving major US and Canadian cities offer connecting flights from their European hub cities to Tunisia, and depending on your ticket, you may be able to take a stopover en route.

In many ways the most convenient **airline** for Tunisia is Air France, which serves most major US and Canadian hubs, and offers frequent connecting flights (two daily) to Tunis. Most overnight services from North America arrive at Paris in time to connect with their morning flight to Tunis. Air France may not however be the cheapest option. Alternatives include British Airways via London, who serve more North American cities. The problem with BA is that most of their North American services arrive at London's Heathrow airport, whereas their Tunis service departs from London's other main airport, Gatwick – fine if you are stopping over in London, but a major hassle if you want an immediate connection. BA services from Atlanta, Baltimore, Boston, Dallas/Fort Worth, Denver and Orlando do however fly into Gatwick, arriving in good time to pick up an onward flight at least three times a week (and from Houston). Swissair via Zurich, Alitalia via Rome or Iberia via Madrid are other possibilities, and you may

AIRLINES IN THE USA AND CANADA

Aeroflot in US ☎ 1-888/340 6400, in Canada ☎ 514/288-2125, ⊛ www.aeroflot.com.

Air Canada ☎ 1-888/247–2262, ⊛ www.aircanada.ca.

Air France in US ☎ 1-800/237-2747, in Canada ☎ 1-800/667-2747, ⊛ www.airfrance.com.

Alitalia in US ☎ 1-800/223-5730, in Canada ☎ 1-800/361-8336, ⊛ www.alitalia.com.

American Airlines ☎ 1-800/433-7300, ⊛ www.aa.com.

British Airways ☎ 1-800/247-9297, ⊛ www.british-airways.com.

Canadian Airlines ☎ 1-888/247–2262, ⊛ www.aircanada.ca.

Delta Air Lines ☎ 1-800/241-4141, ⊛ www.delta.com.

Iberia ☎ 1-800/772-4642, ⊛ www.iberia.com.

KLM/Northwest in US ☎ 1-800/447-4747, in Canada ☎ 514/397-0775, ⊛ www.klm.com.

Lufthansa in US ☎ 1-800/645-3880, in Canada ☎ 1-800/563-5954, ⊛ www.lufthansa-ca.com.

Royal Air Maroc ☎ 1-800/344-6726 or ☎ 212/750–6071, ⊛ www.royalairmaroc.com.

United Airlines ☎ 1-800/538–2929, ⊛ www.ual.com.

US Airways ☎ 1-800/622-1015, ⊛ www.usairways.com.

Virgin Atlantic ☎ 1-800/862-8621, ⊛ www.virgin-atlantic.com.

DISCOUNT FLIGHT AGENTS IN THE USA AND CANADA

Air Brokers International ☎1-800/883-3273 or ☎415/397-1383, ⊛www.airbrokers.com. Consolidator and specialist in RTW tickets.

Council Travel ☎1-800 226 8624 or ☎617/528 2091, ⊛www.counciltravel.com. Nationwide organization that mostly, but by no means exclusively, specializes in student/budget travel.

Educational Travel Center ☎1-800/747-5551 or ☎608/256 5551, ⊛www.edtrav.com. Student/youth discount agent.

High Adventure Travel ☎1-800/350-0612 or ☎415/912-5600, ⊛www.airtreks.com. Round-the-world and Circle Pacific tickets. The website features an interactive database that lets you build and price your own RTW itinerary.

New Frontiers/Nouvelles Frontières ☎1-800/677 0720 or ☎212/986 6006, ⊛www.NewFrontiers.com. French discount-travel firm.

Skylink US ☎1-800/AIR-ONLY or ☎212/573-8980, Canada ☎1-800/SKY-LINK. Consolidator.

STA Travel ☎1-800/777-0112 or ☎1-800/781-4040, ⊛www.sta-travel.com. Worldwide specialists in independent travel; also student IDs, travel insurance, car rental, etc.

TFI Tours International ☎1-800/745-8000 or ☎212/736-1140. Consolidator.

Travac ☎1-800/872-8800, ⊛www.thetravel-site.com. Consolidator and charter broker.

Travelers Advantage Cendant Membership Services, Inc ☎1-877/259-2691, ⊛www.travelersadvantage.com. Discount travel club; annual membership fee required (currently $1 for 3 months trial).

Travel Avenue ☎1-800/333-3335, ⊛www.travelavenue.com. Full-service travel agent that offers discounts in the form of rebates.

Travel Cuts in Canada ☎1-800/667 2887, in US ☎416/979 2406, ⊛www.travelcuts.com. Canadian student-travel organization.

Worldtek Travel ☎1/800-243-1723, ⊛www.worldtek.com. Discount travel agency for worldwide travel.

Worldwide Discount Travel Club ☎305/534-2642. Discount travel club.

TOUR OPERATORS

Adventure Center ☎1-800/228-8747 or ☎510/654-1879, ⊛www.adventure-center.com. Fifteen-day overland adventure holiday including a three-day camel trek.

Adventures Abroad ☎1-800/665-3998 or ☎604/303-1099, ⊛www.adventures-abroad.com. About fifteen itineraries for cultural tours, some including Libya, Malta, Morocco or Italy.

Archeological Tours ☎212/986 3054. Run an annual tour of major archeological sites in Tunisia, with lectures by an archeological historian.

Cross Cultural Adventures ☎703/237 0100. Runs tours with an emphasis on culture and archeological sites. Specializes in customized trips for individual travellers and private groups.

Tunis USA ☎1-800/474 5500 or ☎610/995 2788, ⊛www.tunisusa.com. Tunisia specialists, with an emphasis on culture and history, running seven different tours for small groups with expert local guides, including a two-week culture and history tour, and one-week tours on themes such as deserts and oases, Roman Tunisia and Jewish Tunisia. Also run customized tours for groups and individuals, and can arrange contacts between travellers and Tunisians with similar personal or professional interests.

be able to connect onto Tunisair fllights from other European airlines.

Flying **from the US** in low season, and particularly if you qualify for student or under-26 youth fares, you should be able to get a through ticket from New York to Tunis for around $750 before tax, and maybe for as little as $650. In high season, you are looking at a fare of around $1000. Fares from Chicago, Boston and Miami will be slightly higher than those from New York. From the West Coast, a ticket to Tunis out of LAX will cost anything from $850 upward, rising to $1150 in high season.

From Canada, fares are typically CDN$1190 in low season around Toronto or Montreal rising to CDN$1390 in high season. The equivalent fares from Vancouver are CDN$1570/1750.

FLIGHTS FROM AUSTRALIA AND NEW ZEALAND

There are no direct flights from Australia or New Zealand to Tunisia, and your best bet is to travel via either Europe or the Middle East.

From Australia, one of the cheapest tickets is with Egyptair via Cairo, with a year-round price of A\$1944 return. Other airline prices vary with the season, costing around A\$400 more in winter (Tunisia's summer). Possible options include Alitalia via Rome or Swissair via Zurich – Alitalia's off-season price currently matches Egyptair's. Alternatively, British Airways and Qantas combine with Turkish Air or Royal Jordanian to take you via Asia to Amman or Istanbul, and thence to Tunis, for A\$2050–2400. You can get a similar combination with Thai or Singapore and Royal Jordanian, but it tends to be pricier.

AIRLINES IN AUSTRALIA AND NEW ZEALAND

Air France Australia ☎02/9244 2100, New Zealand ☎09/308 3352, ⊛www.airfrance.fr.

Air Malta Australia ☎02/9244 2011, ⊛www.airmalta.com.

Air New Zealand Australia ☎13 2476, New Zealand ☎0800/737 000 or ☎09/357 3000, ⊛www.airnz.com.

Alitalia Australia ☎02/9244 2400, New Zealand ☎09/302 1452, ⊛www.alitalia.it.

British Airways Australia ☎02/8904 8800, New Zealand ☎09/356 8690, ⊛www.british-airways.com.

Egyptair Australia ☎02/9267 6979, ⊛www.egyptair.com.

Garuda Australia ☎13 1223 or ☎02/9334 9900, in New Zealand ☎09/366 1862 or ☎1800/128 510, ⊛www.garuda-indonesia.com.

Gulf Air Australia ☎02/9244 2199, New Zealand ☎09/308 3366, ⊛www.gulfairco.com.

Japan Airlines (JAL) Australia ☎02/9272 1111, New Zealand ☎09/379 9906, ⊛www.japanair.com.

Malaysia Airlines Australia ☎13 2627, New Zealand ☎09/373 2741 or ☎008/657 472, ⊛www.malaysiaair.com.

Olympic Airways Australia ☎1800/221 663 or ☎02/9251 2044, ⊛www.olympic-airways.com.

Qantas Australia ☎13/13 13, New Zealand ☎09/357 8900 or ☎0800/808 767, ⊛www.qantas.com.au.

Royal Jordanian Airlines Australia ☎02/9244 2701); New Zealand agent: Innovative Travel ☎03/365 3910; ⊛www.rja.com.jo.

Singapore Airlines Australia ☎13/10 11 or ☎02/9350 0262, in New Zealand ☎09/303 2129 or ☎0800/808 909, ⊛www.singaporeair.com.

Swissair, Australia ☎02/9232 1744 or ☎1800/221 339, New Zealand ☎09/358 3216, ⊛www.swissair.com.

Thai Airways in Australia ☎1300/651 960, in New Zealand ☎09/377 3886, ⊛www.thaiair.com.

TRAVEL AGENTS AND TOUR OPERATORS

Accent on Travel Australia ☎07/3832 1777

Adventure World Australia ☎02/9956 7766 or ☎1300/363 055, New Zealand ☎09/524 5118, ⊛www.adventureworld.com.au.

Africa Bound Holidays Australia ☎08/9361 2047, ✉africabound@citysearch.com.au.

Africa Travel Centre Australia ☎02/9249 5444 or ☎1800/000 447, New Zealand ☎09/520 2000, ⊛www.travel.com.au.

Anywhere Travel Australia ☎02/9663 0411 or ☎018 401 014, ✉anywhere@ozemail.com.au.

Budget Travel New Zealand ☎09/366 0061 or ☎0800/808 040, ⊛www.budgettravel.co.nz.

Explore in Australia ☎02/9857 6200 or ☎1300/731 000, ⊛www.exploreholidays.com.au, in New Zealand ☎09/524 5118.

Flight Centre Australia ☎02/9235 3522 or ☎13/1600, New Zealand ☎09/358 4310, ⊛www.flightcentre.com.

STA Travel Australia ☎13 1776 or ☎1300/360 960, ⊛www.statravel.com.au, New Zealand ☎09/309 0458 or ☎09/366 6673, ⊛www.statravel.co.nz.

From New Zealand, the best way to reach Tunisia is also with a combination of Asian and Middle Eastern airlines. A typical one is Malaysian and Royal Jordanian, with two-week return tickets from Auckland to Tunis available from discount agents for around NZ$2765 in high season (NZ winter/Tunisian summer), or NZ$2475 in low season.

RED TAPE AND VISAS

Canadian and EU citizens need no visa for a stay in Tunisia of up to three months, and US citizens for up to four. Australians and New Zealanders need visas, however. Australians can get them at borders and ports on entry, though check this in good time, as these things have a habit of changing. New Zealanders must obtain visas in advance; applications usually take three weeks to process. Visas cost around £4/$6 and you'll need to provide three photos, your passport and fill in two forms. Tunisians holding dual passports may be expected to enter and leave the country on a Tunisian passport.

VISA EXTENSIONS

The practice for **extending a visa** varies, but is rarely easy. If your visa is close to expiry, go to the police in good time, with some proof that you have a reason for staying in the country and evidence that you can support yourself (take along all your exchange slips). Extensions usually take between two weeks and a month to process.

TUNISIAN EMBASSIES AND CONSULATES ABROAD

Algeria 11 rue du Bois de Boulogne, El Mouradia, Algiers ☎02/601388; 23 av 28 Janvier, St Thèrese, Annaba ☎08/864568; 150 bd Col Mahmoud Cherif, BP 280, Tébessa ☎08/484832.

Australia Level 5, Edgecliff Centre, 203 New South Head Rd, Edgecliff, Sydney, NSW 2027 ☎02/9363 5588.

Canada 515 O'Connor St, Ottawa, ON K1S 3P8 ☎613/237 0330; 511 Place d'Armes, Suite 501, Montreal, PQ H2Y 2W7☎514/844 6909.

Egypt 26 Sharia al-Jazira, Zamalek, Cairo ☎02/340-4940.

Libya Sharia Bashir al-Ibrahim, PO Box 613, Tripoli ☎021/333 1051; Sharia al-Khadra, al-Fouihet, Benghazi ☎061/222 6683.

Malta 144 Tower Rd, Flat 2, Sliema SLM 08 ☎345866.

Morocco 6 av de Fès/1 rue d'Ifrane, Rabat ☎03/773 0636.

Netherlands Gentsestraat 98, 2587 HX, The Hague ☎070/351 2251.

Norway Haakon VII'sgt 5B, 0161 Oslo ☎2283-1917.

South Africa 850 Church St, Arcadia 0007, Pretoria, PO Box 56535 ☎012/342 5282.

Sweden Narvavâgen 32, 11522 Stockholm ☎08/5458 5520.

UK 29 Prince's Gate, London SW7 1QG ☎020/7584 8117.

USA 1515 Massachusetts Ave NW, Washington, DC 20005 ☎202/862 1850.

Once granted, they usually give three months' residence. An alternative means of getting a renewal is to pop over to Libya, Malta or Sicily, so that you can get a new tourist stamp on re-entry.

Foreign embassies and consulates can be found in the major towns. Britain, Canada and the US have embassies in Tunis (see p.105), and Britain has an honorary consul in Sfax (see p.249). As well as embassies in Tunis (see p.105), Libya has a consulate in Sfax (see p.249), and Algeria has consulates in Le Kef (see p.281) and Gafsa (see p.303), although travel to Algeria is extremely dangerous at present (see p.185) and visas may not be issued.

CUSTOMS REGULATIONS

The **duty-free allowances** into Tunisia are 400 cigarettes, a litre of spirits plus two litres of wine, 250ml of perfume and a litre of toilet water. Tunisian duty-free shops (often open at airports on arrival as well as departure) do not take dinars, so don't bother to save any for a bottle on your way home. They sell wine, but not the best, and no cheaper than in shops in Tunisia. Their rates for cigarettes and spirits are reasonable, however, and they also sell *chicha* tobacco at good prices.

INFORMATION, WEBSITES AND MAPS

The Organisation Nationale de Tourisme Tunisien (ONTT) have a main office in Tunis

British Tunisian Society, c/o Tunisian Embassy, 29 Prince's Gate, London SW7 1QG. Council for the Advancement of Arab–British Understanding, 21 Collingham Rd, London SW5 0NU (☎020/7373-8414). Maghreb Studies Association, c/o The Maghreb Bookshop, 45 Burton St, London WC1H 9AL (☎020/7388-1840). These organisations can supply you with additional information and books.

at 1 av Mohamed V (☎01/341077, ⓕ341997; ⓦ www.tourismtunisia.com) and others throughout the country, but you can pick up most of their material in advance before you reach Tunisia if coming from the UK, USA, Canada and much of Europe.

In Tunisia, you'll find a locally run tourist office, or **Syndicat d'Initiative**, in many towns, and

ONTT OFFICES ABROAD

Canada 1253 McGill College, Bureau #655, Montreal PQ H3B 2Y5 (☎514/397 1182).

France 32 av de l'Opéra, 75002 Paris (☎01/4742 7267); 12 rue de Sèze, 69006 Lyon (☎04/7852 3586).

Italy Via Calabria 25, 00187 Rome (☎06/4201 0149); Via Baracchini 10, 20123 Milan (☎02/8645 3044).

Netherlands Muntplein 2111, 1012 WR Amsterdam (☎020/622 4971).

UK 77a Wigmore St, London W1U 1QF (☎020/7224 5561; ⓦ www.tourismtunisia.co.uk).

USA c/o Tunisian Embassy, 1515 Massachusetts Ave NW, Washington, DC 20005 (☎202/466 2546; ⓔ ezzeddine@ix.netcom.com).

USEFUL WEBSITES

American Tour Association
🌐 www.grouptravels.com/tunisia
/tunisia_info.html
A good round-up of facts and figures about Tunisia, with statistics on the country's geography, economy and infrastructure.

Amnesty International
🌐 web.amnesty.org/ai.nsf
/countries/tunisia
Amnesty's reports on human rights and prisoners of conscience in Tunisia. Their findings have not made Amnesty popular with the Tunisian authorities.

Australian Department of Foreign Affairs
🌐 www.dfat.gov.au/geo/tunisia/index. Travel advice from the Australian government's Foreign Affairs Department, with a Tunisia fact sheet you can download in PDF.

British Foreign and Commonwealth Office
🌐 www.fco.gov.uk/ Constantly updated advice for travellers on circumstances affecting safety in over 130 countries.

Kerkennah Islands 🌐 www.kerkennah.com Run by two Kerkennians resident in the US, with features on history, on the jslands' various villages, and on traditional fishing techniques, plus photos of the islands and samples of Kerkennian music to download.

Miftah Shambali
🌐 www.i-cias.com/m.s/tunisia/index.htm
The Tunisia section of a site on North Africa, with a small write-up by Norwegian journalist Tore Kjeilen on each of over seventy places around the country, accompanied by photos, and usually containing an interesting comment or two on each place covered.

ONTT – Tunisian National Tourist Office
🌐 www.tourismtunisia.com
An online brochure featuring regional lists of hotels and restaurants the ONTT consider suitable for tourists, and glowing descriptions of Tunisia's tourist resorts plus, more usefully, a list

of festivals held in the country, though it may not be up to date.

Scorpion Venom
🌐 www.sunflower.singnet.com.sg/~chuaeecc/ve
nom/venom.htm
Descriptions and photographs of creatures you might prefer not to encounter in Tunisia.

Star Wars Locations in Tunisia
🌐 www.infomaniak.ch/~lionel/starwars
/default.htm
🌐 www.toysrgus.com/travel/tunisia.html
For serious Star Wars buffs – a couple of sites to help you track down every location used in every Star Wars movie shot in Tunisia, complete with photos.

Tunisia Online
🌐 www.tunisiaonline.com
Very much an official site, with features on the constitution, the president, the economy, and investment opportunities, plus latest news updates. One of the best sections is that on mosaics, with a selection of some of the best Roman mosaics from around the country.

Tunisian Jews
🌐 www.harissa.com/accueileng.htm
A site covering all aspects of Tunisian Jewish culture, including history, arts, customs, recipes, musical samples, and a photo gallery.

Tunisian Post Office
🌐 www.pttnet.gov.tn/stamps/english/index.htm
A site for philatelists, illustrating every stamp issued in the country since the first in 1888.

US Government Travel Advisory
🌐 travel.state.gov/tunisia.html
A cautionary warning sheet on matters such as crime and health, with words of warning for drivers and for Tunisian-Americans travelling on their US passport.

Weather in Tunisia
🌐 weather.noaa.gov/weather/TN_cc.html
The US government National Weather Service page on the latest weather conditions in Tunisia.

---

even some villages, and they are invariably friendlier and more helpful than the state-run ONTT; tourist office addresses and opening hours are quoted in this guide under the "Arrival" section of each town.

From these offices you can get specific local information, including listings of leisure activities, bike rental, laundries and countless other

things. And always ask for the free town plan. Many tourist offices also publish hotel and restaurant listings and give advice on the best places to go. They may even conduct free town tours.

There are a fair few **websites** on Tunisia, run from both inside and outside the country, mostly in French rather than Arabic, with a handful in

English too. There are also an ever-increasing number of internet offices in the country, where you can browse the Web, send email, or check your own if you have a Hotmail or similar account. Places where you can do this are detailed under "Internet access" in the "Listings" section for each major city in this book. Foreign websites, especially in French, may be blocked if they contain any criticism of the Tunisian government, and Hotmail is also frequently blocked for no apparent reason.

MAP OUTLETS

Included in the guide are maps and plans of the main towns, cities and sites – and most other places where we think you'll need one. They can be supplemented with free handouts from the ONTT, who print a reasonable general map of the country and a number of local town plans. Also available, though to be read with occasional irony, are a range of glossy pamphlets and reasonably full lists of hotels (usually including most of the unclassified ones).

Free touring **maps** of Tunisia are available from tourist offices around the country on a scale of 1:1,000,000, and are adequate for most purposes. If you intend to do a lot of driving around the country, on the other hand, or if you just want a better map, it is best to buy one before you arrive, although the Service Topographique (Survey Office) produce an excellent 1:750,000 map, which is usually available at their offices. These are located in most big cities, but usually out of town and hard to find; Sousse is the most convenient. If buying a map abroad, the best ones to go for are Michelin's (no.956) or Freytag and Berndt's, both on a scale of 1:800,000. Kimberley and Frey's 1:1,000,000 map is slightly less clear, as is Cartographia's on the same scale, but Cartographia's shows a number of rough desert pistes that the others leave out, which is handy if you plan on taking a jeep or landrover around the far south of the country. All of these maps make some attempt to show relief, but the only maps with contour lines as such are the Institut Géographique 1:1,000,000 African series, rather expensive and covering the country in three separate maps. For readers in the UK, the best selection of maps is available at Stanfords in Covent Garden, London, who also do mail order.

UK AND IRELAND

Blackwell's Map and Travel Shop, 53 Broad St, Oxford OX1 3BQ ☎01865/792792, ⊛www.bookshop.blackwell.co.uk.

Daunt Books, 83 Marylebone High St, W1M 3DE ☎020/7224 2295, 193 Haverstock Hill, NW3 4QL ☎020/7794 4006.

Easons Bookshop, 40 O'Connell St, Dublin 1 ☎01/873 3811, ⊛www.eason.ie.

Heffers Map and Travel, 20 Trinity St, Cambridge, CB2 1TJ ☎01223/568 568, ⊛www.heffers.co.uk.

Hodges Figgis Bookshop, 56–58 Dawson St, Dublin 2 ☎01/677 4754, ⊛www.hodgesfiggis.com.

John Smith and Sons, 26 Colquhoun Ave, Glasgow, G52 4PJ ☎0141/552 3377, ⊛www.johnsmith.co.uk.

James Thin Melven's Bookshop, 29 Union St, Inverness, IV1 1QA ☎01463/233500, ⊛www.jthin.co.uk.

The Map Shop, 30a Belvoir St, Leicester, LE1 6QH ☎0116/247 1400.

National Map Centre, 22–24 Caxton St, SW1H 0QU ☎020/7222 2466, ⊛www.mapsnmc.co.uk.

Newcastle Map Centre, 55 Grey St, Newcastle upon Tyne, NE1 6EF ☎0191/261 5622, ⊛www.traveller.ltd.uk.

Stanfords, 12–14 Long Acre, WC2E 9LP ☎020/7836 1321, ⊛www.stanfords.co.uk; maps by mail or phone order are available on this number and via ⊜sales@stanfords.co.uk. Other branches within British Airways offices at 156 Regent St, W1R 5TA ☎020/7434 4744, and 29 Corn St, Bristol BS1 1HT ☎0117/929 9966.

The Travel Bookshop, 13–15 Blenheim Crescent, W11 2EE ☎020/7229 5260, ⊛www.thetravelbookshop.co.uk.

Waterstone's, 91 Deansgate, Manchester M3 2BW ☎0161/837 3000, ⊛www.s1.waterstones .co.uk; Queens Bldg, 8 Royal Ave, Belfast BT1 1DA ☎028/9024 7355; 69 Patrick St Cork ☎021/276 522.

Adventurous Traveler Bookstore, PO Box 64769, Burlington, VT 05406 ☎1-800/282-3963, ⓦwww.AdventurousTraveler.com.

Book Passage, 51 Tamal Vista Bd, Corte Madera, CA 94925 ☎415/927-0960, ⓦwww.bookpassage.com.

Elliot Bay Book Company, 101 S Main St, Seattle, WA 98104 ☎206/624-6600 or 1-800/962-5311, ⓦwww.elliotbaybook.com.

Forsyth Travel Library, 226 Westchester Ave, White Plains, NY 10604 ☎1-800/367-7984, ⓦwww.forsyth.com.

Globe Corner Bookstore, 28 Church St, Cambridge, MA 02138 ☎1-800/358-6013, ⓦwww.globercorner.com.

GORP Adventure Library online only ☎1-800/754-8229, ⓦwww2.gorp.com.

Map Link Inc., 30 S La Patera Lane, Unit 5, Santa Barbara, CA 93117 ☎805/692-6777, ⓦwww.maplink.com.

Phileas Fogg's Travel Center, #87 Stanford Shopping Center, Palo Alto, CA 94304 ☎1-800/533-3644, ⓦwww.foggs.com.

Rand McNally, 444 N Michigan Av, Chicago, IL 60611 ☎312/321-1751, ⓦwww.randmcnally.com; 150 E 52nd St, New York, NY 10022 ☎212/758-7488; 595 Market St, San Francisco, CA 94105 ☎415/777-3131; around thirty stores across the US – call ☎1-800/333-0136 ext 2111 or check the website for the nearest store.

Travel Books & Language Center, 4437 Wisconsin Av, Washington, DC 20016 ☎1-800/220-2665, ⓦwww.bookweb.org/bookstore/travellers.

The Travel Bug Bookstore, 2667 West Broadway, Vancouver V6K 2G2 ☎604/737-1122, ⓦwww.swifty.com/tbug.

World of Maps, 118 Holland Av, Ottawa, Ontario K1Y 0X6 ☎613/724-6776, ⓦwww.itmb.com.

World Wide Books and Maps, 1247 Granville St, Vancouver V6Z 1G3 ☎604/687-3320, ⓦwww.worldofmaps.com.

The Map Shop, 6 Peel St, Adelaide SA 5000 ☎08/8231 2033, ⓦwww.mapshop.net.au.

Mapland, 372 Little Bourke St, Melbourne Vic 3000 ☎03/9670 4383, ⓦwww.mapland.com.au.

Mapworld, 173 Gloucester St, Christchurch, NZ ☎03/374 5399, ⓦwww.mapworld.co.nz.

Perth Map Centre, 884 Hay St, Perth WA 6000 ☎09/9322 5733, ⓦwww.perthmap.com.au.

Specialty Maps, 46 Albert St, Auckland, NZ ☎09/307 2217.

Travel Bookshop, Shop 3, 175 Liverpool St, Sydney NSW 2000 ☎02/9261 8200.

Worldwide Maps and Guides, 187 George St, Brisbane Qld 4000 ☎07/3221 4330, ⓦwww.worldmaps.com.au.

INSURANCE

You'd do well to take out an insurance policy before travelling to Tunisia for cover against theft, loss and illness or injury. Before paying for a new policy, however, it's worth checking whether you are already covered: some all-risks home insurance policies may cover your possessions when overseas, and many private medical schemes include cover when abroad. In Canada, provincial health plans usually provide partial cover for medical mishaps overseas, while holders of official student/teacher/youth cards in Canada and the US are entitled to meagre accident coverage and hospital in-patient benefits. Students will often find that their student health coverage extends during the vacations and for one term beyond the date of last enrolment.

After exhausting the possibilities above, you might want to contact a specialist travel insurance company, or consider the travel insurance deal we offer (see box). A typical travel insurance policy usually provides cover for the loss of baggage, tickets and – up to a certain limit – cash or cheques, as well as cancellation or curtailment of your journey. Most of them exclude so-called dangerous sports unless an extra premium is paid: in Tunisia this can mean scuba-diving and windsurfing, though probably not jeep safaris. Many policies can be chopped and changed to exclude coverage you don't need – for example, sickness and accident benefits can often be excluded or included at will. If you do take medical coverage, ascertain whether benefits will be paid as treatment proceeds or only after return home, and whether there is a 24-hour medical emergency number. When securing baggage cover, make sure that the per-article limit – typically under £500 – will cover your most valuable possession. If you need to make a claim, you should keep receipts for medicines and medical treatment, and in the event you have anything stolen, you must obtain an official statement from the police (called a *constat de vol*).

ROUGH GUIDE TRAVEL INSURANCE

Rough Guides offers its own **travel insurance**, customized for our readers by a leading UK broker and backed by a Lloyds underwriter. It's available for anyone, of any nationality and any age, travelling anywhere in the world.

There are two main Rough Guide insurance plans: **Essential**, for basic, no-frills cover; and **Premier** – with more generous and extensive benefits. Alternatively, you can take out annual **multi-trip insurance**, which covers you for any number of trips throughout the year (with a maximum of 60 days for any one trip). Unlike many policies, the Rough Guides schemes are calculated by the day,

so if you're travelling for 27 days rather than a month, that's all you pay for. If you intend to be away for the whole year, the **Adventurer** policy will cover you for 365 days. Each plan can be supplemented with a "Hazardous Activities Premium" if you plan to indulge in sports considered dangerous, such as skiing, scuba-diving or trekking.

For a **policy quote**, call the Rough Guides Insurance Line in the UK freefone ☎0800/015 0906, or, outside the UK on ☎(+44)1243/621 046. Alternatively, get an online quote, or buy your policy online, at ⊕www.roughguides.com/insurance.

HEALTH

Inside the country, most medicines are available but they're also expensive, so take any basics you might need, including stomach pills and suntan lotion. Travel insurance, especially to cover medical emergencies, is an essential precaution. Doctors differ in which jabs they advise for travellers to Tunisia. Most GPs like to keep their patients up to date with polio and tetanus, but few nowadays would suggest inoculation against typhoid, hepatitis A or cholera, and most visitors survive quite happily without having any injections at all, though vaccinations are a small price to pay for the security they provide.

COMMON COMPLAINTS

Two complaints particularly liable to afflict pampered constitutions are stomach upsets and heat. Most people experience some kind of **stomach problem** during a visit, but short of starving there's little you can do to avoid it, as there are unfamiliar microorganisms present in everything you consume. Some people drink only bottled water or use water purifying tablets and still have trouble; others drink tap water and come through unscathed. The best policy is to avoid obviously dirty food, wash all fresh fruit and vegetables, and always wash your hands before eating.

If you do go down with **diarrhoea**, it's essential to replace the fluid which is lost, since dehydration can strike very quickly. In serious cases, or with children, remember that dissolving rehydration salts in water helps your body absorb it. Failing that, half a teaspoon of table salt with four of sugar in a litre of water per day should see you all right. Some say prickly pears and bananas are good if you have diarrhoea, but other fruit is best avoided, as are greasy foods, dairy products, heavy spices and caffeine. If symptoms persist for several days – especially if you get painful cramps, or if blood or mucus appear in your stools – seek medical advice.

Never underestimate Tunisia's **heat**, especially in the south. A hat is an essential precaution and you should take a suntan lotion with the highest screen factor, as the sun really is higher (and therefore stronger) in Tunisia than in northern latitudes. Resulting problems include **dehydration**

– make sure that you're drinking enough (irregular urination such as only once a day is a danger sign) – and **heatstroke**, which is potentially fatal. Signs of heatstroke are a very high body temperature without a feeling of fever, but accompanied by headaches and disorientation (irrational behaviour by your travelling companions may be due to this); lowering body temperature, with a tepid shower or bath, for example, is the first step in treatment.

If you're visiting places on foot, especially in summer, take appropriate precautions – wear a sunhat, take frequent rests in the shade and carry plenty of water.

MEDICAL CARE IN TUNISIA

Medical care is of a high standard in Tunisia, with most doctors trained in France or Belgium. But state hospitals are filthy and overcrowded and basic services like food are not provided. Minor problems can be dealt with by any **infirmerie** (a surgery with a nurse), of which there's one in every town, and several in bigger ones. The larger towns all have hospitals and **cliniques** (small private hospitals that are usually more pleasant than state-run ones). **Pharmacies** administer most kinds of medicine, including some only available on prescription in Europe, and can often advise you about minor ailments. Pharmacists usually speak French but rarely English, so you should learn a few appropriate phrases if you have special needs. In any town of reasonable size, there will be a night pharmacy, open from evening till morning when others are closed.

The latest advice on health in Tunisia can be found on the British government's travel health website at Ⓦwww.24dr.com/reference/travel/index.asp, or the US government's equivalent at Ⓦwww.cdc.gov/travel/nafrica.htm.

HIV INFECTION

Sexual encounters between Tunisians and tourists are not particularly common (although see p.49), but it's as well to know that the incidence of **HIV infection** and full-blown **AIDS** in Tunisia is almost certainly far higher than officially declared. From the point of view of travellers, a holiday affair with another tourist or with a Tunisian beach gigolo (see p.50) are the most likely areas of risk. Take condoms with you (local ones are less reliable) and insist on using them if you have casual sex.

BITES AND STINGS

Rabies exists in Tunisia, and it's wise to give certain animals a wide berth. Dogs can be very fierce, especially if you're walking or cycling; as a last resort, throwing stones (or even just threatening to) should get rid of them. A bite, scratch or even lick from an infected animal could spread the disease; wash any wound immediately but gently with soap or detergent, and apply alcohol or iodine if possible. Find out what you can about the animal and if it's known or thought to be infected, get treatment *immediately* – rabies is invariably fatal once symptoms appear. There is a vaccine, but it is expensive, serves only to shorten the course of treatment you need and lasts no longer than three months.

Other animals to be avoided are **snakes and scorpions**. Both will be as keen to avoid you as

you are them, and won't bite or sting unless disturbed. Don't go around barefoot in areas where there may be snakes or scorpions, wander through undergrowth in sandals, or poke about under or between rocks. If camping in desert areas, shake out your shoes before putting them on in case a scorpion has crept in. Most snakes are non-venomous, and few are life-threatening, but one or two species can be dangerous, most notably the horned viper. All scorpions sting, and a sting can be extremely painful, especially if you have an allergy to it, but again, not many are life-threatening (see box). In fact, even in the case of potentially lethal species, death from snake bites or scorpion stings is rare, and a victim should be in no danger if treated within a reasonable time. Nonetheless, if you or a companion are bitten by a snake or stung by a scorpion, you should seek treatment immediately. Try to remember what it looked like to assist identification when you get treated. Keep the victim calm and still, since moving may spread the venom. In the case of a snake bite, apply a tourniquet if possible above the wound, relieving it for ninety seconds every fif-

SCORPIONS

Looking like some horrific alien creature, complete with claws and deadly sting, **scorpions** are the stuff of nightmares. At often more than 10cm from head to tail, they are the largest land invertebrates, and belong to the arachnid family, along with spiders. As well as being nocturnal, scorpions glow under ultra-violet, so you can see them in the desert at night with the aid of a black light. The pincers are used for self-defence, digging burrows, holding prey and also courtship. Famously, when mating, the male grabs the female and the two perform what looks like a dance. In fact, the male is manoeuvering the female into a position where his genitalia can make contact with hers. Once impregnated, she may well have him for dinner unless he can make himself scarce. She does not lay eggs, but carries the young inside her until they are born, a rarity among invertebrates.

Scorpions are ideally adapted for the desert. They can survive the extremes of both heat and cold, and their exoskeleton protects from dehydration. Like cockroaches, they are among the species most capable of surviving a nuclear holocaust. They eat insects, spiders, and occasionally larger animals such as lizards and even mice, and find their prey with the aid of fine hairs on their

pincers which detect vibrations in the air. They only sting their prey when it's necessary to immobilize it, and only 25 out of over 1000 species in the world have a sting that can be fatal to humans. Children and older people are the most vulnerable, and it is said that Berber women in some Tunisian desert communities used to capture scorpions and boil a certain number up in milk, to give to newborn infants to build up their immunity.

The most deadly species of scorpion in Tunisia is the yellow fat-tailed scorpion (*Androctonus australis*), which is 4–10cm long. It is typically found under stones and in cracks and crevices, including cracks in the walls of houses, and is responsible for the majority of scorpion fatalities in Tunisia. Other dangerous native scorpions include the death stalker (*Leiurus quinquestriatus*), which can also reach up to 10cm and ranges from light yellow to almost orange, the blacktip scorpion (*Buthus occitanus*), up to 7cm in length and light yellow to black, the black fat-tailed scorpion (*Androctonus bicolor*), black and over 9cm long, and *Androctonus amoreuxi*, 6–9cm long and light to dark brown. Other species can give you a nasty sting, but are not dangerous.

teen minutes. Don't bother trying to suck the venom out – that only works in movies, and attempting it may spread the poison. In the case of a scorpion sting, clean the site gently with soap and water, and apply a cold compress if you have one to hand; in most cases, the effects will subside within an hour, but always seek treatment in any case.

The other poisonous animals you may fall foul of are **jellyfish**, now increasingly common in the Mediterranean due to the demise of sea turtles that were their main predators. Jellyfish stings are unlikely to be life-threatening, but are extremely painful, and again should be treated immediately.

COSTS, MONEY AND BANKS

The cost of travel in Tunisia compares well with southern Europe – and especially with Italy. You can get by quite easily on £100/$150 a week, with good meals, reasonable hotel rooms and a fair amount of transport, while on £150/$230 you move into relative luxury. At the bottom end, camping out or staying in the cheaper hotels, you could survive on as little as £70/$100. In general, the south of the country will be slightly cheaper than the north, and untouristed areas rather cheaper than resorts. Food, accommodation and souvenirs in Sousse, for example, can work out at almost double the price of equivalents in Sfax.

Rooms are the most variable factor. A basic (unclassified) hotel will generally charge around £3–7/$5–11 single and £4–10/$7–15 double, while one-star places may be in the £6–20/$9–30 range for a single, £8–25/$12–40 a double, and

three-star tourist hotels are £20–45/$30–65 for a single, £35–70/$55–100 a double in high season, though in beach resorts they may drop to less than half that price off-season. A set **meal**, with (excellent) wine, in a good local restaurant will only set you back around £8/$12 a head, and you can fill up in a cheap diner for less than half that. **Transport** costs are moderate, and distances are not very great: Tunis–Sfax, a journey of 270km, costs around £4.20/$6 by second-class train, £5.50/$8 by bus, first-class train or louage (shared taxi – see p.24), or £24/$36 by plane.

THE TUNISIAN DINAR

The **Tunisian dinar (TD)** is a soft currency (unstable in exchange value), and illegal to export from (or import into) the country. The **exchange rate** is fixed daily on a national basis (you can find it in local newspapers under *Cours des Devises*); at present one dinar is worth about 50p sterling, 75¢ US, FF5, or €0.80, which makes prices generally low for overseas visitors.

An initial source of confusion is the way the dinar is written. It is divided into 1000 millimes and small, fractional prices are usually expressed in terms of **millimes** – 1,500, for example, instead of 1.5. "Whole" dinar prices, however, are usually written as "1TD", rather than "1,000mill". For the sake of clarity, prices in the guide are all expressed in dinars so that, for example, seven hundred millimes appears as "0.7TD".

Banknotes are issued in denominations of 5TD, 10TD, 20TD and 30TD, with silver **coins** of 5TD, 1TD and 0.5TD, and brass coins of 10, 20, 50 and 100 millimes – all identical in design, the last two confusingly similar in size. Aluminium coins of 5 millimes exist, and are easy to confuse with 0.5TD ones; small aluminium 1 and 2 millime coins are rare and useless.

BANKS AND EXCHANGE

Bank **opening hours** are limited. In summer (July & Aug) they are Monday to Friday 8–11am, and the rest of the year Monday to Thursday 8–11.30am and 2–5pm, Friday 8–11am and 1.30pm–4pm, except during Ramadan, when it's Monday to Friday 8am–11.30pm and 1–2.30pm. In tourist areas, banks will sometimes open outside standard hours for **money exchange**, and you can often fall back on hotels; the bigger, posher ones are naturally most likely to change money. Always retain the receipts from your transactions for re-exchanging when you leave the country.

Away from tourist areas, exchange facilities can be few and far between, and you'll sometimes find banks don't have the essential exchange rates, especially first thing in the morning. The local STB (Tunisia's "national" bank) is generally most reliable, and some banks will let you draw cash on Visa or Access/Mastercard. As a very last resort, if you have hard cash, you could try asking around the local louage (shared taxi) station, especially if it runs to destinations beyond Tunisia's borders.

Carrying some **foreign currency** in cash (French francs and US dollars are best, but sterling will do) is a good idea; any bank will take it, and occasionally individuals. Post offices will also often change cash. Banks and post offices take most major currencies, but not Australian or New Zealand dollars. They claim to accept Scottish and Northern Irish sterling banknotes, though they may not do so, so it's best to change your cash into English notes before leaving the UK.

Finally, it's as well to know that the **black market** offers rates only marginally better than official ones. You are unlikely to run across black market currency dealers except on roads close to the Libyan border, where they wave wads of Libyan dinars at passing motorists (if you're really caught short, Libyan louage drivers may also change cash for you, especially dollars, if you are in a place where louages run to Libya), but street money changers also exist in Sfax. When buying

something expensive like a carpet, you may be able to get the price down by offering foreign exchange instead of dinars. ONA craft shops (see p.44) often offer a discount for foreign currency.

CASH AND TRAVELLERS' CHEQUES

You are allowed to bring in unrestricted amounts of **foreign currency** in cash or travellers' cheques. In theory, you should declare it on entry if you intend to re-export more than 1000TD-worth (£500/$750), but tourists are not usually checked for currency on departure.

Thomas Cook, Visa and American Express are the best-known **travellers' cheques** and are accepted at most banks and many hotels, whether in sterling, US dollars, euros or (usually) Canadian dollars – Australian and New Zealand dollars are not recognized. Banks in Tunisia charge a fee of 0.3TD for changing each cheque. You are supposed to keep the receipt and a record of cheque serial numbers safe and separate from the cheques themselves. However, some banks will refuse to change travellers' cheques unless you show the receipt. In the event that cheques are lost or stolen, the issuing company will expect you to report the loss to their office in Tunisia; most companies claim to replace lost or stolen cheques within 24 hours.

A new option from Visa (and competitors will no doubt soon be offering the same kind of service) is **Visa travel money**, a disposable pre-paid debit card with a PIN that you can use in ATM machines worldwide. It's a sort of electronic version of travellers' cheques, where you can buy as much credit as you think you'll need, and dispose of the card when it runs out. You can carry up to eight spare cards in case you lose one, or for a family or group with a common pool of money. There is a 24-hour toll-free global customer assistance services centre in Baltimore, which you can in theory call collect (☎001-410/581 9091). The card is available from, among other places, Thomas Cook in the UK and Colombus Bank in the

---

24-HOUR EMERGENCY NUMBERS FOR LOST TRAVELLERS' CHEQUES

American Express ☎0044-1273/571600.
Thomas Cook/MasterCard ☎0044-1733/318950.
Visa ☎0044-20/7937 8091.

US, and can be ordered in the United States on ☎1-877/394 2247. For further information, check Visa's website at ⓦ www.visa.com.

CREDIT AND DEBIT CARDS

Credit and debit cards are of limited use in shops and restaurants outside tourist resorts, though they can be used for cash advances from banks, and are handy for items of major expense such as car rental – in fact, they're sometimes essential for car rental deposits. They are also accepted by most hotels of two or more stars, and by the more upmarket restaurants. Diners Club, American Express, Visa and Mastercard are all usable in the right places. Visa and Mastercard can also be used to draw cash from most banks and ATMs – your bank's international banking department should be able to advise on this. Make sure before you leave that your personal identification number (PIN) is valid overseas. Remember that cash advances on credit cards are treated as loans, with interest accruing daily from the date of withdrawal; there may also be a transaction fee on purchases made with plastic.

WIRING MONEY

Having **money wired** from home is not cheap, and is best treated as a last resort. Funds can be sent via Western Union to any major post office in the country. Fees depend on the amount being transferred, but, as an example, wiring £700/$1000 will cost around £40/$60. The funds should be available for collection (usually in

dinars) within minutes of being sent (which can be done in person or over the phone using a credit card). A similar service is available from rival firm MoneyGram – funds sent with them can be collected from any branch of Banque Nationale Agricole (BNA) nationwide.

It's also possible to have money wired directly from a bank in your home country to a bank in Tunisia, although this is more complicated because it involves two separate institutions. If you go this route, the person wiring the funds to you will need to know the telex number of the bank the funds are being wired to.

LEAVING TUNISIA

There are strict regulations about the quantity of dinars that you can **change back when leaving** the country. You're allowed to reconvert up to thirty percent of the total amount you can prove you have changed since being in Tunisia – with an upper limit of 100TD. This means keeping an eye on the number of dinars you're likely to have on you when you leave, particularly if you've changed large amounts. It also means you should keep all the **exchange receipts** you're given. You cannot use dinars at the airport duty-free shop, but you can use them in the departure lounge café.

Note, too, that if you leave by air or sea on a ticket purchased in Tunisia with cash you will require a **bon de passage**, which is a slip of paper certifying that the ticket was bought with money changed in a bank. You will first have to get a form from the ticket agent to give to the

MONEY-WIRING COMPANIES

IN NORTH AMERICA

American Express Moneygram ☎1-800/926-9400, ⓦ www.moneygram.com.
Western Union ☎1-800/325-6000, ⓦ www.westernunion.com.
Thomas Cook US ☎1-800/287-7362, Canada ☎1-888 /8234-7328, ⓦ www.us.thomascook.com.

IN AUSTRALIA

American Express Moneygram ☎1800/230 100, ⓦ www.moneygram.com.
Western Union ☎1800/649 565, ⓦ www.westernunion.com.

IN NEW ZEALAND

American Express Moneygram ☎09/379 8243 or 0800/262 263, ⓦ www.moneygram.com.
Western Union ☎09/270 0050, ⓦ www.westernunion.com.

IN THE UK AND IRELAND

Western Union UK ☎0800/833 833, Ireland ☎1800/395395 ⓦ www.westernunion.com.
Moneygram UK ☎0800/018 0104, Ireland ☎1800/205800 ⓦ www.moneygram.com.
Thomas Cook ☎01733/318922, Belfast ☎028/9055 0030, Dublin ☎01/677 1721.

bank. But before changing your money, make sure the bank in question will issue you with the *bon*, as you cannot buy the ticket without it. The money you change when getting a *bon de passage* can- not count as part of the sum from which you're allowed to reconvert thirty percent, so it's best not to change money for other business in the same transaction.

GETTING AROUND

Many visitors to Tunisia are discouraged from exploring the country by the high cost of car rental – around £170/$250 a week – but it's possible to reach nearly every town detailed in this guide by some form of scheduled transport or by service taxis, known as louages. Admittedly, the train lines are not very far-reaching, and other forms of transport may be slow, infrequent or occasionally very crowded, but it's a reliable enough system, and distances within Tunisia are relatively short.

The one general warning to bear in mind is that transport services tend to stop at around 5pm – except in the far south, where local transport can dry up even earlier, though there may be a night bus to Tunis via either Sfax and Sousse or Kairouan. On remote routes your only choice may be the early-morning market bus.

Trains are generally a little faster than the SNTRI (national) bus, and cost slightly less in second class, more in first. SNTRI buses are faster and more comfortable than SRT (regional) buses, but also more expensive, and usually only ply routes to and from Tunis. Louages (service taxis) are faster than buses, and only slightly more expensive, but are considered more dangerous. Buses and louages have the disadvantage of stopping for an hour's lunch in the middle of any journey if it happens to be over lunchtime. A plane journey will cost about five times as much

as train, bus or louage, and of course will be much quicker, airport to airport, though you still have to check in, collect bags at the other end, and travel to and from the airports, which can be time con- suming.

BUSES

Buses are Tunisia's most popular form of trans- port. They're comprehensive but complicated to master. They are run by different companies, including the **SNTRI** (Société Nationale de Transport Rural et Interurbain) and several region- al rivals known as **SRTs** (Société Régionale des Transports). Most have predictable names such as SRT Béja, or SRT du Gouvernorat de Medenine (SRTGM), but one or two have less obvious names such as SORETRAS (Sfax) and SOTREGAMES (Gabès).

SNTRI run services in and around Tunis, linking Tunis to almost every town in the country at least once a day. Each SRT runs local services within its own region, and some northern ones also run ser- vices to Tunis. A few long-distance services don't pass through Tunis (Sousse–Le Kef, for example), but in general it is easier to move towards or away from Tunis than across the country. Given the choice, SNTRI services are invariably better than SRT ones: faster, more comfortable, and much more likely to depart and arrive on time, although they also cost slightly more.

The different companies often refuse to recog- nize each others' existence, so it's important to ask at each individual office to be sure of finding all the buses on a given route. Some bigger towns have a central bus station, sometimes called the *gare routière*, but often the companies operate from their own separate locations, which are detailed throughout this guide. SNTRI generally display departure lists in both Arabic and French, but most others post them only in Arabic if at all, so unless you read Arabic, it will be a case of persistent questioning.

When travelling in the daytime, especially in summer, it's a good idea to consider which side of the bus the sun will be on, and choose a seat to avoid it.

LOUAGES

Louages – large shared taxis, usually battered Peugeots for five passengers, but increasingly minibuses taking eight – are the fastest form of long-distance transport, operating nonstop along fixed routes. They leave as soon as the full complement of passengers has appeared, or when the driver gets tired of waiting. If the car moves off without a full complement and you are the only passenger(s), make sure the driver realizes you are paying only the rate for one *place* – though you may agree with other passengers to split any empty places between you. Choice of seats is on a first-come, first-served basis; most people find the back seat of the Peugeots uncomfortable, but you'll probably be lumbered with it if you are fourth or fifth to arrive. It's best to make it clear which of the remaining seats you want as soon as you find your louage. Although routes are fixed, you can, of course, rent a louage privately to go to a specific destination. If you think a louage driver is overcharging you, ask to see the official *tarif* (price list), which all louages must carry by law. Fares are usually slightly more than the bus fare for the same route.

Louages operate from informal **stations** that are liable to be elusive to the uninitiated foreigner – often a particular garage or backstreet yard. In larger towns, there are different terminals for different destinations. There is now a trend towards building a single louage station and a single bus station next to each other, out of town if need be, and these are being planned or installed in certain major towns. Once you've found the right place (they are detailed in the text, but they often change), ask for your destination – the signs on the cars only indicate where they are licensed, not necessarily where they are going. If you make enough noise, someone will find you a car or show you where to wait. Early morning is the best time to look for a louage – on many routes, they can get scarce at lunchtime and as the day goes on.

Usually, you will turn up to find a louage waiting. If there are a lot of passengers waiting and no louages, competition for seats can be fierce when one does eventually turn up, and you may find yourself joining a tense group of twenty people awaiting the next arrival – the time-honoured technique is to sprint for the car when you see it in the distance, grab a door handle and hang on until the car stops. If you're carrying luggage, your only chance in this situation is to abandon it in the struggle for a seat then load it when the dust has settled. If this is too much for you, someone may get you a place for a little baksheesh. Louages will only stop for you on the road if they have a spare seat – the police are tough on drivers who carry more than the legal limit of passengers.

Some people regard louages as too **dangerous** a form of transport. Certainly, louage drivers can be frighteningly reckless, frequently overtaking on blind curves or the crest of a hill, for example, and definitely not obeying speed limits. The reason is that, with tariffs fixed by law and the number of possible runs in a day limited, profit margins are low and the best way for a driver to make a little extra is to squeeze in an extra run. Unsurprisingly therefore, louages have an even higher accident rate than Tunisian cars in general. Louage passengers in the front seat usually wear a seat belt, if only because of police checks, and it is strongly advisable to wear one in the back seat too. In the new minibus louages, all seats are fitted with belts, and again you are strongly advised to use them.

In addition to intercity louages, local **camionettes** (pick-up trucks) run from large towns to the surrounding villages. These don't always have a limit on passenger numbers and are very cheap, but rather uncomfortable. Occasionally, ordinary **taxis** may run a set route for a fixed fare per place like louages; this will usually be for local routes and may operate at peak times only.

TRAINS

Only a small proportion of Tunisia's train lines (built by the French) have passenger services. They're run by the **SNCFT** (Société Nationale des Chemins de Fer Tunisiens) and cost about the same as louages or SNTRI buses, slightly more than SRT buses and usually run more or less on schedule. Except at Gafsa, they have the advantage that stations are usually very near the centre of town. The disadvantage is that the network is very limited (a lot of towns that have rail lines see only freight trains on them), as is the number of daily services. Some **routes**, like the air-conditioned service down the coast, are excellent – and a real boon in summer. **Prices** are graded according to the type of service, and all trains have first and second class. First costs twenty to fifty percent more than second, and there's also a *Grand Confort* class, much the same as first but less crowded and ten to fifteen percent more expensive again. A return ticket costs fifteen percent less than two one-way tickets. Note that, even if you already have a ticket (on the return leg of a return trip, for example), you'll have to buy a 0.75TD platform access ticket to board your train.

Most long-distance services, especially air-conditioned (*climatisé*), can get crowded in midsummer and should be booked in advance if possible. Even for ordinary services, turn up early to be sure of buying a ticket – if you board without, you have to pay double. Thomas Cook's *Overseas Timetable* (the blue volume) gives a complete and up-to-date list of services. You can consult it in any public reference library. One difficulty is that most stations only have one sign, usually at one end of the platform, so you'll have to keep a sharp eye out to know where you are. Another thing to bear in mind is that trains going in different directions often pass each other at stations, there being only single track in between, and are therefore in the station at the same time – make sure you get the right one.

As well as SNCFT services, there is a local train service called the **TGM** from Tunis to some of its suburbs (see p.108), and a metro in the city itself.

You can buy a one-, two- or four-week train pass called the **Carte Semaine**, which offers unlimited train travel around Tunisia and costs per week just over twice the single fare from Tunis to Sfax, or slightly less than a return fare from Tunis to Gabès. If you plan to do a lot of travelling by train in a short time, it might be good value, at 19.5TD for a week second class, 27.3TD for first; for two- or three-week passes, multiply these figures by two or three. The pass can be bought at stations and travel agents and you need to bring a passport photo. Students under 28 years of age can buy a 10TD **Carte Jeune**, valid for a year, which entitles them to reductions of 25–35 percent on the standard fare.

HITCHHIKING

Hitchhiking is generally good in Tunisia, for men at least. There are no problems with officialdom

and, although there is remarkably little traffic, in remote areas almost anything that passes will stop. In some of these areas, hitching is an informal kind of public transport – especially in the ubiquitous **camionettes** (Peugeot 404 pick-up trucks) and a small contribution is expected. If there are other passengers, watch how much they pay. If you're on your own, you can either try to agree on a price in advance or risk disagreement at the end should the driver try to overcharge you; in fact this is very unlikely and waiving payment is much more common. There are no hard-and-fast rules, but the fare should be a little less than you would pay on a bus. On main routes Tunisians usually only hitch to or from places where there is no louage service, but traffic will probably stop for you anyway.

It can be hard to hitch out of Hammamet, and you have to walk a long way out of Tunis and Sfax, but other **routes** are fairly unproblematic. Market days can be good for travel if you get up early enough. Transport usually heads out to a market first thing in the morning, returning late morning or afternoon. Hitching can be an excellent way of getting to meet Tunisian people. However, although **women** hitching alone or together can pick up lifts with car-renting tourists around Cap Bon or Jerba, it is extremely inadvisable.

BIKES

Tunisia's terrain and climate are ideally suited most of the year to **bicycles and motorbikes**, though you may get soaked in winter and spring, and strong winds can make cycling hard work. The only drawback is the lack of maintenance facilities, as there are very few motorbikes in the country (though thousands of mopeds), and bicycles are common but basic, so you'll have to bring any specialized spare parts along. Bicycles and occasionally mopeds can be rented in big towns but, frustratingly, only for use in the town or along the beach. If you're staying some time in Tunisia and want a motorbike for transport, it's cheaper to buy abroad and import than buy locally. **Trains** will carry a bicycle for about the same fare as a passenger; **buses** usually charge about half the passenger fare.

DRIVING AND CAR RENTAL

In such a small country **driving** ought to be the ideal way to get around. If you can afford to bring a car with you, this is true. Unfortunately **car rental charges** in Tunisia are phenomenal –

among the highest in the Mediterranean. Even the smallest Citroën will set you back 450TD a week in summer and, officially at least, it's illegal to carry more than three passengers. To rent a car, you'll need to be over 21 and have held a licence for at least a year. You should also check the insurance and the small print very thoroughly. From this point of view, if not for price, it might be a good idea to go for one of the big agencies listed below. Hotels often have arrangements with reliable local firms. There are cheap private local companies, although they tend to offer no decent bargains; if a car is cheap to rent it may not be very well maintained. One thing always to check when renting a car is the spare wheel, jack and wrench, since suffering a flat tyre on Tunisia's ragged roads is a strong possibility. Another thing to check is the fuel tank – usually this should be full, and you will be expected to return it full, though some companies give you the car with a nearly empty tank, and you can return it the same way.

Despite these hassles and expenses, driving has many advantages. You can visit the smaller and remoter villages seen only through dusty windows by those trapped in public transport, and you can make rewarding contacts with local people, especially if you pick up hitchhikers.

To bring **your own vehicle**, you will have to be over 21 and carry documents proving your ownership of the vehicle, a valid driving licence or an international one, and a green card covering Tunisia (if it doesn't, you can buy insurance at the frontier).

DRIVING CONDITIONS

Main **roads** are straight and surfaced and often lined with shady eucalyptus trees; A-roads are called *Grands Parcours* (GP) and B-roads *Moyennes Corniches* (MC). Tunisia **drives on the right**, with priority from the right, and vehicles coming onto a roundabout or traffic circle have right of way over those already on it. **Speed limits** are (in theory, and unless otherwise indicated) 90km/h (55mph) in open country and 50km/h (31mph) in built-up areas, 110km/h (68mph) on the country's only motorway from Tunis to just south of Sousse, and 70km/h (43mph) on the island of Jerba. However fast you're going, though, it's customary to slow down when passing **highway patrols**. It's a good idea to have your papers available because there are frequent road checks, especially in the south and around Gafsa – usually, it's your passport rather than your driving licence that they'll want to see. If they check your vehicle, it'll be the lights and horn that they are most interested in. There are also speed traps, and seat belts are compulsory for the driver and front-seat passenger. If you get stopped for speeding you have to pay on the spot. One practice that's initially disconcerting is that the police often flag down drivers to get a lift. It's best not to argue, and if you're not going their way they won't force the matter. As far as parking goes, red and white stripes painted on the kerb tell you that it is prohibited, and in Tunis and one or two other places, wheel clamps are used to enforce this. Be aware also that in town, where left or right turns are banned, there may well not be a "no left turn" or "no right turn" sign at the junction, just a "no entry" sign in front of the turning.

Tunisian drivers are not the safest in the world, and the roads can be quite hazardous. In fact, Tunisia has one of the highest rates of road accidents in the world. Always drive defensively, and

---

CAR RENTAL RESERVATION NUMBERS

Avis US & Canada ☎1-800/331 1084; UK ☎0870/590 0500; Ireland ☎01/874 5844; Australia ☎1800/225 533; New Zealand ☎0800/655 111 or 09/526 2800, ⓦwww.avis.com.

Budget US & Canada ☎1-800/527 0700; UK ☎0800/181181; Ireland ☎0800/973159; Australia ☎1300/362 848; New Zealand ☎0800/652 227 or 09/375 2270, ⓦwww.budgetrentacar.com.

Europcar US & Canada ☎1-800/800 6000; UK ☎0845/722 2525; Ireland ☎01/874 5844;

Australia ☎02/9223 1444; New Zealand ☎0800/486 677, ⓦwww.europcar.com.

Hertz US & Canada ☎1-877/940 6900; UK ☎0870/848 4848; Ireland ☎01/676 7476; Australia ☎1800/550 067; New Zealand ☎0800/655 955 or 09/309 0989, ⓦwww.hertz.com.

National US & Canada ☎1-800/CAR RENT; UK ☎0870/536 5365; Ireland ☎1800/301401; Australia ☎13 1908; New Zealand ☎09/537 2582, ⓦwww.nationalcar.com.

be wary coming up to blind curves and the tops of hills, since it is quite commonplace for Tunisians to overtake approaching these. Also beware farm vehicles travelling unlit at night. Another hazard, especially when passing through towns, is the lack of road sense among pedestrians, cyclists and moped riders, who all seem to meander quite happily down the middle of the road as if they'd never heard of the automobile; you will almost certainly end up using your horn more than you do at home, but you will also have to reduce speed and keep your eyes peeled, especially at dusk. Dipping headlights is a novel concept to most Tunisian drivers and you will be dazzled by the glare from oncoming traffic. Another potential problem is the state of some of the **rougher roads**, especially in the south. Some are obviously difficult, while drifting sand on others can be dangerous. Also, tarmac can be rather narrow and oncoming trucks tend to force cars off the edge of the road, accepted practice but a little worrying at first. The latest problem in highly touristed areas (approaching Kairouan or Matmata for example) is "guides" posing as hitchhikers, who will want to thank you for giving them a lift by inviting you for tea at their home, except that it turns out to be a carpet shop and you will have to worm your way out of, or endure, an hour or so of hard sell.

In the south, many of the routes are **unsurfaced roads**. Their condition varies and many are passable in any ordinary car, while others require a 4WD vehicle. In any case, you will not be able to drive on them at the same sort of speed as on tarmac; even if it seems quite easy, remember that the surface can change unexpectedly, and boulders can appear as if from nowhere. Car rental firms don't permit their vehicles to be driven on unsurfaced roads, and can hold you liable for "any damage caused to the vehicle through driving on dirt tracks". If you intend driving into the desert, see the box on p.415.

Fuel prices are fixed, so they are the same at all petrol stations. Fuel is cheaper in Tunisia than in the UK, but more expensive than in the US. At last check, a litre of petrol cost roughly £0.35/$0.52 a litre. Unleaded fuel is available at most, but not all, petrol stations.

In case of **breakdown**, always carry a good supply of water and, if you're planning a long journey, food and blankets. There are plenty of places that will repair a flat tyre or more serious problem cheaply – look out for workshops with tyres outside, especially on the way into and out of towns.

Car rental companies should refund the cost of any necessary repairs, so long as you have kept the receipt.

FLIGHTS

Tunisia's size makes **internal flights** rather a luxury, even though tickets are relatively cheap (under £30/$45 from Tunis to Jerba); to be sure of a flight, it's wise to book well ahead. Internal flights in Tunisia are run by Tunisair, who have offices in all major towns (their addresses can be found in the Listings sections of this book), and Tuninter, whose tickets are available through Tunisair or any travel agent.

ORGANIZED TOURS

If time is short, you might consider an **organized tour** by Land Rover or even bus. These are offered by travel agents and hotels in most large Tunisian towns and resorts, and can generally be found in our Listings sections under "Tours". Their main advantage is that they are relatively good value (£85/$130 for three days is typical), and allow you to see far more in the way of sights than you could on public transport. Disadvantages are that they rather isolate you from the country, may move on more quickly than you would like and stop for meals at places whose prices go up when you arrive. Organized excursions in Tunisia are usually termed "safari", but note that this does not involve wildlife-spotting.

CITY TRANSPORT

The cheapest way to get around big towns is by **bus**. These can be very crowded (you often have to fight your way on and off) and stops are not always signposted. Useful routes are indicated in the text of the guide, but it's often easier and more interesting to walk. Tunis has a so-called **metro** system that's an articulated tram rather than an underground train, and subject to most of the same provisos as buses.

Taxis are very good value for small groups. They all have meters, so there's no need to fix a price before you go, though this may not apply at night – officially, they should run on the meter and charge you fifty percent extra from 9pm to 6am. You can arrange a tour (around several sites, for example) by renting the taxi for the day. In this case, fix the price first. By law taxis can only take four people, but if there are more of you it is possible to use a larger (and more expensive) estate car, a louage for example (see p.24).

In towns with a large tourist presence, horse-drawn carts known as **calèches** provide a more picturesque alternative to taxis. Though slower and more expensive (and given to stopping off at souvenir stalls, where the driver gets a commis-sion on anything you buy), calèches are a fun ride, especially for children. Also purely for holiday-makers are the frankly ridiculous **tourist land trains**, known as Noddy trains, which have spread like an epidemic to almost all of the country's resorts.

ACCOMMODATION

Tunisia's more expensive hotels are geared primarily to the package holiday trade. The country is adapting to the growth in independent travel – but it's a slow process. In all the main tourist centres and in larger towns in the interior, you can find hotels in every price range, but in smaller places there may only be a choice between a very basic establishment with dirty sheets or a fairly expensive hotel with air conditioning and pool. In midsummer, any kind of room in the more popular towns can be hard to find on the spot – though if you get really stuck someone local will probably invite you to stay rather than see the country's reputation for hospitality diminished.

High season usually means the summer (mid-June to mid-Sept, sometimes only July & Aug); **low season** is over winter (Nov–March), and **mid-season** in between (April–June & Sept–Oct). Not all hotels have seasonal price changes (unclas-sified and city hotels usually do not); some charge the same prices in mid- and high season; and one or two in the **desert** have high season in winter and low season in the summer. **Christmas** and **New Year** tariffs are likely to be even higher than the normal high-season price.

HOTELS AND PENSIONS

Classified hotels, officially approved for tourist use, are graded from one-star to five-star, with wide-ranging prices and standards within each category. The classification of a hotel depends on things like the size of rooms, windows and bath-rooms, and the presence or absence of facilities (such as a swimming pool): it is not a reliable indi-cation of the price or quality of service. Indeed, things like room service – which you might expect in Western hotels with a rating – can be slapdash or nonexistent, and even in a three- or four-star hotel in Tunisia, rooms may have only a shower, no bath; the Western practice of adding drinks from the bar to room bills is rare.

Below the one-star category, there is a range of hotels suitable for budget travellers, even if not officially regarded as appropriate for tourists. These **unclassified hotels**, usually concentrat-ed in a town's medina – just ask for an auberge (inn) or *Hôtel Tunisien* – differ widely. The best of them, often colonial relics, have high ceilings and creaking fans, and are very respectable, and charging 10–20TD for a double room, though in winter they may be cold and draughty with no heating. Many of the cheapest ones (4TD per per-son), though, can be rougher – and they're some-times closed to, or dangerous for, unaccompanied women. In this type of place you may be expect-ed to share a room, or fill it, or even pay for any beds (as many as four) which remain empty. However, there are good (and perfectly safe)

ACCOMMODATION PRICE CODES

All the hotels and pensions listed in this book have been price-graded according to the following scale and, although costs will rise slightly overall with the life of this edition, the relative comparisons should remain valid.

The codes represent the **cheapest available double room in high season**, although many places will have pricier rooms with a higher grade of facilities or maybe a sea view. In the case of hostels, we quote the exact price per person for a dorm bed. Remember that prices are often seasonal and places that are expensive in the summer may have bargain-basement prices off season when business is slack, and that prices may be negotiable, especially out of season or if you're staying for a week or more. All hotels must by law display their official maximum prices in reception, usually in the form of a price per person in a double room, with a supplement for single occupancy. Categories ❸ and higher tend to include breakfast.

❶ Under 10TD. Usually for bed only in a basic unclassified hotel.

❷ 10–20TD. Bed only or bed and breakfast in a good unclassified or cheap one-star hotel.

❸ 20–40TD. Average one-star or a cheap two-star.

❹ 40–70TD. Expensive two-star, cheap three-star.

❺ 70–100TD. Standard three-star, cheap four-star.

❻ 100–150TD. Expensive three-star, standard four-star

❼ 150TD upwards. Deluxe four- or five-star.

places even in this range and, for men at least, they're a useful standby as you can nearly always find a bed.

Women will have to play it by ear much of the time. If Tunisian women are staying in a hotel, that should be a good sign; if all the clientele are men, think again. Male fellow travellers may be prepared to help out by posing as "husbands" or "brothers", but this may not excise some nuisances such as the presence of Peeping Toms when you use the hotel's shared shower – and relying on male tourists can, obviously, plunge you into just the compromising situations you were trying to avoid. Another problem in sharing a room with a man who is clearly not your husband (or even if you are in fact married but retain different surnames) is that you are then assumed to be "generally available", and Tunisian men may treat you accordingly.

Hotels are supplemented by family-run **pensions**, found mainly in the Cap Bon area and varying widely in both price and standard. At their best they really are cheap and friendly *pensions familiales*, and at their worst they're still quite adequate, and one or two are even deluxe, with prices to match.

YOUTH HOSTELS AND CAMPING

There are some 34 **youth hostels** in Tunisia, five of them run by Tunisia's Youth Hostel Association

and the rest attached to youth centres (*Maisons des Jeunes*) run by the Ministry of Culture. Some of these, more specifically designed for accommodation, have been designated *Centre des Stages et des Vacances*. These charge 4–5TD a night, as much as a cheap hotel, and are usually situated on the edge of town near the municipal stadium. They tend to look like barracks and feel like changing rooms, operate curfews and turf you out early in the morning. Some of them seize your passport on arrival, so you have to track it down before you can leave, and can't easily use it for changing money while there. YHA hostels tend to be better run than *Maisons des Jeunes*, less heavy-handed with rules and regulations, more central and often housed in interesting old buildings. Recommended in particular are the hostels in **Tunis Medina** and **Houmt Souk** (Jerba). Those at **Rimel** (Bizerte), **Kélibia**, **Remla** (Kerkennah) and **Aïn Soltane** (near Ghardimaou) are also a cut above the norm. Only the hostel in Tunis requires YHA membership. Men and women have separate accommodation in all youth hostels.

There are only a handful of **campsites** in the country, but their number is growing. Some youth hostels – even a few hotels – also allow camping in their grounds. Unofficially, and especially in remote areas, **camping sauvage** ("wild", meaning off-site, camping) is another option. While sleeping out on the main tourist beaches like Hammamet, Nabeul, Sousse or Monastir is either expressly forbidden or likely to be cut short by the police, there should be few problems elsewhere, and it's common at certain places around Bizerte, Raf Raf and Jerba. In the interior it's a good idea to ask the permission of the landowner. If you can't find the owner, ask the local police, who are very unlikely to say no, or will suggest an alternative site. Informing the police of your presence will also help avoid misunderstandings, especially if you're in a sensitive area, such as an international frontier.

Campsites vary in their **prices**, how they charge, and the facilities they provide. A typical charge would be 3–4TD per person per night, with an extra charge, maybe 5TD, for a campervan, slightly less for a car, and sometimes 2–3TD per night to pitch a tent, in addition to the per-person charge. Some campsites rent out tents, or provide huts to sleep in for those without their own canvas, and in the south they may also offer the option of sleeping in a Bedouin tent.

MUSLIMS, ARABIC SPEAKERS AND JEWISH PILGRIMS

For **Muslims** or anyone who **speaks Arabic**, the opportunities for cheap accommodation are wider. Most likely you will move from one hospitable family to another, but if you're ever stuck try the **local mosque or zaouia**. They often have hostel accommodation where pilgrims can stay – always an interesting place to meet people. **Jews** on pilgrimage, particularly in Jerba (see p.381), may find similar help from the local Jewish community.

EATING AND DRINKING

"*Chilis were essential to the full glory of Kuss Kussu; but he did not expect mere Europeans to rise to such heights. And yet he'd known one really great Englishman, a certain Captain Gordon, who could eat more chilis than any Arab.*"
Reginald Rankin, Tunisia (1930)

Eating out is not really an Arab tradition, but the French presence, along with the effect of tourism, have made their marks and there are now three distinct levels of eating establishment. In big cities and tourist centres you'll come across smart and essentially **French restaurants** offering meals of several courses; these can be excellent and are usually very good value. Every town also has less elaborate restaurants serving main dishes which are virtually indistinguishable from one place to the next – simple meat, chicken, fish and vegetables kept warm throughout the day. You soon learn to recognize these places, known throughout Tunisia as **gargotes**. Last and cheapest are the **rôtisseries** which, despite their name, do more frying than roasting – if you have a low tolerance for grease, you'll probably prefer the restaurants.

Rôtisseries are usually open all day, their food laid out behind the counter so you can just point at what you want. Most restaurants however, and almost all posh ones, usually open only for lunch and supper, and most restaurants display a menu – if it's in Arabic you can ask to go and look at the dishes; cheaper restaurants begin to close around 9pm, and the most popular dishes are often finished sometime before then. As for **prices**, a typical meal in a *gargote* will be very cheap, with starters at around 1.5TD, main courses at 2–3TD, and a whole meal including mineral water for about 5TD (£2.50/$3.75). Moderately priced places will have main courses at 4–7TD, and meals for 7–12TD per head. Once you are paying over 15TD (£7.50/$11.50) a head, or over 8TD for a main course, you are in what in Tunisia is an expensive restaurant, although it is not unusual for restaurants aimed specifically at tourists in the big resorts to charge 15TD for a main and 25TD (£12.50/$18.50) or more for a meal. Outrageous by local standards, such prices are still of course extremely low compared with what you'd pay for an equivalent meal in the West. In resorts, bear in mind that anywhere worth eating in will not need to have a waiter outside hustling for business.

Women travellers may find that restaurants and cafés are some of the worst places for pestering. Your best bet, unfortunately, is to use the more cosmopolitan and expensive places in the towns and avoid those in rural areas. You will also be less conspicuous drinking coffee in a patisserie than in a café. Some restaurants have separate rooms for women diners and the waiter will automatically show you in there when you arrive. There are also one or two cafés where only women can drink, but they tend to be well hidden.

TUNSIAN MEALS

If there is a **starter** at a restaurant it will probably be soup (*chorba* – oily and very spicy), Tunisian salad (basically a finely chopped green salad), or a more specifically Tunisian dish such as *brik à l'oeuf* or *salade mechouia*.

There are two levels of **main course**. The simplest is a starch-based dish (couscous, spaghetti or beans) with a little meat and hot peppery sauce. Unexciting but very filling, this is what most families eat at home. Paying a little more, you get more meat or fish, usually served with salad and chips. Both grilled meat (*brochettes*) and fish can be delicious. Bread (*khobs*) is always included, usually with a little plate of hot red sauce (*harissa*) and oil to dip it into; the *harissa* and oil is sometimes not served to tourists, who are assumed to have an aversion to chilli, but you can always ask for it if you don't get it. There is rarely much to follow the main course except perhaps seasonal fruit or a crème caramel.

If you are invited into a **Tunisian home**, you will probably eat from a communal dish into which you dip bread to soak up the sauce. When handling pieces of food, remember to **use only your right hand** – the left is used for "unclean" functions such as wiping your bottom or washing

your feet – and, if there is only a little meat, not to eat more than your fair share. Men and women eat separately in a Tunisian household, but visiting Western women will probably eat with the men, especially if accompanied by one. Contrary to the popular myth, you are not expected to belch loudly to show your appreciation of the food, nor are you likely to be served sheep's eyes. Should you wish to offer your host a gift, something from home unavailable locally will go down really well, or take a box of sweets from a high-class patisserie.

VEGETARIAN AND OTHER SPECIAL DIETS

How you fare as a **vegetarian** in Tunisia depends on how strictly you avoid animal products. If you are completely vegan, you're going to have a very hard time of it. About the only things you'll be able to eat ready-cooked are chips, spaghetti in tomato sauce and *lablabi* (and even then, you'll have to watch that no eggs or tuna get into it). You can get pizzas made up without cheese or you could live on a diet of bread and olives, but you're best advised to take a spirit stove or book self-catering accommodation to take care of yourself. Staples such as rice, dried beans and pasta are available at grocers and supermarkets, fresh vegetables are easy to find in markets, and "burning alcohol" (*alcool à brûler*) is widely available at hardware shops (camping gas canisters much less so).

If you eat **eggs and dairy products**, you're increasing your range considerably: *ojja, chakchouka, brik, tajine* and omelettes all become possible, and you have even more choice if you are prepared to eat fish and cheese. Even so, you will have to be watchful as the concept of vegetarianism is completely alien to most Tunisians, who may not understand what you want.

Tunisians eat **meat** with every meal (or aspire to) and you won't meet any Tunisian vegetarians. Nor is there much concern about animal welfare: at *Aid el Adha* most families will slaughter their own sheep and in abattoirs and markets animals are slaughtered *halal*, their throats cut without being stunned. So when you try to explain that you don't want meat with your couscous, don't be surprised if you get a blank look. And don't be surprised either if you find meat added to vegetable dishes to "improve" them. Hard boiled eggs and canned tuna fish are added liberally to all sorts of things, especially salads, so it's almost always worth specifying if you don't want them. You may

GLOSSARY OF TUNISIAN FOOD

French, Arabic, and the English translations are given where appropriate.

BASICS

L'addition	El fatura/el hisaab	Bill, check	Huile	Zit	Oil (invariably olive)
Bouteille	Darbooza	Bottle			
Pain	Khobs	Bread	Poivre	Filfel	Pepper
Beurre	Zibda	Butter	Salade	Salata	Salad
Oeufs	Adhma	Eggs	Sel	Melha	Salt
Fourchette	Farchita	Fork	Cassocroûte	Cassecroûte	Sandwich
Verre	Keson	Glass	Cuillère	Mirafa	Spoon
Couteau	Sekina	Knife	Sucre	Sukar	Sugar
Olives	Zitoun	Olives	Table	Taula	Table

FISH (POISSON/SAMAK)

(in general, the French name is used, even when speaking Arabic)

Calmar	Subia	Squid	Mulet	Bowri	Grey mullet
Clovisses	Babush	Clams	Poulpe	Qarnit	Octopus
Crevettes	Qambri	Prawns	Rouget	Trilya	Red mullet
Dorade	Jerrafe	Bream	Roussette	Kalb el-bahr	Dogfish (rock salmon)
Langouste	Fakrun b'har	Crawfish (rock lobster)	Sépia	M'dass	Cuttlefish
Loup de mer	Karus	Sea bass	Sole	Sabidaj	Sole
Merou	Manani	Grouper	Thon	Ton	Tuna

MEAT AND POULTRY (VIANDE/LAHMA)

Biftec	Habra	Steak	Foie	Kibda	Liver
Boeuf	Bakri	Beef	Mouton/agneau	Houli	Mutton/lamb
Brochette	Safud	Small kebab	Poulet	Djaj	Chicken

VEGETABLES (LÉGUMES/KHADRAWAT)

Haricots	Loobia	Beans	Pommes frites	Batata	Chips (French fries)
Oignons	B'sal	Onions	Pommes de terre	Batata	Potatoes
Pois chiche	Houmous	Chick peas (garbanzo beans)			

TUNISIAN DISHES

Brik à l'oeuf	One of Tunisia's great culinary curiosities – an egg fried inside a pastry envelope, the eating of which demands considerable ingenuity to avoid getting egg on your face. Sometimes made with tuna or vegetables, *briks* vary in quality, and are best when freshly cooked and piping hot.
Chakchouka	Vegetable stew based on onions, peppers and chick peas, usually topped with a fried egg.
Chorba	Soup. There are many varieties, but most are spicy and delicious.
Couscous	The classic North African dish – steamed semolina grains, served with meat or fish, and vegetables.
Deglet Fatima	Fingers of filo pastry with egg or other filling.
Gargoulette	A special earthenware pot, and the lamb casserole that is cooked in it.
Harissa	Red chilli and garlic sauce added liberally to almost everything.
Kamounia	Meat (lamb, beef and/or liver) stewed in a thick cumin sauce.

Keftejii	A vegetable stew like a spicy rata-touille, often served with meatballs.	
Koucha	Lamb and potatoes in tomato sauce.	
Lablabi	Bread soaked in chick-pea broth, usually with a raw egg scrambled into it to cook, and spices added on top, sometimes with tuna. Very cheap – the worker's staple – and made in front of you so you can ask them to hold back on this or that.	
Mechoui	Grilled meat.	
Merguez	Spicy sausage – eat it well cooked!	
Mermez	Mutton stew.	
Mloukhia	Jew's mallow, a green leaf vegetable cooked with meat to make a green stew with a distinctive slimy	

texture that some people love and some people hate.

Ojja	Similar to a chakchouka, with egg scrambled into it.
Salade mechouia	Not a salad in the usual sense, but a mashed, spicy mix of roasted vegetables served cold.
Shawarma	Marinaded lamb kebab on a vertical spit, carved and served in a pitta bread. Looks like a doner kebab but is insulted by the comparison.
Tajine	No relation to its Moroccan namesake, Tunisian *tajine* is a kind of baked omelette.

SWEETS (PATISSERIES/HALAWIYET)

Baklava	Honey-soaked flaky pastry with a syrup-soaked nut filling – hazelnut is best.
Draw (sahlab)	Milk thickened with orchid root, sometimes topped with halva or cake. Increasingly rare, but some times served by cafés, especially in winter.
Ftair	A Ghoumrassen speciality – deep-fried batter pancake, some-where between a doughnut and a fritter, usually available in the morning.

Halva	Sesame-based sweet common throughout the Middle East.
Kab el ghazal	A Tataouine speciality – (*corne de gazelle*) pastry horn stuffed with chopped almond filling.
Loukoum	Turkish delight.
Mesfuf	Sweet couscous.
Millefeuille	French cream pastry.
Makroudh	A Kairouan speciality – syrup-soaked semolina cake with a date centre.
Youyou	Ring doughnut.

FRUIT AND NUTS (FRUITS/FAWAKIA)

Abricots	*Mishmash*	Apricots	*Fraises*	*Fraulu*	Strawberries
Amandes	*Louze*	Almonds	*Grenade*	*Rouman*	Pomegranate
Cacahuètes	*Kakwiya*	Peanuts	*Melon*	*Battikh*	Melon
Cerises	*Hbmluk*	Cherries	*Noix*	*Zouze*	Walnuts
Citron	*Limon*	Lemon/lime	*Orange*	*Burkutal*	Orange
Dattes	*Tamar*	Dates	*Pomme*	*Tufah*	Apple
Figues	*Kermus*	Figs	*Pêche*	*Khoukh*	Peach
Figues de Barbarie (Barbary figs)	*Hendi*	Prickly pears	*Pistaches*	*Fozdok*	Pistachios
			Raisins	*Ainab*	Grapes

DRINKS (BOISSONS/MASHRUBAAT)

Bière	*Birra*	Beer	*Citronade*	*Asir limon*	Real lemonade
Thé	*Té or shai*	Tea	*Lait de poule*	*Halib djaj*	Milkshake with egg white
Café	*Qahwa*	Coffee			
Eau	*Ma*	Water	*Jus*	*'Asir*	Juice
Vin	*Sharab*	Wine	*Vin de palme*	*Laghmi*	Palm wine
Lait	*Halib*	Milk	*Lait fermenté*	*Rayeb (leben)*	Soured milk

also ask for a dish without meat, only to find that it's a meat dish with the lumps of meat (but not the gravy) removed. The fussier you are about this sort of thing, the harder it will be for you to eat out and the more you should consider taking a stove and cooking for yourself. In recent years, a small number of restaurants in tourist areas have started to cater for vegetarians, and may offer a specifically vegetarian option (usually vegetable couscous with no added meat stock), but such places are still few and far between.

Also be aware that **hospitality** is an extremely important part of Arab civilization, and if you enter a Tunisian home you're bound to be offered something to eat. Moreover, your host may be insulted if you don't eat it. Do bear this in mind if invited into someone's house.

The Tunisian sweet tooth may be a problem for **diabetics**, especially where drinks and snacks are concerned. Artificial sweeteners are not widely used in Tunisia, diet versions of soft drinks are unavailable, and fruit juice is usually sweetened, though unsweetened juice is now available in supermarkets. Your only recourse otherwise is to drink water. You might consider taking some flavoured concentrate with you to mix with it, as well as some savoury crackers, since these are unavailable in Tunisia too. Sugar will usually be added unrequested to coffee unless you're quick to point out that you don't want it, and the same applies to pomegranate served broken up as a dessert in restaurants, and often to orange juice. You probably won't find sugarless tea at all.

If you only eat **kosher** meat, you'll have to stick to fish and vegetables most of the time, although one kosher restaurant exists in Tunisia – a small *gargote* in Hara Kebira on Jerba (see p.382).

PATISSERIES, SNACK FOOD AND BREAKFAST

Cafés are beginning to merge with **patisseries**, French-style pastry shops which serve elaborate cakes along with almond milk and *citronade*, a refreshing drink made by putting whole lemons, through a blender with sugar and water and straining the result. *Citronade* is a lifesaver in the summer heat, but only as safe as the water that goes into it. Some patisseries also serve other fresh fruit drinks made with a blender, including *lait de poule* ("chicken's milk"), a fresh fruit milk-shake with egg white. If you don't want sugar in juices or milkshakes, make it clear from the start.

Patisseries usually serve French-style cakes, though these are often filled with artificial cream, and are at their best in the morning when fresh, as well as more traditional Arab and Berber sweets such as *baklava* and *makroudh*, which are usually soaked in sticky syrup. Patisseries and cafés are also becoming the place to eat **breakfast** – a croissant or dry cake with coffee. In less sophisticated areas some cafés still provide the traditional *ftair* and *draw*. Most hotel breakfasts consist of a pot of filter coffee served with bread and jam. Those who prefer a more substantial and savoury breakfast could go for a bowl of *lablabi*, bread broken up and soaked in chick-pea broth with *harissa*, cumin, egg, olive oil and often tuna, a very cheap option that's Tunisia's answer to a fry-up.

The perennial **snack meal** is a *cassecroûte*, a thick chunk of French bread filled with vegetables, olives, oil, and either egg, tuna or sausage. It's automatically spread with *harissa* sauce, a concentrate of garlic and red chilli peppers which makes the average curry taste anaemic; if you prefer to go without, specify *sans piquant* or *bilesh harissa*. *Cassecroûtes* can be bought at most rôtisseries and many bakeries. Snack bars at bus and louage stations often sell them too.

Alternatively, grocers will often make up a **sandwich** for you when you buy the ingredients. Cheese is generally disappointing, though the soft white sheep's milk *maasoura*, similar to Italian ricotta, is worth a try, and sardines or tuna are other possible fillings.

The other essential for picnic meals, **fruit**, is one of Tunisia's greatest delights. Depending on the season you can gorge on fresh oranges, figs, grapes, melon, dates, pomegranates, prickly pears, strawberries and cherries. Pomegranates are often served as a dessert, broken up in a dish with the bitter yellow pith removed; if you don't want sugar on top, say so when you order. The prickly pear, or "Barbary fig", was introduced into North Africa by the Spanish in the sixteenth century, after they brought it over from the Americas. In summer they are sold by the thousand from barrows. Though they are immensely refreshing and the first remedy to try for upset stomachs, you should beware of picking them or holding them unpeeled, as they are covered in very hard-to-see spines that get into your skin and are difficult to remove.

If you want to snack while you're out and about, **nuts** and similar snacks, such as roasted sunflower or watermelon seeds, are available from shops everywhere – usually open quite late.

DRINKING

Wine, when available in restaurants, is usually good. Vieux Magon is the best red, full-bodied and comparable to an Australian shiraz. Haut Mornag, Sidi Rais and Koudjat are all excellent table wines; Grombalia and Tordi very rough standbys. Clairet de Bizerte is the best rosé, but Gris de Tunisie is more widely available and also pretty drinkable. Cristal is a reasonable white, and Kélibia in Cap Bon produces a distinctive and unusual **dry muscat**. Except in the tourist hotels, wine is not served in restaurants on Fridays for religious reasons.

Other local drinks include the ubiquitous **mineral waters** (Safia, Aïn Garci or Aïn Oktor), and sodas such as Coca-Cola, generically known as *gazouz*, which are extremely popular. The local **beer** is called Celtia, and is as drinkable as any British or American bog-standard lager. French brand Löwenbrau is made here under license, but is also nothing to write home about. There is however one microbrewery, in Port el Kantaoui (see p.209), which does serve excellent German-style beer. Tunisia also produces two **strong spirits**. Unless you have a throat of steel, it's best to drink *boukha* – a spirit derived from figs – in the standard combination with Coca-Cola; *thibarine*, a date liqueur, is more palatable. **Laghmi** (palm wine) is the sap of the date palm milked from the tree, and fermented for 24 hours. Both fresh and fermented versions are available around the oases in season. The unfermented version is sweet and tastes a little like barley sugar. If you're offered *laghmi* down south, be sure it's OK before drinking as it is sometimes mixed with water of dubious origin, or left too long (it goes off as quickly as it ferments). *Sirops*, distilled from fruit (pomegranate, orange, lemon, fig and even pistachio), are rather sickly in taste and garish in colour but make interesting mixers.

You may find alcohol at a few Westernized cafés, but most Tunisian drinking, in big cities at least, is done in **bars** – exclusively male and still with an air of the bootleg about them, dense with smoke and invariably deafening. Still, they often serve excellent little snacks (melon, olives, even *brochettes*). In the European-style bars of the bigger hotels the drinks are more expensive but the atmosphere more relaxed and even Tunisian women can sometimes be seen. If you're a lone drinker you can buy alcohol in liquor stores – usually hidden away in the back streets of large towns – and larger supermarkets, but you should not carry the bottles around town in public view. Prices displayed do not include the deposit on the bottle.

COFFEE AND TEA

Coffee drinking in the ubiquitous card-playing cafés is a national pastime. The coffee (*qahwa* in Arabic, *café* in French) varies from good to horrible, and comes in several forms. *Express* is espresso; it can sometimes be good, but is usually rather bitter, a fact generally disguised by the addition of large amounts of sugar. *Café au lait*, *café crème* or *qahwa bi halib* usually means filter coffee (served from an urn, bitter and not very nice), and comes with a lot of milk; with less milk it is called *shtar*. *Café filtre* is the same without milk. An espresso with milk (like a cappuccino or French *café crème*) is called a *café direct* or *crème express*. *Capucin* is not a cappuccino, but an espresso with a little milk, like a Spanish *cortado* or Italian *macchiato*. *Capucin nouveau* is the same with condensed milk added. Finally, *qahwa arbi* is Turkish coffee – finely ground coffee brought to the boil and served with the grounds still in it, often perfumed with rosewater or orange blossom water. Not all cafés serve it, but when they do, it is usually well made and very tasty – invariably the best coffee by a long chalk. Two spoons of sugar are usually assumed – to avoid them, ask for *nakas sukar* (a little sugar) or *bilesh sukar* (without sugar).

Tea is either black (*té ahmar* in Arabic, *thé rouge* in French) or green with mint (*té akhdar* in Arabic, *thé vert* in French). Unfortunately, it is most commonly made by boiling the leaves in water, adding massive quantities of sugar and leaving it to stew for hours on a charcoal stove (*canoun*), which every household possesses for the purpose. The result is a powerful brew of almost pure tannin and sugar – said to result in cases of "tea poisoning" and even death – and too pungent for most unhabituated tastes. Green tea is not usually as stewed as black and is sometimes served with pine nuts and almonds. Tea with milk is virtually unheard of, but you may get it in expensive hotels or package tour centres; anyone used to British or Irish tea, however, will not be happy with it.

Most Tunisian cafés still supply the traditional **hookah pipe** or *chicha*, filled with low-grade tobacco mixed with molasses (not hashish, as some tourists seem to think). It is something of an acquired taste, but if you smoke you should certainly try it. Once strictly an old man's pastime, *chicha*-smoking has gone through something of a renaissance of late, and flavoured tobacco is now available instead of the traditional *ma'azil*; the nicest is apple-flavoured (*bitufaah*), with strawberry and mint among the other popular flavours.

RAMADAN

One thing that will probably throw your eating routine is the month of **Ramadan**, when Muslims fast from sunrise to sunset – see p.41 for specific dates. Cafés and restaurants, save those that particularly cater for tourists, are likely to close during daylight too, and bars will close altogether. Food shops are open so you can still buy things to eat, but, although Tunisia is not as strict about Ramadan as some Muslim countries, you may feel it rude and inconsiderate to eat, drink or smoke in public when most people are committed to fasting. An alternative is to observe the fast, wholly or partly, and join local people in breaking it at sunset, hanging out late into the night, enjoying the special feel that cafés have only at this time of year.

TRADITIONAL COSMETICS

Tunisians use a number of natural products as cosmetics, make-up and grooming aids, and you will see them on sale in markets nationwide, and often in use in the hammam. Among natural cosmetics used are:

Chab Alum (aluminium potassium sulphate), a white mineral used as an anti-perspirant and to stop shaving cuts bleeding.

Henna Powdered leaves made into a paste and used for conditioning hair, and for colouring hair, hands and feet. The best henna comes from Gabès.

Kohl Eyeliner made from ground antimony or lead sulphide, sometimes with the addition of other materials.

Suek Walnut bark or root, used for cleaning teeth and reddening lips and gums, giving a slight, and not unpleasant, burning sensation.

Tfal Fine earth used as shampoo and traditionally kept in a container called a *tafalla*. Mixed with rose or orange blossom water, it can be used as a whole-body mudpack. The best *tfal* is said to be from Chebika.

COMMUNICATIONS

Post and telecommunications in Tunisia are up to international standards and you should have little cause to complain. Letters arrive reasonably quickly and rarely go astray, while international calls are relatively easy, with direct dialling, immediate connection and reasonable charges, so long as the public phone offices are open. Emails can be sent from any of a growing number of public internet offices, and it's a good idea to set up a web-based account before you leave home so that you can pick up messages easily. Unfortunately, however, internet connections are slow in most places, and certain web-based email services may be blocked from time to time.

MAIL

Post offices (PTT) in large towns tend to follow **city opening hours** (Sept–June Mon–Sat 8am–6pm, Sun 9–11am; July & Aug Mon–Fri 7.30am–1pm & 5–7pm, Sat 7.30am–1.30pm, Sun 9–11pm; Ramadan Mon–Sat 8am–3pm, Sun 9–11am), while branch offices and those in villages and small towns follow **country opening hours** (Sept–June Mon–Thurs 8am–noon & 3–6pm, Fri & Sat 8am–12.30pm; July & Aug Mon–Thurs 7.30am–1pm, Fri & Sat 7.30am–1.30pm; Ramadan Mon–Thurs & Sat 8am–1.30pm, Fri 8am–12.30pm). Which hours each office follows is specified as appropriate throughout the text. When the post office is closed, stamps can often be obtained from shops

selling postcards, and occasionally from certain authorized taxiphone offices, which will have a sign outside to that effect.

Postal services are very reliable; **letters** to Europe rarely take more than a week, and to North America and Australasia, around two weeks. The parcel service is slower but equally reliable. For inland post, you have the choice of ordinary mail or *lettre prioritaire*, which is guaranteed faster delivery. Postboxes are usually light yellow in colour, are freestanding or set into walls at around shoulder height on the streets.

For **poste restante**, address letters clearly "Tunis R.P., rue Charles de Gaulle, Tunis" (the main post office) or to any local post office, marked "R.P." (for *Recette Postale*). To collect it, you'll need some form of identification, preferably a passport.

TELEPHONES

It is almost as easy to make an **international phone call** as a local one. In most towns you can dial direct on a coin phone at the post office or a "taxiphone" office. The latter is a sort of shop where you can phone Tunisian or international numbers; they're usually open later than the post office and have plenty of change on hand. In some post offices, you make the call without coins and then pay on completion. Some shops also have a public phone, occasionally operated with a phonecard that can be bought at the same shop, and used nationwide. However you do it, it's rarely difficult. Calls cost 0.980TD a minute to the British Isles, 0.882TD cheap rate (8pm–7am and all day Sunday), 1.500TD/1.350TD to North America, and 1.750TD/1.575TD to Australasia. An occasional problem in larger towns is waiting for a booth: in summer, demand should be less at siesta time, 2–5pm. Calling from hotels is much more expensive than using a taxiphone office.

To make a **collect call**, dial ☏ 17 for the international operator and ask for "un appel en PCV" (pronounced *pay-say-vay*).

Internal calls are not expensive: you will need hundred-millime coins, combined perhaps with half-dinar coins for long-distance or calls to mobiles if you intend to speak for longer than just briefly. The system is fairly efficient, with area codes used in the normal way (see box).

DIALLING CODES

DIALLING TUNISIA FROM ABROAD

Australia ☎ 00 11 216 + local code (without zero) + number

New Zealand ☎ 00 216 + local code (without zero) + number

Republic of Ireland ☎ 00 216 + local code (without zero) + number

United Kingdom ☎ 00 216 + local code (without zero) + number

USA and Canada ☎ 011 216 + local code (without zero) + number

DIALLING ABROAD FROM TUNISIA

Australia ☎ 00 61 + local code (without zero) + number

New Zealand ☎ 00 64 + local code (without zero) + number

Republic of Ireland ☎ 00 353 + local code (without zero) + number

United Kingdom ☎ 00 44 + local code (without zero) + number

USA and Canada ☎ 00 1 + local code + number

USEFUL NUMBERS WITHIN TUNISIA

Emergencies ☎ 197

Speaking clock ☎ 191

Directory enquiries ☎ 12

International operator ☎ 17

TUNISIAN DIALLING CODES

All Tunisian numbers are now made up of six digits. Old five-figure numbers have added an initial digit as shown in the brackets below.

☎ 01 – Tunis region

☎ 02 – Bizerte (4), Nabeul (2), Zaghouan (6)

☎ 03 – Mahdia (6), Monastir (4), Sousse (2)

☎ 04 – Sfax region (2)

☎ 05 – Gabès (2), Kebili (4), Medenine (6), Tataouine (8)

☎ 06 – Gafsa (2), Tozeur (4), Sidi Bou Zid (6)

☎ 07 – Kairouan (2), Kasserine (4)

☎ 08 – Béja (4), Jendouba (6), Le Kef (2), Siliana (8)

☎ 09 – all mobile phones (7)

Older payphones may not take more than one coin at a time, so you will have to continue feeding them. Tunisian phone numbers seem to change very frequently, so don't be surprised if numbers given in this book or elsewhere are out of date. Often the first two or three digits will change for all the numbers in town to standardize them, so you may be able to guess the new number from others in town, though this does not always work.

MOBILE PHONES

Mobile phones can be used in most of Tunisia, but not in remote desert areas. Coverage extends to all the towns and villages in this book with the exception of Ksar Ghilane and the area south of Remada.

In the UK, for all but the very top-of-the-range packages, you'll have to inform your provider before going abroad to get international access switched on. You may get charged extra depending on your existing package and also for incoming calls when abroad, as the people calling you pay the usual rate. If you want to retrieve messages while you're away, you'll have to ask your provider for a new access code, as your home one is unlikely to work abroad. For further information about using your phone abroad, check out ⓦ www.telecomsadvice.org.uk/features/using _your_mobile_abroad.htm.

EMAIL

The internet is relatively new in Tunisia, but is expanding fast. Some large hotels, and even one or two small ones, now have email reservation facilities, but they remain a minority. Few people have computers at home, but as a result, most towns have **internet offices** where you can access the Web, usually for around 2–3TD per hour. These are often advertised under the name "Publinet", with a purple and white sign. The downside is that connections can be painfully slow, and pages are often timed out before they appear on the screen. The obvious solution is to go late at night when connections are faster. Some towns, such as Sousse and Tataouine, have offices open 24/7, and most are open until mid-

night or later, usually depending on the number of customers. At night they often have the feel of an underground kind of club, the only thing in town that is open when all godfearing citizens are safely tucked up in bed. At such times however, they tend to be all-male preserves.

If you intend to use a **web-based email service** in Tunisia, it is worth noting that the government occasionally closes off access to Hotmail for hours and even days at a time, and most Tunisian residents therefore use alternatives such as Yahoo.

THE MEDIA

Tunisia is almost completely bilingual, so if you're competent in either French or Arabic you can keep informed about what's happening. You should have little trouble following international news in the local newspapers or on radio or TV – though censorship is heavy and the quality of reporting and analysis is not high. Foreign newspapers, and even TV, are available in any case.

NEWSPAPERS AND MAGAZINES

The **English-language weekly newspaper**, the *Tunisian News*, has some interesting features and a small amount of international news, but what it does say about Tunisia would be better described as PR. The daily **French-language newspapers** *La Presse* and *Le Temps* stay close to the RCD Party line as, unsurprisingly, does the Party's own daily paper, *Le Renouveau*. *Le Temps* is perhaps the most substantial. Each paper lists cultural events, exchange rates, bus, train and plane departures from Tunis, and television and Tunis cinema listings.

Periodicals, less restricted than the daily press, carry interesting items from a more radical standpoint: *Jeune Afrique*, published weekly in France but with a Tunisian editor, is excellent (its credibility enhanced by occasional government bannings).

Foreign newspapers can be bought, a day late, at newsagents and big hotels in all tourist areas (*Le Monde* almost everywhere). In the

resort areas, most British national dailies are available, as are the *Herald Tribune*, *Time* and *Newsweek*.

RADIO AND TV

There are plenty of **French-language radio stations**, and Radio Tunis (93.1FM) is one of the more popular for music. If you have a short-wave radio, you can pick up the **BBC World Service**, which is broadcast on various frequencies through the day. The most consistent reception is generally on 12,095kHz (24.8m), 9410kHz (31.88m) or 6195kHz (48.4m) – details and schedules at ⓦ www.bbc.co.uk/worldservice. The **Voice of America** can be found during the day on 1197kHz, at night on 15,205kHz, also afternoons on 1548kHz, and evenings on 9760KHz, among other frequencies – details and schedules at ⓦ www.voa.gov. **Radio Canada** can be picked up at 6–6.30am local time on 13,755kHz, and at 7–7.30pm on 21,570kHz (ⓦ www.rcinet.ca).

There are four **local TV channels**: one in Arabic, three in French. One of the latter is a Tunisian version of the French France 2. The news programme, Téléjournal, is at 8pm. The Italian station Rai Uno is also available, and other French and Italian channels can sometimes be picked up. Use of satellite dishes is increasing (most tourist hotels have them), giving access to many more channels in various languages, notably German, plus CNN and Eurosport in English.

FESTIVALS, HOLIDAYS AND ENTERTAINMENT

The great national festivals of Tunisia are all related to Islam and so their dates are calculated according to the Muslim calendar. This is a lunar system, and dates recede against the Western calendar by about eleven days a year.

Ramadan, the month-long sunrise-to-sunset fast required of all good Muslims every year (see p.457), would seem like a disastrous time to travel, and you certainly won't go anywhere for at least half an hour when the sun sets and everyone makes a mad dash for food as the call of the *muezzin* or the boom of a cannon marks the end of the day's fasting. Finding food or drinks during the day can be hard outside the resorts, but you may in any case feel it inconsiderate to eat or smoke when others are committed to fasting. Ramadan is also an exciting time. If those observing the fast sometimes get a little sluggish and short-tempered during the day – especially smokers deprived of their hourly fix – the riotous night-time compensation more than makes up for it. Eating, drinking and smoking – with a day's consumption packed into a few hours – go on until two or three in the morning, and, for the only time in the year, café nightlife really takes off. Lights are strung up and you'll find music, occasionally belly dancing, and even puppet shows. In Tunis, the best places to experience this are Place Bab Souika and Bab Saadoun. If you're lucky enough you'll see a puppet show, enacting a tradition that arrived with Turkish rulers in the sixteenth century. Ramadan ends with a flourish in a feast called the **Aïd el Fitr**, or **Aïd es Seghir**, a public holiday on which pretty much everything closes.

The other great national festival, the feast of Abraham known as **Aïd el Adha** or **Aïd el Kebir**, is more of a family affair, the equivalent of a Western Christmas perhaps. Every family that can afford it celebrates the willingness of Abraham to sacrifice his son Ishmael by slaughtering its own sheep and roasting the meat: you can tell the Aïd is approaching by the appearance of sheep tethered by almost every house. There's a gradual movement away from actually slaughtering to just buying the meat, but the festival is still the time when families are reunited and transport is packed all over the country, and it is also a universally observed public holiday, when you will find almost nothing open.

Other religious festivals are less widely observed, though the Prophet's birthday, **Mouled**, is a great event at Kairouan (see p.226), and is also a public holiday, as is Ras el Am, or El Hijra, the Islamic new year. Marabouts (local holy men) also have their own festival called a *moussem* or *ziara*, and centred around the tomb or zaouia where they are buried.

It's impossible to predict **festival dates** in the lunar calendar exactly since they are set by the religious authorities in Mecca, where the new moon is sighted. **National secular holidays**, however, are fixed. These are all to some extent celebrations and this generally means the closure of banks, most shops and offices (see box, opposite). Other secular holidays are **local events**, some traditional, but most of them recent creations designed to bolster tourism or agriculture. These are covered in the relevant chapters but, again, see the box opposite. Latest details can be found on the ONTT website at Ⓦ www.tourism-tunisia.com/festivals.

WEDDINGS

Weddings are extraordinarily public celebrations – one of the few chances people get to really let their hair down, and they make the most of it. Cavalcades of pick-up trucks loaded with people playing pipes and drums drive round the town (in Tunis, Mercedes hoot up and down avenue Bourguiba); a solemn procession carries the bride's dowry through the streets; and the celebrations, dancing and feasting can go on for several days. You can now sign up at the big hotels

APPROXIMATE DATES FOR THE MAIN RELIGIOUS FESTIVALS

Festival	2001	2002	2003	2004	2005
Aïd el Adha	March 5	Feb 22	Feb 11	Jan 31	Jan 19
Ras el Am	March 26	March 15	March 4	Feb 21	Feb 10
Mouled el Nabi	June 4	May 24	May 13	May 1	April 20
1st of Ramadan	Nov 16	Nov 5	Oct 25	Oct 13	Oct 2
Aïd el Fitr	Dec 16	Dec 5	Nov 24	Nov 12	Nov 1

ANNUAL SECULAR HOLIDAYS

January 1	New Year	**May 1**	Labour Day
March 20	Independence Day	**July 25**	Republic Day
March 21	Youth Day	**August 13**	Women's Day
April 9	Martyrs' Day	**November 7**	New Era Day

LOCAL FESTIVALS AND HOLIDAYS

February Olive Festival, Kalaa Kebira (near Sousse, see p.210).

March Hammam Festival, El Hamma de l'Arad (see p.343); Festival of the Ksour, Tataouine (see p.405).

April–May Orange Blossom Festival, Menzel Bou Zelfa (see p.148); Nefta Festival (see p.327).

May Matanza, Sidi Daoud (see p.145); Jewish pilgrimage, Hara Sghira, Jerba (see p.381).

May–June Drama performances in Roman theatre, Dougga (see p.272).

June Falconry Festival, El Haouaria (see p.143).

July Sidi Bou Makhlouf Festival, Le Kef (see p.281); International Jazz Festival, Tabarka (see p.170); Malouf Music Festival, Testour (see p.269); Plastic Arts Festival, Mahrès (see p.251).

July–August Various tourist-oriented "cultural" festivals at resorts and Roman sites around the country; Carthage International Festival (see p.115).

August Festival du Borj, Gafsa (see p.303).

September Wine Festival, Grombalia (see p.147); Wheat Festival, Béja.

October Liberation Day, Bizerte (see p.159).

November Tozeur Festival (see p.320); Date Festival, Kebili (see p.331); Carthage Film Festival (biennial, mainly in Tunis) (see p.103).

December International Festival of the Sahara, Douz (see p.336).

for an evening at a rather sad tourist version of a "typical Tunisian wedding". These are as tacky as you would expect, but if you do receive an invitation to a real wedding – and it is far from unusual to invite complete strangers, especially foreigners – it is well worth taking up.

WEEKLY MARKETS

The rest of the year, life in the country revolves around a cycle of weekly **markets**, often colourful affairs. The Sousse and Nabeul markets have been comprehensively "discovered"; but it's well worth timing a visit to other towns to coincide with the weekly event, which for many of them is the mainstay of the economy. Testour and El Fahs are particularly worthwhile. Market days in each region are listed in a box at the beginning of each chapter.

CINEMA

Tunisians like going to the **movies**. French films and English-language films dubbed into French are especially popular in Tunis. Arabic films, mainly from Egypt, are usually a mixture of American-style soap and musical; they're more popular in rural areas and in the cities' cheaper cinemas and, even if you don't understand the plot – sometimes an advantage – they can be fun.

Indian movies are usually subtitled in French and Arabic, but British, American and Hong Kong films are invariably dubbed into French. Longer films are not so much cut as slashed, leaving out whole reels.

Tunisia's own **film industry**, though hardly prolific, has produced some fine movies, tending to deal with serious subjects, and more influenced by France than by Egypt, India or the United States. The first wholly Tunisian-produced feature (there had previously been a couple of Franco-Tunisian co-productions) was Omar Khliifi's *The Dawn* (1966), a drama about the struggle for independence. Perhaps predictably, Independence and its aftermath remained the most popular theme in Tunisian cinema for some time, but other subjects included the experience of Tunisian emigrants abroad in Naceur Ktari's *The Ambassadors* (1976), social attitudes to homosexuality in Nouri Bouzid's *Man of Ashes* (1986), and rural migration to the cities in Taïeb Louhichi's *Shadow of the Land* (1982). The ill effects of tourism are well dealt with in Ridha Behi's *Sun of the Hyenas* (1977), portraying the effect of a hotel development on a small fishing village, and Nouri Bouzid's *Beznez* (1992), about a beach gigolo. Bouzid returned to the big screen in 1997 with *Bent Familia*, looking at three women and their relationships with men. Another Tunisian director whose films have achieved recognition outside the country is Ferid Boughedir; his best-known work, *Halfaouine* (1990), is a good-humoured coming-of-age tale set in the Tunis faubourg of the title. The social position of women is another subject popular in Tunisian cinema. Tunisia has a growing number of fine **women directors**, yet to achieve recognition abroad, notably Selma Baccar, who broke the male mould with *Fatma 75* in 1978, and has continued to deal with gender issues in films like *Habiba Msika* (1996; see p.269).

Tunis hosts the world's most important annual Afro-Arab **film festival** every other year, with Ouagadougou in Burkina Faso hosting it the years in between (see p.103). It will be in Tunis in 2002, 2004 and 2006.

FOOTBALL

Tunisia is as **soccer-mad** as every other country in the world (North America and Antarctica excepted). While the best local players go to European leagues, Tunisia's top twelve domestic **clubs** contest a league championship and cup each year. The clubs are: Espérance Sportif de Tunis (EST), Club Africain (CA; also from Tunis), Club Sportif de Hammam Lif (CSHL), Club Athlétique Bizertin (CAB), Olympique de Béja (OB), Étoile Sportive du Sahel (ESS; from Sousse), Jeunesse Sportive Kairouannaise (JSK), Club Sportif Sfaxien (CSS), Espérance Sportive de Zarzis (ESZ), Stade Tunisien (ST), Union Sportif Monastir (USM) and Association Sportive de Djerba (ASD). Apart from Espérance and Club Africain, they're usually referred to just by their initials. As you might expect, the clubs from Tunis and more prosperous towns are the most successful.

Tunisia's national team was one of the early African World Cup successes when it qualified for the 1978 finals in Argentina. They qualified again in France in 1998, when, though failing to reach the second round, they achieved respectable results against some of the world's top teams. Although Tunisia has yet to win the African Nations' Cup, Tunisian teams have been prominent in African club competitions since CAB took the African Cup Winners' Cup in 1988. Rival Tunis teams Club Africain and Espérance won the African Champions' League in 1991 and 1994 respectively, while ESS took the CAF Cup (equivalent of UEFA) in 1995. Tunisian teams won two of the three African competitions in 1997 – when ESS won the Cup Winners' Cup and Espérance the CAF Cup – and 1998 – when Espérance took the Cup Winners' Cup and CSS the CAF Cup, a mark of the dominance of North African clubs over the rest of the continent. ESS brought the CAF Cup back to Tunisia for the third year in succession in 1999.

In 2000 however, Espérance made world sports pages in sensational fashion when it lost the Champions' League final. Their opponents, Hearts of Oak, were 2–1 ahead after winning the first leg at home in Accra, Ghana, but with just fifteen minutes to go of the second leg in Tunis, Espérance were 1–0 up and looked like winning overall on the away goal rule. At that point, Ghanaian fans started throwing missiles at one of the linesmen, and police responded by lobbing teargas canisters into the crowd, aiming one at the VIP enclosure just for good measure. Fans of both teams poured onto the running track surrounding the pitch, and one of them passed something to Espérance goalkeeper Chokri el Ouaer, who drew it across his forehead, ran from the goal with his head streaming blood, and fell to the ground. Since pretty much everyone had seen him deliberately inflict the injury, presumably aiming to have the match abandoned, the referee did not accept that he had been hit by a projectile, and sent him off. Rather than bring on their reserve

goalie, Espérance moved midfielder Hassan Gabsi into goal, and when play resumed, Hearts of Oak scored three times to win 5–2 on aggregate. In the aftermath, Hearts were banned from playing at home in African competitions for a year, while Chokri el Ouaer was suspended for a year.

CRIME AND PERSONAL SAFETY

You are unlikely to run into any trouble in Tunisia. The police are invariably polite and helpful to tourists. Thieving, though it obviously goes on, is a lot less common than in most of Europe or North America.

THE POLICE

There are two main **types of police**: the blue uniformed ordinary police (*sûreté* in French, *shurta* in Arabic) and the green uniformed National Guard. The ordinary police have jurisdiction within town limits, and are generally the people to see to report a crime. They usually speak good French and should be able to give you directions if you're lost. The National Guard have jurisdiction in rural areas and guard the country's borders. They may stop you if you're driving, especially near the Algerian border, and will ask to see your passport and question you about where you're going and why, but they won't give you any trouble. The National Guard are the people you should inform before driving to remote desert areas, and in some places there is a special National Guard office specifically for tourists.

It is just possible, though unlikely, that you will be stopped and asked for **identification** on the street (Tunisians are issued with state identity cards, which they carry at all times), but you'll be OK if you can take a police officer to your hotel and show your passport.

THIEVING

Tunisians are generally honest and law-abiding and **stealing** from a visitor is considered shameful. Nonetheless, foreigners are obvious targets for theft when it does occur, the main hot spots being Sousse, Hammamet and Jerba. The most common forms of theft are stealing possessions on the beach while you sleep (sometimes even from bags used as pillows); pickpocketing, especially by young kids in Hammamet, where the usual method involves an accomplice distracting your attention by asking you to change a foreign coin; bag-snatching, especially in the Medina in Sousse; and leading tourists deep into the medina (Sousse and Kairouan the main ones) so that they are lost and nervous, then charging them to be led out again. Even mugging and rape, though rare, are not unheard of, so it is best to avoid unlit and deserted areas of towns late at night. Less nasty, and still relatively rare, is the practice of offering someone a gift, and then demanding an exhorbitant payment for it; food or drinks offered by people you have just met may come into this category.

Many hotels operate a deposit for valuables; otherwise, wearing a body belt might be good for your peace of mind.

If you have to **report a crime** to the police, make sure you go to the police station covering the area where the crime was committed. You'll probably have to go in office hours and you may have to put up with a certain amount of buck-passing and time-wasting, though the police are usually kind and helpful to distressed tourists who have been the victims of crime. Wearing your best clothes is a good idea (and "modest" ones if you are a woman). You will need a **receipt** from the police in order to get your insurance to pay up for anything lost or stolen, and for your passport in order to get a replacement; they might ask you to call back for the receipt, but should issue one for a passport immediately – if you have to insist, do so very politely. You will not get a receipt for stolen cash. Whatever you do, stay calm and do not get angry or shout, no matter how much they give you the run-around. For a serious charge, such as assault, they may take you with them to try and locate your assailant, and will also expect you to come in and identify suspects face to face – this is not pleasant and they will not be happy if you back out of it, so make sure you are prepared to do this when you report the crime. Also be aware if you are a woman and sexual assault

is involved that all police officers in Tunisia are men, though they are usually sympathetic and the prosecution process is fast (two days on average).

DRUGS

This is not Morocco or Egypt. There is hardly any tradition of hashish or other drug use though *takrouri* (marijuana) was smoked during the Ottoman period, and remained legal until the 1950s. With Independence however, harsh laws against cannabis were introduced, and very few people now smoke it. Those who do tend to be rich, and may feel that they have enough influence to get away with it. But use of cannabis is frowned on, both officially and popularly, and is extremely clandestine, with very stiff penalties in force, and imprisonment is the norm for possession of hashish, marijuana or any other illegal drug, even for personal use.

SHOPPING

The most popular souvenirs are soft toy camels – useful for young relatives perhaps, though they have metal wire inside. Traditional craftwork, such as carpets and ceramics, has more lasting appeal, but you may find that items of everyday Tunisian life domestic and otherwise, make better, cheaper and more impressive souvenirs of the country.

If you're going to buy arts and crafts, it's probably worthwhile paying a visit to the local **crafts shop** run by the **ONA** (Organisation Nationale de l'Artisanat Tunisien, also called SOCOPA) the Tunisian crafts organization. They have a number of workshops and a showroom and shop in most big towns – listed in the guide under Practicalities, or in the town Listings. Their goods are generally of a high quality, if a little overpriced, but it's worth visiting to get an idea of what sort of crafts are available and how much they should cost, and to help you weed out the impostors in the field – like the cheap Moroccan pottery sold as "Souvenir of Tunisia". Indeed, quite a few things sold as souvenirs are not in

fact Tunisian at all: as well as Moroccan pottery, there are Egyptian perfume bottles and inlaid boxes, and stone eggs from around the world.

As for **opening hours**, most shops open seven days a week, roughly from 8.30am to noon and 3pm to 6pm during the winter, and daily 8.30am to noon and 4pm to 7pm during summer. Some shops close one day a week, usually Friday or Sunday, occasionally Monday, but this is unlikely to be true of tourist souvenir shops, which are also unlikely to close for lunch.

POTTERY AND CERAMICS

Of the two main pottery centres (whose wares you can find throughout Tunisia), **Nabeul** on Cap Bon specializes in pottery glazed in the Andalusian style, for which tourists are the main customers. Good buys include plates, vases and tiles which can be made up into a wall panel. In the other main centre, **Guellala** on the island of Jerba, ordinary Tunisians are still the main customers, and the best buys are more utilitarian. If you can cart it home, you might go for a huge "Ali Baba" jar – with room to hide at least one thief.

Otherwise, you could buy a "magic camel" water jug, which is filled from the bottom, but can be poured only through the spout. An alternative souvenir from here is an octopus trap (see p.378), but if you'd prefer a used one you should have no trouble persuading a fisherman to sell it to you. Tunisia's third ceramics centre is **Sejnane**, with its own style of "naive" ceramic sculpture available in the region or at El Hanout in Tunis (see p.104).

CARPETS, RUGS AND BLANKETS

There are two main regions of **carpet production** in Tunisia: Kairouan in the centre and Gafsa and the Jerid in the south. In **Kairouan**, where carpets are more finely knotted (quality being measured in knots per square metre – see p.225), they usually have geometric designs and deep colours. **Jerid** carpets are more psychedelic, with bright colours and stylized images. In **Tozeur** you may find carpets with the same distinctive designs used in the traditional brickwork of the houses. Other places where carpets are sold include Gabès and Jerba. **Kilims**, sold particularly in the south – Toujane near Matmata is one village with a tradition of kilim making – are woven rather than knotted. Before buying a knotted carpet, check to see that it carries the government seal of approval, which guarantees its quality, although be aware that Tunisian carpets have no special value outside the country, whatever their quality.

JEWELLERY

Tunisia's **jewellery** trade was traditionally run by Jews, most of whom have now emigrated. Nowadays, the jewellery shops of Houmt Souk on Jerba, often still in Jewish hands, are the best places to buy silver or gold pieces or to have them made up. The Berber regions of the south also specialize in chunky silver jewellery, often set with semi-precious stones. This, however, is less openly on sale, and you may have to ask around to find something good. One typical piece is the **khlal**, a buckle consisting of a pin attached to a silver crescent that's used to fasten clothes. **Hallmarks** exist for silver and gold in Tunisia, though you don't often see them. On gold, a ram's head means 18 carat (75 percent gold), a goat's head is 14 carat (58.3 percent) and a scorpion is 9 carat (37.5 percent). Silver hallmarks include grapes with a figure 1 (90 percent silver), with a figure 2 (80 percent), and an African head looking to the right (less than 80 percent).

Common **motifs** in Tunisian jewellery include the Hand of Fatima and the fish. Both are good-luck symbols used to ward off the evil eye (see p.457), though some say the fish was originally a phallic fertility symbol.

In Tabarka, you'll find a lot of **coral** jewellery on sale, though perhaps you should consider the plight of its source before buying (see p.169).

WOODWORK, BASKETWORK AND METALWORK

There are masses of woodcarvings around, but the nicest buys are made of **olive wood**, which comes mostly from Sfax, at the centre of the main olive-growing region. Especially attractive here are salad bowls, with the added bonus that they're not made at the expense of Southeast Asia's teak forests. **Basketwork** is common throughout the country, made from esparto grass, rushes or palm fronds, and with baskets, hats and table mats among the items produced. Another craft worth investing in is **hammered metal**. There are some excellent plates and trays available, but also a lot of shoddy rubbish. Rather than buying from tourist shops, seek out places where Tunisians might buy and check the artistry involved.

CLOTHING AND LEATHER

Traditional Tunisian **clothes** can look rather silly on foreigners. **Chéchias** (red felt hats) are one possibility, or a handsome camel hair **burnouse** (heavy men's cloak), but these are expensive. If you go for a **sifsari** (light women's shawl and head covering), get a cotton one. A cheaper way to obtain clothes is to buy the fabric and have a tailor make something to order. Alternatively, you could try the **secondhand clothes markets** in most medinas – although much of the clothing is European, there are some outrageous garments to be found. Also available are the blue jackets (called *blusa*) that are the trademark of the Maghrebi working man.

Leather can be good but it can also be awful, so check the quality before buying, especially any stitching. Western-style gear such as jackets and handbags can be very shoddily made; more traditional items such as poufs and *babouche* slippers are usually better. Even then, any dye on them is very likely to run if they get wet. **Sheepskins** are also widely available – make sure they're well cured.

ODDS AND ENDS AND DOMESTIC ITEMS

Often the things which will best remind you of Tunisia are everyday items sold in ordinary shops and markets. A **canoun** (charcoal stove), while not much use back home, can't fail to remind you of all those cups of stewed tea you drank while waiting for louages. Alternatively, you could get a Tunisian **teapot** or a pot for making Turkish coffee (very finely ground coffee traditionally brought to the boil three times), or a *chicha* (water pipe). Failing that, esparto mats, used in pressing olives, can be used as table mats or even doormats. Olive oil and *harissa* (chilli sauce) are almost required purchases and cooks could try their hand at some real Tunisian cookery with a *couscoussier* (couscous steamer). Spices are widely sold as souvenirs, but be aware that things sold as saffron are in fact safflower or turmeric – real saffron consists of fine red strands with no orange or yellow in it at all, and

is rarely if ever available in Tunisia. If you own a car, you could buy some Hand of Fatima stickers to plaster it with.

There are all sorts of other odds and ends you might go for, from the ornate **birdcages** sold especially in Sidi Bou Saïd to **sea sponges**. Other possibilities include **darbouka drums**, typical of Tunisia. Try the drum souk in Tunis for these (see p.104), though if you need one good enough for a serious musician you will probably want it made to order. **Desert roses**, bizarrely shaped crystals of gypsum that look a little like petrified flowers (see box p.325), are the commonest souvenirs sold down south, and very cheap, especially around Nefta, Tozeur and Douz. They can be rather bulky but all sizes are available and you can get several very small ones for a dinar.

In the way of **antiques**, there are a lot of colonial remnants about, but nothing especially cheap. In Tunis, rue des Glacières by place de la Victoire, along with the market area around Souk des Armes and place du Marché du Blé, are likely hunting grounds for this sort of thing (see p.93). Around Roman sites, hawkers offer "Roman" and

---

CARPET CAPERS

Veterans of countries like Morocco, Egypt and India will find Tunisia tame by comparison. In general, you won't be hassled endlessly by salesmen, nor will people attach themselves to you and then demand payment for having been your "guide". Similarly, shoppping in most of Tunisia is relaxed, pressure-free and often conducted over a no-strings-attached cup of tea. However, some **hard selling** has crept into some of the more touristed areas, notably the tourist ghettos of Cap Bon and the medinas of Kairouan and Sousse. If you're going to play the game, it pays to know the rules.

A salesman invites you into his shop, maybe "for tea" because it's his birthday, or even "the birthday of the shop". You make it quite clear (and this is fundamental) that you don't want to buy anything, even if you half think you might. The salesman insists you come in just to have a look. Of course, you may not want to go in. The Arabic for "no, thank you" is *la shookran*, and if you say it with a smile, no one can take offence. A more definitive tactic is to say you already have whatever is being offered.

A **typical scenario**, if you do enter, begins as he shows you the ceiling to demonstrate what an old house he has – a "museum" of carpets (or

carvings, or silver, or antiques); he will show you people at work, then sit you down and call for tea. A large number of carpets are brought and rolled out in front of you. He shows you examples of the different styles, tells you how much they would be worth in your country, shows you the government seal of approval, tells you how little it will cost to send one home and demands to know why you don't want one. He brings out smaller and cheaper examples and keeps up the fluent spiel. Unless of course you do want to buy one, you will have to be insistent in declining to offer a price, and reminding the seller that it was he who insisted you "just look".

Finally, as you apologize and make to leave, he demands to know, of the carpets he has shown you, which you like. He will now probably tell you his **final price**, but any sign of interest on your part will raise it: if you're genuinely interested, you can always shop around and return any time you like. Hostility or abusiveness at this stage is still unusual, but it happens. If so, ignore it, or if you feel strongly enough report it to the local ONTT and enter it in their complaints book, naming the shop concerned.

"Byzantine" coins and "old" oil lamps. Some of them are genuine (coins are sometimes found after rain and left overnight in a glass of fizzy cola to clean them), though worthless; most, however, are artificially aged fakes.

BARGAINING

Whatever you buy, you will often be expected to **haggle** over the price. There are no hard-and-fast rules – it's really a question of how much something is worth to you. It is a good plan, however, to have an idea of how much you want to pay. Don't worry too much about initial prices. Some people suggest paying a third of the opening price, but it's a flexible guideline; you may end up paying only a tenth or less of the opening price, or, on the other hand, not be able to get the seller much below it. If you bid too low, you may be bustled out of the shop for offering an "insulting"

price, but this is all part of the game and you will no doubt be welcomed as an old friend if you return the next day. Prices for food, cigarettes, buses and hotels are usually fixed. All hotels display government-regulated maximum tariffs, but you can try haggling anyway, especially off-season. You can sometimes get a better price for souvenirs by bartering – Levi's and the latest trainers are always in demand.

There are certain rules of the game to remember. Never start haggling for something if in fact you do not want it, and **never** let any figure pass your lips that you are not prepared to pay. It's like bidding in an auction. Having mentioned a price, you are obliged to pay it. If the seller asks how much you would pay for something, and you don't want it, say so. And never go shopping with a **guide**, who will get a commission on anything you buy, which means a higher price for you.

CULTURAL HINTS

As a tourist in Tunisia, you will no doubt be keen to visit archeological sites, museums, mosques and religious buildings, or experience a Turkish bath (hammam). Most mosques are closed to non-Muslims, but if you do visit a religious building, there are certain cultural rules you should observe. A visit to a hammam can be a little daunting for the first time, but it's an experience not to be missed and you'll soon get the hang of it.

MOSQUES, MUSEUMS AND SIGHTS

Tunisian history has left a substantial legacy in the form of religious and other monuments, archeological sites and museums. The authorities are keen to promote Tunisia as more than a cheap beach, and emphasis on Tunisia's monumental heritage has resulted in sights being well maintained and accessible. Be aware, though, that the dominance of organized tourism in Tunisia means that certain mainstream sights are liable to be crowded at peak hours, while other places, lying even slightly off the beaten track, are harder to get to and often barely visited at all.

When it comes to religious monuments still in use, the general rule in Tunisia – in contrast to

Egypt or Turkey, say – is that **non-Muslims** may not enter at all, except for a few very major tourist attractions.

VISITING ISLAMIC BUILDINGS

Visiting **mosques** and **religious buildings** in Tunisia is a frustrating business if you are not Muslim. At a few major tourist attractions, during strictly regulated hours, you can legitimately enter the complex but not the prayer hall. Mosques that are disused (one or two on the island of Jerba for example) can also be visited by non-Muslims. Elsewhere however, if you are not Muslim, you won't usually be allowed to enter at all. The reason for this is that a mosque is an area set aside for praying only, and should not be used for any other purpose. Sometimes, especially if you have a local guide, you may be able to enter the courtyard, but not the prayer hall. It is a bad idea to try to visit mosques against the will of local people, as religion is taken very seriously here. Muslims of course may enter any mosque freely, though you may be challenged to demonstrate that you are Muslim if you do not look it.

In mosques where access into the courtyard is allowed to non-Muslims, you are expected to respect the religious nature of the building and to dress appropriately. According to **religious regulations**, a woman entering a mosque should be covered from her neck to her ankles and wrists; she should also cover her hair and wear a skirt, not trousers. A man should be covered from below the shoulder to below the knee (so T-shirts, but not shorts, are all right for men). Women are also not supposed to enter a mosque during menstruation. Mosques are ritually clean and no-one is supposed to enter without washing hands, feet, eyes, ears, nose, mouth and head in a specifically prescribed manner. Muslims can enter the prayer hall, but should always take off their shoes first.

Zaouias, also called *marabouts*, the tombs of holy men (see p.40), are slightly different in that they are private institutions. Unless Arabic-speaking or Muslim, you're most unlikely to be allowed into a *zaouia* still in use, but many are now either deserted or used as domestic residences. This goes too for **medersas** – Islamic colleges. How much you impose on the occupants of secularized buildings is a personal decision; a courteous enquiry, however, can't do any harm, and many people are only too pleased to show visitors around. One or two *zaouias* are now museums or house the offices of local conservation groups (ASMs) or similar organizations, and are thus open to the public at large.

ARCHEOLOGICAL SITES AND MUSEUMS

Opening hours for **archeological sites and museums** vary. In general, they open at 8–10am and close at 4–6pm (typical hours are 9.30am–4.30pm); some close for lunch from noon or 1pm to 2–3pm, while others open longer during the summer (July & Aug). Most are closed one day a week, usually Monday, but sometimes Sunday or Friday. For **photography** in museums, you are supposed to buy another ticket, and tripods (and any other professional-looking equipment, including sometimes flash) can only be used with special authorization (write to the Institut National d'Archéologie, Dar Husayn, Tunis). Many of the **lesser sites** out in the country have no entry charge, though almost all have a *gardien* (official guardian), who may be eager to show you around for a tip, and even some of the larger ones are only nominally fenced off, so outside official opening hours you can just walk in. There are reductions for students under 32 at most sites and museums.

In the south of the country, there is now a profusion of small **museums of everyday life**, usually housing a motley collection of old pots and pans, household utensils and agricultural implements. These vary from being a waste of time to extremely interesting, and the deciding factor is usually not the exhibits themselves so much as their explanation, which will usually be in French, rarely in English. Occasionally, the exhibits are very well labelled, but more often it depends on the enthusiasm of the staff, a factor which can easily change.

In the large towns and tourist centres, something that calls itself a museum may well turn out to be a shop, so don't be surprised if you are sweet-talked into a "museum" (usually of carpets) where all the exhibits are on sale and the sales spiel starts as soon as you have agreed to accept a cup of tea (and cannot then politely leave until it is served).

HAMMAMS

It's difficult to understand the horror of the English woman in the 1850s who wrote that "a Moorish bath is one of the tortures with which the traveller in the East must make acquaintance". A hammam, or Turkish bath, is not only civilization at its most refined, it's also a bargain at around 70p/$1 for a steam bath, and £2–3/$3–4 with a massage. You could easily pay twenty times as much for the same treatment in the West.

Most Tunisians have at least one hammam a week, and for men Friday night at the hammam is the great social gathering. Most hammams have different hours for men and women, with women usually bathing in the afternoon and men in the morning or evening. Sometimes, especially in Tunis, hammams are exclusively for the use either of males or females, and thus accessible all day. One or two beach hotels have mixed hammams that are rather pricey and for tourists only. To find a hammam, just ask around, as plenty of them tend to be well hidden and they usually have signs only in Arabic, if at all ("hammam" is written حمام in Arabic). Some of them have a distinctive red and green front door.

Bear in mind that in Islam cleanliness is often quite literally next to godliness, and foreigners tend not to be welcome in hammams attached to mosques – which are used for ritual washing before prayer.

Like Roman baths of old, hammams consist of a series of rooms gradually getting hotter, with hot and cold water permanently on tap, with buckets provided so that you can take and mix as much of each as you want. Not everyone uses soap or shampoo but you're welcome to do so. Hammams usually have secure lockers in which to leave any valuables. Always remember that total nudity is not acceptable in Tunisia – you have to change discreetly, and wrap a linen towel (a *touta*, which is provided) around your waist. Once you're suitably attired, you head for the hot room to sit in or around a very hot bath. Before long, people start scratching, using the sweat that's being induced to rub off as much dead skin as possible. This process is finished by the masseur or masseuse, who first gives an expert massage then uses abrasive gloves to remove every last particle of dead skin and dirt. You can also buy and use the gloves yourself – the best are made from loofah. After your bath, you may care to wrap yourself up in several *foutas* and relax for a while in the cooler entrance.

For more on traditional cosmetics see p.36.

SEX AND GENDER ISSUES

Because of the importance of sexual segregation in Islam, even though Tunisia is rather less strict about this than other Arab countries, male and female visitors will probably have somewhat different experiences of the country and, in general, it will be much easier for travellers of both sexes to meet Tunisian men than Tunisian women.

Sex roles and the **division of labour** are much more clearly defined in Tunisia than in the West, and Tunisian people may express surprise at seeing women travelling independently. For women, the main problem will be harassment, although men may also experience unwanted sexual advances from men. These are symptoms of sexual repression in a society where, officially at least, any kind of sex outside marriage is frowned upon. Kissing, cuddling and even holding hands in public may offend people (even if they don't say so), as may going around skimpily dressed.

WESTERN WOMEN AND TUNISIAN MEN

While some women compare it favourably with southern Europe, there's no doubt that general **harassment in Tunisia** is much more commonplace than in northern Europe. It can range from comments as you pass by in the street to persistent chatting, following you or touching; on occasions, however, friendly overtures may suddenly give way to demands for sex. You'll probably face a lot of minor hassles rather than anything seriously threatening, but it can be relentless and fairly persistent. If you do feel you're in danger,

don't be afraid to ask for help from passers-by or make a scene. No Tunisian man would get away with treating a Tunisian woman in this way; the Arabic word *shooma*, meaning "shame on you!" should – if shouted loudly in a public place – embarrass any man into leaving you alone.

Tactics to avoid harassment include wearing dark glasses, which prevents eye contact, including accidental eye contact on your part, hiding your hair – especially if blonde – in a scarf, and covering yourself from top to toe, which should not only cut down on harassment but also put passers-by more definitely on your side if you do have any trouble. Mentioning a husband waiting for you nearby may also put off someone who looks likely to start. Also be aware of your body language, and remember that members of opposite sexes do not touch each other in Tunisia, except close family.

Do be aware, however, of the Tunisian male's point of view. It genuinely is difficult for Tunisian men to know where they stand with Western women. In particular, they are often unable to distinguish between ordinary civility and making a pass. There's a cultural difference here: Tunisian women are generally coy or aloof towards men, any other attitude being taken as a come-on (two areas where this is *not* the case are the big cities, notably Tunis and Sfax, where European sexual attitudes are emerging, and in parts of the far south).

The best solution is to be as standoffish as possible, even if your attitude may be misunderstood as an insult – and even if, as occasionally happens, you're accused of racist sexual preferences (this misunderstanding is often deliberately disingenuous).

For more in-depth coverage of these issues, three **personal accounts** by Western women resident in Tunisia are included in the "Women in Tunisia" section in Contexts (see pp.464–470), as is some background on issues facing Tunisian women in modern society.

WESTERN MEN AND TUNISIAN WOMEN

Generally, men experience few problems in Tunisia related to their sex. There are one or two issues to be aware of, however, which affect your relations with members of both sexes.

Men should **beware of talking to Tunisian women alone**, especially in more traditional communities. All might seem well at the time, but the family may regard it as a breach of confidence and afterwards make life difficult for the woman. Male English teachers, for instance, are requested not to talk to female students alone behind a closed door.

Tunisia is not a country where **sexual relations** with local women are likely – you may be able to meet Tunisian women, especially in big cities, and you may even be able to take them out, especially if accompanied by other Tunisians, but virginity at marriage is far too important for sex to be on the cards. A Tunisian woman caught sharing a hotel room with a Western man, for example, faces very serious trouble indeed, as it's a criminal offence for a Muslim to be caught in a hotel room with a member of the opposite sex other than their spouse, sibling, parent or child. Remember too that Tunisia is a police state where people do keep an eye on each other's comings and goings – and report them – and a lot of Tunisian men are likely to be hostile to a Tunisian woman consorting with a foreign man. If you do go out with a Tunisian woman, you can expect dirty looks, and she can expect the occasional hissed insult, though this will not be so bad if you are also accompanied by other Tunisians as chaperones.

Male tourists and travellers can expect the occasional **sexual proposition** by Tunisian men. A polite refusal should put an end to the matter. If you find it annoying, remember that women tourists have to put up with far more, and that homosexuality is seen somewhat differently than at home (see next column). Don't be paranoid, either: Tunisians are very tactile and same-sex touching does not usually have a sexual connotation.

BEACH GIGOLOS

A relatively recent phenomenon in Hammamet, Sousse, Monastir and Jerba is that of the **beach gigolo** scene, known as *beznez*, from the English word "business" and the French word *baiser*, meaning "to screw". Gigolos cruise the beaches looking for punters of either sex who will wine and dine them and give presents of money in return for sex and company. If a beach gigolo attaches himself to you and follows you into a bar or restaurant, he will expect you to pay, so make it clear if you do not intend to. If, on the other hand, you are interested in what they have to offer, be sure to use a condom, as risk of HIV infection from beach gigolos is extremely high.

The phenomenon was highlighted in Nouri Bouzid's 1992 film *Beznez*, which caused something of a stir in France, where journalists even accused Tunisia of having a sex industry akin to that of Manila or Bangkok. This was something of an exaggeration, to say the least, but it has prompted the authorities to clamp down on the industry. Female prostitution is a good deal more discreet, somewhat downmarket and kept well away from tourists.

GAY AND LESBIAN TUNISIA

Because of the sexual segregation endemic to Islam, **homosexual** activity is very widespread (though anal intercourse between men is illegal) but almost nobody considers themselves gay, and gay people are not identified as a group in Tunisian society. Friendships are far closer than in the West and much more physical – while it is not usually acceptable for a man and a woman to kiss or hold hands in public, it is perfectly normal for two men or two women to do so.

The less positive aspects are that to be a passive partner in such acts has connotations of femininity and weakness and is considered a disgrace, yet no such stigma attaches to the other role, and men will boast quite openly about their prowess in this position. Caution is nonetheless advised, and you should be aware that calls for money or presents in return for sexual favours are more common than sincerity and that blackmail is a possibility.

Gay women are not likely to find any hint of a community in Tunisia. **Lesbianism** is more or less invisible and its existence denied, but what we have said about friendship between men applies doubly between women. As a Western woman,

CONTACTS FOR GAY AND LESBIAN TRAVELLERS

IN THE UK

⊕ **www.gaytravel.co.uk** Online gay and lesbian travel agent, offering good deals on all types of holiday. Also lists gay- and lesbian-friendly hotels around the world.

Dream Waves, Redcot High St, Child Okeford, Blandford, DT22 8ET ☎01258/861149, ⓔ Dreamwaves@aol.com. Specializes in exclusively gay holidays, including skiing trips and summer sun packages.

Also check out **adverts** in the weekly papers *Boyz* and *Pink Paper*, handed out free in gay venues.

IN USA AND CANADA

⊕ **www.gaytravel.com** Gay online travel agent, concentrating mostly on accommodation.

IN AUSTRALIA AND NEW ZEALAND

Gay and Lesbian Travel ⊕ www.galta.com.au. Directory and links for gay and lesbian travel in Australia and worldwide.

Parkside Travel, 70 Glen Osmond Rd, Parkside, SA 5063 ☎08/8274 1222 or 1800/888 501, ⓔ hwtravel@senet.com.au. Gay travel agent associated with local branch of Hervey World Travel; all aspects of gay and lesbian travel worldwide.

Pinkstay ⊕ www.pinkstay.com. Everything from visa information to finding accommodation and work around the world.

Silke's Travel, 263 Oxford St, Darlinghurst, NSW 2010 ☎02/9380 6244 or 1800/807 860, ⓔ silba@magna.com.au. Long-established gay and lesbian specialist, with the emphasis on women's travel.

Tearaway Travel, 52 Porter St, Prahan, VIC 3181 ☎03/9510 6344, ⓔ tearaway@bigpond.com. Gay-specific business dealing with international and domestic travel.

however, your chances of making contact are virtually zilch.

Responses to the dangers of **HIV infection** have so far been limited, but there's little doubt the problem is as grave in Tunisia as almost everywhere else in the world and the need for safe sex is no less pressing (see p.18).

TRAVELLERS WITH SPECIFIC NEEDS

Travelling in Tunisia may require some extra consideration if you are disabled or travelling with children. Senior citizens may want to travel with members of their own age group, or take tours that cater particularly for older travellers, and list organizations that can help you with your trip.

TRAVELLERS WITH DISABILITIES

Facilities for people with disabilities are relatively undeveloped in Tunisia, and disabled Tunisians are often reduced to begging, although families are usually very supportive. Blindness is more common than in the West, and sighted Tunisians are generally used to helping blind people find their way and get on and off public transport at the right stop. Wheelchairs, though often ancient, do exist, and access ramps are gradually appearing at the entrances to hotels, post offices, museums and other public buildings, though it's a slow process, and the ramps are sometimes too steep and narrow to be of much use.

Bus and train **travel** will be difficult because of the steps that have to be negotiated, but louage travel is more feasible if you can stake a claim on the front seat, assuming there is a helper to get you in and out. You should also be able to get on

CONTACTS IN THE UK AND IRELAND

Disability Action Group, 2 Annadale Ave, Belfast BT7 3JH ☎028/9049 1011.

Holiday Care Service, 2nd Floor, Imperial Building, Victoria Rd, Horley, Surrey RH6 7PZ ☎01293/ 774535, Minicom ☎776943, ⓦwww.holidaycare.org.uk. Provides an information sheet on North Africa including a short list of accessible accommodation in Tunisia. Information on financial help for holidays available.

Irish Wheelchair Association, Blackheath Drive, Clontarf, Dublin 3 ☎01/833 8241, ⓔiwa@iol.ie. National voluntary organization for people with disabilities, including services for holidaymakers.

Tripscope, The Vassal Centre, Gill Ave, Fishponds, Bristol BS16 2QQ ☎08457/585641, ⓦwww.justmobility.co.uk. A national telephone information service offering free transport and travel advice for those with mobility problems.

CONTACTS IN THE USA AND CANADA

Access First, 239 Commercial St, Malden, MA 02148 ☎1/800-557-2047 or 781/322-1610. Current information for disabled travelers.

Jewish Rehabilitation Hospital, 3205 Place Alton Goldbloom, Chomedy Laval, Quebec H7V 1RT ☎450/688-9550, ext. 226. Guidebooks and travel information.

Mobility International USA, PO Box 10767, Eugene, OR 97440 ☎541/343-1284; ⓦwww.miusa.org. Information and referral services, access guides, tours and exchange programs. Annual membership $35 includes quarterly newsletter.

Society for the Advancement of Travel for the Handicapped (SATH), 347 5th Ave, Suite 610, New York, NY 10016 ☎212/447-7284, ⓦwww.sath.org. Non-profit travel-industry referral service that passes queries on to its members as appropriate; allow plenty of time for a response.

Travel Information Service Moss Rehabilitation Hospital, 1200 West Tabor Rd, Philadelphia, PA 19141 ☎215/456-9603. Telephone information and referral service.

Twin Peaks Press, Box 129, Vancouver, WA 98666 ☎1-800/637-2256 or ☎360/694-2462, ⓦwww.pacifier.com/twinpeak. Publisher of the *Directory of Travel Agencies for the Disabled*, listing more than 370 agencies worldwide; *Travel for the Disabled*; the *Directory of Accessible Van Rentals* and *Wheelchair Vagabond*, loaded with personal tips.

Wheels Up!, ☎1-888/389-4335, ⓦwww.wheelsup.com. Provides discounted airfare, tour and cruise prices for disabled travellers, also publishes a free monthly newsletter and has a comprehensive website.

CONTACTS IN AUSTRALIA AND NEW ZEALAND

ACROD (Australian Council for Rehabilitation of the Disabled), PO Box 60, Curtin ACT 2605, ☎02/6282 4333; 24 Cabarita Road, Cabarita NSW 2137 ☎02/9743 2699. Provides lists of travel agencies and tour operators for people with disabilities.

Barrier Free Travel, 36 Wheatley St, North Bellingen, NSW 2454 ☎02/6655 1733.

Consultancy service for disabled travellers; can draw up individual itineraries for a fee.

Disabled Persons Assembly, 4/173–175 Victoria St, Wellington ☎04/801 9100. Resource centre with lists of travel agencies and tour operators for people with disabilities.

CONTACTS IN TUNISIA

Association Générale des Insuffisants Moteurs (AGIM), 22 rue Jbel Bargou, Tunis

☎01/848117. The main Tunisian organization for people with impaired mobility.

and off planes with a lift, but check this with the airline or tour operator.

You're likely to find travelling on a **package tour** much easier than full independence. Thomson run a client welfare service (☎020/7391 0170), which can advise people with disabilities on specific travel arrangements with them. You should contact any tour operator and inform them of your exact needs before making a booking. You should also make sure you are fully covered by the insurance policy you take out. Read your travel insurance small print carefully to make sure that people with a pre-existing medical condition are not excluded. And use your travel agent to make your journey simpler: airline or bus companies can cope better if they are expecting you, with a wheelchair provided at airports and staff primed to help.

A number of large hotels, usually at beach resorts, have ramps and step-free access to some or all areas for the benefit of people in wheelchairs. Many of these are designated as "wheelchair friendly" in this book, but note that even in these hotels, the bathrooms are unlikely to be specifically designed for wheelchair-bound guests, and you may not be able to enter the bathroom with a wheelchair, still less manoeuvre it once inside, so always check that a hotel can meet your specific needs before making a booking. Again, you should check with them before booking. If you use a wheelchair, beach hotels are generally much more practical than cheap city-centre ones, which tend to have steep staircases and narrow corridors.

If you do not use a wheelchair all the time but your walking capabilities are limited, remember that you are likely to need to cover greater distances while travelling (often over rougher terrain and in hotter temperatures) than you are used to.

The following hotels all make some provision for disabled travellers and are worth contacting, as well as several hotels in Sousse (see p.196). **Cercina**, Kerkennah ☎04/489600, ✉hotel.cercina@planet.tn – the Sfax–Kerkennah ferry also has wheelchair access.

Chems, Gabès ☎05/270547.

Festival, Monastir ☎03/467555.

Hilton, Tunis ☎01/782800; toll-free numbers worldwide.

Kilma, Hammamet ☎02/227777.

Kuriat Palace, Monastir ☎03/521200, ✉kuriat.palace@gnet.tn.

Médi Sea, Borj Cedria (Greater Tunis), ☎01/293030.

Nafrawess, Hammamet ☎02/288077, ✉nafrawess@planet.tn.

Le Prince, Nabeul ☎02/285470.

Residence, Gammarth ☎01/910101, ⊛www.lhw.com.

Sheraton, Hammamet ☎02/280555, or toll-free numbers worldwide.

SENIOR TRAVELLERS

Age and experience are respected in Tunisia much more than in the West. Older members of the family generally continue to live with their children (usually sons), care for their grandchildren and strongly influence family decisions. There are no state and few private pensions, so social security is a family responsibility.

In Tunisia, people look after their parents just as their parents looked after them, and in return they

---

CONTACTS FOR SENIOR TRAVELLERS

American Association of Retired Persons, 601 E St, NW Washington, DC 20049 ☎1-800/424-3410, membership hotline ☎1-800/515-2299 or 202/434-2277, ⊛www.aarp.org. Can provide discounts on accommodation and vehicle rental. Membership open to US and Canadian residents aged 50 or over for an annual fee of US $10 or $27 for three years. Canadian residents only have the annual option.

Elderhostel, 75 Federal St, Boston, MA 02110 ☎1-877/426-8056, ⊛www.elderhostel.com. Runs an extensive worldwide network of educational and activity programs, cruises and homes-

tays for people over 60 (companions may be younger). Programs generally last a week or more and costs are in line with those of commercial tours.

Saga Holidays, Saga Building, Enrook Park, Sandgate High St, Sandgate, Folkestone, Kent CT20 3SE ☎01222 Berkeley St, Boston, MA 02116 ☎1-877/265-6862, ⊛www.sagaholidays.com. Specializes in worldwide group travel for seniors.

Vantage Travel ☎1-800/322-6677, ⊛www.vantagetravel.com. Specializes in worldwide group travel for seniors.

get the benefit of experienced knowledge and advice on matters ranging from business to childcare, not to mention a live-in babysitter. In this country, age is associated not so much with frailty and vulnerability as with wisdom and a lifetime of input into the family and the community. This means that older people are treated with a certain amount of deference, and shown the respect due their years.

Tunisia is a **popular destination** for older travellers. It's refined, quiet and safe, with all the exotica of North Africa. The country is used to tourists from the West, with hotels generally up to Western standards and all the amenities you would expect.

A number of package tours are geared especially to the needs of older travellers, and many firms run special packages. As well as tailoring their tours and accommodation more to the needs of mature travellers, these offer the opportunity to travel and meet up with people of your own age group.

When planning a beach holiday, you might – depending on your mobility – opt for a hotel that is actually on the beach rather than a walk away, and ask for a ground-floor room when booking. If you are going for a sightseeing package tour, it is a good idea to check on the pace of the itinerary, and consider opting for a more relaxed one with plenty of free time, rather than one which packs the maximum number of sights into the shortest possible period. Highly recommended are the usually twice-yearly art and archeology tours run by firms like Martin Randall and Andante (see p.6).

TRAVELLING WITH CHILDREN

Tunisians, even more than other Mediterranean people, love kids. Travelling with small children in Tunisia, you may find that people will frequently come up to admire them, to compliment you on them and to caress them, which may be uncomfortable for shyer offspring. Children are very important, and numerous, in Tunisian society, and people are not really considered complete adults until they have at least one child. In Tunisian families, children stay up late until they fall asleep and are spoiled rotten by older family members. The streets are pretty safe and even quite small children walk to school unaccompanied or play in the street unsupervised.

Hotels in Tunisia usually give a reduction of thirty to forty percent for children aged under 8 or 10, though this varies with each hotel and you may have to negotiate: obviously, a child staying in your room will cost much less than a separate room. You won't find baby changing rooms in airports, hotels or restaurants, and will have to be discreet if breastfeeding – find a quiet corner and shield infant and breast from view with a light cloth over your shoulder. Beach hotels often have facilities such as playgrounds and children's pools; city hotels are far less likely to cater specifically for children.

Children may well enjoy a number of things that we have not particularly recommended for adults, notably calèche rides and the tourist Noddy trains found in resorts. Short camel rides should also go down well. Buckets and spades are now available at some shops in big beach resorts, but **toys** in general are poor quality, expensive and in short supply, so bring along any you may need.

Of items you might consider taking, **disposable nappies** – Peaudouce is the commonest brand – are available at most pharmacies for prices similar to what you pay at home. You may want to take along some **dried baby food**; any café will supply you with hot water. Bear in mind that Tunisian food can be very spicy, and you will probably want them to hold back on the *harissa* when serving your children. **Baby cots**, when supplied, tend to have low bars, making it easy for the more determined infant to get out. **Child car seats**, when available, are likely to be most uncomfortable unless you pad them well with something soft.

In the US, Travel With Your Children, 40 Fifth Ave, New York, NY 10011 (☎212/477 5524 or 1-888/822-4388), publish a regular newsletter, *Family Travel Times* (✇www.familytraveltimes.com), as well as a series of books on travel with children including *Great Adventure Vacations With Your Kids*. From Britain, you may want to try a holiday with Club Med, whose purpose-built holiday resorts feature kids' club, entertainment and sports facilities on site. Panorama (see p.6) runs kids' clubs at four hotels at Hammamet, the Kerkennah Islands and Port el Kantaoui, which are also open to children booked on Panorama holidays at nearby hotels in the same resort.

DIRECTORY

Cigarettes Tunisian brands are cheap but rough, with 20 Mars strong, Caravanes medium and Cristal milder. Western brands, widely available, cost about four times as much.

Clothes Two things to bear in mind are the heat, especially in the desert, and the modesty demanded by Islam. You will certainly want a light sunhat, especially in summer, and light, loose-fitting cotton clothes. In winter, especially in the north, you will want at least one warm sweater. Be aware that many people, especially older people, can feel seriously intimidated or affronted by scantily dressed tourists wandering around town. Don't walk around the medina in a swimsuit or bare-chested, nor in shorts or short skirts.

Contraceptives Known as *préservatifs*, condoms are available from most pharmacies in large towns, but ones brought from home are more reliable. Some brands of the Pill (*la pilule*) are also available, but remember that if you get diarrhoea oral contraceptives may not stay in your system long enough to be absorbed and may thus become ineffective.

Electricity Generally 220v 50Hz, as in continental Europe, with double round-pin sockets. British, Irish and Australasian plugs will need an adaptor (double round-pin electric shavers will be all right though). American and Canadian appliances will need a transformer too, unless multi-voltage. One or two old places, especially in Tunis, still have 110v voltage – check before plugging in.

Emergencies Police ☎197; Fire brigade (*Protection civile*) ☎198; Ambulance 190.

Laundry There are very few self-service laundries, but many towns have places which do washing by weight. Tourist hotels usually have an in-house service, usually expensive; other hotels may be able to arrange something. Dry cleaners ("pressings") are quite common, but obviously an expensive way to get your socks and undies washed.

Left luggage (baggage deposit) Large train stations take left luggage (ask for the *consigne*), and many hotels – especially cheap ones – have a safe room where you can leave belongings while you are away. Tourist offices may also be able to help for a short period of time, and staff at bus stations or even cafés are often willing to keep an eye on your baggage for you while you wander around town between buses – often just as a favour, without charge.

Photography Avoid taking photographs of government buildings, people in uniform, airports or anything even vaguely military. If in doubt, ask first or you may end up having your camera confiscated. Most of the major brands of camera film are widely available, but speeds other than ISO 100 are hard to come by. Videotape for cameras is expensive, if available at all.

Stoves Camping gas stoves are widely available, but the refills (*cartouches*) much less so. Ironmongers (*quincailleries*) and supermarkets should stock them, but supplies are sporadic. Street sellers sometimes have them when the shops have run out. In Tunis, rue al Jazira is the place to look – especially place Cheikh el Bourzouli. Much more sensible is to take a spirit stove, since burning alcohol (*alcool à brûler*) is widely available. A petrol stove is also a possibility, though somewhat messier.

Time Tunisia is on GMT+1 all year round, which means that it is an hour ahead of Britain and Ireland, six hours ahead of the US East Coast (EST), ten hours ahead of the West Coast (PST), seven hours behind Western Australia, ten hours behind east Australia and eleven hours behind New Zealand. Daylight Saving Time in those places will, however, vary the difference by an hour. Crossing from France or Italy, there is no time difference in winter, but you will have to put your watch back an hour in summer. Flying from Britain, on the other hand, there is no time difference in summer, but you will have to put your watch forward an hour in winter.

Tipping In smarter hotels and restaurants tipping follows Western practice: service is often included, and ten to fifteen percent is the standard tip for waiters. Porters and chambermaids expect something, depending on the price bracket of the hotel and the length of your stay. Café waiters usually get a 0.1TD tip. Taxi drivers do not necessarily get a tip, but always appreciate one. Baksheesh is also expected for small services such as loading your baggage onto buses or finding you a place in a louage.

Toilet paper For reasons that soon become apparent, it's a good idea to carry a stock of toilet paper around with you – it can be bought in most towns. An alternative is to use the Tunisian method (water and left hand), especially in crouching as opposed to sit-down toilets.

Work A work permit is officially required for all foreign citizens working in Tunisia: with the economy in its present state, permits are hard to come by. English teaching is expanding rapidly, though: try writing to the British Council, 10 Spring Gardens, London SW1A 2BN, or to the Bourguiba School of Modern Languages, 47 av de la Liberté, Tunis (☎01/282418). Private conversation classes are sometimes possible to arrange on an informal (and illegal) basis. For almost anything else you will need at least competent French; but because the tourist industry is so highly organized there's little of the fringe market found elsewhere.

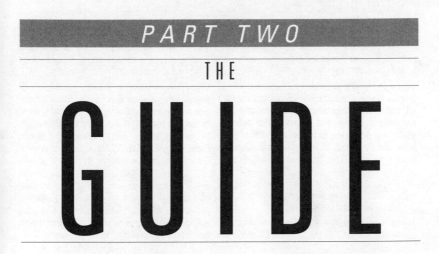

PART TWO

THE

GUIDE

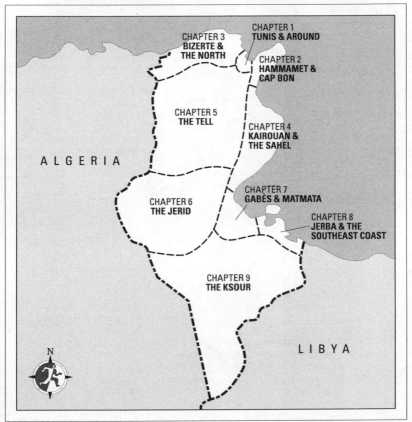

CHAPTER 3
**BIZERTE &
THE NORTH**

CHAPTER 1
TUNIS & AROUND

CHAPTER 2
**HAMMAMET &
CAP BON**

CHAPTER 5
THE TELL

CHAPTER 4
**KAIROUAN &
THE SAHEL**

ALGERIA

CHAPTER 7
GABÈS & MATMATA

CHAPTER 6
THE JERID

CHAPTER 8
**JERBA & THE
SOUTHEAST COAST**

CHAPTER 9
THE KSOUR

LIBYA

N

CHAPTER ONE

TUNIS AND AROUND

T
unis is very much a capital city: home to over a tenth of Tunisia's population, the
base of government and power, and the centre of virtually all that happens in the
country. On first impressions it's not that attractive, as the old colonial centre
becomes increasingly submerged by indistinguishable housing suburbs, and
the streets have a rather Westernized air. But stay a few days and you'll find some allure
behind this unexceptional facade. Few package tours include Tunis, and day-trippers
from the beaches tend to confine themselves to one or two standard streets and monuments in the old Arab town of the **Medina**. The rest is left to the people of Tunis and
anyone else who cares to explore the narrow lanes, busy markets and unrestored monuments, including huge mosques, religious schools and impressive crumbling palaces.

The Medina shelters monuments spanning one thousand years of Arab and Turkish
endowment, and the French-built **New Town**, lying between the small hills of
Belvedere Park to the north and Jellaz cemetery to the south, is beginning to acquire
a period value of its own. These distinct phases of the city's development are intricately linked in a manner which is somehow symbolic of Tunisia's ability to blend cultures.
Moving from ninth-century mosque to eighteenth-century Turkish palace to nineteenth-century French boulevard seems almost a natural progression.

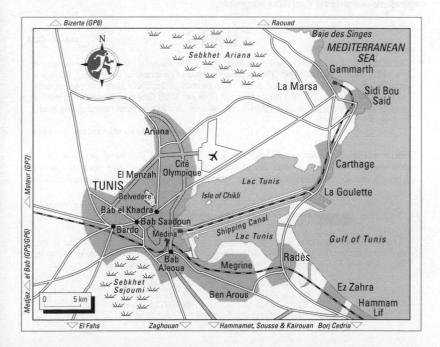

Away from the centre, but easily reached by public transport, are three more major attractions. The **Bardo Museum**, housed in a former regent's palace, has one of the finest collections of Roman mosaics anywhere in the world, best visited before seeing the Roman sites elsewhere in the country. In the other direction, overlooking the Gulf of Carthage, are the remains of **Carthage**, ancient Great Power and the enemy of Rome, and a little further in the same direction, the picturesque resort of **Sidi Bou Saïd**. Carthage can be somewhat underwhelming: the Roman invaders and then time itself were such thorough conquerors that you have to go prepared to use your imagination to a large extent. On the other hand, the views over the turquoise gulf – especially those from Sidi Bou Saïd – easily make up for any lingering disappointment.

Any free time in Tunis can be used up on a trip to the other, less well-known, suburbs. **La Goulette**, with its Spanish fort and fish restaurants, and **Hammam Lif**, nestling below Jebel Bou Kornine – the mountain which stands guard at the bottom of the gulf – both make for worthwhile outings. The gulf shore, north from La Goulette and south from **Radès**, is virtually one beach, but not a very pleasant one. In summer even **Raouad Beach**, the furthest out beyond Gammarth, is crowded, and unofficial reports claim the whole gulf is polluted. Alternatively, catch a bus or a train to one of a range of destinations within easy reach of the capital. With Tunis as your base, almost anywhere in northern Tunisia is accessible.

TUNIS تونس

We arrived at Tunis, object of all our hopes, focus of the flame of every gaze, rendezvous of travellers from East and West. This is where fleets and caravans come to meet. Here you will find everything a man could desire. You want to go by land? Here are endless companions for your journey. You prefer the sea? Here are boats for every direction. Tunis is a crown whose every jewel is a district, its suburbs are like a flower-garden constantly refreshed by the breeze.

El Abdari, thirteenth-century traveller

TUNIS is rooted firmly in an Arab medieval past. For a thousand years before the establishment of Islam, it was an insignificant neighbour of the port of Carthage (although founded earlier) and its only historic role was as a base for invaders laying siege to the larger city. The Arabs, however, preferred Tunis's less exposed site, and as early as the ninth century the **Aghlabids** built the Great Mosque that still stands at the heart of the Medina. In the last years of their rule, from 894 to 909 AD, Tunis served as the Aghlabid imperial capital.

Largely ignored by the **Fatimids**, who ruled from Mahdia in the tenth century, the city really came into its own following the **Hilalian** invasion of the eleventh century, when Abdelhaq Ibn Khourassane established a principality here. Amid the chaos of the time, this **Khourassanid** state was such an island of stability that by the time it fell to the **Almohads**, a hundred years later, it had become the country's natural power centre. When the **Hafsids** declared complete independence in 1236, it was a capital once again.

Under the Hafsids, and especially after the fall of Baghdad to the Mongols in 1258, Tunis became the western Arab world's leading metropolis – a great Mediterranean marketplace at a time of expanding trade between Christian Europe and the Muslim East. Culture flourished in the cosmopolitan atmosphere, and the university in the Great Mosque – the Zitouna Mosque – was rivalled only by those of al-Azhar in Cairo and the Kairaouine at Fez. The Hafsids' own building programme included the first *medersas*, or Islamic colleges, many of the purpose-built souks, or markets, around the Great Mosque, the Kasbah with its mosque, and the city walls.

As Arab rule wavered before the **Ottoman Turks**, Tunis changed in appearance – becoming enclosed by fortifications – and in character, as a more foreign-dominated era emerged. Wealth from trade and piracy poured into the city, financing the building of more mosques, *medersas* and palaces. Christian traders were allowed to settle, and since many of the "Turkish" officials ruling the new **regency** were *mamelukes* – slaves of Greek or Eastern European origin taken as children – several of the buildings and even a few mosques have a strong European flavour.

Until the nineteenth century, Tunis still consisted essentially of the **Medina** and faubourgs – poor suburbs outside the walls – with a few elaborate palaces, such as the Bardo, set in gardens further away. But by the 1860s, several thousand European traders and advisers were living in Tunis and their presence was influential. The International Financial Commission set up by the colonial powers virtually ran the government, and newly found wealth gave merchants considerable power over the impoverished Beys, or Ottoman rulers. At this time a new European city – the **New Town**, or Ville Nouvelle – began to develop outside the city walls, and with the **French occupation** in 1881 the French set about draining the marshy land on the edge of the lake to extend this new colonial domain. Today its wide avenues, jammed with traffic and beginning to crumble, still feel thoroughly *belle époque*, with their pavement cafés, iron balconies and fancy stuccowork.

Orientation

Tunis lies on the shore of the large, shallow **Lac Tunis**, which stretches between the town and the Gulf of Carthage. Along the gulf shore, north and south of the narrow entrance to the lake, stretches a chain of suburbs easily reached by public transport from the city centre. An independent light train line, the **TGM** (Tunis, La Goulette, Marsa), crosses the lake on a causeway to the northern shore's suburbs, which include **Carthage** and **Sidi Bou Saïd**. A mainline train runs from the mainline station to the less attractive southern suburbs of **Radès**, **Hammam Lif** and **Borj Cedria**.

Once in the city itself, orientation couldn't be simpler. **Avenue Bourguiba**, the great central artery, flanked by ministries, smart hotels and shops, and divided by a tree-lined promenade, links the **Medina** in the west to the lake in the east. To either side stretches the grid plan of the French-built **New Town**, bounded by the hilltop

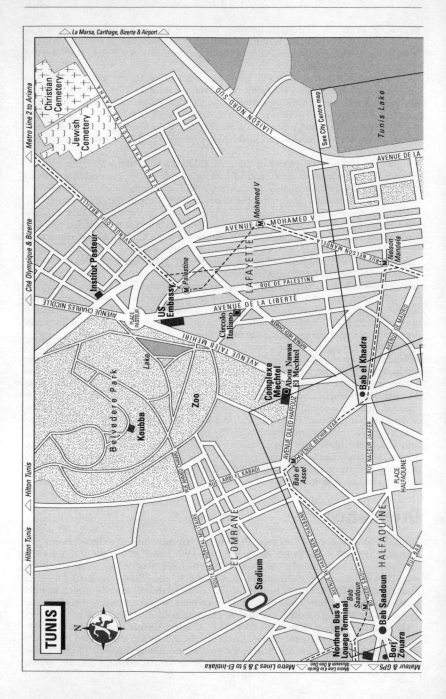

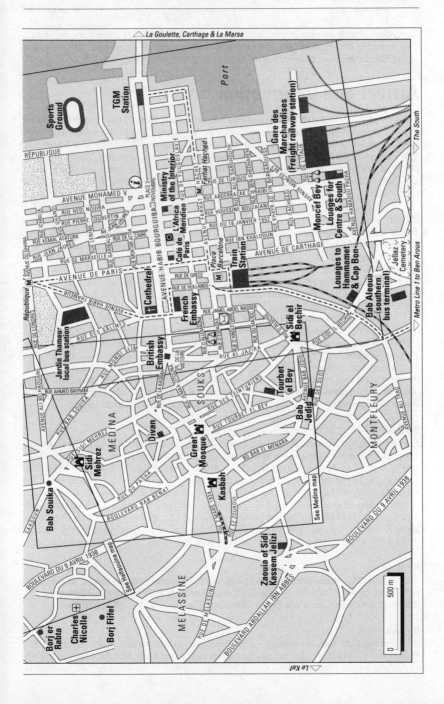

Belvedere Park to the north and the sprawling **Jellaz Cemetery** to the south. Everything in this central area is within easy walking distance and, with the exception of the **Bardo Museum**, there's little to be seen in the straggling suburbs.

Arrival and information

The best place to head on arrival is **avenue Bourguiba**. Most of the reasonably priced hotels are scattered within walking distance in the streets just to the south. The main **ONTT tourist office** is at its eastern end, on 1 av Mohamed V (Mon–Sat 8am–6pm, Sun 9am–noon; ☎01/341077, ⓦwww.tourismetunisien.com), and can supply you with plenty of free maps and booklets as well a list of hotels and their prices but that is about all. There are tourist offices also at the airport (☎01/754000), port (☎01/738 688) and train station.

By air

Tunis Carthage Airport is a fifteen-minute drive northeast of the centre, 8km away on the shore of the lake, and has a tourist office, a number of exchange bureaux, several travel agencies which offer an accommodation booking service, and **car rental** firms. If you're flying in at night, it's best to join the currency exchange queue inside customs immediately, and leave baggage collection till later. The bureaux are supposedly 24-hour, but if they're closed, take a taxi to the *Majestic* or *Carlton* hotels to change cash.

The easiest way into the centre from the airport is by yellow **taxi**, (not the extortionate louages), which should cost less than 4TD during the day or as much as 8TD at night or during rush hour – if you're heading to La Marsa or Gammarth, the fares are roughly double. Otherwise, the #35 and #635 **buses** both leave from the airport (straight ahead and to the left as you leave the terminal) between 6.30am and 8.30pm, taking around half an hour to reach the Tunis Marine bus station on avenue Bourguiba; other drop-off points are the bottom of avenue Habib Thameur where it meets avenue Bourguiba, and place Palestine, behind the République métro station.

By sea

Ferries from Sardinia, Sicily, Genoa, Marseille, Naples and Malta dock at La Goulette, a port in the city's eastern suburbs over the other side of Lake Tunis. The cheapest way into town is by TGM train across the lake to avenue Bourguiba. To find the TGM, come out of the ferry terminal, go straight ahead past the CTN/BNT bank and bear left at the roundabout. From here it's more or less straight on past the Kasbah (on your right) and another 300m or so down to the line. Turn right here and the station is 100m ahead. If your baggage is too heavy, you can always take a taxi – there are a number of them waiting at the port. In a car, head for the TGM but, instead of turning right for the station, cross the line and take a left across the causeway into town.

By train

Tunis's mainline **train station** is on place Barcelone, right at the centre of the main hotel area, south of avenue Bourguiba (métro lines #1, #3, #4 and #5). Most train services run every day but a few do not operate on Sundays and public holidays.

By bus

Both the intercity **bus terminals** – **Bab Saadoun**, at the bottom of rue Sidi el Bechir and avenue de Carthage, for the north of the country and **Bab Aleoua**, also called **Bab el Fellah**, for the centre and south – are well connected to the centre. Bab Saadoun is close to the métro station of the same name (lines #3, #4 and #5) and Bab Aleoua (line #1) is south of place Barcelone. City buses (#50, #72 and #74) run constantly between the two terminals, though they stop by the Bab Saadoun city gate rather than outside the northern bus terminal.

By louage

Louages, or service taxis, arrive at three different locations depending where you are coming from. Services from the **north and northwest** arrive outside Bab Saadoun bus station; coming from **Hammamet and Cap Bon**, you'll find yourself opposite Bab Aleoua bus station, and all other louages use a vast warehouse hangar adjacent to Souk Moncef Bey, fifteen minutes' walk south of avenue Bourguiba. International louages from Libya and Algeria, have their main stops at **Garage Ayachi** at Bab Souika (Libya) and **rue al Jazira**, just off place de la Victoire (Algeria).

City transport

Walking isn't just the most interesting way of getting around the city centre. In summer, when the traffic seizes up in the streets and the atmosphere in the buses is as steamy as in any hammam, it's often the quickest and most comfortable way to get somewhere.

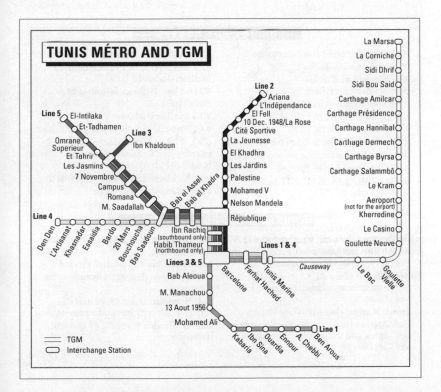

Bus rides in the city generally cost around 0.3TD and tickets can be purchased as you enter the rear door of the bus. If you plan to do a lot of travelling by bus, buy a book of tickets from the office at the Tunis Marine bus station at the end of avenue Bourguiba, near the TGM station; otherwise, pay on board. The other main urban **bus stations** are at Jardin Thameur, place Belhouane (near Bab Souika) and place Barcelone.

More an overgrown tramway, the fairly new **métro** system runs down the middle of the street and obeys traffic lights. Outside rush hours and lunchtime, it's not as frequent as it might be, and its lines are so arranged that most journeys require at least one change (same ticket). Tickets cost about the same as buses.

The central Tunis **TGM train station** is at the port end of avenue Bourguiba, next to Tunis Marine bus and métro (line #1) stations. Trains from here run every twenty minutes or so across Lake Tunis, linking the city with La Goulette, Carthage, Sidi Bou Saïd and La Marsa, at the end of the line and around forty minutes away. The last service is at around 1am. It's also possible to buy a sheet of TGM tickets at the TGM station, but there's no discount. A suburban overland train line runs every twenty to thirty minutes from place Barcelone station to Radès (20min), Hammam Lif (30min) and Borj Cedria (45min).

Taxis in Tunis are hailed in the street in the conventional way, and are metered. By day you'll rarely pay more than 2–3TD for a ride in the city centre. They cost more after 7pm when meters are off and you have to negotiate the price right at the start.

USEFUL BUS ROUTES

#1 circles the Medina anticlockwise
#2 Tunis Marine–Kasbah
#5, #5c and **#5d** Tunis Marine–Belvedere Park
#8 Tunis Marine–Montfleury
#16b, #42 and **#42a** Belhouane–Tebourba
#20b Jardin Thameur–Gammarth
#20c Jardin–Carthage
#23 Thameur–Borj El Amri
#23a, 23b, 23c, 23d, 23T Jardin Thameur–Bardo

#26a and **#26b** Barcelone–Mornag
#27 and **27b** Rabt 10 Decembre–El Menzah–Raouad
#31b Place Belhouane–Kalaat El Andalous
#35 635 Tunis Marine–Airport
#44 Place Belhouane–Kalaat El Andalous
#50, #72 and **#74** connects the two intercity bus terminals (Bab Saadoun–Bab Aleoua)
#52 La Marsa (Ennassin)–Gammarth
#116 Barcelone–Tebourba

USEFUL METRO STATIONS

Barcelone (all lines): train station and main métro interchange
Bardo (line #4): Bardo Museum
République (lines #2, #3, #4 and #5): métro interchange, Habib Thameur local bus station
Tunis Marine (line #1): TGM station
Bab Aleoua (line #1): southern intercity bus station and louages for Hammamet and Cap Bon

Palestine (line #2): Algerian consulate, US embassy
Jeunesse (line #2): football ground
Cité Sportive (line #2): Olympic swimming pool
Bab Saadoun (lines #3, #4 and #5): northern intercity bus and louage station
Bab el Khadra (lines #3, #4 and #5): Halfaouine

Accommodation

The ONTT tourist office is of limited use in helping you find **accommodation**, and though they provide a list of hotels they're unable to handle bookings. Many travel agencies – particularly those at the airport – offer a booking service, usually for the more expensive, classified hotels, with a few selected one-star choices at the lower end of the scale. But if you haven't booked from home the best way to find a room is to just start walking.

Central Tunis has dozens of cheap hotels, though in midsummer the more popular ones tend to fill up disconcertingly quickly and it's wise to start looking as early as possible. If everything appears to be full, it's worth knowing that at the height of the season a few hotels let people sleep on the roof. It's cheaper and makes the humidity more bearable, but is officially illegal. The only real alternative to a hotel here is the rather good **youth hostel** in the Medina – again, try to book ahead. The hotels listed below are unclassified unless stated – though classification is rarely an indication of value for money. The **cheapest hotels** of all are in the Medina and at its edges, but can be extremely insalubrious and insecure; women travelling alone are advised to steer clear of ones not explicitly recommended in the listings.

New Town hotels

The densest concentration of hotels – though they're also the most likely to be full – lies in the French **New Town**, between the Medina and avenue de Carthage, which cuts across avenue Bourguiba about halfway down. Most of these are mid-range to luxury, with a few cheaper dives scattered among them. If you have the energy there are other cheap places to check out further south around **Bab Jazira**, especially on rue d'Algérie and avenue Bab Jedid.

All the hotels below are keyed on the City Centre map (see pp.68–69), except for the Abou Nawas El Mechtel and the Hilton Tunis (see Tunis map, pp.62–63).

Rue Charles de Gaulle and around

Hôtel de l'Agriculture, 25 rue Charles de Gaulle ☎01/326394. Friendly and offering clean, pleasant rooms with showers. ❸

Hôtel de France, 8 rue Mustapha M'barek ☎01/326244, ℱ323314. Clean, big, old-fashioned rooms in a 1940s building, many of which are en suite (about 2.4TD extra). Recommended. ❷

Hôtel Rue de Russie ★★, 18 rue de Russie ☎01/328883, ℱ321685. Brand new and surprisingly smart for the area. The better rooms have balconies over the street; all have baths, TV and phone. ❹

Splendid, 2 rue Mustapha M'barek ☎01/242844. Renovation is long overdue but the rooms are quite clean if somewhat sombre and have a certain seedy charm. An extra 2TD buys you an en-suite bath. ❷

Around avenue de la Gare

Asma, 17 rue du Boucher ☎01/332918. Cheap but very basic accommodation. Women steer clear. 1TD per shower. ❶

Excelsior, 7 rue du Boucher ☎01/342917. No-frills budget option popular with students. Not a place for women. 1TD per shower. ❶

Hôtel de la Gare, 25 av de la Gare ☎01/256754. Friendly, with clean but rather bare rooms with sinks in a fume-choked avenue. ❷

El Mouna, 64 rue de la Sebkha ☎01/343375. Although newish this hotel has already fallen on hard times, but it is spacious if not spotless – rooms without a shower are the best value. ❶–❷

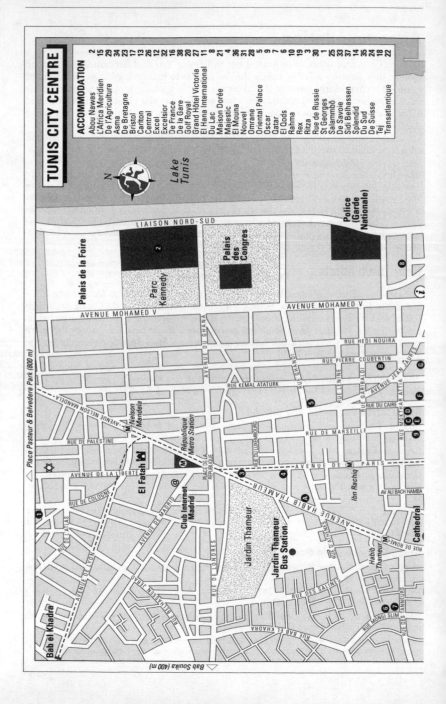

TUNIS CITY CENTRE

ACCOMMODATION	
Abou Nawas	2
L'Afrique Meridien	15
De l'Agriculture	29
Asma	34
De Bretagne	23
Bristol	17
Carlton	13
Central	26
Excel	12
Excelsior	32
De France	16
De la Gare	38
Golf Royal	20
Grand Hôtel Victoria	27
El Hana International	11
Du Lac	8
Maison Dorée	21
Majestic	4
El Mouna	36
Nouvel	31
Omrane	28
Oriental Palace	5
Oscar	9
Qatar	7
El Qods	6
Rahma	10
Rex	19
Ritza	3
Rue de Russie	30
St Georges	1
Salammbô	25
De Savoie	33
Sidi Belhassen	37
Splendid	14
Du Sud	35
De Suisse	24
Tej	18
Transatlantique	22

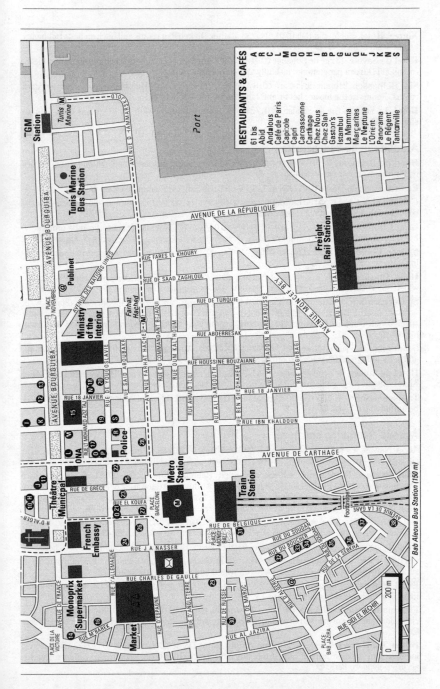

RESTAURANTS & CAFÉS

61 bis	A
Abid	R
Andalous	L
Café de Paris	M
Capitole	D
Capri	O
Carcassonne	H
Carthage	I
Chez Nous	B
Chez Slah	P
Gaston's	G
Istambul	E
La Mamma	Q
Marçarites	F
Le Neptune	J
L'Orient	K
Pano'rama	N
Le Régent	S
Tantonville	

Bab Aleoua Bus Station (150 m)

Nouvel Hôtel, 3 pl Mongi Bali ☎01/345283. Rather Dickensian rooms and big iron beds but handy for the train station. ❶–❷

Hôtel de Savoie, 13 rue de Boucher ☎01/253780. Another cheapie with basic and small, but clean, rooms (1TD extra per shower); tasefully and colourfully painted throughout. ❶

Sidi Belhassen, 21bis av de la Gare ☎01/343409. Cheery sort of place, but with small, rather dark rooms. Rooms at the top are better and have use of the kitchen. ❷

Hôtel du Sud, 34 rue du Soudan ☎01/246916. Cheap and basic with double rooms only, without showers. ❶–❷

Around rue de Yougoslavie

Hôtel de Bretagne, 7 rue de Grèce ☎01/252146. Dirty and unfriendly and without much security, but the rooms are good and cheap. ❷

Central, 6 rue de Suisse ☎01/320 422. A bit on the seedy side but quite clean. ❶

Golf Royal ★★★, 51–53 rue de Yougoslavie ☎01/344311, ⑤348155. Business-class place with air-conditioning and TV, but not many other facilities. ❹

Grand Hôtel Victoria, 79 rue Farhat Hached ☎01/342863. Not that grand and can be unfriendly, but it has large rooms and is right on place Barcelone, so it's handy for bus, train and métro. ❷

Maison Dorée ★★, 3 rue el Koufa ☎01/240632, ⑤332401. Spotless but rather formal place backing onto rue d'Hollande. ❸

Hôtel Omrane ★★★, 65 av Farhat Hached ☎01/345277, ⑤354892. Very well-run 1930s place which still retains a touch of grandeur. Satellite TV and phones in all rooms. ❹

St Georges ★★, 16 rue de Cologne ☎01/781029. If you can live with the location (20min walk north of avenue Bourguiba), this dilapidated colonial house may be the best value in Tunis, with spacious, air-conditioned rooms (10TD extra), some with baths at moderate prices and safe parking. ❷–❸

Salammbô ★, 6 rue de Grèce ☎01/334252, ⑤337498. Airy, spick and span rooms, some en suite, and a TV lounge and breakfast room. Recommended. ❷

Hôtel de Suisse ★, 5 rue de Suisse ☎01/323821. In an alley joining rue d'Hollande and rue Jamel Abdel Nasser. Pleasant rooms but a slightly grubby communal kitchen. ❶

Transatlantique ★, 106 rue de Yougoslavie ☎01/240680. Pleasant, colonial-style rooms and a beautifully tiled lobby. ❸

Avenue Bourguiba and north

Abou Nawas ★★★★★, av Mohamed V ☎01/350355, ⑤352882, ⑤tunis@abounawas.com.tn. The city's newest luxury establishment and by far the best, offering restaurants, health clubs and pool. ❼

Abou Nawas El Mechtel ★★★★ av Ouled Halfouz ☎01/783200, ⑤784758, ⑥elmechtel@abounawas.com.tn. Business-class place well out of the centre towards Belevedere Park. Smart rooms with all you'd expect. Outdoor pool, nightclub, five restaurants and the rest. Same price as the *Abou Nawas*, and unless you have business in this area, you'd be better off there. ❼

Hôtel l'Africa Meridien ★★★★★, 50 av Bourguiba ☎01/347477. A monstrous carbuncle, but the best hotel on avenue Bourguiba with superb views from the upper floors. ❻–❼

Bristol, 30 rue Lt. Mohammed el Aziz Tej ☎01/254835. Basic, but well located and dirt cheap. ❶

Carlton ★★★, 31 av Bourguiba ☎01/330644, ⑤338168, ⑥carlton@planet.tn. Friendly and well-situated business-class hotel, extensively renovated and consequently rather dull. ❺

Excel Hôtel, 35 av Bourguiba ☎01/355088, ⑤341929. Less classy than the *Carlton* but as comfortable and includes bar and satellite TV. ❹

El Hana International ★★★★★, 49 av Bourguiba ☎01/331144, ⑤341199. Not what you'd call a classy joint, in spite of the deluxe rating, but popular with package tourists and businesspeople alike. ❻

Hilton Tunis ★★★★★, av de la Ligue Arabe, Notre Dame ☎01/782800, ⑤797133. Despite its inconvenient location around 5km from the city centre, this luxury hotel has wonderful views across Belvedere Park. ❼

Hôtel du Lac ★★★, av Mohammed V ☎01/336100, ⓕ342759. Discreet and tasteful it is not, but the inverted pyramid is now a landmark on the Tunis skyline and offers a bit of luxury. It's been suggested that this hotel inspired the sand crawler in *Star Wars*. ➎

Majestic ★★★, 36 av de Paris ☎01/332848, ⓦwww.ahlan.tourism.tn/majestic. Elegant colonial architecture, especially the foyer, but the hotel in general is getting a bit shabby despite the polished brass buttons on the doorman's uniform. ➍

Oriental Palace ★★★★★, 29 av Jean Jaurès ☎01/348846, ⓕ350327. This place has style. The decor is Oriental kitsch and worth taking in even if you're just passing by. There is a pool and two restaurants. ➐

Oscar, 12–14 rue de Marseille ☎01/344755, ⓕ345558. Central, business-class hotel with little character, but a late night bar. ➎

Qatar, imp 6, rue des Tanneurs ☎01/342522. Basic but clean rooms with showers. More friendly than next door *El Qods*. ➊

El Qods, imp 6, rue des Tanneurs ☎01/340404. Next door to the *Qatar*, ask for a room with balcony. Not particularly clean and not suitable for single women. ➋

Rahma, 5 rue Qadiciyah (or Kadissa) ☎01/255566. Reasonable place with small rooms, some with sinks and bathrooms, in an alley behind La Parnasse cinema. ➋

Ritza, 35 av Habib Thameur ☎01/255428. Friendly place whose manager speaks English. Basic, clean doubles, some with showers. ➋

Rex, 65 rue de Yougoslavie ☎01/257397. Another colonial leftover that has seen better days but remains adequate value. ➋

Tej ★★, 14 rue Lt Mohamed el Aziz Tej ☎01/342629, ⓕ342666. Expensive but there is good service even if the rooms don't match up. Check the rooms before handing over your passport. ➍

Accommodation in the Medina and Halfaouine

Hotels in the **Medina** tend to be the cheapest, but also the dirtiest, and very stuffy in the summertime and damp and cold in winter. The rooms are typically without attached bathrooms, and cost an additional 1TD for a hot shower, with breakfast not included. Except where otherwise stated they are not recommended for women travelling on their own. On the other hand, a stay in the Medina throws you headlong into a world that would completely pass you by in some hotels in the New Town.

Medina hotels

Hôtel les Amis, 7 rue Monastiri ☎01/565653. Basic but clean and friendly, with Kung fu videos in the TV room.There are no sinks or showers but there is a hammam close by. ➊

Hammami, 12 rue el Mechnaka ☎01/560451. Large grubby rooms in a huge and very impressive mansion near place Bab Carthajana. ➊

Marhaba, 5 rue de la Commission ☎01/354006, ⓕ325452. Basic but cleaner than most, and friendly and safe for women. Arrive early in summer. ➊

El Massara, 5 bd Bab Menara ☎01/563734, ⓕ565265. On the western edge of the Medina and safe for women but the rooms are minuscule if clean. ➋

Medina, 1 pl de la Victoire ☎01/327497, ⓕ325452. Reasonable hotel on the edge of the Medina – relatively clean, conveniently situated and naturally popular. OK for women. ➊

Souk Hôtel, 101 rue des Teinturiers ☎01/347398. Small clean rooms. Friendly and fine for women guests. ➋

Hôtel de la Victoire, 7 bd Bab Menara ☎01/261224. Neighbour to the *El Massara*. Cool and airy, if rather noisy, but with friendly management and a painting in every room. ➊

Medina youth hostel

IYHF youth hostel "Dar Saida Ajoula" (Tunis Medina), 25 rue Saida Ajoula ☎01/567850. Clean, friendly and well run but still subject to rules and curfew (10pm winter; midnight in summer, closed 10am–2pm year round). The building is a former palace and fills up quickly in summer, so book ahead. Dorms for 5TD.

Halfaouine

Hôtel des Amis, 136 rue el Halfaouine, between Bab Souika and place Halfaouine ☎01/566105. Good basic rooms around inner courtyard. Relatively clean and secure. ❶

Hôtel 20 Mars, 9 rue Sidi Alloui ☎01/566924. Basic – and not recommended for women – but friendly in a gorgeously dilapidated building by the Sahib et Tabaa mosque. Minimum rent is by the month (28TD). ❷

The New Town and Belvedere Park

The area now occupied by the modern colonial **New Town** consisted mainly of uncultivated land until the French took control in 1881, when they immediately set about reproducing a French provincial capital. **Avenue de France** and its continuation, **avenue Bourguiba**, run down the middle from the Medina to the port; to either side, the streets more or less follow a grid pattern. The city's main chunk of greenery is the massive **Belvedere Park**, which overlooks it from the north.

Although this isn't the most fascinating part of Tunis, it's where you're likely to spend a lot of your time eating or sleeping, since it contains the city's best hotels, most restaurants and other facilities. Incidentally, for a fantastic **aerial view** of Tunis, as well as Sidi Bou Saïd, the lake and sometimes as far as Djebel Zaghouan 50km to the south, take the lift in *Hôtel El Hana International* to its tenth-floor rooftop café and bar. If you're there at dusk, on any day, you can see the flocking acrobatics of avenue Bourguiba's immense (and noisy) starling colony.

Avenue Bourguiba and around

Avenue Bourguiba is the centre of Tunis in every way. People converge here from all over the city to sit in cafés, stroll under the trees, buy a posy made of jasmine buds – above all, just to see and be seen. There's something very continental about it that's quite at odds with the Medina's cramped narrow streets.

The first landmark along the avenue is the **Cathedral**, built in 1882 and a monstrous, bizarre mixture of Romanesque, Byzantine and Oriental styles. Just across from the cathedral, the **French Embassy** is quite modest by contrast. Built in 1862 as the advance guard of growing French influence, and as the *Résidence Générale*, the centre of the Protectorate administration from 1881, many of the important decisions of Tunisia's recent history have been made within its still heavily guarded walls. A few blocks east, the old French **Théâtre Municipal**, with its bulging layers of white stucco and fantastic carved figures supporting the balcony, plays host to regular and highly recommended Arabic and classical music concerts.

South of the avenue is French Tunis's most lively area, with many of the city's restaurants, nightclubs and cinemas. There's also a huge **food market** on rue d'Allemagne, selling every conceivable kind of produce. The **Musée de la Poste** (Mon–Thurs 8.30am–1pm & 3–5.45pm, Fri & Sat 8am–1.30pm; free), a dark and dusty room in the main post office in rue d'Angleterre, is for ardent philatelists only, while the **Musée des Finances** (Mon–Thurs 8.30am–1pm & 3–5.45pm, Fri & Sat 8am–1.30pm; free) at 27 rue de Rome in the foyer of the Contrôle Générale des Finances, will similarly appeal to numismatists. Beyond the train station, the grid plan begins to go awry near the Medina, and the same thing happens north of the avenue, where the area immediately adjoining rue Mongi Slim and rue Bab Souika – the old **Maltese and Jewish quarters** – is agreeably chaotic. The thirteenth-century **Zaraia Mosque**, on the corner of

COLONIAL ARCHITECTURE

Three early examples of the new French rulers trying to stamp their presence on the city are the main Post Office, and the Cathedral and French Residence, facing each other on avenue Bourguiba. Subsequently, architects prefered the fussiness of provincial wedding-cake elaboration, such as the theatre on avenue Bourguiba and *Hôtel Majestic*, with occasional forays into "Moorish" kitsch.

By far the most exciting facet of the colonial heritage, however, is the wealth of **Art Deco** from the 1925–40 period. An architectural study has identified over four hundred buildings, ranging from luxurious urban villas, to apartment buildings and tenements, to functional office blocks, many of which can still be seen within the grid-plan districts of the modern city.

Art Deco arrived at the Paris Exposition of 1925. Although the term is usually associated with the decorative arts, it also relates to buildings that feature exuberantly stylized decoration and clean geometric forms. To the home-grown architects of colonial North Africa, these characteristics made Art Deco seem an appropriate and modern departure from inherited styles, as well as being up with the latest trends in France.

The masterpiece of Tunis' Art Deco period is the Villa Boublil, a magnificent building near the Belvedere Park at 16 rue d'Autriche, designed by J.G. Ellul, a member of the local Maltese community. Even in its semi-abandoned state, it's well worth a special visit for its rippling lines and elaborate metalwork. A couple of years later, Ellul also designed an office building (the Omnium Immobilier Tunisien, 12 av Habib Thameur) whose discreet elegance would not be out of place in a chic contemporary development. It remains a prestigious address.

Not all the buildings are up to this standard, and many verge on blandness. But it's worth casting your eye above street level every now and then for the telltale semicircular balconies, crowning pylons, elaborate geometric reliefs and above all the metalwork on balconies, doors and windows. Hallway interiors are also sometimes elaborately decorated. Sometimes the effect is minimal: a hint of waviness in the metalwork of a balcony. Other times, you find a grand statement: three apartment buildings by the same designer filling one whole side of a city block (Q. Riccardini, west side of rue du 18 Janvier 1952, south of rue Ahmed Tlili; P.P. Ancona, north side of rue Ghedhahem, east of rue Ibn Khaldoun).

The densest concentration of buildings can be found north of avenue Bourguiba, and colonial archiecture can also be found in Montfleury, the suburb south west of Bab Aleoua bus station. Particularly fine examples are listed below, with street junctions shown in brackets where appropriate.

NORTH (OF AV DE LONDRES)
16 rue d'Autriche (Ibn Tafragin)
20 rue de L'Inde (Asdstrubal)
2, 43 (Syangogue), 45, 131 av de la Liberté
1 (Hotel Madrid)

CENTRAL (AV DE LONDRES TO AV BOURGUIBA)
12 av Habib Thameur
56 av de Paris

SOUTH (OF AV BOURGUIBA)
22 rue d'Algérie (Al Jazira)
34 av Farhat Hached
13 rue Oum Khalthoum

MONTFLEURY
21 rue Allal el Fassi (Sadok)

rue Zarkoun and rue Mongi Slim, is the main sight. The further you go along avenue Bourguiba from the Medina, the stronger the European influence on the architecture. Both avenue de Paris and avenue de la Liberté have some wonderful examples of colonial building, although things get more sombre towards the end of avenue de la Liberté, as you move into a zone of embassies and government buildings. Just off avenue de Paris, the **Jardin Habib Thameur** provides a small amount of greenery but is tiny and fume-laden.

Belvedere Park

Tunis is not a city greatly endowed with parks, and it is really the cemeteries – especially Jellaz (see p.94) – that provide much-needed open spaces. The exception is **Belvedere Park**, which provides an excellent reason for coming this far north. Breathing space has always been a problem in Tunis. An anonymous "English lady" of the 1850s, author of *Letters from Barbary*, reported asking to be shown a garden. Her guide led her some way through the streets, then "halted before two trees, growing against a wall, and surrounded by a plot of about four foot wide, perhaps: and this, he told us, was the biggest garden in the town". Most people today escape the summer humidity by catching the TGM to Carthage or Sidi Bou Saïd, but Belvedere Park, with its green lower area kept heavily watered, is a peaceful and accessible alternative. Vegetation grows much more sparsely as you climb the hill, but there's an excellent view from the top over Tunis to Bou Kornine (see p.120). The elaborate **koubba**, or dome, standing about halfway up, was built in 1798 for a palace in the suburbs and transplanted here in 1901.

At the bottom of the park (just above its main entrance), the old abandoned casino has been converted into a **Museum of Modern Art and Cinema**, due to open in summer 2001. Its terrace is used for theatrical performances in summer as part of the Carthage Festival. Further round to the south is the **zoo** (daily: winter 9am–4pm; summer 9am–7pm: 0.3TD), where some distressingly small cages provide an eyeball-to-eyeball perspective on the fiercer species. Also here is the **Midha**, an early seventeenth-century fountain for pre-prayer ablutions, brought here from its original site at Souk et Trouk in the Medina. The **cafés** in the middle of the zoo and on the lake just outside are two of the most relaxed in the city.

The Medina

"White, domed, studded with minarets, honeycombed with tunnel-like bazaars" – until the nineteenth century, the **Medina** *was* Tunis: an oval-shaped walled city little changed from its days as a great Mediterranean trading power. In the eighth century AD, the conquering Arabs were the first to prefer Tunis's site to Carthage, exposed out on its peninsula, and set about building the monuments that still form the heart of the Medina, most notably the ninth-century **Zitouna Mosque**, still surrounded by the central souks. Along the narrow, winding streets – typical of medieval Arab cities – subsequent generations left their own distinctive legacies: mosques, tombs, palaces and marketplaces. Most of them feature a blend of styles that mirrors the city's cosmopolitan history, although occasionally there is a more straightforward statement, such as the Mosque of Sidi Mehrez's Ottoman domes, which would not look out of place in Istanbul. Because of all this it's no surprise to learn that the Medina is classed by UNESCO as a **World Heritage Site**. Entrance to the monuments theoretically requires a ticket that is available only at the Zitouna Mosque (tickets sold 8am–noon, except Fri) and the Dar Ben Abdallah Museum, though in practice this is rarely enforced.

When the French began to build their new capital on reclaimed land east of the Medina in the late nineteenth century, they made no deliberate attempt to eradicate local culture as they had done in Algiers, but the Medina inevitably declined. After Independence in 1956, a plan was raised to drive a continuation of avenue de France through the heart of the Medina to the government offices on the far side, which would have destroyed the quarter for ever. Fortunately, this idea was abandoned after

WALKS IN THE MEDINA

There are many different ways to approach a visit to the **Medina**. Perhaps the most attractive – if not the most practical – is just to wander at random, stumbling on unexpected sights. At the other extreme, the tourist authorities have created and signposted an itinerary that includes many of the major monuments and provides a quick tour (1–2hr) for visitors – a leaflet showing this route is available from the tourist office at 1 av Mohamed V, but don't count on the signs themselves being easily visible (most are hidden behind doors and shopfronts).

We have divided the Medina into three areas – the **central, southern** and **northern Medina. Halfaouine** and the **western districts** are suburbs, dating back several hundred years to the Hafsid era, and are outside the walls of the Medina proper and covered under a separate heading. Each itinerary covers the main historic sights in each section and many lesser monuments.

Each **walk** on its own probably takes a couple of hours or they can easily be combined to create a longer outing. In terms of monuments, the centre and the souks form the densest area, followed by the south and north.

the Association de Sauvegarde de la Medina was set up to try to preserve the old city's heritage. But the Medina remains the most tangible evidence of Tunisia's immediate precolonial past and of the "decadence that made colonization possible", to quote a senior government official in 1961. As such, it has continued to be treated as a political football: historic buildings have been allowed to deteriorate and the authorities have even been slow to recognize the Medina's potential tourist value. Recently these trends seem to have been reversed, but still few of the monuments are geared up for visitors. Many have been converted to municipal facilities of some kind, while others remain *ukalas* – large buildings subdivided for many families or businesses. The most distinctively Tunisian element are the magnificent doorways which, according to El Bekri, were already famous in the thirteenth century: blue or beige, set with black studs and a "hand of Fatima" knocker, and surrounded by intricately carved stone frames.

Avoid wandering around **after dark**, when the Medina is deserted, ill-lit and sometimes dangerous, with incidents of mugging not unknown. Although old men are hired as watchmen, huddled around fires with baseball bats, they hardly inspire confidence for nocturnal jaunts. (Ramadan is a different story and the main streets are crammed with shoppers and families until near midnight and the cafés do a roaring trade.) Another danger in the Medina after dark is being hit by flying rubbish. It's flung from windows in the evenings for night-time street cleaners, to brush it all up, as there's not much space for garbage trucks down in the narrow streets. During the day, beware of **pickpockets** in the crowded main thoroughfares, rue de la Kasbah and rue Jemaa Zitouna.

The central Medina

With the Great Mosque and souks set squarely in the middle, the **central Medina** was once the heart of the old city. Here, the concentration of streets, shops and people is at its greatest. At certain times of day, the main streets into the Medina from place de la Victoire are so chock-a-block you can hardly move down them. The Medina's main industry nowadays is tourism, usually of the day-trip variety, with most tour groups "doing" the same streets, the same sights and the same souvenir shops. The result is that the centre of the Medina can feel very commercial, even artificial, and the streets like a gauntlet of traders, albeit mostly amiable ones.

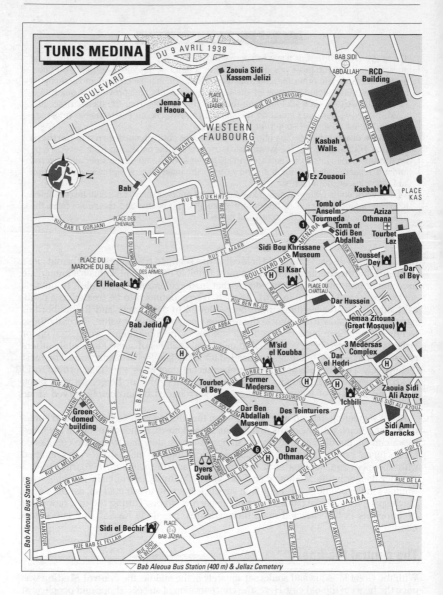

On **place de la Victoire** at the western end of avenue Bourguiba, you'll notice the difference between Western symmetry and Eastern bustle. **Bab el Bahr**, the Sea Gate, stands alone in the middle of the square; before development of the European city began in the middle of the nineteenth century, it opened from the Medina onto more or less empty ground, which led down to the naval arsenal on the shores of the lake. Once the French took over, they inevitably attached particular value to Bab el

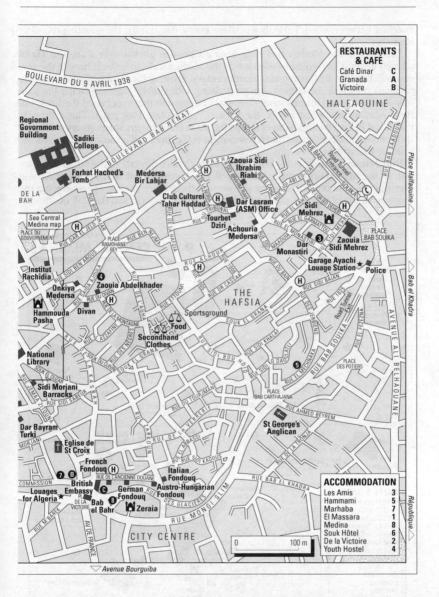

Bahr as the focal point of the meeting between Medina and European city. Ever the symbolic town planners, they knocked down the gate's surrounding houses as well as its walls so as to isolate it in a square, renaming it Porte de France. Then they erected an evangelical statue behind it where the houses had been – now long gone – of Cardinal Lavigerie, founder of the White Fathers. Just outside the gate, until as late as the first half of the nineteenth century, the Beys used to sponsor wrestling matches between oiled Turkish wrestlers every day during the month preceding Ramadan.

This area of the Medina had long been a Christian ghetto, ever since the Turks allowed the first foreign embassies inside the Medina walls to be built here in the seventeenth century. By the mid-nineteenth century, growing European influence saw the positions reversed; the large Italianate building with shabby columns facing the gate was the office of the International Financial Commission that supervised the bankrupt Beys' administration just before the French Protectorate (see p.61). These French, Italian and British commissioners forced the government to grant foreigners privileges and concessions that caused much resentment at the time, and on several occasions the building was attacked by mobs.

Rue Jemaa Zitouna leads from place de la Victoire directly to the Great Mosque, and, as the main tourist route, has turned into a cauldron of overflowing stalls and overeager proprietors. You can buy almost everything more cheaply elsewhere, but the shops are a useful training ground for bargaining techniques, and the stall on the cor-

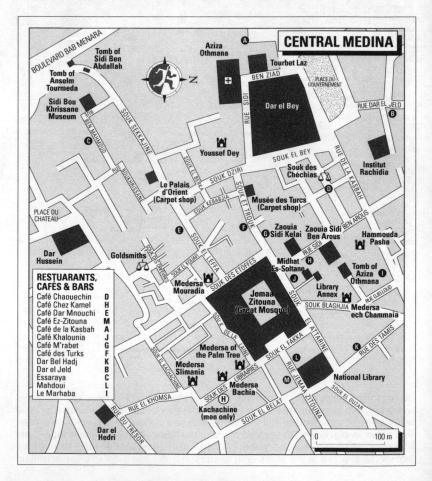

CENTRAL MEDINA

RESTUARANTS, CAFÉS & BARS

Café Chaouechin	D
Café Chez Kamel	H
Café Dar Mnouchi	E
Café Ez-Zitouna	M
Café de la Kasbah	A
Café Khalounia	J
Café M'rabet	G
Café des Turks	F
Dar Bel Hadj	K
Dar el Jeld	B
Essaraya	C
Mahdoui	L
Le Marhaba	I

ner of rue Sidi Ali Azouz often has interesting old metal lamps, chandeliers and pen cases. At no. 12 is the **Church of St Croix**, the first to be built in Tunis, in 1662. In the 1860s it became a sanctuary, protected by the French, and the source of repeated confrontation between them and the Beys. Time after time the Beys had to back down and accept that the criminals and enemies who escaped here were outside their jurisdiction.

The fine door at no. 55 belongs to the **Sidi Morjani Barracks**, the third of five sets of barracks built by Hammouda Bey (1777–1813) after his Ottoman troops mutinied in 1811. Hammouda was forced to recruit tribal warriors from among the Zouaoua Berbers as auxiliaries, and built them five sets of barracks. At the end of rue Jemaa Zitouna, the **National Library** at no. 73 was originally the second barracks; entrance to the library is through the Souk el Attarine. The first of Hammouda Bey's barracks is now Aziza Othmana Hospital, near place du Gouvernement (see p.81); another is in **rue Sidi Ali Azouz**, just off rue Jemaa Zitouna (see p.84); and the fifth has since been demolished.

The Great Mosque

Bringing rue Jemaa Zitouna to an abrupt halt is the **Great Mosque** (daily 8am–noon, closed Fri; 1.6TD, camera 1TD; ticket covers other sights on the official Medina route), known as the Zitouna (olive tree) because it stands on the site of the tree under which its founder, Hassan Ibn Nooman, taught the Koran.

The mosque's massive size is exaggerated by the cramped alleys around it, an effect that must have been even greater when it was completed under the Aghlabids in the ninth century. While the mosque is still the heart of the Medina, for hundreds of years it was the central point of reference for the entire city: the surrounding souks were positioned deliberately around it, as well as a host of secondary buildings such as the *medersas* that housed students who had come to study at the mosque.

Successive additions over the centuries make its exterior appearance today something of a composite. In the seventeenth century Spanish architect Ibn Ghalib – who also designed the mosque complex of the second Turkish ruler, Youssef Dey – was responsible for the spacious entrance portico hanging over the Souk el Fakka (dried fruits) along the mosque's east side; the minaret at the northwest corner, which seems such a perfect fit, actually dates back only to the nineteenth century, when a new minaret was modelled directly on that of the 1235 Kasbah Mosque (see p.92). In the cramped surroundings of the Medina, little else is visible of the exterior except for massive blank walls. It's worth timing a visit for the morning so that you can go inside and see the courtyard, which retains its original form – a vast empty space of polished marble. It is strongly reminiscent of the Great Mosque at Kairouan, built slightly earlier, and has the same wonderfully soothing effect after the bustle of the souks outside. As at Kairouan, the courtyard is surrounded on three sides by simple arcades, while the prayer hall occupies the fourth.

In its day, the **university** based in the mosque was one of the greatest in the world and its library (entry to academics only) still contains one of the world's great collections of Arabic literature. Hundreds of years before European universities had even been thought of, students were coming to Tunis from throughout the Islamic world. Tradition records that each professor had his own column, next to which he always did his teaching. Even in the 1950s there were students here, but during the 1960s the university was brought into line with the national educational system and theological students moved elsewhere.

Coming out of the mosque, turn right along **Souk des Librairies**, one side of which is lined by a series of interconnecting *medersas* built in the early eighteenth century – the **Medersa of the Palm Tree** (no. 11), the **Bachia** (no. 27) and, on the corner, the **Slimania**, which you can visit (times are uncertain but if you ask at the nearby barbershop they usually know where the custodian is). The *medersa* is a type of residential Islamic college of Turkish origin found all over the Muslim world, and here each has the classic form of a courtyard surrounded by students' cells. These three are part of a series founded in Tunis in the eighteenth century, and the story behind two of them typifies the instability of the Husaynid dynasty. The Bachia was founded in 1752 by Ali Pacha, and only two years later he dedicated the Slimania to the memory of his son Suleiman, who had been poisoned by a younger brother. There's also a **hammam** here at no. 30, Hammam Kachachine (daily 5am–5pm, men only).

The main souks

The close link between Islam and commerce could hardly be better represented than by the purpose-built **souks** around the Great Mosque. Hierarchy was symbolized by position: the closer to the mosque, the more "noble" the trade, thus the Souk des Étoffes (cloth) and Souk el Attarine (perfume) were right next to it; messier and noisier businesses such as dyeing and metalwork were relegated to the suburbs.

At the Great Mosque, turn left along the **Souk de la Laine** – Wool Market – which runs up the near side. There's not much wool here any more, but a few traditional tailors and, at **no. 21**, a doorway into the mosque improvised out of Roman blocks. Opposite no. 9 is the **rue de Béjà**, where most of the wool and cotton weaving seems to have moved to. It's interesting to watch the weaving – most of the textiles are still made on hand looms. At the end of Souk de la Laine, a brief detour takes in some of the further souks.

Left along **Souk des Femmes**, you cross the Souk du Coton to a junction with **Souk el Kachachine**, with its noisy wholesale bargaining for rugs and garments. Turn right at this corner, first right onto Souk el Kouafi, then first left into **Souk des Orfèvres**. True to its name, this is still the home of gold jewellers, whose tiny shops on narrow streets reflect their need for security. The souk and its surrounding streets are still protected by heavy wooden doors, which are closed at night and on Sunday afternoons. Left to the junction with Souk el Leffa and then a right downhill will take you to **Souk des Étoffes**, or Cloth Market, recognizable by its red and green columns. With its deep stalls, this is the most spacious souk in the Medina; elegant and refined, it comes

---

THE TUNIS SLAVE TRADE

Slaves were brought to Souk el Berka in Tunis – the most unfortunate from their dungeons in the Kasbah at La Goulette – where they were displayed to prospective buyers, who would first check the strength of their teeth because unskilled slaves ended up working the corsair galleys and being fed entirely on hard biscuits. Most of the slaves were captured at sea, as far away as the English Channel – but there were also frequent raids on coastal towns in Italy, France and Spain. It was a brutal business, though Western tradition has been happy to overlook the equally ferocious Christian corsairs supplying the great slave markets at Pisa, Genoa and other European trading cities. Piracy and slavery were generally accepted (even if not officially) as a lucrative adjunct of Mediterranean trade.

By the end of the eighteenth century, European fleets had forced the corsairs from the sea. Initially the Trans-Saharan trade compensated for the declining Mediterranean supply, and in the 1790s as many as six thousand African slaves were sold in Tunis every year. Over the following decades, however, taxation, along with competition from Tripoli's markets and wars in the south, ruined the trade. Then in 1846, Ahmed Bey, building his reputation as an enlightened ruler, abolished the slave trade and the markets were closed. The Africans have remained. In the past they suffered discrimination and were often reduced to the status of domestic servants, but today they are an integral part of Tunisian society.

to an end at the far west corner of the mosque. At no. 37, the **Mouradia Medersa** was built in 1673 by Mourad Bey, son of Hammouda Pacha, whose mosque is covered on p.83.

Unfortunately, the **Souk el Attarine**, which slopes down the north-western side of the mosque, no longer specializes in perfume, although you'll find plenty of perfume amongst the ubiquitous copper ashtrays, handbags and stuffed camels; in the sixteenth century it used to stay open until midnight in order to serve women, who took their hammams in the evening. On the left of this street as it descends, steps lead up to the **Midhat es Soltane**, a fifteenth-century bathing facility attached to the Great Mosque and renowned for its beauty. It's rarely accessible, so you're unlikely to see more than the facade of the main entrance at the top of the steps, with its dramatic use of black and white marble. Reminiscent of Cairo and Syria, this technique confirms Tunis's position as a meeting place for influences from both east and west Islam. Unlike Dar Othman in the south of the Medina, though, in whose courtyard Western tilework blends with Eastern marble, the Midhat's interior limits itself to stark marble in an Eastern style.

Turning back up Souk el Attarine, continue up the hill along **Souk et Trouk**, built in the seventeenth century for Turkish tailors but now populated mainly by tourist emporiums, past the Musée des Turcs carpet shop at no. 45, with its terrace view over the Medina. Twenty metres from the top, turn left into Souk Kebabjia. The open space a little way along here is the **Souk el Berka**, once the marketplace for Tunis's slave trade.

Around place du Gouvernement

Close to the Souk el Berka, the **Mosque of Youssef Dey** dates back to 1616 and was designed by the Spanish architect who added the portico to the Great Mosque. Blending local features with influences from the East, from Christian Italy and from Islamic Spain, the result is an accurate reflection of the many historical and social currents to which Tunisia's geography has always made it subject. Compared with the massive simplicity of the Great Mosque, it has a more airy, complex feel.

Most obvious here is the octagonal minaret on a square base, recalling Ottoman Turkish designs and signalling the arrival of the new Turkish rulers. The shape of the lantern, with its hanging balcony from which the muezzin (a mosque official) would originally have issued the call to prayer, is not only the first of its kind but immediately established a standard that was to appear again and again in Tunis. Next to the minaret, the **square mausoleum** also incorporates Spanish, Eastern and Italian influences, with a green-tiled pyramidal roof recalling the Alhambra in Granada; the elaborate patterns of black and white marble, Eastern in origin, had already appeared in Tunis in the Midhat es Soltane (see above) and the palace of Othman Dey (p.85). However, the form of the **prayer hall**, with eight rows of six columns, is more purely North African.

Continuing up past the mosque, you emerge from the Medina into **place du Gouvernement**, an open space on what was once the western edge of the Medina proper. Formerly a royal guest house, the **Dar el Bey** is now the prime minister's office, which means that government in Tunis has returned to its original site – since the Hafsids' thirteenth-century Kasbah stood just above here. You can see the excavations over the road, and above them the gleaming PSD Party building, while to the left is the Kasbah Mosque (see p.92). The western suburb walk (p.92) begins here, running up the hill and then around to the southern end of the Medina.

Also in the place du Gouvernement is the **Tourbet Laz**, the tomb of a seventeenth-century Bey and his relations, now occupied by a family who may let you look inside. These *tourbets* (tombs) were very fashionable among rich Turkish families of the time and Tunis has several – the **Tourbet of Ahmed Kouja Dey** is just across the street from here.

Heading back past Youssef Dey's mosque, the street on your left behind the Dar el Bey is the **Souk el Bey**, suitably grand with its broad, pillared arcade. The third and

---

CAFÉS IN THE MEDINA

Recent years have seen a surge in popularity for the Medina's gently mouldering cafés, both as daytime refuges in between sightseeing and shopping, and in the early evenings – and much later during Ramadan – when the *chicha* pipe-smoke becomes a fog. The best are reviewed below and marked on the map on p.78.

Café Chaouechin, Souk des Chéchias. Tunis's oldest café, which occupies the main crossroad of the covered hat-makers' souk. As well as serving excellent Turkish coffee in the morning and fresh black tea in the afternoon, there are impromptu nocturnal music sessions during Ramadan.

Café Chez Kamel, 18 rue Sidi Ben Arous, small, friendly and lacking in tourists with a cosy den upstairs and tables outside. The best *chicha* in town and fine fragrant tea.

Café Dar Mnouchi, the door at the corner of Souk el Leffa and Souk Kebabjia. Unpromising entrance takes you into a wonderfully calm tiled courtyard.

Café Dinar, place de la Victoire. At the Medina's main entrance this basic place has all the essentials with pleasant outdoor tables. It's always packed and cheaper than the *Medina Hotel*'s adjacent café.

Café Ez-Zitouna, rue Djemaa Ez-Zitouna, on the left 50m before the mosque, with Turkish decor and good *chichas*. Also, it gets packed when the football's on the telly.

Café de la Kasbah, place de la Kasbah. Facing the Kasbah Mosque, not the nicest view thanks to traffic, but breezy and with plenty of afternoon sun.

Café Khaldounia, Impasse Khaldounia off Souk el Attarine. Rather basic, but the tables outside give you an undisturbed view of the passers-by on Souk el Attaine.

Café M'rabet, Souk et Trouk, in the *driba* entrance hall of this old palace-turned-restaurant. The tea is sickly but the setting is superlative, with its simple but stately red and green pillars and mat-covered stone benches. During the 1930–50s this was the haunt of Tunisia's anti-colonial literary elite.

Café des Turks, Souk et Trouk. Good Turkish coffee, *chichas* and a pleasant tiled upstairs hideaway.

---

fourth doors on the right are entrances to the **Souk des Chéchias**, another eye-catching market, selling the characteristic Tunisian skullcaps made from wool by a complicated process of carding, moulding and dyeing. During the early eighteenth century this was one of Tunisia's most important industries, but in the mid-eighteenth century European factories flooded the market with cheap imitations and the Tunisian industry was ruined. By the 1920s the remaining manufacturers faced another recession as the wealthy turned to Western dress. Until recently it was a disappearing industry with few Tunisians under the age of 40 owning or wearing a *chéchia*, but recently it's been revived as young Tunisians discover their cultural past. In its centre, Tunis's oldest café, the *Chaouchin*, sells thick Turkish coffee and fine black tea (see box above).

Rue Sidi Ben Arous

Running along the east side of the Souk des Chéchias is **rue Sidi Ben Arous** an attractive little street with a *chéchia* seller, a poky little café (no. 18), a bookshop (Espace Diwan) and a strange apicultural shop (no. 38) selling all manner of bee products, including jars labelled "bee venom". To the south rises the Great Mosque's minaret. In the shadow, at the end of the souk at 23 rue Sidi Ben Arous, is the **Zaouia of Sidi Ben Arous**, a fourteenth-century native of Cap Bon who brought back Sufi teaching from Morocco (see p.84). Built in 1437, this particular *zaouia*, the meeting place of a religious fraternity, quickly became too popular with women for the authorities' liking and was closed – only to be promptly reopened in the face of an ensuing uproar. On the opposite side of the street is the late fifteenth-century Hafsid **Zaouia of Sidi Kelai**, with inscriptions and panels of leaning keystones above its entrance. By contrast, the shocking-pink facade of the nearby **Tourbet of Hammouda Pacha** clearly belongs to a later period. With the **mosque** of the same name, it forms a complex built in 1655 and clearly modelled after the 1616 mosque of Youssef Dey, with the same octagonal minaret and detached square mausoleum.

In the other direction, the northern continuation of Sidi Ben Arous on the other side of rue de la Kasbah is lined by the imposing doorways of what were once senior Turkish officials' houses, which are mostly inaccessible.

Heading east down **rue de la Kasbah**, the other main street running across the Medina, you come to a crossroads. To the left is **rue Saida Ajoula** running past the youth hostel and into the northern Medina. To the right, however, is the **rue Jellous**, a further right brings you to the Impasse ech Chammaia, which surprisingly contains two important monuments. At no. 4, the **Medersa ech Chammaia**, founded by the Hafsid Sultan Abu Zakariya in 1249, was the first *medersa* built in Tunis. For all its simplicity – a one-storey courtyard surrounded by students' cells, built in plain, undecorated limestone – it is a fine example of classic Hafsid style. Nearby, but entered via the Zaouia of Sidi Ben Arous, the **Tomb of Aziza Othmana** belongs to a princess renowned for her generosity. Just before her death in 1669, she liberated her slaves and left her estate to charitable causes – funds to liberate slaves and prisoners, and a fund for poor girls who couldn't otherwise afford to marry. She's buried next to her grandfather, Othman Dey (who built the Dar Othman in the south of the Medina), and the tomb itself was built by Husayn, founder of the Husaynid dynasty and Aziza Othmana's son-in-law. The world of the Tunisian ruling classes was a small one.

The foreign fondouks

Rue de la Kasbah continues downhill and out of the Medina. Just before emerging into place de la Victoire, a tiny alley on the left – rue de l'Ancienne Douane – leads to the site of the first **French Consulate and trading post** (marked by a plaque on the wall just before the Guersin baths). Along the same street are the former Italian, Austro-Hungarian and German embassy buildings, whose first-floor balconies still bear their national insignia, the only clue to their erstwhile importance. Originally known as *fondouks* (trading posts where foreign merchants were obliged to live), they're today all *ukelas*, houses divided up into rented accommodation for several families. This is one of the most run-down areas of the Medina although the ASM is busying itself with the renovation of such *ukelas*. At the end of the alley, rue Zarkoun is a kind of flea market and just beyond you'll find yourself in a street of brothels. The only consular building left is the **British Embassy** on the corner of place de la Victoire. When other nations were moving out to the suburbs the British obstinately stayed in the centre of town. The current embassy was built in the 1860s by Sir Richard Wood, an influential British consul in the days when Britain and France were still jockeying for position here. Wood was instrumental in obtaining for a British firm the concession for the TGM, the first rail company in Tunisia, which he then succeeded in routing through the garden of his residence in La Marsa.

It was Hammouda Pacha in 1659 who gave permission for the *fondouks* to be built. These were still dangerous times for foreigners in Tunis: in 1678 Francis Baker, the English consul, reported that one Sidi Mohammed Bey "did . . . forceably and violently seize on Charles Gratiano, Consul for the French, together with ourselves . . . swearing by the Soule of his deceased he would cutt us to pieces". Fortunately Mohammed Bey fled when his brother Ali Bey returned, and the consul lived to tell the tale.

From place de la Victoire, the **rue des Glacières** leads north. Here, in the eighteenth and nineteenth centuries, huge blocks of ice, shipped from the Alps, were stored to be sold at vast profit during the summer months. Today, the street's main attractions are the shops selling secondhand furniture and bric-a-brac, most of it left by the French in the mid-1950s – Art Deco statuettes and nineteenth-century portraits of long-forgotten soldiers. If you're tempted to buy something, bear in mind that the prices asked are astronomical.

Southern Medina

Next to the central section of the Medina, the **southern area** has the greatest concentration of monumental interest, with two highlights in Dar Othman and the Dar Ben Abdallah Museum. As with all the non-central walks, though, it is the combination of continuing local life – children at school, vegetable markets – with hundreds of years of historical legacy that makes it so worthwhile getting off the main routes. This itinerary takes you from place de la Victoire down to the southern end of the Medina and then back up to finish on its western edge, not far from the beginning of the western suburb walk (see p.92).

Climbing up rue Jemaa Zitouna from place de la Victoire, you come to **rue Sidi Ali Azouz** and, turning left, at no. 7 a nineteenth-century **zaouia** of the same name. Sidi Ali Azouz was born in Fez in Morocco in the seventeenth century and settled in Zaghouan after returning from a pilgrimage to Mecca. Like Sidi Mehrez, he is one of the patron saints of the city of Tunis. Just after the *zaouia* (next left, an unnamed impasse off rue Sidi Ali Azouz) is an opportunity to see a Medina palace unaffected by the riot of decoration that covers every surface of later residences. **Dar Bayram Turki**, named after a senior official of Youssef Dey who lived here at the beginning of the seventeenth century, would originally have been approached through a typical crooked *skifa* or passage. Nowadays a simple doorway leads into a plain courtyard built of undecorated limestone, where two shallow three-arch porticoes face each other, mirrored by blind arcades on the other two sides. Compared with later courtyards, the effect is almost monastic – though far from artless: note the spaced dark stones picking out the shape of each arch, and the characteristic loop motif above. Currently the ground floor is occupied by small **workshops**, including (on either side of the entrance) a ceramics outfit which was involved in restoring Dar Othman.

A little further on, rue Sidi Ali Azouz runs past the brooding bulk of the **Sidi Amir Barracks** – one of the five built by Hammouda Bey at the beginning of the nineteenth century (see p.79). Now virtually abandoned, it feels like a massive police station – which, of course, is what it was built as. Continuing, the street merges with a dark tunnel of the **Souk el Belat**, selling mainly food. To your right, on the corner of Souk el Belat and rue du Trésor, is the tenth-century **Ichbili Mosque** with its squat fourteenth-century minaret set well back. If you're interested in another lovely palace like Dar Bayram Turki, take a brief detour behind the Ichbili Mosque to **Dar el Hedri** at 12 rue du Trésor, easily identifiable by its Hafsid slanting arch-stones above the door and an open gallery running above the courtyard. Because it's now used as shared housing rather than workshops, this palace retains a more serene feeling. As in Dar Bayram Turki, the three-arched courtyard is in honey-coloured limestone, enlivened only by loop motifs (single and double). Instead of black arch-stones, a black design picks out the centre of the courtyard: a simple statement of the theme presented much more elaborately in the courtyard of the *zaouia* of Sidi Kassem Jelizi and on Dar Othman's facade.

Along rue Sidi Ali Azouz, the street forks just after a crossroads. Bear left and you're on **rue des Teinturiers** (Street of the Dyers). Ahead rises the minaret of the **Mosquée des Teinturiers**, also known as the New Mosque and centre of a sizable complex. The octagonal minaret recalls those of Youssef Dey and Hammouda Bey near the Great Mosque, though it was built a century later than Youssef Dey's, in 1716. The mosque was commissioned by Husayn Bin Ali, founder of the Husaynid dynasty, as his own memorial, and he lavished great expense on it, importing tiles for the prayer hall from Iznik in Turkey. In the *tourbet* attached to the mosque, Husayn buried two holy men, Sidi Kassem Sababti and Sidi Kassem el Beji, reserving the space between them for his own use. Things didn't quite work out, however, and Husayn was driven from power by his nephew Ali Pacha, who buried his own father in the position of honour. A *kouttab* and a *medersa* were added to the complex later, making it an impressive, if abortive, memorial. You can see the tombs through a window, if it's open, in rue Sidi Kassem.

Dar Othman and Dar Ben Abdallah

Almost opposite the mosque, down the passage-like rue el M'Bazaa, stands the superb doorway of **Dar Othman**, an attractive palace built by Othman Dey (ruled 1598–1610) to escape the intrigues and insecurities of life in the Kasbah – the gates closed off the street so that the palace could be defended if necessary. Its monumental facade consists of a welter of black and white marble patterns – an effect that was common further east in the Islamic world and may have been imported by the Turks. You may find it a little overdone here: in the *skifa* and the courtyard beyond, decoration continues unabated in the form of coloured tiles, offset by an attractive garden featuring three tall cypress trees in the corners and a lemon tree. If the garden feels out of place, that's because it's a twentieth-century addition. Dar Othman is officially covered by the Medina tour ticket, though it is still in use as offices.

From rue des Teinturiers, turn right into rue Sidi Kassem, then left through an arch onto Impasse Ben Abdallah, where you'll find the **Dar Ben Abdallah** (Tues–Sun 9.30am–4.30pm; 1.6TD, camera 1TD), one of the finest old palaces in the Medina. The palace was originally called Dar Kahia after its builder, one Slimane Kahia el Hanafi, who achieved prominence under the reign of Hammouda Bey (1781–1813) by marrying the daughter of the next ruler, Mahmoud Bey. Slimane was a senior government official and led the ruler's vital twice-yearly *mahalla* (tax-collecting expedition) to the tribes of the interior. With up to eight thousand participants, the summer *mahalla* marched to Béja and fanned out from there across the north; in winter, its base was Tozeur. When Slimane moved to live in the Bey's entourage at the Bardo, his Tunis residence was bought by the rich landowner and silk merchant whose name it carries now.

The palace has a classic design. A *driba* (entrance hall), lined with stone benches for waiting guests, opens onto a *skifa* leading into the house proper and distancing it from the outside world. The florid decoration of the door that leads from *driba* to *skifa* is once again typical of the Italianate styles that became increasingly popular from the eighteenth century – as, too, is much of the ornamentation in the courtyard (look out for the grotesque little dolphins hanging upside down on the fountain). T-shaped reception rooms open off the courtyard; the cupboard-like rooms at the angles were sometimes used as bedrooms.

The palace has been converted into the **Musée d'arts et de traditions populaires** (Museum of Popular Arts and Traditions), with each T-shaped room off the main courtyard devoted to an area of traditional upper-class urban life: childhood, marriage, the men's quarters. After the white stucco and light tiles of the airy courtyard, the rooms' heavily painted ceilings make for a strange contrast. Some of the rooms contain dummies dressed in traditional nineteenth-century costumes and engaged in traditional pastimes, like drinking coffee. All these displays show how even the simplest of everyday items are imbued with an elaborate sense of geometric design.

The Souks of the Dyers, the Tourbet el Bey and Bab Jedid

Returning to rue des Teinturiers, there's an old **hammam** on the left, which proclaims itself the "most elegant establishment of bathing baths in marble". Opposite nos. 92 and 104 open the **Souks of the Dyers**, after whom the street is named. At one time, as part of the clothing industry, dyeing was a vital part of Tunis's economy, but now it's just one more threatened traditional craft. The first of the souks has been taken over for making drums, and piles of clay bodies line the walls waiting for skins to be tanned before being stretched over them. The other souk is still used for a limited amount of (rather gaudy) dyeing.

Continue along rue des Teinturiers, turn right on rue Sidi el Benna, then right again on rue Sidi Zahmoul, past a huge palace with lazy palm trees to the **Tourbet el Bey**. As its name suggests, this royal mausoleum, built by Ali Bey II (1759–81), contains most of the Husaynid dynasty that followed him. Leaden, ornate and uninspired, it is one of the least successful examples of Tunisian Cosmopolitan building in the capital – perhaps because it suffers from too strong a European influence. Nearby, 44 rue Sidi Essourdou was once a **medersa** founded in the eighteenth century by Husayn Bin Ali, the first Husaynid Bey.

Turning right from the Tourbet el Bey onto the street named after it, a small detour can be made by taking a left down rue des Juges and then the third right up **rue des Forgerons** (since the thirteenth century the blacksmiths' souk), bringing you out of the Medina at **Bab Jedid**, a gate built in 1276 as part of the Hafsid city wall. Up some stairs next to it is a tiny mosque, the **Khalouet Sidi Mehrez**, where the Hafsid sultans used to pay homage to the city's patron saint. You could, if you wanted, leave the Medina through Bab Jedid and join the western suburb itinerary (see p.94).

Returning to rue Tourbet el Bey and continuing north along it, you'll pass at no. 41 the tiny **M'sid el Koubba Mosque** where the great historian Ibn Khaldoun used to teach. Born in 1332 at no. 33 of the same street, Ibn Khaldoun anticipated a dominant theme in modern political thought by suggesting that history repeats itself in cycles (see p.485).

A little further on rue Tourbet el Bey, just north of no. 20 and on the right as you emerge from underneath a **sabat** (a room located over the street), a decrepit stone archway leads into impasse du Jasmin. This was originally built in the seventeenth century as a weavers' workshop by the Spanish community, whose wealthy citizens lived on this street. Three and a half centuries later, a silk weaver is still making *sifsaris* in the workshop at no. 7.

Sidi Bou Khrissane and around

Backtracking slightly, turn right onto **rue du Riche**, then right into **rue des Andalous**, both streets having a scattering of magnificent doorways. This is where wealthier Andalusian immigrants settled while the less well-off had to petition for land in order to found towns like Testour (see p.267). At the end a left turn onto rue du Dey then another on rue Mohsen will bring you into a small square. On your left is the **Dar Hussein**, a palace built originally in the twelfth century and enlarged in the eighteenth. Once the town hall, then the French army headquarters during colonial rule, it's now used by the National Institute of Archeology, who will be pleased to let you have a look at the elaborate tiling and stuccowork inside – something well worth doing. Across the square is the **El Ksar Mosque**, founded around 1106 by the Emir Ahmed Ibn Khourassane. The minaret, an interesting blend of Ottoman and Andalusian styles, was added in 1647.

Ibn Khourassane's family, the Khourassanids, who ruled Tunis from 1059 to 1159, have their mausoleum just around the corner. Turn right out of the square into rue Sidi Bou Khrissane then left into rue Ben Mahmoud. On your left is the **Sidi Bou Khrissane Museum** (Mon–Sat 9am–noon & 2–5pm; donation of around 2TD expected). Part of a cemetery dating back to the ninth century, it is really more a garden full of old tombstones than a museum. The Khourassanid emirs are interred under a cupola at the back.

Rue Ben Mahmoud finally runs out into Souk Sekkajine. Buried in a red and green box in the middle of the street on your left is **Sidi Bou Abdallah**, who died on this spot while defending Tunis against the invading Spanish. A Spaniard, however, is buried only a few metres further on, originally under an olive tree but now in a gaudy shrunken *koubba* dating from 1987, at **Bab Menara**, where Souk Sekkajine emerges from the Medina. He is Anselm Tourmeda (aka Abdallah Tourjman), a fourteenth-century Majorcan who came to Tunisia, converted to Islam and wrote religious propaganda in Arabic and Catalan.

Northern Medina

The **northern Medina** is largely free of sightseers and the shops here are geared for local residents. There are fewer sights as such, though the Mosque of Sidi Mehrez is as familiar to Tunisians as the Zitouna Mosque, but this is a much better part of the Medina if you just want to wander. This walk leads up to the northern end of the Medina, where you could take a detour into Halfaouine (see p.89); otherwise, it returns back to place de la Victoire.

Turning off rue de la Kasbah onto rue Saida Ajoula, the first left is rue Onk el Jemal, where no. 5, the **Onkiya Medersa**, was founded by a Hafsid princess in 1341. Backtracking, duck left off rue Saida Ajoula into rue du Divan. At no. 3 on the right is the **Divan** itself, home of the Divan council, which at first played a major role in the power structure of the sixteenth- and seventeenth-century Turkish Regency of Tunis. As authority gradually passed into the hands of individual Beys, though, the council's function became more that of a religious court. Further on at no. 16 is the **Zaouia of Sidi Abdelkader**, built in 1851 by the Qadriya (or Kadria) *sufi* brotherhood as a gathering place for their adepts.

A right at the end of rue du Divan down rue de l'Agha will bring you to an area of **secondhand clothing stalls**. Prices are ridiculously low – you can get virtually brand-new clothes for next to nothing, as well as some superb 1970s *haute couture*. Nearby, at 9 rue des Nègres, is the **Mustansiriya medersa**, founded in 1435 by the Hafsid Sultan el Mustansir and in a state of extreme disrepair. The seventeenth-century **Zaouia of Sidi Braham**, around the corner in rue el Azafine, is famous for its collection of ceramic tiles.

Back at the junction with rue du Divan, follow rue de l'Agha up to the left into little place Ramdhane Bey and have a quick look up at the elaborate set of **Ottoman windows** through the arch ahead of you in rue Bir el Hajar, – a startling sight in the streets of blank exterior walls. Then head off to your right, down **rue du Pasha**, a tidy cobbled street that was the main thoroughfare of the Turkish residential quarter, with graceful doorways befitting the homes of important officials. No. 40, on the left, is the eighteenth-century **Medersa Bir Lahjar**, which hosts frequent concerts with the best-known being the month-long Festival de la Médiane (held during Ramadan). Opposite no. 64 in the same street, follow a passageway into **rue de la Noria**, which has to be the narrowest lane in the Medina. On the left as you bear left into rue du Tribunal is **Dar Lasram**, home of the Tunis Association de Sauvegarde de la Medina (ASM) and built for the Lasram family, an old Kairouan clan that claimed a direct line of descent back to the Arab conquest in the seventh century. This family palace dates originally from the mid-eighteenth century, a date reflected in the exuberant decoration to be seen inside. Next to the Dar Lasram is the **Club Culturel Tahar Haddad**, an active cultural venue for exhibitions, evening recitals and concerts. Opposite, at no. 27, is the nineteenth-century **mausoleum** of the landowning Dziri family, which is now the Maison de la Poésie and hosts mainly Arabic poetry readings.

Rue Sidi Mehrez and around

At the end of rue du Tribunal runs rue Sidi Ibrahim. Just to the left at no. 11 is the **Zaouia of Sidi Ibrahim Riahi**. Originally from Testour, al Riahi was a leading member of the Tijaniya *sufi* brotherhood at the beginning of the nineteenth century. Although successful as a teacher in Tunis, where religion offered greater social mobility than any other profession, he still needed a sponsor because he was not earning a decent living. Into the breach, so as to keep him in Tunisia, stepped Youssef Sahib et Tabaa, the prime minister under Hammouda Bey who later met a brutal end (see opposite).

Follow the street the other way and a dogleg to your left at the end brings you into rue el Monastiri. Around the corner in rue Achour is the seventeenth-century **Achouria Medersa**. Rue el Monastiri runs down into **rue Sidi Mehrez**, the last incarnation of one of the main north–south arteries of the Medina. A busy shopping street, to the left from rue el Monastiri, it houses the **Zaouia of Sidi Mehrez**, fronted by a long passage. At 9 rue el Monastiri is the entrance to Dar Monastir, a restored early nineteenth-century palace.

Sidi Mehrez is still revered as a patron saint of Tunis for his efforts in the tenth century. After the city's sufferings during the revolt of Abu Yazid, it was he who oversaw its revival. The original tomb has shared many of Tunis's ups and downs, and the present building is mainly eighteenth- and nineteenth-century. Traditionally, boys come to drink from its well before their circumcision ceremony.

Opposite the *zaouia*, though not visible from the street, is the **Mosque of Sidi Mehrez**, one of Tunis's most distinctive landmarks. (You can get a good view from the north side of place Bab Souika from rue el Halfaouine and from the southern end of rue Dr Cassar.) A little beyond the *zaouia* on the right, you can climb some steps into a new arcade for the best look at its heap of white domes. Dotted with pigeons, they stand out for kilometres in any rooftop view of the Medina and are the city's only example of the Imperial Ottoman building style. Presumably Mohammed Bey, who founded it in 1696, wanted to stamp a truly Turkish presence on the city, but after his early death, the assassination of his brother and the rise of the Husaynids, the mosque was left unfinished. Instead of the four circular minarets that would have conferred a fully

---

THE HAFSIA AND THE JEWS

Recently reconstructed, and winning an Agha Khan award for Islamic architecture, the Hafsia, Tunis's erstwhile Jewish ghetto, occupies the northernmost corner of the Medina, between rue Achour and rue Bab Souika. At one time the enclave was separated from the rest of the town by a wall and its gates were closed at night. Before the status of Jews was regularized in 1861 there were many other petty restrictions: Jews had to wear black clothes of a traditional style, as European dress was forbidden; they were not allowed to ride horses or own land outside the Hafsia. Jews had their own civil courts, but in their dealings with Muslims were subject to Islamic law, and faced burning at the stake if found guilty of a capital offence. Although protected as a "people of the book" (those who share with Islam a reverence for the Old Testament), many Muslims regarded them as heathen and treated them as such. Occasionally riots broke out and the Hafsia was wrecked by Muslim mobs, but for most of the time the Jews lived in peace, however restricted.

It was the immigration of Maltese and Italian Jews, citizens of powerful European states, that allowed the Jews to escape these repressive laws. By the 1870s their wealth and connections with European governments had given them considerable power and new freedom. Then, under the Protectorate, they joined the middle class and many left the Medina for the suburbs. Nevertheless, when the Germans arrived in 1942 the Hafsia was still very crowded. Fortunately, though they imposed punitive measures, the Nazis did not pursue a policy of mass extermination against Jews in North Africa. After the war many emigrated to Israel and the ghetto was finally pulled down in 1953. The remainder of the Jewish community dispersed into the suburbs.

Ottoman look, it got a small, square North African one; it's even named after the *zaouia* opposite rather than its own founder. The **pottery shops** at nos. 96 and 97 warrant a quick look. Although they don't sell the fancier souvenir products, they do have a wide range of plates, cups, pots and ashtrays, all at very low prices.

Rue Sidi Mehrez emerges from the Medina into **place Bab Souika**, once a place of public execution, and the area of the liveliest cafés during Ramadan nights. Unfortunately, controversial redevelopment, which also included the Hafsia project (see box p.88), has destroyed much of its character.

A right turn out of rue Sidi Mehrez along the eastern edge of the Medina and down rue Bab Souika takes you past the Anglican **Church of St George** on the corner of rue Ahmed Beyrem (formerly rue des Protestants). Look out for the plaque commemorating John Howard Payne, a nineteenth-century US consul better known as the author of the song *Home Sweet Home* whose body had a brief sojourn in the cemetery until 1883 when a US navy frigate arrived and took him home.

The faubourgs

As well as an inner wall around the Medina, the Hafsids built an outer rampart to enclose the city's residential suburbs, or **faubourgs**, which have managed to retain a strong sense of local character and community. They are often referred to by the names of former Medina gates, thus **Halfaouine** is in the Rbat Bab Souika and **Montfleury** in the Rbat Bab Jazira. As in the Medina, the streets of the faubourgs are often deserted and ill-lit at night, and not particularly safe to wander round after hours.

Halfaouine

Halfaouine is one of Tunis's most fascinating areas, with a style completely its own. Originally a settlement outside the walls of the Medina, it was endowed with its own well and fortifications under the Hafsids. Recently, the suburb achieved a certain fame through Férid Boughedir's film of the same name, which ran away with most of the prizes at the 1990 Carthage Festival and still draws the crowds in even today.

On the north side of place Bab Souika, a vaulted entrance leads into the **food markets** of rue Halfaouine. On the right beyond place Bab Souika is the **Abu Mohamed Mosque**, a fine example of architecture from the Hafsid era, erected by public subscription. Associated with this mosque is a tradition of religious meetings during Ramadan to discuss the subject of the *hadiths* – sayings of Mohammed.

Rue Halfaouine eventually gives onto **place Halfaouine**. Having begun life as one of the commodity markets common on the edges of the old city, this square had become the heart of an exclusive district by the eighteenth century, thanks largely to the efforts of Youssef Sahib et Tabaa, Hammouda Bey's last prime minister. Youssef rose from Hammouda's *mameluke* (slave intended for high office) at the beginning of his reign to the post of Sahib et Tabaa, the second most powerful man in the country. He owned ships in his own name and became wealthy through piracy and international trade, using some of his fortune to commission the mosque here as well as the neighbouring Souk el Jedid, site of his personal palace. Unfortunately, Youssef's forthright personality made him vulnerable after Hammouda's death, and in January 1815, only thirteen months after his master's death, Youssef was assassinated after a rival Tunisian-born official called Larbi Zarrouk convinced Hammouda's successor, Mahmoud Bey, that Youssef was a threat.

With its trees and benches, place Halfaouine retains an air of decaying quasi-European elegance, belying the fact that this quiet backwater was once notorious for nationalist demonstrations against the French. Facing the square, the **Youssef Sahib**

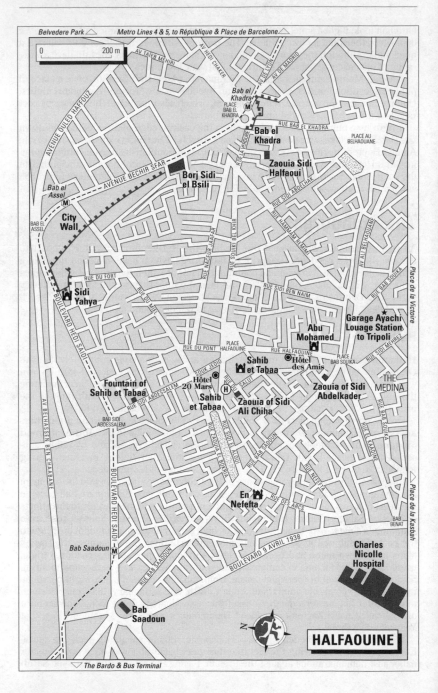

Belvedere Park △   Metro Lines 4 & 5, to République & Place de Barcelone △

0   200 m

AV TAIEB MEHIRI

AV HEDI CHAKER

AV DE LYON

AV DE MADRID

AVENUE OULED HAFFOUZ

Bab el
Khadra
PLACE
BAB EL
KHADRA

**Bab el
Khadra**

**Zaouia Sidi
Halfaoui**

PLACE AU
BELHAOUANE

RUE BAB EL KHADRA

RUE EL FOUR?

AVENUE BECHIR SFAR

**Borj Sidi
el Bsili**

RUE SIDI ABDELHAK

Bab el
Assel

RUE HAMMAM REMIMI

AV ALI BELHAOUANE

**City
Wall**

BAB EL
ASSEL

RUE NACEUR JAAFAR

RUE SOUK BEL KHIR

AV BAB SOUIKA

Place de la Victoire ▷

RUE SIDI BEN NAIM

RUE DU FORT

**Sidi
Yahya**

RUE DU MIR

RUE DU PONT

PLACE
HALFAOUINE

**Abu
Mohamed**

**Garage Ayachi
Louage Station
to Tripoli**

RUE SIDI MIHREZ

RUE HALFAOUINE

PLACE
BAB SOUIKA

**THE
MEDINA**

BOULEVARD HEDI SAIDI

SOUK JEDID

**Fountain of
Sahib et Tabaa**

**Hôtel
20 Mars**

**Sahib
et Tabaa**

**Hôtel
des Amis**

RUE SIDI ABDESSALEM

BAB SIDI
ABDESSALEM

**Sahib
et Tabaa**

RUE DU SALUT

**Zaouia of Sidi
Ali Chiha**

**Zaouia of Sidi
Abdelkader**

RUE EL KAMINE

AV BELHASSEN BEN CHAABANE

RUE SIDI EL ALOUI

RUE ZAOUIA EL BORRIA

RUE BAB SAADOUN

**En
Nefefta**

RUE DES ARCS

RUE NEFETTA

BAB
BENAT

BOULEVARD HEDI SAIDI

Bab Saadoun

BOULEVARD 9 AVRIL 1938

**Charles
Nicolle
Hospital**

RUE BAB SAADOUN

**Bab
Saadoun**

N

HALFAOUINE

▽ *The Bardo & Bus Terminal*

et Tabaa Mosque, begun in 1812, is one of the most beautiful and unusual in Tunisia, closer to a Venetian palazzo than the Great Mosque of Kairouan; perhaps the finest example of Tunisian Cosmopolitan building. The blend of local and Italian elements is at its most successful here, with metal railings, Neoclassical columns and flamboyant black marble – all of them foreign – made to seem perfectly in place. The minaret was only half finished when Youssef met his premature end – which perhaps contributed to a story that the same would happen to the person who completed the minaret. It was finally completed in 1970.

Behind the mosque, at 9 rue du Salut, is the crumbling **Zaouia of Sidi Ali Chiha**, off rue Sidi el Aloui, which leads into an elongated square full of palm trees. Beside the *zaouia* is one of Tunisia's most atmospheric hammams, the **Hammam Sahib** (men in the mornings and evenings; women in the afternoon), a spectacular place full of pillars and horseshoe arches where much of Boughedir's film was shot. Cross rue Bab Saadoun at the other end of the square and in front of you is the **En Nefefta Mosque** on the corner of rue des Arcs and impasse de la Mosquée. The building you see is modern, but the mosque was founded in the fifteenth century and parts of the interior structure date back to that period.

In the northwest corner of place Halfaouine is the **Souk Jedid**, a vaulted passage leading out onto rue Zaouia el Bokria to your left and rue de Miel on your right. The souk, commissioned by Sahib et Tabaa, now specializes in clothes. As you emerge, keep straight ahead along **rue Sidi Abdessalem**. A small room known as a **sabat** crosses the street here at first-floor level; it houses a *kouttab* (Koranic school) attached to the *masjid* (small mosque). This complex of buildings is characteristic of old medina quarters – the local elementary or primary school attached to the parish church, as it were. Right at the end of rue Sidi Abdessalem on a sliver of open space stands the bulbous-domed **fountain of Sahib et Tabaa**, another of his municipal works in this quarter. The fountain was originally located just inside one of the Hafsid city gates, Bab Sidi Abdessalem, so that travellers arriving from the country could refresh themselves, and nowadays it's usually surrounded by a flea market.

Boulevard Hedi Saidi to Bab el Khadra

Beyond the fountain of Sahib et Tabaa runs **boulevard Hedi Saidi**, where you can pick up a bus or the métro (line #4) going west to the Bardo Museum (see p.94). A few hundred metres to the left, **Bab Saadoun**, once one of the city's outer gates but now a traffic island at a major road junction, looks rather lost. Beyond it is the bus station serving the north of the country. South of Bab Saadoun is Rabta Hill, site of two Ottoman forts, **Borj Flifel** and **Borj er Rabta**, both built in the mid-eighteenth century. Nearby, yet another fort, **Borj Zouara** (or Borj el Andalous), dates back to the seventeenth century.

Heading east from Bab Sidi Abdessalem, boulevard Hedi Saidi takes you to **Bab el Assel**, yet another of the city's gates. As you approach it, you'll see the **Sidi Yahya Mosque** on your right. Built as a *masjid* in the fourteenth century by the saint whose name it bears, it was elevated to the status of *jemaa* (Friday mosque) by the Hafsids because of its strategic position. Turn right just before the mosque and have a look round behind it, and you will see the entrance to the old **Bab el Assel fort** at 25 rue du Fort, now a private house. A plaque above the doorway dates it at 1216 AH (1801 AD).

Here, too, begins a huge chunk of the **old wall**, currently undergoing restoration. It starts just past the Sidi Yahya Mosque, and then runs by the Bab el Assel sports centre, where you get a good view of it through the perimeter railings. Follow the pavement round into avenue Bechir Sfar and take the first right into rue du Miel. The entrance to the sports centre is on your right if you want a closer look; otherwise take a left down the little street full of carpenters' workshops. You'll be walking parallel with the wall, still there behind the school buildings on your left. The street emerges at another of the old forts, **Borj Sidi el Bsili**, again dating back to the turn of the nineteenth century. The Ministry of Culture has plans to restore it and open it to the public.

A left and a right turn here down avenue Bechir Sfar brings you, after 100m or so, to perhaps the city's oddest gate, **Bab el Khadra**. This double-doorwayed piece of a fairytale castle is not the fourteenth-century original, but a rebuilt version dating back to 1881.

Behind the right-hand doorway is **rue de la Verdure**, a name referring, like that of the gate, to the "greenery" of the countryside which used to start outside it. Halfway along rue de la Verdure, the impasse de Sidi el Halfaoui (on the left) leads to the **Zaouia of Sidi el Halfaoui**, containing the tomb of the seventeenth-century saint after whom the Halfaouine district is named. Non-Muslims can't enter, but you can glimpse the saint's tomb through a grille by the door.

Rue de la Verdure runs onto a square from where rue Hammam Remimi and a right at the end along avenue Ali Belhouane will take you straight back to Bab Souika. Much better, however, is a stroll down **rue Souiki Bel Khir**, straight ahead, which runs past various interesting cul-de-sacs and under the odd *sabat* (room crossing the street at first-floor level) to end up back in place Halfaouine.

Western districts

As with Halfaouine in the north, the Medina's western and southern fringes are occupied by ancient districts dating back to Hafsid times. Directly west, the **Kasbah district** was the former seat of government, while **Montfleury**, also known as **Rbat Bab Jazira**, further south, was a residential quarter.

Place de la Kasbah, on the western edge of the Medina, is always crowded with civil servants from the various government departments located hereabouts (this makes it a good place to catch a taxi). Sweeping north around the Medina, **boulevard Bab Menara** passes **Sadiki College** with its two domes, founded by Khereddine in 1875 and inevitably described as Tunisia's Eton, where Bourguiba and other future leaders were educated. Right below it, next to the street, is the **tomb of Farhat Hached**, the trade union leader murdered by reactionary French colonialists in 1952 (see p.439).

Place de la Kasbah gets its name from the fort that stood here above the Medina in Hafsid times, which has almost completely disappeared except for the **Kasbah Mosque** and parts of the wall to the south along rue el Zouaoui which are presently being guarded by air-force troops who occupy most of the site. More than seven hundred and fifty years after it was built, though, the mosque still sets a standard for Tunisia. Arriving as part of an Almohad empire based in Marrakesh, the Hafsids wanted to make a clear statement of their origins, and this mosque's minaret – square, with decorated lozenge designs in relief – is immediately identifiable as part of the same family as the Kutubiyya in Marrakesh, the Hassan in Rabat and the Giralda in Seville. When a new Malekite minaret was needed for the Great Mosque in 1834, this was the model that the architects used. Notice that the lozenge design is more subtle than it at first looks, with a different design on the north and south faces from the one on the east and west. Perhaps because of its elevated position, the mosque signals to the rest of the city for the call to prayer: five times a day a white flag is hung out from the scaffold protruding from the minaret.

The rest of the Hafsid kasbah stood on the other side of rue 2 Mars from the mosque, where a stark modern monument and plaza recently replaced the last excavations. Its last occupant was a French barracks installed in 1881 and levelled in 1957, but the Hafsid kasbah really lost its importance after the Turks moved the seat of government

into Dar el Bey in the early seventeenth century. Unfortunately, the historical significance of the site has made it a favourite place for architects trying to express the more
grandiose aspirations of the newly independent state: the current RCD headquarters
building on top of the hill was recognized as a mistake as soon as it was erected in 1974
although it has thankfully been totally obscured by the brand-new seat of local government, a weird mix of pink stone, concrete and blue bulletproof glass. Incidentally, the
RCD headquarters are set to move to a lakeside site by the *Hôtel du Lac*. The best thing
to do is move quickly up rue 2 Mars, passing ministries on the left.

At the top of the hill, you pass a surviving stretch of kasbah **wall** and an old city gate,
Bab Sidi Abdallah, before hitting boulevard 9 Avril 1938; bear left here for a couple
of hundred metres until a tree-lined square opens up to your left, with the green pyramidal roof of the Zaouia of Sidi Kassem Jelizi at the near corner (see below). Fume-rid-
den city artery though it may be, boulevard 9 Avril 1938 runs along the top of a ridge
here and offers a fine view down over Sebkhet Sejoumi, round to the Jellaz Cemetery
and beyond to Lake Tunis. From this viewpoint, it's easy to understand the city's
appalling climate – as the eighteenth-century traveller James Bruce put it, "low, hot and
damp".

The Zaouia of Sidi Kassem Jelizi and around

Fortunately, the **Zaouia of Sidi Kassem Jelizi** (daily 8am–4pm; free) is more than
adequate compensation for coming this far: the most accessible piece of late Hafsid
architecture in the city, with a strong flavour of Spain and some Eastern influence as
well. Abou el Fadl Kassem Ahmed as-Sadafi al-Fasi came originally from Fez, but he is
thought to have learned the trade that earned him the title Jalizi (Potter) in Spain.
When his mausoleum was built, in 1490, it would have enjoyed a prominent position
crowning this ridge at the edge of the Hafsid city. It begins with an entrance hall leading past a small prayer hall on the right into a courtyard. Rooms on three sides,
designed originally for pilgrims and visitors but now displaying pottery exhibits, give
way on the fourth to the tomb itself, whose pyramidal green-tiled roof – reminiscent of
Granada and built at the time of Granada's fall to the Christians – gives the building its
Spanish feel. Looking to the other end of the Islamic world, the courtyard paving's bold
geometric patterns in black marble – found elsewhere in Tunis in the Midhat es Soltane
and in palaces of a slightly later date – are more reminiscent of Cairo. No one is sure
whether the patterns here and in the Midhat are original or whether they were added
later under the Turks. Inside the tomb, however, the tone is all Spanish. In particular,
don't miss the star-patterned tiles in the flat niche opposite the tomb-room entrance.
Outside the mausoleum proper, a small yard shelters a large collection of headstones,
the Hafsid ones having plain columns and the later Turkish examples crowned with a
turban. Opposite the *zaouia*, across the place du Résidence du Leader, where
Bourguiba once lived, stands the strangely squat minaret of the **Jemaa el Haoua**,
founded in the thirteenth century by Queen Atif, wife of the Hafsid Sultan Abu
Zakariya.

Make your way to the bottom right-hand corner of place du Résidence and out along
rue Abd el Wahab. This shortly comes to a junction with rue Gorjani and rue Boukris.
Across from here and slightly to the right, **place aux Chevaux**, with its miniature football pitch, leads on to become **place du Marché du Blé**, the start of a great junk market, where you can pick up anything from old shoe buckles to metal utensils. In the
past, these two areas were the markets where city merchants would deal with farmers
bringing in grain and animals from the countryside. Turn sharp left here into rue Et
Tohma, following the junk, and head downhill. At the bottom of the hill, Saida
Manoubia emerges into the broad **Souk des Armes**, formerly the weapons market,
under the squat minaret of the **Mosque of El Helaak**, traditionally held to have been
founded in 1375 by a freed black slave who sold his gold jewellery to pay for it. Down

to your right, **Souk el Asser** is a babble of eateries and food stalls. A left here will take you to **Bab Jedid**, the Medina gate visible down the hill, where you could hook up with the southern Medina tour (see p.86).

To continue, go straight ahead into the pillared tunnel of rue Hajjamine (forking right after emerging from the tunnel to stay on Hajjamine). When Hajjamine hits rue Abou Kassem el Chabbi, cross the road and continue past a green-domed tomb, down into a small open space surrounded by tombs of eighteenth- and nineteenth-century worthies. Take the lower, left-hand fork out of here and continue on Hajjamine to where rue En Naial comes in on the right – immediately opposite on the left, rue Sidi Mansour heads off downhill, passing a *masjid* with a weedy green-tiled roof at rue Er Raia, and eventually hitting **rue Bab el Fellah** – recognizable as a main drag of the old quarter stuffed with food stalls.

Left on Bab el Fellah will take you back up to **Bab Jazira**, the southern gate out of the Medina, which is dominated by the minaret of the **Mosque of Sidi el Bechir**. A right on Bab el Fellah will take you further south to Bab Aleoua bus station and the **Jellaz Cemetery**, a huge and very pleasant hillside burial ground founded in the thirteenth century. According to legend, the founder was a saint whose servant bought the land from a Jew so that poor Muslims could be buried there. In 1911 it was the scene of the first mass demonstration against the French, when the municipal council threatened to requisition the land for development. A shot was fired – some said by an Italian spectator, others by a French officer – killing a young boy. In the riot that ensued, nine Frenchmen, five Italians and over thirty Tunisians died.

The cemetery is dominated by the seventeenth-century **Borj Ali Rais**, an Ottoman fortress visible from the whole city but, unfortunately, closed to the public. It's also known as Borj Sidi Bel Hassen after the nearby **Zaouia of Sidi Bel Hassen**, which was built in 1815 but dedicated to a thirteenth-century marabout said to have introduced coffee to Tunisia.

The Bardo Museum ﻣﺘﺤﻒ اﻟﺒﺎردو

Housed in the former Beylical Palace (the royal palace of the Bey, or Regent) west of the city centre, the **Bardo Museum** (Tues–Sun: April–Sept 9am–5pm, Oct–March 9.30am–4.30pm; 4.2TD, camera 1TD) is one of those museums that is almost too well endowed. Its encyclopedic collection of Roman mosaics is really too much to take in on a single visit, but even a glimpse of some of the designs will flesh out the Roman sites in the country, and a second visit afterwards will complete the picture. The building itself is spectacular, built up over centuries and surrounded by gardens full of Roman and Punic stones; as you wander around the collections, note the ceilings especially.

The easiest way to get here is on the métro. Line #4 runs to the museum's own station, Bardo métro. It's a thirty-minute journey from the city centre by bus #3 from avenue Bourguiba, bus #3c, #4, #4c, #4d, #23, #23b, #23c or #23t from Jardin Thameur, or several others from Bab Saadoun.

Confusingly, rooms in the Bardo are sometimes numbered and other times named after the particular sites most of the exhibits come from (and sometimes both). The ground-floor and second-floor rooms are numbered but the first-floor rooms are generally known by their name. There is also a tendency to juggle the exhibits about, particularly the Islamic, folk-art and traditions exhibits, many of which are being moved to the Museum of Islamic Art at Reqqada, near Kairouan (see p.227). In summer you might think about starting at the top of the building, so that you don't get up there just as it receives the full attention of the midday sun. English-language guidebooks (8TD) are on sale at the **bookshop** at the museum exit.

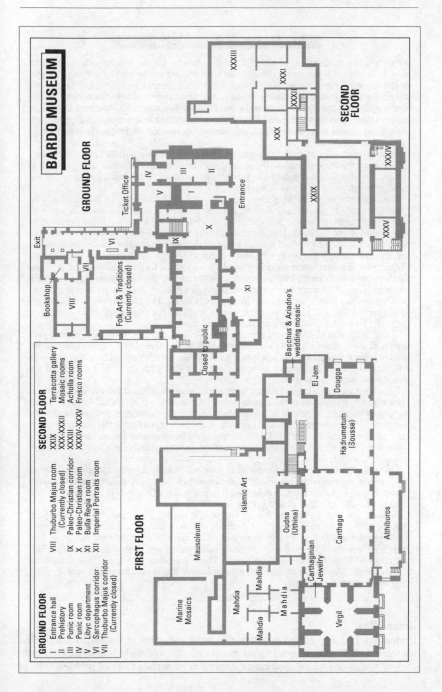

BARDO MUSEUM

GROUND FLOOR

Exit

Ticket Office

Bookshop

VII

VIII

Folk Art & Traditions
(Currently closed)

IV

V   III

X   II

IX   I

Entrance

VI

XI

Closed to public

Bacchus & Ariadne's
wedding mosaic

SECOND FLOOR

XXXIII

XXXII

XXXI

XXX

XXIX

XXXIV

XXXV

FIRST FLOOR

Marine
Mosaics

Mahdia

Mahdia

Mahdia

Mahdia

Mausoleum

Islamic Art

Oudna
(Uthina)

Carthaginian
Jewelry

Virgil

Carthage

Althiburos

Hadrumetum
(Sousse)

El Jem

Dougga

GROUND FLOOR
I   Entrance hall
II   Prehistory
III   Punic room
IV   Punic room
V   Libyc department
VI   Sarcophagus corridor
VII   Thuburbo Majus corridor
         (Currently closed)
VIII   Thuburbo Majus room
         (Currently closed)
IX   Paleo-Christian corridor
X   Paleo-Christian room
XI   Bulla Regia room
XII   Imperial Portraits room

SECOND FLOOR
XXIX   Terracotta gallery
XXX–XXXII   Mosaic rooms
XXXIII   Acholla room
XXXIV–XXXV Fresco rooms

ROMAN AND ISLAMIC ART

Africa's **Roman mosaics**, of which the Bardo has by far the largest collection in the world, are arguably the most colourful and vivid images left behind by a Roman Empire better known for its monumental engineering feats. Like an album of colour snapshots, they offer a direct and beautiful visual record of what was considered important by this extraordinarily powerful civilization. Native Romans at home in Italy painted their walls so colourfully that they preferred floor mosaics to be black and white. In Africa, though, wall painting was never widespread, and mosaics developed as almost the only form of domestic decoration.

Seeing the mosaics in such exuberant quantity makes it easy to take them for granted. These were the Persian rugs of the ancient world, requiring enormous time and skill to lay out, and the fact that most were privately commissioned for homes reflects the status-conscious social structure of the time.

The **subjects** were probably also chosen by the commissioner, so the emphasis on (broadly speaking) entertainment is significant. Hunting, fishing, the amphitheatre and, to a lesser extent, theatrical themes are all indicative of the leisure activities enjoyed by the wealthy. Even the mythological and religious scenes have a strongly hedonistic slant: **Bacchus**, the god of wine and sensual pleasure in general, features heavily, often shown triumphant over the forces of evil. **Venus**, goddess of love, usually has her vampish side strongly emphasized. Most noticeable of all, though, is the feeling of abundance. The **sea** is always shown crammed with endless varieties of fish (including the lobsters which wave in the god Ocean's hair), rural **farming scenes** are a constant, and lush vines weave their way through and around almost every scene. The mosaics evoke a life of sensual gratification and plenty, neatly summed up in an inscription found at Timgad in Algeria: "To hunt, to bathe, to gamble, to laugh, that is to live."

Towards the end of the Roman era, and into the Byzantine, the increasingly tense stylization of the mosaics reflects a less carefree society, permeated by a stricter spiritual discipline intended to preserve it in a hostile world. Although there's nothing here to match the early Byzantine mosaics of Ravenna, the tauter styles can come as a relief after the more florid imperial mosaics.

Because it had to be imported at great expense, **marble statuary** was less common in Africa than in other parts of the Roman world. Carthage, though, was richly stocked with figures of all types, primarily important men and women: generals, senators, sponsors, emperors and other worthies. The museum has a fine, though typically damaged selection: it's worth pointing out that the systematic **de-nosing and emasculation** of male statues was the routine work of invading Vandals, mutilating and castrating their enemies in stone as well as flesh.

There is also a stunning collection of bronze and marble figures and domestic furniture, recovered from the so-called **"Mahdia wreck"**. In 1907 fishermen off Mahdia found this ancient shipwreck, dating from the first century BC. Its cargo gives an impression of the style in which contemporary Romans lived.

Islamic art, which shuns the human image, is at the other extreme. For the most part, Islamic artists have concentrated on decorative pattern and colour, a combination most brilliantly exemplified in a room of ceramic **tiles** taken from inside old mosques. The best are those brought by the Turks from Iznik, with their vegetal designs and bright colours still fresh after hundreds of years. There are other tiles from Tunisia itself, in characteristic blues, greens and yellows, and from Morocco, distinguishable by their tighter geometric patterns.

Ground floor

Prehistory (II) The gallery begins with a small collection of Capsian Neolithic flint blades, mostly from southern Tunisia (see p.298). The highlight is an apparently ordinary pile of stones which upon closer inspection comprises chipped pebbles, balls of flint and bones: this monument found at El Guettar near Gafsa, is considered by some to be the oldest human-made structure in the world.

Punic rooms (III–IV) Clay **statues** reflect the influence of Greece on Mediterranean culture but retain an Eastern flavour – those from the eighth century BC look like stiff Egyptian figures; by the third century BC you find a seated **Demeter** with drapery used in Greek style to allow the figure to break into three dimensions; but as late as the first century AD, a **Tanit** from Thinissut (just above Hammamet) still has a lion's head and the two-dimensional pose of an Egyptian or early Greek figure. Grotesquely **grimacing masks** from the seventh century BC, used to frighten evil spirits away, are distinctively local.

Libyc department (V) The Libyc or Numidian civilization, which followed the Punic, was one of the rare periods of Tunisian "independence", and the exhibits here – notably two **bas-reliefs** of Numidian gods and **bilingual stelae** in Libyc and Punic, and Libyc and Latin, are mere glimpses of what archeologists now realize was a far more advanced culture than had previously been thought. Excavations at the marble quarry of Chimtou (see pp.186–187), long thought to be entirely Roman, have revealed the existence of a formidable Numidian industry there.

Sarcophagus and stele corridor (VI) In the long corridor between the Paleo-Christian Room and the gift shop leading out to the garden, look for an unusual and engaging **third-century AD statue** found at Borj el Amri (Inv 3047) of a hooded man with a face like a gloomy Fred Flintstone, depicted in the realistic style common at the time; otherwise he is little more than a tailor's dummy festooned with symbols: his lion-skin hood and the club he originally held in his left hand are attributes of Hercules; the drape of his tunic suggests female breasts; and in his right hand he holds a bouquet of poppies and wheat, symbols of the Greek cult of Demeter; the dog at his feet is probably the hellhound Cerberus, captured by Hercules as one of his labours.

Paleo-Christian corridor and room (IX–X) A fifth-century **mosaic** from Tabarka on the wall (A307) shows in cartoon fashion a three-aisled basilica or church similar to many found in Tunisia's ancient cities. Similarly, the sixth-century four-way **baptistry** in the middle of the room (from as far away as El Kantara, in Jerba) was to reappear many times – including at George Sebastian's 1920s villa in Hammamet.

Bulla Regia room (XI) The prize of this collection of monumental marble statuary is a rock star-like Apollo with his lyre, who originally stood in his own temple at Bulla Regia.

Imperial Portraits room (XII) The next room contains some fine portrait heads of Roman emperors, including one ultra-realistic one (Inv 3212) of **Gordian I**, the ill-fated elderly tax collector from El Jem who ruled the Empire for a month before committing suicide.

First floor

Islamic Rooms Now re-opened, although some pieces are on their way to Reqqada. Several tiled rooms featuring displays of traditional female dress and jewellery, predominantly from Jerba, as well as perfume receptacles, ceramics and a coin collection.

Althiburos room Five named bullfighting stars carouse in Inv 3361 at a table that looks like an amphitheatre. Each of the drinkers wears a token identifying him with one of the professional gladiators' guilds. A worried-looking servant runs towards them, finger to his lips, saying "Silentium, tauri dormiant!" – "Quiet, let the bulls sleep!" Sure enough, one of the bullfighters' intended victims is struggling to its feet. After the relaxed sophistication of third-century El Jem, Inv 3618 from Béja, dated to the fifth or sixth century, looks like a child's cartoon.

Carthage room Set in the floor at the far end of this lavish central hall is the first of a series of documentary-like **mosaics** of rural life in Roman Tunisia (A105), dating from early third-century Oudna. Among the numerous pieces of statuary, keep an eye out for a stately full-length **portrait of a robed woman** leaning with one hand on an incense burner. Her pose and drapery are direct descendants from Greek originals of the fourth century BC. Five hundred years later, this fine statue was probably made in Rome to commemorate a woman who lived far away in Haidra, where it was found.

Dougga room The **Cyclopes Baths** in Dougga were named after A261, one of the most vivid mosaics in the museum. Three muscular cyclopes (mythical figures who usually have one eye) wield hammers as they forge thunderbolts for Jupiter. The composition is very sophisticated, with one of the group shown from behind. Originally the floor of a *frigidarium*, perhaps this mosaic's scene was designed to warm up its chilled viewers. A382, also from Dougga, shows how bathers recovered, with two servants pouring wine from amphorae on which are inscribed the message "Drink and you will live."

El Jem room A288 shows third-century hunting scenes to delight the heart of any blood-sport enthusiast.

Hadrumetum (Sousse) room Three semicircular scenes from the same room in fourth-century Tabarka show the components of a large agricultural estate: the owner's house (A25); the farm building (A26); and barns and storerooms (A27). From Carthage in the following century, the famous **Seigneur Julius mosaic** (Inv 1) shows Julius himself sitting at his leisure at bottom right, opposite his wife, who leans against a pillar (in a similar Greek fourth-century BC pose to that of the Haidra statue in the Carthage room). Above them in the middle panel stands their house – the domed roofs suggest a baths complex – surrounded by preparations for a hunt. Agricultural scenes in the top panel include olives being harvested from a tree in the top left corner. Finally, an endearingly crude mosaic from **Byzantine Gafsa** (A19) suggests that the Romans' staple leisure pursuits – like chariot racing – survived the Vandal occupation and continued into the sixth century.

Ship rooms This spectacular collection of **Greek bronze statuary** went down in a shipwreck off Mahdia at the end of the first century AD and lay on the seabed until discovered in 1907. Greek art was highly prized in the Roman world and travelled widely around the Mediterranean – excavations in the Roman city of Volubilis in modern Morocco unearthed a good deal of it.

Marine mosaic room Inv 2884 shows a mosaic of **Ulysses** bound to the mast of his ship and heroically resisting the calls of three sirens. Nearby, Inv 2884A from Dougga has another nautical scene from myth in a more flowing style reminiscent of the Cyclopes mosaic in the Dougga room. Some pirates in the Tyrrhenian Sea have attacked a ship only to find it's carrying the god **Dionysus**. Clad in a tunic and brandishing a lance, he has repelled the boarders, who hurl themselves overboard, pursued by Dionysus's panthers – unnecessarily, since the pirates are already metamorphosing into dolphins. The scene is completely stolen by the balding boozy Silenus, who clutches the steering oar for support.

Mausoleum room Mosaic Inv 1393 once allowed wealthy citizens of Thuburbo Majus (whose floor it was) to indulge twice over in their gourmet pleasures in the *triclinium* or dining room. Munching away at their meal, they could stare at the floor and contemplate the background of a well-stocked ocean filled with various game animals and birds, bound and ready for the pot.

Oudna (Uthina) room On the left side of the door, look for A150 and A152. Remains of a feast lie on a dark background: eggshells, fish heads, lemon peel, bread. Using especially fine tesserae, the second-century artist has left an astonishingly vivid still life – you can almost smell the sauce.

Virgil room This is dominated by the eponymous **Virgil mosaic**, found in Sousse and generally dated to the third century. The author of the *Aeneid* (see p.109) sits between Clio, Muse of History (to his right), and Melpomene, Muse of Tragedy. He holds a scroll of the *Aeneid*, which Melpomene appears to be dictating to him. Just off the Virgil room is a small but spectacular collection of **Carthaginian jewellery**.

Second floor

Mosaic rooms (XXX–XXXII) An unlikely fourth-century scene from Le Kef in room XXX (Inv 2819) shows a herd of ostriches being prepared for the chase in an amphitheatre. Inv 3575 in the same room goes into unusually graphic detail. Beneath the placid gaze of spectators, a lion faces off against a gladiator, who jabs his spear into the lion's chest. Blood drips profusely onto the ground.

Acholla room (XXXIII) Acholla, a Roman port north of Sfax of which little remains today, produced a group of **mosaics** as spectacular as any in the country. One of these, Inv 3588, depicts the Labours of Hercules. The hero himself, equipped with lion skin, club and bow, occupies the central roundel, surrounded by others containing his opponents: triple-headed Geryon above, the River Achelous below, and so on.

Fresco rooms (XXXIV–XXXV) One of a series of rare surviving fragments of wall painting, B84 – like so many mosaics – takes for its theme the good things of life, depicting a bottle of wine wrapped in straw, a bag full of eggs and a leg of ham.

Eating and drinking

The places for **eating and drinking** in Tunis are concentrated in the New Town on **avenue Bourguiba** and the streets to either side. Since the Medina closes down fairly early in the evening, there are fewer restaurants there than you might expect, though **Bab Souika** and **Bab Jazira**, at its northern and southern tips respectively, are pretty lively in the evenings, particularly during Ramadan, with enough cafés and cheap restaurants to satisfy any appetite. For food and other supplies, the covered **market** between rue d'Allemagne and rue d'Espagne has everything you'll need and there are also food markets along rue Babel Fellah, rue Sidi Bou Hdid in the Hafsia and along rue Halfaouine. There's a Monoprix **supermarket** on rue Charles de Gaulle, just off avenue de France.

Restaurants

There are plenty of inexpensive **restaurants** in Tunis, most of which will fill you up for 3–4TD. Cheaper still, almost every street in the city has a rôtisserie, where you can either eat a plate of fried food standing up or take away a sandwich (*cassecroûte*). Several cluster around the junction of rue Ibn Khaldoun and rue de Yougoslavie. There are better-quality mid-range places south of avenue Bourguiba and, on the northern side, the early stretches of avenue de Paris and rue de Marseille. Inside the Medina there is little middle ground between the cheap cafés and a number of good, high-class establishments. With money to spare you can have a meal to remember in one of these high-class places, which can be housed in a variety of restored palaces.

Fine dining is one of the legacies of French rule, and Tunis is peppered with elegant Gallic establishments. The food and ambience in these places is everything you would expect from their equivalents in France, but far cheaper: you can get a memorable meal with wine for about 15TD, or even cheaper with set menus. Foreign cuisines are otherwise thin on the ground – apart from the rather awful and widely available pizzas.

We've included the phone numbers for all restaurants where you need to book.

Restaurants north of avenue Bourguiba

61 bis, 61 av Habib Thameur. Trendy new sandwich bar which serves a variety of "combos" (sandwiches, fries and drink) for around 2TD, as well as a few other dishes. Mon–Sat 7.30am–8.30pm.

Andalous, 13 rue de Marseille. Heavy on the gilt but light on the pocket at 9TD for a three-course meal. Live Tunisian music every night. Mon–Sat noon–3pm & 7–11pm.

Capri, 32 rue Mokhtar Attia. ☎ 01/257695. Decently priced Italian and Tunisian cooking only one street north of av Bourguiba. The 8TD set meal is good value. Seafood recommended. Daily noon–3pm & 6pm–midnight.

Carthage, 10 rue Ali Bach Hamba ☎01/255 614. Smart place serving French, Tunisian and a couple of Italian dishes. Tasty, well-presented food, but a bit too brightly lit for the intimate atmosphere aspired to. The three-course set meal is good value at 12TD. Mon–Sat noon–3pm & 7–11pm.

Chez Nous, 5 rue de Marseille ☎01/254043. Fine food and rather pricey à la carte, but the four-course set menu is excellent value at 9TD and includes a delicious chocolate mousse. Muhammad Ali, Michael York and Edith Piaf are among the celebrities who've patronized it and their photos deck the walls. Book ahead, especially Saturday nights. Daily noon–2.15pm & 7–9.30pm.

Chez Slah, 14 rue Pierre Coubertin ☎ 01/258588. Discreetly tucked away in a small street amidst factories and workshops, this converted private house is well worth investigating. Seafood is the specialty and a three-course à la carte will run to around 25TD. Tues–Sun 12.15–2pm & 7.30–10pm.

Circolo Italiano, 102 av de la Liberté, just after av Heidi Chaker ☎ 01/781101. A fair walk north of the centre, but easily the best Italian restaurant in the city, with prices – 40TD for two, including wine – slightly higher as a result. Reservations are essential as it's officially a private club. Daily noon–3pm & 7.30pm–midnight.

Istambul, 4 rue Pierre Courbertin. In case you wondered if there was anywhere cheaper than the *Carcassonne*, this is it. Huge servings at rock-bottom prices – a three-course meal is only 3.5TD. Daily 11am–4pm & 5.30–8.30pm.

Majestic, *Majestic* hotel, 36 av de la Liberté ☎01/332666. The 10TD set menu remains popular partly due to the slightly decaying colonial opulence of the place. For a sample of the interior you can just come in and have mint tea (0.5TD). Daily noon–2pm & 7–10pm.

La Mamma, 11bis rue de Marseille ☎ 01/332388. A deservedly popular place for reasonably priced pizzas, pasta and similar fare. The seafood tagliatelle is particularly recommended. Daily noon–3pm & 7pm–midnight.

Le Neptune, 3 rue du Caire ☎01/254820. This busy, cheap place serves decent though not outstanding, Sfaxian cuisine, with a 3.5TD set menu. Daily 11am–10pm.

L'Orient, 7 rue Ali Bach Hamba ☎01/252061. Pleasant decor and unfailingly busy, this place specializes in seafood with the *menu touristique* at 9TD. Mon–Sat noon–3pm & 7–10.30pm.

Restaurants south of avenue Bourguiba

Abid, 98 rue de Yougoslavie. Don't let the repro Turkish wood scenes and green lighting put you off: this is no-nonsense food at no-nonsense prices (*plat du jour* 2.7–4TD). Mon–Sat noon– 9pm.

Capitole, 60 av Bourguiba. A reasonably priced, long-established place serving filling food. A three course set meal with extensive choices and a cup of mint tea is a bargain at 4.2TD. Unconnected with the hotel of the same name. Recommended. Daily noon–3pm & 6–10pm.

Carcassonne, 8 av de Carthage. Average food, but cheap and with good service. White linen tablecloths, white jacketed waiters and pleasant surroundings. The 4TD menu will fill you up. Daily 12.30–3.30pm & 6–9.30pm.

Gaston's, 73 rue de Yougoslavie ☎ 01/340417. Specializes in seafood (the *bouillabaisse* is excellent) and has an 8.5TD set menu for weekday lunchtimes. A full à la carte meal will cost around 30TD. Tues–Sun noon–11pm.

Restaurant des Margarites, 6bis rue d'Hollande ☎01/240632. Attached to the *Hôtel Maison Dorée*, this place has an expensive à la carte, but a moderate tourist menu at 5.5TD. Mon–Sat noon–2.30pm & 7–9.30pm.

Le Régent, 16 rue du Lieutenant Aziz Tej ☎ 01/341723. Tucked away at the insalubrious end of the street, this superb classy place (book ahead) is slick and discreet, and 25TD will get you the works. Recommended. Closed August. Mon–Sat 11.45am–2.30pm & 6.30–11.30pm.

Tantonville, 96 rue de Yougoslavie. Once a busy 1940s clattering café and still popular, in its dotage, now serving inexpensive Tunisian dishes – a three-course set meal will cost you 7TD. Mon–Sat 7am–9.30pm.

Medina restaurants

Dar Bel Hadj, 17 rue des Tamis ☎01/336910. Refined and upmarket place set in a seventeenth-century palace and catering to Tunisian elites rather than tourists. Sublime food for around 30TD. Mon–Sat noon–3pm & 8pm–midnight.

Dar el Jeld, 5 rue Dar el Jeld, off pl Gouvernement ☎01/560916. On the western side of the Medina in a lovingly restored aristocratic residence, this is top of the range in both price (45TD) and quality. Reservations essential. Closed August. Mon–Sat 12.30–3pm & 8pm–midnight.

Restaurant Essaraya, 6 rue Ben Mahmoud ☎01/560310, ⓦwww.essaraya.com. Tucked away in the Medina behind Bab Menara, an extremely opulent place housed in a magnificent palace. Service and food match the stunning decor. Try the *m'loukhia*, stewed aromatic green leaves and beef. Expect to pay 30TD for a meal. Recommended. Mon–Sat noon–3pm & 8pm–midnight.

Granada, Bab Jedid, opposite Souk el Asser. Enchanting location under the arches of Bab Jedid. Serves up a range of sandwiches (1–1.5TD), pastas (2TD) and salads, as well as a few Tunisian dishes. Popular with tourists and not adverse to overcharging, so check the prices as you order. Daily 24hr.

Mahdoui, 79 rue Jemaa Zitouna. Right by the Great Mosque, this long-established couscous parlour has resisted the urge to go upmarket and serves good, cheap food (3.5TD). Mon–Sat 11.30am–4pm.

Le Marhaba, 166 rue de la Kasbah. Dirt cheap spit'n'sawdust joint in the mid-Medina.

M'rabet, Souk et Trouk ☎01/561729. Situated in the heart of the Medina and built over the tombs of three holy men. Formerly the most stylish place in town to splurge seriously, but a bit touristy now. A meal and the accompanying show (belly-dancing or similar entertainment) will cost around 20TD a head. The fine café below is cheaper. Mon–Sat noon–3pm & 7–10pm.

Victoire, place de la Victoire. At the corner where rue Jemaa Zitouna emerges. Workaday place (also open evenings) with good food for 3 or 4 dinars; the soups are excellent. Mon–Sat 11am–10.30pm.

Cafés, patisseries and bars

Traditional **cafés**, found all over the city and sometimes equipped with *chichas* (hubble-bubble pipes, currently enjoying a surge of popularity amongst young Tunisians), are crowded places where men drink coffee in various forms and women may not feel very comfortable, especially in the New Town. The **Medina cafés** are something of an exception and where you're more likely to encounter curiosity than a cold shoulder. For a rundown of the best Medina cafés, see p.82. The cafés' territory is being gradually invaded by **patisseries** offering snacks as well as pastries, which is where Tunisian women tend to go for fast food or midday breaks – there are a number on the north side of avenue Bourguiba – where you can get sandwiches and coffee, as well as the more traditional pastries, sweets and citronade.

A more expensive alternative where women can feel relatively comfortable are the **café-bars** in big hotels, or the central *Café de Paris* on avenue Bourguiba, where you can happily sit and watch the crowds passing by. This is also probably the most civilized place to have a **beer**. Try the café-bars at *Hôtel Africa*, 50 av Bourguiba, the *El Hana International*, 49 av Bourguiba (its rooftop bar has superlative views), or the *Majestic*, 36 av de Paris. The best and cheapest café-bars on avenue Bourguiba, however, are the *Capitole*, at no. 60, open 24 hours, and serving excellent crêpes, freshly squeezed fruit juice and *lait de poule*, and over the street at the junction with rue de Marseille, the highly popular *Panorama* which serves similar fare all day and night, as well as *shawarma*.

Tunisian **bars** – small, crowded and very male-dominated – can be found mostly around the train station, though there are others scattered through the New Town on street corners (especially along avenue de la Liberté). Most close around 8pm and throughout Friday and Ramadan. The Western-style bars attached to bigger hotels or cafés tend to be much more expensive. Exceptions are the *Oscar Hotel* bar, which is not too expensive at 2.5TD for a beer, and open late, though not a place for single women, while the *Hotel Omrane* bar is more welcoming and also inexpensive. Alternatively, you can drink in some restaurants provided you order a plate, though this can work out just as expensive as ordering your beer in a posh hotel.

Entertainment and nightlife

Tunis's **nightlife** is fairly low-key, with the exception of **Ramadan**, when the city acquires a new lease of life for a month. At other times, the city closes down at about 11pm and soon after sunset in the Medina. Crowds stroll along avenue Bourguiba, and mill around the streets to either side, but facilities in the city centre are limited. You're more likely to find **live music** at Sidi Bou Saïd (see p.117) than in the city centre, but with money to burn there are cabaret shows at restaurants offering slick pseudo-Oriental-style evenings.

Nightclubs
Discos don't offer a very exciting alternative to just sitting at a café and watching the world go by, but if you feel the urge to get hot and sweaty under the disco lights, try Club 2001 at *Hôtel el Mechtel* at avenue Ouled Haffouz, or Joker Club, at the *El Hana International* 49 av Bourguiba, entrance at rue Bach Hamba. There are more sophisticated places out at the suburbs of La Marsa and Gammarth.

Concerts
Interesting displays of live **traditional music** are provided by some restaurants to accompany your meal: nightly at *La Mamma*, 11 bis rue de Marseille, and *Andalous*, 13 rue de Marseille. *M'rabet*, in Souk et Trouk in the Medina, is pretty touristy, whilst *Dar Bel Hadj*'s is hardly likely to inspire feverish dancing.

Watch out, too, for events such as concerts of Arabic and Western **classical music** at the Théâtre Municipal on avenue Bourguiba. These can be surprisingly cheap, especially if you don't mind sitting in the vertiginous upper circles. Occasional one-off performances by international bands and orchestras can be heard at government venues such as the Maison de la Culture Ibn Khaldoun, 16 rue Ibn Khaldoun, which also mounts seasons of classic movies. Other venues to look out for (daily listings in *La Presse* or *Le Temps*), particularly during the Festival de la Medina held during Ramadan, include: Club Culturel Tahar Haddad, 20 rue du Tribunal in the Medina; the adjacent Dar Lasram; the nearby Medersa Bir Lahjar, 40 rue du Pacha; and the excellent occasional concerts of traditional music held at Sidi Bou Saïd's Dar Ennejma Ezzahra, Baron d'Erlanger's Orientalist palace (tickets and information from Maison de la Culture Ibn Khaldoun). The Rachidia Institute's palatial headquarters at the end of Impasse Dabdaba has monthly concerts of classical *mahlouf* music. The Acropolium (the old Cathedral of St Louis in Carthage) is a classy setting for the international singing stars of the Arab world.

Theatre
Tunis's thespian pride and joy is the ludicrous Art Nouveau **Théâtre Municipal** (☎01/259499) on avenue Bourguiba, which regularly puts on plays as well as some opera and rock concerts. Another venue to look out for is Espace el Teatro, Complexe el Mechtel, avenue Ouled Haffouz (☎01/894313), which stages works of a more modern flavour. La Quatrième Art, avenue de Paris is a converted cinema but is now home

to the Tunisian National Theatre (TNT), directed by the energetic Mohamed Driss. Listings for these and other theatres are found in the daily *Le Temps* and *La Presse*.

Films

Cinema-going is a popular pastime in Tunis, with some twenty cinemas dotted around town. Matinées commence at 3pm (tickets 1TD) and evening shows usually screen at 6pm and 9pm (2.5–3TD); the listings are published every day in *La Presse* and *Le Temps*.

The only arthouse cinema in the city is Maison de Théâtre et du Cinema Ibn Rachiq, at the corner of avenue de Paris and rue Mokhtar Attia, which occasionally screens films with French subtitles. More mainstream cinemas include ABC, 8 rue Ibn Khaldoun, and Le Mondial, 10 rue Ibn Khaldoun. Along avenue Bourguiba, you'll find Colisée at no. 45 (in the arcade), Champs Elysées at no. 37, Capitole at no. 60, Le Palace at no. 54, and Parnasse at no. 63 (in the arcade). The Maison de la Culture at 16, rue Ibn Khaldoun, has film weeks, where it shows a different movie at 6pm every night for 0.8TD.

The **Carthage International Film Festival**, a celebration of Arab and African cinema alternating between Tunis and Ouagadougou (Burkina Faso), takes over the capital's cinemas every second November (2002, 2004) – probably your best chance to see some Tunisian films. Events are listed in *La Presse* and *Le Temps*.

Hammams

For the ultimate in sensory pleasure, perhaps the best way to prepare body and soul for the evening is to take a wash in a hammam. Ubiquitous but mostly well hidden, your hotel can direct you to the nearest one, or consult the Medina map (see pp.76–77). Hammams in Tunis are usually single-sex, which means that you can use them throughout the day. The most atmospheric, if not always the cleanest, are in the Medina and in Halfaouine, of which the most spectacular is undoubtedly Hammam Sahib et Tabaa, close to place Halfaouine (men mornings and evenings, women in the afternoon). The Hammam Kachachine at 30 Souk des Librairies (daily 5am–3pm) is almost as atmospheric, but unfortunately for men only. There's a women's hammam at 1 rue Noria (daily 6am–9pm). Always remember to bring your own towel (big enough to change under) and a pair of summer shorts, as the authorities periodically ban the traditional *foutas* as being unhygienic. If you want to be scrubbed by the masseur (*tayyeb*) you often have to get a *jeton* (token) at the cash desk. For more information on the hammams, see p.48.

Ramadan

During the month of **Ramadan** (see p.41 for dates), there's plenty of eating, drinking and merriment until the early hours of the morning, especially over the last two weeks. The uncontested centre of all this activity is the Medina, which has cafés jam-packed till well after midnight and impromptu concerts given in the Souk des Chéchias. *La Presse* covers daily listings of the numerous artistic and musical events held city-wide during the Festival de la Medina (pick up a brochure from the Théâtre Municipal on avenue Bourguiba).

Shopping

Tunis's **souks** not only form a fascinating area of warren-like lanes and passageways to explore, but they still function as the backbone of Tunis's trading community. Souk el Kachachine (p.80) is the place to come for wholesale **rugs** and **clothes**, and Souk et

Trouk (p.81), built in the seventeenth century for Turkish tailors, is where you'll find **carpet** shops. Souk de la Laine (p.80) no longer trades much wool, but has a few traditional **tailors**; one typically Tunisian article, the characteristic red *chéchia*, or skullcap, can be bought in the **Souk des Chéchias** (p.82). The Souk des Orfèvres (p.80) is still home to **gold jewellers**, but the Souks of the Dyers (rue des Teinturiers) (p.85), once part of the clothing industry, now houses a **drum-making workshop**, along with a limited amount of **dyeing**. Souk el Belat (p.84) and Souk el Asser (p.94) have **food** stalls, as does the southern end of rue des Teinturiers, which specializes in fish. **Copper and brasswork**, as well as **chicha pipes**, are best bought on Souk du Cuivre, and you'll also find chichas at the southern end of rue Sidi el-Morjani.

A good place to start shopping if you're interested in buying locally-made crafts is the official **ONA** showroom on the ground floor of Le Palmarium shopping centre, corner of avenue Bourguiba and avenue de Carthage. Prices here are high, but you can get a good sense of the range of goods available before entering the maelstrom of the Medina's central souks, which are bewildering not only for the streaming crowds but for the assortment of merchandise available. Another hassle free place to buy quality pieces (pottery, rugs and jewellery) is Phenecia, out at Carthage Byrsa (see p.113). If you're after genuine antiques, Yousef Ayoub at 27 av Bourguiba is worth a look.

If you prefer to buy everyday **craft goods** that Tunisians use, and at much lower prices, hold your fire until you get to the further reaches of the Medina – the stalls outside the Mosque of Sidi Mehrez, for example (see p.86). More unusual shopping ideas might include **olive wood crafts** from a shop in rue Sidi Ben Arous (see p.82), or leftover **colonial kitsch** from the bric-a-brac and furniture shops in rue des Glacières (see p.83).

Standard tourist fodder is available on **rue Jemaa Zitouna** by the Great Mosque (see p.78), which has turned into a cauldron of overflowing stalls and shops that tend to be more expensive than elsewhere, but there's also the odd stall selling interesting old metal lamps, chandeliers and pen cases. There are some good **pottery** shops on rue Sidi Mehrez, near the Mosque and *zaouia*, with a good selection of low-priced plates, cups, pots and ashtrays, and you'll find Sejnane pottery figurines and animals at El Hanout on rue Jemaa Zitouna.

Listings

Airlines Aeroflot, 42 av Hedi Chaker ☎01/845831; Air Algérie, 26 av de Paris ☎01/341888; Air France, 1 rue d'Athènes ☎01/355422; Alitalia, imm. Maghrebia bd 7 Novembre ☎01/940494; British Airways, 17 av Bourguiba ☎01/330588; Egyptair, 49 av Bourguiba, in the back of the *Hôtel El Hana International* ☎01/341182; Iberia, Imm. Galaxia, c/o Arabia Saudia, Belvedere ☎01/840238; Libyan Arab Airlines, 49 av de Paris ☎01/341646; Lufthansa, Imm. Maghrebia, bd. 7 Novembre ☎01/941344; Sabena, Imm. Maghrebia, bd 7 Novembre ☎01/940940; Swissair, Imm. Maghrebia B, bd 7 Novembre ☎01/705311; Syrian Air, 2 av Carthage ☎01/341127; Tuninter, airport ☎01/701717; Tunisair, 48 av Bourguiba ☎01/336500; Turkish Airlines, Complexe El Mechtel, av Ouled Haffouz ☎01/787033.

American Express c/o Carthage Tours, 39 and 59 av Bourguiba ☎01/240066. The mail service is very efficient (Mon–Sat am only), the exchange service less so.

Arabic courses The Bourguiba School (Institut Bourguiba des Langues Vivantes), 47 av de la Liberté ☎01/832418 or 832923, 𝔽833684, runs a four-week intensive Arabic course (early July–early Aug; enrolments mid-May to mid-June; 380TD), with the possibility of renting accommodation in the university (80TD for the duration), and eating in the college canteen. Alternatively, the school offers non-intensive courses of 4hr per week during the academic year (enrolments mid-July to end Sept).

Art galleries Tunis has a wealth of exhibition space, including state-owned, commercial, religious and private galleries. All are worth a look, especially during one of Tunis's many thematic city-wide festivals, such as Photography Month (Dec) or the Festival de la Medina (Ramadan). You'll find listings of what's on in the dailies *Le Temps* and *La Presse*. Palais Kheireddine, rue du Tribunal (near Dar Lasram in the Medina) has a superlative setting, but some exhibits disappoint. Galerie Yahia/Palmarium, 3 av de Carthage, is a commercial gallery, strong on photography and modern plastic arts. One of the most energetic venues is Club Culturel Tahar Haddad, 20 rue du Tribunal (Medina), which is highly regarded for both Tunisan and international art. For a strictly Tunisian feel there's the Dar Hussein, place du Château, near Bab Menara, a wonderful old mansion with month-long exhibitions. El Teatro/Mechtel Complexe, avenue Ouled Haffouz, by Belvedere Park, puts on avant-garde works by Algerians in exile. Finally, the Medina Gallery, rue el Jeldis in an old Medina town house, displays occasional retrospectives and generally modern paintings. Also worth checking out is the Maison de la Culture Ibn Khaldoun, 16 rue Ibn Khaldoun, which, as well as staging a variety of exhibitions, has a theatre/cinema and information on musical events at Sidi Bou Saïd's Dar Ennejma Ezzahra (see p.117).

Banks and exchange Visa and MasterCard ATMs are scattered along avenue Bourguiba, in place Barcelone and also in the Medina near the mosque. The banks on avenue Bourguiba tend to get crowded in summer. Less packed locations include the Franco-Tunisian Bank, 13 rue d'Alger; Banque du Sud, 45 av de la Liberté, next to the Bourguiba School; and BIAT, 21 rue d'Algérie, by Bab Jazira. The STB next to the *Hôtel Africa* opens late and at weekends. Outside banking hours, you can change cash at the post office and at *Hôtel Majestic*. You can change foreign notes at BIAT near the Théâtre Municipal, the UBCI on the same block, the Amen Bank at 13 av de France, and Banque de Tunisie at 3 av de France. Travellers' cheques are trickier out of hours but you could ask around the big hotels. You are supposed to be able to change money at the airport all night, but don't count on it.

Bookshops There's a limited selection of English-language novels at: Librairie Ben Abdallah, 17 av de France opposite Magasin Général; Claire Fontaine, 4 rue d'Alger; Mille Feuilles in La Marsa, just off the end of the TGM. For books in French about Tunisia and Maghreb, try Claire Fontaine, Mille Feuilles, Espace Diwan at 9 rue Sidi Ben Arous, just up from the Great Mosque in the heart of the Medina, or Éditions Alif at 3 rue d'Hollande. Alif is well worth a visit for its pop-up books, Corsair strip cartoons, and beautiful reprints of ancient maps. Secondhand books in English can be found at Abdessattar M'zoughi, 10 rue d'Angleterre; secondhand French books are sold on the street stalls on rue des Tanneurs.

Bicycle rental There's no official bicycle rental shop but there are many bicycle shops on avenue de Madrid, to the north of the New Town, that may consent to an informal deal; 10–12TD for a full day is reasonable.

Car rental There are several agencies on avenue Bourguiba and in the big hotels. The main ones also have a desk at the airport. The smaller, rather dubious, agencies are usually cheaper but their cars may be older. Reputable city centre offices include: Avis, 90 av de la Liberté ☎01/788563 – also in the *Hilton*; Ben Jemaa, 53 av de Paris ☎01/240060; Budget, 17 av Kheireddine Pacha; Europcar, 1 rue hedi Nouira ☎01/340313; Express, 49bis rue Hedi Nouira ☎01/354099; and Hertz, 3 rue Hedi Nouira ☎01/256451.

Car repair Any French make, and Land Rovers, can be handled at most garages. British and American dealers are in very short supply. If you need towing, call SOS Car Haul ☎01/801211.

Doctors For minor complaints or injuries, an *infirmerie* should be able to sort you out. A wound dressing and tetanus jab, for example, will cost around 3TD. There are *infirmeries* at 20 av de la Liberté, 32 av Bab Jedid, 59 rue al Jazira and 150 rue Bab Souika. There are two recommended *cliniques*, the Ettaoufik ☎01/800211 and the El Manar ☎01/885000. For specialized treatment, ask your consulate or embassy for a list of doctors.

Embassies Algeria, 18 rue de Niger ☎01/780055 or 786740; Australia, c/o Canadian Embassy; Canada, 3 rue de Sénégal ☎01/796577; Egypt, rue 8007, Montplaisir ☎01/791181; France, 79 rue de Yougoslavie ☎01/358000; Ireland, c/o UK Embassy; Libya, 48 bis rue de 1er Juin ☎01/780055 or 786740/visa section 74 av Mohammed V ☎01/842202; New Zealand, c/o UK Embassy; UK, 8 pl de la Victoire ☎01/341444; US, 144 av de la Liberté ☎01/782566. To arrange a visa for Libya, you'll need two passport photos, 20TD, an invitation to visit the country from a Libyan tourist agency, business or friend, and some patience. The visa should be issued within two days and is valid for 15 or 30 days; office hours for visas at the Libyan embassy are Mon–Sat 9am–2pm.

Emergencies Police ☎197; Tourist police, Ministry of the Interior, 32 av Bourguiba ☎01/830802; Fire brigade (*Protection civel*) ☎198; ambulance ☎190.

Football Tunis has two main clubs, Espérance Sportif and Club Africain, who between them scooped most of Tunisia's, as well as Africa's, club trophies in the 1997–98 season. They share the

El Menzah ground up in the Cité Olympique, where they play at home alternate weeks, usually Sunday at 2pm or 4pm, depending on the time of year. The best way to get up to El Menzah is by métro to Jeunesse or Cité Sportive (line #2). To avoid the mad scramble for tickets, you're advised to arrive well before the match. Other metropolitan teams are Avenir Sportif de la Marsa (ASM) and Club Sportif de Hammam Lif (CSHL).

Hospitals The best hospital is the Hôpital Charles Nicolle, bd 9 Avril 1938, northwest of the Medina by Bab Benat ☎01/578000.

Internet There are a number of internet places dotted around the city centre, although they generally don't serve drinks or snacks: Club Internet Madrid, 1st floor, 1 av de Madrid (daily 8.30am–10pm; 1.6TD/hr); Cyber Barcelone, 1st floor, 14 rue de Grèce (daily 9am–10pm; 2TD/hr). Publinet offices are at 28 av Bourguiba (daily 9am–midnight; 2TD/hr), 158 rue Bab Souika (daily 9am–1am; 2TD/hr), with another signposted off rue d'Algérie just west of the intersection with rue Charles de Gaulle (daily 9am–midnight; 2TD/hr).

Laundry Laverie, 15 rue d'Allemagne, charges by the kilo (closed Sun).

Newspapers A wide range of foreign papers can be bought at the stands under the trees in the middle of avenue Bourguiba.

Passport photos A lot of places do these fast and cheaply. Try 23 rue Jemal Abdel Nasser (near the post office), 32 rue al Jazira (on the corner of rue Écosse), 59 rue Mongi Slim, avenue de France (next to the Cathedral, on the corner of rue de Rome), or several places up avenue de la Liberté on your way to the embassy zone.

MOVING ON FROM TUNIS

For a rundown of destinations and journey times, see Travel Details on p.120.

BY AIR

As almost everywhere in Tunisia is within twelve hours of the capital by land, **internal air travel** is rather a luxury, although not overly expensive; *Le Temps* and *La Presse* list the departure times. To get to Tunis Carthage Airport (☎01/754000) you can take bus #35 or #635 from Tunis Marine Station (30min, 5am–8.30pm). By taxi the journey costs 4–8TD depending on the time of day. The confusingly named Aeroport Station on the TGM line from Tunis Marine to La Marsa has nothing to do with the airport. For **international travel**, remember that you need a *bon de passage* (see p.22) if you buy an international air ticket with cash in Tunisia. Note also that the **duty-free shop** at the airport only takes hard currency, so don't save any dinars to spend in it. For airline offices, see Listings, p.104.

BY SEA

If you're leaving Tunis by **sea**, get off at Goulette Vielle on the TGM line heading to La Marsa, and follow the track back for 100m to the main road, turn left and continue for some 300m, past the Kasbah (on your left) until you come to a roundabout. Turn right here and continue, following the road to the left past the CTN building and BNT bank to the ferry terminal (☎01/735932). Services run to Cagliari in Sardinia and to Genoa, Naples and Trápani in Italy. There are also very occasional services to Toulon and Nice. Remember you will need a *bon de passage* (see p.22) if you buy an **international ferry ticket** with cash. **Ferry schedules** and **ticket office addresses** are given in Basics on p.8 or consult "the Guide" section of *Le Temps* for departures. In the summer, things can get hectic at the offices, so it's wise to leave plenty of time for queuing, or get your ticket in Bizerte, Sousse or Sfax instead.

BY TRAIN

The Tunisian **train** service is not comprehensive and you'll find yourself relying heavily on buses – especially as trains over a longer distance are slower, less frequent and not much cheaper than buses. Tunis's mainline station is on place Barcelone (☎01/334444),

Pharmacies All-night pharmacies in the centre include: Jenane, av Bab Jedid ☎01/240994; Karray, 20 av de la Liberté ☎01/243520; and Khabthani, at Le Colisée, 43 av Bourguiba ☎01/252507.

Post office The main post office, for stamps and poste restante, is on rue Charles de Gaulle. Mail is kept in poste restante for only two weeks and there is a 0.35TD charge for each item; mail can go missing. Local and international calls can be made from Publitel and Taxiphone offices which are dotted all over the city. Some of these also send and receive faxes and have photocopiers. The parcels office (*Colis Postaux*) is on avenue de la République, just off av Bourguiba. There is a branch at 1 av Habib Thameur, and a very helpful one in Bab Aleoua bus station.

Swimming The most accessible pool is the Cité Olympique in El Menza (métro line #2 to Cité Sportive). You have to buy a monthly ticket (12TD). Hotels such as the *El Hana International* have first-rate pools and may permit non-residents to use them.

Travel agencies The many travel agencies that line avenue Bourguiba are all very similar, offering combinations of car rental, organized tours, flights, ferry tickets, hotel bookings and so on. As for student travel agents, there is STAV, 2 rue de Sparte ☎01/348011, but its special deals are not spectacularly cheap. Many ordinary agencies will give a 25 percent discount for a student card, as will Tunisair and some other airlines if you're under 31.

Visa extensions If your ninety days are coming up, you either need to leave Tunisia briefly to get a fresh entry stamp (the cheapest and easiest way is to go by ferry to Trápani in Sicily) or else begin a tedious and time-consuming paper chase that will start at the Ministry of Interior at 32 av Bourguiba.

right at the centre of the main hotel area, south of avenue Bourguiba (métro lines #1 and #2). Staff at its helpful information desk hand out accurate timetables for all of Tunisia's passenger services. To secure a seat, it's a good idea to turn up at the station an hour or so before departure to stake your claim as soon as the train arrives.

BY BUS
Buses leave Tunis regularly for all the country's main towns and there are also direct services to Libya and Algeria (see warning on p.185). There are two intercity **bus terminals – Bab Saadoun** (☎01/562532), at the bottom of avenue Bougatfa, for the north of the country and parts of the Tell, and **Bab Aleoua** (☎01/399440), on rue Sidi el Bechir, for the rest – both connected to the centre by bus and with métro stations fairly nearby, although Bab Aleoua, especially, is close enough to the centre to walk. The circular city bus routes #50, #72 and #74 run between the two terminals, but stop by the Bab Saadoun city gate rather than outside the northern bus terminal. With few exceptions (some long-distance buses to Jerba and the Jerid), departures for the following destinations are during daylight hours. Services are greatly reduced during Ramadan.

BY LOUAGE
Louages, or service taxis, follow set routes (often the same as buses) and arrive at and depart from locations near the bus terminals – journey times are roughly three-quarters less than the equivalent bus journey. Bab Saadoun's louage station, for services to the north and northeast, adjoins the bus station. Services to Hammamet and Cap Bon depart opposite Bab Aleoua's bus station. All other louage destinations can be picked up at the vast warehouse adjacent to Souk Moncef Bey on avenue Moncef Bey. For international louages to Tripoli in Libya, use **Garage Ayachi** at Bab Souika, whilst services to Algeria leave **rue al Jazira** at place de la Victoire for Annaba, Constantine and Port de France. Louages depart from about 4am until about 6pm (the later departures are mostly local), and it's better to start earlier the further your destination. One or two important destinations (like Sfax) have louages all night, but you have to wait for them to fill up before leaving, which can take a long time in the small hours.

If you are considering crossing the Algerian border – strongly inadvisable considering the current political climate – please read the **warning** on p.185.

GREATER TUNIS

On a hot summer evening, there's no better way of enjoying Tunis than to get out of the city centre by catching the TGM train line across the lake to one of the suburbs on the shore of the gulf, where the sea breezes clear away the city's oppressive humidity.

Modern-day **Carthage** is the suburb built over and among the remains of the ancient capital of the Carthaginian Empire, second city of the Roman world. The physical extent of the ruins can be disappointing, but not the sense of history nor the scenery. Moving up the coast from Carthage, you move towards upmarket resorts that tend to cater for French tourists seeking a more refined alternative to staying in Tunis – **La Goulette**, with its Kasbah fortress and fish restaurants; **Sidi Bou Saïd**, a cliff-top village of considerable charm; **La Marsa**, **Gammarth** and **Raouad** for swimming and nightlife. Remember, however, that half of Tunis converges on these places in summer, especially at weekends. The TGM will get you as far as La Marsa, but past there you will have to depend on buses if you do not have your own car. Both the green TCV buses, and the regular #40, will take you along the coastal road through Gammarth, the latter service continuing onto Raouad.

The suburbs of the southern shore are distinctly downmarket, with *bidonville* (literally, "oil-drum town") shanties spreading out beyond the boulevard du 9 Avril 1938. But **Hammam Lif**, a turn-of-the-century resort dominated by **Jebel Bou Kornine**, retains some character of its own despite a minor reputation for – rare in Tunisia – drug-related problems. This should not, however, put you off visiting, as the streets remain as safe as any.

Lac Tunis

The **causeway** on which the TGM crosses **Lac Tunis** was built in the 1870s, when the suburbs that now run from La Goulette to Sidi Bou Saïd barely existed. The train was originally routed directly to La Marsa (through the British Consul's garden, see p.83) along the mainland north of the lake.

Lake Tunis offers the chance to see some of Tunisia's more exciting **birds**. Forget the northern half of the lake, whose edges are now being reclaimed for hotel and other developments, and head instead for the southern half, which attracts flamingos, waders, gulls and terns. Numbers are particularly high in spring and autumn, when they're swollen by migrants. The best vantage point is the lake's southeastern corner; take the TGM to La Bac and the ferry across to Radès port, from where you can stroll 3km down into Radès along the lakeshore.

On the **Isle of Chikli**, north of the causeway, **Fort St Jacques** sits mysteriously, built by the Spanish in the sixteenth century. Once used as a prison, it is now a stopover for migrating birds.

If you have the time or inclination to **walk**, some of the fields just north of the lake between Carthage and Sidi Bou Saïd have wonderful **wildflower** displays in spring; look for yellow chrysanthemums, scarlet poppies, blue borage and pink campions. Brilliant goldfinches are common in the area, while butterflies include swooping swallowtails and orange tips and, in spring, hundreds of migrating painted ladies feeding on the sea stocks at the back of the beach.

La Goulette   حلق الوادي

LA GOULETTE (meaning "the gullet", or "throat") is the port of Tunis and increasingly a dormitory suburb for the capital, easily reached by the regular TGM services (every 20min; 20min). However, it still has a lively atmosphere of its own, as well as some excellent fish restaurants – the main reason for coming here, along with the ferries. The cheaper restaurants line the main avenue, with the more expensive ones down quieter side streets.

The road from the causeway and TGM towards the port (from Goulette Vieille TGM station, head back towards Tunis for 100m then turn left at the Esso garage) passes, on the left, a rather run-down area reminiscent of a poor district in southern Europe, complete with church – the area is unsubtley shielded from the main road by a series of enormous billboards. In the middle of the same road is La Goulette's **city gate**, part of the Spanish king Charles V's walls but now standing alone, shored up with concrete.

The **Kasbah**, a massive fortress built in 1535 by Charles V to defend his bridgehead in Tunisia, is a little further on the left and really the only monumental sight here. As a key strategic point in the sixteenth-century struggle for control of the western Mediterranean, it saw some torrid times, finally falling in 1574 to "four hundred and seventy-five thousand" Turks, Moors and Arabs – the figure quoted by Miguel de Cervantes, author of *Don Quixote*, who fought in its defence. Despite being captured, he and many others were glad to see the Kasbah lost – it was a "breeding-place and cloak of iniquities, a glutton, sponge and sink" of all the money spent on it in a futile policy of prestige. Over the next centuries the Kasbah was used as a dungeon for prisoners, who would be taken from here to the Souk el Berka in the Medina to be sold into slavery.

The **International Museum of the Ram** (April–Sept only, irregular hours; 1.1TD) has been installed in two of the rooms in the Kasbah. Its literature proclaims it "probably unique in the world" – though mainly for an unrivalled collection of miscellaneous kitsch, including a shocking depiction of a group of Romans using a battering ram against the besieged Jews of Masada in Palestine.

Continuing straight on from the museum takes you to the port (see p.106), but, to go into La Goulette **town**, take a left up avenue Farhat Hached immediately after the Kasbah to place 7 Novembre. This is the main area for **fish restaurants** and there's a great variety, from very cheap to upmarket. *Restaurant Lucullus* (℡01/737310) at the corner of place 7 Novembre and avenue Bourguiba is one of the smarter, charging around 30TD a head. From place 7 Novembre, avenue Bourguiba splits to the left and avenue Franklin D. Roosevelt to the right. Franklin D. Roosevelt is better for food, with cheap places like the *Stambli* and the *Guitoune*, where meals cost around 5TD, alongside smarter establishments such as the *La Victoire*, *Le Café Vert* and *Le Chalet*. If you feel the need to stay in La Goulette, whilst there are no budget options, two new hotels, the three-star Lido (℡01/738045; ➎) and the soon to be four-star *La Jetée* (℡01/736000, 🖷738396; ➎) which has a pool, are both on the seafront, and are more than adequate.

Carthage and around قرطاج

> *Aeneas looked wonderingly at the solid structures springing up where there had once been only African huts, and the gates, the turmoil, and the paved streets. The Tyrians were hurrying about busily, some tracing a line for the walls and manhandling stones up the slopes as they strained to build their citadel, others siting some building and marking its outline by ploughing a furrow . . . At one spot they were excavating the harbour, and at another a party was laying out an area for the deep foundations of a theatre; they were also hewing from quarries mighty pillars to stand tall and handsome beside the stage which was still to be built . . . Aeneas looked up at the buildings. "Ah, fortunate people," he exclaimed . . .*

Ever since Virgil wrote the *Aeneid* in the first century BC, the ancient port of **CARTHAGE** has been suffused in a legendary aura of romance, power, cruelty and decline. "Any man who could survey the ruins of Carthage with indifference", wrote

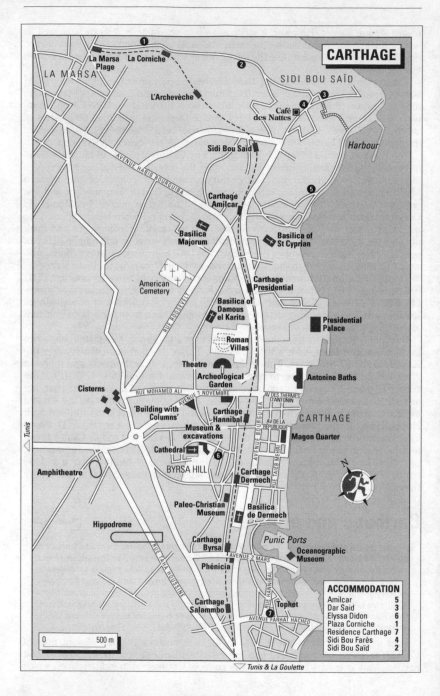

CARTHAGE

La Marsa Plage
La Corniche
LA MARSA
L'Archevèche
SIDI BOU SAÏD
Café des Nattes
Harbour
AVENUE HABIB BOURGUIBA
Sidi Bou Saïd
Carthage Amilcar
Basilica Majorum
Basilica of St Cyprian
American Cemetery
RUE ROOSEVELT
Carthage Presidential
Basilica of Damous el Karita
Presidential Palace
Roman Villas
Theatre
Archeological Garden
Antonine Baths
Cisterns
RUE MOHAMED ALI
AV DES THERMES D'ANTONIN
'Building with Columns'
AVENUE 1 NOVEMBRE
AV DE LA RÉPUBLIQUE
Carthage Hannibal
CARTHAGE
AVENUE BOURGUIBA
Museum & excavations
Magon Quarter
Cathedral
BYRSA HILL
RUE TAIEB MEHRI
Carthage Dermech
N
Amphitheatre
Paleo-Christian Museum
Basilica de Dermech
Hippodrome
RUE TAYA HOUSSINE
Carthage Byrsa
Punic Ports
Oceanographic Museum
AVENUE 2 MARS
Phénicia
RUE HANNIBAL
Tophet
Carthage Salammbo
AVENUE FARHAT HACHED
Tunis & La Goulette

0   500 m

ACCOMMODATION

Amilcar	5
Dar Saïd	3
Elyssa Didon	6
Plaza Corniche	1
Residence Carthage	7
Sidi Bou Farès	4
Sidi Bou Saïd	2

Tunis

one Edward Blaquière, a typical nineteenth-century traveller, "or not call to mind the scenes of its past glories and misfortunes must, indeed, be devoid of sensibility". The image is made that much more potent by the yawning gap between the myth and today's reality. The remains consist of a series of widely spaced sites, with only a little standing above ground level, lurking among the plush villas of Tunis's wealthier commuters.

Still, if you approach Carthage with some imagination and a willingness to be impressed, it has a good deal to offer – not least the wide views over the Gulf and back to Tunis. It only takes a moment's thought to bring the bare bones to life, and judicious use of the TGM train line allows you to see as much or as little as you want; if you get tired, just go on to Sidi Bou Saïd for the evening, where the mood of dusk falling over the Gulf often revives the romance.

Some history

Remarkably little is known about the appearance of **Carthage**, except that it grew up around the ports on the shore and the acropolis on the Byrsa Hill, where today's museum and cathedral now stand. The first detailed accounts come from the Romans, who gleefully describe how thoroughly they destroyed the city in 146 BC.

Having left Carthage in ruins, the Romans made Utica capital of their African province, but in 46 BC **Julius Caesar** refounded Carthage as a symbol of the planned resurrection of Africa, and it grew to a huge size – the second city of the Empire after Rome. Estimates of its population range from 200,000 to 700,000, and it was as cultured as it was cosmopolitan, with a large university. As the Empire's moral and military foundations began to tremble, Christianity became the voice of the establishment, but it was too late to halt the decline. Regarded as a typically decadent Roman city, Carthage was a natural target for Christian abuse. St Augustine lambasted a group of its citizens: "Up to very recently these effeminates were walking the streets and alleys of Carthage, their hair reeking with ointment, their faces powdered white, with enervated bodies moving along like women, and even soliciting the man on the street for sustenance of their dissolute lives."

Although the Vandals and Byzantines tried to keep up the imperial lifestyle, time was running out. The Arab invaders made almost as thorough a job of destroying Carthage

---

CARTHAGE IN LEGEND

Carthage (*Qart Hadasht*, or "New City") was founded, according to legend, in 814 BC by Phoenicians from the eastern Mediterranean. One of a number of such settlements on the North African coast, it gradually became the most important, especially after a 507 BC treaty with Rome banned foreign shipping from the others.

According to a myth that plays on the Phoenicians' celebrated commercial astuteness, their queen, **Dido**, landed on the North African coast and requested as much territory as could be enclosed by an ox hide. The request willingly granted, she proceeded to cut the hide into a long strip that gave her room for a city. According to Books 1 and 4 of Virgil's epic poem the *Aeneid*, **Aeneas** – sole survivor of the Greek destruction of Troy and charged by the gods with a mission to found a new Troy in Italy – turned up while she was building the city. Taken in and sheltered by Dido, Aeneas became increasingly torn between his divine mission and his love for the Carthaginian queen. All this was probably intended as high-class propaganda to explain the rivalry between Rome and Carthage, and Rome's superiority. But Virgil found himself unable to depict Aeneas as the sort of brainless Roman hero required by the official line, and the episode became the first classic tragic love story in European literature. Historically there's no chance of it being true, as Troy was destroyed five centuries before Carthage was built.

as the Romans had done, and what was left was carted away over the next centuries for buildings in Tunis, Kairouan and elsewhere. "In the beginning of the sixteenth century," according to Edward Gibbon, "the second Capital of the West was represented by a mosque, a college without students, twenty-five or thirty shops, and the huts of five hundred peasants, who, in their abject poverty, displayed the arrogance of the Punic senators."

The sites

The two main obstacles to excavating Carthage have been that the original city was thoroughly destroyed by the Romans in 146 BC – and what was left of the Roman city after the Vandal and Arab invasions was used either for building material or, more recently, buried under suburban housing. Nonetheless, a UNESCO-inspired project involving Tunisian, French, German, British, Canadian and American archeologists has excavated areas of the Carthaginian and Roman cities for over 5km along the shore on either side of the TGM train line.

Carthage's many sites lie scattered over an extensive area, so visiting them all on foot makes a good day's ramble. Though perfectly feasible, this can be quite forbidding in midsummer. An alternative would be to pick and choose, using the TGM wherever possible (trains run about every 20min), and perhaps combining Sidi Bou Saïd and La Marsa with a couple of sessions at Carthage. For a worthwhile abbreviated visit, you could take the TGM to Carthage Dermech for the **Carthage Museum**, which also offers a wonderful view over the Gulf; wander north to the **Villas Romaines** or **Antonine Baths**; then catch the TGM again at Carthage Hannibal to move on to Sidi Bou Saïd or back to Tunis.

Southern sites

From Carthage Salammbo station on the TGM, head down towards the sea on avenue Farhat Hached. About 200m down, rue Hannibal leads off to the left, and 50m down that on the right are the remains of the **Tophet**, or sanctuary, of the Carthaginian divinities Tanit and Baal. A rare patch of undeveloped suburban land, dug down into deep pits and scattered with Punic stelae (headstones), this conceals a lurid past. According to legend, the Carthaginians eagerly and frequently brought their children here to be ritually slaughtered. Urns containing the ashes of children have been found on the site, but the practice was almost certainly not as common as Roman propagandists would have had people believe.

The **Punic Ports** sit just 500m away, at the end of rue Hannibal (or straight down avenue 2 Mars from Byrsa TGM station). Once the foundation of Carthaginian prosperity and power, these harbours were a source of fascination, second only to Hannibal's elephants for the envious Romans. What you see today looks like two suburban ponds: the northern, circular one was the naval harbour, linked by a narrow channel (the sea opening is modern) to the rectangular merchant harbour. The best

---

CARTHAGE GLOBAL TICKETS

Entry to all the major Roman sites spread for around 6km along the coast at Carthage, as well as the Carthage and Paleo-Christian museums, is by a 5.2TD **global ticket** (camera 1TD). This is only currently available at four places: the Tophet, Carthage Museum, Antonine Baths and Villas Romaines. The sites are all open daily from 8.30am to 5.30pm in winter and 8am to 7pm in summer. The ticket is only valid for one day, so unless you're happy rushing about, you'll have to buy another to complete the tour of the sites.

way to get a sense of what it all meant is to make your way to the small building on the edge of the naval harbour, where the British excavating team have left behind a detailed scale model (times variable; free). This shows the island as one big shipyard, surrounded by slipways. One of these, left uncovered on the far side of the island, seems surprisingly small considering the awe in which Carthage's fleet was held, suggesting that a Carthaginian naval vessel was only around 34.5m long by 5m wide. There's little to see at the merchant harbour, although excavations there unearthed a wealth of the kind of trade-related material that is now displayed at the Carthage Museum.

Cross the bridge over the channel joining the two ports and you come to the recently modernized **Oceanographic Museum** (Tues–Sat 10am–1pm & 3–6pm, Sun 10am–6pm; 1TD), which first opened in 1924. The US$2.25 million refit, however, has been a sea change, with nifty interactive computer consoles as well as the usual tanks of perennially grumpy groupers and melancholic turtles. Inland on avenue Bourguiba, between Byrsa and Dermech TGM stations, is the **Paleo-Christian museum** (daily: summer 7am–7pm; winter 8am–5pm; 1.1TD), so called after some early Christian remains were unearthed here. It includes excavations and a building housing some fragments of mosaic and a statuette of Ganymede, with Jupiter in the form of an eagle, taking him heavenward to be cupbearer for the gods. There are explanations in English.

Also by Byrsa station lies Phenecia, at 27 av Bourguiba (☎01/734144, ✉katedaoud@yahoo.fr; Mon–Sat 9am–1pm & 3–7.30pm, Sun 4–7pm), a shop run by an ex-pat British woman who has lived in Tunisia for thirty years, and tries to preserve Tunisian handicrafts by travelling to remote communities where traditional arts are losing out to modern materials. The shop stocks fabulous pottery, rugs and re-invented traditional jewellery, and some great photographs.

Byrsa Hill

Byrsa Hill, where the cathedral and museum now stand, was the heart of Carthage under Punic rule and the result of Roman fury, when they sacked the city so thoroughly in 146 BC.

Outside the museum building itself, on the southern edge of the hilltop, some meagre remains are nonetheless the most extensive remnant of pre-Roman Carthage. Ironically, it was the Romans' decision to refound the city a hundred years later that helped preserve at least this much; to provide a platform for their civic centre they levelled the top of the hill, and the Punic quarters clustered around the top were buried under the rubble tipped over the sides, and saved for the meticulous French **excavations** that you can see on the southeast side. The French have uncovered a domestic quarter similar to that at Kerkouane, though here the buildings were as much as five storeys high and the streets narrow, as in the Medina. Each house had its own cistern and a rudimentary drainage system. The scorched material found above these foundations has proved that vindictive Rome did indeed burn Carthage to the ground after the siege.

You can get up the hill quite easily from Dermech or Hannibal TGM stations. From Dermech, stop for a breather on the terrace of the *Elyssa Didon* hotel, from where you can survey the whole area. Dominating the hill is the pseudo-Oriental heap of the **Cathedral of St Louis** (daily 9am–5pm; 2.5TD), built in 1890 and dedicated to the thirteenth-century French king who died at Carthage while laying unsuccessful siege to Tunis in the hope of converting the Hafsid ruler El Mustansir. "Instead of a proselyte, he found a siege", wrote Gibbon, "the French panted and died on the burning sands; Saint Louis expired in his tent". In 1930 the French Catholic Church held a grandiose conference here to proclaim a revival of Africa's great Christian tradition, which is said to have played an important part in arousing Bourguiba's nationalist feelings. The cathedral has now been leased by a private entertainments company, and is known officially as the **Acropolium**, which has already hosted a series of fascinating traditional music concerts. For details contact the Maison de la Culture Ibn Khaldoun (see p.102).

Carthage Museum

Beyond the cathedral and housed in the former headquarters of the White Fathers missionaries of wine and "Thibarine" fame (see p.35), the **Carthage Museum** (Musée National de Carthage; daily April–Sept 8am–7pm; Oct–March 8.30am–5.30pm) provides a substantial and informative display, with labels in English, detailing life at Carthage over more than a thousand years. Beware of guides here charging outrageous rates for their services.

The museum's **ground floor** contains Carthaginian and Roman sculpture, a room devoted to Christian remains, and – unusually and interestingly – a room that illustrates the complexity of current conservation techniques. You'll find the museum's prize exhibits lying side-by-side at the end of the sculpture room: a life-size man and woman, carved around the fourth century BC, each lying on top of a stone sarcophagus. The man's naturalistic head would not be out of place on the statue of a fourth-century Greek philosopher, and the fall of the woman's peplos over her upper body is similarly Greek. But the way both lie on top of the sarcophagus suggests an Etruscan influence, while the woman's coiffure and the bird's wings protectively wrapped around her lower body are both reminiscent of old Egypt. This striking blend of different Mediterranean influences is a theme that recurs throughout Tunisian culture.

Upstairs, the **Punic room** contains many similarly pan-Mediterranean items, as well as a *tophet* in which child sacrifice was carried out, a solely Carthaginian custom. There's also a case devoted to the Punic Ports, which makes an adequate substitute for a visit to the actual site by the shore if it's too hot or you have limited time. Look out in a corner of the upstairs corridor for a pair of rare early **mosaics** which demonstrate the transition from plain pink Carthaginian floors towards the Romans' later, more elaborate work. In the fourth-century BC example, found in a house near the theatre, the band of simple square tesserae is the earliest example known of true mosaic technique in the Mediterranean. Next to it, an attractive first-century AD example incorporates a black panel decorated with sections of coloured marble. In the upper floor's final room, an excellent exhibit succeeds in bringing to life the apparently dull subject of amphorae across the centuries. A garden outside the museum is crammed with architectural bric-a-brac, including – incongruously – the tombstone of Mathieu Maximilian Prosper de Lesseps, French consul general in Tunis in the early nineteenth century and brother of the builder of the Suez Canal.

Behind the hill

The **amphitheatre** below the hill, in sketchy but recognizable condition (free entry), was the site of numerous early Christian martyrdoms. Perhaps most notorious were those of SS Perpetua and Felicitas, who were brought into the arena in 203 AD, stripped naked and placed in nets. Even Romans were horrified when they saw that "one was a delicate young girl, and the other a woman fresh from childbirth with the milk still dripping from her breasts", so they were taken out to be brought back in again, dressed in unbelted tunics; Perpetua was killed by a heifer, Felicitas by a gladiator's sword.

Just over the road is a collection of huge **cisterns**, some inhabited and others decaying, which once received part of Carthage's water supply from the Zaghouan aqueduct.

The Magon Quarter and Antonine Baths

Heading directly seawards from Hannibal TGM station or up the shore from the Punic Ports, cross avenue Bourguiba and you will find the **Magon Quarter** on your right. The German excavations here are neat, tidy and well laid-out, but not really very inter-

The **Carthage International Festival** is Tunisia's biggest cultural celebration, running from June to August every year. Events of all sorts – dance, cinema, music, theatre – are staged at the restored Roman theatre (and on the terrace of the old casino in the Belvedere Park in Tunis). The events are largely in French and are well advertised on hoardings and in the press – tickets can be bought at the theatre. For details of the biennial **Carthage Film Festival**, see p.103.

esting. This residential quarter, located next to the water's edge, is named after Mago, an early king of Carthage.

A couple of blocks north, and signposted from Hannibal TGM, the **Antonine Baths** are the most extensive example of their kind in North Africa, and were once the largest in the Roman world. The entrance to the site takes you through a park full of flowers and date palms, with paths following the streets of the Roman city. You enter along Kardo 16 (a *kardo* is a north–south Roman street). Nos. 17, 15 and 14 run parallel, and all are crossed after two blocks by Decumanus (east–west street) 4. Left from the entrance is the bunker-like doorway to a little seventh-century Christian **chapel**, complete with mosaics, which has been moved here from elsewhere. The contrast between this secret cave – built about the time that the Arabs swept in from the east – and the expansive self-confidence of the Roman baths down on the beach needs no further comment. Further on, a *schola*, or young men's club, is identifiable by an unusual mosaic showing children at some sort of ritual exercise; and further still up the hill is the Byzantine **basilica of Douimes**, in which was found a poignant inscription from the Epistle to the Romans: "If the Lord is with us, who can be against us?"

The **baths** themselves are down on the beach. Once again it's a case of using your imagination, since what remains is only the basement level of a massive complex – it's almost impossible to convey the original size. The central pool alone was as big as an Olympic swimming pool, and when the curved public latrines were first discovered they were taken for a theatre. None of the original mosaics or statuary decorating the public areas have survived, but the complex remains a potent symbol of Roman imperial presence.

Next to the site is a modern **presidential palace**, whose soldiers do not like cameras to be pointed at it.

The Villas Romaines and northern sites

Heading inland from the baths, cross avenue Bourguiba, carry on under the train line and the **Villas Romaines** site is 50m up on the right. It's really little more than a series of foundations of Roman villas and an "Antiquarium" where a few stunted columns and statues have been collected to make a foreground for photographs of the gulf. The sight of modern villas below is hardly new – over 1500 years ago wealthy Tunisians and expatriates were already making this idyllic stretch of coast their own. Right on top of the hill are the bare foundations of the Roman **Odeon**, a type of theatre.

A little further up the road on the same side is the Roman **theatre**, extensively restored for the modern Carthage Festival (see box) and bearing scant resemblance to the original. Carthage's theatres became infamous for the immorality they portrayed and encouraged; several hundred years later a Christian critic wrote of the last days of the African Empire: "The arms of Barbarian people were resounding against the walls of Carthage; and yet the Christian population was going wild in the theatres and enjoying itself in the circuses. Some were having their throats cut outside the walls; others were fornicating inside the walls."

Across the street, a small **archeological garden**, with a few Roman odds and ends, might be a good place for a breather. Further up, a **"building with columns"**, or what's left of it, may be the Baths of Gargilius where St Augustine called a conference of bishops in 411 to trick the dissident Donatist church into being a party to its own prohibition.

Taking a right at the building with columns – or, from the Villas Romaines site, climbing over a fence on the far side of the Odeon and cutting across the fields – brings you to the **Damous el Karita Basilica**, at 64.5m long and nine aisles wide, the largest ancient church known in North Africa. Though little more remains than a ground plan and rows of broken grey columns, there is at least a superficial similarity between this forest of columns and the one built only a few hundred years later in the prayer hall of the Great Mosque at Kairouan – perhaps even incorporating material from here. Another example of continuity is this site's name: an Arabic transliteration of the Latin *Domus Caritatis* (House of Grace).

The **American cemetery** (daily 8am–5pm) beyond – cross the road and take a short cut between the fields on the other side – presents an interesting contrast in style to the British, French and German cemeteries elsewhere in the country. Most Americans killed in action in Tunisia during World War II are buried here and, in contrast to the Commonwealth cemeteries, it goes all out for size and grandeur. The caretaker is something of an authority on the war in Tunisia. Close by, to the northeast, are the scant ruins of an old Byzantine church, the **Basilica Majorum**, and, east of here across the train line, another old Byzantine basilica, alleged to be the **Basilica of St Cyprian**.

Practicalities

The Roman sites lie between Carthage Salammbo and Carthage Amilcar stations on the **TGM** line that runs parallel to the coast, with regular twenty-minute services that take around thirty minutes from Tunis. There are not many places to **stay** in Carthage, and nowhere cheap at all. Most inviting is the two-star *Résidence Carthage* (☎01/731799, 🖷720135; ➎) at 16 rue Hannibal, near the Tophet, which has a rather classy restaurant. You might consider full board, which is only 7.5TD more. The three-star *Hôtel Elyssa Didon*, rue Mendès France, on Byrsa Hill (☎01/733433; ➎) is a much more grandiose affair, priced accordingly, but only worth the difference for the view. The three-star *Hôtel Amilcar* (☎01/740788; ➏), on the beach up towards Sidi Bou Saïd, enjoys a good location, but is mainly used for package tours.

Sidi Bou Saïd and around   سيدي بو سعيد

Somehow, **SIDI BOU SAÏD**, a few kilometres north of Carthage, shrugs off its two and a half centuries as a tourist trap and remains a place of extraordinary charm. Today, it's a favourite retreat for the wealthy, but even on summer evenings you can have Sidi Bou to yourself by wandering through the silent backstreets past white, cubic houses and their blue studded doors.

You certainly won't see such a concentration of wealthy residents and visitors anywhere else in Tunisia, as Sidi Bou is as chic as they come. It seems that every artist and every writer who has visited Tunisia spent some time here, including Cervantes, Paul Klee, Simone de Beauvoir, André Gide and Jean Foucault. In 1939 Sacheverell Sitwell was told that Sidi Bou Saïd was the finest town in all Tunisia in which to see harem ladies in their silken dresses, but gold jewellery and tanned flesh are more the style now, especially around the expensive and rather snooty *Café des Nattes* in the main square.

The first building on this strategic cliff-top was a ribat or monastic fortress built in the early years of Arab rule, part of the chain stretching through Sousse and Monastir to Tripoli in Libya and over whose foundations a modern lighthouse is built. The village grew up around the tomb and *zaouia* of the thirteenth-century holy man Sidi Bou Saïd, still celebrated in the central **mosque** and during the August festival in his honour. According to one inventive but unlikely story, the saint was none other than St Louis, fresh from defeat at Carthage (see p.113), who retired here incognito to marry a local girl. Around the beginning of the twentieth century the village was discovered by wealthy French and other expatriates, who bought houses and went to great lengths to "preserve" the town's character. As a result, there's very little here that is not Tunisian in origin – and nowhere else in Tunisia quite like it. One of the grandest of these houses is **Dar Ennejma Ezzahra** (1912–22; Tues–Sun: summer 9am–noon & 4–7pm; winter 9am–1pm & 2–5pm; 3TD) the French Baron Rodolphe d'Erlanger's monumental and exquisitely beautiful folly which now houses the Centre of Arab and Mediterranean Music. Beside the gardens and architecture, a mixture of "pure" Tunisian and Romantic Orientalism, the main attraction is its collection of musical instruments, though you have to buy their guidebook (20TD) to put them into context. A dedicated musicologist, the Baron was one of the moving spirits behind the important inaugural Congress on Arab Music, held in Cairo in 1932, which was the first time that Arab music had been treated as a whole and as a cultural heritage worthy of both study and preservation. For those interested there's a research institute here, but for a more immediate example there are sometimes rare performances of "endangered" music. Information about performances can be obtained from the Maison de la Culture Ibn Khaldoun in Tunis (see p.102). Another opulent Tunisian house that can be visited is **Dar el Annabi** (Tues–Sun 9am–6.30pm; 3TD). It's on the left hand side half way up from place 7 Novembre to the *Café des Nattes*. Originally owned by a local *mufti* (religious leader), the house passed to his son who served as a minister under Bourguiba. Some of its 55 rooms are still lived in by the present owner, the *mufti*'s grandson, a cardiologist. The house has a wonderful terrace from which you can enjoy panoramic views over the town and gulf, a pleasant courtyard garden in which to sip mint tea and several beautiful rooms complete with eerily realistic mannequins in everyday poses.

A left off place 7 Novembre up rue Dr H. Thameur takes you to the town's main square, from where rue Hedi Zarrouk continues on to end at **Cap Carthage**; on a clear day, you can see right across the bay to Korbous. Below, the rain has exposed several fragments of **Punic flooring**, indicating the presence of villas here even in the third century BC.

Practicalities

The **TGM** from Tunis (every 20min; 35min) leaves you a five- to ten-minute walk from the town centre uphill towards the sea. Turn right from the station and walk until you reach place 7 Novembre; just off the square is a **bank**, the **post office** and a Magasin Général **supermarket**. From place 7 Novembre head up the hill to the small square dominated by the steps of the *Café des Nattes* and the minaret rising picturesquely behind it. There's no budget **accommodation** in Sidi Bou Saïd, but you'll find some excellent little retreats in pleasant contrast to the noise and grime of Tunis. Be aware, however, that everywhere here is booked up months in advance in season, so plan ahead. The most economical option is the unclassed *Hôtel Sidi Bou Farés* (☎ & ℱ01/740091; ❸), in the stairway of the same name off the main square. It's set around a fragrant fig tree branching over a peaceful patio and its owner is something of a musician. Also off the main square, on rue el Hedi Zarrouk, is the recently renovated and excellent four-star former palace, *Dar Said* (☎01/729666; ❼), with charming rooms, wonderful views and a small pool. Another four-star, the *Hôtel Sidi Bou Saïd* (☎01/740411; ❻), around the cape past the lighthouse and about a 1km out of town, has high-class accommodation and enjoys good views.

Eating in Sidi Bou Saïd isn't cheap. For budget meals you'll have to trek to place 7 Novembre and its *gargotes* and sandwich bars, especially the *Bagatelle,* 9 av Bourguiba, which has good local specialities. The cheapest choice in the old town is the reasonable *Restaurant Chergui* (daily: winter noon–6pm, summer noon–midnight), rue el Hedi Zarrouk, with a pleasant rear terrace, where you can enjoy a meal for around 10TD. Otherwise, *Au Bon Vieux Temps* (daily noon–3pm & 6–10pm), further along at no. 56, is swish and expensive, with meals for around 20TD, and offers superb views from its dining room. The *Dar Zarroukh* opposite the *Dar Said* hotel is currently being renovated, but will, no doubt, be expensive, and worth a visit when it re-opens. *Pirates* (daily noon–3pm & 6–9pm, later in summer), by the harbour, is set amongst pleasant gardens and serves up a variety of dishes, though specializes in seafood (meals 15–20TD); if you're staying in town the walk back up will easily burn off any calories acquired during the meal. For hanging out with the beau monde, the *Café des Nattes* in the main square may be at the heart of the scene, though the café at the bottom of its infamous steps is cheaper. But the place to really chill out is the *Café Sidi Chabaane,* further on along rue el Hadi Zarrouk. A steep series of narrow terraces set spectacularly in the cliff overlooking the gulf, it's the perfect place in town to relax in romantic company with a glass of pine-nut tea. Doughnut fans should try a *bonbalouni* from the stall just past the *Café des Nattes.*

La Marsa

المرسى

LA MARSA, next in the long chain of suburbs along the northern shore, is a place of some antiquity. In past centuries, when transport was less easy, the entire court moved out here for the summer. "It is adorned with a royal palace, and pleasant places," wrote John Ogilby in 1670, "whither the rulers of Tunis in the summer go to take their pleasure, and keep their court." Behind the post office are the remains of an early **palace**, but in the nineteenth century, when the last of Tunisia's independent Beys favoured La Marsa, many other Beylical palaces and those of their ministers were built inland – two of the best are the residences of the British and French ambassadors, both sadly inaccessible.

Today La Marsa is easy to get to on the TGM and, in summer, has become a weekend resort for all of Tunis, or so it seems. The long **beach**, with an attractive palm-lined corniche road, is what draws the crowds and, though it is slightly less crowded than those further down, you still feel like a lemming.

Practicalities

La Marsa is quite a large town compared with Sidi Bou Saïd. From the **TGM station** (services from Tunis every 20min; 45min), at the southern end of the corniche, follow the road up to avenue Bourguiba, heading off to the left to place 7 Novembre, where you'll find the **post office**, **banks**, Tunisair, **pharmacies**, and **buses** #20, #20d and #20g to Tunis. Bus #40 for Gammarth leaves from the TGM station and can be picked up along the corniche. If you want to surf the net whilst you're in La Marsa, Le Net Club (Mon–Sat 10am–midnight, Sun noon–midnight; 2TD/hr) on rue Cheikh Zarroukh, 200 metres down towards the sea off avenue Bourguiba, will serve the purpose.

Should you want to **stay** here, options are limited. *Pension Prendl,* 7 rue Mohamed Salah Melki (☎01/749529; ❸), is off avenue Bourguiba about 300m from place 7 Novembre. Not the easiest place to find, it compensates with the cosiest family atmosphere of any pension in Tunisia. Alternatively, there's the *Hôtel Plaza Corniche* at 22 rue du Maroc (☎01/743577; ❺), five minutes' walk from the station back towards Sidi Bou Saïd. Officially also a pension, it gets booked solid in season, so call ahead. There's also a *Maison des Jeunes* (☎01/774074) at the northern end of the beach.

La Marsa's cheap **restaurants** are off the corniche around the avenue 20 Mars arcade. The restaurants *el Hana* and *du Peuple* are budget-priced (daily 8am–9.30pm), as is *La Plage* (daily 10am–9pm) on rue Mongi Slim. Twenty metres further up, just beyond where the Corniche crosses above, the *Restaurant Mexicane* serves up moderately priced pizzas and the like (Tues–Sun noon–3pm & 6–9pm) amidst bits and pieces of americana and a mounted wild boar's head, though nothing particularly Mexican. Where rue Mongi Slim meets the sea is the *Koubet El Haoua*, an amazing piece of art deco that looks like it escaped from Brighton pier; it's currently closed for renovations but should re-open as a Tunisian speciality restaurant sometime in the future. Next to the TGM is a *Baguette & Baguette* (daily 8am–8pm), part of a trendy new sandwich chain where you can get a combo (sandwich, fries and a drink) for around 3TD. Upmarket places include the *Hôtel Plaza Corniche*'s restaurant. The most interesting place in town for a mint tea or Turkish coffee is the *Café Saf Saf*, opposite the mosque at the end of avenue 20 Mars, whose terraces surround a public well dating back to the Hafsid period. If you're lucky you might see a camel working the wheel, but the *Saf Saf* has clearly declined since the memorable performances of the tragic chanteuse Habiba Msika in the 1920s (see p.269).

Gammarth and Raouad Beach

GAMMARTH (bus #20b from Jardin Thameur in Tunis, or #40 from La Marsa, 6TD by taxi from Tunis) is the next instalment of suburb along the northern coastline. It grew up around the series of beaches dubbed **Baies des Singes** (Bays of the Monkeys) by local fishermen – reputedly after the Europeans who sunbathed in the nude there in the 1950s. Up on the hill is the **cemetery** of the Free French killed during World War II.

Gammarth's **hotels** are fairly expensive and, really, if you want to spend several days by the beach Hammamet, Sousse or Jerba are better destinations. It's a strange mixture of average package-tour places and hideous five-star carbuncles. There's no budget accommodation. Least offensive is the small five-star *Abou Nawas Gammarth* just out of town on the coast road to the headland of Cap Carthage (℡01/741444; ❼) with all the creature comforts. By the shore, the three-star *Megara* (℡01/740366; ❻) is in a nice location but slightly dilapidated and rather overpriced. One kilometre further on, and rounding the cape, is the five-star *Le Palace* (℡01/912000, ℻911442; ❼), rigged with all the state-of-the-art fittings and eight restaurants if you can stomach the impersonal architecture. Further along, the main road turns inland whilst the potholed old Route Touristique veers off back to the coast. Here are cheaper package-type three-star options, including the *Cap Carthage Méditerranée* (℡01/740064, ℻741980; ❹), which has tennis courts and a host of activities, and the slightly more personable *Hôtel Karim* (℡01/742188, ℻741200; ❼). In Gammarth itself there is the one-star *La Tour Blanche* (℡01/271697, ℻747247; ❹), which is the cheapest of the lot.

For restaurants there's the *Les Dunes*, a lovely villa with seaviews up towards the Cape from *Hôtel Megara*, or the fractionally cheaper but equally good *Les Ombrelles* just before *Les Dunes* on the beach; The *Sindbad*, just next door, is popular with young chic folk (all three are open daily noon–3pm and 6pm until at least 10pm, and will cost upwards of 20TD for a meal). For real budget fare the no-frills *gargotes* are your best bet.

Beyond Gammarth, civilization is almost at an end. The road runs between a salt flat and **Raouad Beach** (#40 bus from La Marsa or Gammarth), a broad expanse of sand where families camp en masse in summer. As there are few, if any, facilities, the water becomes almost visibly unhygienic in the peak season. You could camp out or look for a place at a holiday village such as *La Noria* (℡01/746348, ℻743337; ❹), but frankly there are much more attractive places in Tunisia to do this.

The southern suburbs

Easily reached by **train** from Tunis's main station on place Barcelone (daily every 20–30min; 5am–midnight), the suburbs along the **southern shore** of the gulf are for the most part shapeless areas of less affluent commuter housing, with warehouses and light industry filling the gaps between what were once smart resorts. **Hammam Lif**, however, retains a down-at-heel allure and the **German World War II military cemetery** at Borj Cedria is a curiosity.

Hammam Lif   حمام النف

Once the last stage on the caravan route from the south, where merchants paid tax before entering the capital, **HAMMAM LIF** was a popular spa in Carthaginian and Roman days, and emerged again as a resort under the Protectorate. By far the busiest and most established of Tunis Gulf resorts, it's a pleasant place to pass a few days in. Palm-lined avenues and an old seafront casino give the town a seedy sort of allure in its dramatic setting under Jebel Bou Kornine, but it rarely throws off its rather listless, Sunday-afternoon feel – except on Sunday, the market day, which is the busiest time of the week. The *Casino* is now a **bar/restaurant** – an excellent place to pop in for a beer and where women need have no worries. As for the decor, as one writer remarked, it's like "Elvis on acid". If you want time to inspect this display, you can **stay** at the unclassified *Bon Repos*, 14 rue Ibn Rochd (☎01/291458; ❷).

Jebel Bou Kornine   جبل بو قرنين

The imposing two-pronged mountain of **Bou Kornine**, heavily forested lower down but with a more open maquis vegetation at the top, is theoretically a national park. In practice, it has become a military zone and you are liable – though unlikely – to be arrested if you try to go further than the *Chalet Vert* restaurant, about 1km up the hill and with a fine view north over the Gulf of Tunis. A road leads up to the restaurant from the main Tunis road, a few hundred metres towards Tunis from Hammam Lif. Walking beyond the restaurant, it's another hour or so along good paths to near the top before the paths begin to lose themselves and disappear.

Borj Cedria   برج السّدريّة

BORJ CEDRIA is the last desultory resort before Soliman Plage. Just beyond it, turning off the main road, there's a discreet sign pointing a few hundred metres inland to the **Deutscher Soldaten Friedhof**, a German military cemetery from World War II. Built in 1975 on a slight rise near the site of the final German surrender, this grim collection of rectangular lockers represents yet another approach to the issue of the World War II dead, a stark contrast to British pastoral, American razzmatazz and French militarism.

travel details

Trains

Tunis to: Béja (6 daily; 1hr 50min–2hr 10min); Bir Bou Regba (7–12 daily; 50min); Bizerte (4 daily; 1 hr 25min–1hr 40min); Borj Cedria (every 20min; 45min); Bou Kornine (every 20min; 20min); Dahmani (3 daily; 3hr 50min); El Fahs (4 daily; 1hr

30min); El Jem (4–6 daily; 2hr 50min); Enfida (4–6 daily; 1hr 15min); Ez Zahra (every 20min; 25min); Gaafour (3 daily; 2hr 15min); Gabès (2–3 daily; 6hr 20min–6hr 40min); Gafsa (2 daily; 7hr 45min); Ghardimaou via Medjez el Bab (4 daily; 1hr–1hr 15min); Hammam Lif (every 20min; 25min); Hammamet (2 direct daily and 4–6 daily connecting at Bir Bou Regba; 1hr 15min–1hr 45min); Jendouba (4 daily; 2hr 30min–2hr 45min); Kalaa Khasbah (1 daily; 5hr); Mahdia (2 daily; 3hr 40min–4hr); Mateur (4 daily; 1–1hr 25min); Metlaoui (2 daily; 8–8hr 30min); Monastir (4 daily, 2hr 30min–3hr 10min); Nabeul (1–2 direct daily and 4–6 daily connecting at Bir Bou Regba; 1hr 20min–1hr 50min); Radès (every 20min; 20min); Sfax (6–8 daily; 3hr 25–40min); Sousse (10–12 daily; 1hr 50min–2hr 20min); Tinja (4 daily; 1hr 20min).

TGM line (every 20–30min) to: Carthage (20min); La Goulette (15min); La Marsa (40min); Sidi Bou Saïd (30min).

Buses

The terminals in Tunis at Bab Aleoua (or Bab el Fellah) and Bab Saadoun serve almost every town of any size in the country at least once a day. **Bab Saadoun** mostly serves the north and parts of the Tell; **Bab Aleoua** serves the rest of the country, principally the south, and international destinations.

Tunis Bab Saadoun to: Aïn Draham (4 daily; 4hr); Béja (14 daily; 2hr); Bizerte (every 30min; 1hr 30min); Ghar el Melh (2 daily; 2hr); Jendouba (6 daily; 3hr); Le Kef (12 daily; 3hr); Mateur (hourly; 1hr 30min); Medjez el Bab (every 30min; 1hr); Menzel Bourguiba (hourly; 1hr 30min); Raf Raf (2 daily; 2hr); Ras Jebel (5 daily; 2hr); Tabarka (16 daily; 4hr); Téboursouk (6 daily; 2hr 20min); Testour (hourly; 1hr).

Tunis Bab Aleoua (Bab el Fellah) to: Douz (3 daily; 8hr); Enfida (hourly; 1hr 30min); Gabès (18 daily; 6hr 30min); Gafsa (10 daily; 5hr 30min); Grombalia (every 20min; 1hr); Hammamet (hourly; 1hr 30min); El Haouaria (7 daily; 3hr); Jerba (4 daily; 8hr 30min); El Jem (5 daily; 3hr 45min); Kairouan (10 daily; 2hr 30min); Kasserine (8 daily; 5hr); Kebili (3 daily; 7hr); Kélibia (hourly; 2hr 30min); Korba (every 30min; 2hr); Korbous (4 daily; 3hr); Maktar (4 daily; 3hr); Mahdia (2 daily; 4hr); Matmata (1 daily, summer only; 7hr); Medenine (8 daily; 8hr); Nabeul (every

30min; 1hr 30min); Nefta (2 daily, summer only; 7hr 30min); Ras Ajdir (1 daily; 10hr); Sbeïtla (4 daily; 4hr); Sfax (11 daily; 5hr); Sidi Bou Zid (4 daily; 5hr); Sousse (7 daily; 2hr 30min); Tozeur (5 daily; 7hr); Tripoli in Libya (1 daily; 15hr); Zaghouan (7 daily; 1hr).

Louages

Louage journey times are roughly three-quarters the time taken by buses on the same route. Frequency depends on demand, but morning is always the best time to get a louage, especially for longer journeys.

*Services to Hammamet and Cap Bon leave from opposite **Bab Aleoua** bus station. Northern destinations depart from the louage station next to **Bab Saadoun** bus station. All other destinations leave from the vast warehouse adjacent to Souk Moncef Bey on avenue **Moncef Bey**. International louages to Tripoli in Libya depart from **Garage Ayachi** at Bab Souika (see Medina map pp.76–77), whilst services to Algeria leave from **rue al Jazira** at place de la Victoire.*

Tunis Bab Saadoun to: Aïn Draham (4hr); Béja (1hr 45min); Bizerte (1hr 30min); Ghar el Melh (2hr); Jendouba (3hr); Mateur (1hr 30min); Medjez el Bab (1hr); Menzel Bourguiba (1hr 30min); Raf Raf (2hr); Ras Jebel (2hr); Tabarka (4hr); Testour (1hr).

Tunis Bab Aleoua to: Enfida (1hr 30min); Gabès (6hr 30min); Gafsa (5hr); Grombalia (1hr); Hammamet (1hr 30min); El Haouaria (1hr 45min); Jerba (8hr 30min); Kebili (7hr); Kélibia (2hr 30min); Korba (2hr); Korbous (3hr); Maktar (3hr); Matmata (7hr); Medenine (7hr 30min); Nabeul (1hr 30min); Ras Ajdir (10hr); Sbeïtla (4hr); Sfax (4hr 30min); Sousse (2hr); Tozeur (6hr).

Tunis Moncef Bey to: Kairouan (2hr); Kasserine (5hr); Le Kef (3hr); El Jem (occasional, 2hr 45min); Monastir (2hr 20min); Sidi Bou Zid (4hr); Tataouine (8hr); Téboursouk (2hr); Zaghouan (45min); Zarzis (9hr).

Tunis rue al Jazira to: Annaba in Algeria (5hr 30min).

Tunis Garage Ayachi to: Tripoli in Libya (13hr).

Ferries

Tunis La Goulette to: Cagliari (1 weekly; 21hr); Genoa (1–5 weekly; 27hr), La Spezia (summer only, 1 weekly, 24hr), Marseille (2–4 weekly; 24hr), Naples (1–2 weekly; 19hr), Nice (occasional; 24hr), Toulon (occasional; 24hr), Trápani (2–3 weekly; 8–12hr).

Flights

Tunis Carthage Airport to: Gafsa (40min; 2 weekly); Jerba (1hr; 6 weekly); Sfax (45min; 4 weekly); Tozeur (1hr; 1 daily).

CHAPTER TWO

HAMMAMET AND CAP BON

Protruding like a crooked finger into the Mediterranean, the Cap Bon peninsula is Tunisia's main resort area. Indeed, glancing at the brochures – with their staggering hotel capacities – it looks a little ominous, particularly along the coast from Hammamet to Nabeul. But although Hammamet, the best-known resort in the country, has been heavily developed, images of a Spanish-like *costa*, with tourists crowded in like cattle, don't apply. The beaches, for a start, are too big and too luxuriant, and the hotels are kept discreetly down to a few storeys, strung out along the tree-lined shore. Half an hour away, Nabeul has less perfect beaches and a less glamorous image, but cheaper places to stay, and good transport links for visiting other areas of the peninsula.

Among these areas, one of the most worthwhile targets is **El Haouaria**, a village at the end of the peninsula with the twin attractions of a remote white strand and a cavern full of bats. **Kerkouane**, around the coast from here, is the largest Carthaginian site yet uncovered, while **Kélibia**, a few kilometres on and dominated by a massive Spanish castle, is the quietest beach resort on the east coast. Over on the north coast of the peninsula, the ancient spa of **Korbous** is the best-known lure, but it's now heavily commercialized; if you're after seclusion and have transport, however, the coast beyond is literally one long and as yet undiscovered beach.

The peninsula is at its best in spring, when it becomes a mass of colour with its fruit orchards and vineyards. If you can make it in April or May, try to coincide with the Orange Festival at **Menzel Bou Zelfa**. By September the ground is parched – although liquid compensation is afforded by the wine festival at **Grombalia**.

Nabeul is the main centre for **road transport** in Cap Bon and anyone visiting the peninsula will probably pass through here. Alternative access is by **rail**: both Grombalia and Bir Bou Regba are on the main Tunis–Gabès line, the latter having a branch-line connection at Nabeul and Hammamet.

MARKET DAYS

Monday – Kélibia
Tuesday – Menzel Temime
Thursday – Hammamet, El Haouaria, Maamoura (near Nabeul), Menzel Bou Zelfa

Friday – Nabeul
Saturday – Soliman
Sunday – Béni Khiar (near Nabeul), Dar Chaâbane (also near Nabeul), Korba

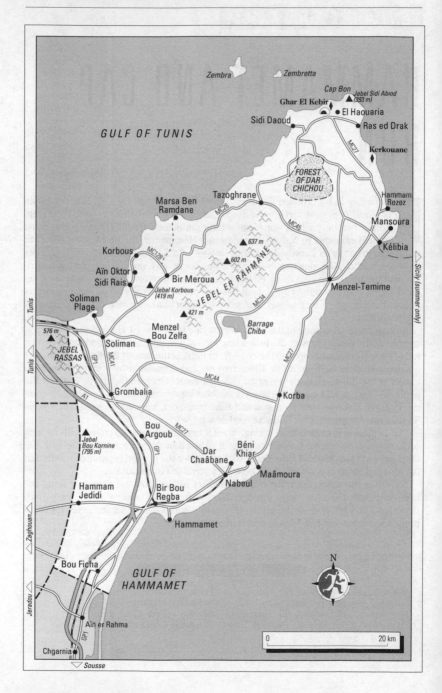

ACCOMMODATION PRICE CODES

The hotels and pensions listed in this book have been price-graded according to the following scale. The prices quoted are for the **cheapest available double room in high season**. For more on accommodation prices and categories, see Basics, p.29.

❶ Under 10TD
❷ 10–20TD
❸ 20–40TD
❹ 40–70TD
❺ 70–100TD
❻ 100–150TD
❼ 150TD upwards

Hammamet

At the beginning of the twentieth century **HAMMAMET**, some 60km southeast of Tunis, was a small fishing village making some extra money by selling lemons from its dense citrus groves to Sicily for export to America. It was not until the 1920s, with the arrival of Romanian millionaire Georges Sebastian, that the town found its true vocation. Sebastian built a fabulous villa just above the beach, described by Frank Lloyd Wright as the most beautiful house he knew. Others followed, and soon Hammamet was part of the Orientalist legend of a sensual Tunisia – somewhere between an intellectual resort and a luxurious bohemia for Europe's prewar moneyed classes. Today, with more than eighty hotels and almost thirty thousand beds, Hammamet is considerably less exclusive. If you're not bothered by being surrounded with burger bars, pizza joints and carpet shops, then there's a lot to be said for Hammamet as a beach resort. However, if tourist zones like this turn you off, then give it a wide berth and head further south – to Mahdia, for example – or else into the Cap Bon peninsula, for less crowded beaches.

Arrival, information and accommodation

Hammamet's two main streets begin at the Medina, with **avenue de la République** heading towards Nabeul, and becoming **avenue de la Libération** further along, and **avenue Bourguiba** going inland towards the **train station**. The **bus station** is right opposite the **post office** on avenue de la République. Arriving by **louage**, you'll be dropped in a triangular square 50m west of *Hôtel Khella* and avenue de la République. If you're heading straight for Hammamet Sud (see below), buses and louages also stop near the motorway turn-off on the P1 Tunis–Sousse road by *Hôtel Samaris*, which means a short taxi ride. The Syndicat d'Initiative **tourist information office** is in a small building on avenue Bourguiba facing the beach (Tues–Sun: July & Aug 7.30am–10pm, rest of the year 9am–noon & 3–6pm; ☎02/262891). A larger ONTT office (Mon–Sat: July & Aug 7.30am–7.30pm, Sept–June 8.30am–6pm; ☎02/280423) is round the corner on avenue de la République. Neither is all that helpful, though both have maps and the ONTT has accommodation price listings.

Most of Hammamet's **hotels** are spread out for kilometres along the beach in both directions from town in the *zones touristiques* of Hammamet Nord, Hammamet Plage (just south of town) and Hammamet Sud. Places in town are cheaper and more convenient for transport if you want to do more than lounge on the beach, and prices for all plunge spectacularly in winter, sometimes a third of high-season rates.

About 2km west of the town centre the most attractive patch of beach begins to curve away from Hammamet Sud, with a view of the Medina on its point. In the opposite direction, it's about 17km northeast to Nabeul, the route lined with hotels in the same way,

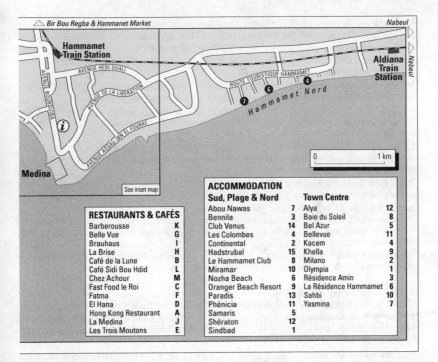

ACCOMMODATION

Sud, Plage & Nord		Town Centre	
Abou Nawas	7	Alya	12
Bennila	3	Baie du Soleil	8
Club Venus	14	Bel Azur	5
Les Colombes	4	Bellevue	11
Continental	2	Kacem	4
Hadstrubal	15	Khella	9
Le Hammamet Club	8	Milano	2
Miramar	10	Olympia	1
Nozha Beach	6	Résidence Amin	3
Oranger Beach Resort	9	La Résidence Hammamet	6
Paradis	13	Sahbi	10
Phénicia	11	Yasmina	7
Samaris	5		
Shératon	12		
Sindbad	1		

RESTAURANTS & CAFÉS	
Barberousse	K
Belle Vue	G
Brauhaus	I
La Brise	H
Café de la Lune	B
Café Sidi Bou Hdid	L
Chez Achour	M
Fast Food le Roi	C
Fatma	F
El Hana	D
Hong Kong Restaurant	A
La Medina	J
Les Trois Moutons	E

although we've listed fewer, as the beach here is more exposed and less attractive. Most hotels will organize excursions, many of which are rather antiseptic, but still the easiest way to see the sights of the town if time is limited. Outside Cap Bon, trips can range from a half-day to several days to the usual destinations of Kairouan, Sousse, Tozeur and Matmata.

Hotels and pensions

The three-star (and above) beach hotels generally offer good, en-suite rooms equipped with satellite television, telephones and air conditioning, as well as reasonable restaurants serving international rather than Tunisian cuisine. Unless otherwise mentioned, hotels include breakfast in their room prices.

HAMMAMET CENTRE

Alya ★★, 30 rue Ali Belhouane ☎02/280218, ℱ282365. A tastefully done place, but overpriced in summer. Ask for a room with a view of the nearby Medina. **④**

Baie du Soleil Vacation Village, av Assad Ibn el Fourat ☎02/280298. Quiet, leafy and right on the beach just east of the centre. Consider taking half- or full board, which isn't much more than paying for the rooms. **④**

Bel Azur ★★★, av Assad Ibn el Fourat ☎02/280544, ℱ280275. Part of the Sol Azur Beach Complex and more expensive than most three-stars, but high-quality, with landscaped gardens and its own beach, and offering boat trips and water sports. **⑥**

Bellevue ★★, av Assad Ibn el Fourat ☎02/281121, ℱ283156. Seafront location close to the Medina, with most rooms overlooking the sea. Pleasant, modern, and newly renovated, but fills up in season. **④**

Kacem ★★★, av Bourguiba ☎02/279580, Ⓕ279588. Smaller than *Yasmina*, with whom it shares the beach, and cheaper, with the advantage of small kitchenettes in the rooms as well as fridges. Facilities include two pools, a gym and a rooftop barbecue area. ❺

Khella ★★, av de la République ☎02/283900, Ⓕ283704. A new place, similar to the *Sahbi* and just north of it on the same street. Fair value. ❹

Milano, rue des Fontaines ☎02/280768. A small, newly renovated pension not far from the beach west of the centre. Clean and more personable than the larger package places. ❹

Olympia ★★, av du Kowait ☎02/280662. Rather package-oriented and on a busy road, but perfectly adequate and quite inexpensive by Hammamet standards. The closest hotel to the train station. ❹

La Résidence Hammamet ★★★, 72 av Bourguiba ☎02/280406 or 280733, Ⓕ280396. Only 300m from the Medina and even nearer to the beach. Four people sharing one of the larger rooms get a better deal. ❺

Résidence Amin ★★★, av de la Libération ☎02/278397. A new place run by the affable Ramdane Kochkache with enormous and tastefully decorated rooms that sleep two to five people. ❹

Sahbi ★★, av de la République, opposite the bus station ☎02/280807, Ⓕ280134. One of Hammamet's cheapest, and described in their brochure as "Moorish style" (no doubt referring to its colossal carpet shop). The rooms are big, clean, prettily furnished and good value. Fills up with package tourists in summer. ❹

Yasmina ★★★, av Bourguiba, opposite *La Résidence Hammamet* ☎02/280222, Ⓕ280593. Rather expensive with modern en-suite rooms and a nice garden. ❻

HAMMAMET PLAGE

Hammamet Plage, the nearest southern "resort" of the town centre, beginning 2km and stretching 4km from the Medina, is within walking distance if you can stand the heat. Hotels here are generally more downmarket, and cheaper than at Hammamet Sud.

Bennila ★★, av des Nations-Unies ☎02/280356. Small pension beyond the International Cultural Centre. Set well back from the beach, but rooms are clean and cheap, and there's a pool. Closed Nov–April. ❹

Continental ★★★, av des Nations-Unies ☎02/261894, Ⓕ281667. Right on the beach. Early 1970s package hotel now showing its age, but close enough (under 2km) to the town centre to walk. The restaurant serves reasonable international fare, but the pool is indoors. ❺

Le Hammamet Club ★★★, rue des Hôtels ☎02/280366, Ⓕ280366. Between the *Oranger Beach Resort* and the *Miramar*, this hotel has no beach frontage, but is good value, especially in winter and with half board. Facilities include two pools (indoor & outdoor), fitness centre, spa pool and sauna. ❺

Miramar ★★★★, rue des Hôtels ☎02/280344, Ⓕ280586. Three hotels in one; the oldest, dating from 1959, is slightly worn and thus cheaper than the two much nicer new wings, comprising bungalows and apartments with cooking facilities. The garden leads to the beach, where you'll find a full range of aquatic activities and boat trips. ❼

Sindbad ★★★★★, av des Nations-Unies ☎02/280122, Ⓕ280004. Five-star comfort west of the centre, before the International Cultural Centre. Horse rides and boat trips are offered along with all mod cons as well as a Moorish bath and tennis courts. ❼

HAMMAMET SUD

This is the most extensive run of hotels, 5–7km from the centre, most blessed with maturing, shaded gardens. The more exclusive hotels have courtesy buses into town; otherwise you can catch a taxi. Even further south, 10–12km or so from town, is the fledgling purpose-built resort of Yasmine (confusingly also called Hammamet Sud), where construction is underway on a 700-berth marina, due to open in 2003. There are already several massive hotels, but the profusion of cranes and building sites (around twenty hotels are currently under construction) means you should give them all a miss until this work is complete.

Club Venus ★★★, rte Touristique Hammamet Sud ☎02/227211, ℱ 226304. Relatively new and very well endowed for its three-star rating: three pools, sauna, mini crazy golf, boules court – plenty to keep you occupied. Good value. **❼**

Hadstrubal ★★★★★, Hammamet Yasmine, 12km from the town centre ☎02/248800, ℱ 248923, ℮ adstrubal.thal@gnet.tn. Hammamet's premier hotel and a member of the Leading Hotels of the World group, but miles out and costs a packet. **❼**

Oranger Beach Resort ★★★★, rte Touristique Hammamet Sud ☎02/280144, ℱ 281077. Very pleasant family-oriented complex. Water sports, including windsurfing and sailing, are available. **❻**

Paradis ★★★, rte Touristique Hammamet Sud ☎02/226300, ℱ 226860. Tackiest and cheapest of Hammamet Sud's establishments, stuffed with package-holiday guests in summer – it's a good laugh with no pretensions. Extensive range of activities, and the outdoor pool has a waterslide (there's a heated indoor pool too). **❻**

Phénicia ★★★★, rte Touristique Hammamet Sud ☎02/226533, ℱ 226337. With its own beach, this place lives up to its four-star rating, and is a darn sight cheaper than its co-stars. The usual facilities, plus three swimming pools, and activities that include boat trips and horse-riding. **❻**

Samaris ★, 6km west on P1 Tunis–Sousse road ☎02/226353. Strictly speaking not part of Hammamet Sud, but this is a gem of a place. Friendly, with a nice lounge and good food. The only disadvantage is that it's a couple of kilometres down to the beach. Self-catering apartments, sleeping up to three people, are available too, and the hotel runs the campsite next door (see below). **❹**

Shératon ★★★★, av Moncef Bey ☎02/226555, ℱ 227301, ℮ reservations_hammamet_tunisia @sheraton.com. A cut above its business-class namesakes elsewhere in the world, with accommodation in Greek-style chalets and the full range of water sports offered. Some rooms suitable for disabled guests. **❼**

HAMMAMET NORD

This area is slightly cheaper than Hammamet Sud, although it also contains many pricier five-stars. The beach, however, isn't as nice. The more easterly hotels can be reached by train – all services from Hammamet to Nabeul call at Aldiana station. Otherwise, it's taxi time again.

Abou Nawas ★★★★, rte Touristique Hammamet ☎02/281344, ℱ 281089 ℮ hammamet @abounawas.com.tn. Up to the chain's usual high standard and right on the beach. Mod cons include spa pool, tennis court, pools and shops, and ample gardens to lose the kids in. **❼**

Les Colombes ★★★, rte Touristique Hammamet ☎02/280049, ℱ 280899. Built in 1970 and slightly tacky, this is very much package-tour heaven (or hell): right on the beach, watersports, an embarrassing disco and plenty of cheerful holidaymakers from all over Europe. **❻**

Nozha Beach ★★★, rte Touristique Hammamet ☎02/280510, ℱ 280157. Large 1980s hotel, with the usual facilities and a good restaurant, but also well equipped for sports such as tennis as well as a range of aquatic activities. Bicycles for rent, and camel and horse rides available. Half- or full board only. **❻**

Youth hostel and campsite

Maison des Jeunes, by the louage station ☎ 02/280440. The usual concrete bliss, but a good fallback if you don't wish to pay high-season rates elsewhere. Dorms 5TD.

Samaris campsite, on the P1 Tunis–Sousse road ☎ 02/226353. Six kilometres southwest of town near the motorway turn-off, in the grounds of the one-star *Samaris Hôtel*, whose pool you can use.

The Town

Hammamet's centre is a little cape sticking out into the sea with the **Medina** standing neatly on its point, the newer quarters spreading out behind, and most of the hotels spaced to either side along the beach. The tiny walled Medina has unfortunately all but been swamped by tourist emporia, although Boutique Fella (daily 9am–1pm & 3–6.30pm) at 9 bis place Pasteur, has good quality locally made traditional clothes at

---

PETTY THIEVING

Stuffed as it is with tourists, petty thieving is common in Hammamet. Take care of your valuables, both on the beach (never leave things unattended) and on the street, where small children might try to distract you with posies of flowers or other objects whilst another runs off with whatever is accessible.

---

fixed prices. The fifteenth-century **Great Mosque** has an attractive minaret, while the over-restored twelfth-century **Kasbah** (daily 8am–6pm; 1.6TD) in the Medina's north-western corner is of little interest apart from its views.

From the Medina, avenue de la République heads towards Nabeul, passing what used to be the **municipal museum** at no. 21. Although it has long since closed down, the building is sometimes still used as a gallery: entry is free, and one or two relics remain inside. On the street corner next to it is an old olive oil press. The **town hall** on avenue Bourguiba, in the very centre facing the beach was formerly the *Hôtel de France*, once popular with Europe's rich and famous.

The main business of Hammamet, of course, is the **beach**. Even with the fast-food stalls, the forests of sunshades and the herds of bored-looking camels, the sheltered curve of the bay – backed by luxuriant greenery which conceals the low-built hotels – still manages to look even more beautiful than the brochure pictures. If you want a very slow ride along the coast, via all the big hotels, there's a tacky toy-town **tourist road train** from outside the Kasbah.

There's little more to the seashore than that, but at some point it's well worth following the signs on the road west of town to **Sebastian's villa** (daily 8am–6pm; 1TD), originally built by the Romanian millionaire in the 1920s and now a State-owned **International Cultural Centre**. You can look around the house and assess Frank Lloyd Wright's impression of its beauty – it really is fantasy material, with an arcaded swimming pool, a baptistry-like bath in solid marble built for four, and a black marble poolside table. During the war, the villa was used by General Rommel as his headquarters in the North African campaign. If you can't make the visiting hours, wander into the grounds and look around the garden and the mock-Greek **theatre** built for the **Festival de Hammamet** during July and August. Although geared primarily for tourists, many of the events are very interesting and it's worth looking at a programme from the ONTT here or in Nabeul to check out what's on. Most events are in French or Arabic. Out beyond the train station on the road to Bir Bou Regba, a weekly **market** is held every Thursday.

For kids there's Fabiland at the western end of avenue Moncef Bey, a small funfair with a few rides. Lastly, 6km along the beach south from town, just next to the *Hôtel Samira Beach*, is the Roman site of **Pupput** (daily April–Sept 8am–7pm, Oct–March 8.30am–5.30pm; 1.1TD). Although the limited remains of baths and houses aren't terribly impressive, some of the Christian tomb mosaics displayed on a wall are attractive.

EATING AND DRINKING

As you'd expect, **restaurants** in Hammamet are plentiful, both in the town and in most of the hotels – and if you're on a budget it's still surprisingly easy to find a cheap Tunisian meal around the town centre. Most of the places on avenue Bourguiba between the Medina and the tourist office are solely geared for tourism, and their fare is overpriced.

Barberousse, on the Medina wall next to *La Medina*. Typical fare and seafood for around 10TD, with good views. Daily 10am–10pm.

Belle Vue, at the southern end of av Bourguiba. Usually dependable with seafood dishes priced at 4–12TD. Daily 8am–11pm.

Herb stall in the Tunis Medina

The Tunis Medina

Wall tiles in the Tunis Medina

Great Mosque, Tunis

A statue in the Bardo Museum

The ruins of Carthage

Sunset at Hammamet

Symbol of Tanit, Tophet, Carthage

Bizerte Medina

War graves at Medjez el Bab

Mosaic at Sousse

Great Mosque, Kairouan

Amphitheatre, El Jem

Brauhaus, facing the Medina. Fantastically Teutonic, more Bavarian than lederhosen, complete with its *bockwurst*, litre steins of beer brewed on the premises, and filled with Germans. A basic meal with a beer will set you back 10–15TD. Daily 10am–1am.

Restaurant la Brise, 2 av de la République. Basic in appearance, but serves tasty and decent-sized traditional dishes for 10–15TD. Daily noon–8pm.

Restaurant Chez Achour, hidden at the end of rue Ali Belhouane. The best seafood in town at 15–20TD for a full meal. Daily noon–midnight.

Fast Food Le Roi, at the northern end of av Bourguiba by the train station. Cheap, basic and tasty, if a little removed from the action. Daily 10am–2am.

Fatma, at the southern end of av Bourguiba. More expensive than its neighbour the *Belle Vue*, but serving similar fare. Daily 8am–11pm.

Restaurant El Hana, at the north end of av Bourguiba. Big portions for the lowest of prices, another cheapie out of town. Open 24hr.

Hong Kong Restaurant, av des Nations Unies, near the Hammamet Plage turn-off ☎ 02/242825. If you fancy Chinese food, this restaurant serves up pricey, but tasty, predominantly Cantonese cuisine. Daily noon–3pm & 6.30–11pm.

Café de la Lune, in a *koubba* in the Cultural Centre grounds. A pleasant café that operates only in season.

La Medina, next door to the *Barberousse*, on the Medina wall. Good views and the usual offerings for around 10TD. Daily 10am–10pm.

Les Trois Moutons, in the Centre Commercial ☎ 02/280981. Refined and quite pricey (20–25TD for two courses and wine) with excellent lobster and shellfish dishes. Daily noon–3pm & 7pm–midnight.

Café Sidi Bou Hdid, on the beach outside the Medina walls. Pleasant place to sip tea or coffee and watch the world go by.

Nightlife and entertainment

As you'd expect, outside the more "respectable" hotels, who put on the usual anodyne entertainment, **nightlife** involves large quantities of alcohol and sexual advances in a number of sweaty nightclubs. You'll find most of these on avenue Moncef Bey, inland from Hammamet Sud: currently popular are *Calypso* and the *Ranch Club*. Also on avenue Moncef Bey is *La Pacha*, which puts on spectacles of snake charmers, *gargoulette* dancers and belly dancers, as does *Sahara City* at the far end of Hammamet Sud near *Hôtel Club Venus*.

If high-season room rates or carpetbaggers haven't skinned you of all your cash, there are two **casinos** in which to tempt Lady Luck. The newest and swishest is the Cleopatra Casino, in the five-star *Hôtel Occidental* complex, in the new extension to Hammamet Sud, *Yasmine*. Much closer (so you can walk back) is the Grand Casino, just beyond *Hôtel Bel Azur*, in the *Hôtel Solazur* complex, to the north of town on avenue Assad Ibn el Fourat. Fans of European football can indulge their passion at the *EuroPub*, next to Fabiland at the western end of avenue Moncef Bey, which also serves pints.

Listings

Banks and exchange There are several banks on avenue de la République and avenue Bourguiba, many of which have ATMs that accept Visa, Mastercard and in some cases Cirrus. The BIAT next to the *Belle Vue Restaurant* has a note exchange machine, and many shops and hotels (the *Alya*, for instance) will change money outside banking hours. The larger hotels have their own exchange services, though sometimes only for the use of residents. The Tunisian Welcome Service agency, in the Centre Commercial on avenue Bourguiba, also provides a Sunday service (9am–noon) as well as at normal times. There are also exchange shops near concentrations of hotels in Hammamet Plage and Sud.

Car rental Avis, avenue du Koweit ☎ 02/280164; Hertz, rue des Hôtels ☎ 02/280187; Topcar, avenue du Koweit ☎ 02/281247. Operators down avenue des Nations-Unies on the hotel strip include Budget ☎ 02/280606, a little beyond the rue des Hôtels turning, and Europcar ☎ 02/280146, a couple of hundred metres further west. Locamob ☎ 02/280339, on rue Dag Hammarskjöld, rents out mopeds.

Car repairs There are a number of garages and spare parts shops on avenue du Koweit near the *Olympia Hotel*.

Cinema Centre Commercial, av Bourguiba, screening mainstream releases from the West, dubbed into French.

Diving Trips can be arranged through many of the hotels – *Club Venus* (see p.129) charges 15TD for an introductory dive, 37TD for an exploratory dive and 40TD for a night dive. Longer courses are also available.

Golf courses Hammamet has three eighteen-hole courses; two at Golf Citrus (☎ 02/226500, courtesy cars from the hotels *Abou Nawas*, *Phénicia* and *Sindbad*), and one at Golf Yasmine (☎ 02/226722).

Hammams There is one in the Medina, opposite the mosque, one at 82 av Bourguiba, and another at avenue Bourguiba's junction with avenue Hedi Ouali. In general they're open for women in the afternoon and for men in the morning and evening.

Infirmeries by the police station at 29 av Bourguiba ☎ 02/282333 and at 29 av de la République ☎ 02/280223, and an emergency doctor's surgery ☎ 02/282333 opposite the *Hotel Bel Azur*.

Internet Publinet on rue Taieb el Azzabi (daily 9am–midnight) and the Public Internet Centre, 117 av de la Libération (daily 9.30am–11pm), both charge 3TD/hr.

Newspapers English-language newspapers are available on avenue de la République near the Medina, and at L'Artisane by the *Résidence Hammamet* on avenue Bourguiba.

ONA No matter what the touts tell you, there's no official craft shop in Hammamet: Nabeul is the nearest, if you need an unhurried idea of price and quality.

Pharmacy All-night pharmacy at 138 av de la République.

Police avenue Bourguiba ☎ 02/280079.

Post office avenue de la République near the centre. Open country hours, but also Sunday mornings. No phones.

Supermarket Magasin Général on avenue de la République opposite the Medina (Tues–Sat 8am–12.30pm & 3–7pm, Sun 8am–1.30pm). There's also a large grocery store at 1 av de la Libération.

Telephones You'll find coin-operated taxiphones in the Centre Commercial on av Bourguiba, in the Kaly Centre opposite the bus station, and the *Berbère* restaurant opposite the Medina. There are also numerous taxiphone and Publitel offices at intervals along the strip.

Tours If your hotel doesn't offer excursions around Cap Bon, they're available from any number of travel agents along av de la République. The Tunisian Welcome Service ☎ 02/280924 in the Centre Commercal is as good as any. Apart from most of the package-type hotels, tour operators include:

MOVING ON FROM HAMMAMET

For a rundown of destinations and journey times, see Travel Details on pp.148–149.

Buses stop on avenue de la République opposite the post office. There are departures every 30min or so to Nabeul, where you can change for other Cap Bon destinations, though there are also some direct buses. **Louages** gather in a small triangular piazza off avenue de la République near *Hôtel Khella*, and serve Tunis, Nabeul and sometimes Sousse. Yellow metered **taxis** wait in front of the Medina.

The **train station** (☎ 02/280174) is on avenue Bourguiba, near the junction with avenue Hedi Ouali. There are frequent services to Nabeul and Bir Bou Regba, from where you can connect for Tunis or for points south. There's only one direct train to Tunis (Mon–Sat 6.10am).

Carthage Tours, rue Dag Hammarskjöld ☎02/281926; CT Tours, 7 av Assad Ibn el Fourat ☎02/281322. Boat trips are available from Hammamet Travel Service on rue Dag Hammarskjold ☎02/280193.

Nabeul and around   نابل

NABEUL, 15km east along the coast from Hammamet, is the seat of the Governorate of Cap Bon, a market centre and the pottery and stonework capital of Tunisia, with a busy working atmosphere quite different from its near neighbour. With its easy access to the fertile hinterland of Cap Bon, Nabeul has always been an industrious place. The inhabitants of Roman Neapolis supported themselves by manufacturing *garum*, a sort of fish sauce used as basic seasoning in almost every savoury dish. "Take the entrails of tunny fish", a second-century recipe instructs, "and the gills, juice, and blood, and add sufficient salt. Leave it in a vessel for two months, then pierce the vessel and the *garum* will flow out." Potteries, too, are long established in this area and remain the principal industry – along with tourism.

Hotels dot the beach between Hammamet and Nabeul, and more continue to be built. Though the sand here is just as extensive as to the west of Hammamet, the beach lacks Hammamet's gentle curve and lush green backdrop, and on a windy day can feel distinctly exposed.

Arrival, information and accommodation

Avenue Habib Thameur leading east into avenue Farhat Hached, is the main east–west through road, bisected by avenue Bourguiba, which leads down to the beach. There are two combined **bus** and **louage** stations: buses and louages arriving from Hammamet or outside Cap Bon use the station 400m west of avenue Bourguiba on avenue Habib Thameur. Arriving from places within Cap Bon other than Hammamet, you'll be dropped at the station 600m east of avenue Bourguiba on avenue Farhat Hached, or opposite the Friday **market** site. A few blocks seawards is place 7 Novembre and the **train station**. The **post office**, also on avenue Bourguiba, is north of the junction of avenues Habib Thameur and Farhat Hached.

The ONTT regional **tourist office** is on avenue Taïeb Mehiri, not far from the beach (July & Aug daily 7.30am–1.30pm; rest of the year Mon-Thurs 8.30am–1pm & 3–5.45pm, Fri & Sat 8.30am–1.30pm; ☎02/286800), and can supply details of the **festival** held in the open-air theatre at the beach end of avenue Bourguiba during July and August.

As a major tourist resort, Nabeul is not short of **hotels**, most of which are closer to standard European package resorts than Tunisian in feel. The big ones are on the beach, but the town has acquired an unusual and welcome sprinkling of *pensions famil-iales*, along with two youth hostels and a campsite. As with Hammamet, prices for the bigger places take a plunge off season, sometimes only charging a quarter of the price.

Hotels and pensions

Hôtel Byzance ★★★, bd de la Corniche ☎02/271000, ℗287164. One of the newest, in a prime location 100m from the beach, with pool, spa pool and karaoke evenings provided. ❺

Hôtel Club Med ★★, rte Touristique, on the beach ☎02/285777, ℗285682. Establishment with full facilities, fortified against any possible intrusion by anyone or anything remotely Tunisian. Closed Nov–Feb. ❻

Hôtel Fakir ★★, rte Touristique ☎02/285477, ℗287616. A small and newish place, just outside the Roman remains and within easy reach of the beach. ❹

Pension el Habib, av Habib Thameur ☎02/224785. On the road to Hammamet by the *oued*. Clean and friendly pension with a small library of left-behind paperbacks. Recommended. ❷

△ Kélibia △ ❶ (first right)

Oued Sidi Moussa

NABEUL

RUE EL ARBI ZARROUK

Friday Market Site

Cap Bon Louage Station ★ Taxi Rank

AVENUE ALI BELHAOUANE

AVENUE MONGI SLIM

❷

RUE DE FRANCE

AV. HABIB EL KARMA

❸

Great Mosque

AVENUE FARHAT HACHED

RUE DU 18 JANVIER

AVENUE TAIEB MEHIRI

❹

ⓘ

❻

SOCOPA

B 5

A

@ Publinet

C

AVENUE HEDI CHAKER

Museum

Supermarket

D

E

PL 7 NOVEMBRE

❼

AVENUE BOURGUIBA

AVENUE BOURGUIBA

F

G

Potted Tree

Train Station

❽

Industrial Fairground (Foire de Nabeul)

AV DE LA RÉPUBLIQUE

R MARBELLA

H

❾

RUE SIDI MAAOUIA

❿

Taxi Rank

Giant Orange Bowl

AVENUE HABIB THAMEUR

RUE DE SFAX

RUE JEDIDA MAGHREBIA

AVENUE MOHAMED V

⓫

Bus & Louage Station

@ RUE DE L'ESPOIR

ONAT

MEDITERRANEAN SEA

N

Oued Souhil

⓬

⓭

Neapolis Excavations

ROUTE TOURISTIQUE

RESTAURANTS

Les Arcades	E
Le Bonheur	B
Le Bon Kif	H
Café Errachidia	F
Café le Petit Chef	A
Fast Food	D
De l'Olivier	G
Sabrine	C
Slovenia	I

Camping les Jasmins

AVENUE HABIB THAMEUR

⓮

⓯

16

RUE ABOU EL KACEM CHABBI

Oued Esseghir

ACCOMMODATION

Auberge de Jeunesse	2
Byzance	6
Club Med	13
Fakir	15
Pension el Habib	12
Pension Hafsides	10
Les Jasmins	16
Kheops	8
Lido	1
Monia Club	14
Pension Mustapha	3
Les Pyramides Complex	9
Résidence Imene	7
Pension les Roses	5
Saf-Saf	11
Youth Hostel	4

0 ————— 300 m

△ Grombalia & Tunis

Hammamet via C28 ▽   ▽ Hammamet via hotels

Pension Hafsides, rue Sidi Maaouia ☎ 02/285823. Another low-key pension, though its town-centre location can make it noisy. The singles are good value. Closed Nov–Feb. **②**

Hôtel les Jasmins ★, av Habib Thameur ☎ 02/285343, ⓕ 285073. The hotel itself is not unreasonably priced and is liable to be booked up in season. **⑤**

Hôtel Kheops, ★★★★, av Mohamed V just off av Habib Bourguiba ☎ 02/286555, ⓕ 286024. Nabeul's top choice, swapping the usual package-tour atmosphere for a slightly more business look. All facilities and an Olympic-sized pool. **⑤**

Hôtel Lido ★★★, 3km east of town on the beachfront, turn right off av Ali Belhouane after Oued Sidi Mouusa ☎ 02/285135, ⓕ 285487. Nabeul's biggest complex after *Les Pyramides* and much better value, with two- and four-bed bungalows also available. All the amenities you would expect, plus water sports. **⑤**

Hôtel Monia Club, on the Hammamet beach road, opposite the site of Neapolis ☎ 02/285713. Officially a pension, this is really more a restaurant and bar with staying guests. Breakfast not included. **③**

Pension Mustapha, av Habib el Karma ☎ 02/222262. A lovely little place, clean and welcoming. Recommended. **③**

Hôtel Les Pyramides Complex, av Bourguiba ☎ 02/285444, ⓕ 287461. Large complex consisting of the main overpriced hotel and two sets of apartments, each with their own kitchens. Of these, *Résidences Les Pyramides* is much better value than the expensive *Les Jasmins* apartments. **④–⑤**

Résidence Imène ★★★, 28 av Bourguiba ☎ 02/222310, ⓕ 272380. Very comfortable, with big rooms, but rather impersonal and fraying slightly at the edges. **⑤**

Pension les Roses, 3 rue Sidi Abd el Kader, just off av Farhat Hached ☎ 02/285570. The cheapest of the pensions and not at all bad. **②**

Hôtel Saf-Saf ★★, av Mohamed V ☎ 02/286044, ⓕ 286198. Newish place in the hotel district that's smaller and less impersonal than most others. **④**

Youth hostels and campsite

Auberge de Jeunesse – Nabeul Plage, av Mongi Slim ☎ 02/285547. The hostel's location right by the beach is great. Its dorms (5TD) fill up in summer, but are empty the rest of the year. You must pay for at least one meal during your stay. Closed Feb.

Maison des Jeunes, av Taïeb Mehiri ☎ 02/286689. The usual concrete splendour, mainly intended for schoolkids on weekend courses, but there is no age limit. Check-in after 5pm only – you can't leave your bags there in the meantime. Dorm beds 5TD.

Hôtel les Jasmins campsite, rue Abou el Kacem Chabbi ☎ 02/285343. The only official site in Nabeul is attached to the hotel (see above).

The Town

The centre of town is where avenue Habib Thameur crosses the Tunis road, **avenue Bourguiba**, which runs straight through the town almost to the beach – around a fifteen-minute walk. A couple of blocks towards the sea, an unsubtle giant pot built around a pine tree in the middle of the road at **place 7 Novembre** proclaims Nabeul's major industry. If you're a die-hard kitsch fanatic, then the giant ceramic bowl of oranges nearby should have you in raptures – it's at the junction of rue Sidi Maaouia and avenue Habib Thameur.

Nabeul's **beach** is what a lot of people come here for. Like Hammamet's shoreline, it is increasingly hotel-strewn but still attractive, with nothing except tourist-oriented cafés and restaurants, as well as the ubiquitous water sport facilities – (see Listings).

The town's weekly Friday **market** out on rue el Arbi Zarrouk, a continuation of avenue Farhat Hached, has become one of the country's biggest tourist attractions, with busloads of shoppers arriving from all over the country to pick up the local crafts (see box p.136). There's nothing out of the ordinary about it except size and convenience – since the tourists have been coming it's sprouted an additional section spe-

NABEUL POTTERY AND OTHER CRAFTS

Many of the souvenirs on display in Nabeul, in shops with names like Sinbad's Palace and Aladdin's Cave, are standard wares available all over the country. But there's a special emphasis on **pottery** in Nabeul because, along with Jerba, this is the national centre of the craft. In fact, the potters of Nabeul originally came from Jerba, attracted perhaps by the quality of the local clay. Another important influence was the arrival in the seventeenth century of Andalusian refugees, bringing with them the artistic traditions of Muslim Spain. The same traditions were carried to Fez in Morocco, and Nabeul's ceramics often resemble those of Fez.

Pottery has a long history in Tunisia – the Roman province of Africa exported standard red tableware all over the Empire – and thanks to the tourist trade it's one traditional craft that appears to have a healthy future, even if some of the products are in highly dubious taste. Most shops will be happy to show you to the workshop of one of their suppliers if you ask about an *atelier* (craftsman). Two particularly good workshops that welcome visitors are Kedidi, 1500m down route de Tunis (☎02/287576), and Poterie Gastle, a little further on (☎02/222247). The industrial potters, who make bricks, are not as glamorous or well known, but are no less interesting. The small humps dotted around the eastern edge of the town, especially near the market, are the ovens in which the bricks are fired, and when they're in operation (usually in the evening) they produce a thick black pall of smoke. You'll probably be invited to clamber down into the inferno-like subterranean chamber where the oven flames are kept fired through the night.

Other crafts are worked in and around Nabeul. **Beni Khiar**, a village 2km east (walk up avenue Ali Belhouane), specializes in **wool products**, possibly a legacy of Hilalian nomads who first settled here in the eleventh century. The village centres around its little daily fish market. Before this, on the left-hand side of the road, you'll find a weaving co-operative, with jackets and carpets a third cheaper than the same stuff in Nabeul's emporia. The workers are happy to show you their craft. Another nearby village, **Es Somaa**, just inland, specializes in **straw mats**. But the big craft, after pottery, is **stonecarving**. This is less amenable to souvenir production, but flourishes thanks to the policy of incorporating traditional elements in modern buildings, including hotels and houses. Doorways, columns and benches in Tunisia have long been carved with intricate geometric patterns – witness the Tunis Medina – and it's fascinating to watch the process. Most of the stonework is done in **Dar Chaâbane**, a small village to the east that is now virtually a suburb of Nabeul. Its main street is lined with workshops clinking to the sound of chisels, while a pile of raw stone on the pavement outside announces the trade. Its weekly market, where you'll find the results on sale, is held on Sunday mornings.

In Nabeul, the **ONA crafts shops** at 144 av Farhat Hached and 93 av Habib Thameur have a good selection of officially priced and selected items.

cializing in holiday souvenirs. Despite its nickname of "Camel Market", the only dromedaries you're likely to see are of the cuddly-toy variety. You can avoid the crowds by coming on Thursday evening for an early start next day.

The Regional Museum and Roman Neapolis

Nabeul has a small and somewhat desultory **Regional Museum** at 44 av Bourguiba, by the tree in the pot (Tues–Sun: April–Sept 8am–1pm & 4–7pm; Oct–March 9am–4pm; 1.1TD, camera 1TD). Along with some Roman mosaics discovered at **Roman Neapolis**, it also has a collection of Carthaginian pieces from Kerkouane and from Thinissut in the hills just above Hammamet. Dating from the third century BC, the Kerkouane statuettes display the usual combination of Greek and Eastern influences. Three hundred years later, in the first century AD, the terracotta figures from Thinissut

– like their companion pieces now in the Bardo – show these cross-cultural influences surviving even into the Roman era: the Punic goddess Tanit's lion head, for example. A long-planned renovation of the museum was in progress at the time of writing, closing it to public view.

Eating and drinking

It's a shame that, given Cap Bon's richness in fruit and vegetables, meat and fish, cooking is hardly the high point of Nabeul. With only a few exceptions, most restaurants are of the greasy-spoon variety and you might be better off getting half- or full board in a hotel, or else self-catering: *Les Pyramides* and *Hotel Lido* both have apartments with kitchens. The daily **market** is on rue de France.

Les Arcades, av Bourguiba, diagonally opposite the train station. Cheaper and less adventurous, with fresh food in pleasant surroundings for under 10TD. Daily 8am–8.30pm.

Restaurant Le Bon Kif, corner av Marbella and av Habib Thameur ☎02/222783. In the same league as *Restaurant de l'Olivier*, its seafood is especially recommended; they have a set menu at 12TD, and *à la carte* at 15–20TD. Daily noon–3pm & 7pm–midnight.

Restaurant le Bonheur, at the bend in av Farhat Hached by the *Pension des Roses*. The best of the cheapies, with good-value set menus at around 5TD. Daily 11am–5pm.

Café Errachidia, corner of av Bourguiba and Habib Thameur. The fanciest place for mint tea; also serving delicious cakes.

Fast Food, corner av Bourguiba and Farhat Hached. This simply named place serves up decent sandwiches and vast salads (1–3TD) in a fastidiously clean environment. Daily 11am–11pm.

Restaurant de l'Olivier, 6 av Hedi Chaker ☎02/286613. Still the best of Nabeul's restaurants, a classy French-style place with matching prices (full meals 20–25TD and they accept Visa and Mastercard). Daily noon–3pm & 6.30–11.30pm.

Restaurant Sabrine, 11 rue Abdesselem Dimassi. One of a bunch of reasonable options between avenue Farhat Hached and Hedi Chaker, this one offers pizzas, pastas and lasagnes among other dishes for 1–4TD. Daily 10am–11pm.

Slovenia, av Habib Thameur, next to *Hôtel les Jasmins* ☎02285343. Serving up a range of international dishes prepared by Rafik Tlatli who is rated as one of Tunisia's best chefs; a full meal should set you back no more than 25–30TD. Daily noon–2.30pm & 6–11pm.

Listings

Banks There are lots on and around avenues Bourguiba and Habib Thameur, and at least one should be open in the morning at weekends. A few also have ATMs which accept Visa, Mastercard and Cirrus, including BIAT on avenue Bourguiba.

Bicycle rental The youth hostel on avenue Mongi Slim and the gatekeepers at *Hôtel Les Pyramides* and *Hôtel Nabeul Beach* rent out bicycles. The set (but negotiable) prices are 2TD per hour, 6TD for a half-day or 10TD for a full day.

Car rental Express Car, 148 av Habib Thameur ☎02/287014; Hertz, av Habib Thameur ☎02/285327; Nova Rent-a-Car, 54 av Bourguiba ☎02/285967.

Cinema Palace Cinema, 43 av Hedi Chaker. Films and some theatre are also staged on Sundays by la Maison de la Culture, 75 av Hedi Chaker. Dubbed into French.

Diving Diving Aquamarine ☎02/287457 in the Sidi Slimane building on av Mohammed V will take you out, though probably from Hammamet.

Festivals The summer festival, a programme of cultural events for tourists, takes place over July and August in the open-air theatre at the beach end of avenue Bourguiba, the only time it's ever used. Nabeul International Fair is more of an industrial affair, held in the Foire de Nabeul site between avenue Bourguiba and avenue Taieb Mehiri in early April.

Hammams There's one at 42 av Hedi Chaker (men mornings, women afternoons), another at 37 rue Sidi Bel Aissa, and a women-only one, Bain Sidi Maaouria, at 19 av Habib Thameur.

MOVING ON FROM NABEUL

For a rundown of destinations and journey times, see Travel Details on pp.148–149.

Nabeul is the main transport centre of Cap Bon, and it's easy to reach most parts of the peninsula from here via regular bus services run by SRTG Nabeul, or by louage. There are several daily trains from the **train station** (☎02/285054) on place 7 Novembre through Hammamet to Bir Bou Regba on the main Tunis–south mainline, with daily connections to Sousse, Monastir, Mahdia, Sfax and Gabès. There's a direct Nabeul–Tunis train daily at 5.50am (excluding Sun & holidays). **Buses** and **louages** to the **Cap Bon peninsula** leave from rue el Arbi Zarrouk, a continuation of avenue Farhat Hached, about 500m east of avenue Bourguiba. Note that there are no buses or louages through to El Haouria; you have to change at Kélibia. Buses and louages for the rest of the country depart from the **bus station** (☎02/285873) on avenue Habib Thameur, five minutes' walk down from avenue Bourguiba. Buses leave every half hour during the day and louages travel the same routes (☎02/286081), some even go as far as Sfax.

Internet Publinet on the corner of av Hedi Chaker and Taieb Mehiri (daily 8am–midnight) and Internet, av Habib Thameur opposite the bus station (Mon–Sat 8.30am–11.30pm), both charge 2TD/hr.

Hospital The large hospital ☎02/285633 in the centre of town only deals with casualties, for other complaints you'll need to visit the regional hospital ☎02/285022 5km out of town on the road to Hammamet. *Infirmeries* are at 80 av Hedi Chaker and 10 rue Ibn Badis, and *cliniques* on av Mongi Slim (☎02/285199) and on the Hammamet road (☎02/286183).

Newspapers English-language papers can be found at the Librairie de l'Avenir, 86 av Hedi Chaker, and Imprimerie Boussan, 131 av Farhat Hached.

ONA craft shops 144 av Farhat Hached and 93 av Habib Thameur.

Pharmacy The night pharmacy is at 37 av Habib Thameur.

Police av Taïeb Mehiri, just off av Ali Belhouane ☎02/285474.

Post office av Bourguiba, north of the junction with av Habib Thameur (city hours), and you can make international phone calls there. There's also a branch on av Habib el Karma.

Supermarkets There's a large supermarket at 30 av Bourguiba, next to *Résidence Iméne*, and another one opposite the hospital on av Habib Thameur.

Taxis Allo Taxi Express ☎02/222444.

Telephones At the post office, or the taxiphone offices at 168 av Habib Thameur (daily 7am–midnight) and avenue Habib el Karma, up from *Pension Mustapha*.

Tours For tours around Cap Bon and further afield in Tozeur and Matmata, contact Delta Travel, 113 av Bourguiba ☎02/271077, but your hotel will most likely also arrange tours.

Water sports Windsurfers and other aquatic gear can be rented at *Hôtel Lido*, *Hôtel le Prince* and *Hôtel Les Pyramides*.

North of Nabeul

North of Nabeul the coast is one endless stretch of white beach backed, as far as Menzel Temime, by unsightly salt flats, and after that by rich farmland. There are few towns, fewer places to stay, and little reason to stop off except for a minimal change of beach scenery.

   KORBA, the next town north from Nabeul, is a large agricultural centre with a Sunday *souk* and minor Roman remains. Birdwatchers should find it worth a stop in passing, as there are lagoons and a salt marsh just to the north, which hold flamingos, spoonbills and avocets in the spring, a good range of migrants in spring and autumn, and ducks over the winter. Another kind of song can be heard at the **Amor Yedess**

Festival where Sufi liturgical chants, specifically of the Soulamia brotherhood and otherwise almost impossible for an infidel to hear, are performed. Generally more sober than the often hypnotic and bizarre Aissawiya chants, the Soulamia are a good introduction to the form. It's held around the third week of Ramadan. The tourist office in Nabeul may have dates nearer the time. If you want to stay, your only option at present is a *Maison des Jeunes* youth hostel (☎02/289296), which closes erratically so phone ahead. Otherwise the former *Club Mediterranée* is currently being redeveloped into a 650-bed behemoth villa complex, which should be ready for the year 2002. Korba has a **post office** (country hours), a number of fast-food places on the Kélibia road up from the bus station, and a couple of **banks** on the main Nabeul–Kélibia road through town.

Another 25km further along the coast is **MENZEL TEMIME**. It has no special attractions except for its **beach** (which is rather windy and some way from town), but it's a feasible alternative to the tourist ghettos of Nabeul and Hammamet. The town **bus and louage station** is a roundabout on the Kélibia road, avenue de la République. Buses and louages head to Nabeul, Kélibia, Menzel Bou Zelfa and Tunis; early morning services from Kélibia to destinations further afield such as Kairouan, Mahdia, Monastir and Sousee also stop here. Running off the roundabout is **avenue Bourguiba**, along which the residents at nos. 41 and 45 have put a lot of work into the design of their front doors. The **post office** is at no. 39, and beyond that are two **banks**, with another on the main square at the end. On the square, next to a cavernous café, the two-star *Hôtel Temim* (☎02/298262, ☎298291; ❷) offers pleasant, clean rooms (with a choice of bath or shower) but closes sporadically, so phone ahead. The only other accommodation is the *Maison des Jeunes* **youth hostel** behind (☎02/344116), signposted only in Arabic and also prone to occasional closure. There's a **cinema** next door and a couple of cheap **restaurants** on the market square beyond that. On a Tuesday, turn left at the square for the **souk**, spread out down a wide boulevard and, if you're in need of supplies at any other time, the opposite direction (the continuation of avenue Bourguiba) takes you to the Monoprix **supermarket**.

Kélibia and around   قليبية

With all the ingredients for resort development, **KÉLIBIA**, 50km along the coast from Nabeul, has so far resisted tourist development and remains an agricultural centre with a major fishing port nestling under a huge sixteenth-century fortress. Be aware that a building project north of town, Kélibia la Blanche, may change things over the next few years. For the time being however, both the port and neighbouring **Mansoura** remain pleasantly unspoilt with stunning white sand coves that feel very removed from Hammamet. You can combine the beaches with a visit to Kerkouane (see p.142) by taking some food and strolling back along the shore, though be warned that it's about four and a half hours' walk.

As part of its agricultural heritage, Kélibia produces a **dry muscat wine** which is worth trying. Another Kélibia curiosity is the number of locals who bear the name *el Ingliis*, meaning "Englishman" or "Englishwoman". By one account their common ancestor was an Englishman who came to work here during the Ottoman era, converted to Islam and stayed. Another story has it that they are all descendants of shipwrecked sailors.

The Town

Part of Kélibia's charm is the feeling that it's something of a backwater, but this hasn't always been the case. Some fine remains, including mosaics, which can be seen in the various patchy **excavations** around the town (free entry; you may be asked for a photo

fee but this is just a scam), bear witness to a sizable Roman presence and, for the Byzantines, who built the first **fortress** here, Clupea (Kélibia) was reputedly the last place of refuge after the Arab invasion. Later, the town and fortress were sacked three times by the Spanish between 1535 and 1547.

The fortress has recently been restored (daily: summer 8.30am–6.30pm; winter 8.30am–5.30pm; 1.1TD) and, although there's little to see in itself (apart from the *gardien*'s impressive collection of domestic fowl), the views are superb. At the foot of the towering fortress lies the **port**, consisting of little more than a few scattered shops and houses, as well as the State Fishing School. Kélibia is the best natural harbour before Sousse – which explains the fortress. For **water sports** in Kélibia, the municipal club by the harbour rents out windsurfers.

The main **beach** lies south of the fishing port at the end of avenue Erriadh, but unfortunately it's covered in seaweed and gunk from the port and is not that attractive.

Practicalities

The town centre itself is some 2km west of the fortress and port. You'll most probably arrive in town at the **bus and louage station** on avenue Ali Belhaouane. The **post office**, which has Western Union money transfer, is on avenue Bourguiba (country hours) and there are Publitel and taxiphone offices on avenue des Martyrs near the centre, as well as a couple out beyond the *Hôtel Palmarina*. For internet acccess there's a Publinet on avenue des Martyrs not far along from place de la République (daily 9am–4am; 1.5TD/hr). There's a **bank** on avenue Bourguiba, one on rue Ibn Khaldoun and one on place de la République. The **night pharmacy** is at the beginning of avenue des Martyrs, around the corner from the post office. There's a small food **market** where avenue Erriadh meets avenue des Martyrs. The **Monday souk** takes place just north of avenue Ali Belhaouane but also has stalls set up all the way to the food market. Daily necessities can be bought at the Tam **supermarket** on rue Ibn Khaldoun, or at Magasin Général, on avenue des Martyrs by the food market. There is **no tourist office** in town. The **police** (☎02/296343) are on avenue Bourguiba on the way out towards Nabeul.

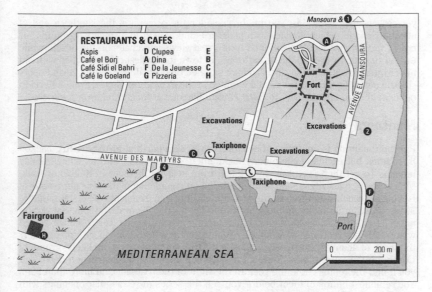

Accommodation

There's a reasonable selection of medium-priced **accommodation** in town, notably the old favourite, though now rather shabby, 1940s *Hôtel Florida*, down the grubby beach by the harbour (☎ & ⓕ02/296248; **③**). Its rooms (with sea views) and bungalows (without) cost the same, but the bungalows have en-suite bathrooms. Next door is the new three-star *Hôtel Palmarina* (☎02/274062, ⓕ274055; **⑤**), which is expensive in spite of its pool and mod cons. The *Pension Anis* (☎02/295777, ⓕ273128; **③**), off avenue Erriadh between the town centre and the beach, has spotless, airy rooms and shared – but squeaky-clean – bathrooms. The more expensive, package-type holiday village *Mamounia* (☎02/296088, ⓕ296858; **④**) some way along the beach has little in common with its Marrakesh namesake. If you're on a budget, there's the drab, but unusually friendly *Maison des Jeunes* **youth hostel** (☎02/296105) on the Mansoura road by the port. You can sometimes **camp** in the grounds, which have a small, unearthed Roman site in front.

Eating and drinking

There are plenty of **restaurants** in Kélibia, though the more obviously touristic ones have an unwelcome tendency to overcharge – check the price before ordering. In the town itself, the *Anis* (daily noon–3pm & 7–11pm) is the classiest (and priciest) choice but with service to match. Budget options include the very good *Dina* (daily 8am–11.30pm) on rue Ibn Khaldoun, with tasty pizzas and excellent fish *chorba*, and another pizza joint, *Restaurant Aspis* (daily 9am–11pm), a pleasant place on avenue des Martyrs, just round the corner from *Pension Anis*, with smartly-dressed staff serving cheap pizzas and big, tasty sandwiches. Out by the port, *Restaurant de la Jeunesse* (daily 10am–2am), avenue des Martyrs just after *Hôtel Palmarina*, has reasonable seafood dishes for 6–12TD. The *Palmarina* itself has an expensive restaurant (daily noon–2.30pm & 7–10pm), strong on shellfish and with a decently-priced *menu touristique* at 7.5TD. Further on, *Café Sidi el Bahri* (daily 6am–midnight) has good views but rather ordinary and overpriced fare. *Le Goeland* (daily 8am–midnight) next door is more reliable and cheaper with mains at 5–7TD, but serves food only in summer. If you're travelling with kids, you might consider the pizzeria at the southern end of avenue Erriadh, which doubles as a patisserie and is next to a small fairground. For **cafés**, the two previously mentioned have great views and chairs on the beach, while *Café el Borj*, up by the fort, has good views. In town the busiest cafés are filled with old men arguing over games of cards and are situated on place de la République and opposite the post office. **Drinkers** can take refuge in the *Restaurant Clupea*, avenue Erriadh opposite the food market, in the *Hôtel Florida* bar, and at *Restaurant de la Jeunesse*.

Mansoura

Far more alluring is the series of beautiful coves 2km north at **MANSOURA**, backed by a small but exclusive community nicknamed "Little Paris", with its fancy holiday houses. To get there, you can catch a taxi from near the harbour in Kélibia or walk. Mansoura's exclusivity is soon to be shattered on completion of the *zone touristique* of Kélibia la Blanche, however. In the meantime, there's an excellent café-restaurant, the *Mansourah*, on its rocky promontory (Mon–Fri noon–3.30pm & 6–10pm, Sat & Sun noon–11pm). The *Hôtel Mansoura*, 1.5km further along the road (☎02/295992; closed winter; ❺) has reopened after lengthy renovation as a "vacation village", presumably the first of many. Immediately opposite is the entrance to an unlikely group of **Carthaginian rock tombs**. Take a track leading alongside a construction depot and you'll find the tombs cut in the rock to the right of the road after no more than 50m. You're almost on top of them before you see the series of rectangular openings with steps heading down, so clean cut that they look twenty years old, not twenty centuries. North of Mansoura, the shore runs in deserted and tempting swaths of white beach to the end of Cap Bon.

Kerkouane كركوان

Halfway between Kélibia and El Haouaria, a signposted sideroad runs about 1.5km down to the Carthaginian site of **Kerkouane** (daily: summer 9am–6pm; winter 9am–4pm; 2.1TD, camera 1TD), discovered in 1952 and classed by UNESCO as a World Heritage Site. Punic jewellery and other artefacts are displayed in a small adjoining **museum** (Tues–Sun same hours), whose most notable exhibit is a wooden Punic statue found nearby. There's also a clay *tabouna* oven, very similar to bread ovens still in use today in some Cap Bon villages.

There was much excitement at first about the character of the streets and housing, and the curious absence of public buildings, giving rise to an eccentric theory that this

---

MOVING ON FROM KÉLIBIA

For a rundown of destinations and journey times, see Travel Details on pp.148–149.

All buses and louages leave from the **bus station** (☎02/296208) on avenue Ali Belhaouane. Note that the early-morning daily bus departures for Mahdia, Monastir, Sousse and Kairouan, all pass through Hammamet. All other buses change at Nabeul for Hammamet. **Louages** tend to follow the bus routes but with a much reduced journey time. Note that there are no louages to El Haouaria, but standard yellow taxis perform the same function on a price-per-place basis (*par plassa*).

It's worth noting that a summer **hydrofoil** service sometimes runs from Kélibia port to Trápani in Sicily, usually a four-hour journey but unpredictable, especially in rough weather; timetables vary from year to year. For information and tickets, contact Select Travel on rue Ibn Khaldoun (☎02/273117).

was a fifth-century BC holiday resort – a sort of Carthaginian *Club Med*. It is now understood that the town's main industry was manufacturing a purple dye for which Carthaginians and Phoenicians were famous, named after a species of shellfish called *murex*. Hundreds of these creatures were collected and left in large pits in the ground to rot; the smell must have been overpowering, but the decomposed mess was somehow made up into the dye known by the Romans as "Tyrian purple" (after the Phoenician capital, Tyre), much beloved as the imperial colour.

Almost all the **houses**, whose foundations line the easy-to-follow streets, follow the same plan: a narrow corridor leading into a small courtyard, with a water well and sometimes an altar to the household gods. Kerkouane's houses are most famous, however, for their private **baths**, neatly lined with reddish cement, some of them covered with plain pink and white mosaic. Virtually every house has its own, which says something about Carthaginian society – while the Romans spent vast sums on public baths, the Carthaginians kept a private, low-key profile. The town was abandoned sometime in the second century BC, after the destruction of Carthage, and never reoccupied by the Romans – which explains its remarkable state of preservation.

If Kerkouane, the largest Carthaginian site yet discovered, seems like a meagre remnant of a major civilization, it's worth remembering that outsiders were as impressed by the Carthaginians' agricultural prowess as they were by their navy. A description of the interior of Cap Bon by Diodorus Siculus, a historian writing in Rome in the first century BC, but drawing on earlier accounts, still holds true today.

It was divided into market gardens and orchards of all sorts of fruit trees, with many streams of water flowing in channels irrigating every part. There were country houses everywhere, lavishly built and covered with stucco, which testified to the wealth of their owners . . . Part of the land was planted with vines, part with olives and other protective trees. Beyond these, cattle and sheep were pastured on the plains, and there were meadows filled with grazing horses.

To **get to Kerkouane**, if you don't have your own transport, you can take a bus or louage from Kélibia to the turn-off (0.8TD); take a taxi (for around 4TD – settle the price before you start); or even walk or hitch – the latter is certainly possible. Leaving the site, you'll probably have to take potluck and hitch, or hail a passing bus or louage.

El Haouaria and around   الهوّارية

Just below **Jebel Sidi Abiod**, the defiant last hump of Cap Bon, is the pretty village of **EL HAOUARIA**, best known as the centre of falconry in Tunisia. In an annual festival held in mid-June, young birds are caught on the mountain, trained for a month, then used for hunting game birds on the mountain and the heaths below. Two species of birds of prey are involved – sparrowhawks, which are trapped in nets on the mountain as they migrate, and female peregrine falcons, which are taken as young from the nests on the rocky cliffs. The males, it is said, soon die of a "broken heart". The number of birds each falconer can catch is supposed to be strictly limited; they may not be sold, and the sparrowhawks are later returned to the wild, but what happens to the peregrines is uncertain. About 500m out of the village, there's an extremely helpful and informative **wildlife information centre**, with particularly good information on birds of prey, run by the Cellule Nature et Oiseaux. The building is called the *Aquilaria*, after the Latin for "eagle", and the name of the town is thought to have derived from the same word. The village itself is a sleepy agricultural centre that turns its back on the Mediterranean to focus on Cap Bon's rich hinterland.

BIRDLIFE AROUND EL HAOUARIA AND THE CAPE

The rocky hillsides around the mountain of Jebel Sidi Abiod and the walk to Ras ed Drak beach are rich not only in flowers but also in **birdlife**. The fields have abundant finches, buntings and warblers, along with stonechats – the black-headed males perching prominently on bushes and telegraph wires. Down on Ras ed Drak, the scrub behind the beach is often full of migrating birds, with the unusual blue rock thrush and Moussier's redstart both relatively common residents.

The sea is worth watching too, and vast numbers of breeding pairs of the stiff-winged Cory's shearwater, as well as gulls and gull-billed and sandwich terns, can often be seen flying past, the last two species occurring as winter visitors and passage migrants.

The actual headland of Cap Bon is special because it is the last jumping-off point for migrating birds of prey before they cross the Mediterranean. April and May are the peak spring passage months, with lesser numbers coming back each autumn. Honey buzzards are the dominant species, although black kites, marsh harriers and common buzzards also occur in good numbers, together with a variety of migrating eagles, sparrowhawks and hobbies (the small, rather dashing falcons, midway in size between kestrel and peregrine, that prey mostly on swallows and the like – they follow the migrating swallow flocks up from Africa). The best place for viewing the migration is the top of Jebel Sidi Abiod. This requires a **permit** during the migration season; write in advance to the Direction des Fôrets, 30 rue Alain Savary, Tunis (☎01/258118).

El Haouaria is pleasantly out of the way and its villagers will assume you've come to see the two sets of **caves** just outside the town. One of these, the **Ghar el Kebir** (daily: summer 8am–7pm; winter 9am–5pm; 1.1TD), is a complex of quarries right on the shore, reached by following the road straight through the village past the cemetery and beyond the *Pension les Grottes*. To your left you'll see electricity-generating windmills, from which a walk of 30min brings you to a group of pyramid-shaped chambers poised above crashing breakers. Quarrying operations started here by the Carthaginians were continued by the Romans and Byzantines – the latter installing a military garrison – and the stone was used for buildings all around the Gulf of Carthage. The locals here recount vivid stories of slaves who spent their whole lives working inside the caverns.

The other complex, up on the mountain – **La Grotte des Chauves-Souris** – is full of bats. A four-kilometre track leads from the village, but you'll need to ask around for a guide in El Haouaria itself. You'll also need a torch to make close acquaintance with the creatures. If bats don't appeal, the mountain is still a wonderful place for long windy walks, where you can reflect on the strategic position that played such a large part in Tunisia's history, with Sicily just 150km away.

Southeast of El Haouaria, at the very beginning of Cap Bon's south coast, hides the area's most beautiful and least-known beach, **Ras ed Drak** – known as El Haouaria Plage these days. The white sands are sheltered here and given an extra dimension by the mountain's craggy shoulder. A signposted four-kilometre road leads from El Haouaria over heathland to the assortment of villas and farms on the slopes behind the beach where, in season, there's a small shop on the sand. The futuristic complex on the shore to the south is a station on a gas pipeline running between Algeria and Italy.

Practicalities

If you need to change money, El Haouaria has a **bank** in the main square. There's a **louage** service from the main square to Kélibia every hour or so and less frequently to Grombalia, Soliman and Tunis. There are four buses a day to Nabeul via Kélibia, seven to Tunis and one to Sousse and Mahdia (5.45am). For information on buses call (☎02/297012). For local destinations such as Kerkouane, or the Sidi Daoud turn-off, you could share a **taxi** (2–3TD to the Sidi Daoud turn-off). There is no tourist office here, but good budget **accommodation** in the form of the *Pension Dar Toubib* (☎02/297163; ②), tucked away down the side streets but well signposted (follow the blue signs). If you'd prefer more comfort, the only alternatives are the two-star *Hôtel l'Épervier* (☎02/297017, ⓕ297258; ③), on the main street, and the *Pension les Grottes* (☎02/297078; ③), at the top of the hill leading down to Ghar el Kebir, with en-suite a/c rooms, and nothing special other than its views. **Camping** on Ras ed Drak is feasible if you're happy with water from wells and food bought from the farms. Across the street from the *Épervier* in El Haouaria, the *Restaurant de la Jeunesse* serves basic **meals**. The *Épervier*'s restaurant is priced in line with its rooms (set meals for 6 or 8TD with *à la carte* more expensive). *Pension les Grottes* also has a restaurant, but it fails to take advantage of its beautiful location. By far the best place is *Restaurant la Daurade* (☎02/269080; daily noon–3pm & 7–11pm), right on the seashore next to the caves, with its cosy indoor section and series of outdoor terraces. Their speciality is, unsurprisingly, daurade fish. A three-course meal can be enjoyed for around 20TD, quite a bit cheaper if you don't have seafood as a main, they don't serve alcohol though.

Sidi Daoud and around سيدي داود

Seven kilometres on past El Haouaria, heading west along the north coast of the peninsula, a turning on the right leads 2km to **SIDI DAOUD**, the sleepiest of sleepy fishing villages. Almost totally dormant for ten months of the year, it bursts into life around May for the **Matanza**, a spectacular if gory tuna harvest with a technique going back to Roman times. A huge net is laid about 4km out to sea, stretching from surface to seabed to catch the fish as they migrate around the coast to spawn. The net forms a series of chambers of decreasing size, and when the final one – the *corpo*, or death chamber – is full, it is closed. Then the boats converge around the net and raise it from all sides until the fish are virtually out of the water, at which point the fishermen jump into the net and set about the fish (some of which weigh as much as 250kg) with clubs and knives.

It used to be possible to get a **permit** from the National Fisheries Office to watch the Matanza from one of the boats but, after disagreements with the tourist authorities, this scheme has lapsed. If you're interested, it might be worth checking the permit situation with the Commissariat Général de la Pêche in Tunis at 30 rue Alain Savary (☎01/258118) before you come up here. Failing that, the local office is at the dockside. If you do get permission and decide to try it, be warned that the smell of fish lingers for some days afterwards.

Off the coast north of Sidi Daoud, the islands of **Zembra** and **Zembretta** are now off limits, having been declared a nature reserve under army protection. Zembra, with sea birds, beautiful scenery and excellent snorkelling, used to host a scuba-diving centre run by the Centre Nautique de Tunisie. If you want to try for a permit to visit, you could write to the Direction des Forêts at 30 rue Alain Savary in Tunis, well in advance of your trip, stating reasons; don't expect success, but, if you do get permission, access to the island is by fishing boat from Sidi Daoud. There's nowhere to stay on the island so it'll have to be a day-trip.

The only other diversion around Sidi Daoud is the **Forest of Dar Chichou** to the southeast. A road runs inland from Sidi Daoud, through the forest to emerge on the south coast between Kerkouane and Kélibia. On the way, you pass a fenced-off **nature reserve** devoted, strangely enough, to **gazelles**; you should be able to glimpse some from the road, especially if you stop and wait quietly for a while.

From Sidi Daoud down the Cap Bon's northern coast to Bir Meroua, the road stays several kilometres inland, skirting country that is surprisingly mountainous – even reminiscent of Scottish heathland. For most of the way, the coastline is one deserted beach, backed by farmland with any number of possible tracks down to the shore but no facilities once you are there.

There is no **public transport** from Sidi Daoud itself, but you may be able to pick up a bus or louage along the main road. Buses from El Haouaria to Soliman and Grombalia run along here (local people will know current times), but louages are likely to be full and you might have to consider hitching.

Korbous and around قربص

Protruding like the knuckle of Cap Bon's finger, the massif of **Jebel Korbous** looms over the ancient thermal resort named after it. Apparently these waters are good for curing arthritis, rheumatism, hypertension, obesity and cellulite. Famous since Roman times as *Aquae Calidau Carpitanae*, and heavily developed by the French, **KORBOUS**, 30km along the coast from Sidi Daoud, has seen better days and now exudes a seedy, turn-of-the-century air reminiscent of Hammam Lif (see p.120). It remains a popular weekend excursion, though, and the scenery is dramatic – especially if you have transport that will take you all the way round the mountain. There are four daily buses from Tunis's Bab Aleoua station, which also stop at Aïn Oktar (see opposite).

Korbous is set in a steep ravine where the Romans first came to take the waters. At the end of the nineteenth century the spa was redesigned by a French civil engineer, who then retired to the precarious villa – now a presidential palace – perched on the rock overlooking the main street. There isn't a great deal to Korbous apart from its main street lined with souvenir stalls for daytrippers on Sundays, the spa and two **hotels**: the fancy three-star *Hôtel les Sources* (☎02/284540; ❺), for those who can afford the supervised thermal cure – "the largest dose will be taken first thing in the morning while fasting in several successive swallows", according to ONTT literature – and the *Résidence des Thermes* (☎02/284520; ❸), five minutes from the spa on the main road, with good rooms and a restaurant opposite. It's best to ring and confirm that they're open. The ancient and suitably grotty **hammam** (daily 8am–4pm; men in the morning, women in the afternoon) is thought to have origins in Roman times. Between the presidential palace and the hotel, the **Zarziha Rock** has been polished smooth by generations of women sliding down it to cure infertility. It's a pretty enough place, with waves crashing onto rocks below the Jebel Korbous's craggy green slopes. Facilities are limited, but the *Café-Restaurant Dhrib*, on the main street, is pleasant and moderately priced, as is the *Résidence des Thermes*'s restaurant.

Once you've seen Korbous, you'll need your own transport if you want to follow the new road around Jebel Korbous. One kilometre beyond the village past the *Café-Restaurant Dhrib*, a spring called **Aïn el Atrous** (Goat Spring) shoots out of the mountain through a pipe below the road. Following the steep steps beside it down to the sea, you'll find a narrow strip of beach beyond which people **camp** (though it looks very exposed). At the point where the hot sulphurous spring water meets the salty Mediterranean, a small pool containing both waters has formed, which is wonderfully relaxing and good for skin complaints and rheumatism. A track extends off back up the road, then hundreds of metres up the mountain's north shoulder and down onto a high plain and the village of **Douela**, before meeting the main road south to Soliman at the small settlement of **Bir Meroua**. If you can get down the steep hill, the long, pristine white beach of **Marsa Ben Ramdane** is one of the most spectacular in the country: take the track (signposted "Bekakcha") to the right about 3km outside Bir Meroua on the road to Korbous. About 11km further sits a magnificent white beach. Dominated by a fort that's been converted into a private house, the only permanent inhabitants down here are a few fishermen who operate from a wooden pier. In season, you might be able to rent one of the reed shacks on the beach.

South of Korbous, the coastal road skirts the foot of the mountain for 3km before hitting the diminutive spa town of AÏN OKTOR. The four daily buses to Tunis pass this way. Three kilometres further south, the road drops down into the tiny, rickety settlement of SIDI RAIS. Once a fashionable seaside resort, it now comprises just a row of wooden houses on stilts and a restaurant, *La Brise* (variable hours), serving good fish dishes. One kilometre back towards Korbous, the *Hôtel Chiraz* (☏02/398143; ❸) has eight rooms around an orchard but ring first to check that they're open. Four kilometres south of Sidi Rais, you rejoin the C26, which takes you south to Soliman.

Soliman and Soliman Plage سليمان

Eighteen kilometres south of Korbous is SOLIMAN, a seventeenth-century Andalusian settlement whose mosque is almost the only remnant of that time. Today the town is a prosperous agricultural centre with an attractive tree-filled square next to the mosque, whose semicircular Spanish roof tiles can just be made out. Look out, too, for a fountain surrounded by colourful ceramic work.

Rue Habib Thameur runs from the town centre around the mosque to end up near the bus station. As well as several bus services (see pp.148–149), there are also louages to Tunis and Grombalia, which leave from near the bus station. There are no buses or louages for Soliman Plage; taxis leave from place 7 Novembre, the other side of the town centre, or you could walk. The post office (country hours) is at 35 rue Habib Thameur. As for accommodation, there are no hotels in town itself, only at Soliman Plage.

Isolated on the edge of an empty marshy plain, SOLIMAN PLAGE (also known as Plage Ejjehmi) is Soliman's beach resort, 3km away. The sand is white enough and there are good views of the mountains – Jebel Bou Kornine to the west and Jebel Korbous to the east – but the desolate stretch of beach makes for one of the least attractive resorts in Tunisia. At the end of the road from Soliman is a café, and two hotels a few hundred metres up the beach to your left (to get straight to them, turn off the Soliman road 500m before hitting the beach). Between the café and the hotels, straw beach cabins are used by Tunisian holidaymakers during July and August, when the beach is packed solid. The rest of the year they're abandoned and anyone could use them for a night on the beach.

Of the two hotels, both catering for European package tourists, the one-star *Hôtel el Andalous* (☏02/290199; ❹) is the cheaper and has waterskiing and riding, but no pool and may be closed in winter. Posher and rather Teutonic is the large two-star *Hôtel Solymar* (☏02/290105, ℻290155; ❺). Beyond the *Solymar*, the beach continues round to Borj Cedria (see p.120).

Grombalia and around قرمبالية

Heading south from Tunis, the highway and the old P1 cut through the fertile bottom end of Cap Bon. Originally settled by Spanish Muslim immigrants in the seventeenth century, the region was later popular with European farmers under the French regime, who left behind the many red-tiled farms and crumbling gateposts scattered among its vast vineyards and orchards.

There's little enough reason to stop here, unless you happen to coincide with one of the seasonal festivals. GROMBALIA, straddling both GP1 and the main north–south train line, is the largest market town in the area and celebrates a wine festival every September to coincide with the harvest – though, that aside, there's little reason to come. There are frequent buses and louages to Menzel Bou Zelfa, Nabeul, Soliman and Tunis. Grombalia's train station serves Mahdia, Monastir, Sousse, Bir Bou Regba (with connections to Hammamet and Nabeul) and Tunis; there are also hourly **buses** to Menzel Bou Zelfa, Nabeul, Soliman and Tunis.

MENZEL BOU ZELFA, 8km east of Grombalia, has an **Orange Festival** to celebrate the appearance of orange blossom in April or May, as well as an important seventeenth-century **zaouia**, a multi-domed structure in the centre of town.

If you're mobile, and fancy an excursion into the hills west of Grombalia, take the road opposite the Société Tunisienne de Banque on the main road, which leads 8km over the motorway up to the village of **AÏN TEBOURNOK**. Just before Aïn Tebournok, look out north of the road for a grotesque **colonial mansion**, a fantasy Moorish pile, with a quasi-minaret for a central tower staring out over the plain. Aïn Tebournok itself sits in a bowl of hills, built around an ancient spring where Roman remains lie forlorn and deserted.

Some 10km south of Grombalia on the road to Hammamet is **BOU ARGOUB**. There's little enough to this tiny village apart from a **villa** built by the Fascists of Tunisia's Italian community for Mussolini. Relations between Mussolini and the French were never good: the Italians always felt they had been cheated out of Tunisia in 1881 and had to settle for second best with Libya. Mussolini was continually preparing to invade Tunisia and, with more Italian colonists in the country than French, this appeared no empty threat. Ultimately, however, the Abyssinian campaign distracted "Il Duce" and the villa, now a girls' school, was never occupied by him.

travel details

Trains

Grombalia to: Bir Bou Regba (4–7 daily; 15–20min); Gabès (1 daily; 6hr 10min); Mahdia (1–2 daily; 3hr 20min); Monastir (2–4 daily; 2hr 50min); Nabeul (1–2 direct daily; 50min); Sfax (1 daily; 4hr 5min); Sousse (2–4 daily; 1hr 25min–1hr 40min); Tunis (4–6 daily; 35min).

Hammamet to: Bir Bou Regba (8–10 daily; 7min); Nabeul (8–10 daily; 20min); Tunis (1 direct daily; 1hr 10min; connections via Bir Bou Regba 7–10 daily; 1hr 10min).

Nabeul to: Hammamet (8–10 daily; 25min); Bir Bou Regba (8–10 daily; 30min); Tunis (1 direct daily; 1hr 20min; connections via Bir Bou Regba 7–10 daily; 1hr 30min).

Buses

El Haouaria to: Kélibia (4 daily; 30min); Nabeul (4 daily; 1hr 30min); Soliman (7 daily; 1hr 15min); Tunis (7 daily; 2hr).

Grombalia to: Menzel Bou Zelfa (hourly; 15min); Nabeul (hourly; 45min); Soliman (hourly; 15min); Tunis (hourly; 45min).

Hammamet to: Kairouan (2 daily; 2hr 15min); Mahdia (1 daily; 3hr); Monastir (1 daily; 2hr);

Nabeul (every 30min; 15min); Sousse (2 daily; 1hr 45min); Tunis (4 daily express; 1hr; regular service every 30min; 1hr 30min).

Kélibia to: El Haouaria (hourly; 30min); Hammamet (4 daily; 1hr); Kairouan (1 daily; 3hr 30min); Korba (hourly; 45min); Mahdia (1 daily; 4hr); Menzel Bou Zelfa (hourly; 1hr); Menzel Temime (hourly; 15min); Monastir (1 daily; 3hr); Sousse (2 daily; 2hr 45min); Nabeul (hourly; 1hr); Soliman (hourly; 1hr 15min); Tunis (hourly; 2hr 30min).

Menzel Bou Zelfa to: Grombalia (frequent; 15min); Kélibia (hourly; 1hr); Menzel Temime (hourly; 45min); Soliman (frequent; 15min); Tunis (hourly; 1hr).

Nabeul to: Borj Cedria (every 30min; 1hr); El Fahs (3 daily; 1hr 45min); Grombalia (every 30min; 45min); Hammamet (every 30min; 15min); Kairouan (4 daily; 2hr 30min); Kélibia (hourly; 1hr); Korba (every 30min; 15min); Mahdia (3 daily; 3hr 30min); Menzel Temime (every 30min; 45min); Monastir (3 daily; 2hr 30min); Sousse (3 daily; 2hr 15min); Tunis (every 30min; 1hr 30min); Zaghouan (3 daily; 1hr 30min).

Soliman to: El Haouaria (7 daily; 1hr 15min); Grombalia (frequent; 15min); Kélibia (frequent;

1hr 15min); Korbous (4 daily; 15min); Menzel Bou Zelfa (frequent; 15min); Tunis (hourly; 45min).

Louages

Louage journey times are roughly three-quarters the time taken by buses on the same route. Frequency depends on demand, but morning is always the best time to get a louage, especially for longer journeys.

El Haouaria to: Grombalia (1hr 15min); Kélibia (yellow taxis serve as louages for this route and leave every hour or so; 20min); Soliman (1hr); Tunis (1hr 45min).

Hammamet to: Nabeul (15min); Sousse (15min); Tunis (1hr 45min).

Kélibia to: El Haouaria (20min); Korba (30min); Menzel Temime (10min); Nabeul (45min); Tunis (2hr).

Nabeul to: Enfida (1hr 30min); El Fahs (1hr 30min); Hammamet (15min); Kélibia (45min); Tunis (1hr); Zaghouan (1hr 15min).

Soliman to: Grombalia (15min); Menzel Bou Zelfa (15min); Menzel Temime (45min); Tunis (45min).

Hydrofoil

Kélibia to: Trápani in Sicily (summer-only, services vary).

CHAPTER THREE

BIZERTE AND THE NORTH

S parsely populated and with few roads, Tunisia's **northern coast** has played little part in the country's touristic development until recently. **Bizerte**, the one town of any size, is still more of a port than a resort, despite the excellence of the beaches in the area. Even if you get no further, Bizerte is worth a few days of your time – easily reached from Tunis, and with a monumental heritage covering centuries of strategic importance. Closer to the capital, and very much the preserve of Tunisians, are the superlative long white strands of **Raf Raf** and **Ras Sidi el Mekki**. Beaches with few equals in Tunisia they are cut in two by the steep green flanks of **Cap Farina**, with its crumbling old pirate base of **Ghar el Melh**. **Utica**, a Roman city famous for its part in the civil war between Julius Caesar and Pompey, lies not far from Ghar el Melh on the road from Tunis. Inland, **Lac Ichkeul** and its national park form an ornithological highlight.

West of Bizerte along the coast, buses are infrequent and often erratic, but it's possible to reach some beautiful and remote beaches poised between deep forested headlands. **Cap Serrat** and **Sidi Mechrig** are both feasible targets; **Tabarka**, long popular as a resort for independent travellers and a recent target for major tourist development, is perhaps best of all, overlooked by a spectacular island-castle. Just inland from here, **Aïn Draham** is reckoned the coolest point in midsummer; and around, in the **Khroumirie Mountains**, there are some impressive hikes.

In contrast to the coast, the **Medjerda Valley**, formed around the country's one permanently flowing river, has always had a considerable urban population. **Béja** is the most attractive of the modern centres, though more intriguing is the Roman city of **Bulla Regia** with its underground villas, unique in the ancient world.

THE COAST

To visit anywhere other than the major centres along the north coast without a car means either hitching or fighting for a place in the occasional louage. Trains only run along the **Medjerda Valley**, with a branch line up to Bizerte; otherwise the whole

---

MARKET DAYS

Monday – Aïn Draham
Tuesday – Béja, Bizerte, Ghardimaou, Souk es Sebt
Wednesday – Jendouba, Menzel Bourguiba, Nefza
Thursday – Bou Salem, Sejnane

Friday – Tabarka, Ras Jebel
Saturday – Bizerte, El Alia, Hammam Bourguiba, Mateur
Sunday – Bezina, Fernana, Menzel Bourguiba, Thibar

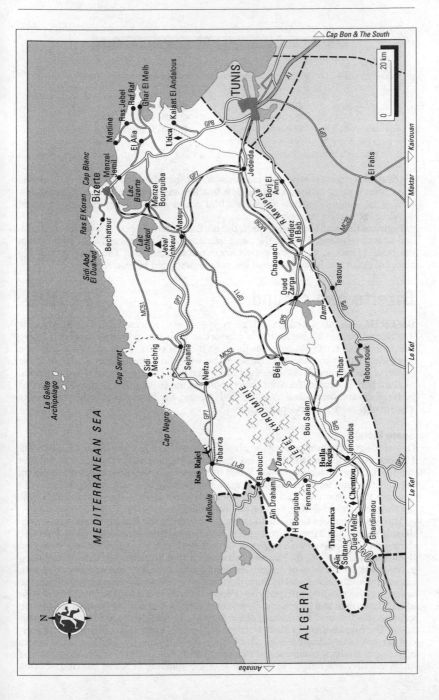

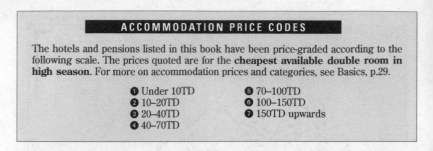

north coastal region is somewhat inaccessible. The payoff lies in the rugged, unspoiled shoreline. Soaking up the sun on the best beaches and stopping off to explore the historic sights could fill several weeks; it's best not to hurry, taking leisurely trips and avoiding the searing summer heat.

Between **Raf Raf beach** and Tunis, the northern shoreline consists of barely inhabited alluvial farmland. Beyond, the coast becomes thickly populated and culminates in the port of **Bizerte**, where the population thins out again until **Tabarka**, recently the object of major tourist development but not yet despoiled beyond recognition.

Bizerte and around   بنزرت

BIZERTE, also called Benzert or Bizerta, is the most underrated of Tunisia's resorts – perhaps because it's not so much a resort as a historic port that happens to have beaches. These aren't as opulent as those on the east coast, but if you're looking for a town with both swimming and character you won't find much better. It stands at the mouth of **Lac Bizerte**, a saltwater lake connected to the sea by a canal, along which the modern port is located. An older outlet connects the fishing port to the sea. Guarded by two forts and overlooked by a dignified mosque, the fishing port is the place to get a sense of Bizerte's pre-colonial identity.

Some history

One of the great natural ports of the Mediterranean, Bizerte was exploited early by the **Phoenicians**, who improbably called their town Hippo Diarrhytus and dug the first channel linking the lake to the sea. When the Romans arrived they improved the existing facilities, and imperial prosperity gave the town its first taste of popularity – the Younger Pliny described it as "a town where people of all ages spend their time enjoying the pleasures of fishing, boating and swimming".

The Arabs changed the name to Benzert, and under the Hafsids its prosperity continued, when it had a great hunting park. Bizerte inevitably found itself in the front line during the Turco-Spanish struggles of the sixteenth century, and Charles V punished the town for supporting the corsair Barbarossa with a brutal raid in 1535. It continued to absorb large numbers of Andalusian immigrants, however, and was rewarded with considerable attention from the Turkish rulers, who developed its amenities during the seventeenth and eighteenth centuries. **Piracy** was rife at this time but, with the demise of the slave trade and increasing European domination of the Mediterranean, Bizerte went into decline until the opening of the Suez Canal brought renewed strategic importance. The French then set about building up the port's facilities – strictly for commercial purposes, they claimed. Even after World War II, Bizerte inspired lust in the hearts of Western strategic planners, and following Independence the French simply stayed on. When they still refused to evacuate after the bombing of Sakiet Sidi Youssef (see

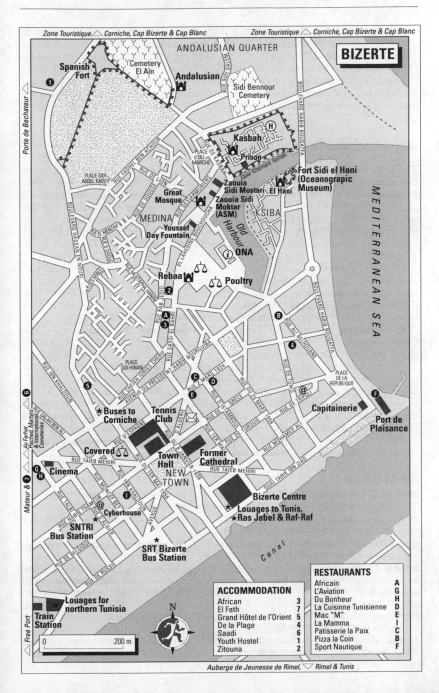

Zone Touristique △ Corniche, Cap Bizerte & Cap Blanc   Zone Touristique △ Corniche, Cap Bizerte & Cap Blanc

ANDALUSIAN QUARTER

BIZERTE

Spanish Fort

Cemetery El Aïn

Andalusian

Sidi Bennour Cemetery

BOULEVARD HABIB BOUGATFA

Porte de Bechateur

PLACE SIDI ABDEL KADER

Kasbah

Prison

H

Quai Khemais Ternan

Fort Sidi el Hani (Oceanograpic Museum)

PLACE 'DU MARCHE

RUE DE KASBAH

Zaouia Sidi Mostari   El Hani

Great Mosque

Zaouia Sidi Moktar (ASM)

KSIBA

MEDINA

Youssef Day Fountain

Old Harbour

i ONA

PL. LAHEDINE BOUCHOUCHA

Rebaa

Poultry

A
2
3

B

4

PLACE SIDI HINAN

PLACE DE LA RÉPUBLIQUE

5

C
2 Mars 1934
D

E

Buses to Corniche

Tennis Club

Capitainerie

Port de Plaisance

Covered

Town Hall

Former Cathedral

NEW TOWN

G
H

Cinema

J

Bizerte Centre

Louages to Tunis, Ras Jebel & Raf-Raf

Cyberhouse

SNTRI Bus Station

SRT Bizerte Bus Station

Canal

M E D I T E R R A N E A N   S E A

Mateur & ▽   Av Farhat Hached, Martyrs & International Cemeteries

Free Port

Louages for northern Tunisia

Train Station

N

0   200 m

ACCOMMODATION

African	3
El Fath	7
Grand Hôtel de l'Orient	5
De la Plage	6
Saadi	4
Youth Hostel	1
Zitouna	2

RESTAURANTS

Africain	A
L'Aviation	G
Du Bonheur	H
La Cuisinne Tunisienne	D
Mac "M"	E
La Mamma	I
Patisserie la Paix	C
Pizza la Coin	B
Sport Nautique	F

Auberge de Jeunesse de Rimel, ▽ Rimel & Tunis

p.440), Tunisian forces blockaded the military base in 1961. The French responded by trying to break the blockade, and Tunisia's army undertook its first military action. More than a thousand Tunisian lives were lost before the French finally withdrew on October 15, 1963 – no longer a national holiday, but still a day of celebration in Bizerte.

Thanks to the French legacy (and departure), the main thrust of Bizerte's development has been industrial, and its naval arsenal has been converted into a vast complex, including what was once North Africa's first blast furnace. Tourism comes second place.

Arrival, information and accommodation

The **train station** is by the docks at the western end of rue de Russie and rue de Belgique, a ten-minute walk to the centre. Outside is the **louage station**, where more regional services (from Mateur, Sejnane, Menzel Bourguiba and Béja) will drop you. If you're coming from Tunis, the louages drop you at the corner of quai Tarik Ibn Ziad and rue du 8 Mai 1938, next to the lift bridge. The SRT Bizerte **bus station** is at the bottom of avenue d'Algérie and rue Ibn Khaldoun, at the end of quai Tarik Ibn Ziad. Other buses, from Kairouan, Sousse, Sfax and Jerba, stop at the SNTRI depot in rue d'Alger.

You'll find the **tourist office** above ONA at quai Khemais Ternane in the old port (July & Aug Mon–Thurs 8am–1.30pm & 4–7pm, Fri & Sat 8.30am–1.30pm; Sept–June Mon–Thurs 8.30am–1pm & 3–5.45pm, Fri & Sat 8.30am–1.30pm; ☎02/432897). Note that **street names** in Bizerte are mainly posted in Arabic and locals tend not to number buildings and houses, so locating specific places can be a problem.

In Bizerte you can **stay** in the town centre, on the beaches to the north, or at Rimel beach, south of town. The choice depends on what kind of hotel you want: most of the cheap (and generally tawdry) places are in town (watch they don't overcharge you). The more expensive and modern starred hotels are found just north of town in the newly developed **zone touristique de Sidi Salem**, whilst older and somewhat cheaper package-type places are strung out beyond along the Corniche for 5km to Cap Bizerte. The *zone touristique* hotels are within walking distance from the city centre; for the Corniche, take a bus from the "Cheikh Idriss" bus stop at the corner of boulevard Hassen en Nouri and avenue Bourguiba. Prices for most places drop spectacularly out of season, with rooms at thirty percent of high-season rates not uncommon. **Camping** out on the main northern beaches is usually tolerated.

Hotels in town

Africain, 59 rue Sassi el Bahri ☎02/434412. Recently renovated, this basic place is clean and friendly and favourable to the nearby *Zitouna,* although both are noisy due to the street market. ❷

El Fath, av Bourguiba ☎02/430596. A recent addition that's more upmarket than most of the other town alternatives, and a good deal better, too. ❸

Grand Hôtel de l'Orient, 38 bd Hassan en Nouiri ☎02/421499. Recently renovated modern place and a good bet in summer with its air conditioning. ❸

Hôtel de La Plage, 23 av Mohammed Rejiba ☎02/444792. Newest of the town hotels and only 50m from the seafront. Rooms range from basic, clean doubles, to triples and family rooms, both with and without facilities. Also has a rooftop terrace and satellite TV lounge. Run by the same management as the *Africain.* ❷–❸

Saadi, rue Salah Ben Ali ☎02/422528. Out by the sports stadium this cheapie is reasonably clean, if basic and without hot showers. ❷

Zitouna, pl Slahedinne Bouchoucha ☎02/438769. Definitely dingy and without hot water, but cheap. Ask for a room with a window. ❶

Hotels in the zone touristique

Résidence Aïn Mertem, 1km up the Corniche ☎02/422615, ℱ432459. New, huge upmarket *apart'otel* offering a range of self-catering studios sleeping three, five or seven, as well as apartments and chalet-villas, which are only a bargain if you're in a big group (five or seven people). ❻

Corniche ★★★, 2km up the Corniche ☎02/431844, ℱ431830. One of the smarter of the Corniche hotels – gleaming marble and chrome, with prices to match. ❻

Jalta ★★, 1.5km up the Corniche ☎02/443100, ℱ436888. Friendly and well-run package place offering horse-riding, windsurfing and other facilities. ❺

El Khayem, 5km up the Corniche ☎02/432120 or 434277. Cheapest of the beach hotels, and furthest from town right at the tip of Cap Bizerte. Accommodation is in , apparently "typical", concrete windowless huts. The showers don't always work but it's friendly. ❷

Nador ★★, 2km up the Corniche ☎02/431848, ℱ433817. Mainly geared to German package tours. Offers water sports. ❺

Petit Mousse ★★, 3.5km up the Corniche ☎02/432185. Dating back to 1946 and exceptionally friendly, this is the pick of the *zone touristique* hotels, and you'll need to book ahead. ❺

Youth hostels and campsite

Auberge de Jeunesse de Rimel and campsite, Rimel ☎02/440819. Signposted from the road near the #8 bus stop (20min from the SRT Bizerte bus station). Sylvan and peaceful place smelling of pine and eucalyptus, with dorm beds for 5TD. The sea is 300m through the trees and over a dune. See p.158 for more on Rimel Plage.

Maison des Jeunes, Complexe de Jeunesse, bd Hassan en Nouri ☎02/431608. The usual charmless monolith, located just to the west of the Spanish Fort. There's a sports hall and a covered pool. Check in after 6pm; dorms 5TD.

The Town

Modern Bizerte begins with a shipping canal built in the 1890s. Crossed via a **lift-bridge**, the canal runs from the Mediterranean into Lac Bizerte, a large stretch of saltwater. The bridge looks pretty impressive when raised, its middle section towering straight up and visible right across Bizerte. Bizerte itself still consists of a grid-pattern **French new town** – a wholly unscenic place that has a curious gritty charm, with a green and spacious central square and grandiose buildings along the seafront. The new town sits alongside the remains of the old walled town with its harbour, the **Old Port**, built to serve as a major Mediterranean naval and military base, and guarded at the entrance by the twin forts of the **Kasbah** and **Fort Sidi el Hani**. Next to the harbour are the narrow streets and monuments of the **Medina**, overlooked from the top of the hill behind the town by the so-called **Spanish fort**, begun by the Spanish but finished by their enemies, the Turks.

Until the end of the nineteenth century, Bizerte was a compact city straddling a natural channel leading from the Mediterranean into the lake, its centre standing on an island in the middle and heavy fortifications punctuating its surrounding walls. When the French colonial planners arrived they filled in most of the channel, built their new town east of avenue Bourguiba on reclaimed land and dug the modern canal to provide superior access to the lake. You can still get a sense of the historic town, though, by heading for place Lahedine Bouchoucha, on the edge of the Old Harbour.

The Old Harbour

Surrounded by cafés, narrow streets and forts (and one particularly hideous block of apartments), the **Old Port** is the heart of Bizerte. Originally it split into two arms, one running along what is now place Lahedine Bouchoucha and one continuing around today's ONA building. Reuniting on avenue Bourguiba, the channel went behind an island and continued into the body of Lac Bizerte. The island in the channel – nowadays the area around the ONA, the market and the Rebaa Mosque – lay within the city walls, and in pre-colonial times, this was where the European population lived in detached splendour. Most of old Bizerte lay west of the channel, making up what is now known as the Medina. Its western wall followed the path of boulevard Hassan En Nouri up to the Spanish fort on the hill behind town, before returning back down the hill to the Kasbah.

It's a long time since any fishing boats or corsair privateers sailed all the way through town, along the channels and below the minarets, on their way to and from Lac Bizerte. But the Old Port retains a magical feeling, especially in the evening. Café tables are set out along the quay and, as darkness falls, illuminated boats chug off for the night's fishing, accompanied by the call to prayer from the minaret of the great mosque that stands just next to the harbour. In the daytime, the quaysides are a peaceful retreat where you can have a coffee or wander up to the prosaic modern bridge between the twin fortifications of the Kasbah on the left and Fort Sidi el Hani on the right.

The Kasbah and Ksiba

Standing at the mouth of the port, the **Kasbah**, with its massive walls, is hard to miss. Although its general form suggests an originally Byzantine foundation, like many of Bizerte's monuments, it dates mainly from the seventeenth century. Virtually untouched by the modern city outside, it's a wonderful place to wander around, as beyond its single, heavily defensive gate lies a miniature old town of passages, arches and walls painted in pastel shades. Outside, through an entrance in the southeast bastion facing the port, you can also reach a promenade running around the top of the Kasbah **walls** (Tues–Sun 9am–12.30pm & 3–6pm, till 8pm in summer; 0.5TD). A café operates up here on most summer evenings, but at any time of day it's the best place to get a view of the historic town's layout and to imagine fishing boats and privateers alike making their way through the town into Lac Bizerte.

Facing the Kasbah on the other side of the harbour channel, the smaller **Fort Sidi el Hani**, is the other half of what must have made a formidable defensive ensemble, though the effect is now somewhat muffled by the modern bridge over the channel. Parts of the fort – the round tower and the wall facing the channel – date back to Byzantine times. It is now a small **Oceanographic Museum** (same times and price as Kasbah walls), though aside from a few glum turtles and forgetful fish it's not up to much. The area immediately behind the fort is called the **Ksiba** (the diminutive of the Kasbah, meaning "little fort"), and still houses local fishermen, who moor boats outside their doorsteps.

The Medina

Overwhelmed by the colonial town and bombed during World War II, the **Medina** is nonetheless a good place for a wander – despite a sparsity of monuments and souks, in parts the overused adjective "labyrinthine" really does apply. To save you getting lost, its most impressive monuments lie conveniently next to the old port in what was once the heart of the town. Walk up place Lahedine Bouchoucha towards the port. To your left, stands a great horseshoe in alternating black and white marble which once belonged to a **fountain** erected in the seventeenth century by Youssef Dey, second of Tunis's Turkish rulers and founder of the mosque in Tunis's Medina. Like the mosque, this fountain was designed by an architect of Spanish origin – he is identified in its inscription as El Andaloussi. The fountain's inscription advises passers-by in both Arabic and Turkish to use its water until such time as the waters of Paradise become available to them. Originally the water would have been fed by a *nouria* waterwheel powered by a camel, like the one in Kairouan, but sadly both camel and water are long gone.

Bizerte's **Great Mosque**, built in 1652, lies a little way beyond the fountain. Its minaret is visible either from the cramped rue des Armuriers or – even better – from the other side of the port, where you can watch its reflection jostling in the water with brightly coloured fishing boats, while the walls of the Spanish fort loom on the distant hillside behind. Dating, like the fountain and Youssef Dey's mosque in Tunis, from the first years of Turkish rule, the minaret belongs recognizably to the same school, its octagonal shape (signifying Hanefite sympathies) and hanging balcony reminiscent of contemporary Tunis monuments.

Just north of the Great Mosque, on a corner, the **Zaouia of Sidi Moktar** is now the headquarters of the local ASM (Association de Sauvegarde de la Medina), who sometimes use it to put on exhibitions about the Medina and their work in restoring and maintaining it. The ASM also has a fascinating map of Bizerte, drawn to show the city as it was in 1881, before the new town and canal were built. A little further still towards the Kasbah on rue des Armuriers is the seventeenth-century **Zaouia of Sidi Mostari**. To explore the old streets of the Medina, you can head back down rue des Armuriers, which twists the length of the old town as rue Bab Jedid, and take any number of side alleys to your right.

Just below the walls of the Kasbah, a small open square makes a pleasant place to sit at a café table. Beyond it, outside the old city wall, lies the former **Andalusian Quarter**, populated by Spanish Arab and Jewish immigrants who arrived following the Christian reconquest of Spain. There are some old streets and a whitewashed mosque, flanked by two **cemeteries** – Sidi Bennour, on empty ground outside the Kasbah walls, and El Aïn, whose gravestones sprinkle the hillside below the Spanish fort.

Like its contemporary at La Goulette outside Tunis, the massive **Spanish fort** dates back to the sixteenth century, when Tunisia was the front line in the war between Christian Spain and Ottoman Turkey. On taking control of Tunisia in 1535, the Spanish dismantled Bizerte's existing fortifications. Later, as their struggle with the Turks continued, they realized that they would need defences in this key port and began building the fort in 1570, probably not even completing it before the Turks ejected them in 1573. Since then it has undergone significant alterations and additions; in its original form, it was a star-shaped polygon with a central courtyard and one huge entrance gateway from the town. Although occasionally used as an open-air theatre – for which a mock amphitheatre is under construction just below – all it really offers now is the view from its battlements, a couple of World War II Italian guns and some rusty old cannons that were mentioned by Alexandre Dumas on his visit in 1848.

Echoes of past battles can be found in two other cemeteries which are poignant memorials to those who died while liberating or defending Bizerte. The Martyrs Cemetery, dedicated to Tunisians who fell during the 1963 liberation from the French, can be found by taking avenue Farhat Hached northwest out of town for a kilometre, then bearing left and uphill at the fork in the road; you'll see the ten-metre-high monument ahead and the pristine cemetery lies across the main road. In contrast, the International Cemetery at the end of rue Pasteur is ramshackle, but contains some grand tombs (especially those of the Italians). To get there, follow avenue Bourguiba west out of town to where it meets rue Hedi Chaker, with a post office on the corner. Turning right up rue Pasteur, with a large military installation on your right, you'll find the cemetery at the end.

The beaches

Bizerte's main beach is the **Corniche**, a strip of sand varying in width and crowdedness as it stretches the 5km from Sidi Salem, by the old port bridge, north towards Cap Bizerte. Beyond lies the pretty and secluded small beach of Les Grottes; to get there you'll either have to walk the last 2km from where the bus stops, or take a taxi from town (around 2TD). Buses up the Corniche stop in town at "Cheikh Idriss", a bus stop on boulevard Hassan en Nouri by the corner of avenue Bourguiba. Buses #1 and #2 also go up the Corniche from just north of the old port.

Three kilometres southeast of town, the beach of **Rimel** (meaning "sand") is definitely lusher, if a little exposed. This is where Bizerte's other youth hostel is situated, reached by bus #8 from the Menzel Jemil stop at the bus station. The **shipwrecks** on Rimel beach can be seen from the bridge over the canal, and are about a fifty-minute walk down the beach from the hostel and campsite, away from town. Both hulls are from Italian vessels wrecked in 1940. For beaches further afield, see p.166.

Eating and drinking

Because Bizerte is so undeveloped for tourism, its **restaurants** are rather thin on the ground, especially the mid-range ones. On the other hand, there are enough cheap *gargotes* to keep you satisfied, and Bizerte is one of the best places in Tunisia for a real splurge too, with several places to treat yourself along the Corniche. The hotels *Corniche* and *Jalta* both have **bars** serving alcohol, as well as **discos**. The *Café Venizia* on the first floor of the Bizerte Shopping Centre on quai Tarik Ibn Ziad, has a good view over the canal and modern lift-bridge.

Restaurants in town

Restaurant Africain, rue Sassi el Babri, next to *Hôtel Africain*. Limited menu but good and cheap (around 3TD). Daily 8am–9pm, later in summer.

L'Aviation, av Thaalbi and av Bourguiba. A good stand-by if you balk at the pricier places, with good couscous and grilled meats for under 5TD. Daily 7am–10pm.

Restaurant du Bonheur, av Thaalbi, near the corner of av Bourguiba ☎02/431047. Mid-range prices in a smart restaurant (set menus at 12 & 13TD, à la carte costs a little more). Daily 11.30am–3pm & 6pm–midnight.

Restaurant la Cuisine Tunisienne, rue 2 Mars 1934, near the corner of rue de Constantinople. You can silence a grumbling stomach for around 2TD in this *gargote*. Daily noon–11pm, Sun noon–3pm only.

Restaurant Mac 'M', rue 2 Mars 1934. A cheap and modern *gargote*, also serving, you guessed it, pizza. Daily 11am–11pm.

La Mamma, rue Ibn Khaldoun. Good, affordable (3–5TD) Italian (and Tunisian) food in pleasant surroundings. Daily noon–11pm.

Patisserie la Paix, corner of rue 2 Mars 1934 and rue Constantinople. Bizerte's best sweet paradise, well-known for its excellent ice cream.

Restaurant de l'Hôtel Petit Mousse, Corniche ☎02/432185. An excellent meal here will set you back around 15–20TD including wine. Daily noon–3pm & 7–10pm.

Pizza Le Coin, corner of rue de Tunis and rue Farhat Hached. Cheap pasta and pizzas. Daily 9am–9pm.

Sport Nautique, bd H Bougatfa, at the harbour mouth in the Port de Plaisance ☎02/432262. A posh restaurant which offers a nice terrace to enjoy a plate of oysters over a bottle of wine and costs 25–30TD for a meal. Daily noon–3pm & 7–10pm, closed Ramadan.

Restaurants in the zone touristique

Restaurant Belle Plage, on the beach, beyond the *Petit Mousse* ☎02/431817. Mid-range prices (around 15TD for a full meal) and a reasonable menu selection. Daily noon–3pm & 6.30–10pm.

Restaurant Eden, 3km from town on the Corniche ☎02/439023. A fairly classy joint specializing in seafood and charging 15–20TD for a full meal. Daily 12.30–3pm & 6.30–11pm.

Listings

Airlines Tunis Air, 76 av Bourguiba ☎ 02/43220.

Banks Spread around the new town, they include UIB on av Taïeb Mehiri at rue Moncef Bey; L'Habitat on av Bourguiba at av Taïeb Mehiri; BIAT on rue Moncef Bey at rue 2 Mars; Du Sud on rue H Thameur at av Taïeb Mehiri; BNA on rue Mongi Slim at pl 7 Novembre; BT on rue Ibn Khaldoun at av d'Algérie.

Bicycle rental The *Hôtel Jalta* rents out bicycles (6TD/day). Otherwise, you may be able to strike a deal at one of the many bicycle shops on av Bourguiba, between rue Ibn Khaldoun and rue du 1er Mai. Bicycles are ideal for exploring the otherwise hard to get to (and around) Lac Ichkeul National Park (see p.163).

Car rental Avis, 7 rue d'Alger ☎ 02/433076; Hertz, Bizerte Centre ☎ 02/438388; Mattei, 27 rue d'Alger ☎ 02/431508.

Car repairs Bd Hassan en Nouiri, just down from the *Maison des Jeunes*, has a string of garages, mechanics and spare parts shops.

Cinemas Casino, pl des Martyrs; Colisée on rue 1 Mai at av d'Algérie; Majestic, rue de Tunis; Paris, 43 av Taïeb Mehiri at av Bourguiba.

Consul Italy's honorary consul is Ahmed Kamel Ouadhour, in an office on rue 2 Mars 1934 on the same side and block as *Hôtel Continental*.

Festivals Street celebrations and a carnival of sorts celebrate the city's 1963 liberation from the French on October 15. The Festival de Bizerte, held annually from mid-July to mid- or the end of August, sees international music hosted at the Spanish Fort. The Saints Day of Sidi Selim was formerly tied to the Islamic calendar, but may now be incorporated into the Festival de Bizerte.

Football The local club is CAB Bizerte, 1987 African Cup winners, but currently only bobbing around the first division. Their ground is up by Porte de Bechateur. Matches usually kick off at 2pm on Sundays.

Hammams The best hammam in town is the Hammam de la Régence on pl Lahedine Bouchoucha, opposite Rbaa Mosque. Another is in the Kasbah, and there's one in rue Salah Ben Ali, near the *Hôtel Saadi*. Hours at all of these are 6am–noon and 6–9pm for men, noon–6pm for women.

Hospital The regional hospital is up rue Ibn Khaldoun, at the roundabout, bear up into rue Saussier ☎ 02/431422, with the 24hr Infirmerie Chida at 5, rue de Théâtre ☎ 02/434640 or 09/440035.

Internet Cyberhouse on av Habib Thameur (daily 9am–2am; 2TD/hr) has good connection and plenty of posts, while Internet at 14 rue de Tripoli (8am–12.30pm & 3–11pm; 2.5TD/hr) has only a couple of posts. Internet access is also available at Publinet, corner of rue d'Espagne and rue de la Goulette (10.30am–midnight; 2TD/hr).

Pharmacy There's a night pharmacy at 28 rue Ali Belhouane ☎ 02/432461.

Police Rue du 20 Mars 1956 ☎ 02/431200 or 431065.

Post office Av d'Algérie at rue 1 Mai (city hours); it changes cash, has Western Union money transfer and has phones in the side entrance.

ONA crafts shop, quai Khémais Ternane. Behind the market, facing onto the Old Port (Mon–Sat 8.30am–1pm & 3–5.15pm).

Supermarkets Monoprix, rue 2 Mars 1934, at rue Ibn Khaldoun.

Swimming There's a municipal pool on the Corniche near the *Maison des Jeunes*. Otherwise, try the Corniche hotels.

Taxis Call Allo Rapide Taxi ☎ 02/421200.

Telephones There are coin-operated Publitel offices at rue Habib Thameur, one block east of the post office, and on rue 2 Mars 193, near the junction with rue de 8 Janvier. There are other taxiphone and Publitel offices throughout the city.

Tours Some of the big hotels, notably the *Hôtel Jalta*, run trips – for example, half a day in Raf Raf and Utica, a day in Kairouan or a three-day "safari" in the south (not a wildlife trip as such, but a whirlwind tour of the key sites), or you could try Aphrodite Tours, 12 rue Ahmed Tlili ☎ 02/436195, or Via Bizerte, 1 rue de 1 Mai ☎ 02/432901.

MOVING ON FROM BIZERTE

For a rundown of destinations and journey times, see Travel Details on p.188.

Buses to Tunis leave more or less half-hourly from the SRT Bizerte bus station at the western end of quai Tarik Ibn Ziad (☎02/431371 or 431736); there are also frequent services to Ras Jebel, where you can change for Raf Raf. Outside the bus station building is the stop for Menzel Bourguiba via Rimel. There are other buses from SNTRI's unpromising-looking depot in rue d'Alger (☎02/431222), on the corner of rue Habib Thameur, to Houmt Souk on Jerba, and daily departures for Kairouan, Sfax and Sousse.

Louages have two sites. Those to Tunis (red stripes), Ras Jebel and Raf–Raf (blue stripes) leave from the corner of quai Tarik Ibn Ziad and rue du 8 Mai 1938, next to the lift-bridge. For other departures to locations within this chapter, the stop is outside the train station. There are very occasional louages to Tabarka. The **train station** (☎02/431071) at the end of rue de Russie and rue de Belgique by the docks has services to Tunis via Tinja and Mateur.

Menzel Abderrahman and Menzel Jemil

South of Bizerte, the villages of **Menzel Abderrahman** and **Menzel Jemil** (short journeys from Bizerte's main bus station along the Tunis road) were both founded by the Aghlabids in the ninth century and make attractive places from which to view the lake. Menzel Abderrahman is right on the shore, while Menzel Jemil – now virtually a suburb of Bizerte – perches on a hillside, its a dapper old central **square** dominated by a fortress-like whitewashed **mosque**.

The Raf Raf coastline

A beach of legendary beauty, **Raf Raf**, just 30km east of Bizerte, is the best-known attraction on a stretch of coast that remains surprisingly undeveloped. Conventional tourist facilities are sparse in this area of conservative farmers, but the rewards are greater if you make the effort to explore, with some beautiful beaches and cliff-top scenery towards **Cap Farina** and the fledgling resort at **Ras Sidi el Mekki**.

Transport to the area can be confusing until you master the local geography. All buses from Bizerte go through Ras Jebel before backtracking to Raf Raf town and then down to the beach (specify "Raf Raf Plage"), and there are plenty of buses and taxis plying solely between Ras Jebel and Raf Raf. As for transport from Tunis, only one bus a day serves Raf Raf direct (Bab Saadoun station), but five go to Ras Jebel, and during summer you can usually get a louage direct to the beach, though you'll have to fight for a seat at weekends.

Ras Jebel   رأس الجبل

At the centre of the region is **RAS JEBEL**, a farming town which makes few concessions to visitors and is really only useful as a transport connection. The road into town divides before reaching the centre, with the main square and its towering minaret straight ahead, and the **bus stop** to the left – there are departures from here to Ghar el Melh, Raf Raf and Tunis, and frequent **louages** to Bizerte. A street drops to the right, passing a large **café** and the **market** on the left before reaching a basic **hotel** further round to the right. The town's single other notable feature is a Lee Cooper jeans factory.

Although Ras Jebel has its own **beach**, 2.5km down a signposted road, it's small and gets crowded in July and August, when families camp there on a long-term basis and conditions become less than hygienic. To avoid this, just walk along to the west until you find a deserted cove, though note that you'll have to bring water supplies.

Raf Raf beach

رفراف

The real attraction on this part of the coast is **Raf Raf beach**, an almost endless curve of white sand backed by dunes, forest and steeply sloping fields of figs, vines and rustling cane. At its eastern edge is the long claw of **Cap Farina**, with the cliffs of its ridge hidden in shadow or gleaming in the sun, to the west a small, knobbly hill, and out in the bay, the rocky islet of Pilau. If you feel an urge to do other than swim, sunbathe and eat grapes and figs (some of the best in the country), Cap Farina makes a spectacular walk. The easiest way up is from Raf Raf, along a track to the watchtower. More daring is to climb the gash of sand visible on the mountain from the beach, from the top of which the whole coast opens out, west to Raf Raf's curve, east down to the lagoon of Ghar el Melh and Ras Sidi el Mekki beach.

The beach is popular, formidably so at weekends, but even then it's easy to escape the crowds. If you want to **stay** here, there's the friendly *Hôtel Dalia* (☎02/441668; ❸) with good self-contained rooms (the more expensive ones have sea views); and possibly some **villas** for rent (ask around), but you may prefer to rent one of the straw shacks (in season), or you can sleep out if you're discreet.

Ghar el Melh

غار الملح

GHAR EL MELH, 4km along the coast from Raf Raf beach, means "Cave of Salt", perhaps a reference to the lagoon which the River Medjerda has created around the town, ruining the harbour facilities that once made Porto Farina (as it was then called) a notorious haunt of pirates. In 1654 the English Admiral Blake, in an action described by Lieutenant Colonel Sir Lambert Playfair (see p.484) as "one of the most brilliant victories in the history of the British Navy", attacked and destroyed the port. By the next century, however, it had been rebuilt with three forts and an arsenal. Piracy and smuggling continued to be the town's main source of revenue well into the nineteenth century – carried out, for the most part, by the British and the Maltese. The government only clamped down in 1834, when a huge arsenal – kept by one of the Maltese smugglers in his basement – exploded, taking many of the surrounding houses with it. Ahmed Bey tried to turn the port to more legitimate trade, building new jetties and forts. But by this time the estuary had started to silt up, and today Ghar el Melh is a small farming town, half asleep under the green flank of the mountain, where the **forts** and the crumbling walls of the **old port** are steeped in a sense of nostalgic melancholy. Buses to Ghar el Melh operate through Ras Jebel.

Ras Sidi el Mekki

رأس سيدي المكي

Ghar el Melh should really be left to slumber gently, but its peace will be forever destroyed if long-standing plans to develop the beach at **RAS SIDI EL MEKKI**, 6km beyond, at the tip of Cap Farina, are ever fulfilled. The authorities like to call this beach "Polynesian", which does at least convey the stillness of the water and the isolation. It's little known for the moment, though, and its facilities consist of just a few straw huts, a **café-restaurant** with good fresh fish, and a few holiday **villas** for rent (ask around), so camping is the ideal solution.

Just over 2km beyond Ghar el Melh, a track turns off left, while the road veers right to a new fishing **port**. The beach is another 3km from the town. If you don't have your own transport, you'll have to hitch or end up walking from Ghar el Melh, where the bus stops.

Utica and around

أوتيقا

The ancient site of **Utica** lies in the broad alluvial plain of the **River Medjerda**, whose banks, so British traveller Sir Grenville Temple (see p.484) reported in the nineteenth century, "were witnesses to the well-known combat between the forces of Attilius Regulus and an enormous serpent, in 225 BC". The river – the only permanently flowing one in the country – plays a vital part in irrigating the north, but for centuries it has also been silting up this section of the coast, locking in what were once great ports. Utica lies off the main Tunis–Bizerte road, a two-kilometre walk from the village of Zana, and just over 30km southeast from Bizerte.

Some history

Now a smallish site marooned 10km from the sea, **Utica** predated Carthage as the first Phoenician trading post on this coastline. It never really reconciled itself to Carthage's supremacy, backing the losing mercenary army in its revolt against Carthage in 240 BC and then supporting Rome in the 146 BC campaign which ended in Carthage's destruction; a century later it supported Pompey against Julius Caesar in the Roman Civil War. One of Pompey's backers, Cato the Younger, was in control of the city when he heard of Caesar's decisive victory at Thapsus, near Mahdia. Having decided to kill himself rather than surrender, he fell on his sword in time-honoured fashion; and when doctors tried to repair the damage, he thrust them aside and rent his innards asunder with his bare hands. This was the sort of gesture which went down well with the Romans: they immediately erected a statue of Cato, facing heroically out to sea, and enshrined him in national myth. With the resurrection of Carthage as the new Roman capital, though, Utica began a decline that was then accelerated as silt from the river gradually put an end to the city's port and *raison d'être*.

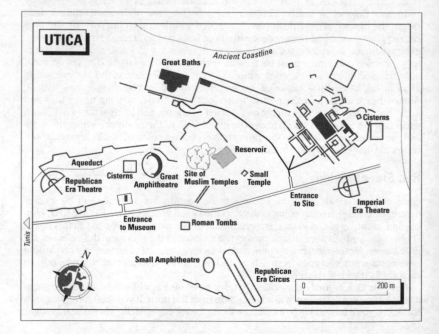

The site

Despite the size and wealth of the Roman city, its **site** is not extensive. The central feature is the **House of the Cascade**, whose doorway still stands. The private residence of some very well-off citizen, it gives an impression of staggering affluence even without walls or decoration. The ground floor was almost entirely devoted to entertaining, with the main complex of rooms to the right of the pool in the centre of the house. In the middle of this side, the *triclinium* (dining room) is identifiable by the U-shape of its floor decoration. Couches, on which Romans lay to eat their meals (Cato was a source of amazement because, Stoic that he was, he actually ate sitting up), occupied the three sides around the walls. Of the orange and green paving in the middle of the floor, the orange "Numidian" marble came from Chemtou (see p.186), while the green was imported from Euboea, today's Evvia, in Greece. On either side of the *triclinium* is a garden well and another reception room: one well contains the running fountain arrangement (all in mosaics) which gives the house its name. The other rooms around the central pool are smaller reception chambers, except for a stable to the left of the entrance; note the feeding troughs. The stable for the horse-drawn carriage is on the other side of the entrance, with a wide doorway.

The residences surrounding the House of the Cascade are less affluent, but still part of an exclusive district. The **Forum** was only a block away to the north, beyond the **Punic necropolis** excavated at a lower level, and the sea was not much further. A little way west along the ancient shoreline – reminiscent of Carthage's Antonine Baths (see p.115) – stood Utica's own massive **baths complex**, whose remains are still visible. It is not certain where the shore was when the Medjerda started silting it up, but it would have been close to the bottom of the slope – from the House of the Cascade's roof you could watch ships sailing in from Spain, Carthage and Alexandria.

The **museum** (Tues–Sun: April–Oct 8am–7pm; Nov–March 8.30am–5.30pm; 2TD, camera 1TD) lies just before the entrance to the site. It contains mainly domestic and funerary objects illustrating the life led by Uticans for more than a thousand years. The Punic pottery and grave reliefs (note the angular Punic script) in the early rooms date from its first six hundred years. The Phoenicians were traders and merchants, and when they weren't fighting the Greeks they were doing business with them; look out for a fine Greek *skyphos* (wine goblet) painted with a Maenad chasing a Satyr. The Roman relics, as so often, are prosaically domestic, and the quantity of marble statuary is a clear indication of the city's wealth. None of it is of particularly high standard – the Reclining Ariadne and Satyr (recognizable by his tail) are poor versions of stock garden figures – and, because North Africa has no white marble of its own, all this had to be imported at great expense from elsewhere in the Mediterranean.

Kalaat el Andalous   قلعة الاندلس

KALAAT EL ANDALOUS, 5km from Utica, is the village just visible to the northeast of Utica, on what was once another headland in the sea. Not much is left now of the original village founded by Spanish immigrants during the seventeenth century, but it's a pleasant walk across the rich river plain and there's a magnificent view from the steep cliff on the far side, ranging from Bou Kornine and Sidi Bou Saïd in the south, to Cap Farina in the north. Buses #31b and #44 from place Belhouane in Tunis pass through here regularly.

Lac Ichkeul National Park   بحيرة إشكل

The sixty-square-kilometre **Lac Ichkeul**, linked to Lac Bizerte by a narrow channel near Tinja, is too shallow to be navigable, making it an ideal habitat for fish and bird life. In winter it's an ornithologist's delight as a haven for birds migrating from northern Europe. Non-tidal but slightly saline, the lake provides a unique ecosystem that the government has protected as a **nature reserve** (daily 7am–6pm, though these are flexible and not enforced; free). Unfortunately it's under threat due to the heavy demand on its water, with two dams already constructed on its feed rivers and a further four planned, although a recently constructed water pipeline to Bizerte from the mountains behind Tabarka may forestall their purpose. The combined effect of the dams and the low rainfall has lowered the water level in the lake, causing saltwater from Lac Bizerte to flow back into it. This, together with evaporation, means that the lake is growing more saline, killing off the water plants on which its delicate ecosystem depends.

Apart from its famous ornithological attractions (see box opposite), the lake abounds in **frogs** and **toads,** including a very handsome, vocal species with green stripes down the back; there are **terrapins** too. The Sejnane marsh on the lake's north side is a good place to look for these.

Getting to the park is not easy by public transport, and it's a good idea to first visit the tourist office in Bizerte (see p.154) for advice and information. From Bizerte, the bus or louage to Mateur passes the southeastern corner of the lake, with the turning for the park 7km beyond Tinja, just after the road crosses the train line. Alternatively, you can catch a bus or louage to Menzel Bourguiba, and then a louage or taxi to "Ichkeul", the settlement by the park gate. A track leads off here across a marsh to the park entrance, where a *gardien* should come to greet you. If he's not there, you're perfectly all right to continue. The track beyond the gate skirts around the bottom of the mountain, past some domed bathhouses, to a sign for the **ecomuseum** (daily 7am–6pm; free), which sits above the ridge – be prepared for a steep climb. The museum is really of interest only to keen ornithologists and geologists with a good collection of stuffed birds and explanatory maps and diagrams of the lake's ecosystem. It's 9km from the Mateur road to the museum, so prepare for a long walk if you don't have transport. Alternatively, for viewing the northern shore of the lake, the bus from Bizerte to Sejnane skirts the water's edge, passing both the Douimis and Sejnane marshes. If you're staying at the *Ichkeul Hôtel* in Guengla, outside Menzel Bourguiba, take the local bus from Guengla (see p.166) to Tinja, and you can hitch from there either along the north or, with more promise, the south side of the lake to the gate mentioned above. Finally, note that a **bicycle** would really come into its own here (see Listings on p.159 for details on renting one).

Jebel Ichkeul

جبل إشكل

A superb limestone mountain, **Jebel Ichkeul** rises directly from the southern edge of the lake. It was a royal hunting park in the thirteenth century and **wild boar** and **jackals** still live on its flanks, as do **porcupines, mongooses, otters, tortoises** and a small herd of **water buffalo** – descended, it's said, from a pair given to the Bey of Tunis by the king of Sicily in 1729. During the war, US troops stationed nearby developed a taste for the meat and the herd was virtually wiped out.

The **flowers** up on Jebel Ichkeul are utterly dependent on the winter rains and you can walk through a carpet of colour or over barren straw, depending on the weather. As well as on the mountain, interesting flowers grow around the rivers feeding the lake – around the Douimis River on the north shore, for instance, you'll find a white Star of Bethlehem and a delightful, tiny narcissus. The **agricultural weeds** are spectacular even in a dry year, since many of the fields to the north of the lake are irrigated. Look out for fields ablaze with poppies and wild chrysanthemums, and for various colourful convolvulus species around the edges. Honeywort, with its strange pendulous yellow and brown flowers, is also common by the roadside, and there's a shocking-pink soapwort in the fields.

BIRDWATCHING ON THE LAKE

Waterfowl are Lac Ichkeul's high spot. Ducks feed on the extensive beds of pondweed and greylag geese on the club rush. These plants, together with the sheer size of the lake, make it North Africa's principal wildfowl wintering ground, with up to 150,000 birds at its peak.

Although huge flocks are present only between October and February, ducks remain in good numbers until the spring, with a few staying on and occasionally breeding over the summer. The birds move around the lake depending on the distribution of the plants they feed on, but in general the best viewpoints are from the coast north of the mountain (there's a good track along it starting from the museum), or from the Douimis and Sejnane marshes on the north side. The latter marsh requires a walk along the river from the road.

As well as ducks and geese, the lake supports a variety of **wading birds** around its fringes. If the water level is high enough, both the Douimis and Sejnane marshes are good all year round for waders, with sizeable populations of avocets, black-winged stilts and Kentish plovers. These are augmented in winter by black-tailed godwits, redshanks and the smaller sandpipers. If it's wet, the edge of the Joumine marsh closest to the level crossing outside Tinja is a great spot to watch waders, but beware of the dogs around here. Herons and egrets breed among the reeds, the grey heron a resident and purple heron a summer visitor, and there's sometimes a colony of night herons in the reeds at the north edge of the mountain. The unmistakable white storks don't breed in the park but they nest close by and often feed around the lake's edges.

The lake's **speciality birds** include the purple gallinule, a rarity rather like a huge red-billed coot; the marbled teal, a small, shy duck with a mottled brown plumage; and the white-headed duck, a universally rare bird which winters in small numbers.

With all these water birds about, as well as small mammals, reptiles and amphibians, the lake also attracts **birds of prey**. Marsh harriers are the most dominant species, identifiable by their upturned wings as they drift over the reed beds and surrounding fields in search of small prey. Of the falcons, peregrine, lanner and kestrel all breed on the mountain, Bonelli's and short-toed eagles wheel high in the sky, and long-legged buzzards breed here too.

Don't ignore the **smaller birds**, either. Reed warblers and great reed warblers breed here in summer, nightingales are common, and bee-eaters breed in the river banks. Quail, the smallest game bird, breed in the park too; listen for their "whic whic" call from the surrounding fields in spring – they're notoriously hard to spot. Moussier's redstarts are common among the scrub on the mountain, and Sardinian warblers are everywhere. Woodchat shrikes perch on telegraph wires and lone trees in summer, and a related and very rare species, the black-headed bush shrike, breeds here in very small numbers. Nightingales, known in Arabic as **bulbuls** – like drab blackbirds but with a loud and mellifluous song – reach the most northerly part of their range in Tunisia (they're primarily Asian and African birds). Incidentally, if you've come with weighty telephoto lenses and other **photographic equipment**, be discreet, as officially photography is not permitted in the park due to a number of military and air bases around it.

Menzel Bourguiba and around   منـزل بـورڨيبـة

On the south side of Lac Bizerte, **MENZEL BOURGUIBA** (formerly the French garrison town of Ferryville) is itself uninteresting, but is a reasonable base for exploring the Lac Ichkeul National Park, whose main gate is 7km away.

The centre of Menzel Bourguiba is a pleasant square with a bandstand. The only **hotel** in town is the *Moderne* (☎02/460551; ②) in rue d'Alger, which runs off the bandstand square towards the train station. Cheap but very basic and somewhat grubby, it has no showers – though there are three hammams nearby. The *Moderne* is also an inexpensive eatery and the town's main bar and social focus, a pretty lively place in the evenings (except Friday), when cold beer and wine are served until late. During World War II, soldiers on both sides had occasion to drink here, and the venerable *patron* who served them still runs the place.

The other hotel in the area is the one-star *Hôtel Ichkeul* (formerly *Younès*), some way out of Menzel Bourguiba in **GUENGLA** (☎02/461606; ❸), right on Lac Bizerte. To get there, you could take a taxi or (infrequent) bus from Menzel Bourguiba town centre, or follow avenue de Palestine from the bandstand past the hospital and the craft centre opposite, turning left with the tarmac at the barracks entrance, and straight on for another 2km. The hotel is signposted on the right and you can get a pleasant room with a high-class restaurant in a tranquil setting. The proprietor also runs the Tardi wine company, which bottles many of the region's wines and arranges visits to the cellars at **AÏN GHELLAL**, 10km to the south. **Wildlife** enthusiasts should note that the hotel is ideally placed for exploring Oued Tinja, the river that connects Lac Ichkeul with Lac Bizerte.

The **train station**, down rue d'Alger from the bandstand, no longer has any passenger services – the nearest passenger **train station** is Tinja, 6km west on the Tunis–Bizerte line; louages outside the station run there. Turn left just before the station and continue for 100m to find the **Tunis louage station**, or cross the tracks and turn right to the site of Menzel's Wednesday and Sunday **market**, where you can pick up **louages to Mateur**. To find the **bus station**, and **louages for Bizerte**, go back up rue d'Alger, turn left at the bandstand and go straight on past a six-way roundabout and standard-issue monument to the November 7, 1987 "chargement", where you'll also find the **post office** and Monoprix **supermarket**. There are regular buses to Tunis and Bizerte, plus two or three daily for Tabarka, Aïn Draham and Béja.

Fifteen kilometres southwest on the main GP7, **MATEUR** has little of interest apart from its transport connections, although its very busy Saturday market is entirely devoid of tourists. SRT Bizerte runs the **bus station**, but other services stop here, and one way or another there are plenty of departures for Tabarka, Sejnane, Béja, Bizerte and, of course, Tunis. **Louages** run from here, too. There are also four daily trains in either direction to Bizerte (35min) and Tunis (1hr 15min).

West of Bizerte

West of Bizerte, the beaches run in shallow curves until the hump of **Cap Blanc**, 8km along the coast. Often said to be the northernmost point in Africa, though its most northerly point is actually a few kilometres west at **Ras Angela** (aka Ras Ben Sekka). Like all the beaches on the north coast, when the wind blows here they can feel slightly exposed, but in summer it's never unpleasant. The Roman writer Pliny the Younger tells how a boy out swimming here was befriended one day by a dolphin so tame that it carried him out to sea for rides. The dolphin soon acquired a cult following, but this was too much for the local bureaucrats of the Roman Empire, who had the dolphin killed. More conventional water sports are available today at the big hotels.

For a distant view of Cap Blanc, catch a #6 bus from boulevard Hassan en Nouri in Bizerte to the village of **BECHATEUR** – a side trip which reveals some of the unexpectedly bleak scenery behind the coast at this point. Bechateur itself is a tiny hamlet on a windswept hilltop which was once inhabited by the Romans, and blocks of their masonry can be seen in the walls of the village here and there. The bus stops at Bechateur, but a track continues for 15km to the beach of **Sidi Abdel Waheb** – worth exploring, if you have some means of getting down. The area still yields unexpected discoveries – between Cap Blanc and Ras Angela, at **AÏN DAMOUS**, a recently discovered underwater cave is said, rather implausibly, to be an entrance to Roman catacombs leading all the way to Utica.

From here, the coastline consists of a series of isolated coves, backed by increasingly heavy forests, whose inaccessibility pays dividends to those in search of wilder shores. Most of the coves are uninhabited, putting them beyond the reach of all but the most dedicated, but a few are viable even if you don't have your own transport. In order to get to them, though, you'll need plenty of time, and you'll probably have to negotiate a taxi or charter a louage from **SEJNANE**, 40km west of Mateur, and the best base for accessing the beaches. It's a peaceful country town, living off agriculture and mining, with its own unique style of pottery. Pots and beaches aside, there's little reason to stop here (unless for the Thursday market) except to enquire about transport out again – which is mainly back to Mateur.

Due north of Sejnane are the remote beaches of the promontory of **Cap Serrat**, down a well-signposted fifteen-kilometre track that turns off the GP51 and runs steadily down through heavily forested land. At the end of the track the mountains subside into a broad valley with a scattered settlement and a spectacular empty **beach**. If you have a 4WD, you might want to head west along a rougher track to the next named beach, **Sidi Mechrig**, which boasts a small settlement, and a **hotel**, *Hôtel Sidi Mechrig* (no phone; ❷), on the beach, as well as some scanty but picturesque **Roman ruins** of a bathhouse. For an easier approach to Sidi Mechrig, continue along the GP7 to just before Tamra, where a signpost indicates a seventeen-kilometre track. Next in the line of named beaches along the coast is **Cap Negre**, reached by a track signposted about 6km after the Sidi Mechrig turning. It's barely inhabited except for a National Guard post occupying the remains of a French coral-fishing establishment, sacked in 1741 by the same expedition that ejected the Genoese from their fort at Tabarka. West of Nefza, 15km beyond the Cap Negre turning, a track leads down to yet another beach, **Zouiraa**.

Just before Ras Rajel, 10km east of Tabarka, the road passes a **Commonwealth War Cemetery**, whose green pastures face a petrol station on the other side of the road. From the middle of Ras Rajel, a new road runs 2km north to the long-promised international **airport**, whose arrival is a sign of changing times in the Tabarka area. Currently an echoing hall that welcomes perhaps four flights a week from Monastir, Italy, Belgium and Germany, and this only in summer, if the airport becomes successful it will be at the expense of the area's reputation as a charming backwater.

Tabarka   طبرقة

The setting of **TABARKA** is all that anyone could ask for – the **Khroumirie mountains** subside suddenly into a fertile plain, and in one corner is the natural harbour first used by the Carthaginians, dominated by an offshore rock that's crowned by a **Genoese castle**. Tabarka's success as a resort has taken what was basically a sleepy country town by surprise. Independent travellers used to arrive in July and early August, making the atmosphere like a big easy-going campsite. When they left, the town would settle back to being a market centre (Friday **souk** on the Aïn Draham road just out of town) and small fishing port. Alas, the tourist authorities and developers are trying to recreate in Tabarka the perceived success of resort development like Sousse. Along with the new airport, five massive hotels and a golf course have been conjured out of the previously pristine beach running east of town, and three more hotels are under construction; downtown, the fishing port has been endowed with a luxury development called **Porto Corallo** complete with a 100-berth marina, reminiscent of a downmarket Port el Kantaoui. Throughout the town, construction workers are busy tearing down old buildings and replacing them with grim four- and five-storey apartments. Clearly, Tabarka is undergoing significant change and you're inevitably going to find yourself sharing it with more and more fellow visitors.

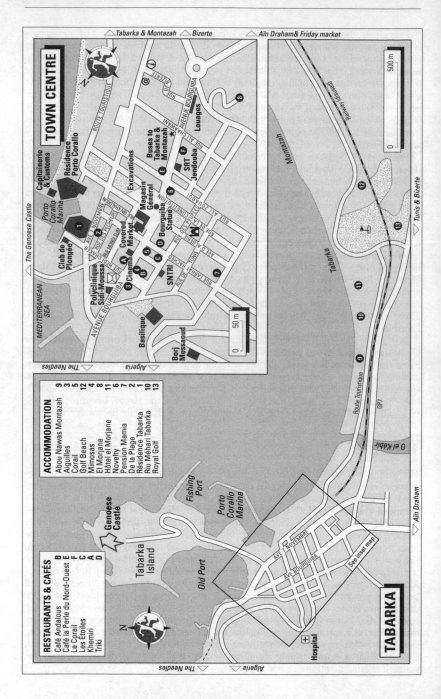

TOWN CENTRE

Tabarka & Montazah — Bizerte — Aïn Draham & Friday market

The Genoese Castle

MEDITERRANEAN SEA

Porto Corallo Marina

Capitainerie & Customs

Residence Porto Corallo

ROUTE TOURISTIQUE

RUE BIZERTE

@

i

8

Club de Plongée

Excavations

Magasin Général

Buses to Tabarka & Montazah

Lounages

AVENUE BOURGUIBA

RUE AÏT ZOUAOUI

RUE ALI DRAHAM

SRT
Jendouba

F

E

6

Polyclinique Sidi-Moussa

1

2

3 Cinema

A

B

4

5

C

D Bourguiba Statue

SNTRI

7

AVENUE BOURGUIBA

RUE DE LA CONSTITUTION

RUE DU FARHAT HACHED

AVE DE GABÈS

AVE DE L'ALGÉRIE

Basilique

Borj Messaoud

0   50 m

The Needles — Algeria — Algeria

Montazah

Tabarka

12

13

11

10

9

Route Touristique

GP7

0 el Kébir

Railway (disused)

Tunis & Bizerte

0   500 m

ACCOMMODATION

Abou Nawas Montazah	9
Aiguilles	3
Corail	5
Golf Beach	12
Mimosas	4
El Morjane	8
Hôtel el Morjane	11
Novelty	7
Pension Mamia	6
De la Plage	2
Résidence Tabarka	1
Riu Méhari Tabarka	10
Royal Golf	13

Genoese Castle

Fishing Port

Porto Corallo Marina

Tabarka Island

Old Port

RESTAURANTS & CAFÉS

Café Andalous	B
Café la Perle du Nord-Ouest	E
Le Corail	F
Les Etoiles	C
Khemiri	A
Triki	D

TABARKA

AVE 7 NOVEMBRE

AVE BOURGUIBA

AVE BOURGUIBA

See inset map

Hospital

Tunis & Bizerte

Aïn Draham

The Needles — Algeria — The Needles

N

Some history

Roman Thabraca was the main port of exit for Chemtou marble from south of the mountains (see p.186), and thanks to this and grain exports it became a substantial town, wealthy enough to produce the fine early Christian mosaics on display in the Bardo Museum in Tunis. Decline set in after the fall of the Empire, but the eleventh-century geographer El Edrisi was still impressed by "ancient monuments of fine construction", and by the twelfth century trade was sufficiently brisk to convince the commander of a shipwrecked Genoese boat in the service of the Knights of St John to stay, whose descendants kindly bought the island in 1542 (see Genoese Castle, p.171). Like everywhere else along the North African coast, ownership of the town was fiercely contested over the next two centuries. The French colonials used Tabarka as a hunting resort (wild boar and game birds) in a small way, but it was still considered remote enough in 1952 to be a suitable place of exile for Bourguiba. After Independence, the isolation and charm remained, until recently, quite intact. **Coral** diving, and **cork** growing in the mountain forests behind the town, as well as fishing, farming and tourism, provide the area its industry and income today.

Arrival, information and accommodation

Ignoring the sprawling modern "Medina" – something of a slum – the town itself is tiny, with just a main street, avenue Bourguiba, and a few blocks on either side. Right in the middle of avenue Bourguiba is Tabarka's main square, where you'll find a covered market and the town hall. From the main square, avenue Bourguiba runs northwest towards the fishing port and Porto Corallo marina, and in the other directions towards Aïn Draham and Bizerte. Running parallel to avenue Bourguiba, next to the beach, is avenue 7 Novembre, which passes the regional **tourist office** at the corner of rue de Bizerte (July & Aug Mon–Thurs 8am–8pm, Fri & Sat 8am–2pm; Sept–June Mon–Thurs 8.30am–1pm & 3–6.45pm, Fri & Sat 8.30am–1.30pm; ☎08/673555) and continues on to the new Tabarka Montazah *zone touristique*.

The **airport** is a few kilometres east in Ras Rajel (see p.167), though it's currently used only by summer Europe charter flights and a weekly flight to and from Monastir. You'll have to get a **taxi** into town (around 10TD), or hitch a lift with a hotel bus. Otherwise, walk 2km straight ahead to the main road and catch a louage or bus. In town there are two **bus stations**: SNTRI at 12 rue des Peuples, and SRT Jendouba at 72 av Bourguiba. SRT Béja buses stop in Tabarka's main square. **Louages** arrive at the southern end of avenue Bourguiba, by the *Hôtel Mimosas* turn-off and the Esso petrol station. Incidentally, the **rail track** from Mateur to Tabarka shown on many road maps is well and truly defunct.

The old town, on and around avenue Bourguiba, is the best place for budget **accommodation**. The comparatively small *zone touristique* of **Tabarka Montazah** east of town is a source of more upscale alternatives and is gearing up for a second phase of con-

---

CORAL

Coral, Tabarka's favourite souvenir, was one of the luxury items exported from North Africa to Europe, and avenue Bourguiba is lined with shops selling jewellery made by local artisans out of the coral brought up by divers. Prices here are considerably lower than in Tunis. The coral is Mediterranean coral, a species which has been collected for jewellery use for centuries, with the result that it is now fast declining and has been listed as an endangered species – think twice, therefore, before sanctioning this process by buying a coral souvenir in one of the many shops throughout northern Tunisia.

struction. The inevitable **tourist train** links the *zone* with the town (avenue Bourguiba) in summer. All these hotels, are within forty minutes' walking distance. There are also hourly **buses** at a quarter to the hour (more in summer) to the hotels and Cité el Morjane beyond, which leave from outside the BNA bank on the corner of avenue Bourguiba and rue Ali Chaawani. Hotels are substantially cheaper in the low season, if they are open.

Hotels in town

Aiguilles ★★, av Bourguiba ℡ 08/673789, ℱ 673604. One of the new independents, smart and pleasant if a little overpriced. ➍

El Morjane, corner of av Bourguiba and rue Tazerka ℡ & ℱ 08/643082. Recently renovated, large rooms with clean beds and sink. No hot water or showers but not bad for the price. ➋

Mimosas ★★★, up the hill above town ℡ 08/673028, ℱ 673279. The elegant old-fashioned alternative to the newer hotels. The old wing's sea views are stupendous; less so those in the modern wing, though the rooms are better. Singles are well priced. Small pool, pool table and terrace café. Recommended. ➎

Novelty ★★, 68 av Bourguiba, just east of the central square ℡ 08/670176, ℱ 673008. Reasonably smart and comfortable though the rooms can be a little dark. Low-season rates are overpriced. ➍

Pension Mamia 3 rue de Tunis ℡ 08/671058. A friendly place with basic but clean rooms set around a courtyard. ➌

Hôtel de la Plage, 11 av 7 Novembre ℡ 08/670039. Bright and clean, and even though it has been recently extended and renovated it remains a good best cheapie but the a/c rooms with shower are overpriced. ➌–➍

Résidence Tabarka, Porto Corrallo ℡ 08/670840. Recently built time-share block, its studios with kitchenettes are for rent by the day, but book ahead in summer. Use of pool, sauna, hammam and gym. ➍

Hotels in the zone touristique

Abou Nawas Montazah ★★★, ℡ 08/673532, ℱ 673530. The hotel nearest town, with a plethora of facilities including an Olympic-sized pool, four tennis courts, horse-riding and a thalassotherapy centre. Bargain in low season. ➏

Golf Beach ★★★★, ℡ 08/673002, ℱ 673918. Formerly the *Paradise*. The furthest (so far) of the *Montazah* hotels and on the other side of the road from the beach. This opulent place has all you'd expect for its stars and rooms either have views of the ocean or the hills behind. ➏

Riu Méhari Tabarka ★★★★, ℡ 08/6714444, ℱ 671923. The alley's top cat, part of a Spanish group, with all the facilities you'd expect. It also has roomy bungalows, set well back from the beach, but within a birdie of the golfing greens. Hotel and bungalows. ➏–➐

Hôtel Morjane ★★★, ℡ 08/673411, ℱ 673888. The grandaddy of the lot, dating from 1968 and, like most '68 veterans, its ideals and standards have slipped a bit. But it's still good value. Horse-riding available. ➎

Royal Golf ★★★, ℡ /673899, ℱ 673838, ℮ royal.golf@gnet.tn. Set back a little way from the beach this place was built in 1994 and is already starting to look the tiniest bit shabby. Nevertheless it has all the usual facilities and great ocean views from some rooms and is a good deal cheaper than most of its neighbours. ➎

The Town

Tabarka is built on a simple grid plan, with the **main square** and its town hall making a focal point. Some interesting Roman remains have been unearthed on the square, watched over by a statue of Habib Bourguiba and his dog. **Avenue Bourguiba** forms the town's main artery, running from the roundabout by the louage station through the main square and on towards the Needles on the coast (see opposite).

Many of the events during the annual six-week July and August **Tabarka Festival,** and the **Jazz Festival** which follows at the end of August, are put on in the garden of the so-called **Basilique**, just uphill from the *Café Andalous*. This was actually a cistern supplying the Roman town, which the White Fathers converted into a church. The building itself is currently closed for renovations and its small museum is being transferred to the castle (see below). Other patches of Roman excavation are dotted around the town, including the **Borj Messaoud** halfway up the hill behind the Basilique, also originally a Roman cistern but converted into a fort by French and Italian merchants in the twelfth century.

Compared with the **Genoese Castle**, a twenty-minute walk from avenue Bourguiba along avenue Hedi Chaker, these minor monuments seem rather feeble. The castle's origins were as dramatic as its appearance is now: in 1541 the Turkish corsair Khair ed Din Barbarossa surrendered it to Charles V of Spain in return for his colleague Dragut, who had been languishing in a Christian jail, and the next year Charles sold the coral fishing rights and the island to a Genoese family called Lomellini. Having built the castle and enough of a town to support twelve hundred inhabitants, they managed to stay, despite Turkish control of the mainland, for two centuries. One of their main sources of income came from acting as agents for ransoming slaves in Tunis, a service for which they charged a three-percent commission. Then in 1741 they found themselves in need of agents when an Ottoman expedition sacked the outposts here and at Cap Negre, selling the Christian inhabitants into slavery in Tunis, where the name Tabarchini still survives.

The romance of this place was dealt a blow when the French built a causeway to the castle's island after World War II, but the silhouette on its rocky pinnacle has lost none of its allure – it's a fabulous place, especially at sunset when the sun sinks gingerly over the Needles and glints in the other direction off the cliffs of La Galite (see p.173). After a long period of military use, the castle itself is now being prepared to house a **museum** which will hold the collection, formerly in the Basilique, of mosaic reproductions, objects from local excavations and a few old anchors.

West of town, the coast is a series of rocky coves whose beginning is marked by the grotesquely shaped **Needles**, jagged blades of rock standing in a row that juts out towards the castle.

In the other direction, the **beach** stretches 4km round the bay. A kilometre or so down towards the *zone touristique* hotels, a few remnants of World War II wrecks just protrude from the water. You should be able to find some space on this beach, even at its most crowded. The presence of the coral makes for some of the best snorkelling in the Mediterranean. Above the beach loom the big tourist hotels, together with the golf course.

A new curiosity, perhaps created to feed the demands of the new tourist crowds, is the **Cork Museum** (Musée du Liège), a couple of kilometres outside town on the Aïn

---

CORK

Cork is made from the outer bark of the cork oak, which grows all around the western Mediterranean. The first cork harvest, when the tree is about fifteen to twenty years old, is achieved by making a careful cut – so as not to damage the layer of inner bark beneath the cork – around the trunk just above the ground, and another just below where the branches begin. Four vertical cuts are then made and the oblong panels of cork carefully removed. The outer bark regrows and can be harvested every eight to ten years. Trees continue producing cork for about 150 years. Cork's springy lightness is due to millions of tiny air pockets trapped within it, which also make it waterproof and pretty well soundproof. It wasn't used to make bottle corks until the fifteenth century, and that was almost its only use until the veritable explosion – life buoys, table mats, cigarette tips and, of course, floor and wall tiles – of recent times.

Draham road (Tues–Sun, summer 7am–1pm & 3–6pm; winter 8am–noon & 2–5pm; free). Here you'll find the source of the extraordinary cork souvenirs that are now sold in town along with the ubiquitous stuffed camels, as well as some background to the Mediterranean cork industry. With three percent of world production, Tunisia is a small player compared with Portugal and Spain, which together account for 83 percent.

Eating and drinking

Fish is the main source of sustenance in these parts, and excellent it is too, with large, whole succulent specimens being the rule in cheap places as well as the more expensive ones. Among the bargains, the *Restaurant Triki* (daily 8am–9pm) at 43 rue Farhat Hached is one of the best, with meals for under 5TD. For similar prices, try the *Restaurant des Étoiles* (daily 8am–9pm) at 11 rue du Peuple, or two more places at nos. 29 and 33 on the same street. The *Restaurant Le Corail* (daily 9am–10pm) on avenue Bourguiba has a small, but good menu and a filling set meal for 6.5TD.

Worth a try, is the homely and mid-priced *Khemiri* (daily noon–3pm & 7–10pm) at 11 av Bourguiba, which is slowly going to seed but may still conjure up the odd gem. The set menu at the *Hôtel Mimosas* (daily noon–3pm & 7–10pm) is a little more expensive at 9TD, but the views are unsurpassed, and it's also good for a quiet drink or a game of pool. Also in this range is the excellent, if touristy, *Café la Perle du Nord-Ouest* (daily 11am–midnight), at the corner of avenue Bourguiba and rue Ali Zouaoui, serving good seafood specialities à la carte for around 15TD, unless you snap up the lobster (50TD a piece). Restaurants attached to the hotels *Novelty* and *Aiguilles* (both daily 11am–3pm & 7–10pm) are more expensive, but anodyne and charmless.

For tea or coffee and a *chicha*, don't miss Tabarka's trendiest rendezvous, the *Café Andalous*, on the corner of rue du Peuple and Hedi Chaker, with its bizarre, and rather atmospheric, collection of bric-a-brac. As for **nightclubs**, hotels *Abou Nawas Montazah* and *Royal Golf*, both in the *zone touristique*, have discos where local boys try out their latest chat-up lines on holidaymakers. Nearer town is the disco attached to *Hôtel Mimosas* (summer only).

Listings

Banks You'll find banks on the main square, at 30 av Bourguiba, at 12 av Hedi Chaker, and at the corner of av Bourguiba and rue Ali Chaawani. The Habitat on av Bourguiba next to the *Aiguille* hotel has an ATM which accepts Visa, Mastercard and Cirrus.

FLORA AROUND TABARKA

The Tabarka region is one of the richest natural habitats in Tunisia, with the cork oak forests around Aïn Draham dropping down to the "coral coast" around Tabarka.

For a good **walk** to the west of Tabarka, go up rue Farhat Hached from avenue Habib Bourguiba, and then take a track off to the right, which scrambles up to the road by the army camp. Turn left along this road, and follow it as it winds up through shrub-covered hillside. The sandy rock doesn't support a great variety of flowers, but there are some unusual species – the Mediterranean **medlar tree** (a species of hawthorn) and heavily grazed **mastic trees** and **Kermes oaks**. Turn right off the road and head towards the coast. Look closely under the **white-flowered rockroses** on the hill and you'll find the extraordinary parasitic plant **cytinus**: with red and yellow waxy flowers and no green leaves, it gets its energy from its host plant, and is particularly common around here. In between the shrubs is **romulea**, an abundant and very beautiful tiny purple relative of the crocus. You can return along the cliffs to Tabarka, passing above the Needles. Blue rock thrushes are common on this stretch of cliffs.

For a rundown of destinations and journey times, see Travel Details on p.188.

MOVING ON FROM TABARKA

The **airport** (℡08/680005) is a few kilometres east in Ras Rajel, but flights out are infrequent (charters to continental Europe and once weekly to Monastir in summer). The town has two **bus** stations: SNTRI at 12 rue du Peuple (℡08/670404), with services to Tunis via Nefza (for louages to Béja), Sejnane and Mateur, via Béja, and SRT Jendouba at 72 av Bourguiba (℡08/670087), which serves Aïn Draham, Jendouba, Le Kef, Bou Salem and Bizerte. SRT Béja runs buses to Béja, which stop in Tabarka's main square; check also with SNTRI to see who has the next bus out. **Louages** – most of them for Jendouba, via Aïn Draham – leave from avenue Bourguiba by the roundabout at the southeast of town. Otherwise, **hitching** to Aïn Draham is pretty standard practice.

Car rental Hertz has an office in the Porto Corallo development ℡08/670670, as does Europcar ℡08/670834. *Hôtel Morjane* in the *zone touristique* has an activity centre which also hires out quad bikes.

Diving Just before the beginning of the causeway to the castle, a turn-off leads to the Club de Plongée ℡08/671478, part of the yachting club facing the fishing port, where the local coral divers are trained. The club also offers a *baptême* (first dive) to outsiders for 15TD and training to the first grade for 265TD with 10TD membership and a medical certificate, which both the club or the Polyclinique Sidi-Moussa on av Bourguiba can provide. The course lasts 7–10 days and includes up to ten dives. You must be over 14. They rent out boats and diving equipment and train up to the third grade. The *Hôtel Riu Mehari Tabarka* ℡08/671444 also has a dive centre which offers introductory dives for 15TD and a range of courses up to instructor level.

Golf The entrance to the brand-new eighteen-hole golf course ℡08/670028, ℻674026 is 4km east after *Hôtel el Morjane* in Tabarka Montazah *zone touristique*.

Hammams There are two hammams in rue Farhat Hached (daily: men 5am–noon & 5–10pm; women noon–5pm).

Hospital At the western end of rue Farhat Hached ℡08/673661.

Internet Publitel, near the tourist office (8am–midnight; 2TD/hr).

Medical facilities A 24hr Polyclinique Sidi-Moussa is at the northern end of av Bourguiba ℡08/671200.

Pharmacy There's a night pharmacy, Noureddine, at 5 rue Ali Zouaoui ℡08/673314.

Police Rue du Peuple ℡08/671021.

Post office Rue Hedi Chaker (country hours). There's also a smart new taxiphone in *Résidence Tabarka* from where you can make international calls.

Supermarket Magasin Général on the main square (Tues–Sat 8am–12.30pm & 3–7pm, Sun 8am–12.30pm).

Taxis AlloTaxi ℡08/673636.

Tours The *Mimosas* and the big hotels in the *zone touristique* all organize day excursions. Boat trips in a glass-bottomed boat are run by Aquamarin ℡08/673508, next to *Résidence Tabarka*.

La Galite   جزيرة جالطة

La Galite is a small volcanic archipelago 60km off the coast. The largest of the islands is only 5km long, with a tiny seasonal population that at one time included Bourguiba (on yet another bout of exile). The sea here is rich in fish, with great snorkelling in summer if you get the chance, and this is the only place in the Mediterranean where it's possible to see the exceedingly rare Mediterranean monk seal – numbered in the very low hundreds at most. La Galite is now a strictly protected area and in theory closed to all except genuine scientific expeditions, although it is just possible that the

Club de Plongée in Tabarka could organize a trip if you wrote to them well in advance – contact the Secrétaire, Club de Plongée, Port de Pêche, BP49, 8110 Tabarka (☎08/671478, ✉bessassi@planet.tn). There's talk of "repopulating" the islands with a view to expanding tourism; hopefully, if the environmentalists win the day, this will remain just talk.

Aïn Draham and the Khroumirie mountains

In summer the mountain air is refreshing in **AÏN DRAHAM**, 20km south of Tabarka, and 800m above sea level, and the town has become an unassuming resort, though there is little to see in the way of sights. The French tried to recreate here a small Alpine village in what was the equivalent of the British Shimla in India, and many of the older buildings appear to have been spirited out of Switzerland and the Jura mountains in France and plumped down on this remote mountain in North Africa.

Today Aïn Draham is popular with Tunisians who can afford to escape the heat of the capital – which means that prices have been pushed a little higher than usual (its name means "Springs of Silver"). Most holidaymakers are here for a longish stay and rent out villas on the outskirts of the village, leaving the centre mostly unspoiled. The steep main street, **avenue Bourguiba**, lined with a few cafés and general stores – as well as the town's prettiest building, the **police station** – runs down the flank of **Jebel Bir** (Well Mountain), the highest point in the area at 1014m. It doesn't quite have the full Swiss Alpine atmosphere sometimes claimed, but the combination of forested slopes, fresh air and red-tiled roofs is European enough for a minaret to look incongruous.

Coming here in summer, it's almost a shock to find exercise suddenly a pleasure instead of a penance. There are two standard **walks** around town: one is to the **Col des Ruines**, the ridge opposite the village, which you can either scramble up directly, or gain access to from a sideroad 2km down the main Tabarka road north of Aïn Draham. The other is the hike to the summit of **Jebel Bir**, which offers great views: east over mountains shaved with firebreaks like a reverse Mohican hairdo, north to Tabarka on its plain, and west over more mountains into Algeria – you can make out El Kala as a white smudge on the horizon. A dirt road to the summit runs from the Jendouba road near the *Hôtel Rihana*: the pylon at the top is easy to spot and home in on. Both walks are about a three- or four-hour round-trip from the town and are occasionally steep, but not particularly strenuous.

Practicalities

Most of the necessities of life are to be found somewhere along avenue Bourguiba, including the Syndicat d'Initiative **tourist office** at no. 57 (daily 8am–1pm & 3–6pm; ☎08/655052 or 655115), several **banks**, and the **post office** (country hours) at no. 114, where you can make international phone calls from an open kiosk. On avenue Habib Thameur you'll find the municipal **swimming pool**, the **ONTT** crafts shop and the Clinique Sidi Abdallah (☎08/655101). There is also a regional **hospital** (☎08/655047) not far from the bus station.

The town itself has only a few places to **stay**. The new *Hôtel les Pins* (☎08/656200, ⓕ656182; ❹) on avenue Bourguiba, just round the corner from the bus station, has clean, pleasant doubles with bathrooms and balconies enjoying pleasant views. Further on, the *Hôtel Beau Séjour* (☎08/655363; ⓕ 655527; ❸), near the top of avenue Bourguiba, is a remnant of the French hunting parties, with stuffed boars' heads on its walls. Further still, the *Maison des Jeunes* **youth hostel** (☎08/655027) offers the usual Colditz-like accommodation. More attractive, expensive and remote, are three alternatives in the surrounding forests. The three-star *Hôtel Col des Ruines "Nour el Aïn"* (☎08/655000, ⓕ 655185; ❹) is a brand-new place, 10km east of Aïn Draham in Oved

Zéèn forest: it's signposted off the Tabarka road just north of town. A kilometre beyond the *Maison des Jeunes*, on the road to Jendouba, the three-star *Hôtel Rihana* (☎08/655391, ☎ 655396; ④) is a very pleasant walk from town, and some 5km further is the two-star *Hôtel les Chênes* (☎08/655211; ④), under the same management as *Rihana* and attractively set in the forest, but rather run-down and overpriced.

Aïn Draham is one of the few places in the country where you can eat **pork**, with wild boar available in the *Hôtel Beau Séjour* and other hunting-oriented hotels during the season. The *Beau Séjour* does a set menu. Other town eateries, mostly in avenue Bourguiba, are cheaper and more halal, including the *Restaurant el Qods* and the *Restaurant du Grand Maghreb*, more or less opposite the *Beau Séjour*, and, further down, the cheap and grotty *Restaurant de la Jeunesse* at no. 74, and the *Restaurant des Chasseurs* across the street at no. 113.

Moving on from Aïn Draham

All **buses** leave from the bus station on avenue 7 Novembre, off avenue Bourguiba at the bottom of the hill. There are services to Hammam Bourguiba, Le Kef, Jendouba, Tabarka, Bizerte and Tunis via Béja. The **louage** station is next to the bus station, with most vehicles Jendouba-bound, though you might be lucky and get one to Tabarka. To get to Babouch on the Algerian border, you can take the Tabarka bus, or a taxi.

The Khroumirie mountains   جبل خرومري

The small eruption of forested mountains in the northwest corner of Tunisia is called the **Khroumirie**, but in practice you're more likely to hear the area referred to as Aïn Draham, its one sizeable village and effective capital. The region stretches from Tabarka on the coast to Fernana 50km south, and its mountains rise steeply from the sea to a height of over 1000m, covered with leafy forests of **cork oak** and ferns – and reputedly bristling with wild boar – before dipping down to the Medjerda valley at Jendouba. This sudden mountainous barrier gives rise to enormous amounts of rain which never reach other parts of the country: in winter it's not unusual to find a metre of snow at Aïn Draham.

Looking over the Khroumirie mountains, it's easy to see why the **Khroumir Berber tribespeople** who lived here were virtually independent of the country's rulers. They had a reputation for ferocity, regularly raiding the surrounding tribes and even crossing into Algeria to steal herds. But, despite their strength, they kept clear of the dynastic quarrels that embroiled – and destroyed – other tribes. When Mohammed Bey's disgruntled nephew fled here after an abortive coup in 1867, he was sent packing. Fourteen years later, however, the Bey's inability to stop cross-border raiding provided the French with the excuse they needed to invade Tunisia from Algeria in 1881.

East below the mountaintop of Jebel Bir lies the lake of the Beni M'tir dam, surrounded by forests. A detour south of Aïn Draham leads down here before rejoining the main road just before **FERNANA**, which took its name from the only tree for miles around (now vanished), which stood near this bleak settlement. The tree's singularity gave rise to a legend about its special powers. On their annual tax-collecting rounds the Bey's officials never dared penetrate further into the Khroumirie than here. The story goes that the Khroumiris would consult the tree about how little they could get away with declaring, and it would rustle its answer. According to one tale, it was the tree's error of judgement that caused the French invasion. Just north of the village the newly built four star *Hôtel La Forêt* (☎08/655302, ☎655355; ⑤) has all the mod cons in a pleasant setting.

North from Aïn Draham, the road winds along the edge of the great natural bowl which surrounds the Tabarka plain, the only settlement it passes through being **BABOUCH**, just before the Algerian border. Like Aïn Draham, Babouch was a great hunting centre in colonial times, and the last lion and leopard were shot here eighty and sixty years ago respectively.

Babouch and Aïn Draham are surrounded by cork oak woodland, and almost any walk from either will take you through the forests; the valley leading from Babouch towards Hammam Bourguiba is one especially beautiful and rewarding area, although be aware that the troubles in Algeria have made the border area particularly sensitive and you should not wander too far from the road. This is the only large deciduous **forest** in Tunisia and the wildlife is distinctive. You may notice how individual woodland birds, familiar from northern Europe, are developing differences that will, in tens of thousands of years, lead them to be classed as separate species. The blue tit here has a black head; the chaffinch is pale, without a red breast; the green woodpecker is greyish and lacks the red "moustache"; and the jay is quite different, with a red, black and white head.

Louages run from Babouch to **HAMMAM BOURGUIBA**, a resort used by the expresident, where you can take a thermal cure in the three-star *Hammam Bourguiba* (℡08/632552, ℻632497; ❸); otherwise, try the anti-stress massage or ominous-sounding "*cure d'enveloppement*". As yet unexcavated **Roman ruins** indicate, as ever, that the Romans were the first to discover the water's beneficial effects, believed to be especially good for respiratory conditions.

THE MEDJERDA VALLEY

The **Medjerda valley** is the most fertile and best-watered region of Tunisia. In Roman times it supplied much of the grain that fed Rome, its perennial river, unique in Tunisia, allowing the fields to be irrigated and the grain transported. During the 1930s and 1950s the French improved irrigation by building numerous dams, so harnessing the winter floods for the summer. More recently, their feats were surpassed by Chinese engineers, who built a canal and pipeline that takes water to Cap Bon without a single pumping station en route. Most of the valley's towns are prosperous market centres, but the region's main attractions are its Roman ruins, most spectacularly those of **Bulla Regia**. Inevitably and enticingly, the valley forms a stark contrast to the coastal route, and it's straightforward enough to combine both in a looping, wandering journey starting and ending in Tunis.

Medjez el Bab ‏مجز الباب‎

MEDJEZ EL BAB was a seventeenth-century Andalusian foundation on the Roman site of Membressa, but little remains of either except for the mosque just back from the main square and a few miscellaneous fragments in the garden of the town hall. Today it's a main crossing point over the Medjerda, one of a number of small farming centres dotted along the main roads of northern Tunisia.

Built in the seventeenth century (a plaque in the middle dates it at 1088 AH, or 1677 AD), the **bridge** is the only real reminder of that period, but only by chance did it survive the bitter battles for Medjez in the winter of 1942–43. A **Commonwealth War Cemetery**, 4km west along the Kef road, bears eloquent and emotional witness to the 2904 Commonwealth soldiers killed here. The best way of getting there is by taxi from Medjez louage station, or, if you're in a group, by coming to an agreement with a louage driver. A bus can drop you off, but then you'd have to get another one to pick you up afterwards.

There's no tourist office in town, but, if you want to **stay**, the *Hôtel Membressa* (℡08/460121; ❷), on the west bank of the river, overlooking the bridge, is something

The Imperial War Grave Commission, subsequently renamed the Commonwealth Commission, was set up after World War I to arrange for the burial of Britain's **war dead** in specially designed cemeteries. Its general principle was to bury the dead near where they died, and wherever possible in the countryside. Timeless English Pastoral was the desired atmosphere, and it's something of a shock to find these little pieces of England, with lawns and trees, in the middle of Tunisia. As you move along the seemingly endless rows of names, it's important to recognize the nightmare they represent, yet impossible to fully comprehend it. An unnamed grave means that a body could not be identified from the remains, and headstones are grouped together when several were indistinguishable. The cemeteries are moving, and their spirit is summed up in the words of English war poet Keith Douglas, who fought in Tunisia in 1943 before being killed just after D-Day aged 24: "Remember me when I am dead/And simplify me when I'm dead."

There are Commonwealth **cemeteries** at Medjez el Bab (see opposite), Messicault (1km east of Borj el Amri on the GP5 Medjez–Tunis road, some 30km from Tunis), Ras Rajel (see p.167), Oued Zarga (see p.178), Béja (see p.180), Thibar (see p.181), Enfida (see p.191) and Sfax (see p.250). Indian servicemen are buried at Sfax, Jews at Borgel Jewish cemetery in Tunis, and victims of World War I in Bizerte International Cemetery.

American servicemen killed in action in Tunisia (and a number of Commonwealth soldiers) are buried at Carthage American Military Cemetery (see p.116). There are also French military cemeteries at Enfida (see p.191) and Gammarth (see p.119) and a German one at Borj Cedria (see p.120).

of a dive, frequented mainly by inebriated male clients – its main business, in the rather raucous **bar**. They should have food if you ask them early enough. Buses and louages stop in a square just across the bridge, where there are also two **banks**. There are frequent **buses** to Béja and Tunis, and **louages** to Tunis, Testour and Béja. There's also a **train station**, 2km out of town on the left bank of the river, with trains to Tunis, Béja, Jendouba, Ghardimaou and Oued Zarga.

Around Medjez

After the war graves experience, you might want to clear your head by taking a taxi-truck or bus up the road to Toukabeur and Chaouach, two villages high on the mountain wall to the north, for a magnificent view over the surrounding countryside and a reminder that Medjez was once a strategic point. **CHAOUACH**, at the end of the road, is built on the site of a Byzantine fort on a rocky outcrop, the fort itself assembled from the remains of Roman Sua just below. **TOUKABEUR**, 3km below Chaouach on the same road, has more scant remains – the garage on the main square is a converted Roman cistern. On April 12, 1943, a unit of the British 1st Army captured a hill just north of Chaouach. One member of the unit was Sidney Keyes, among the most promising English poets of World War II. "Algeria is a pleasant enough country," he wrote home, "but Tunisia is like what Scotland must have been in the eighteenth century, a mass of bald mountains, terribly cold at night." Two weeks later, at the age of 20, he was killed just outside Medjez, and he lies buried in plot number 2.K.15 in the Borj el Amri Commonwealth cemetery, on the main road between Tunis and Medjez.

West from Medjez, the road hugs the north side of the Medjerda valley. When the huge **Sidi Salem dam** was completed, the river had to be diverted, and the people of **OUED ZARGA** were entirely rehoused in smart new homes. The old village was the site of a notorious massacre in September 1881, when the French stationmaster and ten other European staff were burnt alive in a sudden uprising by the local people. A conflagration from another era is commemorated at Oued Zarga's **Commonwealth War Cemetery**, left behind in the old village. A track starting opposite the Garde Nationale post leads 2km downhill to the old village.

Béja and around
باجة

Twenty-five kilometres or so west of Oued Zarga, after you climb over a high ridge, **BÉJA** comes into view, spread over the slopes of a mountain rather like Le Kef to the south. It's an important grain town and, although there's little of outstanding interest, it's well worth stopping off here if you're passing through, especially on a Tuesday, when the weekly **souk** is held.

Some history

Since Roman times, Béja has held the biggest **grain market** in the north, and has paid the price of prosperity with a torrid history of destruction and recovery. The first of these cycles began in 109 BC, when a Roman garrison was massacred by a population keen to show its support for the Numidian **King Jugurtha**. The only survivor of the disaster, one Turpilius, turned out to have made a grave error of judgement, because, when his supreme commander Metellus arrived and punished the town by razing it to the ground, he had Turpilius flogged and executed. "A man who in such a calamity could prefer dishonourable survival to an untarnished name must have been a detestable wretch," the historian Sallust explained helpfully.

The town recovered, only to be levelled again by the Vandals in the fifth century, Abu Yazid in the tenth, and the Banu Hilal in the eleventh. By 1154, however, according to El Edrisi, it was a "beautiful city, built on a plain extremely fertile in corn and barley, so that there is not in all the Maghreb a city so important or richer in cereals." It has remained an important agricultural centre ever since, attracting large numbers of Europeans under the French, who left their mark in the form of striking buildings and a well-populated cemetery.

Arrival and information

The **train station** lies on avenue Habib Thameur, with SRT Béja running the city's only **bus station**, also used by SNTRI and a few other regional companies, on the Tunis road. **Louages** can be picked up from a station beside avenue Moncef Ben Kahla. There are **banks** along avenue Bourguiba, where you'll also find the **post office** (city hours) just uphill from the old church, and a night **pharmacy** behind the church; the regional **hospital** (☎08/451431) south along avenue Bourguiba on the edge of town. Magasin Général, next to the market, is the town's **supermarket**. There's no tourist office.

The Town

Béja's backbone is **avenue Bourguiba**, which climbs from a level crossing at the bottom of the hill up to the town's main square. Bisecting the avenue, avenue de France runs east – with the **modern town** beginning from place de l'Indépendance – and rue **Khereddine** runs northwest up towards the Great Mosque, with the Medina behind.

Climbing avenue Bourguiba, you'll come across the huge and extraordinary **church**, built by Béja's large colonial population in a bizarre confusion of dimly remembered European styles, with a few local additions – the tower, for example, looks like a minaret. The church is now a cultural centre. You can study more of Béja's outrageous

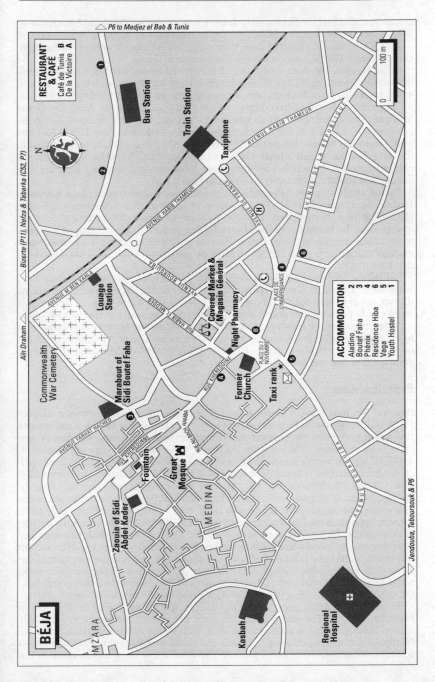

BÉJA

△ P6 to Medjez el Bab & Tunis

RESTAURANT & CAFÉ
Café de Tunis   B
De la Victoire   A

N

Bizerte (P11), Netza & Tabarka (C52, P7) ▷

Aïn Draham ▷

Bus Station

Train Station

C Taxiphone

AVENUE HABIB THAMEUR

AVENUE DE LA RÉPUBLIQUE

AVENUE HABIB THAMEUR

AVENUE DE FRANCE

H

AVENUE BOURGUIBA

AVENUE M BEN KAHLA

Commonwealth War Cemetery

Louage Station

RUE HABIB EL MEDDEB

Covered Market & Magasin Général

Night Pharmacy

C

PLACE DE L'INDÉPENDANCE

6

4

RUE KHEREDDINE

AVENUE FARHAT HACHED

Marabout of Sidi Boutef Faha

3

Former Church

B

PLACE DU 7 NOVEMBRE

5

Taxi rank ★

RUE EL KHEREDDINE

RUE ALI BACH HAMBA

Fountain

Great Mosque

Zaouia of Sidi Abdel Kader

MEDINA

M'ZARA

AVENUE BOURGUIBA

Kasbah

Regional Hospital ✚

▽ Jendouba, Teboursouk & P6

ACCOMMODATION
Aladino   2
Boutef Faha   3
Phénix   4
Residence Hiba   6
Vaga   5
Youth Hostel   1

0   100 m

colonial architecture, at the building (now a row of shops) dated 1912 immediately behind the former church opposite the top of rue Habib el Meddeb. Reminiscent of Tunis's Christmas-cake colonial style, their early date suggests how important an agricultural centre like Béja was in the colonial scheme of things.

Béja's **Medina**, run-down though it is, has survived largely intact. It is unusually full of mosques, as well as old fountains and busy market streets and, with the cool climate which seems to prevail here, it's one of the most pleasant to wander through in Tunisia. Its main street is **rue Khereddine**, running only a block away from the **Great Mosque**, Almohad in style, with an unusual red minaret. Rue de la Mosquée, behind it, emerges into a square as rue Blagui. Ahead, bearing right into place Bab el Aïn, you pass a **fountain** on your left dated 1219 AH (1804 AD). To the left, in another square, the 1843 **Zaouia of Sidi Abdel Kader**, with its green-tiled *koubba* dome, is now a kindergarten, but the people who work there (Mon–Sat 8am–5pm as a rule) are welcoming and will almost certainly let you in to have a look.

Taking a right off place Bab el Aïn, you're back on the main road at **place Khemais Bedda**, the centre of the Medina. A couple of hundred metres further, rue Farhat Hached on the right sweeps round to give an impressive view of the countryside to the east, passing the **Marabout of Sidi Boutef Faha** on the left, before bringing you back to the old church. Between rue Farhat Hached and rue Khereddine is a **secondhand clothes market** where you can obtain all those ghastly 1970s fashions you missed the first time round.

Behind the Medina, the **Kasbah**, dominating the old town, was originally Byzantine, but what little remains is now occupied by the army and is out of bounds. The **Mzara** district, north of here and also above the old town, is said still to have one or two cave dwellings, but this is a very poor part of town and sightseers aren't especially welcome.

At the bottom of rue Habib el Meddeb, a left along avenue M Ben Kahla brings you to a **Commonwealth War Cemetery**, unusual for its position next to a housing estate; on its far side is a typical colonial cemetery, full of dynastic Italian family tombs now smothered in dust and cobwebs.

Practicalities

Béja has five **hotels** and a **youth hostel**. The newest player is the two-star *Aladino* (☎08/455077; ③) on the P6 at the edge of town. Very convenient for buses and louages this bright pink place has pleasant modern rooms with bathrooms, satellite TV and some with balconies. The recently declassed concrete *Hôtel Vaga* (☎08/450818, ⑥456902; ③) on avenue Bourguiba opposite the post office, is friendly, with comfortable, slightly shabby, self-contained rooms – if rather bizarre decor. The unclassified *Hôtel Phénix* (☎/⑥08/456079; ③), at 8 av de la République, just off place de l'Indépendance is adequate, with shared bathrooms, although some rooms are rather dingy with little outside light. If no one is there, try the bar round the back at 37 av de France. Opposite is the *Résidence Hiba* (☎08/457244, ⑥456299; ②), which has a range of characterful, high-ceilinged rooms with sinks, bidets and some with balconies; the management are friendly and speak some English. Far cheaper than any of these, and half-board, is the basic *Hôtel Boutef Faha* (no phone; ①), opposite the marabout of the same name in rue Farhat Hached, next to a large café. Rooms are basic but clean, some with a terrace, and you're at the edge of the Medina. The *Maison des Jeunes* youth hostel, opposite the bus station (☎08/454054), has the usual barrack-like dorms (5TD).

As far as sustenance goes, you're not exactly spoiled for choice in Béja; and in Ramadan even the few places below close for the month, making picnics the only option. Mind you, this is a pleasure in Béja, with its lovely fresh vegetables (in the Medina and market), profusion of sweets and cakes available everywhere, and good selections of olives, cheeses and pickles. There are a few cheap **restaurants** in the

Medina, like the *Restaurant de la Victoire* (daily 8am–8pm) at 25 rue Khereddine, but these are generally pretty basic affairs. Otherwise you're limited to hotel restaurants such as the *Vaga* (daily noon–3pm & 7–11pm), which has à la carte for around 11TD, and the cheaper, but even duller, *Hiba* (noon–3pm & 7–10pm), with a 7TD set meal. The top recommendation, especially for its seafood, is the *Hôtel Phénix*'s restaurant (daily noon–3pm & 7–11pm), where you'll get an excellent meal for around 15TD. The only reservation here is that you sometimes have to enter through the *Phénix*'s rather raucous bar on rue de France, which women may find intimidating. A good place to watch the world go by is the *Café de Tunis* on place du 7 Novembre.

Thibar   تيبار

Eleven kilometres south of Béja, a road turns left towards Téboursouk (see p.275), passing a farmstead that looks like a fort with an egg on top, and runs through the pleasant little village of **THIBAR**, which has a farm and monastery set up by the White Fathers in 1895 that's still in use today. Thibarine date liqueur and Thibar wine are made here and, if you're lucky, you may be able to visit the **wine cellars**. Behind the farm buildings, yet another **Commonwealth War Cemetery**, a small one this time, broods among trees full of birds.

There are some scant **Roman remains** south of the village, not really worth seeing but an excuse for an hour-long stroll. Head past the site of Thibar's **Sunday souk**, taking the right-hand fork in the road, signposted "Bou Salem". At the crossroads 1.5km further on, turn right as signposted. With vineyards on your left, then a peach orchard, you're now on an avenue of eucalyptus trees. After a kilometre or so, you pass a water-pumping station on your left and, 100m beyond, a path to the left takes you around a field and across an *oued*. The remains, such as they are, lie on the other side.

Jendouba and around   جندوبة

JENDOUBA is just about the least interesting town in the whole country. What it does have in its favour, however, is plenty of accommodation, banking and transport facilities, making it a perfect base for visiting the impressive Roman site of **Bulla Regia** in the hills above the Medjerda valley, or the lesser remains of **Thuburnica** and **Chemtou** to the west. There are a few Roman remains in Jendouba itself, but these were lifted from Bulla Regia and now sit in a small garden, along with a monument to Jendoubans who died fighting the French for control of Bizerte in 1961 (see p.154), down rue Hedi Chaker on place des Martyrs.

Arriving in Jendouba by bus or louage, you're likely to find yourself at the main transport focus of place 7 Novembre, a large roundabout on the western edge of town with three columns supporting a clocktower in its middle. On one side, by a level crossing, is the **louage** station for Aïn Draham and Tabarka (you can be dropped at the Bulla Regia crossroads for the site). On the other side are the louage stations for Ghardimaou and Oued Meliz, and beyond them the bus station and louages for Le Kef, Béja, Bizerte and Tunis. There are also buses to Tunis, Béja, Le Kef, Ghardimaou, Tabarka and Bizerte.

To get to the town centre, take rue Hedi Chaker from place 7 Novembre, then turn left down rue Taïeb Mehiri. Here you'll find the **post office** (city hours; international call facilities), **banks** and the easily overlooked **train station**, tucked away in a corner by the police station, with services to Béja, Medjez el Bab, Oved Zarga, Tunis and Ghardimaou on the Algerian border. If you turn left off rue Hedi Chaker, just after place des Martyrs, rue Ali Belhouane takes you past more banks, **pharmacies** (day and night), and the louage station for Tunis. There's no tourist office in Jendouba.

If you're stuck out by the bus station and want to find somewhere to **stay**, the two-star *Hôtel Simitthu*, right by the roundabout (☎08/604043, 🖷602595; ❸), is the best in town. East of the train station up rue 1 Juin, left from rue Hedi Chaker, leads to the two-star *Hôtel Atlas* (☎08/603217; ❸), cheaper and correspondingly less plush than the *Simitthu*.

There are plenty of cheap **restaurants** in the town centre, and the *Simitthu* and *Atlas* hotels both do moderately priced set menus. If your stay in town becomes prolonged, there's also a **flea market** of sorts off place 7 Novembre, at the end of boulevard Khemaïs el Hajera, a **cinema** 100m down avenue Bourguiba from place 7 Novembre, and a Publinet internet office opposite *Hôtel Atlas* on rue 1 Juin.

Bulla Regia   بـولا ريجيـة

Bulla Regia is one of the most extraordinary Roman sites anywhere in the world. The **underground villas** that form its distinctive feature were built by wealthy inhabitants and, though they have their modern parallel at Matmata (see pp.354–357), were unique in the

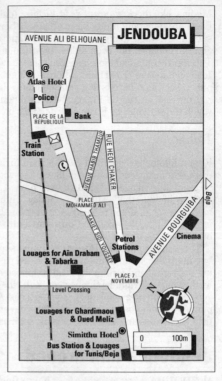

Roman Empire. Equally striking are the intact and beautiful **mosaics** left *in situ*, all too rare now that the museums have taken the best mosaics at other sites.

As with the troglodytes at Matmata, no one knows for certain why Bulla Regians went underground, given that the rock in other hot settlements was also soft and hence easier to excavate. This has always been an important region, though, and Bulla Regia played much the same market-centre role as Jendouba does today. The "Regia" in its name refers to royal connections before the arrival of the Romans, when it was associated with one of the native Numidian kingdoms. Subsequently, it became yet another prosperous Roman town and was still occupied in the Byzantine era, but abandoned after the Arab conquest in the seventh century.

The **site** itself (Tues–Sun: April–Oct 8am–7pm; Nov–March 8.30am–5pm; 2.1TD, camera 1TD) lies just north of Jendouba, 6km along the GP17 Aïn Draham road, then 2km to the right along the minor C59, signposted for Bou Salem. A taxi from Jendouba to the site shouldn't cost more than 2.5TD from the flea market off place 7 Novembre, or there are shared taxis for about 0.5TD. From Aïn Draham louage station, there are minibuses (0.7TD) to the turn-off. Make it clear that it's just the turn-off (*croisement*) that you want; if the driver thinks you want the site itself, he may direct you to a taxi. From the crossroads, you have to walk the last 2km – take the direction signposted "Bou Salem", in the opposite direction from Chemtou. A small **museum**, opposite the site entrance (same hours as the site), has maps illustrating Bulla Regia's position in Roman Africa, pictures of the Numidian kings to whom the town owes its suffix, and some nice neo-Punic stelae.

The Memmian Baths and Treasure House

Bullia Regia's most prominent remains – the **Memmian Baths** – stand just by the site entrance and were named after the wife of Septimius Severus, the first African emperor of Rome; the large central hall was a *frigidarium*. From here, take the track leading north to the Quartier des Maisons; shortly on the left is the first of the buried villas, the **Treasure House**, so called after a cache of seventh-century Byzantine coins discovered inside. The standard pattern for villas built in this curious way was to have a normal ground floor, with a dining room and perhaps bedrooms sunk underground. The relatively small Treasure House conforms to this pattern, with a large dining room downstairs (identifiable by the pattern of the floor mosaic, showing where couches were positioned around three walls), flanked by two smaller rooms. At least one of these was a bedroom, so presumably eating and sleeping were the two daily functions for which the wealthy Roman citizen most wanted to remain cool.

Back at ground level, some columns standing over to the left belong to a pair of basilica **churches**. One of them has a baptismal font at its western end. From here an artificial **mound** in the middle of the site is visible: this gives a good view over the whole area, and especially the residential quarter directly below it.

The Peacock, Hunt, Fishing and Amphitrite houses

Just left of the crossroads next to the mound is the **House of the Peacock,** whose eponymous mosaic has been removed to the Bardo Museum in Tunis, but it's the fully excavated block on the other side of the street that's most fascinating. Almost the whole

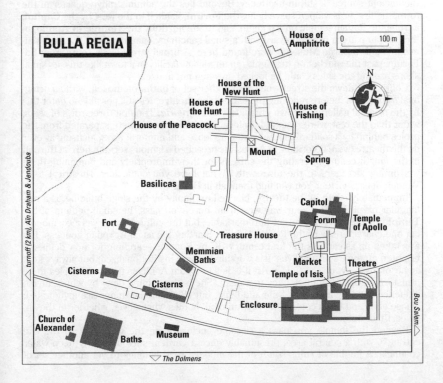

block is occupied by the huge **House of the Hunt**, whose basement even includes its own colonnaded courtyard, off which opens a magnificent dining room with its mosaics still in place. Bedrooms also open off the courtyard. Note, too, the hexagonal holes in the superstructure of the courtyard, designed to lighten the load, and clusters of what are apparently broken clay pipes in the walls – these were piled together, then plastered over, forming a light but strong construction unit which helped make these basements possible. A private baths complex and some latrines on the ground floor suggest that the owner of this house was something of a plutocrat.

Leaving the House of the Hunt, head north along the street running alongside, then take a right at the top of the **House of Fishing**. This has a huge basement built like a bunker, with a semicircular fountain that would have produced refreshing jets of water, which faces a small room containing part of a mosaic depicting fishermen and their prey. Take the street leading north from here to the **House of Amphitrite**, a sea goddess, justly famous for the magnificent mosaics on the basement level. The star of the main scene in the *triclinium* is actually Venus, not Amphitrite, but you have to delight in the attendant Cupid who manages to ride a dolphin and admire his chubby features in a mirror at the same time. When Bulla Regia was first excavated, one disturbing discovery was a skeleton tied to a chair with an iron ring around its neck, inscribed: "Adulterous prostitute: hold me, because I ran away from Bulla Regia." The later building over the street was a **baths** complex.

Around the Forum

Head back down the street, then off left to the **spring** – as at Sbeïtla (see pp.291–293), the ancient source is still in use today. Beyond lies the administrative quarter of the town, the first grassy open space being the **Forum**, flanked to the west by the **Capitol**, a true-blue Roman temple on a podium, and to the north by the **Temple of Apollo**, in the African pattern of a courtyard with a small sanctuary opening off it. The best statues in Tunis's Bardo Museum were found here. A broad street leads south from the Forum, past the **market** on the right – an important facility in a town like this, its small shops around the sides could be locked up when not in use.

Continuing down the street, you pass another set of **baths** on the left, with an octagonal *frigidarium*, before reaching the back of the **theatre**. It's still possible to enter this by the original galleries, known graphically as *vomitoria*. The first three rows of seats, wider than the rest, were reserved for local dignitaries – who were separated from the proles behind by a solid railing. Bulla Regia's loose and immoral ways, focusing as ever on the theatre, were notorious. St Augustine preached a famous sermon here at the end of the fourth century, berating the citizens for their impropriety and imagining them welcoming strangers to the town with "What have you come for? Theatrical folk? Women of easy virtue? You can find them all in Bulla."

Immediately south of the theatre, blocked originally by the stage building, is a rectangular plaza. Making your way west from here, you pass the small podium of the **Temple of Isis**. Its remains are unremarkable, but the cult it served was a cosmopolitan one characteristic of the Roman Empire. Starting life as an Egyptian goddess, Isis was taken up as early as the first century BC by Romans searching for new deities to brighten up their spiritual lives. Isis worship became institutionalized, but always kept an air of mystery; in *The Golden Ass* it is Isis to whom Apuleius turns in his plea to be transformed back from a donkey to a man: "She is the shining deity by whose divine influence not only all beasts, wild and tame, but all inanimate things are invigorated; whose ebbs and flows control the rhythm of all bodies whatsoever, whether in the air, on earth, or below the sea."

Beyond the temple you pass a sizeable enclosure on the way back to the site entrance, with a central area, presumably once a garden, surrounded by deep water channels. A jumble of ruins south of the modern road belongs to yet another set of baths, next to what is now misleadingly called the **Church of Alexander**. An inscription from the Psalms was found over the door here ("May the Lord guard your coming in and your going out, now and for ever more, Amen"), and the trough-like stones (as at Kef, Haïdra and Maktar) were probably connected with the distribution of food and commodities. Half a kilometre or so south of here is an area of pre-Roman **dolmens**.

Ghardimaou and around   غار الدّماء

GHARDIMAOU, 30km west of Jendouba on the GP6, is a small border town and unglamorous in the extreme. Its setting is its only virtue: a misty river plain, overshadowed on three sides by mountains that pile up steeply towards Algeria. If you intend to remain in Tunisia (and at present you have no other option), the only real reason for coming here is to visit the minor Roman sites of Thuburnica and Chemtou, one featuring a miraculously preserved bridge and the other an ancient marble quarry once renowned throughout the Roman Empire. There's also the mountainous **Forest of Feija**, a national park 20km northwest of Ghardimaou, right on the Algerian frontier.

Ghardimaou's **train station** is centrally placed, with services to Jendouba, Béja, Medjez el Bab, Tunis and Oued Zarga. There's a single **hotel** in town, should you want to stay – the *Thuburnic*, overlooking the station (✆08/660043; ❸). There is some activity in its bar and restaurant but, as a depressed resident admitted, "there's no ambience in Ghardimaou". There's a *Centre des Stages et des Vacances* **youth hostel** (no phone) in the village of **AÏN SOLTANE**, which is a good alternative to staying in Ghardimaou if you have the time, but it's been closed for a while – ask around in Ghardimaou before making the trip. You'll also have to get someone to take you there, and since it's very close to the border it's advisable to inform the local police or border officials of your intentions. When you're ready to leave, **louages** to Jendouba depart from along the main road.

This is true border country – never more viciously or tragically so than during the Algerian War of 1954–62. In 1957, the French built the infamous **Morice Line** to prevent the Algerian ALN (Armé de la Libération Nationale), based in "neutral" Tunisia, from reinforcing their FLN (Front de la Libération Nationale) counterparts inside the

---

TRAVELLING TO ALGERIA: A WARNING

Since early 1992, when the government cancelled elections expected to be won by the FIS Islamic party (Front Islamique de la Salvation), Algeria's internal security situation has become virtually a civil war between the forces of the establishment (in essence, the army) and the Islamic fundamentalist movement. In 1995, 30,000 people had already died in the vicious struggle between hardliners on both sides. Victims of the security forces have included ordinary citizens suspected of allegiance to their Islamist opponents, and whole villages thought to have voted for the FIS in 1992, while the Islamists have targeted not just security and government officials, but anyone involved in what they perceive as a West-tainted activity: to date this has included journalists, a *rai* (pop music) star, feminists and sporting officials. Compared to the total number of victims, only a small proportion have been foreigners, but two Islamist paramilitary groups have stated publicly that they are explicitly targeting foreigners and they mean it. Several foreign tourists have been murdered and anyone who visits the country is in extreme danger. Some travellers feel that the far south is safe, and the mid-south relatively so (see p.327), however, no part of the country can be regarded as completely secure. The coastal strip in the north of the country remains a killing field, and travel there would be foolhardy in the extreme. Unless this situation changes drastically, any journey to Algeria, particularly the north, is extremely dangerous: **DO NOT GO THERE**.

country. Three hundred kilometres long, the Morice Line ran from the Mediterranean in the north to the Sahara in the south, where no one could hope to cross the border unnoticed. It was brutally effective. A 2.5-metre-high electric fence, charged with 5000 volts, was flanked by minefields and defended by eighty thousand French troops using the latest in electronic surveillance technology. One three-day assault in April 1958 saw the ALN push eight hundred men at the line just north of Souk Ahras. In a week-long running battle, six hundred of them were killed or captured. After the line was built, the ALN never did succeed in providing significant support across the border.

The **border crossings** here and further north at Babouch are the most heavily used in the country, but have been closed with increasing frequency of late. You are strongly advised *not* to visit Algeria at present: large-scale massacres of Algerian villagers are a regular occurrence, and not confined to the region around Algiers: both Annaba on the coast, and Souk-Ahras – 50km beyond the border – have been targeted in the past. Travelling close to the Algerian border can be problematic; stick to the road and have a hotel and destination in mind if questioned by security forces.

Thuburnica

A visit to the Roman site of **Thuburnica** (free access) on the north side of the river plain gives ample chance to see the district's scenery. Taxi-trucks leave regularly from the turning outside Ghardimaou across the bridge towards Algeria, signposted "Turbournic 13km". The remains are an excuse for the journey, but you'll find a memorable little **bridge** carrying the track over one of the deep stream beds that hurry out of the foothills. The bridge's Roman builders are nearly two thousand years gone, but it still looks as if it might have been put up twenty years ago. The rest of the ancient town is scattered in smallish fragments over the hill to the west – a ruined Byzantine castle stands on top, and a fine two-storey **mausoleum** about halfway up.

Chemtou   شمتو

The other Roman site in this area is **CHEMTOU** (Tues–Sun: April–Oct 9am–6.30pm; Nov–March 9am–5pm; free access to site museum; 2.1TD, camera 1TD), an apparently unremarkable place that was once famous throughout the Roman world as Simithas, the source of Numidian marble, a lurid red-yellow-pink variety much in vogue with imperial builders. Plainly recognizable on an isolated hill on the plain, the site lies 10km east of Thuburnica on the minor C59 Ghardimaou–Jendouba road. There are several ways of getting there, the easiest being to catch a local **louage** from either Ghardimaou or Jendouba, making sure that they take the Thuburnica road and not the main P6 Le Kef–Tunis road. Alternatively, catch a louage or train to the village of Oued Meliz, 3km southwest of the site, from where you have to walk: the signposted turn-off 1km east of Oued Meiz leads 2km down to a ford over the River Medjerda, mocked by the massive remains of a **Roman bridge**. The site is just beyond on the right. Easiest of all is to arrange for a taxi to take you to the site from Jendouba and wait to drive you back; this should cost no more than 8–10TD.

The site and museum

Newly victorious in 146 BC, the Romans used the marble widely and closely identified it with extravagance and luxury. "No beams of Athenian stone rest in *my* house", wrote the poet Horace, "on columns quarried in furthest Africa". As a result, the industry supported a sizeable town which has been excavated by a team from Tunis and the German Archeological School in Rome. The fruits of their findings are displayed in the new US$1.5million **museum** (same hours as the site), which is really the main draw, especially as the site itself isn't really that much to look at. There are four main rooms, each illustrating an aspect of Chemtou's past. The **Salle de Géologie** contains rock samples, and explains the geology and morphology of the region, and so the creation of marble, whilst the **Salle de Marbre** explains the excavation. The **Salle Numide** has a lovely carving of a Numidian mounted God, as well as reliefs dedicated to Baal and other funerary pieces, some from the region of the Berber King Micipsa dating from 148–118BC. The relics are remarkable in that pre-Roman, Numidian excavation of marble was for a long time unknown to archeologists and suggests that Numidian culture, of which very little remains, was more spohisticated than previously thought. But the highlight of the museum is the **Salle de Chemtou la Romaine**. This displays some of the 1646 solid gold coins which were found here, in a hoard, when building the museum, and which most visibly testify to the riches of what was an immensely wealthy town. The mosaics, too, are impressive, set into a stunning reconstruction of their original temple, along with a striking series of massive reliefs showing shields and other accoutrements that decorated the Roman successor to the original Numidian hilltop altar.

Saddling the middle of the hill are the marble **quarries** themselves – just gaping holes in the rock now, but their emptiness seems to preserve an indefinable memory of the skill and sheer hard work of so many men over so many years. The Romans, who declared the quarries imperial property under Emperor Octavius Augustus, a decision which necessitated the building of an entire city, had the industry highly organized, with every single block stamped with the names of the emperor, the consul in office and the local official, along with a production number so that it wouldn't go missing. The effort involved in transporting the stone to its destination on the other side of the Mediterranean was enormous – it was either dragged all the way over the Khroumirie mountains to be shipped from Tabarka, or floated down the Medjerda to Utica – but of course, this only enhanced its power as a status symbol. The emperor Hadrian, a great devotee, once presented a hundred columns to Athens and twenty to Smyrna as marks of imperial favour. As to who actually did the work, excavators have unearthed traces of a mammoth **prison camp**, in which condemned criminals and others were kept, covering some 20,000 square metres and guarded by military installations. A number of remaining miscellaneous blocks illustrate the Romans' particular sense of colour, a taste later shared in turn by the Byzantines and a nineteenth-century operation which revived the workings.

On the top of the eastern summit is a partial restoration of the hilltop **altar**. You can just make out the ancient steps which were hacked into the rock leading up to it. There's something powerful about this high place of worship, which the civic dignity of official Roman religion came to lack.

Below the northern slope of the hill is a broad area of remains, originally a first-century AD military camp but taken over and adapted by some sharp Roman entrepreneur into an on-site factory for products from the quarries. Raw stone was delivered to the southern entrance of the camp and then passed along a production line of workshops, ending up with the polishers. The finished utensils and small statues were dispatched all over the Empire. Also visible north of the hill are stretches of aqueduct heading into the hills, from where they brought the water that fed the town.

South and west of the hill were the residential and official quarters of the town, far away from the prison camp, below which, towards the tumbledown Roman bridge, you can make out the remains of a **basilica** and a half-buried **theatre**. The bridge, whose massive remains bear elegant testimony to the Romans' civil engineering, carried the main Sicca–Thabraca (Le Kef–Tabarka) road, along which much of the stone was hauled for export. Among the tangled ruins on the northern bank, you can see the unusual industrial feature of three parallel grooves – unique in North Africa – which forced the flowing water to drive turbines to grind grain.

travel details

Trains

Bizerte to: Mateur (4 daily; 1hr–1hr 15min); Tinja (4 daily; 1hr 20min); Tunis (4 daily; 1hr 40min).

Ghardimaou to: Béja (4 daily; 2hr); Jendouba (4 daily; 2hr 40min); Medjez el Bab (4 daily; 1hr 10min); Meliz (3 daily; 3hr); Oued Tunis (4 daily; 3hr); Oued Zarga (4 daily; 1hr 30min).

Buses

Aïn Draham to: Béja (4 daily; 5hr); Bizerte (1 daily; 5hr); Hammam Bourguiba (2 daily; 30min); Jendouba (5 daily; 1hr); Le Kef (2 daily; 2hr); Tabarka (5 daily; 1hr); Tunis (4 daily; 3hr).

Béja to: Aïn Draham (5 daily; 3hr); Bizerte (6 daily; 3hr); Jendouba (10 daily; 1hr 30min); Medjez el Bab (frequent; 1hr); Siliana (1 daily; 5hr); Sousse (2 daily; 3hr 30min); Tabarka (4 daily; 1hr 30min–2hr 30min); Tunis (frequent; 2hr).

Bizerte to: Aïn Draham (1 daily; 5hr); Beja (1 daily; 2hr); Ghar el Melh (2 daily; 1hr); Houmt Souk (2 daily; 11hr); Jendouba (1 daily; 3hr); Kairouan (1 daily; 5hr); Menzel Bourguiba (8 daily; 45min); Raf Raf (daily; 1hr); Ras Jebel (frequent; 1hr); Tabarka (1 daily; 4hr); Tunis (half-hourly; 2hr).

Jendouba to: Aïn Draham (5 daily; 1hr); Béja (8 daily; 1hr 30min); Bizerte (1 daily; 3hr); Ghardimaou (4 daily; 1hr); Le Kef (6 daily; 1hr 10min); Medjez el Bab (10 daily; 3hr); Tabarka (4 daily; 2hr); Tunis (10 daily; 4hr).

Medjez el Bab to: Béja (frequent; 1hr); Jendouba (10 daily; 3hr); Le Kef (hourly; 1hr 30min); Téboursouk (hourly; 1hr); Testour (hourly; 30min); Tunis (frequent; 1hr).

Ras Jebel to: Bizerte (frequent; 1hr); Ghar el Melh (6 daily; 45min); Raf Raf (frequent; 30min); Tunis (5 daily; 2hr).

Tabarka to: Aïn Draham (12 daily; 1hr); Béja (8 daily; 2hr 15min); Bizerte (1 daily; 4hr); Jendouba (5 daily; 2hr); Le Kef (2 daily; 3hr); Mateur (6 daily; 3hr); Sejnane (6 daily; 2hr 30min); Tunis (9 daily; 3hr 45min).

Louages

Louage journey times are roughly three-quarters the time taken by buses on the same route. Frequency depends on demand, but morning is always the best time to get a louage, especially for longer journeys.

Béja to: Jendouba (1hr); Medjez el Bab (45min); Nefza (for Tabarka and Sejnane; 45min); Téboursouk (1hr); Thibar (40min); Tunis (1hr 45min).

Bizerte to: Béja (1hr 30min); Jendouba (2hr); Mateur (45min); Menzel Bourguiba (30min); Raf Raf (30min); Sejnane (2hr); Tunis (1hr 30min).

Jendouba to: Aïn Draham (45min); Béja (1hr); Bizerte (2hr); Gharimaou (30min); Le Kef (50min); Oued Meliz (20min); Tabarka (1hr 30min); Tunis (3hr).

Tabarka to: Aïn Draham (40min); Jendouba (1hr 30min).

CHAPTER FOUR

KAIROUAN AND THE SAHEL

Kairouan – the Holy City – is only the most obvious attraction in **the Sahel**, an area that is central in every way to Tunisia. (The Arabic name "Sahel" means "coast or margin" and, in the case of the sub-Saharan Sahel, the edge of the desert.) Ranging back from the east coast, these fertile plains have long been the heartland of the country's agriculture, and a focus during each shift of power. The Romans planted millions of olive trees throughout the region, and under Arab rule it was the base of the great Aghlabid dynasty, which launched a successful invasion of Sicily from the port of Sousse in the ninth century.

Monuments from this and ensuing dynasties grace most of the Sahel's larger towns. **Kairouan**, the first Arab capital in North Africa, is pre-eminent – above all for its Great Mosque, justly Tunisia's most famous building as well as its spiritual centre. But **Sousse**, **Sfax**, **Monastir** and **Mahdia** are each highly rewarding for their architecture, and **El Jem** shelters what is arguably the Roman world's finest surviving amphitheatre.

Add to this an impressive series of beaches and it's easy to understand the region's popularity – and why the **Sousse–Monastir coast** is gradually becoming the country's most highly developed for tourism. Yet there are still places – in particular, parts of the **Kerkennah Islands** – where you can find virtual isolation. Most people invariably find themselves staying longer than originally planned.

Enfida (Enfidaville) and Takrouna   النّفيضة

ENFIDA is the administrative centre for a vast and fertile agricultural estate that was an indirect cause of French colonial intervention in 1881. The estate's original owner, the reforming Turkish official Khaireddin, put it up for sale when he was recalled to Constantinople, and the Franco-African Company immediately submitted the highest bid. The Tunisian government tried to keep the estate out of French hands, but the

---

ACCOMMODATION PRICE CODES

The hotels and pensions listed in this book have been price-graded according to the following scale. The prices quoted are for the **cheapest available double room in high season**. For more on accommodation prices and categories, see Basics, p.29.

❶ Under 10TD	❺ 70–100TD
❷ 10–20TD	❻ 100–150TD
❸ 20–40TD	❼ 150TD upwards
❹ 40–70TD	

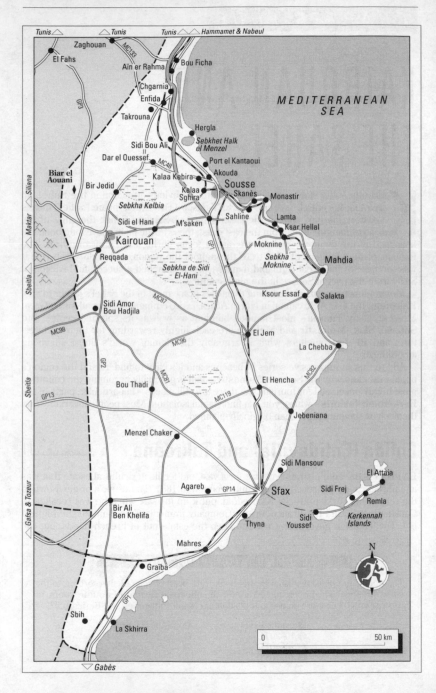

MARKET DAYS

Monday – La Chebba, El Alia, El Jem, Kairouan, Ksour Essaf, Mahres, Msaken
Tuesday – Ksar Hellal, Remla (Kerkennah)
Wednesday – Moknine
Thursday – Bou Thadi, Kalaa Sghira, Sbih, Sidi el Hani
Friday – Kalaa Kebira, Mahdia, Sahline, Sfax, La Skhirra
Saturday – El Hencha, Hammam Sousse, Monastir, Sidi Bou Ali
Sunday – Enfida, Graïba, Ksar Hellal, Sousse

attempt backfired, and helped to convince the French that the time had come to take full control in the country.

The estate is still heavily cultivated, but the town has been bypassed by the coastal road to Sousse, and its dusty streets would hardly be worth a visit were it not for the breathtaking village of Takrouna nearby and the small town **museum**, in the old French church on the main street (daily: May–Oct 9am–1pm & 2–6pm, Nov–April 9.30am–4.30pm; 1.1TD, camera 1TD). The collection of mosaic epitaphs and tombstones vividly illustrates the mix of cultures and values prevalent here in ancient times – Berber, Carthaginian, Roman and Christian. Many tombstones are dedicated to priests of Saturn, a Roman transplant of the Carthaginian god Baal; hence the un-Roman symbols such as crescent moons. When Christianity came, the Berbers adapted once again, and names in the epitaphs like Filocalus, Gududa, Jades and Vernacla show that local people as well as overlords took to the new religion.

The mosaics from the nearby site of Uppena reveal persecution of Catholic Christians by the Vandals, who followed the Arian heresy. One depicts the deaths of sixteen Catholic martyrs, while two more are epitaphs to bishops summoned to a church convention in 484 AD by the Vandal king Huneric, who then kept them here until their deaths.

During World War II, heavy fighting took place around Enfida in the final weeks of the North African campaign, as the retreating Germans attempted to hold a line here against the Eighth Army. A melancholy reminder of this are the two **military cemeteries** – a Commonwealth one on the western edge of town (follow signs for Zaghouan) and, 3km further on, below the looming presence of Takrouna's rocky outcrop, one for the French forces. They make an interesting comparison – the French one is austere and militaristic, with a helmet placed on each grave, while the Commonwealth cemetery is green and rustic.

Between Enfida and Bou Ficha on route GP1, just north of Chgarnia, the **Friguia Safari Park** (Tues–Sun: mid-June to mid-Sept 9am–6pm, mid-Sept to mid-June 9am–4pm; 5TD with own vehicle, 24TD on *Hôtel Kanta* tour from Port el Kantaoui, see p.206) is run in collaboration with the Tunisian forestry commission and the Paris zoo. It runs a breeding and reintroduction programme for threatened species, and also features lions, giraffes, elephants and other African wildlife.

Practicalities

Most of Enfida is spread out along one main street. At the western end is the turn-off for Zaghouan and, less than 100m east of it, the turn-off for Sousse. Beyond, on the northern side of the main street, are the **post office**, **police** and **museum**, with a couple of **banks** and cheap *gargotes* opposite them. A street opposite the post office leads to a square, off which is the main **market**. There are **no hotels** in town and no tourist office.

The main **bus station**, 100m east of the museum across the main road, is where buses and louages heading to or from Tunis can be picked up (see p.258 for details of services). One or two services between Sousse and the north have to be picked up at the relevant turn-off – the people in the bus station should be able to advise you. The **louage station** for Sousse is a few metres down the Sousse road, and there is a bus stop just beyond it. For the **train station**, head east, turn right about 20m after the museum, and continue for a couple of hundred metres. Half a dozen trains stop here daily en route to Sousse, two to Sfax and Monastir, and one to Gabès. In the other direction, four daily Tunis-bound trains stop at Enfida.

Takrouna   تكرونة

The victims lying in the military cemeteries died fighting for **TAKROUNA**, a Berber village 7km northwest of Enfida and perched high on a rock, whose inaccessibility had long made it a natural defensive position. The final Allied assault on it in 1943 was made by thirteen New Zealanders, most of them Maoris, scrambling up the sheer rock under fire from the besieged Nazi troops. Today it can be reached by local minibus-louage, picked up at the Zaghouan turn-off. The Berbers have always cherished their independence, and this site is typical in its isolation and impregnability. It is crowned by a green-domed marabout, and the view from the top is mind-blowing – from the sinister gleaming blade of Jebel Zaghouan behind to the broad sweep of the coastline. All this has placed Takrouna firmly on the tourist map, and busloads are rushed in and out along a specially built road. Unfortunately, Takrouna's touristic exploitation has changed the attitudes of villagers to visitors, and today their welcome comes at a price. The hassle can be quite extreme and off-putting. The road that goes past Takrouna continues to Zaghouan through some lovely remote heathland, passing two more Berber villages – **Jeradou** and **Zriba** – which are similar to Takrouna, but less visited (see p.262).

Sousse and around   سوسة

As a tourist destination, **SOUSSE** seems to have everything going for it: a historic **Medina** containing two of Tunisia's most distinctively beautiful monuments, an excellent **museum** second only to the Bardo, and endless stretches of white **beach**. Little wonder it has become Tunisia's most popular resort. But if the town has become rather a tourist trap of late, one result is that it has plenty of facilities, a number of cultural events, and a wide choice of restaurants and places to stay.

Some history

Founded as the Phoenician colony of Hadrumete probably in the ninth century BC, Sousse was Hannibal's naval base in his struggle against the Romans. Since then, thanks to its natural harbour and central position on the fertile eastern seaboard, it has been a vital port for every civilization occupying this stretch of North African coast, each remodelling it in their own image – Roman *Hadrumetum*, Vandal *Hunericopolis* and Byzantine *Justinianopolis*. *Hadrumete* avoided Carthage's fate by wisely backing Rome in the third and final Punic War (see p.426), and even when the all-conquering Oqba Ibn Nafi, leader of the Arab invaders (see p.430), destroyed the town in the seventh century, it wasn't long before Soussa – the Arabic name still most commonly used – revived. Sousse was the main outlet to the Mediterranean for the Aghlabids ruling in Kairouan and they launched their invasion of Sicily from here in 827. It was later occupied by the **Normans** (then masters of Sicily) in the twelfth century, the **Spaniards** in the sixteenth, and was bombarded in turn by the French and Venetians in the eighteenth century. By the end of the nineteenth century the resilient town was becoming increasingly important to the French colonists. Since then Sousse's growth was impeded only in World War II when, as an important German supply port, it suffered heavy Allied bombing. It is now Tunisia's third largest city, with a 300,000-strong population, and textile production goes some way towards balancing tourism, the biggest industry by far, which at times seems to completely swamp the place.

Arrival and information

Monastir airport is 20km southeast of Sousse, connected to the town by tourist hotel buses, taxis (5TD), city bus #52, and the métro train. A number of **car rental** firms also operate from the airport, and you should be able to pick up a rental car immediately on arrival. The main **train station** is in the centre of town on boulevard Hassouna Ayachi, while speedy **métro** services from Mahdia, Monastir and Monastir airport leave you at Bab Jedid station on boulevard Mohamed V. Arriving by **bus or louage**, you'll be dropped at the new *gare routière* (bus station), or the louage station, diagonally opposite each other some 2km out of town on the Sfax road, by the Sunday market. Avenue 15 Octobre, the straight road between the bus station and the UIB bank, leads after 1km to the southwest corner of the Medina; a taxi into town will cost around 2TD. Only if arriving by bus from Monastir or Mahdia will you be dropped at place Sidi Yahia in the Medina's northeast corner.

There's a quite helpful and well-organized ONTT **tourist office** at 1 av Bourguiba (July & Aug Mon–Sat 7.30am–1.30pm, Sun 9am–noon; Sept–June Mon–Thurs 8.30am–1pm & 3–5.45pm, Fri & Sat 8.30am–1.30pm; ☎03/225157), almost on place Farhat Hached, with useful information, including train and bus schedules and fares. There's also a Syndicat d'Initiative (Mon–Sat: July & Aug 8am–6pm; Sept–June 8am–1pm or 2–6pm) in place Farhat Hached.

Accommodation

Most of the cheaper **hotels** are situated within the Medina, with classier options in the new town. The gleaming white monster beach hotels begin at the northern end of avenue Bourguiba and go on for miles. Almost all of them offer full board and an in-house disco, so you don't actually *need* to go into town at all, and many offer bargain rates in low season and can be warmer at night than the draughty Medina hotels. **Camping** is strictly forbidden on most of the beaches – though it is allowed at the youth hostel.

Medina hotels

Hôtel el Aghlaba, 2 rue Laroussi Zarrouk ☎03/211024. Simple but clean and pleasant, and run by women. Not all rooms have outside windows, and none have their own bathrooms, though each sex has its own showers. Dorm beds (3TD) available for men only. **❶**

Hôtel Ahla, pl du Grande Mosquée, opposite the Great Mosque ☎03/220570. The rooms here are a bit spartan, but clean enough and excellent value, especially considering the location. **❷**

Hôtel Emira ★, 52 rue de France ☎ & ⓕ03/226325. Clean and friendly, each room with its own bath and some with a balcony. Evening barbecues on the roof terrace in summer. **❸**

Hôtel Gabès, 12 rue de Paris ☎03/226977. Friendly, basic hotel with decent doubles (and 6TD singles on the top floor), communal showers with hot water round the clock, and a roof terrace with great views, where you can sleep in summer for 5TD. **❷**

Hôtel Medina ★, 15 rue Othman Osman, by the Great Mosque ☎03/221722, ⓕ221794. Posher than most of the other Medina hotels, with en-suite rooms and breakfast included, but a bit dingy. This is the only Medina hotel used by tour groups. **❸**

Hôtel Mestiri, 19 rue el Aroua ☎03/222120. Simple Tunisian hotel, nothing fancy and poky rooms, but cheap and clean enough. **❷**

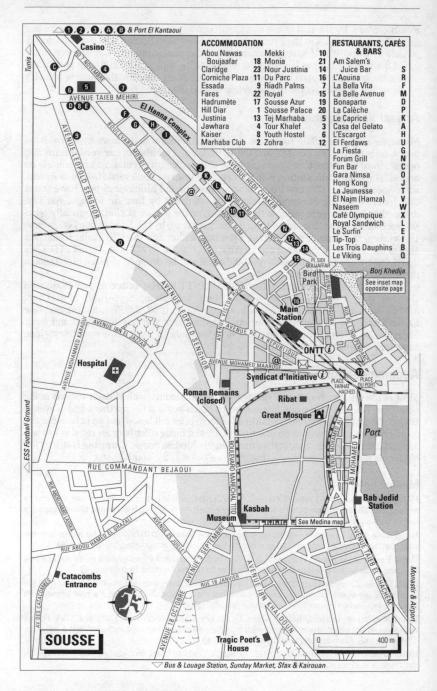

△ ❶ ❷ ❸ Ⓐ Ⓑ & Port El Kantaoui

Casino

ACCOMMODATION

Abou Nawas Boujaafar	18	Mekki	10	
Claridge	23	Monia	21	
Corniche Plaza	11	Nour Justinia	14	
Essada	9	Du Parc	16	
Fares	22	Riadh Palms	7	
Hadrumète	17	Royal	15	
Hill Diar	1	Sousse Azur	19	
Justinia	13	Sousse Palace	20	
Jawhara	4	Tej Marhaba	5	
Kaiser	8	Tour Khalef	3	
Marhaba Club	2	Youth Hostel	6	
		Zohra	12	

RESTAURANTS, CAFÉS & BARS

Am Salem's Juice Bar	S
L'Aouina	R
La Bella Vita	F
La Belle Avenue	M
Bonaparte	D
La Calèche	P
Le Caprice	K
Casa del Gelato	A
L'Escargot	H
El Ferdaws	U
La Fiesta	G
Forum Grill	N
Fun Bar	C
Gara Nimsa	O
Hong Kong	J
La Jeunesse	T
El Najm (Hamza)	V
Naseem	W
Café Olympique	X
Royal Sandwich	L
Le Surfin'	E
Tip-Top	I
Les Trois Dauphins	B
Le Viking	Q

Tunis ▷

AVENUE TAIEB MEHIRI

El Hanna Complex

BD 7 NOVEMBRE

BOULEVARD MONGI BALI

AVENUE LEOPOLD SENGHOR

RUE DE RABAT

AVENUE HEDI CHAKER

BOULEVARD DE LA CORNICHE

RUE CONSTANTINE

Mongi Slim

PL SIDI BOUJAAFAR

Bird Park

Borj Khedija

See inset map opposite page

AVENUE VICTOR HUGO

AVENUE LEOPOLD SENGHOR

Main Station

AVENUE IBN EL JAZZAR

AVENUE MOHAMMED KARAOUI

AVENUE DE LA REPUBLIQUE

ONTT ℹ

Hospital

AVENUE MOHAMED MAAROUF

Syndicat d'Initiative ℹ

PLACE FARHAT HACHED

PLACE DU PORT

RUE DE L'INDEPENDANCE

RUE BOURGUIBA

◁ ESS Football Ground

Roman Remains (closed)

Ribat ▪

Great Mosque 🕌

Port

BOULEVARD MARECHAL TITO

RUE COMMANDANT BEJAOUI

Kasbah

Museum

AVENUE MOHAMED ALI

BD MOHAMED V

Bab Jedid Station

See Medina map

AVENUE TAIEB EL GHACHEM

Monastir & Airport ▷

RUE ABDOU HAMED EL GHAZALI

RUE 25 JUILLET

AVENUE 3 SEPTEMBRE

Catacombs Entrance

N

AV DES CATACOMBES

AVENUE 18 OCTOBRE

RUE 18 JANVIER

AVENUE IBN KHALDOUN

SOUSSE

Tragic Poet's House

0   400 m

▽ *Bus & Louage Station, Sunday Market, Sfax & Kairouan*

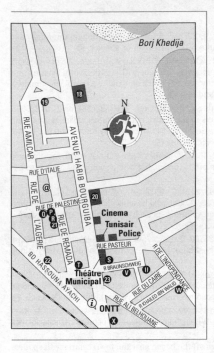

Hôtel de Paris, 15 rue du Rempart Nord ☎03/220564, ⓕ219038. Pristine though small rooms, a large, sunny terrace and friendly management. Shared showers with hot water only 7am–10pm in winter (24hr in summer due to solar power). ❸

Hôtel de Tunis, 19 rue de l'Église ☎03/224350. This once small, grubby place will have re-emerged butterfly-like after a refit, aiming to compete with the nearby *Hôtel de Paris*, and promising bright, en-suite rooms. ❷

Hôtel Zouhour, 48 rue de Paris ☎03/228729. Cheap, but a bit grubby (check the sheets are fresh). Some rooms are en suite, and there are no communal showers for those that aren't. ❶–❷

Town centre hotels

Abou Nawas Boujaafar ★★★★, av Bourguiba, corner of pl Boujafaar ☎03/226030, ⓕ226595,ⓔ abnboujaafar.ssc @planet.tn. A grandiose business hotel known for its seawater "thalassotherapy" centre. ❻

Claridge ★, 10 av Bourguiba, off pl Farhat Hached ☎03/224759, ⓕ227227. An old favourite and city landmark, with central heating and shower or bath (but not toilet) in every room, and room service available, as well as discounts on all stays of three days or more. ❸

Corniche Plaza, bd de la Corniche ☎03/226763, ⓕ226433. A small place with plain but large, clean and airy rooms, all en suite with balcony, and pleasant, efficient staff. ❸

Fares, bd Hassouna Ayachi, corner of rue de l'Algérie ☎03/277800, ⓕ227380. A possible alternative to the *Hadrumète*, with a choice of bath or shower in the en-suite bathroom, and balconies on all rooms, some with good views over the Medina. ❹

Hadrumète, pl Assad Ibn Fourat, off pl Farhat Hached ☎03/226291, ⓕ226863. The Roman torso in the lobby is a remnant of its two-star past, and the rooms are still bright and clean here. On the fourth floor they have balconies, and many have views over the port. Off-season rates are particularly good value. ❸

Mekki, rue 2 Mars ☎03/227127, ⓕ229151. A clean, quiet pension with spacious en-suite rooms with balconies, in a cul-de-sac one block behind bd de la Corniche. ❸

Monia ★★, rue Remada ☎ & ⓕ03/210469. An immaculate little place tucked away behind av Bourguiba, with en-suite rooms complete with TV and a/c. ❹

Hôtel du Parc ★★, rue de Carthage ☎03/220434, ⓕ229211. Comfortable, with friendly staff, but popular for illicit liaisons (so sometimes a dubious clientele). All rooms en suite. ❸

Royal, 4 rue Teboulba la Corniche, near the bird park ☎03/220536, ⓕ260115. A clean, friendly pension not far from the beach with simple but cosy en-suite rooms. ❸

Sousse Azur ★★, 5 rue Amilcar, near the bird park ☎03/227760, ⓕ228145. Spotless, with attached bathrooms and welcoming smiles. Some rooms have balconies, all have a/c. ❹

Sousse Palace ★★★★, 30 av Bourguiba ☎03/219220, ⓕ219230. A 1960s package hotel reborn as a swanky, plush establishment in the heart of town. Rooms tastefully done out in turquoise, a magnificent lobby bar, large pool, fitness centre and gym, plus a children's club to amuse the littl'uns while you hit town. Very nice indeed, and extremely good value off-season. ❻

Beach area hotels

Essada ★★, av Leopold Senghor ☎ 03/219515, ⓕ 227277. A friendly place behind the *Kaiser* and *Soussana*, 700m from the beach. All rooms en suite with either bath or shower. ❸

Hill Diar ★★★, bd 7 Novembre ☎ 03/241811, ⓕ 242836, ⓔ hilldiar@planet.tn. A very pleasant laid-back beach hotel 3km from the centre, set in lovely gardens with a little zoo of aviaries plus sheep, goats and guinea pigs. The rooms are sunny and airy (with bungalows available in summer), and there are flowers all over the place indoors and out. ❺

Justinia ★★★ and **Nour Justinia** ★★★, both av Hedi Chaker, ☎ 03/226381 or 2, ⓕ 225993. Sharing a pool, these are the nearest beach hotels to the centre but are not as smart as those further up the beach. The *Nour Justinia* offers cheap deals off season, especially for full and half-board, with beach views from the roof; the *Justinia* is self-catering. ❺

Kaiser ★★, av Taïeb Mehiri ☎ 03/228030, ⓕ 224683, ⓔ hkaiser@planet.tn. A small, mainly package-tour place near the *Tej Marhaba*, about 400m off the beach, but with a swimming pool. Also has external glass-windowed elevators. ❹

Marhaba Club ★★★, **Marhaba** ★★★ ☎ 03/242170, ⓕ 243867, ⓔ marhaba@planet.tn and **Marhaba Beach** ★★★★ ☎ 03/240112, ⓕ 240688, ⓔ marhaba.beach@planet.tn, bd 7 Novembre. A group of three hotels that share facilities. Good value – especially for single rooms off season – and deservedly popular with British holidaymakers. ❻

Riadh Palms ★★★★, bd 7 Novembre ☎ 03/225700, ⓕ 228347, ⓔ palms.reservations@planet.tn. A large package tour hotel well situated on the best bit of beach in Sousse, but otherwise nothing special. Wheelchair-friendly. ❻

Tej Marhaba ★★★★, av Taïeb Mehiri ☎ 03/229800, ⓕ 229815, ⓔ tej.marhaba@planet.tn. Large and classy with lots of coming and going. Wheelchair-friendly, with a well laid-out pool area, and an indoor pool too, but a walk of 200m and a main road to cross before you're at the hotel's beach. ❻

Tour Khalef ★★★, bd 7 Novembre ☎ 03/241844, ⓕ 243868, ⓔ tourkhalef@planet.tn. Another well-regarded package hotel with full facilities. Wheelchair-friendly, and popular off season with older travellers on longer-stay holidays. ❻

Zohra ☎ 03/227423. A pension, tucked away 50m off the beach near the town centre, with spotless rooms (en suite with balcony) and a sun terrace, popular with Scandinavians, though the Swedish woman who ran it has now left. ❹

Youth hostel

Maison des Jeunes, av Taïeb Mehiri, beyond the *Tej Marhaba* ☎ 03/227548. The cheapest place in Sousse if you're on your own, but with rather barrack-like dorms (5TD) and a midnight curfew. Camping also possible.

The City

The hub of the city is **place Farhat Hached**, a huge "square" – if it can be called that – which becomes, on its outer fringes, variously place des Martyrs, place Sidi Yahia and place du Port. Here all traffic and activity seem to converge, and even the main train line runs straight across it. To the north is the **new town** that's been almost entirely rebuilt since the war, and to the south is the **Medina**. The port is so close that it's unsettling at night to see a large ship, all lit up, apparently being towed across the square – a surreal image heightened when the train to Sfax edges its way through in front. The inevitable **avenue Bourguiba** leads from here up to place Sidi Boujaffar, where the **beach** begins, backed for a kilometre by **avenue Hedi Chaker**. Further along, **boulevard 7 Novembre** follows the coast, separated from the beach by a line of hotels all the way to Port el Kantaoui.

There isn't a great deal to see in the new town, and little in the way of exciting colonial architecture, but Sousse does have a few **Art Deco** buildings that enthusiasts may like to check out. One is the ABC Cinema on avenue Habib Thameur, backing onto avenue Mohamed Ali just to the east of the Medina; another is an office building on the corner of rue Amilcar and rue de Palestine, just across the street from *Restaurant le Viking*. There are also three Art Deco-style private houses on boulevard de la Corniche, one on the west side about 100m north of place Bou Jaffar, opposite the *Hôtel Justinia*, with two others at nos. 31 (near the Cine Nejma) and 85 (opposite the El Hana complex).

The Medina

The monuments in the walled **Medina** testify to the city's long-lasting importance; in particular the Ribat and the Khalef Tower indicate Sousse's strategic significance, especially to the Aghlabids. You might expect the old city in such a resort to have lost all charm and character in a deluge of tacky souvenir shops, but, while there are plenty of these, with a ready spiel for eager punters – and often abuse for less eager ones – the Medina has clung to its individuality. Note that there have been one or two cases of bag-snatching in the shopping areas of the Medina, so keep your eyes open and don't dangle valuables temptingly about the place. If you fancy a spot of shopping, one good place to check out is the Souila Shopping Centre in the northeastern corner of the Medina, where you can browse at leisure without pressure, and where prices are fixed and displayed.

The Medina's **ramparts**, following foundations laid by the Byzantines, were put up under the Aghlabids in 859AD. The gap in the northeast corner by place Farhat Hached was caused by Allied bombing in 1943. Unfortunately, you're not allowed to climb onto the walls except for a very small section within the museum (see p.200).

At the northern end of the Medina, the **Ribat** (daily 8.30am–5.30pm, Ramadan 8.30am–3.30pm; 2.1TD – tickets from a kiosk opposite the main entrance of the Great Mosque in place des Martyrs) was begun by the Aghlabids in 821. It's a well-preserved example of a style peculiar to this period of North African history, when the Muslim inhabitants were under constant threat from marauding Christians based in Sicily. The word ribat is related to marabout, and the buildings served a religious as well as a military purpose, housing devout warrior troops broadly comparable to crusading Christian orders such as the Knights Templar. When necessary, the men would fight, at times of peace they lived and studied in the bare cells around the Ribat's inner courtyard; the simplicity of the fort reflects the men's dedication to their second role. The only large communal room is the **prayer hall** over the entrance. Until superseded by the Khalef Tower at the opposite corner of the Medina, the Ribat's **tower** served as a lookout point and would pass on beacon messages – messages could be relayed from Alexandria in Egypt through to Ceuta in Morocco in a single night. Although the Ribat was primarily defensive, only six years after it was begun the Aghlabids were strong enough to launch a successful invasion of Sicily. The city's defences remained important, however, against both Christians at sea and the Berbers inland – hence the thickness of the Medina walls on the western, inland side. The entrance was built with columns and capitals taken from Roman and Byzantine buildings.

Opposite the Ribat stands the **Great Mosque** (Thurs & Sat 8am–2pm, Fri 8am–1pm; 1.1TD; tickets from kiosk opposite the main entrance; dress with respect for the congregation – free loan of cover-all *jellabas* available – and avoid prayer times), Sousse's other great early Islamic monument. Although founded in the ninth century, like the great mosques of Kairouan, Tunis and Sfax, this has a sparer quality, perhaps because it has received fewer later additions; the original concept of uncomplicated forms remains on view, giving added emphasis to the minimal decoration of the inscription around the wall of the courtyard. The little domed **kiosk** atop the eastern corner was added in the eleventh century to act as a minaret; its wide staircase is a feature more commonly seen further east.

Down a side street near the Ribat you should be able to see a curious open minaret, like stone crochet-work, which belongs to the **Zaouia Zakkak** – Turkish-built, as the

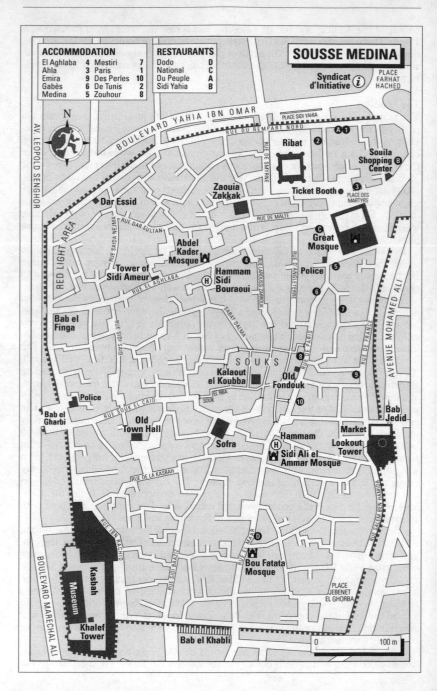

ACCOMMODATION

El Aghlaba	4	Mestiri	7
Ahla	3	Paris	1
Emira	9	Des Perles	10
Gabès	6	De Tunis	2
Medina	5	Zouhour	8

RESTAURANTS

Dodo	D
National	C
Du Peuple	A
Sidi Yahia	B

SOUSSE MEDINA

PLACE FARHAT HACHED

Syndicat d'Initiative

BOULEVARD YAHIA IBN OMAR

PLACE SIDI YAHIA

RUE DU REMPART NORD

AV. LEOPOLD SENGHOR

RUE DE SMYRNE

Ribat

Souila Shopping Center

Dar Essid

RUE DAR SULTAN

RUE SAIDA NEIMA

Zaouia Zakkak

RUE DE MALTE

Ticket Booth

PLACE DES MARTYRS

RED LIGHT AREA

Abdel Kader Mosque

Great Mosque

RUE LAROUSS ZARROUK

Tower of Sidi Ameur

RUE EL AGHLABA

Hammam Sidi Bouraoui

Police

RUE D'ANGLETERRE

Bab el Finga

RUE SIDI SAID

SABAT DALMA

RUE DE PARIS

RUE DE FRANCE

AVENUE MOHAMED ALI

S O U K S

Kalaout el Koubba

Old Fondouk

Police

SOUK EL RBA

RUE SOUK EL CAID

SOUK

Bab el Gharbi

Old Town Hall

Bab Jedid

Sofra

Hammam

Market

Sidi Ali el Ammar Mosque

Lookout Tower

RUE DE LA KASBAH

RUE SALEM BEN HAMIDA

RUE IBN RACHID

BOULEVARD MARECHAL ALI

Kasbah Museum

RUE SIDI BAAZIZ

RUE EL MAR

Bou Fatata Mosque

PLACE JEBENET EL GHORBA

Khalef Tower

Bab el Khabli

0   100 m

octagonal shape reveals. Nearby, rue el Aghlaba climbs to leave the Medina at **Bab el Finga**, passing en route the 1852 **Abdel Kader Mosque** opposite no. 29 and, a little further at no. 52, the square stone **Tower of Sidi Ameur**, like a minaret without a mosque. The area just north of Bab el Finga is a red-light district, which can only be entered here since all other exits have been walled off. On rue du Rempart Nord, just before you get to the walled-off red-light district, **Dar Essid** is a beautifully restored traditional home, now open to the public as a museum (daily: May–Oct 10am–7pm; Nov–April 10am–6pm; 2TD). A stone above the doorway of one room off the inner courtyard appears to date the building at 928 AD, although a closer inspection reveals that the initial digits of "1346 AH/1928 AD" have been erased. Nonetheless, it's worth a visit.

Back at the other end of rue el Aghlaba, rue d'Angleterre leads south past the tourist stalls to an area of covered souks, which is closed up at night. Turn right here onto rue Souk el Rba, and almost immediately on the right is the **Kalaout el Koubba** (Mon–Thurs & Sat 9.30am–1pm & 3–5.30pm, Sun 10am–2pm; 2TD), an eleventh- or early twelfth-century Fatimid building whose original function remains unknown. In the fourteenth century it became a *fondouk*, later a café; now it's a fascinating museum. Tableaux with life-size plaster models illustrate Tunisian marriage customs and household activities, and there's an English-speaking guide to show you around and explain the details. The building itself is also worth more than a passing glance, with a *koubba* (dome) whose design, with its external zigzag fluting, is unique in Africa. You also get a view of the neighbouring souk mosque's twelfth-century tiled octagonal minaret.

Parallel with rue d'Angleterre, running south from the Great Mosque, **rue de Paris** is the main street of tourist souvenir shops, selling the usual goods at not very bargain prices. One place worth a quick look is no. 54, an old *fondouk*. At its southern end, rue de Paris joins rue d'Angleterre to become rue el Maar. Just beyond, on the left at no. 3, you can make out the delicately carved facade of the **Sidi Ali el Ammar Mosque**, which dates to the Fatimid period, next door to the white dome of a hammam. A turning to the right, opposite the hammam entrance, leads past a spice, grain and coffee-grinding shop at no. 16, exuding all kinds of wonderful smells, to a blank and impenetrable wall which surrounds the **Sofra**, an early Islamic cistern complex. Near the end of rue el Maar you pass a small, austere mosque on the left, named after one **Bou Fatata** and built, around 840, in a style that's in marked contrast to the elaboration of the Fatimid buildings. Rue el Maar comes to an end at **Bab el Khabli**, the gate of the southern wall of the Medina. From here, a left within the wall takes you to place Jebenet el Ghorba, whose small, daily market specializes in second-hand clothes, then north up rue Salem Ben Hamida and alongside the eastern rampart up to Bab Jedid. The woman at no. 3, a house with a lookout tower built into the wall, sometimes lets tourists climb it for a small fee.

The Kasbah and Museum

Leaving the Medina at Bab el Khabli and climbing the windswept promenade to your right alongside the southern wall, you come to the former **Kasbah** in the Medina's southwestern corner. The Kasbah grew up around the **Khalef Tower**, built here in 859 at the highest point in the city to improve on the view given by the Ribat tower, put up thirty years earlier. Today the Kasbah houses an excellent **museum** (mid-April to mid-Sept Tues–Thurs 9am–noon & 3–7pm, Fri–Sun 9am–6pm; mid-Sept to mid-April Tues–Thurs 9am–noon & 2–6pm, Fri–Sun 9am–6pm; 2.1TD), whose exhibits – predominantly mosaics – are of a consistently high quality and, unlike those of the Bardo (see p.96), don't threaten to overwhelm by sheer quantity. Many mosaics and tombstones were found in the region's Christian catacombs and, with their familial and domestic epitaphs, are distinguishable by the XP symbol (the "X" is actually a Greek Ch, and the "P" a Greek R, together standing for "Christ"). Entering the museum, you come first into a cloister. Straight ahead, on the wall to your left are a number of epitaphs. One long message reads:

> *This was Eusebia, brothers, a rare and most chaste wife who spent with me a life of marriage, as time tells: sixty years, eight months and twenty days. God himself was pleased with her life, as I say. Truly a gentle wife of the rarest sort: I, Sextus Successus, lawyer, her husband, beg that you always remember her in your prayers, brothers.*

The room diagonally across the cloister from the entrance has a number of striking **mosaics** from the second and third centuries AD. Facing you as you come in is Neptune triumphant in a chariot pulled by mer-horses. To your left on the wall behind you, a large early third century AD mosaic shows Bacchus in Triumph in a chariot pulled by tigers, with a lion and a leopard in the foreground. In the late third century mosaic next to it, four fishing boats sail a sea full of beautifully detailed (and zoologically accurate) fish and other sea creatures. A similar subject is on the same wall at the other end of the room. Facing it, there is a beautiful but sadly incomplete mosaic of different birds and animals, while a little to its left is a yin-yang sign, a Chinese symbol that came to the Romans with the silk trade. As you leave the room, check the mosaic above the door of Venus bathing, surrounded by a group of rather stern-looking portraits.

The next room round the cloister contains some old tombstones, and the next door leads into the courtyard, with other rooms off to the right as you go through. A series of mosaics are displayed in a trio of rooms straight across the courtyard. The first room features theatre scenes and a first-century work containing swastikas, which in those days had no sinister connotation as an Indian sun symbol. Like the yin-yang and the tigers in the other mosaic room, it shows the Roman connection to India and China, just as medieval Europe followed the rise of Islam. The third room has some amazing amphitheatre mosaics of gladiators facing, and preparing to face, all mannner of wild animals. From the courtyard, a small piece of the rampart is accessible, but most of the Kasbah is closed to the public.

South of the Kasbah, along rue Ibn Khaldoun and bearing right at the fork after 200m or so, is the **House of the Tragic Poet**, a tiny Roman site with mosaics of dramatic themes along the lines of its namesake in the ruins of Pompeii in Italy. Another area of Roman remains can be glimpsed from avenue 3 Août, just northwest of the Medina, but is currently closed to the public.

The beach

What brings most tourists to Sousse are its **beaches**. Though inferior to Hammamet's – the shore is more exposed, urban and often windy – they have a more eminent literary history. Somewhere on the sands beneath where the hotels now stand, French novelist André Gide had his first sexual experience, at the age of 23, when he came here in 1893. His partner was his porter, Athman, who appears in Gide's semi-autobiographical novel, *L'Immoraliste*, though the author leaves out any mention of the sexual encounter.

The beach stretches from the centre of town to Port El Kantaoui, 7.5km up the coast. The southernmost part, south of Borj Khedija, is dirty and litter-strewn. North of it is the city beach, also called **Bou Jaafar Beach**, with avenue Hedi Chaker running alongside to form a promenade. This part of the beach is relatively narrow and usually pretty crowded. The choicest bit, with the widest sand, is 500m further along, between the *Hôtel Riadh Palms* and Oued Blibane, beyond which the hotels become sparser. As you round the cape by the *Hôtel Alyssa*, 6km out of town, the beach narrows again, but is now almost free of hotels and their guests until you reach Port el Kantaoui.

Large slices of beach are privately owned by the hotels, with small pockets open to everyone in between them. These **public areas**, especially those with direct access to the road can get very busy in summer as Tunisian families pile in with everything but the kitchen sink in tow. The **private sections** are usually marked by umbrellas and sunbeds, and generally charge a small **fee** (usually 1TD) for their use. It may be worth paying for a chair and umbrella, if only for the **security** of having someone watch over your things while you swim or visit the hotel's snack bar, though of course you should never leave valuables unattended. If you're female, the security in a private section will protect you from the advances of young Tunisian men. The level of vigilance can vary from lax to hawk-like, depending on who's in charge of your particular slice of sand; the *Marhaba* hotel complex is one of the best security-wise. Apart from petty thieving gangs of kids, look out for beach sellers of cigarettes, candied almonds and such sundries. Most are honest, but some will overcharge new arrivals unfamiliar with Tunisian money, and may lift unattended or unwatched valuables.

You can take part in various **beach sports** at one of four posts on public areas of the beach, allocated as franchises by the city council. These are: between the *Jawhara Club* and the *Hôtel Smara Beach* near the casino; by the *Hôtel Tour Khalef*, "Tina's", in front of what was (and probably will again be following reconstruction) the *Hôtel el Ksar*, just south of the *Hôtel Hill Diar*, and to the north of here by the *Hôtel Orient Palace*. Franchisees at all four posts have agreed prices and charge standard rates. Activities available include parasailing (15TD), waterskiing (10TD) and windsurfing (7TD/hr), as well as jet-skis (15TD/hr), and inflatable bananas and doughnuts. **Pedalos** are also available near the *Hôtel Tour Khalef* and at other sites along the beach.

For a change from beach-type activities, just across place Bou Jaffar at the southern end of the promenade, where you can rent calèches (horse-drawn carriages), there is a small **bird park** (daily 8am–5pm; 0.2TD). Nothing very exciting, it is really just a small park with a few aviaries, but it does offer at least a change of scene.

The market and catacombs

Given the large numbers of tourists who come here, it was inevitable that the **market** in Sousse would be "discovered", and images of huge camel sales are used to entice people. Market day is Sunday, and the site is a couple of kilometres out towards Sfax. Unfortunately, camels are no longer sold here, so if you were hoping to buy one you're out of luck.

Another suburban attraction is the **Catacombs of the Good Shepherd**, about 1km southwest of the Medina (Tues–Sun: mid-April to mid-Sept 8am–noon & 3–7pm; mid-Sept to mid-April 9am–noon & 2–6pm; 1.1TD). Take rue Commandant Béjaoui from Bab el Gharbi (the Medina's western gate), turn left after 500m, then right onto rue Abou Hamed el Ghazali and left after 100m. One of four sets of Roman catacombs in Sousse, this was the burial place of early Christians from the third and fourth centuries. A small part of it has recently been restored – perhaps a little too tastefully. It is illuminated with flickering lights and, though most of the tombs are bricked up, one or two are fronted with glass to reveal the skeletons inside. The part open to the public only extends for a couple of hundred metres, but the whole complex has over 5km of catacombs in total, and contains over fifteen thousand tombs.

Eating and drinking

Sousse has plenty of quality **restaurants** and **cafés**. Tourists are catered for with European cooking but Soussis (natives of Sousse) favour haunts that have much less in the way of finesse but serve equally palatable food at a cheaper price. A lot of the beach hotels have buffets and set menus at moderate prices, too. The tourist-driven places in Sousse tend to be tacky and poor value, and generally speaking anywhere that displays its menu outside in several languages, with a waiter trying to hustle you in as soon as you stop to look, is worth avoiding.

Sousse does not really have any licensed **bars** like Sfax or Tunis, but some attached to hotels or restaurants serve alcohol. Of these, the terrace bar of the *Claridge Hôtel*, at 10 av Bourguiba (daily 5am–10pm), is a good place to relax with a beer during the afternoon. The *Palace Brasserie*, 100m up the road by the Palace cinema (daily 1–8pm), is more like an ordinary Tunisian bar. An alternative up in the hotel zone, and more comfortable for women, is the *Rose and Crown*, an English-style pub, as you may guess from the name, which is in the Tej Marhaba shopping centre on bd 7 Novembre, opposite the *Hôtel Jawhara* but belonging to the *Hôtel Tej Marhaba* (daily 11am–midnight or later). As well as beer – Tunisian, not English – the *Rose and Crown* also serves food, including a full English fried breakfast. For a decent pint however, your best bet is to get a taxi up to Port el Kantaoui, where *Golf Bräu* brews and serves the best beer in Tunisia (see p.209); it does in fact have a smaller offshoot slightly nearer town, about 100m north of the Hammam Sousse turn-off at the far northern end of the hotel zone.

Medina restaurants

Dodo, rue el Hajra ☎ 03/212326. A moderately priced establishment at the southern end of the Medina with a fine stone-walled upstairs dining space, serving pizzas as well as other European and Tunisian dishes. Daily noon–9pm.

Restaurant National, rue el Aghlaba, near the Great Mosque. Basic cheapie serving grilled meat, chicken *shawarma*, and basic staples such as pasta, beans and chips. Daily 9am–9pm.

Restaurant du Peuple, rue du Rempart Nord, next to the *Hôtel de Paris*. A very pleasant and well-priced little place, good for breakfast, couscous and tajines. Dessert is free. Daily: April–Oct 6am–midnight; Nov–March 6am–9pm.

Restaurant Sidi Yahia, pl des Martyrs, Medina (name in Arabic only, though it says "Restaurant" in the window). A reasonable *gargote* that's very low-priced considering its prime location. Daily 7am–8pm.

Town centre restaurants

Restaurant L'Aouina, rue de Remada. A low-priced restaurant in a little street behind av Bourguiba and rue Amilcar. Specialities include grilled fish and couscous. Daily noon–10.30pm.

La Bella Vita, bd de la Corniche, near the junction with av Taïeb Mehiri. An immaculate and reasonably priced spot for sandwiches and burgers as well as pizzas and full meals. Daily 11am–11pm.

Restaurant la Calèche, rue de Remada ☎ 03/226489. One of the better posh gaffs in town, and not outrageously expensive, with good-value set meals. Daily noon–midnight.

Restaurant el Ferdaws, rue Braunschweig. Decent food at a reasonably priced cheapie whose staples include pasta, chicken and chips, and sometimes couscous. Near the *Claridge Hôtel*. Daily 6am–9pm.

Forum Grill, av Hedi Chaker ☎ 03/228399. A friendly place on the front with good food and good service; moderately priced. Daily noon–3pm & 6–11pm.

Restaurant la Jeunesse, rue Ali Bach Hamba, just off av Bourguiba. Reasonable food at low prices. Daily 11.30am–10.30pm.

El Najm (Hamza), rue Braunschweig, opposite the juice bar (name in Arabic only). A small, cheap Tunisian diner, known for having the best *lablabi* in town, and also serving excellent *chakchouka*, *merguez* and other traditional specialities. The owner's wife is Irish, and he speaks English. Mon & Wed–Sun 6am–10pm, Tues 6–10am.

Restaurant Naseem, corner of rue Khaled Ibn el Walid and rue de l'Indépendance (name in Arabic only). A busy and popular little place serving couscous, grilled chicken, *chakchouka*, *kamounia* and other typical Tunisian dishes. Daily 8am–9pm.

Restaurant le Viking, rue de l'Algérie ☎ 03/228377. In a side street off av Bourguiba. Another good, central, upmarket option, named for the owner's long sojourn in Nordic climes, and very popular with Scandinavian tourists. Daily noon–midnight.

Beach area restaurants

La Belle Avenue, bd de la Corniche. One of the first – and best – of a host of Western-style fast-food takeaways, with cheap burgers, pizzas, chips and the like. Daily noon–midnight.

Le Caprice, bd de la Corniche. A friendly, moderately priced place with pizzas and a selection of salads. Mon & Tues, Thurs–Sun noon–midnight.

Restaurant l'Escargot, 87 bd de la Corniche ☎ 03/224779. A pleasant upmarket place with great seafood and grilled meats, plus of course snails for starters (with garlic or bacon) for those who like them. Daily 7–10.30pm; sometimes open lunchtimes too.

Restaurant la Fiesta, rue Mongi Slim ☎ 03/225112. A good choice of both fish and meat dishes. A bit pricey à la carte, but good, with a good-value 9TD set menu, and sometimes entertainment in the form of a belly dancer too. Daily noon–midnight.

Hong Kong Restaurant, rue de Rabat, opposite the *El Hana Beach Hôtel* ☎ 03/221366. Sousse's only Chinese, with a 9TD set menu or expensive à la carte dishes, including pork and duck. Daily noon–3pm & 6pm–midnight.

Le Surfin', av Taïeb Mehiri near the corner of rue Mongi Slim ☎ 03/225871. Fixed-price fish dinners, pricey at 17.5TD but worth every penny (half-price for children), including a seven-plate hors d'oeuvre, fish soup and whatever fish is fresh in, plus sorbet for dessert. Choice is limited but it's always fresh and well-cooked. Daily noon–3.30pm & 7pm–midnight.

Tip-Top, 73 bd de la Corniche ☎ 03/226158. Consistently good, moderately priced establishment with great fish dishes, including fish couscous, and also pizzas, with set menus at 6–9TD. Daily 11.30am–10pm or later.

Les Trois Dauphins, bd 7 Novembre, 2km north of town near *Hôtel Tour Khalef* ☎ 03/270397. Excellent upmarket eating out in the hotel zone, with a choice of indoor or terrace dining or, in summer, a barbecue in the beer garden. All sorts of food is on the menu, including English or Continental breakfasts, and there are even Indian dishes of a sort in case you can't survive without a curry. You can also just pop in for a beer or a coffee. Daily 9am–midnight.

Snack bars and patisseries

Am Salem's Juice Bar, rue Braunschweig, by the *Claridge Hôtel*. The best place in town for real fruit juice; very well priced compared to all the tourist places. They only have what's in season but they also do scrumptious cakes. Wed–Mon, 8am–11pm.

Casa del Gelato, bd 7 Novembre, by the *Hôtel Hill Diar*. Delicious ice-cream out in the hotel zone, in a snazzy cubic building with a pizzeria upstairs. Daily 7am–1am.

Gara Nimsa, av Léopold Senghor, near corner of rue de Rabat. Locally renowned baker and patisserie with ice-creams and pizzas too (the neon sign outside just says "Jus – Glaces – Pizza – Gateaux"). Daily 6am–midnight.

Café Olympique, 1 av Bourguiba, corner of pl Farhat Hached. A bit of a tourist trap, but serves passable breakfasts and *shawarma* sandwiches. Check the price before ordering, however. Daily 6am–10pm.

Royal Sandwich, bd de la Corniche, 100m south of rue de Rabat. The best place in town to sample a "chapatti", which is nothing like the unleavened Indian bread from which it takes its name, but a round leavened bread, sliced in half, toasted on a hotplate, and filled with harissa, tuna and an omelette, according to your specifications. Daily 11am–3am.

Nightlife

Avenue Bourguiba and avenue Hedi Chaker are where people eat, drink, meet or simply stroll the promenade in the evenings. The only **nightclub** down here is the *Topkapi* at 65 av Bourguiba, mainly gay and rather seedy, but open as late as 4am. A little further afield, the *Samara King Disco* on boulevard 7 Novembre, about 2km north of the town centre, is very lively, especially on Friday and Saturday nights in summer. Unless you are staying at the neighbouring *Hôtel Samara*, you pay to enter, and the club usually gets going around 11pm, and continues until 3am or later if people are still on the dance floor. The *Maracana Club*, just north of the *Samara King*, is similar, but newer. There is also a reasonably popular disco in the *Hôtel Tour Khalef* called *La Grotte*, which some wags unkindly say lives up to its name. Opposite the *Samara King* is a glitzy **casino** (daily 5pm–5am, take passport to enter; 1TD, chips purchased with hard currency only), doubling as a **cabaret the-**

atre, with a drag show most nights. Also nearby are a couple of trendy **dance bars**: the *Dive Bar* at *Restaurant Bonaparte* on av Taïeb Mehiri, and a more recent imitator, the *Fun Bar* at *Hôtel Rym*, north of the junction of avenue Taïeb Mehiri and avenue Leopold Senghor, not far from the *Samara King*. Both are open 8.30pm until late into the wee hours, and feature funky bartenders in glamrock face-paint.

Listings

Airlines Tunis Air, 15 av Bourguiba ☎03/227955.

Banks There are plenty of banks in av Bourguiba and always one or two open Saturday and Sunday morning. A solution to the summertime queues is to try banks further afield (such as the BNA on av de la République near the corner of av Victor Hugo). There are one or two places in the Medina and on av Mohammed V. After hours, try the big hotels for money-changing.

Bookshops Librairie Farjallah at the corner of rue Ali Belhouane and rue Avicenne has a small selection of English classics, as does Cité du Livre at 3 av Bourguiba; the secondhand bookstalls by Sidi Yahia bus station have the occasional English title.

Car and motorbike rental ATL, bd 7 Novembre, up in the *zone* ☎03/241828; Avis, bd de la Corniche ☎03/225901; Budget, 83 av Bourguiba ☎03/227614; Express/Eurorent, av Hedi Chaker ☎03/229731; Hertz, 77 av Bourguiba ☎03/225428; Europcar, 49 bd de la Corniche ☎03/226252; Topcar, bd de la Corniche ☎03/226070. Motorbikes, scooters and mopeds can be rented at Ali's Motos Rent on bd 7 Novembre ☎03/226519, opposite the *Hôtel Jawhara*.

Car repairs Mechanics and spare parts stores are concentrated on av 15 Octobre, down towards the Gare Routière, and on bd Mohamed V, south of Bab Jedid station.

Cinemas The Théâtre Municipal on av Bourguiba, a block north of the *Hôtel Claridge*, screens arty films (and stages plays and classical concerts). Otherwise, there's the Palace a few doors up, the ABC on av H Thameur or the Ciné Nejma on bd de la Corniche.

Dentists Recommended English-speaking dentists include Kamel Bouslama on av Habib Thameur by the old ABC cinema (☎03/224699) and Hosni Sriha on av Mohamed Maarouf opposite the boys' college, Lycée des Garçons (☎03/211833).

Doctors Big hotels have their own doctors on call, but recommended doctors otherwise include Dr Mounira Kadhraoui Zahra at 1 rue Essarouel 2km north of town in Khezzama ☎03/242251, whose husband ☎09/400838, also a doctor, speaks English and makes house calls for around 20TD.

Ferry companies CTN has an office at rue Abdallah Ibn Zoubeir, off pl du Port ☎03/229436, and Ustica, which sometimes has a hydrofoil service from Sousse to Trápani (Sicily), seem to change their agent yearly, but tickets are best obtained from travel agents in town, such as Chams Tour at 8 rue Ali Belhouane ☎03/225357, or Sahel Voyages at 6 rue de Palestine ☎03/220531 or 2.

Festivals Both Sousse and Port el Kantaoui have high-season programmes of cultural events for tourists known respectively as the International Festival of Sousse and the El Kantaoui Festival. Every 24 or 25 July, there's a carnival in aid of a mythical marabout named Baba Aoussou, featuring a procession of floats with music and dancing making its way down from Port el Kanataoui into town. There's also a regional folk art festival in mid-March, and an Olive Festival in Kalaa Kebira at the end of November.

Football The main local team is Étoile Sportive du Sahel (ESS), whose ground is west of the Medina (out of Bab Gharbi and straight ahead up rue Commandant Béjaoui for 2km), and matches are usually played on Sunday afternoons.

Hammams Hammam Sidi Bouraoui in rue Sidi Bouraoui (off rue Aghlaba by no. 23) is one of the oldest in the Medina (Mon–Wed: men 4am–3pm, women 3pm–midnight). Hammam Sidi Ali al Ammar at 3 rue el Maar, next to the mosque of the same name, is open daily 6am–1pm for men, and 2–9pm for women. A more sanitized (and expensive) version of a hammam is available at the *Hôtel Chams el Hana* on bd de la Corniche, where couples can also go along together in the evening (Tues–Sun: men 7–11am, women noon–7pm, mixed 8.30–10.30pm).

Hospitals Farhat Hached University Hospital ☎03/221411 is on av Ibn el Jazzar, off av Leopold Senghor, behind the Medina. The Clinique des Oliviers on bd 7 Novembre ☎03/242711, opposite the *Hôtel Scheherezade*, is generally preferable. The new Clinique Essalem by the junction of av Leopold Senghor and av Taïeb Mehiri ☎03/210375, is also rated highly, with 24hr casualty admissions.

Internet access The best place is Publinet Sousse Centre in Immeuble Gloulou on av Mohamed Maarouf, 100m west of the post office (24hr; 2TD/hr). Other places include: Cybernet, 1st floor, Immeuble Kassaa, at the north end of rue Remada (daily 8am–9pm; 2.4TD/hr); Publinet Century 21 on rue de Rabat, just west of rue Mongi Slim (daily 8am–midnight; 3TD/hr); and Club Génération Informatique behind *Cala Pi Nou* pizzeria on rue des Jardins in El Khezama, 100m west off bd 7 Novembre by the *Sun Palace Hotel* just south of *Casa del Gelato* (Mon–Sat 10am–8pm, Sun 10am–6pm; 2.5TD/hr).

Massage As well as the version on offer at the hammams, aromatherapy and reflexology are offered for women only, by *Rough Guide* contributor Dee Eltaïef, at 93 bd 7 Novembre, opposite the *Hôtel Jawhara* ☏ 03/227109, currently for 22TD a session.

Newspapers English-language papers can be found at the stall in the main train station, and at Cité du Livre in av Bourguiba at the corner of rue Ali Bach Hamba as well as some of the beach hotels.

Pharmacy There's a night pharmacy at 38 av de la République.

Police The central station is on rue Pasteur ☏ 03/225566, with smaller ones by the Great Mosque's southwest corner, and inside Bab el Gharbi.

MOVING ON FROM SOUSSE

For a rundown of destinations and journey times, see Travel Details on pp.257–258.

Sousse is well connected, with bus, train, louage and air services all close at hand. The new bus and louage stations face each other by the Sunday market, a couple of kilometres out of town on the Sfax road, while for Monastir and Mahdia, bus and train services to have their own stations, the latter also serving the airport.

By bus
All bus services bar local ones to Port el Kantaoui, Hergla, Monastir and Mahdia leave from the new **Gare Routière** (☏ 03/237978) by the Sunday market (ask taxi drivers for Souk el Had or Souk Dimanche). Local bus services depart from **place Sidi Yahia** in the northeast corner of the Medina, serving Hergla (#12 & #18) via Port el Kantaoui and Chott Mariam, Kalaa Sghira (#20), Kalaa Kebira (#15) via Akouda (also served by #14), Monastir (#52) and Mahdia (#30).

By louage
All **louages** leave from a station opposite the Gare Routière bus station. **Hergla yellow taxis** (difficult to spot – they have the word "Hergla" in Arabic on their roof sign where Sousse taxis have a number beginning 09 instead), picked up from place Sidi Yahia, can function as louages at certain times of the day, especially mornings, taking four passengers for a set fare, but make it clear it's just a single place (*plassa*) you want rather than the whole taxi.

By train
Train services leave from the **main station** in boulevard Hassouna Ayachi (☏03/225321). There are ten daily departures for Tunis, including two which are direct and first-class only, four that stop at Kalaa Kebira and Enfida, and five that connect at Bir Bou Regba for Hammamet and Nabeul. In the other direction, trains serve El Jem and Sfax (also served by two direct first-class), continuing to Gafsa and Metlaoui, or Gabès, plus there's a night service connecting at Sfax for Gabès, which runs straight though on Saturdays.

A fairly quick service known as the **métro** runs to Monastir via the **airport**, from 6am to 7.55pm (from 6.45am Sun) from **Bab Jedid station**, 200m south of place Farhat Hached on boulevard Mohammed V. About two thirds of the métro trains continue to Mahdia.

By air
Monastir airport (☏03/460600) is 20km southeast of Sousse, with scheduled flights to various European destinations, as well as Jerba (1 weekly; 40min). The airport is connected to town by the métro train (see above), and bus #52. Taxis cost around 5TD, depending on your bargaining skills.

Post office At the corner of av de la République and bd M Naarouf (city hours), with a bureau de change for cash.

Supermarkets The best supermarket in town is Bonprix on av Victor Hugo, just north of av Mohamed Maarouf, which doesn't close over lunch. Otherwise, there's a Monoprix at the beginning of av Bourguiba by pl Farhat Hached, and two branches of Magasin Général, one on rte de la Corniche and one behind pl Farhat Hached on rue de l'Indépendance. A bright new supermarket has opened up by the *Riadh Palms* hotel, slightly pricier but with a better choice of foods, and open 24hr.

Swimming pools Hotel pools in Sousse are not usually open to non-residents, but there's always the sea.

Telephones There are taxiphone offices on almost every street corner, and most stay open from 7am or 8am to 10pm.

Tours Try the big hotels, or agencies like Cartours on bd de la Corniche ☎03/224092, who do trips such as a three-day "safari" (not a wildlife expedition) around the south for 170TD; other trips include a day in Gabès and Matmata for 55TD, or Kairouan, El Jem and Mahdia for 40TD. You should book a couple of days in advance.

Around Sousse

Sousse is surrounded by the very old and the very new – the latter in the form of a massive tourist development at **Port el Kantaoui**, and the former by the cliff-top village of **Hergla** and a group of timeless hamlets in the hills a few kilometres inland. For naturalists, too, the area is interesting, with marshland, mud flats and saltpans all the way down the Sahel coast and around the bay of Gabès, attracting large numbers of wading birds and associated species. The best areas around Sousse to see these are the **Oued Sed** and **Sebkha Kelbia**.

Port el Kantaoui and around   القنطاوى

Nine kilometres north of Sousse, **PORT EL KANTAOUI** offers Tunisia without tears for the delectation of the international tourist. With the help of Kuwaiti investment, a vast pleasure complex has been conjured out of a stretch of empty coast, including a "genuine" Tunisian yacht harbour in "authentic" Andalusian style. Call it artificial, soulless, even anaemic, it has nonetheless become one of Tunisia's most popular resorts and, if you don't mind being in a tourist ghetto cut off from the rest of the country, it does have a lot going for it. Tunisian people find the place fascinating and come down by the busload in season to see how the other half lives and to join foreigners in dancing the night away.

The **marina** is a popular winter refuge among Mediterranean yachting folk, who come here for its mild climate and very reasonable mooring fees – you'd have to go through the Suez Canal into the Red Sea to beat either – while package tourists flock to the marina for its well-designed hotels and range of facilities. The **SDANEK Diving Centre** (☎03/246374) at the end of the quay offers lessons for beginners and advanced divers, with daytime and night-time dives. Sailing excursions are available along the quayside too, on glass-bottomed boats, fishing boats or imitation galleons.

Other attractions on offer in Port el Kantaoui include the **Oasis Parc**, a garden of birds and of aromatic and medicinal plants (daily 8am–7pm; 2TD), where the road into Port el Kantaoui itself leaves the main road. Just across the way, and still on the main road, **Hannibal Park** (daily 10am–10pm), is a collection of fairground-type rides for children including a train, a merry-go-round and trampolines; entry is free – you pay by the ride. Just across the main road from here is the **Acqua Palace** (daily: April–June & Sept–Nov 9am–6pm; July & Aug 9am–10pm; 10TD, or 8TD after 2pm), a water amusement park featuring chutes, slides, water toboggans, wave machines, spa pools and all sorts of splashy fun for adults and children alike.

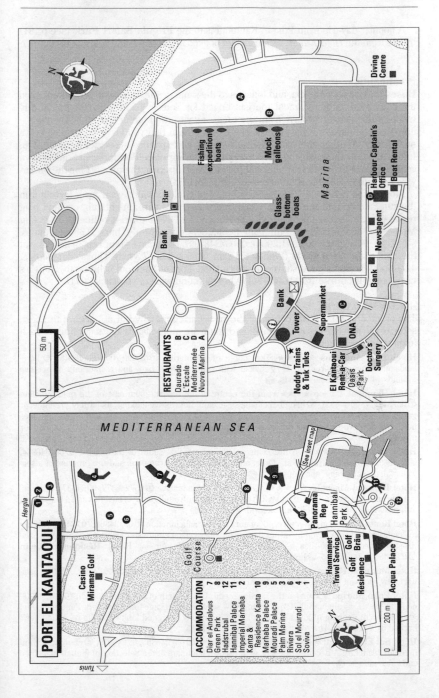

PORT EL KANTAOUI

MEDITERRANEAN SEA

△ Hergla

▷ Tunis

Casino
Miramar Golf

Golf
Course

ACCOMMODATION

Diar el Andalous	7
Green Park	8
Hadstrubal	12
Hannibal Palace	11
Imperial Marhaba	2
Kanta &	
Residence Kanta	10
Marhaba Palace	9
Mouradi Palace	5
Palm Marina	3
Riviera	6
Sol el Mouradi	4
Soviva	1

Hammamet Travel Service
Panorama Rep /
Hannibal Park
Golf Bräu
Golf Résidence
Acqua Palace

See inset map

0   200 m

RESTAURANTS

Daurade	B
L'Escale	C
Mediterranée	D
Nuova Marina	A

0   50 m

Marina

Diving Centre

Fishing expedition boats

Mock galleons

Glass-bottom boats

Harbour Captain's Office
Boat Rental

Newsagent

Bar

Bank

Bank

Supermarket

ONA

Bank

Tower

Doctor's Surgery

El Kantaoui Rent-a-Car
Oasis Park

Noddy Trains & Tuk Tuks

A popular day-trip from Port el Kantaoui is to the **Friguia Safari Park** (see p.191) by bus from the *Hôtel Kanta*, which can be booked at the hotel, and costs 24TD per person.

Practicalities

Buses to Sousse or Hergla, and louages to the same destinations, can be picked up on the main road, although most tourists bound for Sousse seem to prefer the **noddy trains** which leave regularly from the main entry to the marina area (3.5TD return – note that you have to return on the same colour train that you leave on, or else buy a new ticket). Another alternative is the **tuk-tuk**, an expanded six-seater version of an Indian auto-rickshaw, which leaves every half-hour for place Bou Jaffar in Sousse town centre. Two daily buses to Tunis will pick up passengers at the turn-off for the motorway. For **car rental**, try Kantaoui Rent (℡03/241318).

Most of the hotels here have everything you could possibly want for a fortnight in the sun, and around the marina you'll find shops, one bar, a nightclub, car and boat rental offices, banks, a post office, a doctor and an ONTT **tourist office** (July & Aug Mon–Sat 7.30am–1.30pm, Sun 9am–noon; Sept–June Mon–Thurs 8.30am–1pm & 3–5.45pm, Fri & Sat 8.30am–1.30pm; ℡03/348799). Panorama's tour rep, in an office at the back of the *Hôtel Kanta* (Wed & Fri 9am–noon & 4.30–7.30pm, Thurs 9am–noon & 4.30–6pm), is also a good source of information. Port el Kantaoui is home to Tunisia's favourite **golf course** (℡03/348756), where a round will set you back 30TD.

ACCOMMODATION

The original **hotels** in the centre of the resort are generally but not always the best; some of the newer ones to the north and south are more slapdash affairs, built to cash in on the resort's name.

Hôtel Diar Andalous ★★★★★, 1km north of the marina ℡03/246200, ℻246348, ✉ diarelandalous@abounawas.com.tn. Very stylish with comfy rooms, bars and restaurants in massive grounds with twelve tennis courts. ❼

Hôtel Hannibal Palace ★★★★★, in the centre of the resort, 200m east of the main junction ℡03/348577, ℻348321, ✉ hannibal.elhana@planet.tn. Impressive-looking, its largely green decor greets you as you enter the marina area, and was one of Port el Kantaoui's original hotels, but does not really deserve its five-star rating as it has no indoor pool and no coffee served by its outdoor one. ❼

Hôtel Hasdrubal ★★★★, in the centre of the resort, just south of the marina ℡03/348944, ℻348969, ⓦwww.hasdrubal.com. Quiet and restful with its large pool, and the promise of a seawater "thalassotherapy" spa from 2002. ❼

Hôtel Imperial Marhaba ★★★★★, 1.7km north of the marina ℡03/246477, ℻246377, ✉ imperial.marhaba@planet.tn. The most stylish of the hotels, with a full range of facilities and a very swish atrium-style lobby done out in marble, with glass lifts. ❼

Hôtel Kanta ★★★★, in the centre, 400m north of the main junction ℡03/348666, ℻348656, ✉ hotel.kanta@planet.com. Friendly rather than grandiose, with an emphasis on service rather than palatial-style decor. It also has a self-catering annexe, the four-star **Hôtel Résidence Kanta** ℡03/348666, ℻348656, ✉ hotel.kanta@planet.com. ❻

Hôtel Marhaba Palace ★★★★, 300m north of the marina ℡03/243633, ℻243639. With a palatial lobby, pleasant rooms and cheerful service. ❼

Hôtel Palm Marina ★★★★, at the northern end, 1.8km north of the main junction ℡03/246900 or 1, ℻246921, ✉ elmouradi.df@planet.tn. Now served by package-tour operators Panorama, this place is worth popping in just for a look at the beautifully designed lobby with its reception desk backed by a sea view. The rooms are cool and tasteful. ❼

Hôtel Sol El Mouradi ★★★, north of the golf course ℡03/246355, ℻246070, ✉ elmouradi.commercial@planet.tn. A decent three-star with its own hammam and a selection of pinball machines and video games. ❻

Hôtel Club Soviva ★★★, at the northern end, 1.7km north of the marina ☎03/246146 or 7, ℱ246157 or 8. Reasonable for the price, but most notable for its aquapark swimming pool complete with amazing giant slide and water chute, sadly out of bounds for under-10s, but otherwise open for a fee to non-residents who can't face the trek down to the Acqua Palace. **❻**

EATING AND DRINKING

For a change from hotel **food**, there are some excellent restaurants by the quayside, with prices that will make you blench if you are used to typical Tunisian prices, but which still represent extremely good value compared to what you'd pay for the same food in the West. Notable among them are the *Daurade* (☎03/348893; daily except Wed noon–11.30pm), a tip-top fish restaurant offering seafood bisque, fish hotpot and paella, with baked Alaska among the desserts, and the nearby *Nuova Marina* (☎03/348407, daily except Mon 11am–midnight), set back from the quay and rather less pricey, with Italian dishes including pasta, pizza and starters each at 5TD, meat and fish dishes for 6TD, and a limited selection of desserts for 3TD. Across the quay, by the harbourmaster's office, is the *Méditerranée* (☎03/348788; daily except Tues noon–11pm), with a selection of fish or steak cooked to your specifications, as well as vegetarian dishes and a 15TD tourist menu. Near the tower and port entrance, the relatively pricey *L'Escale* (☎03/348791; daily 1–9pm), has some excellent poultry dishes, including duck à l'orange, ostrich medallions and quail with pigeon.

For a **beer**, the best place in Port el Kantaoui, and indeed the whole of Tunisia, is *Golf Bräu*, on the main road junction between Hannibal Park and the Acqua Palace (daily 8am–2am), a German-run microbrewery producing its own pilsner, white beer and black ale, all absolutely delicious, with free bar snacks thrown in (food is also available). The beer costs about double what you'd pay for a *Celtia* in Sousse, but is well worth the difference.

Hergla هرقلة

Fifteen kilometres north of Port el Kantaoui, and 24km north of Sousse, **HERGLA** is a pretty village perched on a cliff which can be reached by bus (#12 or #18, running roughly hourly from place Sidi Yahia in Sousse via the hotel zone and Port el Kantaoui) or by yellow taxis, starting opposite the ONTT in place Farhat Hached. Hergla has a long history, including a time when it marked the boundary between two Roman provincial subdivisions. This romantic setting should have belonged to a pirate's lair, but the inhabitants have always made their living from weaving **esparto grass** – brought from as far inland as Kasserine – into filters used in pressing olives for oil. A fishing harbour has now been built, a spectacular place with whitewashed houses and topped, as in the hill villages, by a mosque. Built in the eighteenth century and named after a local man called Sidi Bou Mendel (who, the story goes, flew back from Mecca in the tenth century on his handkerchief), the mosque overlooks a cemetery and a drop to the deep blue sea. The paltry remains of Roman **Horrea Coelia** (a few mosaics) are 500m down the cliff road to the south: look for a blue metal fence by a junction on the seaward side (daily 8am–7pm, later in summer; free, token payment to the *gardien* at your discretion). To the north of the village is a **beach**, narrow and flotsam-strewn, but deserted. There are also snorkelling possibilities and a scuba diving centre (☎03/231386). Two kilometres west of the village, towards the Tunis–Sousse freeway, is **Hergla Park** (July–Sept daily 9am–2am, Oct–June daily except Tues 9am–7pm; free – you pay by the ride), a collection of fairground rides, but most of all two go-karting tracks, a full-sized one (950m) for adults, and a junior version (450m) for kids.

There is nowhere to stay in Hergla, but there's a **bank** and a trio of **restaurants** – the medium-priced *L'Étoile* on the main square (daily 7am–9pm), and the similar *La Paix* on avenue de Bizerte, the road up to the cliff top (daily 8am–10pm), both serving Tunisian staples such as couscous and spaghetti; and the more upmarket but still not especially pricey *Boumendil*, next door to the *La Paix* (☎03/251299; daily noon–10pm), serving your choice of the day's catch freshly grilled.

South of Hergla

Some 4km south of Hergla, the road crosses the **Oued Sed**, a freshwater and reed-bed area, whose river flows under the main road and eventually ends up in **Sebkhet Halk el Menzel**, a salt lake close to the sea. Any passing bus can drop you off here.

As always, freshwater is a magnet for **birds** and, if there's enough water in the river and the lake, it's well worth a trip, with all the usual wading and waterside birds, including spoonbills, plus occasional sightings of purple gallinule and marbled teal. Peregrine falcons and marsh harriers hunt over the area – the latter feeding on the abundant frog population. **Flamingos** are present whenever there's enough water, and you can sometimes see large flocks of migrating cranes, too.

At **Sidi Bou Ali**, south of Hergla on GP1 rather than the coast road, you can check out a very different kind of avian life at the **Carthage Autruche Ostrich Farm** (daily 8am–6pm; 5TD). Set up by a former German ambassador to Tunisia, the farm was originally a pilot project aimed at encouraging the farming of ostriches in Tunisia, but has become rather a tourist attraction, especially on Sundays, which are its busiest day. The farm is at km120, a few hundred metres from the village, which can be reached by bus or louage from Sousse.

Sebkha Kelbia سبخة الكلبيّة

In the past, **Sebkha Kelbia**, a huge salt lake inland 30km west of Sousse, was a major site for wintering wildfowl and waders, but dams have been built on its feed rivers, and it has been completely dry since 1982. After a very wet winter, though, it would certainly be an outstanding site. The lake can be best explored from the village of **Dar el Ouessef** at the northern tip where the Oued Sed flows out, or (with a bit of a walk) from the village of **Bir Jedid** at the southwestern corner.

The fields around Kelbia are rich in **gypsum** and, in spring, hold a very colourful and characteristic **flora**. Vast areas of the lake itself, in common with all *sebkhas* or salty mud flats, are dominated by species of salt-resistant glasswort. Tamarisk bushes form a shrubby fringe, and birdwatchers will find them worth scouring for small warblers.

Hill villages

Once picturesque, though now rather nondescript, if still quite traditional, are three hill villages just a few kilometres inland from Sousse – **Kalaa Sghirra**, **Kalaa Kebira** and **Akouda** – all of which date back to Aghlabid times. To get to them, take the bus from place Sidi Yahia in Sousse (#20 to Kalaa Sghira leaving half-hourly; #15 to Kalaa Kebira, #14 or #15 to Akouda, leaving every 10min). Kalaa Kebira holds a festival every December to celebrate the olive harvest, with music, dancing and general merrymaking.

Before they became so sprawling, each village stood perched on its green hill topped by a mosque, and this still forms the heart of each one, and preserves a sort of bustling venerability, with ancient winding streets and doorways. In 1864 their tranquillity was shattered when the villagers joined forces with the tribes from the interior in a revolt against the Bey's demands for increased taxation. They came near to overthrowing the government but soon fell out with each other, giving General Zarrouk a chance to gather his troops and defeat them piecemeal. The retribution he exacted was terrible, with heavy fines imposed on the villagers, while those who could not pay were seized, tortured and executed. Landowners with no cash were forced to sell their acres to merchants from Sfax, who had wisely remained loyal to the Bey, and thus the villagers became labourers rather than landowners. Many were totally impoverished. Even today, Zarrouk's name is considered synonymous with cruelty, and historians identify the year 1864 as the turning point in the region's economy. Thereafter a steady decline set in.

Monastir and around المنستير

Coming from almost any other part of the country, it's a shock to discover just how densely populated this small triangle south of Sousse is, with a thriving town every few kilometres. Even in Roman times this was the case, and the coastline is still littered with vestigial remains of their many settlements. But it was under the Aghlabids, when the capital was Kairouan, that this area moved ahead of the rest of the country.

Most of the towns are virtually indistinguishable with crowded streets and a purposeful atmosphere that's very different from the rest of the country. **MONASTIR**, however, has a special appeal. A former fishing port on the Sahel coast just 25km southeast of Sousse, it has never been allowed to forget that **Habib Bourguiba** (born here August 3, 1903) emerged from its industrious middle class, which later provided his power base. With a festival every year on the late president's birthday, along with the Bourguiba family mausoleum, the Bourguiba Mosque, and a presidential palace, Monastir has uneasily adjusted to a role in the national limelight. As well as this attention, the town has also had to cope with the international film industry and a level of tourist development which has all but swamped it. Needless to say, all this detracts somewhat from its older heritage.

Arrival and information

Monastir airport, right in the middle of the country's tourist haven, is connected to Monastir, Mahdia and Sousse by a **métro train**, whose platform is 100m from the air terminal. There are also **buses** (#52) to Monastir. A number of **car rental** firms also operate from the airport, and you should be able to pick up a rental car immediately on arrival. You can catch a **taxi** into Monastir for around 5TD, though you'll have to haggle – taxi drivers are quick to take advantage of tourists. The **train and bus stations** are both on avenue des Martyrs. The ONTT **tourist office** (May–Sept Mon–Thurs 7.30am–1.30pm, Fri & Sat 7.30am–1pm; Oct–April Mon–Thurs 8.30am–1pm & 3–5.45pm, Fri & Sat 8.30am–1pm; ✆03/461960), on place de l'Indépendance opposite the Bourguiba Mosque, has a pamphlet and price list of unlovely hotels and a fairly basic map of the town and the *zone touristique*. There's another tourist office (same times; ✆03/520205) just up the coast in the **zone touristique de Skanès**, near Les Hôtels métro station off the road to the *Skanès Palace Hôtel*, fronted by the helpful and knowledgeable Ayara Moncef.

Accommodation

Hotels in Monastir are almost all reserved for package tours, with the exception of the youth hostel and a trio of cheapish places out on the Ksar Hellal road. For real budget accommodation, you're much better off staying in Sousse or at the *Al Jazira* in Mahdia and visiting Monastir as a day-trip. Prices for all take a nose dive out of season, with fifty to seventy percent lopped off high-season rates. Les Hôtels métro station, for the *zone touristique*, is served by 16–21 trains daily (10min).

Town hotels

Cap Monastir ★★★, Port de Plaisance ✆03/462305, ℱ464999, ⓦwww.caesium.fr/capmonastir. Next to the *Regency*, with two-, four-, six- and eight-bed apartments with TV, a/c, kitchen and bal-

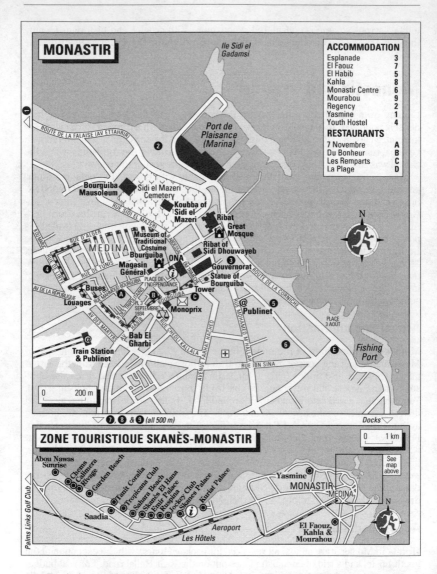

MONASTIR

Ile Sidi el Gadamsi

Port de Plaisance (Marina)

ROUTE DE LA FALAISE (AV ETTAHRIR)

Bourguiba Mausoleum

Sidi el Mazeri Cemetery

Koubba of Sidi el Mazeri

RUE SIDI EL MAZERI

Ribat

Great Mosque

Museum of Traditional Costume

Ribat of Sidi Dhouwayeb

RUE D'ALGER

MEDINA

Bourguiba

ONA

Gouvernorat

Statue of Bourguiba

Magasin Général

RUE DE TUNIS

RUE DE LIBIT

PLACE DE L'INDÉPENDANCE

Tower

ROUTE DE LA CORNICHE

AV DE LA RÉPUBLIQUE

Buses

Louages

PL 3 SEPTEMBRE 1934

Monoprix

@ Publinet

PLACE 3 AOUT

AV DES MARTYRS

Bab El Gharbi

RUE MOHAMED M'HALLAH

Fishing Port

@ Train Station & Publinet

AVENUE FARHAT HACHED

RUE DE CHEIKH KALLALA

RUE IBN SINA

0   200 m

Docks

ACCOMMODATION

Esplanade   3
El Faouz   7
El Habib   5
Kahla   8
Monastir Centre   6
Mourabou   9
Regency   2
Yasmine   1
Youth Hostel   4

RESTAURANTS

7 Novembre   A
Du Bonheur   B
Les Remparts   C
La Plage   D

N

❼, ❽ & ❾ (all 500 m)

ZONE TOURISTIQUE SKANÈS-MONASTIR

0   1 km

See map above

Abou Nawas Sunrise

Chems

Cabimra

Rivage

Garden Beach

Tanit Coralia

Tropicana Club

Sahara Beach

Skanès El Hana

Esmir Palace

Ruspina

Jockey Club

Skanès Palace

Kuriat Palace

Yasmine

MONASTIR

MEDINA

Saadia

Aeroport

Les Hôtels

El Faouz, Kahla & Mourahou

Palms Links Golf Club

N

cony. Past its best and lacking beach or pool, this place is still a good deal if there's a group of you who plan to stay a week more, especially outside summer. ❺

Esplanade ★★★, rte de la Corniche ☎03/460149, ℱ460050. Most central of the hotels, almost within spitting distance of the Ribat. ❻

El Faouz ★★, pl du 7 Novembre ☎03/448280, ℱ448221. A friendly place between *Kahla* and *Mourabou*, and much better, but equally inconveniently situated. Rooms have TV, a/c and private bathrooms. Open to bargaining. ❹

El Habib ★★★★, rte de la Corniche ☎ 03/462944, ℱ 460214. Part of the comfortable *Ribat Complex* which includes the three-star *Résidence el Habib*, where you can rent two-bed apartments in season. ❻

Kahla, av Tareb Mehiri ☎ 03/464586, ℱ 467881. On an busy roundabout about 800m up the Ksar Hellal road from the junction of av Bourguiba and av des Martyrs. Self-catering apartments as well as rooms. ❸

Monastir Centre ★★★, av Habib Bourguiba ☎ 467800, ℱ 467809. This is a new, well-run and very well-equipped hotel in the centre. Within a few minutes of the beach with all the usual activities, and a good restaurant. Recommended. ❻

Mourabou, rte de Khniss ☎ 03/461585. One of those places where nothing works, whether hot water, heating or toilet flush. Still, bring a plug on the off chance that the hot water's running (baths in all rooms). The cheapest in town, and free bus to the beach, once a day in summer. ❸

Regency ★★★★★, Port de Plaisance ☎ 03/460033, ℱ 460727. Monastir's poshest hotel, right by the marina – park your yacht while you pop in for dinner. ❻

Yasmine ★, rte de la Falaise ☎ 03/501546. Clean and does a good breakfast, but 2km out of town, and pricey in summer. Half or full board only. ❹

Hotels in Zone Touristique de Skanès

These are mainly for prebooked package tourists, which means you pay the full whack if you just drop in. Still, they're perfectly decent for a beach break, and you're not missing much by staying out of Monastir.

Abou Nawas Sunrise ★★★, 12km distant at La Dkhila ☎ 03/521644, ℱ 521282, 🌐 www.abounawas.com. Downmarket by usual Abou Nawas standards and very 1970s Ibiza, but with nice two-floor chalet accommodation, and good value by Monastir standards, for full-board, which is all they offer anyway. Closed winter. ❼

Emir Palace ★★★★★, 1km west of Les Hôtels métro ☎ 03/520900, ℱ 521823. The *zone*'s fluffiest kennel. Everything you could want, and totally Tunisia-proof. ❼

Kuriat Palace ★★★★, 5km from town centre, near Aéroport métro station ☎ 03/521200, ℱ 520049, 📧 kuriat.palace@gnet.tn.The most expensive *zone* four-star, but well equipped with loads of restaurants, bars, health centre and good water sports activities. Wheelchair-friendly. ❻

Sahara Beach ★★★, 2km west of Les Hôtels métro ☎ 03/521088, ℱ 520466, 📧 saharabeach @planet.tn. Let's play numbers: 2000 beds means 1000 people to potentially score with. Alternatively play water sports or horse-ride to trim that flab. Cheaper than most. ❺

Skanès el Hana ★★★★, 2km west of Les Hôtels métro ☎ 03/521055, ℱ 520709, 📧 skanes.elhana @planet.tn. More stylish than adjacent *Sahara Beach* and complete with the usual water sports and horse-riding. ❺

Youth hostel

Maison des Jeunes, rue de Libye, near the bus station ☎ 03/461216. Recently renovated, central and the cheapest place in town. Dorms 5TD.

The Town

The heart of the town is the **Medina**, skirted to the north and east by rue d'Alger, to the south by avenue Bourguiba, and to the west by avenue des Martyrs. Some parts of its walls are eighteenth century, others more recent, and there are gratuitous additions in the 1980s Andalusian style used at Port el Kantaoui. The **Bourguiba Mosque** in rue de l'Indépendance follows classic Hafsid design, but the rest of the Medina has been so blatantly gentrified that it hardly even merits a stroll. In fact, the real Medina was originally the area around the Ribat; what is called the Medina today was a walled suburb, like the faubourgs of Tunis. One little curiosity is the **tower**, which protrudes, for no apparent reason, from the wall opposite the post office. Just up from here, it's difficult to miss the **golden statue of Bourguiba** in the square by the Gouvernorat office, which beats even Nabeul's potted tree and giant orange bowl for sheer tackiness. The statue commemorates Bourguiba's schooldays – the school itself was ironically demolished to make way for the monument. Close by, beside the tourist office on rue de l'Indépendance, is the small, dusty **Museum of Traditional Costume** (Tues–Sun: April–Oct 9am–1pm & 3–7pm; Nov–April 9am–noon & 2–6pm; 1.1TD), with its diverting display of local clothes.

To go with its new national prominence, the town centre east of the Medina has had its houses razed and replaced by a bleak esplanade designed to show off Monastir's monuments to the best advantage. The **Bourguiba Mausoleum** (Mon–Thurs 2–4.30pm, Fri & Sun 9am–4.30pm; no shorts; free) is undoubtedly the most eye-catching of these, just to the north, unmistakable with its gilt cupola and twin minarets. Housed within are the tombs of Bourguiba's close family in the two rooms off to the left, and the man himself in a marble sarcophagus in the central chamber, complete with 365 piece crystal chandelier. The mausoleum stands in a cemetery named after the **Koubba of Sidi el Mezeri**, the tomb of a twelfth-century saint. The inscription on the gateway, apparently written by the saint himself, mentions one Princess Mona, who the town is said to have been named after.

Compared to Bourguiba's monuments, the old **Ribat of Harthema**, overlooking the sea, is rather more restrained (Tues–Sun: May–Oct 8am–7pm; Nov–April 8.30am–5.30pm; 2.1TD, camera 1TD), although it was the first ribat in Tunisia to admit female professors and students. Begun in 796, it has undergone so many reworkings that even experts have difficulty in dating its various parts. The core structure follows the same plan as at Sousse, however, with a courtyard surrounded by cells for the fighters, and on one side a prayer hall now used as a rather good **museum** to display ancient Islamic writings, fabrics and pottery – look out here for eleventh-century Coptic fabric from Egypt and an ornate 1774 Turkish marriage certificate. A map of the original Medina shows how comprehensively the old town was levelled in the pursuit of modernity, creating the sterile esplanade outside the Ribat. Traditionally the Ribat has been a favourite backdrop for filmmakers wanting to evoke the biblical world – this is where Jesus trod the battlements in Zeffirelli's *Jesus of Nazareth*, as did Brian in Monty Python's alternative scenario. The ninth-century **Great Mosque** stands next door, and the smaller **Ribat of Sidi Dhouwayeb** lies between the mosque and the Medina.

The **old fishing port** sits 1km to the southeast in a rocky inlet. It must have been a pretty place once, but the corniche is now so loaded with hotels that it looks distinctly out of place. The **house** where Bourguiba was born is in place 3 Août (his birthday), just before the port. Further on, the promenade turns due south and into a more workaday district, with the shore lined with larger modern fishing vessels: a weekly **souk** is held here on Saturdays. In the other direction, the road leads west along the coast past more resort development and Bourguiba's favourite **palace**, where the ex-honcho lived out his dotage.

Eating, drinking and nightlife

Good, cheap **eating** is hard to come by in Monastir, and if you're on a beach holiday you might consider opting for full or half-board in your hotel. You'll find most restaurants and fast-food places on the streets enclosing the Medina, many with reasonable if unexciting tourist menus for 5–7TD. Of these, *Restaurant les Remparts* (daily noon–3.30pm & 6–11pm or later), on avenue Bourguiba near the tower, is the most popular with decent pizza and a range of set menus starting at 10TD; *Restaurant du Bonheur* (daily noon–3pm & 6–11pm) is also good and cheap. Inside the Medina itself, another budget place to try is *Restaurant 7 Novembre* (daily noon–3pm & 6–10pm) on rue 13 Août 1956. If you feel like a splurge, the marina is full of fancy restaurants. You'll find one of Monastir's oldest establishments, *Restaurant la Plage* (Thurs–Sat noon–3pm & 6–11pm), at place 3 Août, serving a fine line in fish; try the *shirkau*, a local speciality of tiny fish made into a kind of patty – expect to pay 15–20TD for a full meal.

From June to August, special **evening events** are held every Thursday and Saturday at various hotels and at the marina. These, laid on by the ONTT and hotels, include donkey racing, mock weddings, orchestras both traditional and less so, and an item billed incongruously as "majorettes". In July and August each year, the **Monastir International Festival** receives a number of international Arab singing stars and orchestras. For the rest of the year nightlife is typically low-key, except for a couple of rather dreadful **nightclubs** at *Hôtel Sahara Beach* and *Hôtel Kuriat Palace,* both in the *zone touristique.*

Listings

Airlines Tunis Air, in the Ribat Hotel Complex ☎ 03/462550; Nouvelair, Zone Touristique Dkhila, near the *Hôtel Sahara Beach* ☎ 03/520600.

Banks Near the post office on av Bourguiba, and more on pl de l'Indépendance in the very centre of the Medina.

Car rental Avis ☎ 03/521031, Budget ☎ 03/520000, Europcar ☎ 03/520799, and Hertz ☎ 03/521300, each have counters at the airport ☎ 03/460300. Master Car ☎ 03/467840 and Nova Rent ☎ 03/467826 are on av Bourguiba.

Cinema Rue Abdessalem Trimêche, opposite the ONA crafts shop.

Diving Monastir Plongée et Loisirs ☎ 03/462509, down at the marina, organizes trips. The minimum charge for a day-trip is 200TD for boat and skipper, so forming a group makes it cheaper. They may be closed out of season.

Golf courses The Flamingo Monastir ☎ 03/500283 is next to the Ouardanine road, which leads from the town centre towards Kairouan. Another eighteen-hole course, Golf Palm Links ☎ 03/521910, is way out along the *zone touristique* hotel strip near the *Sunrise Hôtel.* In season, daily shuttle buses operate between it and the major *zone touristique* hotels; ask at your hotel reception.

Hammam Rue de Tunis, in the Medina (daily: men 6am–1pm, women 1–5.30 pm).

Hospital The regional hospital is on av Farhat Hached ☎ 03/461144 or 1.

Internet There is a Publinet (24hr; 2TD/hr) at the train station and another at rue Mohammed M'hallam (daily 9am–midnight; 2TD/hr).

ONA crafts shop Rue Abdessalem Trimêche, corner with rue de l'Indépendance.

Pharamacy There's a night pharmacy on rue Chedli Kallala, off av Bourguiba and past the market.

Police Rue d'Alger ☎ 03/461431. Tourist police in the Zone Touristique near the *Hôtel Sahara Beach* ☎ 03/521771.

Post office Av Bourguiba opposite the Medina wall (city hours).

Supermarkets There's a Magasin Général on rue de l'Indépendance, and Monoprix on av Bourguiba, which has longer opening hours (Mon–Sat 8am–7pm, Sun 8am–1pm).

Swimming pools Most of the beach hotels will let you use their pools, sometimes also Turkish baths for 3.5–5TD.

Telephones International calls can be made from the taxiphone office diagonally opposite the Central Bank of Tunisia, next to the train station.

Tours Most of the *zone touristique* hotels offer reasonably cheap bus or 4WD excursions to Matmata and other attractions in the south. Otherwise, there are a dozen agencies at the airport, or try Tourafric on av Bourguiba ☎ 03/460048. It's possible to visit the Kuriat Islands, a deserted archipelago 15km off the coast where Phoenician ruins have recently been found. Fishing trips, or days out on a boat can be arranged from the marina – the Sidi Bou will take a group of four out for half a day for 130TD and kids go along free.

MOVING ON FROM MONASTIR

For a rundown of destinations and journey times, see Travel Details on pp.257–258.

Monastir's **train station** (℡ 03/460725 or 460755) is southwest of the Medina on avenue des Martyrs, near Bab el Gharbi, with departures to Enfida, Bir Bou Rekba and Tunis, and regular "métro" services to Sousse and Mahdia (via Ksar Hellal and Moknine). The **bus station** (℡ 03/461059) is a short walk up the street, by the city wall, with services to Le Kef, Kairouan, Kelibia and Nabeul. For all other destinations you must go to Sousse using the #52 bus (every 20min). **Louages** also leave from here.

To get to the **airport** (℡ 03/520000), the métro is the obvious means (every 30–50min from 6.05am, 6.45am on Sun; 10min), although there are also buses. When neither of these are running, you'll have to take a taxi (around 5TD, although you'll be quoted much more).

South of Monastir

There is no direct public transport between Monastir and Mahdia, and any journey involves a change of vehicle at either Ksar Hellal or Moknine (see above). Going by **train** is a much better option, with frequent "métro" trains to Mahdia via Lamta, Ksar Hellal, Bekalta and Moknine. The settlements in this area are constantly expanding and merging with each other, and travelling through them – to the buzz of a thousand *mobylettes* (mopeds) – you get a vivid sense of why this region is such an economic powerhouse.

Two thousand years ago, the area was already industrious and heavily settled. **LAMTA**, 15km southeast of Monastir, was once Leptis Minor, cousin of the much larger Leptis Magna, whose ruins on the modern Libyan coast are among the most spectacular Roman sites in the world. The new **museum** (Tues–Sun: May–Oct 9am–1pm & 4–7pm; Nov–April 9.30am–5.30pm; 1.1TD, camera 1TD) on the northern edge of town, next to the Monastir road and quite a walk from the train station, is worth a visit if you are passing or interested in industrial-type archeology, which seems to be a speciality of this region. Like the British team at Salakta, an American-funded excavation here focused on pottery, as Leptis exported so-called red slipware all over the Mediterranean for five hundred years. The museum explains techniques and processes – with English labels – and also has one unique piece of fine art in a carved Christian sarcophagus found in 1975 and probably imported from France or Rome.

A few kilometres south of Lamta, bustling **KSAR HELLAL** is an old textile centre where silk is still made. The thread is dyed in large vats, and handlooms are used to weave the cloth. Sadly, the resulting article is disappointing – usually plain, with none of the geometric designs that you find on coarser textiles, and very expensive. The town's other claim to fame is as the venue for the 1934 Neo-Destour Party Congress in which Habib Bourguiba emerged as leader. From here disciples went throughout the country encouraging strikes and civil disobedience that came close to overthrowing the Protectorate. Ksar Hellal fades into **MOKNINE**, another sprawling town, which has a small regional **museum** (variable hours; 1TD), 100m to the left on the main road entering town, and housed in a disused **mosque**, with exhibits of coins, manuscripts, pottery and weapons from different periods. If the exhibits themselves fail to entertain, the labelling certainly will.

On the coast 6km east of Bekalta, Roman **Tapsus** was the site of a battle in 46 BC that ended the Roman civil war between Julius Caesar and Pompey.

Kairouan and around

القيروان

"What a Hell of a place to put a Holy City", wrote *The Times'* military correspondent of **KAIROUAN** in 1939; in midsummer, when the town bakes like a brick on its barren plain, it's hard to disagree. But Tunisia's oldest Arab city and Islam's fourth most holy centre – after Mecca, Medina and Jerusalem – is an exceptionally rewarding place. Its architectural interest is unrivalled, and the strong Eastern flavour it has retained comes as a surprise after Sousse.

Some history

Not surprisingly, perhaps, it was divine inspiration that led to the choice of this infernal site. In 670 **Oqba Ibn Nafi**, advancing west, called a routine halt here with his army. A golden cup was found on the ground, which he recognized as one he had lost at Mecca; then a spring was discovered, and declared to be connected to the holy well of Zem Zem at Mecca. Having first banished for eternity the "noxious beasts and reptiles" which had been present in some abundance, Oqba founded his capital on the spot. There was sound strategic sense behind the inspiration, as the new city was a reasonably secure and central base for the new rulers, halfway between the seaborne threats of the Mediterranean and the mountainous homes of the rebellious Berbers. Despite this security, extremist **Kharijite** Berbers took the city in 757, and their behaviour (such as massacring their opponents and stabling horses in the Great Mosque) shocked more moderate Kharijites, who drove them out and installed one Abderrahman Ibn Rustam as their ruler. In 761, Egyptian forces loyal to the Caliph retook the city, and Ibn Rustam set up shop in Tahirt (Algeria), from where his family (the Rustamids) ruled the south of Tunisia.

As the **Aghlabid** capital, Kairouan quickly developed into one of the world's great cities, its monuments surpassed only by the level of its scholarship and its influence, which reached far across the Islamic world. The Kairaouine Mosque in Fez – still the centre of Morocco's religious life – takes its name from the origins of the Kairouan native who founded it in 857. There was a decline under the Fatimids, who moved the capital to Mahdia, and a low point was reached in 1057 when the town was sacked by the Banu Hilal. But although the Hafsids made Tunis their political capital, Kairouan has never lost its ancient, holy status, with seven visits to Kairouan supposedly equivalent to one pilgrimage to Mecca. The town was jealously guarded from infidels and, before the arrival of the French, Christians needed a Beylical permit to enter the walls; and even then personal security wasn't guaranteed. In 1835, Sir Grenville Temple had a permit, and may have exaggerated in reporting that "if we were known to be Christians, whilst walking about, we might be torn to pieces by the infuriated populace". Members of the 1881 **French invasion force** were, indeed, distinctly apprehensive as the tribes assembled in a wide arc around the town. But when it came to the final battle their defence crumbled and, much to the surprise of the French column, the town surrendered without a shot being fired.

Modern Kairouan is a successful market centre for agricultural goods, especially apricots and almonds, and a major producer of carpets and Caravanes cigarettes. But it remains intensely religious – a living centre of Islamic doctrine. Through the post-Independence years, its religious authorities periodically created friction over Bourguiba's attempts at secular reform. In 1960, when he urged national abandonment of the Ramadan fast (see p.457), Kairouan pointedly observed it a day later than the rest of the country and simultaneously with Egypt, in a gesture of Arab–Islamic solidarity. The town's avenue Bourguiba was only named after the president made a visit of conciliation in 1969 and the greater part of it has now been renamed again. Kairouan also

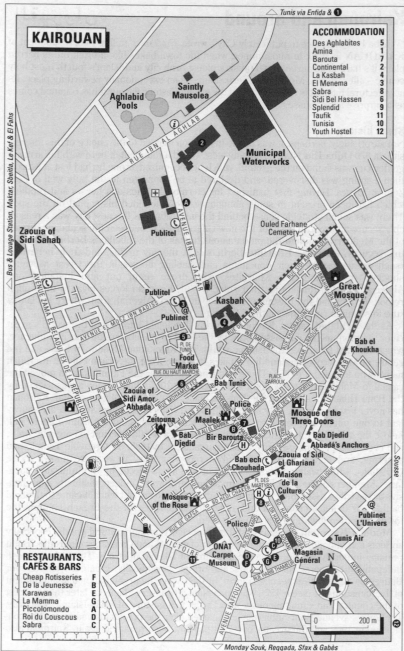

KAIROUAN

Tunis via Enfida & ❶

Aghlabid Pools

Saintly Mausolea

Municipal Waterworks

RUE IBN AL AGHLAB

Zaouia of Sidi Sahab

AVENUE IBN EL JAZZAR

Publitel

Ouled Farhane Cemetery

Bus & Louage Station, Maktar, Sbeitla, Le Kef & El Fahs

AVENUE ZAMA EL BELAOUI

AVENUE EL MOEZ IBN BADISS

Publitel

Publinet

Great Mosque

RUE SIDI ABDEL KADER

RUE IBRAHIM IBN AGHLAB

Kasbah

PL DE TUNIS

Food Market

RUE DU HAUT MARCHE

RUE SIDI GAID

RUE DE LA REPUBLIQUE

RUE IBN ZOUBAIR

RUE ZOUAGHA

RUE MOHAMED FES

Zaouia of Sidi Amor Abbada

Zeitouna

Bab Djedid

RUE DE LA KASBAH

RUE DAR EL BEY

RUE TAHAR ARROUF

RUE KHADDADOUNE

Bab el Khoukha

Bab Tunis

PLACE ZARROUK

PLACE DES PORTES

RUE EL FARAB

Police

El Maalek

Bir Barouta

RUE EL BARBER

RUE DE LA MOSQUEE DES BELAGHJIA

Mosque of the Three Doors

Bab Djedid

Abbadá's Anchors

RUE DE LA MOSQUEE DES TROIS PORTES

Zaouia of Sidi el Ghariani

Bab ech Chouhada

Maison de la Culture

PL DES MARTYRS

RUE SIDI EL GHARIANI

RUE DE LA REPUBLIQUE

Sousse

Mosque of the Rose

RUE DES AGHLABITES

BD HEDI CHAKER

RUE HAMDA

Police

Publinet L'Univers

RUE DE LA VICTOIRE

RUE DE GAFSA

ONAT Carpet Museum

RUE OUZATTA

Tunis Air

Magasin Général

AVENUE DE FES

N

AVENUE HAFFOUZ

RUE HABIB THAMEUR

0   200 m

Monday Souk, Reqqada, Sfax & Gabès

STREET NAMES IN KAIROUAN

Streets in Kairouan seem to change their names even more indiscriminately than elsewhere in Tunisia, and many streets have two or more names. Avenue de la République was formerly called rue Farhat Hached; avenue Zama el Belaoui used to be avenue de la République; avenue 7 Novembre was avenue Ali Belhouane, which itself replaced avenue Bourguiba; and boulevard Hedi Chaker (alongside the city wall between place des Martyrs and rue de Gafsa) was avenue Ali Belhouane. Rue Mohamed Fez is still frequently called boulevard Sadikia, whilst avenue Ali Zouaoui is also called boulevard Driss 1, boulevard Idris Snoussi, or avenue Belaghjie Avenue. To add to the confusion, most maps of Kairouan (including ones in the tourist office) are extremely inaccurate and name streets differently or wrongly in any case. However, the main sights are now prominently signposted, and attempts are being made to translate the old Arabic-only street-name plaques. Where an old street name is still often used, both new and old have been marked on our map.

has a special place in international Islamic consciousness, and representatives from all over the world converge on the city for the Mouled celebration of the Prophet's birthday. The whole city is a UNESCO World Heritage Site.

Arrival and information

The **bus and louage stations** are inconveniently located 1.5km northwest of the Medina: from the bus station turn left out of the main entrance, turning left on to a wide boulevard after 100m with the louage station on your right hand side. Another 200m brings you to the junction with avenue Zama el Belaoui (avenue de la République on most maps). A left here takes you past the Zaouia of Sidi Sahab to the tourist office; a right leads down to the big roundabout by the post office.

The new **French quarter** to the south of the Medina contains the banks and administration, but most of the life of the town remains centred on the main street through the Medina, avenue 7 Novembre (formerly avenue Ali Belhouarne, and before that, avenue Bourguiba), at the north end of which is Bab Tunis, from where avenue Ibn el Jazzar (aka rue des Aghlabites) leads north to the ONTT **tourist office** at rue Ibn al Aghlab by the Aghlabid Pools (Mon–Sat 8am–6pm, Fri 8am–noon; ☎07/231452). The efficient office stocks brochures, guidebooks, has a list of hotels, and is one of the places you can buy the **global tickets** for Kairouan's monuments (see box p.221). There is another tourist office in place des Martyrs (Mon–Thurs 8.30am–12.30pm & 3–6pm, Fri & Sat 8.30am–12.30pm only; ☎07/231897).

Accommodation

Hotels in Kairouan run the gamut from cheap and basic to five-star luxury, though if you're used to coastal tourism standards you may be a little disappointed.

Des Aghlabites, pl de Tunis ☎07/230880. Large, modern and reasonably clean budget place, set around an enormous courtyard popular with Tunisians. Women should feel safe, and some rooms have showers. ❷

Amina ★★★, 2km up the Tunis road from the ONTT tourist office ☎07/226555, ⓕ235411. In spite of its pool and mod cons this place suffers from its location – miles out in a garbage-strewn wasteland. Sees plenty of package tourists from the coast though. ❺

Barouta, opposite *Restaurant de la Jeunesse*, just off av 7 Novembre (no phone). An ultra cheapy with passable cleanliness; not suitable for women on their own and only really worthwhile if you're after the cheapest deal. Cold water only. ❶

Continental ★★★, opposite the tourist office, rue Ibn al Aghleb ☎ 07/231050 or 231135, Ⓕ 229900. Its service doesn't always live up to its star rating, but it's comfortable, clean and has a pool. ❹

La Kasbah ★★★★★, av Ibn el Jazzar ☎ 07/237301, Ⓕ 237302. Kairouan's only topnotch hotel, in the converted Kasbah, is basically a brand new building with the Kasbah's facade. While there are some excellent features such as the fabulous pool in the central courtyard and a café in the former prison, the maze of bland corridors leading to the rooms are unimaginative given the potential of its location. Nevertheless, it has all you would expect for its stars and isn't overly expensive. ❻

El Menema, rue Moez Ibn Badiss ☎ 07/226182, Ⓕ 235033. Clean and pleasant, with large cool rooms, some with private bathrooms and (and heaters in winter). Their card promises "you would find your pleasure, your good freedom and much courtesy". ❸

Sabra, pl des Martyrs ☎ 07/230263. Deservedly popular place, if shabby around the edges. Rooms have sinks and are usually clean, there are hot shared showers (and a hammam next door), but the toilets are only just bearable. You can sleep on the roof (which has excellent views) in summer. Bargainable. ❷

Sidi Bel Hassen, rue Mohamed Fez (formerly bd Sadikia) ☎ 07/230676, turn left just out of Bab Tunis. A mixed bag of rooms, some without windows, others facing the street and Medina wall (which conceals an alley of brothels). The rooms are spacious, usually clean and the front ones are recommended. A bargain. ❶

Splendid ★★★, rue 9 Avril, off av de la République ☎ 07/227522 or 230041, Ⓕ 230829. Kairouan's classiest, with an air of subdued grandeur. Big rooms, all with TV and attached bathrooms, and there's a bar. Recommended. ❹

Taufik, rue de la Victoire ☎ 07/234634. One of the cheapest in town with shared facilities, but not at all bad, and little visited by tourists. ❶

Tunisia ★★, av de la République ☎ 07/231855, Ⓕ 231597. Big, clean rooms with a choice of bath or shower. It's worth comparing with the nearby *Splendid*. ❸

Youth hostel

Maison des Jeunes youth hostel, av de Fes, 1500m southeast of Bab ech Chouhada ☎ 07/230309. With a midnight curfew, but it is open all day. Dorms 5TD.

The Medina

Kairouan's **Medina** stretches east to west, the **Great Mosque** at its far northeastern corner, and its main street, **avenue 7 Novembre** (formerly Ali Belhouane), seeing most of the city's life. The ancient suburbs lie to the north and west, with the new **French quarter** to the south. When planning your route, especially on a hot day, bear in mind that two of the city's main attractions lie some way from the Medina – the Aghlabid Pools, right next to the tourist office, and the Zaouia of Sidi Sahab to the northwest, not far from the bus station.

Although the Medina is smaller than the one in Tunis, it has a mystique which has always affected Western travellers. In 1914, the artist Paul Klee remarked that the Medina was "the essence of *A Thousand and One Nights*, with a 99 percent reality content". Shortly after, he declared euphorically "I am a painter!" and cut short his trip to plunge himself into a frenzy of artistic productivity which lasted to the end of his life.

The Medina **walls** were originally built by the Zirids on foundations dating from 761, but it was only a few years before they were wrecked by the Hilalian invasion, and they have undergone repeated destruction and restoration ever since. The most recent damage was during World War II, when the Germans needed to build an airfield in a hurry. The most impressive remaining walls are those around Bab ech Chouhada at the south end of avenue 7 Novembre, and those around Bab Tunis at the north end, which still protect local sensibility from a cul-de-sac of brothels, nestled just within the walls.

Bir Barouta

Lurking just east of avenue 7 Novembre, the tunnel-like **souks** are surprisingly easy to miss, as is the **Bir Barouta**, which looks more like a mosque than a well. Up some steps is an unlikely camel, clad in a natty set of green fluffy blinkers, tramping endless circles to draw water that you can, supposedly, drink – though strangely enough the guides give it a wide berth. Some say that this is the well connected to Mecca which Oqba found in 670, but its name refers to a holy man of the thirteenth century whose prayers for water were answered when his dog, Routa, scratched the ground until water gushed forth. A taste of the water, it's said, will bring you back one day to Kairouan. Just behind Bir Barouta, on the right of rue Barouta heading to Souk Belaghjia, is ONTT's **Centre des Traditions et des Métiers d'Art** (closed Fri & Sat afternoons & Sun), which houses apprentice workshops at which the finer of Kairouan's crafts are taught: silver- and woodwork, weaving and filigree embroidery. The pupils are usuallly happy to explain and show you their work – an ideal way of getting a feel for the goods before entering the hard sell of the bazaars.

The Great Mosque

At the Medina's eastern end, the **Great Mosque**, or mosque of Oqba (8am–2pm, Fri at noon; prayer hall closed to non-Muslims), in its grand simplicity, is one of the oldest, largest and most important mosques in the country. Compared with the delicate elaboration of later periods, its massive buttressed walls feel more like a fortress, and it's hard not to be impressed by such a powerful and beautiful expression of faith; the best times to visit are early or late morning.

Only one of the several monumental entrances is now used, but the **Lalla Rihana Gate** on the east side, dating from 1294, deserves a quick detour. Typically Hafsid, with the characteristic arches and cupola, the gate was built more than four hundred years later than most of the present mosque, which was erected by the Aghlabid Ziyadatallah in 836 and greatly influenced mosques built at the same time in Sfax, Sousse and Tunis.

Framed by Hafsid and Turkish colonnades, the vast **courtyard** was never just an aesthetic addition. In a town so short of natural water sources, the courtyard was used as a catchment area, with rainwater channelled to the curiously shaped drain in the centre and into huge cisterns below. The curious notches in the **drain** were designed to decant dust from the water before it went down into the cistern. The **wellheads** used to draw from the cisterns are made out of antique column bases, and the grooves in the rims come from centuries of rope friction. The oversized **sundial** in the courtyard is

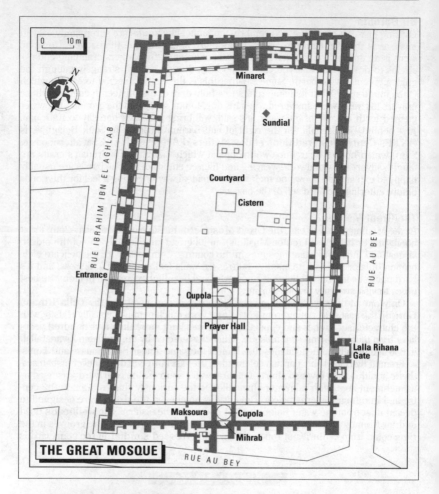

THE GREAT MOSQUE

one of two; the second, a smaller one for afternoon use, is on the superstructure of the eastern colonnade. Although the age of the **minaret** is disputed, its lowest storey is thought to date from 730, a century before most of the present mosque. This might explain why it stands off-centre, and it certainly makes it the oldest surviving minaret in the world. The minaret's blunt form is more imaginative than it first appears, particularly in the way the windows increase in size as ascending storeys grow smaller. Two blocks bearing Roman inscriptions are built into the minaret, one of them upside down.

Neither the minaret nor the courtyard is symmetrical, which emphasizes by contrast the layout of the **prayer hall**, which has six aisles to either side in the colonnade and eight in the hall itself, with the entrance set off by the cupola above. The elaborate wooden doors into the prayer hall date from the nineteenth century. With its roof supported by columns (mainly from Roman sites), the hall has been likened by centuries of pilgrims and travellers to a forest. The central aisle, higher than those on either side, is further marked out by stone reliefs below the ceiling. A transverse aisle, connecting the Gate of Lalla Rihana to another on the far side, is also distinguishable. Wooden pillows separate the capitals from the higher elements of the columns, designed to soak up any shifts caused by earth tremors. There are endless stories about these columns. According to one, anyone who counts them all will become blind; in another, the pairs operate as a sort of Muslim eye of the needle – those who cannot squeeze between them, it is said, will never reach Paradise. Dimly visible at the far end of the central aisle are 130 faïence tiles around the mihrab, imported from Baghdad in the ninth century. The wooden *minbar* just next to the mihrab is another important example of early Islamic decorative art, also carved in the ninth century by order of Ibn Aghlab himself. The wooden enclosure, or *maqsoura*, to the side of the *minbar*, was installed by a Zirid ruler in 1022 so that he did not have to pray among the hoi polloi.

Just outside the wall by the Great Mosque, the little **Ouled Farhane Cemetery** with its whitewashed gravestones makes a pretty backdrop for souvenir snapshots, while at the other end of boulevard Ibrahim Ibn Aghlab, **Bab el Khoukha** is the oldest of the Medina's remaining gates, originally called the "Sousse Gate" when built in 1705.

The Mosque of the Three Doors and the Zaouia of Sidi el Ghariani

Heading south from the Great Mosque, two remarkably photogenic streets – rue Khadraouine and rue Tahal Zarrak – head down to place Zarrouk, left of which you pass though a street of woodcarvers to reach the Mosque of the Three Doors. Closed to non-Muslims, the **Mosque of the Three Doors** is a rare nineteenth-century survivor. In the inscriptions above the three doors, is the top two bands date from the mosque's foundation, the lower band and minaret from later additions. Between the top two bands of inscriptions is a row of stones with floral decorations, of which no two are decorated the same.

A few minutes' walk away is the **Bab ech Chouhada**, the gate at the southern end of avenue 7 Novembre, and the **Zaouia of Sidi el Ghariani**, with its formidable entrance. Although the building dates from the beginning of the fourteenth century, it is now named after a native of Gharian in Libya, who died a hundred years later. In 1891, according to Sir Lambert Playfair, the hereditary governor of Kairouan was still one of Abd el Ghariani's descendants; since then the *zaouia* has seen hard times, but it has been restored and is now the home of the ASM (Association de Sauvegarde de la Medina). Notice especially the green and black columns of the mihrab, and the typically dark wooden ceiling of the tomb. The *zaouia* is not where it's marked on most maps; that spot, about 100m further along the street, is an old Beylical palace, now a carpet shop, Tapis–Sabra. The salesman here may try to entice you inside by asking for your ticket and claiming the shop is a museum.

Outside the Medina

After the bustle of the Medina the tranquillity on the outside comes as some relief. The **Aghlabid Pools** are a keen reminder of the ingenuity of Arab engineering, while the mosques and *zaouia* are rich in architecture. The most important feature here is the **Carpet Museum**, which weaves its way around this knotty subject and comes up with piles of stuff.

The Aghlabid Pools and the Mosque of Sidi Sahab

Around a kilometre from the Medina at the north end of avenue Ibn el Jazzar, the **Aghlabid Pools** (global ticket, or free entry via western gate) were incorrectly ascribed to Roman engineers by blinkered nineteenth-century French historians who imagined that Arabs of the time could not have conceived such a technically complex project. After extensive restoration, the pools (four of a presumed fourteen have been excavated) have the bland feel of a municipal waterworks – not surprisingly, since that's what they were. The vitality of water would have been foremost in the minds of the newly arrived Arab builders as they conjured this city from the desert more than a thousand years ago. The largest pool measures 128m across and the buttresses around its sides have something of the Great Mosque's monumental purity. Water arrived by aqueduct from Jebel Cherichera, 36km to the west, to be settled in the smaller adjacent basins before being stored here. Such utilities were an essential feature of urban life in this area, and there were once as many as fourteen of them. As well as holding the water, it was hoped that the pools would help relieve the town of its summer heat – instead, they were a terrific mosquito breeding ground and consequent source of malaria. The small stand in the middle of the larger pool held a pavilion in which the Aghlabid rulers could recline. Incidentally, the city's modern waterworks – not entirely dissimilar – are only a stone's throw away, next to *Hôtel Continental*.

Following the main avenue to the west (avenue de la République on most maps, though officially rue Ibn al Aghlab), you arrive at the **Mosque of Sidi Sahab**, or more correctly the Mausoleum of Abou Zammaa el Belaoui or **Mosque of the Barber** (entry with global ticket). Its occupant was a companion, or *sahab*, of the Prophet, and his distinguishing characteristic was that he always kept with him three hairs of the Prophet's beard – one under his tongue, one on his right arm and one next to his heart, hence the tendency to call him the Prophet's barber. The mosque and its surrounding complex remain a much-venerated place of pilgrimage, where families – both Berber villagers and prosperous town-dwellers – come to pay their respects. Most of the existing buildings date from the seventeenth and nineteenth centuries, and their elaborateness contrasts with the less fanciful form of the Great Mosque. The entrance to the main complex ducks under an Andalusian-style minaret, where an ornate passage of marble columns and Italianate windows leads to an equally rich courtyard, its walls and ceilings lined with green-blue tilework and white plaster stucco. In a small room to the left of the courtyard is the **tomb of Sidi Sherif Ben Hindu**, the architect of the Great Mosque. Sidi Sahab himself lies buried in the room on the far side (closed to non-Muslims). This central court is a wonderfully peaceful place to sit on a hot afternoon, with the trees outside waving overhead. The mosque is also a popular place to have boys circumcised, and the climax of the ceremony happens in this courtyard. Over the preceding weeks the boy's family will have filled a large jar with sweets and nuts before sealing it. At the moment of the big snip, the jar is smashed in the centre of the courtyard, and the waiting children scramble for its contents.

The Zaouia of Sidi Amor Abbada

Continuing south from Sidi Sahab along avenue Zammaa el Belaoui for 500m or so, a left down either rue Sidi Gaid or rue Ibn Zoubair takes you to the **Zaouia of Sidi Amor Abbada** (Tues–Sun 9am–4pm; global ticket). Sidi Amor Abbada was a nineteenth-century blacksmith, somewhat loopy by all accounts, who nonetheless must have operated successfully enough to build this seven-domed tomb, now a museum of some of his artefacts, mostly giant and rather useless iron objects. Until recently the collection included two enormous, blunt and unwieldy swords, which were supposed to protect Kairouan against the infidel. Alas, they were stolen in 1996. Still, it would seem that Kairouan remains safe, on account of two enormous anchors (another two have disappeared), which Amor Abbada claimed had come from Noah's Ark on Mount Ararat, and which currently fasten Kairouan to the soil in the roundabout outside the city's southern Bab Djedid, just east of Bab ech Chouhada. A rival theory suggests that they came from the silted-up port of Porto Farina, now known as Ghar el Melh (see p.161).

Walking back into the Medina from here, the quarter you pass through to reach the other, western, Bab Djedid, next to over-restored **Zeitouna Mosque**, is one of the town's ancient suburbs, and particularly well endowed with **doorways** painted in dis-

CARPET MAGIC

Carpet making in Kairouan belongs to a tradition going back many hundreds of years. The authorities will tell you that every Kairouan woman – doctor, lawyer or shop assistant – knows how to make them, and that 5000 families in the town are engaged in the industry. However, you can safely discount the vendors' claims to either a carpet's antiquity (which usually means "secondhand") or the claim that the marriage shawls on sale were made by the bride for her own wedding. The ones on sale are mostly made by professional (male) weavers. After all, would you sell your wedding dress to a tourist? Furthermore, many shops offer tempting credit facilities as part of their hard sell (see pp.46 & 47 in Basics for bargaining techniques) – sceptical caution is advisable.

Knotted carpets
All the carpets are handmade, but there are two basic types. The more expensive ones, recognizable by the pile, are **knotted** to either 40,000, 90,000 or 160,000 knots per square metre. These carpets are luxury items produced by a sophisticated urban culture and their designs are based on a central diamond-shaped lozenge derived originally from the lamp in the Great Mosque, but infinite variation is possible. Traditionally, each design is passed on and evolves from generation to generation within the family. An important subdivision is between Alloucha and Zarbia. Alloucha carpets use a range of colours which can be naturally derived from the wool – beiges, browns, whites and blacks – a recent innovation, perhaps in deference to Western "ethnic" tastes; the traditional Zarbia carpets use rich polychrome shades of deep blue and red.

Woven carpets
Woven carpets, or Mergoum, come from a very different culture, the nomadic Berbers. Instead of being urban luxuries, they were literally the roof over a family's flocks. Mergoum use brighter colours, the sort of intense reds and purples which Berber women still wear, and more strictly linear geometric patterns. Because Mergoum are cheaper, they're more open to abuse, and the designs of roofline mosque silhouettes have very little to do with traditional forms. For a look at some traditional designs, call in at the carpet museum, which has a small collection of old Mergoum.

The carpet market
If you're really committed to bargaining, it's possible to buy the carpets direct from the women who make them at the Saturday **carpet market** in Souk Belaghjia. Be aware, however, that the retailers don't like foreigners cutting into their business, and if you don't speak Arabic you'll need a translator. The scene is fairly frenetic, with a row of women sitting on one side of the alley displaying their carpets and a row of merchants standing on the other; in between them runs an independent auctioneer who takes bids for the carpet on offer. The whole thing is done at feverish pitch and the atmosphere is electric. It's well worth a look, even if you don't intend to buy. If you do, then prices can be less than half those in the shops; though watch out – the nicest old lady can be a shark and you could easily pay good money for junk. Around 1–2pm on Monday or Saturday is the best time to go.

turbing colour combinations, featuring the brown and blue that seem to be a Kairouan speciality.

The Carpet Museum
The former ONTT crafts shop on avenue Ali Zouaoui, just up from the post office, no longer sells carpets but functions as a **carpet museum** (Mon–Thurs 8.30am–1pm & 3–6pm, Fri & Sat mornings only), with mostly modern replicas of the many traditional types hung on its walls. It is heavily involved in quality control, and every carpet for sale

is inspected and awarded a rating – *Deuxième Choix*, *Première Choix* and *Qualité Supérieure* – which is then stamped on it. Any carpet without this rating has not been passed.

Eating, drinking and nightlife

Buses between Tunis and the south often have to wait, even in the middle of the night, while all the passengers get off at Kairouan to buy the **sweets** for which it is famous – the best known of which is *makroudh*, a honey-soaked cake with a date filling. The city's foremost patisseries are in the Medina along avenue 7 Novembre.

For something more substantial, the budget-priced *Restaurant de la Jeunesse* (daily 11am–7pm, later in summer) on avenue 7 Novembre, almost opposite Bir Barouta, will feed you for under 5TD; their couscous in particular is recommended. Other options include: *La Mamma* (daily 9am–10pm), on rue Soukeina Bent el-Haussein, where you can enjoy good sandwiches and pizzas for a few dinars; the spotlessly clean and family-run *Karawan* (no set hours, closed Ramadan) next door, which serves up traditional meals for 4–8TD; and any of the dirt-cheap rôtisseries at the post office roundabout, where you can fill up on chicken and chips for 2TD. As with everything in Kairouan, however, ask the price before you tuck in, or you'll get stung. The *Sabra* (daily noon–9pm, later in summer) on avenue de la République serves fairly tasty food, and has a set meal at 6TD, but as prices rise the portions here seem to decrease. Upmarket choices are limited to *Hôtel Splendid* (daily 11am–2.30pm & 7–9.30pm), with a 9TD set meal, and the *Sofra* (daily March–Oct noon–9pm), which is housed in an original part of *La Kasbah Hôtel*, where a wide range of expensive dishes are served in atmospheric surroundings.

As a conservative town, Kairouan has little local **nightlife**, except for some raucous restaurant-cum-bars around the roundabout by the post office, such as the *Roi du Couscous* (closed Fri) at rue 20 Mars. Otherwise, the Aghlabid Pools are a popular summer venue for evening strolls, and if you're peckish you can pick up a cheap pizza at *Piccolo Mondo* (daily 8am–10pm, later on Sat) and take it with you, as many locals do. The most popular **cafés** are those on place des Martyrs, along with an unnamed cavern on the left side of avenue 7 Novembre just before rue Bab Jedid, and another nameless café on rue Dr Hamda Laouani, which offers good *chicha* pipes. More expensively, you could smoke a *chicha* and slurp on a coffee at the *Café Maure* in the former prison of the kasbah in *La Kasbah Hôtel*. For a calm **beer**, try the *Hôtel Splendid*.

Listings

Airlines Tunis Air, rue Khawarezmi, off bd Bourguiba ☏ 07/230422. Harameya Travel, nearby on av Dr Hamda Laouani ☏ 07/234234, serves as an agent for most other airlines.

Banks There are several in the centre between Bab ech Chouhada and av de la République, one of which should be open weekend mornings, but don't rely on it.

Car rental Hertz, av Ibn el Jazzar ☏ 07/224529.

Cinema Maison de la Culture, bd Bourguiba.

Festivals The Mouled Festival, a celebration of the Prophet's birthday, is a big event in Kairouan. A seasonal pudding called *assida* is a speciality of the celebration, whose date varies according to the Islamic calendar (see p.41).

Hammams Men can use the hammam attached to the *Hôtel Sabra* (daily 5am–4pm). Women can only use it by arrangement after 4pm, if there's a group of you. Failing that, you will have to find the women's hammam close by, but it's very well hidden. There is another men's hammam in the Medina near Bir Barouta.

Hospital The Ibn el Jazzar University Hospital is on av Ibn el Jazzar ☏ 07/230036, near the *Hôtel Continental* and the Aghlabid Pools.

MOVING ON FROM KAIROUAN

For a rundown of destinations and journey times, see Travel Details on p.258.

The bus and louage station (☎07/300011 or 303772) is northwest of the Medina, beyond the Mosque of Sidi Sahab: a taxi shouldn't cost more than 2TD, or else walk up avenue Zama el Belaoui, turning left at the last road before Sidi Sahab – turn right 200m on, and you'll see the bus station at the end; for louages don't turn right, the station is up ahead on your left. As the town is pretty central, there are **bus** services to most parts of the country. There are **louages** to Maktar, Sbeitla, Sfax, Sousse and Tunis, but none to El Jem or Mahdia – you have to go via Sousse.

Internet Publitel, next to *Hôtel El Menema* on rue Moez Ibn Badiss, is open 24hr, but is expensive (4TD/hr). Slightly more difficult to find, but much cheaper is Publinet L'Univers (24hr; 1.5TD/hr), nestled amongst a maze of streets northeast of Tunis Air. To get there from the Medina head out to Tunis Air, and take the next left by the sign for the *Maison des Jeunes*. Follow the road round to the left, then right and the Publinet is on your right.

Markets A busy daily food market is held in the streets between Bab Tunis and pl de Tunis, and there's another, which combines with a flea market, just south of the bus and louage stations, best on Sundays. Also well worth heading for is the distinctly untouristy Monday souk, attracting Berbers and others from all around: it's held about 500m down av Haffouz (aka av Beit el Hikma) from the post office on the right.

Pharmacy There's a night pharmacy at 44 av Ali Zouaoui ☎07/230069, less than 100m north of the junction with bd Hedi Chaker, on the right.

Police There's a police station (daytime only) in the Medina on av 7 Novembre by Souk Belaghjia, and another (24hr) on rue du 20 Mars, opposite *Hôtel Splendid*. Call ☎197 for emergencies.

Post office On a large roundabout where av de la République meets rue de la Victoire and av Haffouz (city hours; bureau de change).

Supermarket Magasin Général on bd Bourguiba, just south of Bab ech Chouhada.

Swimming pools The *La Kasbah* and *Amina* pools are for residents only, whilst the one at the *Continental* can be used for 3.5TD.

Telephones There are numerous taxiphone offices in both the Medina and New Town.

Around Kairouan

On the flat plain surrounding Kairouan are the remains of some palace complexes built by the ninth-century Aghlabid rulers, testimony to their feelings of insecurity even in such a prosperous period. The minimal remains are hardly worth a visit for their own sake, but those at **Reqqada** could be combined with a visit to the National Museum of Islamic Art.

Reqqada   رقّادة

The main reason for visiting **REQQADA** (or Rakkada), 11km south of Kairouan, is the **National Museum of Islamic Art** (Tues–Sun 9am–4pm, closes noon on Fri; 1.1TD, camera 1TD; ☎07/223337), which opened in 1994 to great fanfare in a former presidential palace. As it currently stands, the collection – jumbled ancient Koranic manuscripts, old gold and silver coins from the earliest period of Arab rule, and some desultory ceramics, glassware and stoneware – is a bit of a letdown, not helped by the fact that labels are in Arabic only. Furthermore, several rooms are presently closed, and on occasion the museum itself fails to open. The reason for this, however, is that the museum is gearing up to, eventually, receive a wealth of other material formerly exhibited in other museums, such as the exquisite ninth-century Cordoban astrolabe formerly at Monastir, and a good part, if not all, of the Bardo's Islamic collection.

To get there, take the bus for students at the Faculté des Lettres, which leaves every hour between 8.15am and 11.15am from Kairouan's avenue Haffouz (also avenue Beit el Hikma) by a hexagonal kiosk, about 200m down on the right from the post office. Otherwise, there's a bus and louage stop (which start at the main station) 200m further on. When you arrive at the stop, the museum is a kilometre further and signposted to the right. More simply you could take a taxi (3–4TD) from the centre of town.

As you walk towards the museum from the bus stop, you'll find the minimal remains of the **palace**, built in 876 by the Aghlabid sovereign Ibrahim II, in a field on the right. The Aghlabids' reasons for wanting a palace out of town included avoiding troop rebellions and being able to have a reasonably pleasurable lifestyle beyond the withering gaze of Kairouan's religious lobby. Another reason for choosing Reqqada was its agreeable climate, believed to have dynamic powers: "Every time the doctor Zian Ibn Khalfoun left Kairouan for Reqqada," wrote El Bekri, the early traveller, "he took off his turban in order to receive directly on his head the beneficial effects of this atmosphere."

Raqqada's predecessor was **El Abbasiya**, built 5km southeast of Kairouan after a troop rebellion of 809, in which the Kairouanis had joined. Even less remains of this than of the palace in Reqqada, but it has given rise to an intriguing theory. El Bekri's description of a minaret which once stood there fits that of the Leaning Tower of Pisa, itself built in 1174. The theory begs the question of whether this is more than co-incidental, given that Pisan ships took part in the Norman campaign in Tunisia between 1141 and 1160.

Scanty remains of another old palace, **Sabra**, are to the left off the Reqqada road a couple of kilometres out of Kairouan, and not easy to find. The palace was built for the Fatimid ruler El Mansour on the site of his final victory over the Kharijite rebel Abu Yazid (see p.431) in 947. Abu Yazid is said to have died of his wounds exactly a year later.

Biar el Aouani   بيار العواني

The P3, the direct road north to El Fahs and on to Tunis, skirts the southern edge of the Zaghouan massif, last remnant of the Dorsale range, before reaching an easy run across flat empty country all the way to Kairouan. The only diversion on this route, 20km north of Kairouan, is **BIAR EL AOUANI**, with its perfect turreted Byzantine **fort** on the bare hillside, and a little local museum (variable hours) whose curator rushes up to greet any car that stops. The isolation makes the site all the more attractive.

Mahdia and around   المهدية

Georges Sebastian, whose fabulous villa helped launch Hammamet as an internationally famous resort, regarded **MAHDIA**, 50km south along the coast from Sousse, as the only other place in Tunisia which could compare. Until recently, he was right. It was one of the most beguilingly unspoilt towns in the country and had made only a half-hearted gesture towards mass tourism. In the last few years the tourist authorities and big money developers have taken Sebastian's lead and installed a massive *zone touristique* in Mahdia – though this is well outside the old town. However, while this has already spurred a rash of overeager gift shops in the Medina, as well as overcharging taxi drivers and the like, the corner of the historic old town remains remarkably unaffected. This, as well as the light and colour of the place, makes Mahdia well worth a few days' stay.

Some history

Set on a narrow peninsula in the belly-like bulge of the Sahel coast, Mahdia's geographical position has defined its history. After defeating the last of the Aghlabids in

909, the new Fatimid ruler of Tunisia, the self-styled **Mahdi** (see p.233), needed a capital to provide security from the hostility of the Sunni majority. The heretical Fatimids overthrew the complacent Aghlabids with the aid of Berber dissidents, but were neither popular nor concerned to be so. They wanted Tunisia as a base to conquer Egypt and Iraq, the heart of the Arab world. It was with this in mind that the historian Ibn Khaldoun later called Mahdia a "dagger held in the fist".

Mahdia made the ideal capital, its narrow entrance easily closed off by the massive wall begun in 916. Behind the wall the Mahdi built a Great Mosque, a harbour, a palace and other installations, with everything else relegated outside the wall. A few merchants were allowed to trade inside, but had to live outside, and the Mahdi claimed that his aim was to separate them from their wives during the day and from their goods at night.

For the next six hundred years, Mahdia was to be one of the most formidable fortresses in the Mediterranean. Its first test came with a siege in 944–45 by **Abu Yazid**, "the man on a donkey" (see p.431), and his Kharijite revolt from Tozeur, but this was soon beaten off. After the Fatimids left for Cairo in 970, Mahdia shared the chequered fortunes of other coastal towns. In 1057 the **Zirids**, supposedly the country's rulers, were forced to take refuge here by the invading Banu Hilal, and thirty years later a joint Genoese–Pisan force seized the city, and the Zirids had to buy it back. Taken again by the Norman king Roger II of Sicily in 1148, the return to Islamic control in 1160 brought prosperity through trade and piracy and, in 1390, another unsuccessful siege by the French, English and Genoese. The wars of the sixteenth century, however, brought Mahdia's period of greatness to an end. In 1547 the corsair **Dragut** made the town his centre of operations, causing the Spanish to storm it in 1550. Rather than have to return, when they left in 1554 they brought the walls down. Since then – apart from routine pillagings by the Spanish in 1597 and the Knights of Malta in the seventeenth century – Mahdia has been a peaceful fishing port.

Arrival and information

Buses drop you outside the **louage station**, inconveniently located on avenue Belhouane, 3km west of the old town. You can walk to the Medina by turning left out of the station with the railway to your right, then left at the level crossing, right at the end, and left again onto avenue Farhat Hached, with the port to your right. Alternatively, a taxi should cost 0.5TD and less than that to the *zone touristique* hotels. The **train station** is centrally located on avenue Farhat Hached by the port.

Next to the port is a main square, place de l'Indépendance, with the town hall, police station and entrance to the Skifa el Kahla gate-tunnel (see p.231), which joins the new town to the west with the peninsular Medina. There are plenty of **banks** nearby, as well as the ONTT **tourist office** (May–Oct Mon–Sat 8am–6pm; Nov–April Mon–Thurs 8.30am–1pm & 3–5.45pm, Fri & Sat 8.30am–1.30pm; ☎03/681098), just through the Skifa in the Medina. They're helpful, with a list of hotels and prices, though not that well equipped (you have to purchase maps in the tourist shops).

Accommodation

There are only two **hotels** in the Medina (book ahead in summer, especially the *Al Jazira*), with the rest along the beach to the northwest in the 2.8 square kilometre **zone touristique**, which has twenty hotels and several more planned. Most are expensive, though out of season prices plunge, with half- or full-board not much more than a simple bed and breakfast. As a rough rule of thumb, the further out the hotel, the better and more modern the facilities. **Taxis** to the *zone touristique* hotels should cost 1TD. Alternatively, the **Sahel métro** trains from Mahdia to Monastir call at two handy sta-

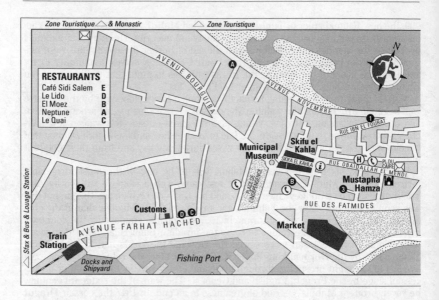

tions: Sidi Messaoud, near *Hôtel Mehdia* and Mahdia Zone Touristique, near *Hôtel Mahdia Palace* towards the end of the *zone*.

If you prefer a beach location without the luxuries, there's also an unofficial **camp-site** between the recently closed *Sables d'Or* and the *Mehdi* hotels. The **youth hostel**, centrally placed near the train, bus and louage stations, is unusually good.

Hotels in town

Al Jazira, 36 rue Ibn el Fourat ☎03/681629,ⓕ 680274. With smallish rooms, shared bathrooms, and heating. It's a bit basic but some rooms have jaw-dropping views over the sea (no.9 especially), just 10m away and, with its friendly and ever-helpful management, it is recommended. ❷

El Medina, rue el Kaem, in the Medina ☎03/694664, ⓕ696384. This new hotel place has pleasant, clean and airy rooms set around a courtyard and a roof terrace. Though lacking the sea views of the *Al Jazira* and more expensive, it's still a good place. ❸

Hotels in the zone touristique

Abou Nawas Cap Mahdia ★★★, 4km from Skifa in the *zone touristique* ☎03/680300, ⓕ696332, ⓔcapmahdia@abounawas.com.tn. Relatively long-established member of the *zone touristique*, offering horse-riding and water sports as well as archery. Recently taken over and modernized by the *Abou Nawas*, which doesn't prevent it from putting on some marvellously tacky evening entertainment. ❼

Cap Sérail ★★★, 5km from Skifa in the *zone touristique* ☎ 03/695011. New, much smaller and intimate than most *zone* hotels, and offers water-sports facilities. ❻

Corniche, av 7 Novembre, just before the *zone touristique* ☎03/694201. Unremarkable modern place, but very good value, next to the beach. ❸

Mahdia Palace ★★★★★, 5.5km from Skifa in the *zone touristique* ☎03/696777, ⓕ696810. Mahdia's swankiest, easily justifying its prices. All mod cons, fantastic outdoor (and indoor) pools, tennis courts, health club and if it gets too much there are five bars. ❼

Thapsus ★★★, 6km from Skifa in the *zone touristique* ☎03/695530, ⓕ695374, ⓦwww.thapsus-hotel.com. The newest, and most distant, on the *zone*, which means that the beach to the north is virtually deserted. Water sports and horse-riding offered. ❻

Youth hostel

Maison des Jeunes, rue Ibn Rached ☎ 03/681559. Follow signs off av Farhat Hached opposite the train station, with dorm beds (5TD) and double rooms available. **❷**

The Town

Mahdia's **Medina,** on a peninsula poking out to sea, is only a tiny quarter now of what's otherwise a typical, thriving Sahel town, but its maritime atmosphere sets it apart from Tunisia's other old cities. The sea provides the dominant smell here, and even the stones of the houses look more seaworn than weather-beaten. The dominant sound, on the other hand, is not the breaking of waves, but the working of looms, since weaving is the main cottage industry here.

Forming the dividing line between the old and new towns is the **Skifa el Kahla** gate, a sixteenth-century reconstruction of what the departing Spaniards blew up in 1554, which dominates the main square. The gate – once the only entrance to the city – stood in the middle of a wall as much as 10m thick, stretching right across the neck of the peninsula. It's staggering to think that the defences destroyed by the Spaniards four hundred years ago were already six hundred years old. The Skifa in particular had quickly become legendary: each section of its vaulted passage could be closed off by lowering an iron grill weighing as much as eight tons; but it was the narrow passage itself, immortalized in the name *Skifa el Kahla*, "The Dark Passage", which became most notorious: "So dark", according to John Ogilby, translating Olfert Dapper's book of 1670, "that it is terrible to strangers, seeming rather a murdering den than an entrance into a city". Nowadays the murdering den is an informal souk, which comes into its own on Fridays with a number of perfume, magico-mineral and jewellery sellers.

Beside the Skifa, on place de l'Indépendance, is the new archeological **Municipal Museum** (Tues–Sun 9am–4pm, summer 9am–1pm & 3–7pm; 1.1TD, camera 1TD). A light and airy place whose ground floor houses Punic, Roman and Christian ceramics, mainly oil lamps (the Christian models are particularly intricate), and *amphorae*, as well as statues and mosaics from Thysdrus (El Jem). The Islamic Art section upstairs includes ceramics, calligraphy, mosaics and examples of traditional local dress together with the looms used to weave them. Labelling is in French and Arabic.

The street on the far side of the Skifa cuts through Mahdia's main tourist drag, with souvenir shops and persistent hard sell. Beyond it, you come to **place du Caire**, one of the most perfect little squares in all Tunisia. Sitting at the café here under the small minaret of the **Mustapha Hamza mosque**, the only reminder of time passing is the tortoise-like movement of old men who shift their seats slowly round the square in pursuit of shade. The two **cafés** here form Mahdia's main nocturnal attraction.

Also worth a visit if you want to learn more about the Medina is the local branch of the **ASM** (variable hours), in an old palatial residence on avenue 7 Novembre east of the *Al Jazira*. It aims to organize projects to renovate the houses within the Medina. If you're interested in **weaving**, the Medina is full of workshops whose loom workers are friendly and usually willing to chat about their craft to passing tourists. Prices range from 4–6TD for a synthetic bedspread, to 35–40TD for a pure silk sash, and up to 600TD for a silk, gold and silver thread bridal wedding shawl made to order. This is some of the most beautiful craftwork you'll find anywhere in Tunisia: have a chat with Karim Khoadja Nasser, whose loom and workshop is around the corner from *Al Jazira* on rue du Caire.

The daily fish **market** by the modern fishing port and the weekly Friday market are both lively; look out especially for octopuses, which are sold by the bunch. They're caught by boys who can be seen any morning picking their way round the shallow rocky pools on the peninsula's shore, armed with spiked canes. Stretching off into the **new town** to the west of the Medina is avenue Bourguiba, running parallel to the **beach** as it curves away to the north. The *zone touristique*, with over twenty massive hotels, doesn't start until some way along.

The Great Mosque

Straight on from place du Caire, beyond another Turkish mosque on the left, the Slimen Hanza, the fortress-like **Great Mosque** dominates the expanse of place Kadhi en Noamine. By the 1960s the whole building was so decrepit that it was entirely reconstructed – what you see now is a modern version of the original built by the Mahdi in the tenth century, incorporating some characteristic Fatimid elements. Most prominent of these is the monumental entrance, a Fatimid innovation which owes its form to Roman triumphal arches and its function to the elitism of Fatimid doctrine. Only the Mahdi and his entourage were allowed to use the main entrance, and the same distinction carried over to the prayer hall, where the central aisle was reserved for those in the ruler's favour. Deep niches, used in the entrance gate and in the prayer-hall facade, represent another Fatimid innovation, and the two bastions at either corner of the north wall were cisterns for collecting water from the roof. The courtyard was used as a cemetery by the Spaniards in 1551, but when they left in 1554 they exhumed the bodies and took them to Palermo. Suitably dressed non-Muslims are usually allowed in outside prayer times, but don't assume this.

Most of the peninsula itself is rocky, but some steps going down from the *Café Sidi Salem* at rue du Borj on the south side of the peninsular 200m beyond the Great Mosque, provide good **swimming** off the rocks below the excavation site. The café itself (see below) has wonderful views.

Cap d'Afrique

Passing the fenced-off Fatimid excavations to your left, the hilltop **Borj el Kebir** (Tues–Sun: May–Oct 9am–1pm & 3–7pm; Nov–April 9am–4pm; 1.1TD, camera 1TD)

THE MAHDI

Just as Jews look forward to the coming of the Messiah, and Christians to the second coming of Jesus, so Muslims look forward to the coming of the Mahdi or "divinely guided one", whose arrival will herald the final victory of Islam. Muslim belief in the Mahdi is based on the *hadith* (sayings of the Prophet), but some *hadith* are more reliably authentic than others, and those that refer to the Mahdi are not in the category considered most reliable. In one of them, Mohammed says that the Mahdi "will fill the earth with fairness and justice as it was filled with oppression and tyranny", while in another he tells that "The Mahdi will be from my family, a descendant of Fatima." Fatima is the Prophet's daughter, from whom the Fatimids claimed descent.

The Mahdi is not a Prophet or Messiah, but a rightful Caliph or Imam, the divinely appointed leader of Islam. The question of who is the rightful Caliph has been disputed by Sunni and Shi'ite Muslims since the time of Ali, the fourth Caliph, who was Fatima's husband and Mohammed's son-in-law. When he died in 661, Shi'ite Muslims refused to accept the legitimacy of the Umayyad Caliphs who succeeded him. Instead, they regarded as legitimate leaders of Islam only Ali's direct male heirs, to whom they gave the title Imam. Most Shi'ites ("Twelvers") recognize twelve Imams, of whom the last, Mohammed al-Muntazar ("the Expected One") disappeared in 873. According to legend, however, al-Muntazar did not die; he is simply "hidden", and it is he who will return one day as the Mahdi, the hidden Imam revealed.

Belief in the coming of Mahdi originated among Shi'ites, but soon spread to Muslims of all schools, although Sunnis and non-Twelver Shi'ites do not accept that it will be al-Muntazar. Throughout history, and especially at times of crisis, leaders and would-be leaders have claimed to be the Mahdi, especially in North Africa. Like most, Obaidallah Said, the "Mahdi" from whom Mahdia takes its name, conveniently ignored certain aspects of the Mahdi legend: the Mahdi, for example, will reign for only seven years, after which comes judgement day and the end of the world.

looms large over the **cemetery** beyond. Dating from 1595, it was first just a simple rectangle, the corner bastions were added in the eighteenth century. As forts go, this one is bleak and uninteresting, but it does offer a great view over the town (mornings are best for photography from this angle, although Mahdia's evening light often takes your breath away). The *gardien* may talk of a subterranean tunnel leading off the narrow entrance to El Jem and describe how elephants were used to transport building blocks for an amphitheatre from the port at Mahdia to the middle of the Sahel. But it is unlikely that there was any Roman settlement here, as the crumbling **port** below the fortress was built by the Fatimids: it once had a tower on either side of the entrance with a chain suspended between (which Christian attackers broke through in 1088). That which once held a Mediterranean strike-force is now used only by a few small, brightly painted fishing boats, themselves left behind by the modern vessels and the new port in town, the old **harbour** and the few confused remains of the Mahdi's **palace** almost breathe melancholy, an impression not helped by the fact that the end of the peninsula is a large cemetery. The red lighthouse at the tip is operated by the military, though there are no problems with photography, or clambering around the very sea-worn ruins right at the end – Cap d'Afrique.

Eating, drinking and nightlife

You don't have to stray far from the main square by the port to get some great **food**, at prices you won't believe if you've just come from Sousse or Monastir. In the *Restaurant el Moez* (daily 8am–7pm, later in summer), in a passage parallel to the Skifa, you can fill up on excellent and very moderately priced fish soup and a deliciously spicy *kamounia* for 2–3TD. For not much more, the friendly *Restaurant de la Medina* (daily 8am–9pm, later in summer) in the same building as the market, does succulent fish and excellent soups served by a handlebar-moustached waiter in a bright-yellow three-piece suit. More upmarket restaurants can be found along the quayside avenue Farhat Hached, best of which are *Le Lido* (daily 11am–11pm) and *Le Quai* (daily 8am–midnight), both offering three courses for around 15TD, but the difference in price and attitude isn't reflected in the quality of the food. Another pricey alternative on the north shore is the *Neptune* (daily 11.30am–midnight), avenue 7 Novembre, 300m from the Skifa. Much the best, however, is *Café Sidi Salem* (daily 9am–11pm or midnight, much earlier in winter), rue du Borj on the south side of the peninsula, which offers superlative sea views, and the food isn't bad either, with sandwiches for 1TD and seafood dishes around 7TD. You'll find the usual unremarkable **nightclubs** at many of the *zone touristique* hotels, namely: *Club César* at *Hôtel Thapsus*, *Mourad* at *Hôtel Mansour*, *Samba* at *Hôtel el Mahdi*, and *El Jem* at *Hôtel Mahdia Palace*.

Listings

Banks There are several at the eastern end of av Farhat Hached, and the eastern end of av Habib Bourguiba. BIAT on the new town side of the Skifa has a Visa ATM.

Car rental Avis, av Bourguiba ☎03/696342; Hertz, av Bourguiba ☎03/695255; ADA/Mattei, av 7 Novembre just before the *Restaurant Neptune* ☎03/696716 have bargainable rates.

Diving The Club de Plongée le Mahdois ☎03/681339 is based at *Hôtel Abou Nawas Cap Mahdia*, and offers diving equipment and lessons.

Festivals The National Festival of Professional Theatre is held in March. April sees the National Festival of Folk Music and Arts; June a fishing festival, and July the "Nights of Mahdi Festival". Information on all of these is available at the tourist office nearer the dates. Most events are held in the Borj el Kebir.

Hammam On rue Obaidallah el Mehdi in the Medina (they provide *foutas* to change under).

Hospital The regional hospital ☎03/681005 is in rue Mendès France.

Internet Cybernet, av Belhouane, near the CNSS College. To get there from the Skifa follow av Bourguiba for a couple of kilometres until the Hertz agency, after which you turn left and it's on the left after 100m (Mon–Sat 9am–midnight, Sun 10am–midnight; 1.5TD/hr).

Pharmacy There are several pharmacies on av Bourguiba and the night pharmacy is on place 1er de Mai ☎03/681490.

Police Place l'Indépendance ☎03/681419.

Post office The main office (city hours) is on av Bourguiba, 500m from Skifa el Kahla on the left. It also has international phones, Western Union money transfer and changes money.

Supermarket Magasin Général is at 63 av Bourguiba (Mon–Sat 8am–noon & 3–7pm, Sun 8am–12.45pm).

MOVING ON FROM MAHDIA

For a rundown of destinations and journey times, see Travel Details on pp.257–258.

Buses stop outside the louage station (☎03/680372), 3km west of town and 0.5TD by taxi. You can walk by turning right 1km down avenue Farhat Hached onto avenue Taîeb Mehiri, then left after 200m, and turning right at the end (before the level crossing) onto avenue Belhouane, from where it's 500m on the right. Note that if you're going to Monastir by louage, you'll have to change at Moknine or Ksar Hellal. For Kairouan, you're best heading to Sousse for a connection. The **train station** (☎03/680177) is centrally placed on avenue Farhat Hached by the docks, and has one daily train to Tunis, and frequent **métro trains** to Monastir, Monastir airport, Sousse, Moknine, Ksar Hellal and Lamta.

Taxis Taxi rank on corner of pl de l'Indépendance and rue de Fatimide ☎03/695900.

Telephones Apart from the post office, international calls can be made from taxiphone offices opposite the market, on rue Obaidallah el Mehdi between the Skifa and place du Caire, and on the west side of the main square.

South of Mahdia

About 10km south of Mahdia, there's little to distinguish **KSOUR ESSAF** from any other textile town in the Sahel, but it's the jumping-off point for **SALAKTA**, a few kilometres south, a small village on the site of Roman Sullecthum. The **ruins** are really only for the enthusiast, though it's a pleasant enough place with a new fishing harbour. Shared taxis ferry to and fro between Ksour Essaf and the shore. Right on the beach is a Roman **cemetery**, next to a **museum** (Mon–Wed: May–Oct 9am–1pm & 3–7pm; Nov–April 9.30am–4.30pm; 1.1TD, camera 1TD) that contains the mosaic of a lion 4.5m long from nose to tail, and the funerary breastplate of a general from Hannibal's army. Also in the museum is an enlarged photograph of a mosaic found in Ostia, Rome's port town, showing ships in front of the office of a group of traders who specialized in trade with Sullecthum – a vivid reminder of how close trade links across the Mediterranean were. If you're interested in archeology of a more industrial bent, much of the museum here is devoted to the work of a British-funded team on Roman pottery from the region.

South along the shore are other vestigial **remains** of baths, houses and walls, some of them actually in the sea. A little further on are the **Catacombs of Arch Zara**. If you want to look for them, follow the coast road south from the museum for just over a kilometre until you come to a junction. Turn right inland, and continue for about 300m until the tarmac turns right again, but instead of following it turn left with the main power lines. After nearly 1.5km of piste, a track to your left heads towards a building with a blue-tiled onion dome on the roof. The path takes you after 100m to three pits, one of which has steps leading down into the catacombs, or Ghar Dhaba, quite an extensive series of niche-lined tunnels, which you'll need a light of some kind to explore. Just before the path, also on your left, an old Roman **cistern** is used by a local family to keep their rabbits in. The piste continues 500m to emerge on the Ksour Essaf–Sfax road by the "Sfax 87/Mahdia 18" marker.

Between here and Sfax the coast is largely bare, but the town of **LA CHEBBA**, 20km south, has beaches of a sort, and a couple of places to **stay**. In town, the *Hôtel Lahmar* (☎03/641805; **②**) is reasonable enough, and there's the *Centre Maison des Jeunes* **youth hostel** (☎03/643815), 5km north of town, 1.5km off the main road; call them to check they're open before traipsing out there. A couple of hundred metres away is a sand and rock beach, full of black seaweed and washed-up garbage, but free of people. You can **camp** at the hostel but meals are only available in the summer.

The peninsula protruding into the sea for 4km east of town ends in the most easterly point in the belly of the Sahel, **Ras Kaboudia**, a corruption of Caput Vada, its ancient name. A **lighthouse** standing here incorporates the remains of a Byzantine fort.

Another Roman site, **Acholla**, lies on the coast between here and Sfax. Originally founded by Maltese Phoenicians, its mosaics have been plundered and hauled off to the Bardo in Tunis, but ruins of a **bathhouse** and two **villas** – one the home of a second-century AD Roman senator – remain.

El Jem الجم

The extraordinary **amphitheatre** at **EL JEM**, 40km southwest of Mahdia, is the single most impressive Roman monument in Africa, its effect magnified by the sheer incongruity of its sudden appearance, surrounded by a huddle of small houses in the middle

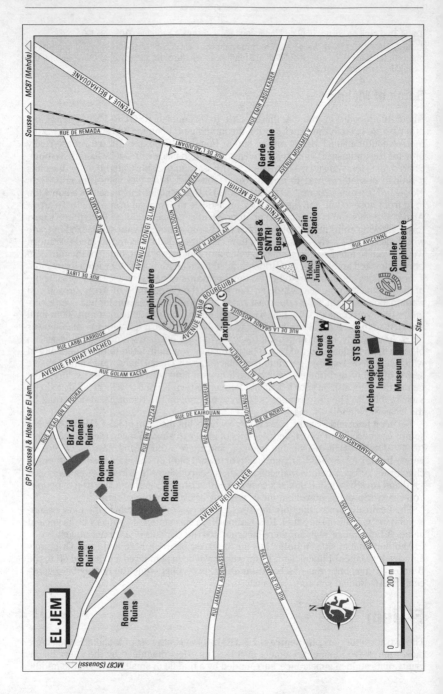

of the flat Sahel plain, halfway between Sousse and Sfax. There are a couple of reasonable hotels here, but transport is good and there's no reason to stay longer than it takes to see the amphitheatre and the museum. A good time to visit is before the tour groups arrive after 8am, or else late afternoon when they've gone.

Some history

Ancient El Jem was probably larger than the modern town, full of luxurious villas owned by men who had grown rich trading olive oil to Rome. As the Romans expanded from grain into oil, the Sahel began to grow rich, and it was during the second century AD that **Thysdrus**, set here at a crossroads of the area, first started to expand so spectacularly. Prosperity brought luxury villas, mosaics and the amphitheatre – but eventually also the town's downfall. The citizens rose in revolt against the level of Roman taxation around 230 AD, killing the collector of taxes and proclaiming the eighty-year-old Imperial official **Gordian** as Emperor of Rome. This action introduced an unsettled period for the Empire and did Thysdrus little good. The one memorial to Gordian's short rule (soon defeated – he committed suicide) is the amphitheatre, begun in his time and left unfinished at his death. According to one legend, the amphitheatre saw the last heroic stand of **Kahina**, Jewish prophetess and leader of **Berber resistance** to the Arab invasion in the seventh century. Certainly it would be even better preserved today if in 1695 Mohammed Bey had not blown up most of one side in order to evict the followers of Ali Bey.

The Town

The remains of the **amphitheatre** (daily: May–Oct 7am–7pm; Nov–April 8am–5.30pm; 4.2TD, camera 1TD) are among the best preserved of its kind – finer than the Colosseum in Rome, and not much smaller. Its original capacity is estimated at around thirty thousand, more than the population of Thysdrus itself. People would have come from all around to watch the games here, boosting the town's civic prestige.

Chambers underneath the middle of the arena held **gladiators**, animals and theatrical scenery, and an elaborate system of lifts delivered them directly to the arena. Animals would be hoisted up in cages, which could then be opened in safety using pulleys from below. Following extensive restorations, you can wander around the underbelly of the complex. To recreate the scene, picture an amphitheatre mosaic you've seen, and imagine the roars and stench of animals and the fear of those about to face them in this claustrophobic space, which was lined with marble so neither combatant nor animal could escape.

The **museum** (same times and ticket as amphitheatre, closes 5.30pm in winter), south of the amphitheatre next to the Sfax road, is worth the effort even on a hot summer day, as its small collection of mosaics includes several that are as fresh and vigorous as any in the country. In the courtyard, two peacocks – almost Art Nouveau in their stylization – look ready to leap off the wall. A metal frying pan in the room to the right is an unusual domestic touch, displayed alongside amphitheatre scenes. But the large room at the far side of the courtyard contains the real masterpieces, with mosaics featuring an almost abstract peacock-tail design, a balding, drunken Silenus being bound by three boys for a nymph, and a child riding a tiger. There's one small field of **excavations** next to the museum, with typical peristyle house plans and some mosaics in place. Work is under way to transport, in entirety, a particularly luxurious **Roman villa** (villa d'Africa) to within the museum grounds from its present site in the middle of modern El Jem. If things go as planned, this should be fascinating in its own right: the villa covers some 3000 square metres and contains a number of excellent mosaics, of which two are currently in a museum in Rome.

ROMAN ENTERTAINMENT

Circus shows were the opiate of the Roman masses, used unashamedly by rulers to keep their huge urban populations happy, and the whole ritual played an important part in cementing the paternalistic relationship between rulers and ruled. A royal box was situated at each end of the arena, from where the charitable sponsor of the show would watch the proceedings and intervene when necessary. The defeated gladiator in a duel had the option of throwing himself on the mercy of the ruling official in his box, which he signalled by lying on his back and raising his left arm. If the crowd thought his courage had earned him his life, they would signal it by giving the thumbs-up sign – but the final decision was the official's alone: if his thumb was pointed down, the victim was killed on the spot. Doubtless, prudent officials tended not to offend the crowd too often.

The only disadvantage of the shows for the rulers was their in-built inflationary spiral. The more spectacular the show, the higher the expectations next time. **Wild animals** played a large part in the proceedings and were plentiful here in Africa. Animals would be pitted against each other or against gladiators, or else unarmed victims would be thrown into their midst. On the day that Rome's Colosseum opened, five thousand animals are said to have perished. But the appetite for blood grew ever stronger, and human life was sufficiently cheap for **armed gladiators** to be in plentiful supply. They were mostly prisoners or criminals, or even bankrupts on a contract to pay off their debts – if they survived. Gladiators were surrounded by a macabre sort of glamour: they had their own fan clubs, and sometimes banquets were put on at which the public could meet the next day's combatants.

Perhaps the most disturbing aspect of all this is that people enjoyed it so much. When a gladiator was on the point of dispatching his victim, the crowd would scream "Bene lava!" ("Wash yourself well [in blood]"), a homely little tag usually found on the doorsteps of houses and public baths.

Over the road from the museum and across the rail line are the remains of a **smaller amphitheatre**, hardly in the same state as the big one but free and open all the time, and less-visited. This small version was built first.

Another patch of **Roman excavations** can be found just outside town; take avenue Hedi Chaker – the Sousse road – west for about a kilometre until you come to the last house on the right. Then turn sharp left up a track that heads straight back towards the big amphitheatre. The excavations begin immediately on the left, with another group 100m straight in front. A left turn there will take you to a third group, and beyond that a fourth. Unless you want a walk in the sun, none of these scattered bits of stone is really worth the effort.

Practicalities

The **train station** lies on the central square, with services to Sfax, Sousse, Tunis, Gafsa, Metlaoui and Gabès. Staff at the train station will store your bags while you visit the amphitheatre and museum (2TD per piece). **Louages** cluster directly opposite, most of them headed for Mahdia, but some for Sousse and the occasional one to Tunis, Sfax or Kairouan (the latter is not an official route: you have to arrange this in complicity with the driver). SNTRI **buses** run services to Sfax, Sousse and Tunis that stop across the square, and STS buses to Mahdia depart from the front of the archeological institute by the museum. Note that there's no direct public transport to Kairouan.

There is a **tourist office** (daily May–Oct 8am–2pm, Nov–April 8.30am–1pm & 3–5.45pm; ☎03/630438) next to the amphitheatre which can provide you with a leaflet about the site if nothing else. There are a couple of **banks** in town, a **post office** (country hours) and a **taxiphone office** (daily 8am–9pm) by the amphitheatre, and a

Magasin Général **supermarket** on avenue Bourguiba near the main square. **Market day** is Monday in the main square. The main festival, the **International Festival of Symphonic Music** (☎03/630438, ⓔfestinter.eljemm@planet.tn), occurs in July with both classical Arabé music (including Mahlouf) and classical European orchestral performances in the amphitheatre. If you want to **stay** in town, the one-star *Hôtel Julius* (☎03/690044; ❸), right next to the station, is friendly and helpful, and a couple of its rooms offer glimpses of the amphitheatre, although the hooting from passing trains may disturb you. **Food** is available at the *Hôtel Julius* after 7pm, and at the *Restaurant du Bonheur* nearby. For something cheaper, there are a couple of *gargotes* around the marketplace by the main square. The hotel is the only place in town where alcohol is served.

Sfax and around

صفاقس

The writer Ronald Firbank once took it into his head to call **SFAX** "the most beautiful city in the world", for which he has been ridiculed ever since by travel writers, their readers and at least one mayor of the town. Granted some exaggeration, Sfax *is* a much more attractive place than is usually supposed. Somehow everything seems a little easier here, from bureaucratic operations to a certain no-nonsense attitude that other Tunisians often dislike. Indeed, with its two excellent museums and consistently underrated Medina, Sfax can claim to be the most sophisticated town in the country. Ferries also run regularly to the **Kerkennah Islands**, another good reason for passing through.

Some history

Sfax's lack of interest in tourism is significant: as the wealthiest, most successful city in the country, it has no need to rely on tourists either for revenues or for self-esteem. Founded in 849 near the site of a small Roman town, Taparura, Sfax took its name from a species of cucumber (*faqous* in Arabic) and made its money from a trading fleet and the products of the Sahel's olive trees. By the tenth century it was already wealthy.

During the **Hilalian invasion**, a member of the Zirid family, one Ibn Melil, set up a principality in Sfax, with hopes of reuniting Tunisia around it, but the Normans already had their eyes on it, and it fell to them in 1148. The Sfaxians plotted their resistance and began manufacturing arms in secret. Posing as beggars, they went from door to door recruiting fighters. As a signal they would be given beans of a number corresponding to the number of combat-worthy men in the house. Then, on New Year's Eve 1156, celebrated by the Christians with fireworks and a procession of bejewelled cows, they mingled with the Normans and surprised them mid-carnival, recapturing the town. With money from the cows' gold, they built the "Cisternes des Vaches" a few hundred metres northwest of the Medina – the site is now a school, but the district still bears the name – and even today New Year's Eve is celebrated in Sfax with beans and fireworks.

In 1546, under the crumbling rule of the Hafsids, Sfax again became a principality under the cruel adventurer **El Mokkani**. It was rescued fifteen years later by the pirate **Dragut**, who reunited it with the rest of Tunisia. Then began the period of Sfax's greatest prosperity, which reached its height in the eighteenth century. When the French came in 1881 they met fiercer resistance here than anywhere else, and the city was bombarded by nine warships and four gunboats. Having taken Sfax, the French proceeded to sack the city, profane its mosques and kill hundreds of its inhabitants. Later it was here that **Farhat Hached**, the UGTT leader, found fertile ground for trade unionist resistance to French rule.

Today, Sfax occupies a unique position in Tunisia. Politically, the Sfaxian lobby is very powerful, its clout deriving from its commercial pre-eminence, which by now is

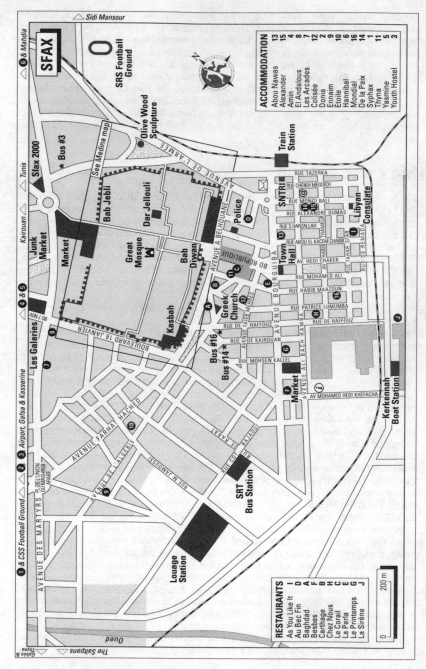

SFAX

ACCOMMODATION
Abou Nawas	13
Alexander	15
Amin	4
El Andalous	8
Les Arcades	7
Colisée	12
Donia	2
Ennaim	9
Etoile	10
Hannibal	6
Mondial	16
De la Paix	14
Syphax	1
Thyna	11
Yasmine	5
Youth Hostel	3

RESTAURANTS
As You Like It	I
Au Bec Fin	D
Baghdad	A
Besbes	F
Carthage	B
Chez Nous	H
Le Corail	C
La Perla	E
Le Printemps	G
La Sirène	J

Tunisian lore. Sfaxians are known as "the Jews of Tunisia" (an indication of residual anti-Semitism), and the stories and proverbs about their competitive nature are endless. Feelings about Sfax in the rest of the country consist of a mixture of admiration, envy and resentment, while the Sfaxians just go about their business.

Arrival and information

Sfax's main thoroughfare, avenue Bourguiba, runs roughly east–west across town. The modern town centre is spread astride it, with the Medina to its north. Arriving by **train** or SNTRI **bus**, you will find yourself at its eastern end, still pretty well in the town centre. Arriving by SRT **bus**, you'll be dropped off at the western end of town, as you will if you arrive by **louage**. The louage station is 200m west of the bus station along the same street. You can take a taxi from the bus or louage stations (1.5TD to most parts of town), or turn right down rue Commandant Bejaoui, and walk a few hundred metres to the western end of avenue Bourguiba. Sfax's **airport** is 7km west of town, from where taxis to the city centre cost around 3TD; the #14 bus also travels into town from the main road outside the airport.

The **ONTT tourist office** is on avenue Mohamed H Khefacha, near the Kerkennah boat station (Sept–June Mon–Thurs 8.30am–1pm & 3–5.45pm, Fri & Sat 8.30am–1.30pm; July & Aug Mon–Sat, and usually also Sun, 7.30am–1.30pm; ☎04/497041). The staff are very friendly, and they have a number of maps, information leaflets and handouts.

Accommodation

The Medina has a variety of cheap and basic **hotels** – mostly very basic and unsuitable for women travelling alone (the *Ennacer* is an exception, and *El Medina* and *Hôtel du Sud* also claim to be suitable for women). There is a better-value budget option, the *La Paix*, in town, as well as a couple of classy joints if you prefer more comfort. Mid-range, you get a slightly wider choice, and if the town-centre hotels are full, there are others further afield, notably to the west of town. A number of upmarket establishments cater mainly for visiting business people. Hotel **prices** in Sfax do not vary with the season, though this may change if, as planned, a *zone touristique* opens up north of town. For the very cheapest Medina hotels, you usually pay per bed rather than per room.

Medina hotels

El Andalous, 64 rue Mongi Slim ☎04/220903. Grotty but friendly. No showers but there is a hammam nearby. Not recommended for women. ❶

Bali, rue Hadstrubal (no phone). Very basic, even by Medina standards. Only one double room available, otherwise pay for a bed, or all in a three- or four-bed room if you want it to yourselves. Not recommended for women. ❶

Besbes, 23 rue Borj el Nar ☎04/210962. Far from luxury, but clean and reasonable for the (very cheap) price. ❶

Ennacer, 100 rue des Notaires ☎04/211037. Bright and clean, the best hotel in the Medina, with spotless communal showers (though hot water can be sporadic) and a roof terrace. ❷

El Habib, 25 rue Borj el Nar ☎04/221373. A cut above most of the other Medina cheapies. Some rooms have their own toilet, though showers are communal. ❶

El Jemia, 89 rue Mongi Slim ☎04/221342. Reasonably clean, with communal showers and hot water at least some of the time. Not recommended for women. ❶

El Jerid, 61 rue Mongi Slim (no phone). Small rooms around a sunny landing above a clothing shop, clean and very cheap. ❶

El Magreb, 18 rue Borj el Nar ☎04/220057. Basic but clean, friendly, and dirt cheap, with shared showers and hot water at least some of the time. **❶**

El Medina, 53 rue Mongi Slim ☎04/220354. Cleanest, friendliest and the most respectable of the rue Mongi Slim hotels. Should be fine for women (indeed the sexes have separate toilets). **❶**

Moktar, 19 rue Borj el Nar ☎04/220892. Friendly though pretty basic – no washbasin in the rooms for example, though there are shared showers with hot water at least some of the time, and rock-bottom prices. **❶**

Hôtel du Sud, 42 rue Dar Essebai ☎04/211324. Family-run with very basic rooms but prices to match, plus spotless toilet and shower facilities, and a nice patio with tiled seats. **❶**

New Town hotels

Abou Nawas ★★★★, av Bourguiba ☎04/225700, ℱ225521, ℰsfax@abounawas.com.tn. Well-placed hotel with all mod cons including a rooftop pool, but rather business-oriented and the service is not all that great. **❻**

Alexander ★, 21 rue Alexandre Dumas ☎ & ℱ04/221613. Next door to the central *La Paix* and rather more sedate, with good value en-suite rooms and friendly, efficient staff. **❸**

Colisée ★, 32 av Taïeb Mehiri ☎04/227800, ℱ299350. Friendly, comfortable and central. All rooms en suite with a choice of shower or tub, plus TV and a/c in some. **❹**

Mondial, 46 rue Habib Maazoun ☎04/226622, ℱ299350. Decent and good-value en-suite rooms, pretty comfortable, though the slightly shabby boudoir-style furniture is a little strange. **❸**

Hôtel de la Paix, 17 rue Alexandre Dumas ☎04/296437, ℱ298463. An old favourite, and cheapest of the city-centre bunch. Safe and friendly if rather sombre, with some rooms en suite. The cheapest single rooms (5TD) on the roof cost no more than a bed in the small Medina hotels, and are far better value. **❷**

Thyna ★★, 35 rue Habib Maazoun ☎04/225317, ℱ225773. A bit run-down but comfortable enough, with en-suite rooms, most with a/c, and all with a phone. **❸**

Hotels out of the centre

Amin ★★, av Mejida Boulila ☎04/245600, ℱ245603. On a busy road north of town near the hospital, and rather better value than the nearby three-stars. All rooms en suite with a/c and satellite TV, though the perfumed air-freshener they spray them out with every day is a definite minus point. **❹**

El Andalous ★★★, av des Martyrs ☎04/405406, ℱ406425. Not to be confused with the hotel of the same name in the Medina, this place is large and efficient, catering for tourists and business-people alike, with quite small but very comfortable rooms, all with a/c and satellite TV. **❹**

Les Arcades ★★★, av des Martyrs ☎04/400700, ℱ405522. A slightly pricier competitor to the *El Andalous*, with quite spacious rooms, bigger at the front but quieter at the back, all with a/c and satellite TV. There's a big garden out back, and underground parking facilities. **❺**

Donia ★★, rte de l'Aéroport ☎04/247714, ℱ248552, ℠www.doniahotel.com. Used as an overnight stop by Land Rover tour groups and by visiting sports teams (with conference rooms for pre-match briefings and team meals). Rather pricey but handy for the sports stadium. **❹**

Ennaim, 46 rue Mauritanie ☎04/227564, ℱ220363. Off av de l'Algérie beyond the *Étoile*. Large, pleasant rooms, some en suite (second floor rooms are better than the first floor ones), and all with a phone. There's no bar, but a café downstairs. **❷**

Étoile ★, 9 rue Mohamed Janoussi ☎04/296091. Off av Farhat Hached west of town, the *Étoile* is quiet, amiable and good value. Some rooms en suite. **❸**

Hannibal, rue Mohamed Rachid Ridha, off rte de Mahdia ☎04/234329. 2km from the centre, Sfax's only pension is a bit tatty but eccentric and characterful, as well as quiet and good value, with spacious rooms, massive bathrooms and the possibility of full board. **❷**

Syphax ★★★★, rte de Soukra ☎04/243333, ℱ245226, ℰsangho.syphax@planet.tn. Way out of town beyond the football ground, and hardly worth the effort considering the price, though the pool and gardens are very pleasant, the staff are efficient and the food is good. **❺**

Yasmine, av 7 Novembre, 200m north of av des Martyrs ☎04/401000, ℱ402004. A new hotel, gleaming and immaculate, of three-star standard, with nice-sized, cosy rooms, a/c and satellite TV, and tasteful red and white tiled bathrooms. **❹**

Youth hostel

Maison des Jeunes, rte de l'Aéroport ☎ 04/243207, ℱ 246745. At the beginning of the airport road. Clean three- and four-bed dorms (5TD), with communal toilet and segregated showers; closed 8am–3pm; 10pm curfew. Camping possible.

The New Town

At first the city seems to vindicate all criticism with its sprawling suburbs of housing and industry, but Sfax's centre is as compact as that of Sousse. The Medina is separated from the port by a French grid-plan **new town** that is pretty light on things to see but contains almost everything you need in the way of facilities. The pedestrianized **boulevard de l'Indépendance** connects the Medina's main entrance at **Bab Diwan** to the thoroughfare that runs through the new town, **avenue Bourguiba**.

The new town was largely rebuilt after heavy bombardment during World War II, and today it's less crowded and more open than the Medina, with paved esplanades, genuinely green spaces and tree-lined streets. Being right on the sea, the climate is also less oppressive, and there's a large port with a busy daily **fish market**. As well as fish, sponges and seashells are landed: there's a warehouse for these at 1 av MH Khefacha, next to the *Besbes Restaurant*, where you can pop in and buy a genuine sponge for your bathroom.

Very stylish, if a touch incongruous, is the French-looking clock tower on the **town hall** in place Hedi Chaker, which houses the musty and rather neglected **Archeological Museum** (Mon–Sat 8.30am–1pm & 3–6pm; 1.1TD). Room 1 (the entrance hall) holds Islamic antiquities including a couple of Korans with beautiful calligraphy. Room 2 has early Christian relics from La Skhirra, including mosaics from the sixth century Basilica, and a nicely executed fifth- or sixth-century mosaic of Daniel in the lions' den. Room 3 contains Roman relics, including a third-century funerary urn painted with scenes of people hunting and fishing, some rare fragments of second-century frescoes, a third-century mosaic featuring two pairs of naked wrestlers, and a collection of oil lamps illustrating their development from Punic through Roman and Byzantine to early Islamic styles. Room 4, an area to the right of the stairs, has one headless statue and nothing else. Room 5, long, thin and ill-lit, houses fragments of mosaics from Thyna that are difficult to see well because there is no room to stand back and look at them. Room 6, with a similar viewing problem, has an interesting mosaic of an amphitheatrical bear hunt. Finally, Room 7, to the left of the stairs, contains prehistoric stone tools and decorated pieces of ostrich egg-shell from near Gafsa, relics of the Capsian culture.

Admirers of **Art Nouveau architecture** will find interest in nos. 39–41 av Bourguiba, a stucco confection on the corner of rue Patrice Lumumba, while the colonial mock-Moorish style of the castle-like building on the corner of avenue Bourguiba and avenue Hedi Chaker (opposite the Town Hall) is worth a second glance, as are the cherub-surmounted windows of no. 10 rue d'Athènes, behind the Greek Orthodox church.

The Medina

Sfax's **Medina** differs from many in Tunisia in that it is still a thriving community. This is no tourist spectacle, but a real city where people live and work, and you won't find souvenir stalls or tour groups trailing after a guide. Not that you'll be made to feel in any way unwelcome; on the contrary, the pleasant reaction you get in the shops where Sfaxians make routine purchases comes as a refreshing contrast to the tedious "Kommen Sie hier, mein Freund" of Tunis and Kairouan's souvenir emporiums. The Medina is changing however, becoming more commercial in fact, as residents move

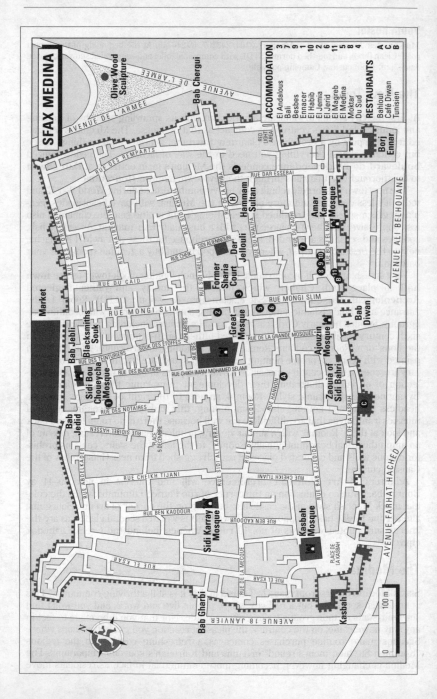

SFAX MEDINA

Olive Wood Sculpture

AVENUE DE L'ARMÉE

Bab Chergui

AVENUE DE L'ARMÉE

RED LIGHT AREA

RUE DES REMPARTS

RUE SID KHELIL

RUE DES FORGERONS

RUE KHAIREDDINE

RUE DE LA DRIBA

RUE DAR ESSEBAI

Hammam Sultan

(H)

Dar Jellouli

SIDI AIENNOURI

RUE CHEIK

RUE DU KHALIFA

Amar Kamoun Mosque

RUE DU CADHI

RUE SIDI KHELIL

Former Sharia Court

RUE DU CAID

3

RUE MONGI SLIM

RUE BORJ EL NAR

7

8 9 10

B 10

Market

Bab Jebli

Blacksmiths Souk

RUE MONGI SLIM

RUE DES TEINTURIERS

2

RUE DS ADRARTES

5

6

RUE MONGI SLIM

Bab Diwan

Sidi Bou Choueycha Mosque

SOUK DES ÉTOFFES

RUE DES BIJOUTIERS

Great Mosque

RUE DE LA GRANDE MOSQUÉE

Ajouzin Mosque

Borj Ennar

Bab Jedid

RUE DES NOTAIRES

RUE CHIKH IMAM MOHAMED SELAMI

A

Zaouia of Sidi Bahri

RUE DE LA MECQUE

RUE SIDI ALI KARRAY

RUE SIDIBEL HASSEN

PLACE 5 DÉCEMBRE

RUE MANNOUN

C

RUE DE LA KASBAH

Bab Gharbi

RUE ABDELKADER

RUE CHEIKH TIJANI

RUE CHEIKH TIJANI

RUE BAB EL JEDIDE

RUE BEN KADDOUR

Sidi Karray Mosque

RUE BEN KADDOUR

Kasbah Mosque

RUE EL KSAR

RUE EL KSAR

RUE DE LA MECQUE

PLACE DE LA KASBAH

Kasbah

AVENUE 18 JANVIER

AVENUE FARHAT HACHED

AVENUE ALI BELHOUANE

N

0   100 m

ACCOMMODATION	
El Andalous	3
Bali	7
Besbes	9
Ennacer	1
El Habib	10
El Jemia	2
El Jerid	6
El Magreb	11
El Medina	5
Moktar	8
Du Sud	4

RESTAURANTS	
Bahloul	A
Café Diwan	C
Tunisien	B

out and businesses move in, but it only serves to make the place even more animated, except for Mondays, when businesses within the walls are closed.

The Medina's near-complete **ramparts** make for a dramatic first impression. In view of the many bombardments the city has endured, they are in remarkable shape, with some parts dating back to the ninth century. If you want to walk around the walls on the inside, you can follow them almost all of the way in the Medina's western corner from Bab Jedid to Bab Gharbi. One curious feature of the Medina is the multitude of first-floor **workshops**: narrow staircases lead up to these cramped rooms, where small businesses – tailors, shoemakers, engravers – beaver away using traditional techniques and equipment. Few of them mind being interrupted, and their terraces offer wonderful rooftop views.

The **Kasbah** in the Medina's southern corner was originally constructed in 1849 as a ribat, and was later the governor's residence and the headquarters of the town's militia. It is now restored as the **Museum of Traditional Architecture** (Tues–Sun 9.30am–4.30pm; 1.1TD), featuring exhibits on private, public and religious buildings, but the best thing about it is that you can climb up the bastions and walk along the battlements. On leaving, check out the attractive tiled doorway of the school across the square. Just north is the whitewashed **Sidi Karray Mosque**, dating back to 1654 and surrounded by some classic Sfaxian doorways decorated in pink Gabès stone, notably that of 31 rue Ben Kaddour. The mosque is the focus of Sfax's Mouled festivities to celebrate the Prophet's birthday.

Rue de la Kasbah runs alongside the southern wall from the Kasbah, past *Le Café Diwan* and into place de la Journée de Tunis. On the corner as you come into the square is the **Zaouia of Sidi Bahri**; note the double inscription above the door, again in pink Gabès stone. If you cross the square from here, the multiple arches of **Bab Diwan**, the Medina's main entrance, are to your right. As at Tunis, Bizerte and Sousse, this main gate into the Medina was once much closer to the sea. Only its westernmost, horseshoe entrance is ancient, going back to the fourteenth century. Along with Bab Jebli, it was one of just two original city gates, both still retaining their iron-clad doors, which were once closed nightly.

The Dar Jellouli Museum and around

To your left, opposite the inward side of Bab Diwan, is the **Ajouzin Mosque**, restored in the nineteenth century. Rue de la Grande Mosquée runs next to it, up towards the Great Mosque. Straight on down rue Borj el Nar, the **Amar Kamoun Mosque** – right, after about 150m – is between nos. 50 and 52. Look out for its small stone minaret. The mosque was rebuilt, like so many of Sfax's monuments, in the eighteenth century, when the city became a major commercial centre. But the style of the minaret gives away its earlier origins.

Another 200m along the same street to the end, then a right, and a right at the end again, brings you to the entrance of the **Borj Ennar** (Mon–Thurs 9am–noon & 3–5pm, Fri & Sat 9am–noon), a fortress built to guard the Medina's eastern corner, now the headquarters of the ASM, and accessible to the public. The area alongside the wall to the north of Borj Ennar is a red light district, best avoided, and in any case walled off so that there is no through access. West of the Borj's entrance, some cobbled steps lead down into a small square where a gateway on the left leads out of the Medina, while on the right, a small archway brings you back into rue Borj el Nar, emerging between nos. 76 and 78. Cross rue Borj el Nar and take rue Dar Essebai, straight ahead of you. At the end, turn left into rue de la Driba, past **Hammam Sultan** on your left, Sfax's oldest bathhouse, restored in the eighteenth century but dating back to Hafsid times; after the hammam you will see the Dar Jellouli Museum just to the right ahead of you, on rue Cheikh Sidi Ali Ennouri.

The **Dar Jellouli Regional Museum of Popular Arts and Traditions** (Tues–Sun 9.30am–4.30pm; 1.1TD) is not to be missed, housed in a seventeenth-century residence as interesting as the exhibits themselves. As in the Dar Ben Abdallah museum in Tunis, these illustrate local life, with costumes, utensils and manuscripts. One exhibit demonstrates how rose water is made, another shows how Tunisian women traditionally prepare their kohl eyeliner. There's even an old kif pipe similar to the ones still used in Morocco (though not Tunisia) today.

Leaving the museum, turn left and continue up rue Cheikh Sidi Ali Ennouri, which brings you to a small square. Rue Sidi Khelil, left off the square under a small archway, takes you past the former courthouse on the left (nos. 36–40). Just beyond, you cross **rue Mongi Slim**, one of the Medina's main thoroughfares and perpetually bustling. Rather than get caught up in the flow, however, carry straight on past **place Souk el Jemaa**, the site of a hectic Friday market, and you come out into rue de la Grande Mosquée, facing the northeastern wall of the Great Mosque.

The Great Mosque

Sfax's **Great Mosque**, though at first sight lower and less imposing than its contemporaries at Kairouan and Sousse, repays closer inspection. Unfortunately, it is not possible to enter unless you are Muslim, but non-Muslims can look in through the windows, which are normally open.

Begun in 849 by the Aghlabids, the mosque was extensively rebuilt in the tenth century under heavy Fatimid influence and remains one of the most distinctive buildings from that era – more so even than Mahdia's own Great Mosque. The most characteristic feature is the series of niches on the east facade, crowned by toothlike rims – a form of articulation quite foreign to both the simple Aghlabid style and the later, more sophisticated calm of the Hafsid styles.

This love of movement in external decoration is even more apparent in the **minaret**, whose wedding-cake layers of decoration are highly unusual for this region; the geometric bands, round windows and religious inscription seem almost frenzied compared to the Kairouan minaret. You can see the minaret from next to its western corner at the junction of rue des Aghlabites with rue Cheikh Imam Mohamed Selami, or climb up to a terrace for a clearer view – the best are from the top of one staircase between nos.59 and 61 rue Cheikh Imam Mohamed Selami, and another in the entrance to the teahouse at 5 rue des Aghlabites, where you can also get an excellent cup of green tea.

A curiosity worth looking out for is the stone embedded above the fourth window from the left in the mosque's northeastern facade. Originally Byzantine, it depicted two peacocks (the ancient Greek symbol of eternity or immortality) surrounded by grapevines and small birds, with a Greek inscription above and probably a cup or fountain between them. Such obvious pictures of animals and plants are very rare in Islamic architecture, but the spirit of the inscription ("Good deeds and happiness accompanying them enrich Your holy abode") was considered sufficiently Muslim for its inclusion in the mosque.

The souks

Heading north from the Great Mosque, you pass under an arch into rue des Aghlabites, on the other side of which is the area of the main souks. More or less straight ahead is the **Souk des Étoffes**, specializing in fabrics, with rich garments all around, gradually giving way to carpets as you move up the souk. Parallel, one street to the left, is rue des Bijoutiers, the **jewellers' souk**. Cross rue Okba at the end of Souk des Étoffes, and follow rue des Teinturiers (once the dyers' souk) until you come to **Bab Jebli**, currently closed, but one of the city's original gates and worth a glance.

Just to the left is the **Sidi Bou Choueycha Mosque**, recently restored. The older of its two prayer halls is Zirid or Hafsid, but the later one, added in 1683, marked a new phase in Sfaxian architecture, establishing a style which was to dominate eighteenth-century construction in the city. If you are Muslim, you should definitely pop in for a look at the stonework and tiled *mihrab*. In the other direction, opposite no. 19 in rue des Forgerons, an archway leads through to the **blacksmiths' souk**, where the smiths are hard at work amid the noise and grime. However, a glance at the upper storey, reached via a staircase to your left as you go through the archway, reveals that this was once a *fondouk* and in fact it dates back to the tenth century. It was associated with Bab Jebli, outside which there was a marshalling point for trans-Saharan caravans, whose passengers would stay overnight at the *fondouk*. More recently, it featured as a Cairo bazaar in the film of *The English Patient*.

Coming out of the blacksmiths' souk, a right turn brings you to the end of rue Mongi Slim, which leads straight back to Bab Diwan. Opposite the end of rue Mongi Slim, crowds squeeze through a narrow Medina entrance in a crush worthy of Cairo. On the other side of it is a large food **market** complex, one of the most successful modern uses of the old vaulted forms to be seen in Tunisia, and, unlike so many other new market buildings, a delight to wander through.

Eating and drinking

As with accommodation, the Medina is the obvious place to go for **budget eating**. On the other hand, if you feel like treating yourself, you'll find the expense well worth it, as Sfax has some first-class restaurants at prices that are very cheap by Western standards, though often quite pricey by Tunisian ones. Sfax is noted in Tunisia for its fish and seafood cuisine, but there are those who avoid the local fish because of sea pollution from the phosphate plant just south of town. Note that many of the best restaurants are closed on Friday.

Medina restaurants

Restaurant Bahloul, 25 rue Hannon. Hidden away inside the Medina, this is a clean and good-value cheap place to have lunch, but unfortunately closes too early for supper. Daily 8am–3pm.

Restaurant Tunisien, 16 rue Borj el Nar. Best of a number of cheap places just inside Bab Diwan, serving spit-roast chicken, couscous and basic Tunisian dishes at very low prices. Daily 9am–10pm.

New Town restaurants

Alexander, in the *Hôtel Alexander*, 21 rue Alexandre Dumas ☎04/221911. The restaurant here is one of the best value eating places in town, with excellent meat and fish dishes (prawn bisque, prawn brochette, stuffed squid) at comparatively moderate prices, with a 7TD set menu. Daily 10am–3pm & 6–11pm.

As You Like It, 19 rue Tahar Sfar, corner of rue Abou el Kacem Chabbi. Offers budget-priced "hot fast food" including pizzas, burgers, spaghetti with seafood, and crêpes for dessert. Mon–Fri 11.30am–8pm, Sat 11.30am–10pm.

Restaurant Au Bec Fin, pl 2 Mars, opposite the post office. Pleasantly situated and with decent, if not very exciting, reasonably priced fare. Mon–Sat noon–3pm & 6–9.30pm, Sun noon–3pm.

Restaurant Baghdad, 63 av Farhat Hached ☎04/223856. Excellent Tunisian cooking, some would say the best in town, a little pricey à la carte, but there is a 7TD set menu. Daily except Fri noon–3pm & 7–11pm.

Restaurant Besbes, 79 av Bourguiba. On the corner of av Mohamed H. Khefacha, with very inexpensive couscous, meat or fish dishes. Daily 8am–10pm.

Restaurant Carthage, 63 av Ali Belhouane ☎04/212299. Handily located, more or less opposite Bab Diwan. Seafood dishes including octopus in sauce and spaghetti *aux fruits de mer* at high but not outrageous prices, though the service is a bit snooty, and you may well hear the ping of a microwave from the kitchen when your dish is ready. Daily except Fri 11.30am–3pm & 6–10.30pm.

Chez Nous, 26 rue Patrice Lumumba ☎04/227128. Good food and meticulous service, at relatively moderate prices. Daily noon–3pm & 6.30–10.30pm.

Le Corail, 39 rue Habib Maazoun ☎ 04/227301. Fairly chic, with fine cooking, but angling for the moneyed tourist market. Mon–Sat 11.30am–3pm & 6–11.30pm.

La Perla, 18 av Bourguiba ☎ 04/229036. Good Tunisian food at moderate prices, with entertainment in the form of a singer from about 8.30pm nightly. Daily noon–midnight or later.

Le Printemps, 55 av Bourguiba ☎ 04/226973. Very smart, with excellent and not too pricey French cooking, and a 10TD set menu available. Mon–Sat noon–2.30pm & 6–10pm.

La Sirène, by the port ☎ 04/224691. Across the train line from the bottom of rue Haffouz, or across the bridge from the Kerkennah ferry port. Excellent, though expensive, fish restaurant – choose your fish and have it barbecued while you wait. Great octopus salad among other seafood entrées. Daily except Fri noon–3pm & 6–11pm.

Drinks and snacks

For a cup of tea or coffee, head for the *Le Café Diwan* off rue de la Kasbah by no. 37 (daily 7am–midnight) – an amazing place, actually inside the city wall. Go upstairs for a better view. With pine-nut tea, rose-water Turkish coffee, a relaxed atmosphere and, arguably, the smoothest *chicha* in the country, it's recommended for women as well as men. Other coffee bars – and alcohol bars – are located around boulevard de la République and in the grid zone south of avenue Bourguiba. These tend to be rather raucous and very male-dominated. A quieter, and more female-friendly, beer can be had at the bars of hotels like the *Alexander*, the *Colisée*, the *Andalous*, the *Arcades*, and the *Donia*. The bars of the *Colisée* and the *Thyna* may also be places to make contacts for gay men.

For those with a sweet tooth, a number of places in rue de la Grande Mosquée in the Medina do waffles with chocolate sauce: try nos. 73 or 77.

Listings

Airlines Air France, c/o Yassine Travel Agency, 15 rue Taïeb Mehiri ☎ 04/224847; Tunis Air, 4 av de l'Armée ☎ 04/228028 also represent Tuninter.

Banks Banks are mainly concentrated on av Bourguiba and bd de la République; STB in bd de la République is probably the best, but they may not change money until the daily rates come in around 9am. One bank will be open at weekends. BIAT by the *Hôtel Abou Nawas* in av Bourguiba has an ATM that accepts Visa and Mastercard. The post office will change cash.

Bookshops Librairie la Caravelle, 22 av Bourguiba on the corner of rue Habib Maazoun has some English titles – mainly classics, but also some recent bestsellers. A bookshop at Arbi Zarrouk with Mohsen Kallel has a very few second-hand titles in English.

Car rental Avis, rue Tahar Sfar, at rue H Maazoun ☎ 04/224605; Europcar, 40 rue Tahar Sfar ☎ 04/226680; Hertz, 47 av Bourguiba ☎ 04/228626. A number of small firms have their offices around the junction of rue Habib Maazoun and rue Tahar Sfar.

Car repairs and spares Mechanics and car spares stores are concentrated along and between av des Martyrs and av Farhat Hached in the area to the east of place de l'Union du Maghreb Arabe.

Cinemas Atlas, 103 av Hedi Chaker; Le Colisée, 27 rue Tahar Sfar at av Hedi Chaker; Étoile, 50 bd de la République. Opposite the Étoile is the municipal theatre, where plays, classical concerts and dance events are held, especially during the summer festival.

Consulates Libya, 35 rue Alexandre Dumas ☎ 04/223332; has been known to issue visas, but at last check was sending people to Tunis to apply. UK, honorary consul: Moncef Sellami, 1st Floor, 55 rue Habib Maazoun ☎ 04/223971.

Ferry companies CTN, 75 rue Habib Maazoun ☎ 04/228022; Sonotrak, Kerkennah boat station ☎ 04/222216.

Festivals The International Festival of Sfax in July and August features cultural events including music, dance and theatre. Also in July, there's a "fantasia" of traditional Arab equestrianism in Agareb, 22km west of Sfax.

Football Sfax's main club, the Club Sportif de Sfax (CSS), has its ground behind the youth hostel near the beginning of the airport road. Sfax Railway Sport (SRS) play in among the railway sidings just south of av 13 Août.

Hammam Hammam Sultan, 78 rue de la Driba, near the Dar Jellouli museum (daily: men 6am–noon & 7pm–midnight, women noon–6pm).

Internet access Publinet offices are at 7 rue Ali Bach Hamba (daily 8.30am–midnight; 2TD/hr) and on rue Ahmed Sikelli, 50m north of av des Martyrs near the *Hôtel des Arcades* (Mon–Sat 9am–11pm, Sun 2.30–11pm; 2TD/hr].

Hospitals The main hospital is on route de l'Aïn, west of the town centre ☎04/244511, with the Polyclinique Ettawfik on bd des Martyrs at the corner of rue Hedi Nouira ☎04/404306, and the Polyclinique Zitouna further east on bd des Martyrs opposite the Sfax 2000 building ☎04/211611.

Newspapers English language papers are available at two kiosks off the southern end of bd de la République: in a little square diagonally opposite the town hall, and in Marburg at the junction of rue Habib Maazoun and rue Léopold Senghor, in front of the *Hôtel Thyna*.

ONA crafts shop 10 rue Lt Hamadi Taj, beween rue Alexandre Dumas and rue Abou el Kacem Chabbi (Mon–Sat 9am–noon & 3–6.45pm).

Pharmacy There's a night pharmacy at 32 Les Galeries, 50m up bd 7 Novembre from av des Martyrs.

Post office Av Bourguiba, by the train station (city hours).

Police Rue Victor Hugo, off av Ali Belhouane behind av de la République ☎04/229700.

Pool halls If you're at a loss for something to do of an evening, there are two pool halls on rue de Haffouz at nos. 51 and 125.

Supermarkets Monoprix has a branch at 12 rue Abou el Kacem Chabbi, and another in the Sfax 2000 building on bd des Martyrs (the latter has more convenient hours: daily 8.30am–7pm with no break for lunch). Also Zeitouna at the corner of rue Kairouan and av de l'Algérie.

MOVING ON FROM SFAX

For a rundown of destinations and journey times, see Travel Details on pp.257–258.

The **train station** is central and easy to find, right at the eastern end of avenue Bourguiba (☎04/221999.

As for **buses**, city bus #16 to the war cemetery and out towards the Thyna turn-off can be picked up in rue Haffouz near the corner of rue Léopold Senghor, and #3 to Sidi Mansour from just off boulevard des Martyrs opposite the Mahdia louage station. Both run every twenty minutes during the day. Otherwise, **SNTRI buses** stop opposite the train station in rue Tazerka (☎04/222355), with regular departures to Tunis and Sousse – via El Jem or Mahdia – and one continuing to Bizerte. The **SRT bus station** is down near the other end of avenue Bourguiba in rue Commandant Bejaoui, opposite the end of rue de Rabat. From here, buses serve Gabès, Gafs, Kasserine, Le Kef, Mahdia, Medenine, Ben Gardane, Jerba, Kairouan, and Nefta (via Tozeur, Moulares and Redeyef). Buses also run to Mahrès, La Chebba, Sidi Bou Zid and Agareb. Note that SRT Gafsa has its own section of the bus station; other firms use the main part, which belongs to SORETRAS.

Louages all now leave from a single station, 200m west of the SRT bus station on in rue Commandant Bejaoui (☎04/220071).

Ferries for the hour-long journey to the Kerkennah Islands are operated by Sonotrak, Porte de Kerkennah, rue M Hedi Khefacha (☎04/222216; passengers 0.5TD, car 4TD, motorbike 1TD), and leave seven times a day for most of the year, with up to fourteen departures a day at the height of summer. There is access if you are in a wheelchair, but you will have to spend the journey on the car deck.

Sfax's **airport** (☎04/278000) is not very well connected, but it offers flights to Tunis and to Paris, as well as charters. The airport is 7km west of town off the Gafsa road (also called route de l'Aéroport), but it is officially a military airport, so procedures are strict, and they won't take kindly to you getting your camera out. Bus #14 from rue de Kairouan, just north of avenue Taïeb Mehiri, drops you at the airport turn-off on the Gafsa road (still nearly a kilometre from the airport itself), so your best bet is to take a cab, which shouldn't cost more than 3TD or so.

Swimming There's a 25-metre municipal pool on rte de l'Aérodrome, near the youth hostel (Tues–Sat 7am–8pm, Sun 9am–1pm; 2TD for 50min, students 1TD).

Around Sfax

The nearest **beach** to Sfax is 12km to the north at **Sidi Mansour** (reached by city bus #3 from avenue de l'Armée and avenue des Martyrs). Sidi Mansour is also home to an annual festival in honour of its marabout, usually held in July or August, with horse-racing, boat-racing and music. On the way is the source of all the **olive-wood** salad bowls, chess sets and other souvenirs that are sold in Sfax's few souvenir shops: the Maison du Bois d'Olivier (☎04/272094), signposted off the road 9km out of Sfax. They usually only have a few things in stock, but you can call in advance to have things made to order, or pop in and see what's in their showroom.

To the south of Sfax, 2km down the Gabès road, the **Commonwealth War Cemetery** is as well kept as ever, next to an ordinary Christian cemetery that isn't. Indian soldiers are segregated off in a little enclosure at the back: Muslims to the right, Sikhs and Hindus to the left, together with a few graves from World War I. The cemetery can be reached from town on city bus #16.

Thyna and the Saltpans طينة

Ten kilometres south of Sfax, **Thyna** (free access) is the site of Roman Thaenae, and the source of some of the mosaics in the Sfax museum. The turn-off from the Gabès road is signposted, but not too conspicuously, so keep your eyes peeled. Any bus bound for Gabès or Mahrès should drop you there (ask for the Thyna *croisement*), and city bus #16 leaves you 300m short. From the turn-off, follow the Thyna road left towards the sea until you see a lighthouse; go straight on past it and take a track off to the right, following the arrow, just after it. The main relic here is the **Baths of the Months**, whose mosaics are still in place but covered with sand. The desultory remains to the south are a smaller **bathhouse**. Inland a little, another track runs alongside the ramparts of the Roman town. On the other side of it are the main buildings so far excavated, including

---

WILDLIFE OF THE SALTPANS OF SFAX

The saltpans south of Sfax support high winter populations of **flamingos**, rare **spoonbills**, and a variety of **herons**, **egrets**, **gulls** and **terns**. The whole area offers exceptional birdwatching, partly because of the sheer numbers and range of species, but mostly because the birds have become used to saltpan workers and shell fishers, making them very approachable. If you're remotely interested in wildlife, it's not a site to pass up.

The little inlet closest to Sfax is magical in the early morning sunlight, with hundreds of wading birds among the shell fishers. Although the biggest numbers of birds are recorded from November to the end of February, many are still present through to April, and some species (such as avocet, blackwinged stilt and redshank) stay on to breed in the coastal salt marshes surrounding the mud flats.

The feeding grounds in the mud flats beyond the saltpans are the actual reason why the birds congregate at Sfax, and a few hours watching the area gives a fascinating insight into their **feeding habits**. You'll see everything from flamingos doing their inverted side-to-side sieving of the shallow water with their huge bills, to spoonbills with their own usefully shaped mouthparts; from herons and egrets standing poised, ready to pounce, to the true waders (stints and dunlins, curlews and godwits) probing the mud, each species to a different depth and for different prey.

As well as the waders, Sfax is a good place to watch for **sea birds**, including the region's largest tern, the Caspian, with its long red beak. In winter, you can also see hundreds of **black-necked grebes**, bobbing on the water like miniature round ducks.

a **temple**, whose mosaics have been carted off to the museum, and a **Roman street** with remains of houses. Chances are, the *gardien* of the site will find you and give you a guided tour.

The **saltpans of Sfax** stretch almost continuously from Sfax to Thyna, and produce some 300,000 tonnes of top-grade sea salt a year. More significantly, they're the Mediterranean's single most important site for **wintering wading birds**, making them a focus of international scientific interest. The combination of a shallow coast and a tidal range of 1–2m – a highly unusual feature in the largely tideless Mediterranean – exposes huge areas of mud flats at low tide that are rich in the small creatures that form the bulk of a wading bird's winter diet.

You can access the southern end of the saltpans from the site at Thyna, and the whole shebang is under development as a national park. In the meantime, you can access the northern end by taking avenue de l'Algérie westward out of town, turning onto the Gabès road (boulevard de l'Environnement), and then the third left, just over the Oued. Walk up that, and the mud flats start on your right. The **entrance** to the saltpans has a gate and a high wire fence and is marked *Cotusal*, but while the mud flats are public land, they're unsafe to walk across, as well as being foully polluted with Sfax's effluent; the best way to see the birds is to wander along the banks on the seaward side of the saltpans – private land, for which you'll need to ask permission to enter at the gate. The birds are found on the mud flats at low tide, and on just a few of the saltpans, depending on their salinity. There are fifteen square kilometres of saltpans, so it may take some time to find the birds' location.

Mahrès
المحرس

Continuing south for 30km or so, you pass through MAHRÈS, an unexciting beach resort with a Monday market and three hotels. The **beach** is not really suitable for swimming, being covered with slimy green seaweed, but there's a very pleasant sandy one at **Chafaar**, 5km north along the shore or 8km up the main road; turn seaward just after a level crossing and continue down a track for 4km. You should be able to **camp** in the open air here.

If you want to **stay** in the centre of Mahrès, simple accommodation is available at the *Hôtel Younga* (✆04/290334; ➋), with the hotel entrance at the back and a very reasonable low-priced eatery at the front – the *Restaurant de la Corniche* (daily 9am–10pm), which also serves pizzas in the summer. Just north of town is the two-star *Marzouk* (✆04/290261, ℱ290866; ➍), with clean rooms, all en suite and some a/c, and a small pool; next door is the three-star *Hôtel Tamaris* (✆04/290950, ℱ290494; ➍), better value with a larger pool, with bougainvillea-wreathed gardens, and paintings in each room by the owner's wife, based on traditional carpet designs. The hotel also has rather a posh and expensive restaurant (daily 10am–3pm & 6pm–1am, musical entertainment in the evenings).

Mahrès's three **banks, taxiphone office** and, bizarrely, the skeleton of a whale, are to be found along the main street. The town hosts an annual **International Festival of the Plastic Arts** at the end of July, and it has a permanent **park of modern sculptures**, including a doughnut man, and a giant metal jasmine seller, with stairs inside his legs up to benches in his belly, which are only open during the festival. The *Caféteria du Festival* opposite is a good place to sit and watch the world go by. **Buses** and **louages** for Sfax can be picked up by the *Hôtel Younga*, and there's a bus station 100m south on the other side of the road and a **train station** inland, with five daily services to Sfax, two continuing to Sousse and Tunis, plus two daily services to Gabès, Gafsa and Metlaoui.

If you're a sucker for ruined castles, you might make the effort to get to **Borj Younga**, a Byzantine fortress rebuilt by the Aghlabids, 11km south of Mahrès. The turn-off is marked only by a stop sign, just before a couple of lone shops in the middle

---

OLIVE TREES

Whether you find the roads out of Sfax scenically appealing depends on your reaction to row upon row of **olive trees** – the age-old industry of the Sahel ever since the Romans introduced them to replace grain. It was in the early nineteenth century, however, that the olive plantations really came into their own. Most of the olive oil was shipped to Europe where, too coarse and strong-tasting for dainty European palates, it was made into soap. The markets seemed bottomless and the price high, encouraging many Sfaxians to occupy lands belonging to the surrounding Methelith tribes in order to plant trees. By the 1830s, the German traveller Prince Puckler-Muskau claimed that the trees already stretched further than the eye could see.

Most of the trees are planted a standard 20m apart, the optimum distance, and the harvest begins in November. As it has to be done by hand, the process is highly labour-intensive, with teams of seven combing the branches, protecting their fingers with hollowed-out goat horns (more recently with plastic substitutes). An average tree around Sfax produces 50kg of olives a year, almost all of them sent to factories on the outskirts of the city.

Unfortunately, recent increases in productivity and production – not only in Tunisia but throughout the Mediterranean – have led to overproduction. In the last decade prices have tumbled, and after a good harvest Tunisia can't sell the bulk of its oil, whatever the price. Now the government encourages farmers to uproot the older plantations and plant cereals, and so history has turned full circle.

---

of nowhere. From there, it's a three-kilometre walk down a track to the fort, the shell of which remains, adorned by graffiti, next to a marabout, a couple of houses and a well. It looks rather more impressive from a distance than it does when you actually reach it. Gabès-bound buses (except SNTRI services) will drop you off at the turn-off.

La Skhirra
الصّخيرة

Forty-five kilometres south of Borj Younga, and 51km north of Gabès, **LA SKHIRRA** has a big oil terminal for pipelines coming from Algeria and Tunisia. Until the second half of the nineteenth century it was simply a summer camp for the Mehadhaba tribes, then, in 1871, the Perry Bury Company of Lancashire began exporting esparto grass for paper manufacture from here. It quickly became one of the region's most important commodities and the town grew up on this British link. In case you should need to stay here, there is a two-star **hotel** 2km south of town, the *Bab Essahara* (☎04/295175, ℱ295223; ❸). The oil terminal is in fact 14km north of town at Hechichina, where there is also an archeological **site**, many of whose finds are now in the museum in Sfax, leaving little to see. Three kilometres offshore here is **Kneiss Island** and, if you're lucky, you might be able to get someone to take you over to it for some isolated birdwatching, but check with the port police first.

The Kerkennah Islands
جزير قرقنة

Throughout history the **Kerkennah Islands**, 20km off the coast of Sfax, have been a place of exile – the Carthaginian general Hannibal, Roman outcasts, adulterous Muslim wives and Habib Bourguiba have all been sent here at one time or another. Now this isolation is an attraction for tourists. Conventionally promoted as the poor folk's Jerba, the islands are distinctively quieter and make an ideal spot for doing nothing for a few days or weeks – even energetic swimming is out of the question as the sea is so shallow, though this does make it highly suitable for young children to play in.

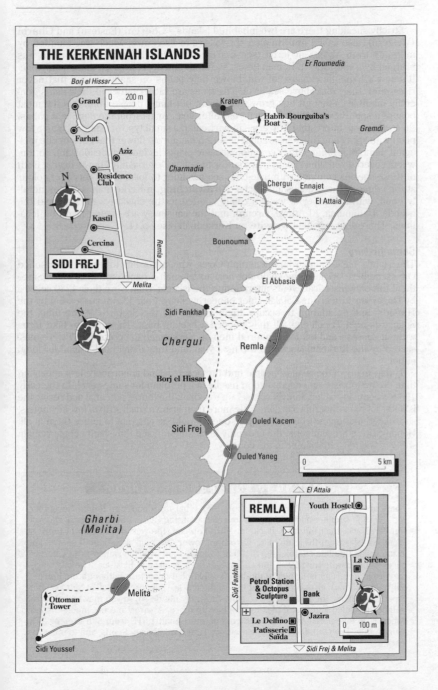

Strictly speaking there are two inhabited islands – **Chergui** (Eastern) and **Gharbi** (Western), also called **Mellita** after the village at its centre, which was founded by migrants from Mellita in Jerba (see p.378) – but the channel between them was bridged by a causeway in Roman times, so for all practical purposes there's only one. It's now a hypnotic expanse of windblown date palms on sandy ground that never rises more than 13m above sea level. The trees are rather tatty and their dates generally inedible (although figs grow well here), but many people think this the most beautiful spot they know and return year after year. Apart from the dominant palms, there are some interesting **flowers** – in particular, a small type of asphodel, and a low plant with sprawling thin leaves and a beautiful flat purple flower that goes by the inelegant name of *fagonia*. Other common seaside plants include dandelions and cottonweed, covered with fine silvery hairs and with yellow "everlasting" flowerheads. Both of these species combine with pale-blue sea lavender to form a fine carpet of colour at the edges of the beaches and rocks. **Birdwatching** in Kerkennah is also generally good, with a number of waders easily spotted in the shallow waters around the islands. Bounouma, El Attaya, Gremdi and the causeway are among favoured locations. There's an excellent **website** on Kerkennah – see p.14.

Some history

The islands' name came from the nymph **Circe** who, according to legend, imprisoned Odysseus here because she could not bear to let such a handsome man leave. Since then, the only historical events interrupting the islands' calm were their 1286 seizure by **Roger de Lluria**, the Catalan ruler of nearby Sicily, their 1335 repossession by the **Hafsids**, and an attempt to occupy them in 1510 by the Spanish. At the time, the Spaniards held Tripoli and felt they needed a backup base. They tried to take Jerba without success, and left four hundred men on Kerkennah to occupy it. All were massacred by the Kerkennians within the next year, and they didn't hold Tripoli for long, either.

Today, many of the islands' people find the desert island atmosphere less appealing than do the tourists, and depopulation has been a problem for some years. In the early 1960s a company called Somvik was set up to exploit the tourist potential and revive the islands' fortunes, but this has done little more than bring a small strip of low-key hotels, so isolated that unless you're staying in one it would be easy not to notice them at all. Happily, there are signs that the economy is picking up, and the island people remain some of the most hospitable in the country.

GETTING TO AND FROM THE ISLANDS

There are seven daily **ferries** to and from Sfax (1hr) from mid-April to mid-November, with eight in summer and as many as fourteen crossings a day at the height of the season. On Kerkennah the ferry docks at **Sidi Youssef**, the westernmost tip of the first island, not far from the crumbling **Ottoman tower**, 3km along the north shore. The island's sole **bus** line rumbles north along a single road over the causeway to Chergui; buses connect with the ferries and run to Sidi Frej, Remla and El Attaia. The other way, they leave Remla an hour before the boat's scheduled departure (although the journey only takes 25min); all except the first bus of the day are supposed to call at Sidi Frej but, especially outside the main tourist season, they may not do so, so you may be better off walking to Ouled Yaneg and picking the bus up there. A surer, and not much costlier, option is to take a **taxi**, which should cost no more than 1.5TD from Sidi Frej, or 2TD from Remla. The *Grand Hôtel* also sometimes runs a minibus to Remla, and to meet the ferries.

Sidi Frej and around   سيدي فرج

A left turning just after the causeway to Chergui leads to Kerkennah's main resort, **SIDI FREJ**, on the west coast. If heading this way by bus, make sure you take the right one when you get off the ferry, otherwise you could get dropped off at Ouled Yaneg and be left with a two-kilometre walk. That said, if you arrive on a ferry in the early morning, there probably won't be a bus to Sidi Frej, so you'll have to take a cab (1.5TD) or walk from Ouled Yaneg anyway.

Sidi Frej is on the island's west coast, and is a very pleasant and low-key place compared to the resorts at Hammamet, Sousse and Jerba, although it is rather isolated, with just a few hotels and very little else. Consequently, much revolves around the swimming pools and organized activities in the hotels.

The **beach** at Sidi Frej is certainly not the best on Kerkennah, and the *Grand Hôtel* really has the only bit worthy of the name, though it also has a **swimming pool**, which non-residents can use for a few dinars; the *Appart-Hôtel Aziz*'s is also open to non-residents for a small fee, as is the *Résidence Club*'s, which is the biggest (you can also swim in these pools free of charge if eating at the hotels' restaurants). The *Grand Hôtel* has the best facilities, including **windsurfing** (free for residents, 5TD/hr non-residents), **pedalos** (8TD/hr non-residents), and a **kids' club** organized by the Panorama tour rep. To see more of the islands, you could rent **bicycles** from the *Cercina* (1TD/hr) or the *Grand* (2.2TD/hr or 11TD/day). One short trip is to **Borj el Hissar**, a ruined fort 2km or so up the coast along a track from the hotel zone, put up by the Aghlabids on a Roman site, later rebuilt by the Spanish, and destined to become a museum. In front of it on the shore, some **Roman mosaics** have been excavated.

Five kilometres further, **Sidi Fankhal** is Kerkennah's finest beach, also accessible by piste across a salt flat from Remla on the other side of the island. Alternatively, Samir's Horse and Camel Hire in Sidi Frej (you should find him outside the entrance to the *Grand Hôtel*) offers rides to Borj el Hissar in summer.

Practicalities

You can **eat** at all the Sidi Frej hotels and, if you're lucky, try local Kerkennah specialities such as *tchich* (octopus soup) and *melthouth* (something between pasta and couscous). The *Grand Hôtel* does a moderately priced tourist set menu; otherwise you'll be paying slightly more at the *Cercina*, more still at the *Aziz*, and slightly less at the *Kastil*, but the *Cercina* has by far the best food, with a restaurant serving excellent fresh fish (daily noon–midnight). For a **drink**, the *Cercina*, the *Aziz*, the *Résidence Club* and the *Grand Hôtel* all have bars worthy of a visit, the *Cercina* for a cool lunchtime beer on the terrace, the *Aziz* perhaps for a relaxed evening. In the way of nightlife, the *Résidence Club* and the *Aziz* have what look to be the best **nightclubs**, though this may depend on your taste in music.

Hotels

Appart-Hôtel Aziz, 700m from the main road junction, on the right ☎04/489932, ⒻTD259404. Offers large, cool rooms or large family appartments, with satellite TV, air-conditioning in the new block, and the possibility of self-catering, although supplies are limited to the shop within the hotel. It too has a pool, plus a jacuzzi, a pleasant bar and what promises to be an "English nightclub", with its DJ box resembling King Kong's head. ❹

Cercina, just off the main road junction ☎04/489600, Ⓕ489878, Ⓔhotel.cercina@planet.tn. The first hotel you come to, with a choice of simple but pleasant en-suite rooms in the old block, mostly with sea views, or spacious, airy rooms without the view but with a/c, phone and satellite TV in the new block, and designed to accommodate wheelchair use. There is also the option in summer of cheaper, rather poky "bungalows" with shared bathrooms in the grounds. The reception also has

FISHING EXCURSIONS

Doing anything energetic on Kerkennah really defeats the object of coming here, but a popular **excursion** is to go out with one of the fishermen, who take people aboard for a small fee, usually cooking a meal of fresh fish into the bargain. The islanders use a curious fishing technique involving screens made of palm fronds set in V-shapes in the waters all around the shore. A trip in one of their small sailing boats, as the sun falls behind the palms and floods the sea a deep blood red, is one of Tunisia's most idyllic experiences. The going rate is about 12TD per person for half a day; contacts are easily made at the *Jazira* in Remla and the *Cercina* in Sidi Frej, or by just asking around the fishing boats. Longer trips of up to a week for up to ten people going round the islands in a *felucca* (the larger boats that took people to the mainland before the ferry service started in the 1970s) can also be arranged through the *Café Restaurant Archipel* in El Attaia. One boatman offering such trips is Samir Bouzida ("Captain Sam"), who can be contacted on ☎04/484330.

displays of local seashells, and of ancient artefacts dredged up from the seabed by local fishermen. ❸–❹

Kastil, 200m from the main road junction, on the left ☎04/489884. A group of small cubic huts with shared washing facilities. Definitely a fall-back option. ❸

Hôtel Farhat, 1.5km from the main road junction, at the end of the road, on the left ☎04/489237 is due to reopen very shortly after a five-year revamp.

Grand Hôtel, at the end of the road, 1.5km from the main junction ☎04/489861, ⨍489866. Has the best facilities of the Sidi Frej hotels, and the best bit of beach, catering for mainly British package tourists. ❺

Résidence Club, 600m from the main road junction, on the left ☎ & ⨍04/489777. Set to reopen after a ten-year closure, with en-suite bungalows, a large pool, poolside bar, and impressive looking nightclub, complete with spherical seating nests to relax in around the dancefloor. Activities on offer include horseback-riding and windsurfing. ❸

Remla   رملة

REMLA, the "capital", lies on the east coast 8km from Sidi Frej and contains about three-quarters of all the shops on the islands. As a beach, it has nothing to recommend it, but as a village it is quiet and amiable, making no attempt whatsoever to jolly along the islands' sleepy way of life. It boasts the islands' only other **hotel** – the friendly *Jazira*, right on the main street (☎04/481058, ⨍482001; ❷), with clean if rather plain rooms and shared washing facilities. New rooms with their own bathrooms are under construction. The hotel also has the only bar in town. The *Centre des Stages et des Vacances* **youth hostel** (☎04/481148), a couple of hundred metres further up the main road and then right down towards the beach, is clean and welcoming, open 24 hours, with a mix of Tunisian and foreign guests and the option of **camping**. Remla also has a **bank** (on the main crossroads), a **hospital** (100m towards Sidi Fankhal; ☎04/481052), a petrol station, police station (☎04/481053), two taxiphone offices and a **post office** (country hours). The *Patisserie Saïda* opposite the *Jazira* sells excellent cheap sandwiches, and the *Delfino* a few doors towards the crossroads (daily 7.30am–7.30pm) does pizzas in summer and baisc Tunisian dishes at other times. Alternatively, you can eat at the *Jazira* (daily 10am–3pm & 6pm–midnight, later in summer), whose meals are cheap to moderate, depending on the current price of fish, or at the slightly more expensive but excellent *Sirène Restaurant* by the beach (☎04/481118; daily 10am–3pm & 6pm–2am), with delicious fish and seafood. Remla is the main centre for the Kerkennah Islands' two annual **festivals**: the week-long Sirène Festival in July, with a series of mainly musical events, and the three-day Octopus festival held either at the beginning or the end of the octopus fishing season (March & Nov), with exhibitions, conferences, and much eating of eight-tentacled sea beasts. A sculpture of an octopus and octopus trap in the centre of town, in front of the petrol station, celebrates the industry.

El Attaia and Gremdi

From Remla, the road keeps straight on for 12km to end at the fishing village of **EL ATTAIA**, reached by four daily buses from Remla (the last returning at 3pm). The village is home to a restaurant, the very reasonably priced *Resto le Regal* (☎04/484100; daily noon–9pm, but hours vary), offering *fruits de mer* such as seafood risotto, and couscous with fish, octopus or cuttlefish. Beyond the village, on the way to the new fishing port, the *Café Restaurant Archipel* is open in summer (June–Sept) for meals and drinks by the sea. A turning to the left on reaching El Attaia leads through some small settlements to the shore near **Kraten**, another fishing village. En route, at **Ennajet**, there used to be a **museum** devoted to Habib Bourguiba's dramatic escape from French custody in 1945, when he passed through the village. The museum is now closed, but the boat he used and the house he sheltered in can still be seen by the shore at a turn off some 5km out of El Attaia.

Across a narrow stretch of water lies the uninhabited island of **GREMDI**, to which local fishermen will row you for a small consideration and come and collect you by arrangement. Together with the beach at **Bounouma**, 6km west of El Attaia, Gremdi is a favourite spot for **camping**. Finally, en route to El Attaia, you might try to find the meagre **Roman remains** near the village of **EL ABBASIA**, 4km north of Remla; the same village was also the birthplace of Farhat Hached, the UGTT leader gunned down by die-hard French settlers in 1952.

travel details

Trains

Enfida to: Gabès (1 daily; 5hr 30min); Grombalia (4 daily; 40–50min); Mahdia (2 daily; 1hr 20min–1hr 30min); Monastir (2 daily; 1hr 10min–1hr 45min); Sfax (2 daily; 2hr 20min); Sousse (6 daily; 45min); Tunis (4 daily, 2 on Sun; 1hr 15min–30min).

El Jem to: Gabès (2 daily; 3hr 25min–3hr 40min); Gafsa (2 daily; 4hr 45min); Metlaoui (2 daily; 5hr 20min); Sfax (5 daily; 45min); Sousse (4 daily; 1hr); Tunis (4 daily; 2hr 45min).

Mahdia to: Ksar Hellal (11–15 daily; 35min), Moknine (11–15 daily; 30min), Monastir (12–16 daily; 1hr); Sousse (11–15 daily; 1hr 30min); Tunis (1 daily; 3hr 45min).

Monastir to: Enfida (2 daily; 1hr 10min–1hr 25min); Ksar Hellal (11–15 daily; 25min); Mahdia (12–16 daily; 1hr 15min); Moknine (11–15 daily; 30min); Sousse (16–21 daily; 30min); Tunis (2 daily; 2hr 30min–2hr 45min).

Sfax to: Bir Bou Regba (4 daily, 2 connect for Hammamet and Nabeul; 2hr 50min); Gabès (2 daily; 2hr 40min); Gafsa (2 daily; 3hr 30min); El Jem (4 daily; 45min); Mahrès (4 daily: 35min); Metlaoui (2 daily; 4hr 10min); Sousse (6 daily; 1hr 45min); Tunis (6 daily; 3hr 45min). Trains from Sfax do not stop at Enfida.

Sousse to: Bir Bou Regba (8 daily, 5 connect for Hammamet & Nabeul; 1hr); Enfida (4 daily; 40min); Gabès (1 direct and 1 connecting daily; 4hr 30min); Gafsa (2 daily; 6hr 30min); El Jem (4 daily; 1hr); Kalaa Kebira (4 daily; 13min); Mahdia (11–15 daily; 1hr 30min); Metlaoui (2 daily; 7hr 15min); Monastir (16–21 daily; 30min); Sfax (6 daily; 1hr 50min); Tunis (10 daily; 1hr 50min).

Buses

Enfida to: Bizerte (2 daily; 3hr); Hammamet (1 daily; 1hr 15min), Kairouan (4 daily; 1hr); Kélibia (1 daily; 2hr 30 min); Nabeul (3 daily; 1hr 30min); Sousse (hourly; 1hr); Tunis (hourly; 1hr 30min).

El Jem to: Mahdia (5 daily; 40min); Sfax (5 daily; 1hr 15min); Sousse (3 daily; 1hr); Tunis (5 daily; 3hr 45min).

Kairouan to: Douz (4 daily; 5hr); Enfida (4 daily; 1hr); Gabès (7 daily; 4hr); Gafsa (7 daily; 4hr); Hammamet (6 daily; 2hr 15min); Houmt Souk (3 daily; 4hr 30min); Kasserine (6 daily; 2hr); Le Kef (3 daily; 3hr 30min); Maktar (3 daily; 2hr); Medenine (5 daily; 5hr); Nabeul (6 daily; 2hr 30min); Nefta (3 daily; 5hr); Sfax (3 daily; 2hr); Sousse (16 daily; 1hr–1hr 30min); Tataouine (1 daily; 5hr 30min); Tozeur (6 daily; 4hr); Tunis (10 daily; 2hr 30min).

Mahdia to: Ksar Hellal (hourly; 30min); Moknine (hourly; 20min); Nabeul (2 daily; 3hr 30min); Sfax (2 daily; 2hr 30min); Sousse (hourly; 1hr 30min); Tunis (2 daily; 4hr).

Monastir to: Kélibia (1 daily; 3hr 30min); Kairouan (1 daily; 1hr 30min); Le Kef (1 daily; 4hr); Ksar Hellal (hourly; 35min); Moknine (hourly; 40min); Nabeul (3 daily; 2hr 30min); Sousse (every 30min; 30min).

Sfax to: Agareb (9 daily; 30min); Bizerte (1 daily; 6hr 30min); Ben Gardane (2 daily; 4hr 30min); La Chebba (10 daily; 1hr 30min); Douz (1 daily; 4hr); Gabès (18 daily; 2hr); Gafsa (5 daily; 3hr); El Jem (5 daily; 1hr 15min); Jerba (4 daily; 4hr 30min); Kairouan (1 daily; 1hr 30min); Kasserine (4 daily; 3hr); Kebili (3 daily; 3hr 30min); Le Kef (3 daily; 4hr 30min); Mahdia (10 daily; 2hr 30min); Mahrès (20 daily; 40min); Medenine (5 daily; 3hr); Nefta (1 daily; 5hr 30min); Redeyef (1 daily; 5hr); Sbeïtla (4 daily; 2hr 30min); Sidi Bou Zid (3 daily; 2hr); Sidi Mansour (every 20min; 30min); Sousse (11 daily; 2hr 30min); Tataouine (2 daily; 4hr); Tozeur (1 daily; 5hr); Tripoli (3 weekly; 12hr); Tunis (11 daily; 5hr); Zarzis (1 daily; 4hr).

Sousse to: Akouda (every 10min; 15min); Béja (2 daily; 4hr) Ben Gardane (2 daily; 7hr); Bizerte (2 daily; 3hr 30min); Chott Mariam (14 daily; 30min); Douz (2 daily; 6hr 30min); Enfida (17 daily; 45min); El Fahs (2 daily; 1hr 30min); Gabès (13 daily; 4hr 30min); Gafsa (3 daily; 5hr); Hergla (14 daily; 45min); El Jem (3 daily; 1hr); Jerba (2 daily; 6hr 45min); Kairouan (16 daily; 1hr); Kalaa Kebira (every 10min; 20min); Kalaa Sghira (every 30min; 20min); Kebili (3 daily; 6hr); Le Kef (3 daily; 4hr); Mahdia (hourly; 1hr 30min); Matmata (1 daily summer only; 5hr 30min); Medenine (5 daily; 5hr 30min); Port el Kantaoui (14 daily; 30min); Sfax (11 daily; 2hr); Monastir (every 20min; 45min); Tataouine (2 daily; 6hr 30min); Tozeur (1 daily; 5hr); Tripoli (3 weekly; 14hr); Tunis (11 daily; 2hr 30min); Zaghouan (2 daily; 1hr 15min); Zarzis (1 daily; 6hr 30min).

Louages

Louage journey times are roughly three-quarters the time taken by buses on the same route. Frequency depends on demand, but morning is always the best time to get a louage, especially for longer journeys.

Enfida to: Sousse (50min); Tunis (1hr 30min).

El Jem to: Mahdia (40min) and Sousse (50min). Tunis (occasional, 2hr 40min)

Kairouan to: Maktar (2hr); Monastir (1hr 15min); Sbeïtla (1hr 40min); Sfax (2hr 30min); Sousse (1hr); Tunis (2hr).

Mahdia to: El Jem (40min); Ksar Hellal (30min); Ksour Essaf (15min); La Chebba (30min); Moknine (30min); Sfax (1hr 30min); Sousse (1hr 30min).

Monastir to: Kairouan (1hr 15min); Ksar Hellal (40min); Lamta (35min); Moknine (45min); Ouardanine (10min); Sousse (20min); Tunis (2hr 20min).

Sfax to: Agareb (30min); Bir Ali (1hr); La Chebba (1hr); Gabès (2hr); Gafsa (2hr 30min); El Hencha (40min); El Jem (1hr); Jerba (4hr 30min); Kairouan (2hr 30min); Kasserine (3hr 30min); Le Kef (4hr 30min); Mahrès (30min); Mahdia (1hr 30min); Maktar (3hr); Medenine (3hr); Sidi Bou Zid (2hr); Sousse (2hr); Tozeur (4hr); Tripoli (9hr); Tunis (4hr 30min).

Sousse to: La Chebba (1hr 20min); El Jem (50min); Enfida (50min); Hammamet (1hr 15min); Kairouan (1hr); Kasserine (3hr 30min); Ksar Hellal (30min); Ksour Esaf (1hr 30min); Mahdia (1hr 30min); Moknine (50min); Monastir (20min); Nabeul (1hr 30min); Port el Kantaoui (15min); Sbeïtla (3hr); Sfax (2hr); Sidi Bou Ali (30min); Sidi Bou Zid (3hr); Siliana (2hr 30min); Tunis (2hr).

Ferries

Sfax to: Sidi Youssef, Kerkennah (7–14 daily; 1hr).

Flights

Monastir to: Jerba (1 weekly with Tunisair; 40min). Also scheduled flights and seasonal charters to Europe, including some charter flights to the UK.

Sfax to: Paris (2 weekly with Tunisair; 3hr); Tunis (5 weekly with Tuninter; 45min).

Sousse to: Jerba (1 weekly; 40min).

CHAPTER FIVE

THE TELL

he Tell begins with fertile plains – good, well-watered farming land – but rises quickly into the **Dorsale mountains**, the highest in the country, forming a barrier from Zaghouan to Kasserine. Beyond, to the south, lie empty and infertile steppes which fade towards the coast into the Sahel. The plains have been heavily populated since Roman times, though the southern parts, over the centuries, were steadily taken over by esparto grass and left to sheep and camel herds. The tribes that lived here in the nineteenth century were notorious for their banditry; the **Hammama**, centred on the tomb of Sidi Bou Zid, used to raid as far as the very gates of Sfax. During the Protectorate large areas of public grazing land were taken over by colonists and the tribes were left to fight over the scraps. Most of the population lived by working on colonial estates and gathering esparto grass.

Despite a number of new mineral plants in the south, the economy remains largely agrarian, and vulnerable to external economic crises. The last and bloodiest of these was in 1984, when the IMF-backed removal of bread subsidies led to nationwide riots, which started in Kasserine and led to the deaths of eighty people (p.441). Nowadays the economy has revived, but the region still lags behind the rest of Tunisia's "economic miracle" so that workers still leave for larger towns like Le Kef and Kasserine. Nonetheless the Tell remains a deeply rewarding, if divided, region to travel through, both in terms of its obvious attractions – landscape and its numerous ancient sites – as well as the striking and unaffected pride of the people.

Tour groups make their way from the coast to the main Roman sites of **Thurburbo Majus**, **Maktar**, **Sbeïtla** and, above all, **Dougga**, but they largely neglect the region's less obvious attractions. To be fair, however, there are very few **hotels** in the region (we've listed almost all of them): wild camping is a good as well as rewarding way around this problem though most sizeable places tend to have at least one "**hôtel populaire**": dirty, hidden away and not suitable for women. **Zaghouan**, an unspoilt market town just an hour from Tunis, sits below the country's most spectacular mountain, **Jebel Zaghouan**, whose foothills harbour a group of isolated Berber villages. **Testour** was built up by Andalusian settlers and retains a very Spanish flavour, with a glorious seventeenth-century minaret more like a Toledo church tower. Over by the Algerian border is **Le Kef**, a historic mountainside town that looks out over landscapes reminiscent of the American West. Hidden here, and virtually unvisited, are **Haïdra**, one of the most majestic Roman sites in the country, and **Jugurtha's Table**, a flat-topped mountain that served as a bandit's lair for many centuries.

MARKET DAYS

Monday – Kasserine, Maktar, Sidi Bou Zid, Tajerouine
Tuesday – Dahmani, Haffouz, Kasserine, El Krib, Sidi Jedidi
Wednesday – Menzel Chaker, Sbeïtla
Thursday – Le Kef, Siliana, Téboursouk
Friday – Testour, Thala, Zaghouan
Saturday – El Fahs, Sidi Bou Zid

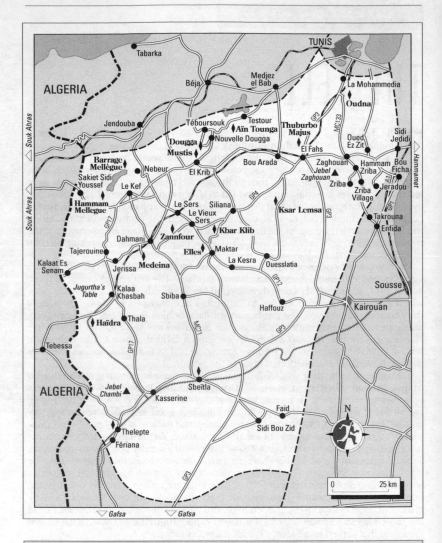

ACCOMMODATION PRICE CODES

The hotels and pensions listed in this book have been price-graded according to the following scale. The prices quoted are for the **cheapest available double room in high season**. For more on accommodation prices and categories, see Basics, p.29.

❶ Under 10TD
❷ 10–20TD
❸ 20–40TD
❹ 40–70TD
❺ 70–100TD
❻ 100–150TD
❼ 150TD upwards

The Tell does not have a very integrated system of **transport**. Le Kef and Kasserine are the main transport centres, reasonably well connected to other parts of the Tell and beyond, and places on the edge of the region often have better connections to other parts of the country. Sbeïtla and Kasserine have train lines but no passenger services.

Zaghouan and around
زغوان

Almost alpine in feel, with its green slopes and the grey crags above, **ZAGHOUAN**, 57km south of Tunis, is perhaps the most refreshing town in Tunisia. The old town's steep, narrow streets crisscross a low ridge of Jebel Zaghouan – not quite the highest mountain in the country, but easily the most spectacular. Cold water gushing from the mountain springs used to supply Carthage via a 132-kilometre Roman aqueduct.

One end of the ridge is punctuated by the old church spire and the new mosque's minaret; nearer the middle are the nineteenth-century **Great Mosque** and the **Mosque of Sidi Ali Azouz**, named after the patron saint of Tunis, where he is also commemorated with his own *zaouia* and mosque (p.84).

The place to head for is a **café** below the Roman remains, which lie about 3km above the town centre – follow signs for the *Nymphes* hotel and turn right at the *Club de Chasse*, past a second-century Roman **triumphal arch** and the Sidi Ali Azouz Mosque. Here you can sit and enjoy the view, extending over the bare plain below and up into the mountain behind. The Roman "temple" here is little more than a backdrop – not a temple at all, in fact, but a grand fountain of the type found in all Roman towns. The twelve niches above the basin once held a statue for each month of the year. Look out, while you're here, for the wild roses for which Zaghouan is famous – actually domesticated, the nurseries were introduced by Andalusian refugees in the seventeenth century and are used to make **attar** rose-water and perfume. There's a **rose festival** held here in May.

If you feel inspired to climb the craggy, limestone ridge of **Jebel Zaghouan**, either take the sixteen-kilometre track leading to the relay station on the summit (from where there are superb views over the countryside), or scramble up directly from the temple in a couple of hours to the lower peak nearer the town. It's very hard going, rough on exposed legs and a good place to twist an ankle, and the mountain is not a place to get caught out on after dark.

Jebel Zaghouan, rising 1300m above the surrounding plains and visible within a seventy-kilometre radius, is the most typical of the ranges that form Tunisia's backbone. From a naturalist's point of view, its highlight is an abundance of **birds of prey**, of which up to a dozen species can be sighted in a few hours, including eagles, vultures, kites and falcons, wheeling around their nest sites, or soaring hundreds of metres before gliding out over the plains in search of food. They're active most of the day, but early morning and evening are the best times to watch.

Public transport around Zaghouan is not that extensive, but interesting excursions can be made west to El Fahs and Thuburbo Majus, or southeast to the Berber villages of Zriba and Jeradou.

Practicalities

Although a fair number of tourists stop by to see the Roman ruins, few stay long, leaving the town surprisingly unspoilt. If you have the choice, come on a Friday for the **market**.

The only **accommodation** options are the *Maison des Jeunes* youth hostel (℡02/676630), a barrack-like affair on top of the next ridge over from the town centre, and the pleasantly located *Nymphes* hotel (℡02/675708; ❸), 1.5km along a shady lane leading from behind the town high up among the trees (signposted – turn left at the *Club de Chasse*). Both are closed for renovation until 2002, so call ahead and check their status if you wish to stay here. The road to the *Nymphes* continues to a café-restaurant just below the remains, where the owners may allow **camping**. In the new town, 100m down from the bus station at the Hammamet exit, the *Restaurant Touristique Les Sources* (daily noon–8pm) is blessed with great views; a meal here will set you back 12–15TD.

Transport in Zaghouan operates from the bottom of the old town near the Roman arch (see p.296 for details of bus and louage services).

South to the Sahel: Berber villages

Southeast towards Enfida and the Sahel, the roads lead past a couple of dramatic **Berber villages** perched in the dying fall of the Dorsale mountains and similar to Takrouna outside Enfida (see p.192).

The most remote is the now abandoned **ZRIBA** (also called Zriba Tunisien), 12km southeast of Zaghouan and confusingly located amidst Hammam Zriba and the French-built Zriba village. You'll need to find your way first to Hammam Zriba – turn right 5km out of Zaghouan towards Enfida on the MC133 road – and continue through the modern settlement to the shops around the **hammam** itself, which occupies the opening of a narrow gorge leading into the hills. You should be able to find a bus or a lift from Zaghouan this far – especially at weekends, when the hammam is a popular excursion. There are communal baths (0.5TD), and a small Jacuzzi-like one that holds four people (6TD/hr) at the end of the entrance to the old hammam. The *Complex Touristique 7 Novembre* (☎02/677533; ③) next door has enormous rooms with bathrooms, and is packed with Tunisian hammam-goers. If you're interested in a scramble, the gorge is apparently where Gustave Flaubert drew inspiration for the massacre of the mercenaries in *Salammbô*. To continue to Zriba, you'll need to find a rough eight-kilometre track that heads southeast past the entrance to an ugly open-cast mine. As you walk or bump over the hills, you'll catch glimpses of the village in the distance, clinging to the edges of an outlying jag of the mountain behind. The village itself is less striking than its setting, with narrow lanes crawling up and down the steep ridge.

Similar to Zriba, **JERADOU** is more accessible if you have transport – less so if you don't. A track (10km) leads east to it from the Zaghouan –Enfida road some 7km south of Zriba village. Like Zriba, Jeradou occupies an outlying pinnacle of a mountain and consists of narrow streets leading up to a saint's shrine on top of the ridge. Look out for Roman remains in the field of olives below the village.

From Jeradou, a minor road heads south through **SIDI KHALIFA**, a small settlement with a multi-domed shrine. A track leads a short way south from here towards a low forested hill, at whose foot lie the unexpected remains of Roman **Pheradi Maius** – baths, a triumphal arch and, on the hilltop above to the east, a temple to Baal. The road through Sidi Khalifa goes on to join the coast road halfway between Bou Ficha and Enfida.

Sidi Jedidi and Oued ez Zit

The direct road from Zaghouan to Hammamet (MC28) leads east off the Bou Ficha road through open countryside, cultivated with wheat, olives and almonds and populated with Berbers and their flocks of sheep and goats. Twelve kilometres on, the village of **SIDI JEDIDI** has become the target of tourist excursions from Hammamet especially to coincide with the Tuesday **market**. The setting, in the shoulder of the hills, ridged with strange, needle-like rock outcrops, is spectacular. From the top of the ridge here you can look down towards the coast, where your first sight of the resort complex is of parasails floating above the beach. There are a few **cafés** and cheap **restaurants** here, but not much else.

The main road back to Tunis from Zaghouan runs northwest to join the GP3 to El Fahs. If you have transport or happen to find a lift, you might want to think about taking the back road to Tunis, which runs east across the fertile plain below Zaghouan to **OUED EZ ZIT** (River of Oil), a small village with some Roman remains. Here the route heads north and enters a lonely pass between Jebel Zit and Jebel Marchana, either of which makes attractive walking country. Towards the end of the pass, the road offers a dramatic view of the back of Jebel Ressas, the lonely trapezoid mountain more usually seen lurking behind Jebel Bou Kornine from Sidi Bou Saïd. Beyond the mountain, the road runs through vineyards towards the straggling southern end of Tunis.

El Fahs and around الفحص

El **FAHS** is a sizeable but nondescript market town, and the only reason to come here is to see the Roman site of **Thuburbo Majus**, 3km north (minibuses 0.5TD, though you might have to wait for one to fill up). The town has few attractions of its own, with the exception of the **Saturday market**, one of the largest in the area and totally devoid of tourist buses. The marketplace is next to the train line near the station, which has three daily services to Tunis, Dahmani (for louages to Le Kef), and one daily to Kalaa Khasbah for Jugurtha's Table. **Buses** stop on the main road, and serve Le Kef, Sousse, Nabeul, Zaghouan, Kasserine, Maktar and Tunis; **louages** also stop nearby on the main road. East and west of El Fahs, good minor roads lead through empty country (with limited public transport) to Zaghouan and Medjez el Bab. More heavily travelled are the main roads south to Kairouan and southwest to Siliana and Maktar. There's no tourist office, nor any hotels, in town.

La Mohammedia and Oudna المحمّدية

Sixteen kilometres from Tunis on the road to El Fahs, Ahmed Bey (1837–56) built a summer palace called **La Mohammedia** that he hoped would surpass even Versailles in its grandeur. Senior state officials had long kept country residences here, including Youssef Sahib at Tabaa, who built the mosque in Tunis (see p.89), and Shakir Sahib at Tabaa, both of whom met early deaths. Ahmed Bey began to build a palace complex here in the 1840s and, following his state visit to France in 1846, aimed to incorporate some of what he had seen in Europe. This included a French optical telegraph system – then the latest in telecommunications – which the French, rulers of Algeria since 1830 and already jockeying for position in Tunisia, were only too glad to provide. Lines were set up linking La Mohammedia to the Bardo Palace and to La Goulette, but the system was barely used before being abandoned after Ahmed Bey's death.

Little but a shell now remains of Ahmed's palace complex. All the roofs have collapsed and most of the tiles have been pillaged, but the site still has the bare outlines of the palace buildings and associated barracks. Tunisia has a large number of redundant and ruined Beylical palaces, perhaps because of the superstition that it was unpropitious for a Bey to rule from the palace of his predecessor.

A few kilometres beyond La Mohammedia, the road runs parallel to the Roman **aqueduct** which carried water from Zaghouan to Carthage. First built in the second century AD, it was reconstructed by the Byzantines after the Vandal invasion, and later by the Fatimids and Hafsids. Where the road meets the aqueduct (free entry), an eight-kilometre track leads directly to the unexcavated remains of Roman Uthina, now called **Oudna**. Unfortunately some excellent mosaics have gone to the Bardo, but a number of surprisingly opulent dwellings have since been uncovered, as well as traces of public baths, cisterns and a theatre.

Thuburbo Majus

طوبوربو مايوس

The ruins of **Thuburbo Majus** (daily April–Oct 8am–7pm; Nov–March 8.30am–5.30pm; 2.1TD, camera 1TD) lie behind a low rise 3km north of El Fahs on the Tunis road, beyond a bridge over the Oued Miliane. Under French rule, El Fahs was known as Pont du Fahs, and as you cross the river you can see the remains of a bridge left behind by the Romans in the riverbed to the east. If you're on foot, ignore the signpost for the site – which seems to take you halfway around northern Tunisia – and walk instead straight up to the dip between two small hills, the eastern edge of the Roman city. There's a small **café** and **toilet** at the main entrance.

Thurburbo Majus was a Berber–Carthaginian settlement long before the Romans arrived. The name was actually based on a common root in the indigenous local language, used in place names like Thuburbo Minus (modern Tebourba), Thuburnica near Ghardimao (see p.186), and Téboursouk near Dougga (see p.269). For the Romans (and later the French) it was an important market centre and grew rich on the proceeds. Like so many other provincial towns, it acquired the trappings of Rome – a Forum, a Capitol, and the semblance of an orderly grid plan at the heart of an older, meandering town. The site was abandoned after the seventh-century Arab invasion and was only rediscovered in 1875. As Roman sites in Tunisia go, it lags slightly behind the likes of Maktar and Sbeïtla but is easier to reach from Tunis and the coastal resorts.

The Forum

The town's public buildings date mainly from the great imperial era of the second to third century AD. The **Forum** – the paved open space at the centre of the site, laid out between the years 161 and 192 AD – was its most characteristically Roman feature, something that any self-respecting imperial town had to have. A colonnade ran around three sides, the fourth left open for the **Capitol temple**, which catered for the imperial cult of Jupiter, Juno and Minerva. The podium and the vertical emphasis of the columns are very much the norm, and if you walk round behind it's easy to see just how much effort had to go into giving the temple a massive base so that it would dominate the Forum in the prescribed manner. In fact, the whole of one side of the Forum had to be raised on an artificial platform to create the required level space – a graphic illustration of the influence of the Roman role model over status-conscious provincial citizens. The area of housing behind the Capitol was later converted into **oil factories**. You can see clearly where one massive circular press was installed so that the oil would drip into a pool originally designed for human bathing – a sad illustration of the change in Thuburbo's circumstances, with industry supplanting leisure. To the north, one of three surviving **triumphal arches** marks the outskirts of town.

The Temple of Mercury and market

Behind the colonnade on the other three sides of the Forum stood temples and municipal buildings. On the right-hand side as you look from the Capitol is a curious **Temple of Mercury**, built in 211 AD to the local and not the Roman pattern, and featuring an outer courtyard – circular, with niches making corners – leading into the sanctuary. Mercury was the god of trade (as well as thieving), and the three split-level courtyards below the temple formed the town's **market**, where stalls can still be made out. The Mercury temple looks out over an area of jumbled streets and houses, predating the Forum, in a layout that was anathema to the Romans. Several hundred metres beyond, towards another triumphal arch in the distance, is a second residential quarter with regular streets, a Roman addition as the town expanded. In many ways, the contrast between the two areas is similar to the difference in modern Tunisia between tradi-

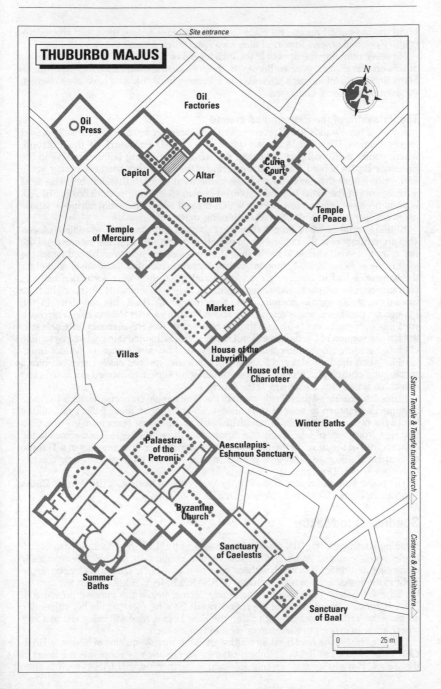

THUBURBO MAJUS

Site entrance

N

Oil Factories

Oil Press

Capitol

◇ Altar

Curia Court

◇ Forum

Temple of Peace

Temple of Mercury

Market

Villas

House of the Labyrinth

House of the Charioteer

Winter Baths

Palaestra of the Petronii

Aesculapius-Eshmoun Sanctuary

Byzantine Church

Sanctuary of Caelestis

Summer Baths

Sanctuary of Baal

Saturn Temple & Temple turned church ▷

Cisterns & Amphitheatre ▷

0   25 m

tional medinas and French grid plans – like the Romans before them, the nineteenth-century colonial powers imported their own ideas when it came to town planning.

However rambling the streets in the quarter below the Forum, though, the houses in this central district were as Roman as their wealthy inhabitants could make them. Some fine colourful mosaics are visible in a house where columns have been re-erected around the central courtyard.

The Palaestra of the Petronii and around

Just east of here stands a well-preserved row of blue-grey columns which still support an entablature. These made up one side of the 225 AD **Palaestra of the Petronii**, where young men took part in boxing, wrestling and running before heading to the **Summer Baths** behind. Carved in the paving of the Palaestra's southern corner, you'll find some letters that make up a Roman game used to learn the alphabet. The most striking part of the baths beyond, confused in plan after being remodelled in 361 AD, is an impressive semicircular portico which housed not statuary but latrines – whose users sat over a still-visible channel of running water.

Nothing could be more Roman than the Palaestra, but three hybrid centres of worship are reminders of the cultural blend in Roman North Africa. In the far corner of the Palaestra is a small **shrine** to the healing god Aesculapius, here worshipped under the joint name of Aesculapius-Eshmoun. An inscription reveals that those wishing to enter the sanctuary had to observe a three-day ritual when they were forbidden bathing, shaving, beans and pork, and sexual relations. A street leads off to the right here towards a small temple podium. This **Sanctuary of Baal**, the top deity in the Phoenician pantheon, was erected in the second century under Roman rule. The courtyard just over the street (with its entrance re-erected) was a **Sanctuary of Caelestis**, the Roman version of Carthaginian Tanit. Later it was fashioned into part of a Byzantine church. Standing among the columns of its nave and two aisles, into the former courtyard between the Palaestra and Sanctury of Caelestis, you can easily make out how a rectangular church plan was imposed on the existing square courtyard. An apse is recognizable at one end, a baptistry at the other.

Ruins discernible on the hillside south of the Baal temple comprise perhaps the most monumental **cistern** to be seen in Tunisia, even boasting an inner gallery around the top of the deep storage tank. An **amphitheatre** above is just recognizable – there's a fine view from here of Jebel Zaghouan dominating the whole region, and across to the eastern **gate** of the town on the next hill. Above this gate are the remains of a **Temple of Saturn**, the Roman equivalent of Baal, whose temples tend to stand near the city boundaries, as at Dougga.

The route from the centre of town to the eastern gate leads past the **Winter Baths** – mediocre except for their impressive facade.

Southwest to Maktar

Heading southwest, the GP4 makes up one side of the El Fahs–Maktar–Kairouan triangle which contains some of the most remote country in the Tell. It's scenically rewarding, but difficult to reach without your own transport. The most obvious single sight is the massive Byzantine **fortress** of **KSAR LEMSA**, 20km down a left turn off the El Fahs–Siliana road towards Ouesslatia. Sitting below the massive presence of Jebel Bargou, it guarded one of the routes north into the more fertile but vulnerable areas of the Tell. Continuing south along the Ksar Lemsa road will bring you to a fork where you can go east to Kairouan or west to Ouesslatia.

Back on the Siliana road heading southwest, a left turn 20km east of Siliana at **BARGOU** (also known as Rabaa or Robaa) offers a scenic one-way route into the heart of the **Jebel Bargou** massif. Twenty kilometres further on, **SILIANA** itself is, like

Ouesslatia, a lowland equivalent of Maktar, a dull modern farming centre where you wouldn't want to stay for its own sake. It is, however, the site of one of the few **hotels** in this area – the *Zama* (☎08/871121, ℻870751; **④**) – and there's a **youth hostel** (☎08/872871), but ring ahead to check whether it's open. Siliana also has reasonable transport connections, which makes it one of the few feasible bases for exploring the El Fahs–Maktar–Kairouan triangle. There's also a daily bus to Béja (3hr; see p.296) but there's a possibility that it stops at every stone before arriving.

Roman remains within reach of Siliana, just accessible down a nine-kilometre track and recommended for enthusiasts only, are the vestigial ruins at **JAMA** of what is thought to be Zama Minor, site in 202 BC of the climactic battle of the Second Punic War, in which Scipio (soon to become Scipio Africanus) defeated Hannibal.

It's uphill most of the way from Siliana to Maktar (see p.287). About 10km outside Siliana, a minor road turns west to cut across for 20km to the Maktar–Le Kef road. About halfway down this lonely road, which bumps up and down over steeply rolling country, you pass two solitary Roman-era monuments, both easy to miss. The first, known as **Ksour Toual Zouamel**, is a two-storey square mausoleum which sits below and to the north of the road, halfway up a hill. About 1km further, the second, known as **Kbor Klib**, is a couple of hundred metres south of the road on the ridge of the same massif. A huge block of masonry, originally 45m long by 15m wide and 6m high, it remains uncertainly identified, and is said to be either a Numidian sanctuary, similar to the one which stood on top of the hill at Chemtou, or a victory altar erected by Julius Caesar to celebrate his Civil War triumph.

Testour and around ‎تستور

Approaching the Tell from Tunis, the main westward route splits at Medjez el Bab, where the northern fork (GP6) climbs over the Téboursouk range (see pp.176–177). The south-ern branch (GP5) follows the Medjerda River before reaching **TESTOUR**, 75km west of the capital and the most undiluted remaining evidence in the country of the Spanish immigration of the early seventeenth century, its modern concrete outskirts aside.

A cluster of tiled roofs on a mound above the River Medjerda, the heart of Testour looks so Spanish that it's no surprise to find that it was built by Andalusian refugees in the 1600s. Its appearance and the local people's way of life have changed very little since, and this, along with the almost pristine rural feel of the place, gives it a particu-lar fascination, the more so if you can coincide with the Friday regional **market**, although the daily souks are crowded nonetheless. At all events, it's worth a stop en route from Tunis to Dougga and Le Kef, an easy enough road to travel by bus or louage.

At **AÏN TOUNGA**, 9km west of Testour on the Le Kef road, there is an ancient site (free access) which includes one of the most impressive **Byzantine fortresses** in Tunisia. Remains of its walls and towers, some half-buried but still enormous, loom over the modern road. Above the fortress are the remains of Roman **Thignica**: a resi-dential quarter crowned by a temple, with the outline of a theatre, baths and an arch hidden away in a garden below to the right.

Some history

Some of the **Andalusian Muslims**, evicted from Spain in the wake of the Christian reconquest, were wealthy enough to settle in Tunis itself, where the rue des Andalous is a reminder of their presence. Others had to petition the authorities for land, and in 1609 were granted the old Roman site of Tichilla, today's Testour.

The new Andalusian communities were renowned throughout North Africa for their commercial abilities and hard work, but were conscious of their outsider status. Both feelings are neatly expressed in a myth about Testour's foundation. According to this story, the first group of settlers originally stopped about 12km north of the current town, where some of them planted vineyards. The Turkish authorities were so impressed when they saw the result that they slapped on taxes at a punitive level – whereupon the disgusted settlers uprooted their vines and themselves and moved on to Testour's current site.

From its foundation, Testour's economy centred on the agricultural activities of the region – for which it still provides an important market – but there were also skilled artisans among the immigrants. The town was long famed for its **chéchias**, skullcaps made from the wool of local flocks. These have almost disappeared, but the other main trade – traditional **roof tile production** – has survived. A factory can be seen down by the river below the Great Mosque, one of only two left in all Tunisia (the other is at Tozeur), where some two thousand tiles are produced every week.

The Town

In Testour, the bourgeois pride and culture of the Andalusian settlers found permanent expression in mosques and public buildings that are redolent of rural Spain. The **Great Mosque**, unmissable with its distinctive tiled octagonal minaret, is the largest and most beautiful of an extraordinary number of mosques built here in the early seventeenth century. It stands at the end of the main street, its walls the texture of crumbled biscuit, surmounted by a ribbed tile roof. Inside, the delicate arcades of the two courtyards – one hung with white jasmine – are in marked contrast to the generally heavier local styles. Yet even here you can see that Roman bits and pieces – doorframes, capitals, columns and oil presses – have been reused in the paving. One corner column in the main courtyard sports a milestone proclaiming "Carthage 66 miles", which, as it happens, is just about right.

The **minaret** dominates the mosque, just as it dominates the town and the surrounding river valley, with its nostalgia for Spain. Most obviously Spanish is the superimposition of an octagonal crowning section, lavishly decorated with tiles, on a square base, which recalls church bell towers in Aragon and Castile. In the base, the builders used a Toledan technique in which rectangular patches of rubble somehow become decorative when surrounded by brick. Least obvious, but perhaps the biggest giveaway, is the clock on the south face, which is standard for a church bell tower but doesn't appear on a minaret anywhere else in the world. Note that the numbers go backwards, allegedly because the Andalusians wanted time to go back so that they could be returned to their homeland.

Testour's Spanish immigrant citizens could hardly have provided a clearer demonstration of their identity than this mosque and its minaret. This is actually the second great mosque that they built. The remains of the first – a floor plan, a bricked-in mihrab and the bottom half of a smaller minaret – lie not far to the northeast of the existing one.

Local legend tells that there were once fourteen mosques here, built on virtually every side street off the main avenue and serving the specific needs of local communities, playing host to business and municipal meetings as well as everyday prayer. Only a handful remain, but almost without exception they consist of a bell-tower-like round crown on a square base. The **Abdellatif Mosque**'s minaret, just north of the main street on rue Kortouba, has some rows of faïence tiles. "Kortouba" refers to Cordoba in Spain; just before it, on the same side of the main street, notice also rue Ichbilia (Seville).

South off the main street, at the end of rue 26 Fevrier 1953, stands another graceful reminder of Andalusian culture – the **Zaouia of Sidi Naseur el Baraouachi**, built around his tomb in 1733. It begins in a lengthy passage and passes through a green door whose studded nails have been painted a hallucinatory red. Inside, however, all is calm, with a tiny paved courtyard surrounded by small chambers under a tiled arcade and almost swamped by an orange tree. The tomb itself, under its green-tiled dome and decorated with stucco and faïence tiles, is still an object of veneration; the stains on its far wall were made by hands coated in henna to ward off the evil eye.

Most of the Andalusian immigrant communities in Tunisia included **Jews** as well as Muslims, though many have left for Israel over the past few decades. Testour was formerly the site of a Jewish pilgrimage from all over Tunisia to the tomb of Rabbi Fraji Chawat, said to be a native of Fez who died here. More recently, the town became tangled in the torrid story of a Jewish woman called Habiba Msika, born in 1895, who became one of the country's best-known singers and actresses during the musical revival in the early twentieth century. She is largely remembered today for her gruesome death in 1930, when her jealous lover Elyaou Mimouni – a wealthy native of Testour – doused her in petrol while she slept, burning her alive. The film *Habiba Msika*, directed by Selma Baccar, tells the story of her life.

Mimouni's house now serves as Testour's **Maison de Culture** on rue Kortouba, beyond the Abdellatif minaret, with an Arabic plaque on the wall in which the fateful year of 1930 is recognizable. If you can find someone to show you round this incongruously lavish 1920s mansion, you can see Mimouni's massive safe, some splendidly vampish photos and even an auditorium that was purpose-built for Msika. The Maison de Culture is also the place to ask about Testour's annual **Festival of Malouf Music**, which takes place in June and July in the large and hideous new café opposite the great mosque.

Practicalities

There have been few incursions into the fabric of the old town – most of the straggle of **new development** flanks the main road heading west to Le Kef. There are no hotels in town, and no tourist office. **Buses** stop at the *Restaurant el Qods*, on the main road west of town, and run hourly to Téboursouk and Le Kef, as well as to Medjez el Bab and Tunis.

Dougga and around   دقَّة

"Dougga very big city" is what the hopeful guides hanging around the entrance will tell you, and they're right (guides request 10TD an hour, but you should be able to bargain down to 6–7TD, especially if it's quiet). The Roman site of **Dougga** (daily: April–Oct 8am–7pm; Nov–March 8.30am–5.30pm; 2.1TD, camera 1TD) is both the largest and most dramatic in Tunisia, and contains what some consider the most beautiful single Roman monument in North Africa. If you see only one Roman site in the country, it should undoubtedly be "these magnificent remains of taste and greatness, so easily reached in perfect safety by a ride along the Medjerda", as the English traveller James Bruce noted in 1765. The city was accorded World Heritage Site status by UNESCO in 1997.

Dougga's name suggests non-Roman origins, as does its site high on the side of the valley – the Romans preferred flatter sites more suited to their standardized urban forms. Here they seem to have adapted well to a town that had already been described in the fourth century BC as being "of an impressive size". By the second century BC it had become the seat of Numidian king **Massinissa**, whose support for Rome in the last war against Carthage gained much credit for the town. From the second century AD, under Roman administration, it began to enjoy a period of great prosperity. At its peak the Roman town had a population of ten thousand and, although the surrounding countryside now looks empty, aerial photography has revealed no fewer than ten other settlements within a ring of just six square kilometres.

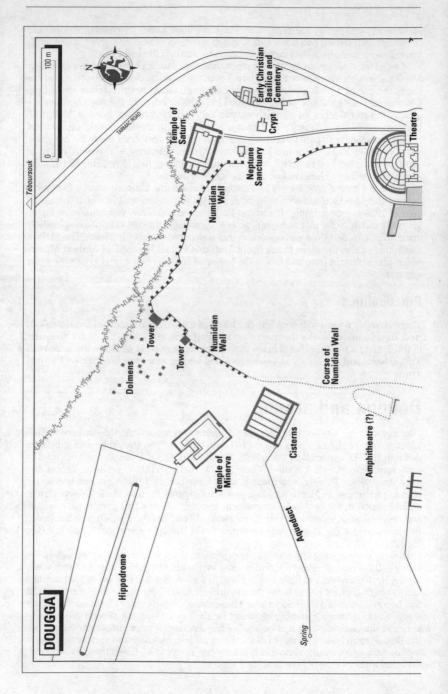

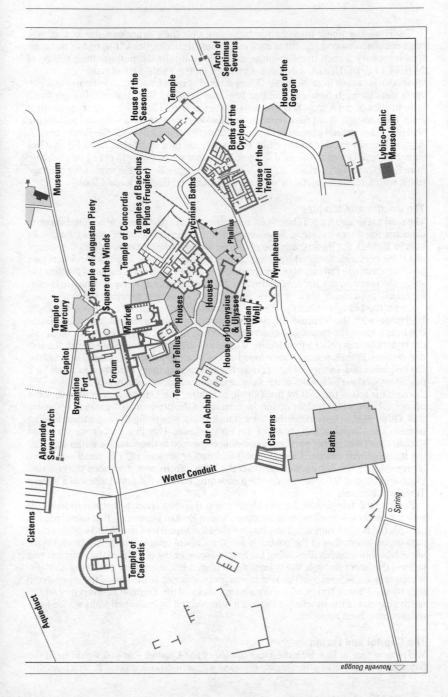

Nouvelle Dougga

Arch of Septimus Severus

House of the Seasons

Temple

House of the Gorgon

Baths of the Cyclops

Temples of Bacchus & Pluto (Frugifer)

House of the Trefoil

Temple of Concordia

Lycinian Baths

Museum

Temple of Augustan Piety

Square of the Winds

Phallus

Temple of Mercury

Market

Houses

Nymphaeum

Capitol

Temple of Tellus

Houses

House of Dionysius & Ulysses

Byzantine Fort

Forum

Numidian Wall

Alexander Severus Arch

Dar el Achab

Cisterns

Cisterns

Water Conduit

Baths

Spring

Temple of Caelestis

Aqueduct

Lybico-Punic Mausoleum

The Byzantines built huge fortifications and, after their departure, the local inhabitants remained among the ruins until excavating archeologists at the end of the nineteenth century forced them to move down the hill into the purpose-built village of **NOUVELLE DOUGGA**, a drab modern place on the Tunis–Le Kef road.

Access is easiest from Nouvelle Dougga: hourly buses from Tunis to Le Kef and vice versa pass through Nouvelle Dougga (the stop is called Brif Brahim), though you'll have to walk or get a taxi (3TD one way) to the site itself (3km). The other approach is from Téboursouk, about 6km northeast of the site, from where a sideroad follows the wall of a valley up and around to Dougga (taxis cost around 8TD for the return trip). A day-trip is easily feasible from Le Kef, or else you can pick up the last Le Kef–Tunis bus from Nouvelle Dougga at around 5.50pm. If you fancy something to eat while you're up here the *Restaurant Mercure*, on the Nouvelle Dougga side, caters mainly for package tours, with a reasonable, if dull, menu at 8TD (9am–midnight; closed Mon).

The theatre and temples

The road to Dougga from Téboursouk winds into the site past a heavily restored **theatre**, almost at the top of the steep slope over which the grey remains are spread. Originally built in 168 AD, the theatre was one of a string of monumental projects from the second and third centuries financed by Dougga's wealthy land-owning families. An inscription proclaims that one Publius Marcius Quadratus erected the theatre, the halls flanking the stage, the porticos, the statue platform and the scene building. Today the theatre is used for occasional summer performances of the French classics in May and June.

Up on the hilltop behind the theatre are some early and peripheral odds and ends, beginning with the **Temple of Saturn**, whose columns overlook the road. These columns formed the facade of a courtyard which in turn led into three inner chambers, the typical African pattern for a temple. This is not surprising, since underneath the second-century Roman remains were found traces of a pre-Roman sanctuary of Baal, the Carthaginian god. In the paving opposite the central sanctuary chamber, look out for a pair of mysterious footprints in the floor, remnants of some unknown ritual.

From the top of the cliff by the Temple of Saturn, you can cut across west to some occupied houses that huddle under the remains of the pre-Roman Numidian defensive wall. Otherwise, return to the theatre and make your way along the main track leading towards the Capitol at the centre of the Roman town. This in turn becomes a paved Roman street that seems narrow and twisting compared to the norm – another sign that the Romans here inherited a well-established earlier settlement. The small semicircular **temple**, on the left as you approach the town centre, was dedicated to Augustan Piety, and beyond it is what used to be a **mosque**, built on the foundations of a Roman Temple of Fortune.

Because this temple stood at an oblique angle, the open space below was rounded off with a semicircle – most unusual for conservative Roman planners – that introduces an unexpected note of intimacy. The plaza is called the **Square of the Winds**, after a compass-based inscription in the paving below the Capitol temple which names all twelve winds. As with mosaics illustrating the four seasons, or the months of the year, this one reflects the important role the natural world played in the imagery of Roman Africans. It's likely that the Square of the Winds was commissioned at the end of the second century by the Pacuvii family, who were also sponsors of the **Temple of Mercury** on the north side and of the **market** to the south, surrounded by individual stalls whose foundations have been restored.

The Capitol and Forum

You're now face to face with the huge temple of the **Capitol** – or you would be, if the Byzantines hadn't built some highly disorienting fortifications around it, which are the reason for the Capitol's excellent state of preservation. The Capitol really is a magnificent sight as it looks out over the town and the valley below, but you have to get close to appreciate just how huge it is. It was a gift to the city in 166 AD – just two years before the theatre was built – from the parents of the proud theatre donor, and an inscription records its dedication to "Jupiter, Juno and Minerva for the safety of Marcus Aurelius and Lucius Verus", joint emperors at the time. Some fragments of the massive cult statue of Jupiter that originally stood 6m high in the *cella* (inner sanctum) – a potent symbol of Roman power – are now in the Bardo Museum in Tunis. The relief sculpture in the temple pediment shows a human figure being molested by a large bird – the previous emperor, Antoninus Pius, undergoing his apotheosis at the hands (or claws) of an eagle, and a singularly uncomfortable reward it looks, too.

The open space west of the temple is the **Forum**, lavishly decorated with columns of polychrome marble, but modest in size because of the lie of the land. Although the Byzantine fortifications make this difficult to appreciate, the Square of the Winds may have been built so as to increase the sense of open space around the Capitol and give it an urban Roman quality.

A track leads west among the olive trees behind the Capitol to the **Triumphal Arch of Alexander Severus**, named after the emperor who reigned from 222 to 235 AD, when the arch was built. Further along, set in the gentle lap of the valley side, is the **Temple of Caelestis**, possibly the most likeable of Dougga's monuments. Built at the same time as the nearby Triumphal Arch, it's dedicated to Juno Caelestis (Heavenly Juno), the Romanized version of the Carthaginian god Tanit, and thus makes a pair with the Temple of Saturn on the far side of the city; but it's the truly Roman cult which is given central position in the Capitol. The temple itself, featuring podium and columns with attractive Corinthian capitals, is nothing out of the ordinary, but the semicircular colonnaded portico behind it is, like the Square of the Winds, unusual in the conservative architectural atmosphere of Roman Africa. Far away at the other end of the Roman Empire (Turkey and Palestine, for instance), this sort of touch was commonplace, but in Tunisia innovation seems to have gone against the grain of the Roman designers. The portico was inscribed with the names of distant provinces of the empire – Dalmatia, Judaea, Mesopotamia, Syria and Laodicea – as well as Carthage and Thugga. They may all have been centres of the Caelestis cult.

An ancient residential quarter

Head back towards the city centre along the track which turns into a Roman street just below the Forum and runs past an imposing doorway to the right. This is now known by the Arab name of Dar el Acheb, and the original function of its courtyard is not known. Beyond Dar el Acheb, the main street cuts through the centre of the town's most exclusive residential quarter. Large houses are crammed into all available spaces on the narrow side streets, and it's hard to imagine how it once looked when the walls stood to their full height. As the street follows the contour of the hill around, one sharp left and a left again leads between houses to the **Temple of Tellus** (Earth), dated to 261 AD and identifiable by a small peristyle (columned courtyard) leading to a sanctuary room with niches in the far wall, a recognizably African temple pattern. Further round the hill, the **House of Dionysus and Ulysses** is named after the famous mosaic of Ulysses tied to the mast of his ship while the Sirens sing; it's now in the Bardo (see p.98).

By now you are below the fortress-like remains of the **Licinian Baths**. Look for a barrel-vaulted passage – originally a tradesmen's entrance – which takes you into the baths from here. The official entrance was down some steep steps into a room on the northwest side of the complex, where mosaics and columns still stand. A headless statue probably represents one of the Licinii family who donated the baths to the city in the third century AD. The large central room was the *frigidarium*, which opened through a smaller *tepidarium* to the southwest on to the *caldarium*, situated above the tradesmen's entrance and facing south to catch the sun. In the other direction, the large peristyle room in the northeast corner was the *palaestra*, a sort of training room for athletes.

Continuing along the main street, then right at its end, the large **House of the Trefoil** has had its history censored – a stone with a relief of a phallus stood outside the door, identifying the town brothel, until it was removed some 1800 years later by authorities concerned for tourist sensibilities. If you'd like to see it look twenty metres away on the terrace above the road, west of the house and behind the Licinian Baths. A staircase leads down between two standing columns to a wide courtyard surrounded by rooms, one (its roof heavily restored) in the clover-leaf shape that provides the building's name – a name that carefully avoids any suggestion of the house's original function.

Beside the brothel stood a small private **baths complex**, now named after the magnificent mosaic in the Bardo of three bodybuilder Cyclopes swinging their hammers to forge Jupiter's thunderbolts. The baths were presumably connected with the brothel and still contain a well-preserved row of toilet seats.

The Arch of Septimius Severus and the Libyco-Punic Mausoleum

Heading down the hill past the baths leads eventually to the **Triumphal Arch of Septimius Severus**, built in 205 AD, a few years before the one near the Caelestis Temple. A track originally left the city through this arch to join the main road below from Carthage. Septimius Severus, who came from Libya, was the founder of the dynasty of Roman emperors which ended with Alexander Severus (dedicatee of the Triumphal Arch near the Caelestis temple). It was Septimius's wife whose accent was notorious in Rome; but not that of the emperor himself, according to one tactful poet: "Your speech is not Carthaginian, nor your dress, nor is your spirit foreign: you are Italian, Italian . . ."

A track to the right, just before the arch, winds down to the **Libyco-Punic Mausoleum**, built in the second century BC for "Ateban, son of Ieptamath, son of Palu", which is important as one of the few surviving examples of pre-Roman monumental building in Tunisia. Although the mausoleum managed to survive the Roman Empire more or less intact, in 1842 it fell victim to the British Empire when the British consul, Sir Thomas Reade, dismantled it to get at the bilingual inscription which provides the names above. The inscription remains in the British Museum in London, where Libyco-Phoenician was deciphered for the first time. Ironically, it was with the help of a sketch by James Bruce that the French authorities reconstructed the mausoleum at the turn of the century.

Like other remnants of immediately pre-Roman North Africa – the sarcophagi in the Carthage Museum (see p.114), for example, and the recently reconstructed temple at Chemtou (see p.187) – the mausoleum is a melange of different influences. Greek culture contributed the Ionic order in the second storey, but most of the elements are more recognizably Eastern, influenced by Carthage's Phoenician links; the overall form is similar to Anatolian and Syrian monuments, and the lotus-flower pilaster capitals on the corners of the first and third storeys speak with an Egyptian accent.

The Temple of Minerva and around

On the summit of the hill behind the Capitol are a few traces of the pre-Roman town, as well as some peripheral Roman structures. A track which veers right, uphill, from the Roman road between the theatre and Capitol leads past a group of seven massive **cisterns** on the right, each 35m long and 5m wide, with newly restored pink roofs. An aqueduct fed water into these from the spring located a little way west. Above the cisterns, a **Temple of Minerva**, built in the second century AD, follows the African pattern, with a colonnaded courtyard leading into a sanctuary room. Beyond the temple, the track runs along what looks like a long, flat field that was once the municipal **Hippodrome**. Two small heaps of rubble facing each other 190m apart were the ends of the *spina*, the central barrier around which the chariot races were run. If this seems like a bleak kind of place to watch a chariot race, sitting on the bare rocks opposite, the man who donated the land to the city in 214 AD knew better – he provided it "ad voluptates populi" (for the pleasure of the people), and numerous mosaics in museums around the country support his judgement.

Back to the east, beyond the end of the *spina*, is an area of **dolmen tombs** dating from the third century BC to the first century AD, sited just below the walls of the Numidian city, of which some remains and even a tower can be seen behind.

Téboursouk

تبرسق

For most tourists, **TÉBOURSOUK**, 30km south of Béja, is simply a point of transit on the way to Dougga. While it's probably not worth visiting for its own sake, there is enough to repay a brief wander – it is a venerable and attractive market town in its own right, with a Thursday **souk** just off the main road to Le Kef, and a Byzantine **fortress** dominated by a **marabout** clinging to the hill above. Like Dougga, just along the valley side, it affords balcony views south over the broad agricultural lands of the Tell.

The only places to **stay** in town are the *Maison des Jeunes* **youth hostel** (℡08/465095), and the rather snooty and overpriced two-star, *Hôtel Thugga* (℡08/466647, ℻466721; ❸), below the town on the main road to Testour, with various Roman artefacts tastefully arranged outside. **Buses** stop by the fort in the centre of town, and **louages** stop opposite (see p.296 for details of services).

Mustis

موستي

Twenty kilometres after Téboursouk, the road to Le Kef runs past a well-preserved triumphal arch standing casually by the side of the road. This was the outskirts of Roman **Mustis** (free access), today a site of middling-to-limited interest whose central ruins sit right by the edge of the road near an attractive **zaouia** a little further along.

Mustis was originally an unremarkable farming town much like modern **Le Krib**, a kilometre further down the road. On the left of the entrance sit remains of the **temples** of Ceres and Apollo. Then a paved Roman street leads uphill through an arch, with two massive pieces from an olive press leaning against a wall at the top of the street; the remains of the structure they came from are recognizable over to the left, beyond the **Temple of Pluto**. Just north of here are traces of a three-aisled Christian **church** ending in an apse.

From here you can already see the walls of the Byzantine **fort** that dominate the site – a sign that Mustis, like so many other similar towns, ended its life as a frontier outpost. From inside, the fort offers a vivid sense of the precariousness of life at the turn of an era. Perhaps this is because it is smaller than the likes of Aïn Tounga or Haïdra, and there is barely room for it to contain everything the inhabitants would have needed, like cisterns, living quarters and defensive walls.

Le Kef and around

الكاف

The first sign of **LE KEF**, just 45km east of the Algerian border, is a gleaming ribbon of rock that twists round Jebel Dyr under the mountain's summit. Clinging just below the southern end of the table top is the old town, while the newer quarters spill ever wider down the hillside below. It's a breathtaking setting – the more so in its isolation close to the Algerian border – and the kind of place where you feel involved just wandering round, contemplating the vistas below. But there's more than just views here:

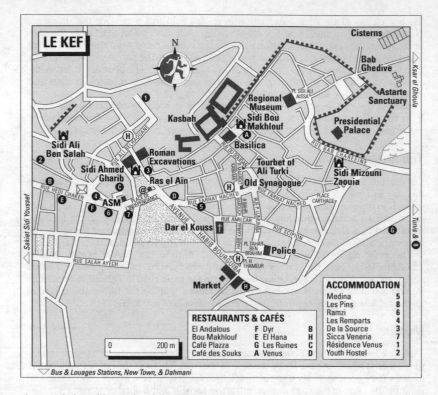

LE KEF

Cisterns

Bab Ghedive

Ksar el Ghoula

Astarte Sanctuary

Regional Museum
Sidi Bou Makhlouf

Kasbah

Presidential Palace

Sidi Ali Ben Salah

Roman Excavations

Basilica

Sidi Ahmed Gharib

Tourbet of Ali Turki

Ras el Aïn

Old Synagogue

Sidi Mizouni Zaouia

ASM

Tunis & 8

Dar el Kouss

Police

Market

Bus & Louages Stations, New Town, & Dahmani

RESTAURANTS & CAFÉS

El Andalous		F	Dyr	B
Bou Makhlouf		E	El Hana	H
Café Plazza		G	Les Ruines	C
Café des Souks		A	Venus	D

ACCOMMODATION

Medina	5
Les Pins	8
Ramzi	6
Les Remparts	4
De la Source	3
Sicca Veneria	7
Résidence Venus	1
Youth Hostel	2

0   200 m

the town's long history has left a legacy of monuments, and it also has an interesting regional culture museum.

Some history

Although still regarded as the unofficial capital of western Tunisia, Le Kef's predecessors enjoyed more prominence. The area was inhabited very early: Neolithic tools have been found nearby and the Numidians built megalithic tombs here. It became the Carthaginian urban centre of **Sicca** after the Second Punic War. Unable to pay its defeated mercenary army, Carthage packed them off here, a move which rebounded when the mercenaries rose in revolt and waged a four-year struggle in which they were only suppressed with the aid of yet more mercenaries. The war – of a legendary brutality – inspired Gustave Flaubert's blood-and-guts novel *Salammbô*. The town was annexed in 46 BC by the Romans, who attached the title "Veneria", reflecting its special appeal. The Arabs, who took it in 688, called it Chakbanaria, but renamed it El Kef (The Rock) in the seventeenth century.

Since the Islamic conquest, Le Kef's strategic position between the Tunisian hinterland and the Algerian interior put it at the centre of so many inter-factional struggles that it never quite regained its former eminence – a process accelerated in the twentieth century when the train line to Algeria was built through Jendouba and Ghardimaou to the north, although it was made provisional capital of Tunisia during World War II. Algerians have, however, had occasion to be thankful for Le Kef, which was the main base and command centre of the FLN (Algerian armed resistance) until 1962.

In the years since Independence the town has felt itself a victim of the national bias towards the Sahel region (both Habib Bourguiba and Ben Ali come from there) – feelings which erupted particularly strongly in the 1984 troubles. For a town of its size it is desperately short of work and recreational outlets and, even though the townspeople are proud to have one of the largest schools in Africa, the pupils it educates find little employment here.

Arrival, information and accommodation

The **bus** and **louage** station is south of the old town in the new town on the road to **Dahmani**, a twenty-minute walk past the modern administrative buildings to the town centre (1TD taxi). The road at the top of the hill heads left towards Sakiet Sidi Youssef, or right to **place de l'Indépendance** at the centre of town. Rue Hedi Chaker heads east from here, and continues down past the **post office** (city hours) to meet the Sakiet Sidi Youssef road. There is no tourist office in town, but the **Association de Sauvegarde de la Médina (ASM) office** (variable hours, weekday mornings best; ☎08/201148), on place de l'Indépendance, promotes interest in Le Kef's history and functions as a tourist office; it also serves as an unofficial social club. If it's closed the excellent **regional museum** (p.279) is also a good source of information.

Le Kef has several **hotels**, mostly low- to mid-range and a decent **youth hostel**.

Hotels

Medina, 18 rue Farhat Hached ☎08/204183. The rooms here aren't as promising as its lobby suggests, but are usually clean and there should be hot water. A decent bet. **②**

Hôtel les Pins, av de l'Environnement, 2km out of town on the Tunis road ☎08/204300, ☏202411. A modern place owned by the same folk as the *Venus*, with superlative views from most rooms, good facilities and very well priced. Recommended if you don't mind staying out of town. **④**

Ramzi, rue Hedi Chaker ☎08/203079. Kef's newest hotel and pretty good. Spotlessly clean tiled rooms with or without bathroom. **③**

Hôtel les Remparts ★, rue des Remparts ☎08/202100. A new purpose-built place, centrally located opposite the post office, with good rooms but less personable than the *Venus*. **③**

Sicca Veneria, av Bourguiba ☎08/202389. Central and with mod cons and a choice of bath or shower. Recently renovated. **③**

Hôtel de la Source, rue de la Source, near the beginning of avenue Bourguiba ☎ & ☏08/204397. Something of a grotty travellers' hotel, and popular with Algerians too. All rooms except one are the usual budget fare, the better ones facing the street. The exception is its legendary four-bed *chambre de famille*, where a huge double bed reposes under an ornate vaulted stucco ceiling; this may be the nearest you'll come to sleeping like an eighteenth-century Tunisian bey, give or take the odd grubby sheet. No hot water unless you pay double. **②**–**③**

Résidence Venus, rue Mouldi Khamessi, off rue Ali Belhouane ☎ & ☏08/204695. A friendly, laid-back pension underneath the restaurant of the same name. It's five minutes' walk north of place de l'Indépendance, up rue de la Source, right at rue Ali Belhouane, and on the second left. If your budget's up to it, this is the best bet in town, with most rooms en suite. **③**

Youth hostel

Maison des Jeunes, 8 rue Mohamed Gammoudi ☎08/204424. Very friendly, and right in town near the post office. Currently not taking guests – call and check.

The Town

Le Kef – or plain Kef as it's usually known – is a great place just to wander at random, catching glimpses, between houses or over the trees in the park, of the plains below. The old quarters huddle below the southern end of the mountain plateau, with the new districts spreading out down the slope below. From the central **place de l'Indépendance**, **avenue Bourguiba** follows the curve of the hill round to the right, a tremendous belvedere for the chequered plains below.

On the uphill side of avenue Bourguiba is the **Medina**, with narrow cobbled streets winding up to the Kasbah at the cliff's edge. The Medina's main street is **rue Farhat Hached**, which begins at avenue Bourguiba near place de l'Indépendance. A third of the way along it is the old synagogue, from where rue Marakit Karama ascends to the Basilica in **place Bou Makhlouf** and to the **Kasbah** beyond that, while in the other direction rue Bahri Barbouch drops to place Habib Thameur, just off avenue Bourguiba above the market.

Place de l'Indépendance and around

Place de l'Indépendance forms the heart of the town, but is little more than a crowded traffic junction bordered on the south side by a park. Just north of here, the **spring** of Ras el Aïn rises in the open space just below the *Hôtel de la Source* on the square; it has always supplied the cities on this site, receiving cult reverence through the centuries. Roman blocks which channelled the water can be made out. Just next to the locked door of the spring proper is a small niche, a **shrine** to the Islamic saint Lalla Mna who was originally a Roman nymph, but was later renamed and Islamicized. She remains a living cult, and there are often recent offerings in the niche.

Back along rue de la Source, past the **Mosque of Sidi Ahmed Gharib**, is a confused area of **Roman remains** which are permanently but slowly being excavated and restored. Above the street is the entrance to a huge Roman **cistern** which stored the water that fed the more interesting complex across the street. Here at the far end is a **nympheum**, or fountain, which would have been lined with statues, and a **baths complex**. The baths were subsequently converted into a church whose geometric mosaics are visible. A wall is lined with the tombstones of Roman worthies. Before emerging onto rue Ali Belhouane, rue de la Source runs through an attractive old **vaulted passage** containing food shops.

The Medina

Le Kef's main attraction is its **Medina**, which has managed to retain not just monuments from successive periods in its history, but also a neighbourhood feeling, away from the bustle of the new town. Closest of the monuments is the well-preserved (if rather dull) fourth-century **Dar el Kouss Church** – take the first right off rue Farhat Hached immediately after it leaves avenue Bourguiba, and the church is on the first corner. A small room in its far right-hand corner has a curiously carved lintel stone combining a Greek cross and a palm frond. The *gardien* (keys) should be found at the ASM office.

From here you can rejoin rue Farhat Hached and turn right to meet rue Marakit Karama going uphill and rue Bahri Barbouch coming down it. At rue **Bahri Barbouch** you leap forward to Turkish times, when the street was reserved for the town's Jewish community. The building on the northeast corner of this junction is the former **synagogue**, recently – and remarkably, here in the distant interior of an Arab country – restored. The synagogue's walls are now lined with items evoking the not-so-distant world of Tunisia's Jewish community, such as Hebrew tablets, photos of local life in the 1950s and a wedding invitation from 1960. The knowledgeable *gardien* who lets you in is usually inside – if not, ask at the ASM office. Incidentally Le Kef's last Jewish citizen died peacefully in 1995.

Le Kef was one of three *ghribas* in the eastern Maghreb – the other two being in Annaba, Algeria (presumably disappeared) and Jerba (see p.381). The town had a sizeable Jewish community, though virtually all left for Tunis, France or Israel in the years following World War II and especially during Independence. Their traditional specialization in jewellery lives on in the shops which line rue Bahri Barbouch, where you will also find spectacular wedding costumes and one small jewellery shop with a fine old painted wooden shade.

Le Kef has also played its part in recent Tunisian history. The father of Husayn Bin Ali, the Husaynid dynasty's founder, is entombed just up the hill. You pass his somewhat derelict **Tourbet of Ali Turki** at the top of rue Bahri Barbouch and rue du Soudan. Ali Turki was born in Crete but came to Tunisia and enrolled in the army during the reign of Mourad Bey. While serving in Le Kef he married two local Tunisian women, each of whom gave birth to a son: one of them was Husayn Bin Ali, founder of the Husaynid dynasty (ruled 1705–35; see p.435); the other was the father of Ali Pacha, Husayn's successor (ruled 1735–56).

If you continue up rue du Soudan you'll come to **place Bou Makhlouf,** an open space below the Kasbah that lay at the heart of the souks of the old town. Here was the town's Great Mosque, the monumental building now known as the **Basilica,** which was used for hundreds of years for Muslim worship. The building now serves as a **museum** of local antiquities (daily 8–11am & 3–6pm; free), although it is more interesting for its own sake – even though very little is known for certain about its origins. Built either in late Roman or Byzantine times, it takes the form of a spacious courtyard (look for columns of unusual green stone) which leads into a cruciform room ending in an apse. Both the apse and the arms of the cross are lined with niches (23 in all), with a carved lintel running above them.

The diminutive **Mosque of Sidi Bou Makhlouf** at the end of place Bou Makhlouf, along with the complex of streets around it, is one of the most captivating spots in Tunisia. The mosque – named after the patron saint of Le Kef, who originally came from Fez – is a small masterpiece, the bare whitewashed courtyard leading into a domed prayer hall resting on antique columns and lined with white stuccowork. On the outside, its dome has an unusual ribbed appearance, similar to the domes of Tunis's Sidi Mehrez. At the beginning of the nineteenth century this complex became home to Le Kef's branch of the Aissaouia *sufi* brotherhood, renowned for some of the more outlandish *sufi* rituals. On one side of the cobbled street leading up to the mosque is a blue door into a former *fondouk* which has a Roman tombstone for a tap in its central water trough. Opposite it is the pleasant *Café des Souks* (daily 9am–9pm, open late in summer), with chairs also in the square. For a magical experience, take your drink up to the Kasbah ramparts above. It's the perfect place to sit and watch the changing patterns of light over the plains and is especially enchanting under a full moon.

The Kasbah

The views from the **Kasbah** above attest to the prime military importance of Le Kef. The smaller and lower of the **forts** here is a legacy of the border struggles under the Beys: Hammouda Bey added it in 1813 to house a guard of ultra-faithful troops, because of Algerian designs on the town. Excavations here during the current refurbishment uncovered the remains of a number of Turkish clay pipes made in Smyrna (now Izmir) on Turkey's Aegean coast. The older, larger fort dates back to 1601 and was converted into a prison for Tunisian nationalists, during the French occupation.

With the exception of the statuary at the top, the Kasbah has now been abandoned by the military, and has been renovated to house a **cultural centre** (variable hours; free, though the guides may expect a tip) in the large fort, where the region's cultural archives – currently in the ASM office – will be housed. The dungeon is to become a small museum, so currently the only cultural activities inside the fort are during the annual two-week **Festival de Sidi Bou Makhlouf** held in mid-July, when there are theatre and music performances.

Following rue el Kasbah round above the Basilica and rue Sidi Bou Makhlouf to place Ben Aissa, you'll find the worthy **regional museum** (Tues–Sun: April–Oct

9am–1pm & 4–7pm; Nov–March 9.30am–4.30pm; 1.1TD, camera 1TD), housed in the restored *zaouia* Sidi Ali Ben Aissa. Its exhibits beautifully evoke the way of life of the nomads, whose tents can still be seen on the surrounding plain. Put up in 1784, the building that houses the museum was originally the headquarters of a *sufi* religious brotherhood called the **Rahmania**. The staff are enthusiastic and knowledgeable and can help you out with general queries if the ASM is closed.

The old town walls run almost continuously from the Kasbah around to the east, finally encircling a **presidential palace**. This is something of a sore point in the town, as it occupies a prime site but is hardly ever used; a swimming pool beckons invitingly in its grounds, while the municipal pool in the park has never been opened. Just below the palace walls is the nineteenth-century **Zaouia of Sidi Mizouni**, which is the local headquarters of the Qadriya *sufi* brotherhood, probably the oldest of the *sufi* brotherhoods.

Bab Ghedive and beyond

Just above the palace, **Bab Ghedive** (Gate of Treachery) gives entrance to the town and earned its name in 1881 when the governor and town notables, having received no orders to fight, opened the gate to the French army on its "temporary mission" – even though the townspeople were prepared for a long siege. They surrendered the most important frontier defences without a shot being fired.

Once through the gate, the transition from town to country is startlingly abrupt. Just ahead, an iron ladder leads down into a vast **Roman cistern** that's twelve gloomy chambers in length and one of the coolest places in Kef – but an alcoholics' den at night.

Over to the right from here, across the road, are more fragmentary remains, the first set of which may be the ancient **Sanctuary of Astarte** – so notorious for its erotic mysteries. Roman moralists professed shock that young Carthaginian girls of noble birth were forced to sacrifice their virginity here to the goddess, ensuring the fertility of the land on which Sicca depended, but it was the Romans who gave the town the suffix "Veneria". Sex still enjoyed a high profile here in Christian times; the second area of remains, below the disused **Christian cemetery**, may have been the **Ksar el Ghoula Basilica**, which reputedly possessed a magic mirror – men who suspected their wives of infidelity could look at the glass and find the face of their rival. Beyond it, a **Jewish cemetery** stretches all the way back to the wall, the part nearest to it being much older than the rest of the Jewish and Christian cemeteries.

Eating and drinking

Food is generally good and cheap in Le Kef with numerous perfectly decent *gargotes* on and around avenue Bourguiba. Best of the cheapies are: the pleasant family-run *Restaurant les Ruines*, (daily 7am–8.30pm, 10 or 11pm in summer), up a dead end by the ASM office; the *Bou Makhlouf* (daily 5am–9pm), which only has the name written in Arabic, but it's just before the Esso station on the other side of the road; *Restaurant el Andalous* (Mon–Sat 6am–8pm, 11pm in summer), in rue Hedi Chaker opposite the post office, which does great couscous and the *Restaurant El Hana* (daily 6am–7pm, 9pm) in avenue Bourguiba above the market. All of these places will fill you up with standard tasty fare including soups, couscous, chicken and steaks for 3–5TD. For a cheap pizza with a view, try *Café Plazza* (daily 9am–9pm, later in summer) a few hundred metres east on the road to Tunis.

For a smarter, more expensive meal, try the *Hôtel Sicca Veneria*'s restaurant (daily 11.30am–3pm & 6–11pm). Alternatively, if you've never had supper at a petrol station, the *Restaurant Dyr* (daily noon–3pm & 6–10pm), above Esso's pumps in rue Hedi Chaker, 50m past the post office, serves a surprisingly good meal for 10–15TD. A final, more upmarket, alternative is the *Restaurant Venus* (daily noon–3pm & 6–9pm, closed Fri) on avenue Bourguiba.

If you want to **drink** in the evening, try the cheap, unnamed bar-restaurant up behind the post office at 4 rue Salya. The *Sicca's* bar is only slightly more refined.

Listings

Banks There are several banks around town, especially at the top of rue Salah Ayech and rue Ali Belhouane; others can be found in av Bourguiba above the market, and opposite the bus station on the hill down into the new town. They run a weekend rota, so there should be at least one open in the mornings. If not, the post office changes money.

Cinemas Ciné Pathe, av Bourguiba (no sign).

Consulates The Algerian consulate is at no. 3 rue Hedi Chaker. You could try them for a visa, but they will probably tell you to go to Tunis and apply there. See p.185 for a warning about travel in Algeria.

Festivals The annual two week Festival de Sidi Bou Makhlouf is held in mid-July, during which time theatre and other performances are held in the Kasbah. The first day sees a procession by the Aissouia *sufi* brotherhood through the streets. Another good date to be in town is the 27th day of Ramadan, which also sees religious parades and music.

Guide An entertaining if not wholly accurate guide for walks in the hills around Le Kef is the polyglot Issaoui Fathi, who you can ask for at the *Hôtel de la Source*. He requires three days' notice.

Hammams The best is on rue Ali Belhouane – follow rue de la Source to its end, past the tunnel and turn right. Others are at pl Habib Thameur, at the bottom of rue Habib Karma, and at 33 rue Farhat Hached.

Hospital On the Sakiet Sidi Youssef road ☎08/420900.

Pharmacy There's a night pharmacy in rue Souk Ahras – turn right just before the post office in rue Hedi Chaker and it's 100m up on your left.

Police Just off pl Tahar Ben Brahim.

Post office Rue Hedi Chaker (city hours); international phones. There's also a taxiphone office on rue de la Source at av Bourguiba.

Supermarket Monoprix is 100m off to the left of the hill down into the new town, about halfway down, just above the bus station.

Around Le Kef

If the view across the plains around Le Kef tempts you, there are several good hiking possibilities and particularly rewarding excursions. One of the best short walks is to **SIDI MANSOUR**, a small village around 4km north of town. Leave Kef by Bab Ghedive and scramble up the rocks below the TV mast. A rough path leads north through a small eucalyptus plantation and onto the top of the plateau, opening out on an immense view over the broken forests along the Algerian border and the glint of the lake behind the Mellegue Dam. The village, a small farming community, is soon reached. Just to the west, beyond a deep river canyon, are wide caves gouged in the rock – a popular picnic spot inhabited in prehistoric times. It isn't far north of the village to the other end of the plateau; or you can climb up to the east, then bend down and around and come back into Kef by the palace.

The artificial **Lake Mellegue** that gleams in the distance from Sidi Mansour was created by damming the River Mellegue. Buses head in this direction from Kef to the attractive village of **NEBEUR**, 17km northeast below the northern tip of the mountain of Jebel Dyr, and then 5km on to **BARRAGE MELLEGUE**, a small cluster of houses on the dam itself. The water crashing out at the bottom has the colour and consistency of liquid chocolate. The reason for coming to the dam, though, is to walk back to Le Kef through open country – a five-hour hike, but a rewarding one. There's no danger of getting lost as Jebel Dyr is always in sight and, once you get to the mountain, Le Kef is only 5km further on.

If you aim for the top of **Jebel Dyr**, then head round its western face below the cliff edge, you should hit a winding tractor track that runs all the way to Sidi Mansour. It climbs through clumps of pines, foothills of the mountain proper to emerge onto broader slopes which sweep up like waves against the rock. The scenery is tremendous, but the hike will also give you an insight into the pace of life in this part of Tunisia, and an appreciation for the value of **water**. When you set out on the walk, take as much water as you can carry, but even so you'll probably need refills. For these you're dependent on the infrequent springs that the isolated local farmhouses rely on for their daily needs. On reaching these, you'll be surrounded by a group of children who have walked several kilometres with donkeys and cans to fetch the day's supply.

At the other end of Lake Mellegue, the restored Roman spa of **Hammam Mellegue** is at the end of a twelve-kilometre piste off the road to Sakiet, 10km west of Le Kef. (Sakiet buses go to the piste junction only.) Hot spring water provides a communal bath (women in the morning, men in the afternoon), which is very popular with people from the surrounding villages. Walking is the only sure way of getting to it, though you might try sticking your thumb out just in case. Alternatively, ask around for a lift at the market in Le Kef.

Thirty-five kilometres west of Le Kef, **SAKIET SIDI YOUSSEF** is the last village before the Algerian frontier. The border post here is sometimes open (see opposite), and accessible from Le Kef by louage, but you should check this before setting out – the main crossing is 30km north at Ghardimaou (see p.186).

There's little other reason for visiting Sakiet, although it does have a historical notoriety. It was here, in the midst of the Algerian War in 1958, that the French bombed the civilian population. The incident was denounced as a "new Guernica" and caused a rapid decline in relations between France and newly independent Tunisia. One outcome was the Tunisian attempt to eject the French navy from their base at Bizerte.

South of Le Kef

The area **south of Le Kef** – before the fertile plains climb up onto bleaker steppes around Kasserine – is right off the tourist routes. Yet, using Le Kef as a base, it's a quietly rewarding region to explore. The scenery, always impressive, becomes eerily compelling around the craggy mountain of **Jugurtha's Table**, and there are two unexcavated but well-preserved Roman sites at **Medeina** and **Haïdra**. Each of these – particularly Haïdra – has an aloof grandeur in its remoteness, inspiring an excitement quite absent from the more domesticated major sites.

Tajerouine and Jugurtha's Table

TAJEROUINE is the first town of any size on the main road, 25km south of Le Kef, and is quite a transport centre. The **bus** station is in the middle of town on the main road, with plenty of buses to Le Kef and Sakiet Sidi Youssef. **Louages** stop nearby, down a road next to the mosque. Tajerouine has a **Monday souk**, and there are **banks** and a Magasin Général **supermarket** opposite the bus station, but no hotel and little character: it's hardly more than an outgrown roadstead.

But beyond the town, you emerge onto the plains – vast open spaces with jutting isolated **mountains** that bob like ships on a calm sea. There is a good deal of mining on the plain, with major producers of iron and phosphates dotted about here.

The place to head for, however, to reap the best rewards of the scenery around here, is **KALAAT ES SENAM**. Just 6km from the Algerian border, this small village sits at the foot of the mountain known as **Jugurtha's Table**, a flat-topped peak like Jebel Dyr to the north but more sharply defined, with its tilting plateau standing out for kilometres around. Louages go to Kalaat es Senam either direct from Le Kef or with a change at Tajerouine. Stock up with water while you can, because it's a good two hours' walk from the village to the steps in the middle of the mountain's north side, though the steps themselves make for an easy ascent.

The name "Jugurtha's Table" refers to the tradition that it was the stronghold of the Numidian king **Jugurtha** in his second-century BC struggles against the Romans; a role echoed in more recent times by the name of Kalaat es Senam – "Seat of Senam" – after a local bandit who made similar use of the mountain against the armies of the Beys. This dramatic past seems very close as you climb the steps to the summit, which are hacked into the rock and lead to a Byzantine gateway. The lunar-like surface is littered with remains, which include troglodyte **caves** and a spooky **marabout**. Romance apart, the mountain also provides a magnificent view and, if you have camping gear, it's an extraordinarily remote place to spend the night.

Kalaa Khasbah and Haïdra Town

KALAA KHASBAH (also known as Kalaa Jerda) is an old Italian mining town retaining echoes of its colonial influence, with tiled houses, profuse greenery and abandoned mining machinery, including an enormous chimney stack. But the real reason for coming here is to find transport to the Roman site of Haïdra, 18km west towards Algeria.

This is the terminal for passenger **train** services, with one a day to Tunis via Le Sers, Gaafour and El Fahs; even though Haïdra is on the train line, there are no passenger trains further than Kalaa Khasbah. There are onward **buses** to Thala, Kasserine, and Le Kef, and **louages** to Thala, Kasserine and Le Kef (see p.296 for details of services). **Hitching** to Haïdra from Kalaa Khasbah is quite easy – there's only one road, so virtually everything that passes will stop. On your way back down this road, look out to the north for glimpses of Jugurtha's Table, ducking above and below the skyline – more than ever reminiscent of the prow of a ship. The modern settlement of **HAÏDRA TOWN** has even more of a dead-end border feel than Ghardimaou, enlivened only by a grotesque **train station**. With its extraordinary combination of Classical order and 1930s Deco, this would look weird anywhere, let alone miles from anywhere on a North African frontier. The **border post** here is usually open, but little used.

TRAVELLING TO ALGERIA

On no account go to Algeria. You should also be aware of heightened Tunisian sensitivities when travelling near the Algerian border – passport checks will be more frequent than normal, and you should think hard before going off the beaten track anywhere near the border. See p.185 for more details.

Haïdra
حيدرة

The Roman site of **Haïdra** (free entry), 18km southwest of Kalaa Khasbah, is remotely positioned by the Algerian frontier and only minimally excavated, meaning that the surviving monuments are exceptionally well preserved. Coming upon them, you feel something of the awe early travellers must have experienced when confronted with remains of a mysterious and magnificent past.

Ancient Haïdra, Roman Ammaedara, was in its way a border post like the modern village of the same name, founded as a base for the Third Augustan Legion, whose job was to protect Rome's new province from hostile incursions. When the Legion was

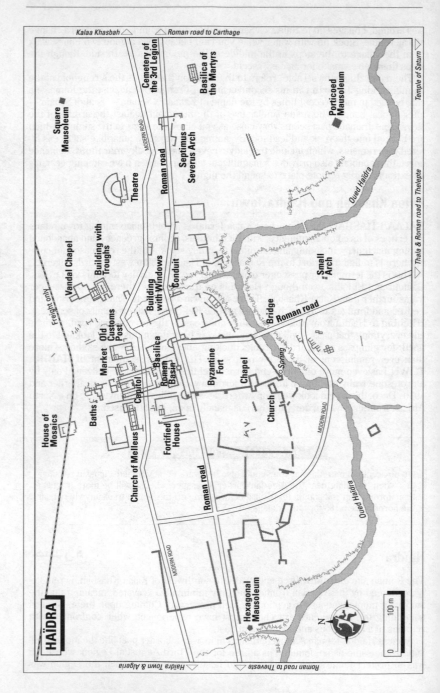

HAÏDRA

Kalaa Khasbah △   △ Roman road to Carthage

Cemetery of
the 3rd Legion

Basilica of
the Martyrs

Temple of Saturn ▷

Square
Mausoleum

Porticoed
Mausoleum

Theatre

Septimus
Severus Arch

Roman road

MODERN ROAD

Thala & Roman road to Thelepte ▷

Vandal Chapel

Building with
Troughs

Building
with Windows

Conduit

Small
Arch

Oued Haïdra

Freight only

Market   Old
Customs
Post

Basilica

Bridge   Roman road

House of
Mosaics

Baths

Capitol

Roman
Basin

Byzantine
Fort

Chapel

Spring

Church of Melleus

Fortified
House

Church

MODERN ROAD

Roman road

MODERN ROAD

Oued Haïdra

Hexagonal
Mausoleum

N

0   100 m

Haïdra Town & Algeria ◁   ◁ Haïdra Town

Roman road to Theveste ▽

moved further west, the camp became an important town – but, after the Islamic conquest, it reverted to its border role.

The ruins sprawl beside the road just to the east of the modern settlement. If you've managed to get a ride in from Kalaa Khasbah, you might want to get dropped off outside the Byzantine fort at the centre of the ancient remains, opposite a French customs post dated 1886, recently vacated by the military to make room for a museum that is still in its planning stages.

The site

East of the customs post, identifiable by a hemispherical arch, are the remains of Haïdra's "building with troughs" (see also p.289). A **Vandal Chapel** behind it is so called because of the crude inscriptions on its paving stones dating it to the reigns of the kings Thrasamund (510 AD) and Ildirix (526 AD), who sound as though they come from an Asterix and Obelix storyline.

On the west side of the customs post, a **market** can just about be made out as a square depression, followed by the **Capitol** temple with only its podium recognizable, and then the more interesting **Basilica of Melleus**, featuring two rows of columns, some in Chemtou marble, clearly defining the nave. Entrance to the church was through three doors at the eastern end, which connected with a courtyard. An apsidal structure at the western end was the *presbyterium*, reserved for clergy. Spidery inscriptions from the sixth and seventh centuries, still visible on the paving stones, suggest something of Haïdra's turbulent history. They include the gravestones of two bishops buried here – Victorinus, a Vandal Arian Christian, and Melleus, a Byzantine Catholic.

Across the road from the Basilica lies a fortifed house, and over to the east the five empty windows of the **"building with windows"**, whose function is not known. Behind looms the northern wall of the mother of all Byzantine **fortresses** in Tunisia. Built to guard an important frontier crossroads when the Byzantines retook Tunisia from the Vandals in 533 AD, its north wall was rebuilt much later under the Turks. Two hundred metres long by 100m wide, with stretches of wall and towers still standing 10m high, the fortress stretches down to the river valley at the bottom of the hill. Roads from Carthage and Tebessa entered through fortified towers at the top of the fortress, while the road from Thelepte crossed a Roman **bridge**, whose remains can still be seen in the riverbed, and then entered through the southeastern tower. The interior presents a jumble of unexcavated remains except for the evocative **chapel**, built against the southwest wall, with its apse and green columns. If smaller Byzantine fortresses such as Mustis reek of panic on the frontier, this one conveys instead the determination,

---

MAN BITES LION

The area around Haïdra was notorious among early European travellers for the lawlessness of its inhabitants. Although James Bruce (see p.484), passing this way in 1765, managed to avoid mortal danger, he did have a curious gastronomic experience. A recent predecessor, one Dr Shaw, had claimed that the inhabitants of Haïdra ate lions, but was promptly accused of "traveller's licence" by the learned doctors of Oxford University, who "took it as a subversion of the natural order of things, that a man should eat a lion, when it has long passed as almost the peculiar province of the lion to eat man". Ever the vigorous empiricist, Bruce was not much impressed by expert opinion, and was glad to be able to report that he had "eaten the flesh of three lions – that is part of three lions – in the tents of the Welled Sidi Boogannim". He found the texture like old horseflesh, palatable except for a strong smell of musk. As for the locals, he sniffed, "a brutish and ignorant folk, they will, I fear, notwithstanding the disbelief of the University of Oxford, continue to eat lions as long as they exist".

however doomed, of a Byzantine empire based thousands of kilometres away to defend what it saw as its rightful inheritance.

The site's eastern outskirts contain two well-preserved square **mausoleums**, the golden-coloured southern one with its four-columned second storey standing in splendid isolation above the river. Between them, next to the modern road, stands the **triumphal arch** of Septimius Severus (195 AD). Like the arch at Maktar and the Capitol at Dougga, this owes its crisp preservation to fortifications that the Byzantines built around it; here, the Byzantine work has been only partially dismantled, and the arch emerging from its casing looks for all the world like a piece of sculpture coming out of a plaster cast. West of the site, again just above the river, stands another well-preserved **mausoleum** – this time hexagonal.

Thala   تالة

Continuing from Kalaa Khasbah to Kasserine, the only village of any size is **THALA**, 10km south of Kalaa, on the steep slope dividing the plains of Kef from the more forbidding steppes around Kasserine. At an altitude of 1017m, it is a refreshing place in summer but a cold one in midwinter. The village's only claim to fame is a notorious incident in 1906, when a marabout, **Amor Ben Othman**, inspired the local Fraichich tribes to take up arms against the colonists who had stolen their lands. In the ensuing riot sixteen men, women and children died, causing an outcry across North Africa. Amor Ben Othman was brought to trial and the press clamoured for his execution. Only Myriam Harry, a reporter on *Le Temps*, cared to look behind the scenes and describe the poverty and deprivation suffered by the Fraichich tribe under colonial rule. "Oh little Joan of Arc of this desert," she wrote, "what pity you inspire in me". Her sympathy could not help the marabout and his accomplices: all were hanged with great ceremony as a warning to others.

There are a few minor **excavations** on the main street in Thala, and a **marble factory** in the lower outskirts of the village, but, unless you arrive on a Friday (market day), there is little reason to linger. Should you want to **stay**, there is the cheap and popular *Hôtel Bouthelja* (℡07/480040; ❷), just off the main street, but it is for males only and basic. There are also a couple of cheap **restaurants**, a **bank** and a **petrol station**. At the **bus station** up the hill, there are regular daily services to Kasserine, Tajerouine and Le Kef; opposite is a **louage stop** for Kalaa Kasbah, Kasserine and Haïdra. The SNTRI stop for the two daily buses to Tunis is down the hill (see p.296 for details of services).

Medeina   مدينة

Medeina, Roman Althiburos, isn't the easiest site in Tunisia to reach. You have to get the bus from Le Kef to Dahmani (also known as Ebba Ksour), a small tree-shaded farming town, and then walk or hitch 7km down the Jerissa road; the turning to Medeina is on the left, and the site about a four-kilometre walk away.

Despite its present remoteness, Medeina once stood on the main Roman road from Carthage to Tebessa. Today its ruins are attractive enough, rambling above a green riverbed, though hardly extensive. The first glimpse is of a third-century AD **Triumphal Arch**, almost hidden in a field to the left. Beyond, towards the centre of the site, the most distinctive building is the **Capitol**, just above the riverbed, to one side of the paved **Forum**, opposite the remains of a **temple**. A street runs southeast through the Forum, and following it you find a well-preserved **fountain** on a street corner. Further in this direction are the remains of a **theatre**.

Back in the Forum, alongside the temple opposite the Capitol is the **House of Sixteen Bases**, whose name refers to the unusual reliefs on the bases of its inner portico. Some way north of here, across a stream bed, is the **Building of Aesclepia**. No one knows its precise function, but having begun life as a private house it seems to have become the home of some sort of cult connected with the healing god Aesclepius. This explains the extraordinary number of baths found here, and the quality of the mosaics – most of them third- or fourth-century AD, and now removed to the Bardo Museum in Tunis.

Maktar and around

مكثر

It's well worth going through the town of **MAKTAR** (or Makthar) for the scenery alone. The road from Le Kef winds 60km through some preliminary foothills to **Le Sers**, a French railway town sitting in the middle of a vast natural land that contains some of the most fertile land in the country. Passing through Le Vieux Sers, a few kilometres further south, are a couple of rough tracks leading to the unexcavated but quite substantial remains of Roman Assuras at **ZANNFOUR** (6km), and of **ELLES** (9km), with megalithic tombs and a meagre Roman settlement that produced the Bardo's bizarre fourth-century mosaic of a stressed Venus being crowned by two female centaurs.

The main road goes on to climb up the side of the bowl, and on neighbouring hilltops beyond the rim are the ancient and modern towns of Maktar, separated by a modern road junction at a Roman triumphal arch.

Modern Maktar, across a ravine from the ancient town, is quite a tempting place to stay. At nearly 1000m altitude, the air is fresh, the scenery tremendous, and the relaxed feel to the town can come as a welcome relief. The only pretence to bustle is **market day** on Monday. **Buses** to and from Le Kef and Kairouan leave from a balustraded road at the bottom of the town, as do **louages** for Kairouan and Sousse. Buses for El Fahs, Kasserine and Tunis, and louages for El Fahs, Siliana and Tunis, all leave from the main street in the centre of town – turn left out of the *Mactaris*, then left again and at the top you'll see the departure point (see p.296 for transport frequencies and durations).

Accommodation is available at the basic but adequate *Hôtel Mactaris* (☎08/826465; ❷), near the bus and louage stop at the bottom end of town. The town's main **bar** and **restaurant** share the ground floor of this hotel.

Ancient Maktar

The site of **ancient Maktar** was only rediscovered in the nineteenth century by the French officer, Captain Bordier, who founded the modern town on a neighbouring hilltop just a short walk away. Dominating the surrounding country, it was founded in the second century BC by a Numidian king trying to protect his domain from Berber incursions. Even after it was Romanized in the second century AD, Maktar kept a strong local tone, and the city wasn't abandoned until the Hilalian invasion of the eleventh century. Today the ruins are of a similar extent to Sbeïtla's, though the mountaintop setting is much more spectacular and the museum is full of objects (tombstones in particular) that illustrate the hybrid nature of North Africa's rural Roman culture.

The site

Entry to the **site** (Tues–Sun: April–Oct 8am–noon & 3–7pm; Nov–March 8.30am–5.30pm; 2.1TD, camera 1TD) is via the **museum**, whose displays of neo-Punic stelae, many dedicated to Baal Hammon, show the enduring local influence over the early colonizers. Although Roman elements gradually appear on the stones (note the family emphasis, increasing depth, and architectural frames), the basic sculptural style is a primitive naivety that makes the figures look like rag dolls.

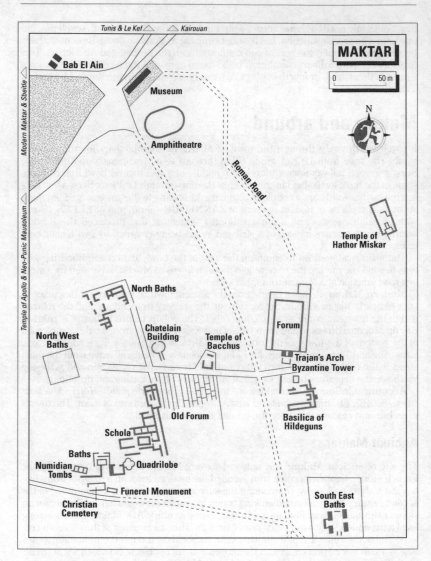

Outside the museum garden, beyond a church built on top of an earlier temple, is a small **amphitheatre** which has been substantially restored. From the middle of the arena, surrounded by gates where you can still see the slots for doors, it has the feel of a Spanish bullring. Following the track up the slope to the level hilltop brings you to a scant **Forum**, built at the same time as the **Triumphal Arch**, dedicated in 116 AD to the Emperor Trajan, whose accomplishments as "Conqueror of the Germans, Armenians and Parthians" sound very impressive. As at Dougga and Haïdra, this arch was fortified by the Byzantines and used again at the turn of the century by Captain Bordier, who installed himself in the Southeast Baths.

At the northeast corner of the Forum, a **marketplace** can be distinguished, surrounded by stalls and with an altar dedicated to Mercury. A short walk further in this direction takes you to the remains of the **Temple of Hathor Miskar**, a local divinity, and the large **House of Venus**. The Hathor Miskar temple is more interesting for the material it contained, revealing that local cults survived well into the Roman era.

Back at the Forum, a solitary tree just south of the triumphal arch stands over two rows of double columns belonging to the fifth-century Vandal **Basilica of Hildeguns**. Its baptistry, hidden behind the apse at its eastern end, is reminiscent of the one in Sbeïtla's Basilica of St Vitalis, though less lavishly decorated. After the Byzantines ejected the Vandals, they buried some of their dead in the church. From here it's a short walk south to the unmissable **Southeast Baths**. Thanks again to Byzantine fortifications, whose remnants can be made out, these are some of the most impressively preserved Roman baths in Tunisia, with massive walls and pillars and some lovely geometric mosaic floors still in place.

Back at the Triumphal Arch, a smooth paved road leads west past a **Temple of Bacchus** on the right (look for the cave uncovered in its cellar) and an irregular paved open space on the left. This is another **Forum**, an older African one that predates the rigid Roman lines of the model next to the Triumphal Arch. The original wasn't any less functional than the new Forum; it's just that custom demanded one in the Roman style.

The **Châtelain Building** at the road junction is named after its excavator but is little understood, while the **North Baths** date from Byzantine times. The **Northwest Baths** date from the second century AD, but were converted into a church in the fifth or sixth century. Roman blocks were cut down (look for an interrupted inscription) to obtain the square posts that define the nave and two aisles.

A path leads southeast from here to the prettily ruined **Schola**, its columns and trees reminiscent of Olympia in Greece. This was basically a clubhouse for a young men's association, where well-born youths of the town would meet both socially and as a sort of police force. Their complex here consisted of the main building, later confused by being turned into a well-defined church with apse and columns, and just to the south the so-called *quadrilobe*, whose windows with troughs make it one of the mysterious **"Buildings with Troughs"** (see p.285). Here the troughs were perhaps used for the collection of contributions by the association's members.

It was this sort of voluntary association, with its implicit faith in the Roman order, that formed the backbone of the Empire. If it had been able to offer the rural Berbers what it offered the urban citizens, it might have lasted longer. A remarkable gravestone found at Maktar, belonging to the so-called "Maktar Reaper", records a rare case of upward mobility. The inscription, thought to date from the second half of the third century AD, tells the "local boy made good" story with relish – how the dead man worked his way up the social scale by the sweat of his honest brow. You too, it concludes encouragingly, can be a success: "Learn, mortals, to lead a blameless life. Those who have lived honourable lives have earned an honourable death."

Behind the Schola, some jumbled remains belong to a **cemetery** that was in use for six hundred years; its earliest tombs were megalithic chambers active before the arrival of the Romans, and still used in the first century AD. Five hundred metres west of here, outside the site wall, beyond a **Muslim cemetery** that surrounds a white-domed **koubba**, stands an Oriental-looking neo-Punic **mausoleum** similar to the one at Dougga. Getting over the site wall is a bit of a scramble – you may prefer to go back to the site entrance and walk up the road. The mausoleum's pyramidal roof and angular design are distinctly un-Roman, though the monument may in fact have been built during the imperial epoch. Another 500m northwest of here is an African-style **Temple of Apollo**. If you come up here by the road, or return down it, don't miss the **herm** (entry stone with phallus) which stands outside the excavation headquarters. A second triumphal arch below the museum is difficult to miss; the square **Mausoleum of the**

Julii, across the road from the museum, is easier to miss. And easiest of all to miss is the tumbledown **dolmen tomb** in the middle of town, on the right of the road on to Kairouan.

The route to Kairouan

The most exciting way out of Maktar is the **road to Kairouan**, which runs through some of the most rugged scenery in the country. After about 10km you enter the vast **Forest of Kesra**, a blanket of bright-green Aleppo pine named after **LA KESRA**, a Berber village clinging almost invisibly to a mountain face at an altitude of 1078m.

Sideroads connect the village to the main route from both east and west, the western one slightly shorter at about 3km – the western junction, with stores and a school, is also where you're more likely to find a lift. If you catch it open (closed during winter), the *Hôtel des Chasseurs*, 1km west of the junction on the main road, offers spectacular **views** up to the village and down onto the plain. Although steep, the climb up to La Kesra offers a foretaste of the *ksour* in the south, as well as a reminder of similar villages further north, such as Chaouach (p.177) and Jeradou (p.262). The houses merge with the slope, leaving no doubts about the defensive necessity which saw settlements like these built, faced with the dangers of open plains to the south – Maktar shared the same vulnerability. Nowadays the only defence is a pair of **cemeteries** at either end of the village, each surrounding a white-domed tomb of a saint.

Back below, at a village called El Garia, the main road soon punches through the last ridge of hills, a final reminder of the Tell before you descend onto the plain of the Sahel. If you're going through to Kairouan, you face another 90km of barren emptiness, broken by only the barest of diversions. Just east of the roadside town of **HAFFOUZ**, 35km east of La Kesra, is an old and neglected French **war cemetery** for Muslim soldiers. Twenty kilometres further, as the road crosses Oued Chnihira, look out to the north of the road for remains of the **aqueduct** which carried water from the mountains to Kairouan's Aghlabid pools (see pp.223–4).

About 15km beyond the tunnel at El Garia, a turning goes left to **OUESSLATIA**, another 10km away. This road offers an alternative route into the exciting El Fahs–Maktar–Kairouan triangle. Another drab modern farming settlement of little interest for its own sake, Ouesslatia is the principal settlement inside the triangle, lying in the broad valley between Jebel Ousselat to the southeast and Jebel Seri to the northwest. In the eighteenth century, and for hundreds of years before, these mountains were the home of the eponymous Ousselatia, a tribe that, like the Khroumirs, remained outside the control of central government in Tunis. In the dynastic quarrel of the 1730s they made the mistake of backing Husayn Bin Ali, and on his death in 1740 the mountain was taken by his rival, Ali Pacha. The chronicler Mohammed Seghir Ben Youssef cut down all the olive trees and exiled the survivors to the corners of the Regency, from where they were never allowed to return.

Despite its fertility, the mountain is still deserted, its empty villages having remained untouched for two hundred years. Like much of the terrain around here, it's good walking country, with limited public transport.

This same road, if followed north all the way, leads past the Byzantine fort at Ksar Lemsa to El Fahs. The other road out of Ouesslatia heads northwest to Siliana, round the flank of **Jebel Serj**, which at 1360m is only slightly lower than Jebel Chambi, outside Kasserine, the highest mountain in the country. Ten kilometres along this road, as it climbs up to enter the mountain massif, the remains of Roman **Aggar** tumble down the slopes to the north of the road. A little further, the massive pillars of a Roman **bridge** march across a riverbed next to a rickety-looking modern equivalent.

Sbeïtla and around

سبيطلة

The dusty modern market town of **SBEÏTLA**, 30km east of Kasserine, is unexciting in the extreme, enlivened only on Wednesdays by the weekly **souk** held mainly on avenue Ali Belhouane. What makes a detour here advisable is its proximity to the site of Roman **Sufetula**.

Very little is recorded about the Roman town, apart from one moment of abortive glory in 646 AD, when the Byzantine Prefect Gregory declared the African province independent in anticipation of the coming Arab invasion. Much good it did him or the province: the Arabs won a famous victory here in 647, making Sbeïtla the shortest-lived of all Tunisia's capitals. What remains of Roman Sufetula sits on a level plain with little scenic interest, but it does boast the best-preserved complex of Forum temples in the country. These have long been famous, inspiring one of Sir Grenville Temple's (see p.484) prints in 1835, an enlargement of which is on display in the museum here. The museum also has some fine Christian remains and the most unadulterated Roman city plan in Tunisia.

The site

The **site** (daily: April–Oct 7am–7pm; Nov–March 8.30am–5.30pm; 2.1TD, camera 1TD) lies along the Kasserine road, northwest of the new town. To get there, walk straight ahead out of the bus station about half a kilometre up rue Taieb Mehiri, past a **triumphal arch** on the right of the road which straddled the main Roman highway east to Hadrumetum (Sousse). A small **museum** (same hours; closed Mon) of archeological finds and explanatory displays recently opened opposite the site entrance. Apart from the Temple print mentioned above, look out for a round fifth-century altar table that looks at first like an olive press, and an attractive mosaic featuring a cross in red and yellow. Touts hanging around outside sell "Roman" coins, some of which may actually be genuine although almost worthless.

You enter the site past a small Byzantine **fort** and an immediate left turn takes you past another on the right. Both were little more than fortified houses, with no door on the ground floor (entrance would have been via a wooden staircase). Climbing up to look down into the second fort, you can see how crammed the rooms are: you wouldn't have wanted to withstand a long siege in here.

Beyond the fort, opposite a plan of the site on the left, are the best-preserved remains of an **olive press** in Roman Tunisia, with massive standing stones that remind you what a serious industry this was in the region. After the olive press, turn right towards the centre of the site. It's immediately apparent that you're already walking along a regular grid plan, suggesting that, unlike most of the other major Tunisian sites, Roman Sbeïtla did not grow out of an earlier African foundation.

After two long blocks, you reach the well-preserved **baths** on the right, with paved pools and hypocaust heating systems visible everywhere. Entrance was down some steps from the street on the north side; the double pillars of a palaestra exercise yard are straight ahead through two rooms, flanked immediately to the left by the *frigidarium* and, beyond, the *caldarium*. Below the baths the sad remains of a **theatre** overlook the river. It's not hard to imagine what a pleasant spot it must once have been. Back on the main road that runs towards the Forum at the centre of the complex, the **Church of St Serverus** is recognizable by the four standing corners of its baptistry. This church was carved out of an existing temple in the African style. Its baptistry was originally the temple sanctuary, reached through a square-porticoed courtyard to the south; the body of the church was laid east–west across the courtyard, with a *presbyterium* apse just recognizable at the west end.

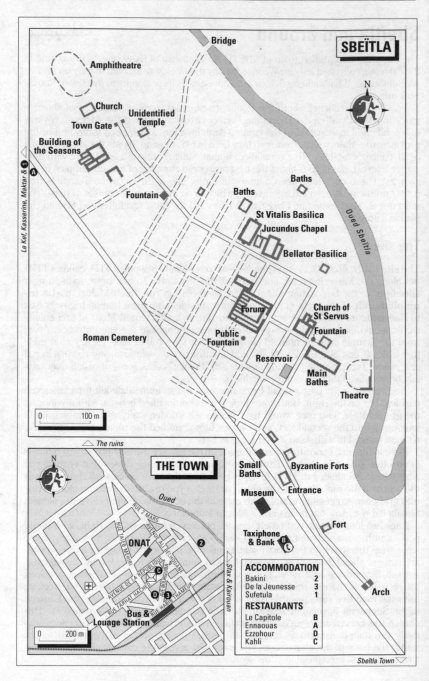

SBEÏTLA

Bridge

N

Amphitheatre

Church

Town Gate

Unidentified Temple

Building of the Seasons

Le Kef, Kasserine, Maktar &

A

Fountain

Baths

Baths

St Vitalis Basilica

Jucundus Chapel

Bellator Basilica

Oued Sbeïtla

Forum

Church of St Servus

Fountain

Roman Cemetery

Public Fountain

Reservoir

Main Baths

Theatre

0   100 m

Small Baths

Byzantine Forts

Museum

Entrance

Fort

Arch

The ruins

N

THE TOWN

Oued

RUE 2 MARS

ONAT

AVENUE ALI BEL HOUANE

RUE TAIEB MEHIRI

2

Sfax & Kairouan

AVENUE DE LA RÉPUBLIQUE

C

RUE BOURGUIBA

AVENUE FARHAT HACHED

D

3

RUE FARHAT HACHED

RUE HABIB THAMEUR

Bus & Louage Station

0   200 m

Taxiphone & Bank

B

C

Sbeïtla Town

ACCOMMODATION	
Bakini	2
De la Jeunesse	3
Sufetula	1
RESTAURANTS	
Le Capitole	B
Ennaouas	A
Ezzohour	D
Kahli	C

The Forum and basilicas

Highly photogenic due to its uniquely well-preserved condition, the **Forum** ensemble – dated to 139 AD by an inscription on the entrance archway – is Sbeïtla's big draw. Although the Byzantines may have made use of the enclosure wall as a defence, it is probably too thin to have been built as a fortification and, in any case, the original Forum was undoubtedly surrounded by a wall, as well as a colonnaded portico inside on three sides. Dedicated to the trinity of Juno, Jupiter and Minerva, the two side **temples** were approached by flights of steps, while Jupiter's in the middle stood on a podium and was accessible only from the side. For the first time here in Tunisia, you get a real sense of the dominant impact of a Roman civic centre.

Passing out of the Forum between the temples, you can turn right towards a complex of Christian buildings, which after being installed on top of existing Roman structures underwent constant shifts in configuration to reflect changes in Christian doctrine. Furthest to the right, with an apse at each end (and tombs visible in the apse nearest the street) is the Basilica of Bellator. In its first Christian incarnation, this was flanked to the west by a freestanding baptistry, later converted into a chapel. You can see where a reliquary column was inserted in the middle of a baptistry basin that was in the curiously elongated shape characteristic of Sbeïtla. The relics in question, which would have resided in the hollow on top of the column, are thought to have been those of Jucundus, a Catholic bishop martyred by the Vandals – hence the building's name, Jucundus's Chapel.

Beyond the chapel lies the largest building in the complex, the Basilica of St Vitalis, with five aisles divided by rows of double columns. Dating from the end of the fifth century, it would have had only fifty years of use before Gregory's defeat by the Arabs in 647. Even so, like Bellator's Basilica, it went through adjustments which produced an apse at both ends of the central nave. In its original form it would have had only the one nearest the street, behind which is hidden a magnificently decorated baptistry basin. The inscription in its mosaic says that the basin was built at the instigation of Vitalis and Cardela. Beyond the northwest corner of the cathedral is a baths complex.

The northern end of the site

In the distance, looking north, you should be able to see a **bridge** over the *oued*. Built by the Romans, the bridge is still used (though heavily restored), providing access to a spring on the far bank whose water is pumped directly to Sfax. Just about level with the bridge, a solitary square ruin known as the "**unidentified temple**" stands over the northwest limit of the town. Both feature in the foreground of Temple's sketch of the ruins in 1835, as the frame for some picturesque Arab hunters standing over a dead lion. Look out here for the foundations of a **Triumphal Arch** over the street, and the attractive **Building of the Seasons** on the far side, its colonnade carved with a vine in typical local style. Beyond, a low mound outside the town is all that remains of the **amphitheatre**.

Practicalities

The modern town of Sbeïtla has a **bank** and a **post office** (country hours) in avenue Farhat Hached, between the bus station and the town centre, but no tourist office. There is another bank and a **taxiphone office** in a new complex next to the museum, which also houses the *Restaurant Le Capitole*. If you want to **stay**, there are two two-star hotels – the clean and comfortable *Bakini* (✆07/465244; ❹), near the mosque on rue 2 Mars, and the pricier *Sufetula* (✆07/465074, ℱ465582; ❹), on the Kasserine road beyond the site, catering mainly for organized tour parties, but more spacious and with a view over the ruins, and a swimming pool (closed in winter) which non-residents can use for 5TD. There's also a cheaper option, the friendly *Hôtel de la Jeunesse* (☎07/466528; ❷) on avenue Bourguiba by the bus station, with clean and basic rooms.

For **food and drink**, the *Bakini* has a sedate bar and restaurant. Rather raucous by comparison, *Café Ezzohour* opposite the bus station, at the start of avenue Bourguiba, is no longer a hotel, but still dispenses beer. Basic food can be found in the *Restaurant Khali* (daily 8am–10pm); it's signed in Arabic only on a yellow sign at the other end of avenue Bourguiba, near the roundabout in the centre of town. The new *Restaurant Le Capitole* (daily 10am–midnight), opposite the site and with views over the ruins, serves three-course meals for around 15TD, is used by package groups during the day and locals for drinking in the evening. The inexpensive *Restaurant Ennaouas* (daily 9am–9pm) is opposite the ampitheatre a few hundred metres out towards the *Sufetela*.

The train station has no passenger services, but the **bus station**, in rue Habib Thameur at the southern end of town, has daily services to Kasserine, Sidi Bou Zid, Tunis, Sfax, Kairouan and Sousse; there are also **louages** to Sidi Bou Zid and Kasserine.

Sidi Bou Zid سيدي بوزيد

Moving on, the road east to Kairouan skirts the eastern edge of the Dorsale range, though there's nothing to entice a stop along the way. Similarly, the route to Sfax fails to provide even this limited interest. If you can get a lift to the first big crossroads. Some 17km east of this junction, then 8km south of the Sfax road, is **SIDI BOU ZID**, a notoriously drab town, most of whose population works in Sfax. About the only thing of interest in town is the **Zaouia of Sidi Bou Zid** and the nearby *zaouia* of his son. Unexciting from the outside (entry reserved for Muslims), this marabout is a centre of pilgrimage and the historical base of the Hammama tribal confederation.

The **bus and louage station** is about 600 metres north of the town centre on the Sfax road (see p.296 for details of services). A clutch of **banks** and a couple of cheap **restaurants** can be found by the bus station, as well as a **market**. The weekly **souk** takes places on Saturdays a few blocks behind near the *zaouias*.

There are two one-star **hotels** in Sidi Bou Zid, both in the direction of Sfax from the bus station and main square. The *Hôtel Chems* (☎06/634465; ❸) on avenue Bourguiba is small, comfortable and welcoming, if over the odds, though its budget-priced restaurant (daily 10am–8pm; 5TD or less) does an excellent *steak au poivre*. *Hôtel Horchani* (☎06/634635; ⓕ633775; ❷–❸) on rue de Meknassy, 400m off avenue Bourguiba down rue de Palestine is also clean and friendly. The *Maison des Jeunes* **youth hostel** (no phone), next to the *Horchani*, is the usual affair; for an extra dinar you'd be better off at *Hôtel Chems*. On the way out of town on avenue Bourguiba you'll pass the **post office** on your right, with a **taxiphone** office opposite and a Magasin Général **supermarket** on the left.

Kasserine and around القصرين

From the edge of the high steppes at Thala, the Gafsa road passes through empty and unrelenting country populated mainly by lonely shepherds and their flocks. Fifty kilometres south of Thala – and just 30km west of Sbeïtla – **KASSERINE** proves a sprawling and unattractive town under the equally uninspiring **Jebel Chambi**, Tunisia's highest mountain, at 1554m. The town centre is focused on a huge barracks and a conspicuously ugly American-aided cellulose factory, which accounts for the periodic stench of chlorine in town; a depressed as well as a depressing place, it's no surprise that the bread riots of January 1984 (see p.441) began here. Although it is the site of the remains of Roman Cillium and a large mausoleum, both are some way from the town centre and barely worth the effort except for enthusiasts.

The main square that marks the town centre boasts trees and flowers, three **banks**, a couple of cheap **restaurants**. **Buses and louages** leave from a site a kilometre out on the road to Sbeïtla (see p.296 for details of services). There's a **hospital** (℡07/474022) out towards the ruins, with buses running from the main square every fifteen minutes. Kasserine has no tourist office. You can access the **internet** at Publinet (24hr; 2TD/hr) in Le Complex, where there are shops and cafés, east of the town centre on the Sbeïtla road.

There are quite a few **hotels** in town, with budget places like the *Hôtel Ben Abdallah* (℡07/470568; ❷), 40 rue Habib Thameur, beside the Magasin Général; and the Colditz-style barracks of the *Maison des Jeunes* **youth hostel** (℡07/474053), 1km from the town centre on avenue Bourguiba, on the left going towards Cillium. Slightly more comfortable is the *Hôtel de la Paix* on avenue Bourguiba, 50m from the main square towards Sbeïtla (℡07/471465; ❷), and the rather officious one-star *Hôtel Pinus* (℡07/470164; ❸), 350m from the main square towards Sbeïtla. Top of the list is the friendliest hotel in town, the three-star *Hôtel Cillium* (℡07/473682; ❹), near the junction with the Thala road, by the ruins of the same name, with huge rooms, nice views of the ruins and a swimming pool (open to non-residents). **Food** is available on the main square, and behind it in avenue Taïeb Mehiri, where there are several patisseries, rôtisseries and cafés. There are a number of **bars** on avenue Bourguiba near the main square, the *Hôtel de la Paix* has one, and there's another next door.

Cillium and the Mausoleum of the Flavii

The remains of Roman **Cillium** are well out of town past the *Hôtel Cillium*. To walk there from the town centre (some 3km), turn right along avenue Bourguiba from the town square (the opposite direction to Sbeïtla), after a kilometre you'll pass the cellulose factory on your left, and a little further on the right, the remains of a Roman Mausoleum. After another 500m you cross a bridge over a wide river. Fork right at the junction beyond and you come to another junction after 100m or so, by the hospital. The left fork here takes you to Cillium, the hotel and ruins. If you don't fancy walking all the way or taking a taxi, get a bus to the hospital and walk from there, taking a left 100m beyond the hotel. The ruins begin a short way up this path, and are spread out over quite an area. The most impressive feature of a not very outstanding site is the third-century **arch**. Nearby is a group of rather pretty whitewashed **marabouts**.

On the way to Cillium, and more engaging than its rather limited remains, is the **Mausoleum of the Flavii**, the best-preserved example of its kind in the country. It stands three storeys high next to the main road (coming from town towards Cillium it's just after the *oued* on your right). The mausoleum is decorated with a 110-line falteringly poetic inscription to the dead Flavius. Four lines sum up the Roman dedication to conspicuous consumption:

> *Who could fail to be mind-blown as he stands here, who would not marvel at this construction and be staggered at the wealth which has caused this monument to rise to the heavenly skies . . . ?*

Onward to Gafsa and Tébessa

There's nothing to stop off for on the road between Kasserine and Gafsa, one of the bleakest in the country. The only town of any size is **FÉRIANA**, 5km after the minimal remains of Roman **Thelepte**, which look more than usual as if someone has just scattered a handful of hefty blocks across the road: the basilicas, baths and a theatre in the home town of St Fulgentius (467–532) are barely visible. If through some mishap you do get stuck in Fériana, it offers the *Hôtel Mabrouk* (☎07/441202; **②**) on the main road, along with a couple of **banks**. A road to Tébessa in Algeria splits off at Thelepte, but the current political situation in Algeria makes crossing the border inadvisable, see p.188.

travel details

Trains

The only train lines in this area run from Tunis to Kalaa Khasbah (1 daily; 5hr), via El Fahs (3 daily; 1hr 20min), Gaafour (3 daily; 2hr 15min), Le Sers (3 daily; 3hr 50min) and Dahmani (3 daily; 3hr 50min). There are no passenger services to Le Kef or Haïdra.

Buses

Kalaa Khasbah to: Kasserine (5 daily; 2hr 30min); Le Kef (3 daily; 1hr 30min); Thala (5 daily; 2hr).

Kasserine to: El Fahs (7 daily; 4hr); Gabès (4 daily; 4hr); Gafsa (4 daily; 1hr 30min); Kalaa Kasbah (6 daily; 2hr 30min); Le Kef (6 daily; 4hr); Maktar (7 daily; 2hr); Sbeïtla (7 daily; 30min); Tunis (8 daily; 5hr).

Le Kef to: Béja (2 daily; 2hr); Bizerte (1 daily; 4hr); El Fahs (2 daily; 2hr); Gafsa (2 daily; 4hr 45min); Jendouba (9 daily; 1hr 10min); Kairouan (3 daily; 3hr 30min); Kalaa Kasbah (3 daily; 1hr 30min); Kasserine (5 daily; 4hr); Maktar (3 daily; 1hr 30min); Medjez el Bab (hourly; 1hr 30min); Nabeul (1 daily; 4hr); Sakiet Sidi Youssef (2 daily; 1hr 10min); Sfax (3 daily; 4hr 30min); Sidi Bou Zid (1 daily; 3hr); Sousse (3 daily; 3hr 45min); Tajerouine (hourly; 30min); Téboursouk (hourly; 40min); Testour (hourly; 1hr); Thala (5 daily; 1hr 45min); Tunis (12 daily; 3hr).

Maktar to: El Fahs (4 daily; 2hr); Kairouan (4 daily; 2hr); Kasserine (4 daily; 3hr); Le Kef (4 daily; 1hr 30min); Tunis (7 daily; 3hr).

Sbeïtla to: Kairouan (2 daily; 2hr); Kasserine (10 daily; 30min); Sfax (3 daily; 3hr); Sidi Bou Zid (4 daily; 1hr); Sousse (2 daily; 3hr); Tunis (4 daily; 4hr).

Sidi Bou Zid to: Gabès (3 daily; 4hr 30min); Gafsa (2 daily; 2hr); Kairouan (5 daily; 1hr 30min); Kasserine (2 daily; 1hr 30min); Le Kef (1 daily; 3hr); Sbeïtla (4 daily; 1hr); Sfax (2 daily; 2hr); Tozeur (1 daily; 4hr 30min); Tunis (4 daily; 5hr).

Téboursouk to: Béja (2 daily; 1hr); Le Kef (hourly; 40min); Medjez el Bab (hourly; 1hr); Testour

(hourly; 30min); Thibar (2 daily; 30min); Tunis (6 daily; 2hr 20min).

Testour to: Le Kef (hourly; 2hr); Mejdez el Bab (hourly; 30min); Téboursouk (hourly; 30min); Tunis (8 daily; 1hr 50min).

Thala to: Kalaa Kasbah (6 daily; 20min); Kasserine (5 daily; 45min); Le Kef (6 daily; 1hr 45min); Tajerouine (6 daily; 30min); Tunis (2 daily; 5hr).

Zaghouan to: Enfida (2 daily; 45min); El Fahs (8 daily; 30min); Hammamet (10 daily; 1hr); Nabeul (10 daily; 1hr); Sousse (2 daily; 2hr); Tunis (7 daily; 1hr).

Louages

Louage journey times are roughly three-quarters the time taken by buses on the same route. Frequency depends on demand, but morning is always the best time to get a louage, especially for longer journeys.

Kalaa Khasbah to: Kasserine (2hr); Le Kef (1hr); Thala (1hr 30min).

Kasserine to: Fériana (45min); Kalaa Khasbah (2hr); Sbeïtla (20min); Thala (1hr 30min); Tunis (4hr).

Le Kef to: El Ksour (50min); Jendouba (50min); Kalaa Khasbah (1hr 15min); Kalaat es Senam (1hr 15min); Tajerouine (20min); Tunis (3hr).

Maktar to: El Fahs (1hr 30min); Kairouan (1hr 30min); Siliana (30min); Sousse (2hr 30min); Tunis (2hr).

Sbeïtla to: Kasserine (20min); Sidi Bou Zid (45min).

Sidi Bou Zid to: Gafsa (1hr 30min); Meknassy (1hr); Sbeïtla (45min); Sfax (1hr 30min); Tunis (3hr 15min).

Téboursouk to: Béja (45min); Medjez el Bab (45min); Nouvelle Dougga (15min); Thibar (20min); Tunis (2hr).

Thala to: Haïdra (50min), Kalaa Khasbah (15min); Kasserine (30min).

Zaghouan to: Enfida (30min); El Fahs (20min); Nabeul (all occasional, 45min); Tunis (45min).

CHAPTER SIX

THE JERID

Rich in the phosphates which play a major role in Tunisia's economy, the Jerid – the parched terrain spreading west from Gabès all the way to the Algerian frontier – is an arid land of bare pink hills punctuated only by mining towns and sporadic oasis-villages built around springs and deep gorges. These take time to explore, but are memorable places to experience the precariousness of oasis life. In contrast, the oasis at **Tozeur**, a popular tourist resort, and the quieter neighbouring oasis of **Nefta** – both reached quite easily – are vast folds of luxuriance, set right at the edge of the **Chott**, a bizarre salt lake of shifting colours and mirages. Nefta has long been a centre of Sufism, whose monuments add an intriguing dimension to its charac-

ter. Across the Chott lie further oases – the scattered centres of the **Nefzaoua**, under constant threat from the dunes of the Great Eastern Erg. **Kebili** and **Douz** are the two main towns, but what supplies the interest is the access they offer to the vastness of the desert.

Gafsa and around

قفصة

For hundreds of years **GAFSA**, 130km northwest of Gabès, has inspired the sort of impression that the Edwardian traveller Norman Douglas (see p.484) quoted from an old Arab song: "Gafsa is miserable; its water blood; its air poison; you may live there a hundred years without making a friend." Douglas agreed – "one dines early in Gafsa and afterwards there's nothing, absolutely nothing, to do". After a brief flirtation with tourist development, the town now seems resigned to its fate as a stopover for tour parties heading south. But it isn't really as bad as people like to make out, and worth a day or two for the scenery alone. Indeed, Gafsa's scenery is its most striking feature, with one long tongue of bleak hills passing behind the town to the west, another parallel in the southern distance. On the edge of this pocket is the **Gafsa oasis**, west of the Kasbah, large but more diffuse than those of Tozeur or Nefta.

Some history

Gafsa's history is one of the longest in the Maghreb, let alone Tunisia. The prehistoric Capsian culture which spread all over Africa is named after implements found near the site of Roman **Capsa**. In 107 BC, the Roman town's Numidian predecessor was famously captured by the Roman general **Marius** from the troublesome Jugurtha. "Except the immediate neighbourhood of the town," wrote the historian Sallust, "the whole district is desolate, uncultivated, waterless, and infested by deadly serpents, which like all wild animals are made fiercer by scarcity of food, and especially by thirst, which exasperates their natural malignity." Not short on malignity himself, Marius sacked the town and slaughtered the population – giving the excuse that the

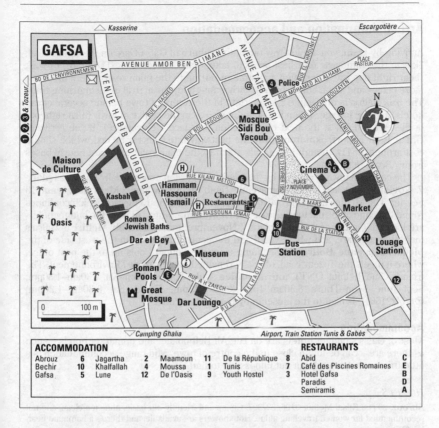

ACCOMMODATION							RESTAURANTS	
Abrouz	6	Jagartha	2	Maamoun	11	De la République	8	Abid	C
Bechir	10	Khalfallah	4	Moussa	1	Tunis	7	Café des Piscines Romaines	E
Gafsa	5	Lune	12	De l'Oasis	9	Youth Hostel	3	Hotel Gafsa	B
								Paradis	D
								Semiramis	A

inhabitants were a "fickle and untrustworthy lot". An important Roman colony, Capsa was heavily fortified by the Byzantines and renamed **Justiniana** after the emperor – neither of which moves proved any deterrent to Arab **Oqba Ibn Nafi**, who captured the city and took 80,000 prisoners in 668. Despite the conquest, and large-scale conversion to Islam, El Edrisi reported Latin still being spoken here in the twelfth century.

Gafsa's most recent world headlines were in January 1980. On January 27 a mysterious group of unidentified soldiers took over the town in a night-time operation. It took several days for the army to evict them, after 48 deaths; of the 60 captured, 13 were hanged on April 17. To this day the incident remains shrouded in mystery. Rumour has it that the leader was a native of Gafsa who had fled to Libya in the wake of the Ahmed Ben Salah purges of 1969, and the common thread in suggested explanations seems to be that the men came from Libya. As to their purpose, however, nothing is clear; if the Tunisian south was expected to rise spontaneously and declare allegiance with Libya, its mood had been severely misjudged. But it is significant that Gafsa was chosen as the target. As the economic and administrative capital of the Jerid, whose phosphates play such a large part in the national economy, there is some resentment among the citizens that they don't benefit more from the industry. True or not, the common view in the town, that the profits all go to rich businessmen in Sfax, suggests considerable disenchantment.

Arrival, information and accommodation

Arriving by **train**, you are left way out in the suburb of Gafsa Gare on the Gabès road, 3km to the southeast. Your best bet is to take a taxi into town (1.5TD or so), or walk (bear right opposite the station and straight on) up to the main road, where there are more taxis – and some buses, but not early enough for the arrival of the morning train. The **bus** station is off avenue 2 Mars, right in the centre of town behind several cheap hotels, and the **louage** station is also more or less in the centre of town (turn right out of the exit and left at the next road junction for place 7 Novembre). If you arrive at **Gafsa Ksar** airport, 5km from town, the best way into Gafsa is by taxi, which should cost around 1.5TD, though if you walk 100m to the main road there are hourly buses from 7.30am to 6.30pm.

The centre of town is marked by the triangular garden now officially known as **place 7 Novembre**, tucked in between avenue Taïeb Mehiri, avenue 2 Mars and avenue 13 Février. The Medina lies to the west of here, across avenue 13 Février, which continues round the edge of the old town as **rue Ali Belhouane**, where most of the budget hotels are located. On the east side of place 7 Novembre, **avenue Taïeb Mehiri** is Gafsa's main thoroughfare, and where you'll find the central **market**. On the west side of the Medina is **avenue Bourguiba**, running from the Roman Pools up to the post office, where it meets the Tozeur road, officially renamed boulevard de l'Environnement. The friendly and helpful ONTT **tourist office** (July & Aug Mon–Sat 7.30am–1.30pm; Sept–June Mon–Thurs 8.30am–1pm & 3–5.45pm, Fri & Sat 8.30am–1.30pm; ☎06/221664), is next to the museum by the Roman Pools.

Accommodation

Most of Gafsa's budget **hotels** are on rue Ali Belhouane, and upmarket hotels – such as there are – can be found close to the centre of town. Mid-range accommodation is a little thin on the ground, but not impossible to find.

HOTELS

Abrouz, 29 rue Kilani Metoui ☎06/227357. Cheap and friendly but basic, none too clean, and not recommended for women travelling alone. Hot showers are available, and there's a hammam nearby. **①**

Bechir, 40 rue Ali Belhouane ☎06/223239. Very cheap but the rooms are small, and there are no showers, so you'll have to use the hammam. **②**

Gafsa ★★, 10 rue Ahmed Snoussi ☎06/224000, ⓕ224747. Catering mainly for tour groups, but quite classy nonetheless, with the best rooms in town, large with gleaming bathrooms, a/c and satellite TV. **③**

Jugurtha ★★★★★, Sidi Ahmed Zarroug ☎06/224411, ⓕ226400. Four kilometres west of town in a small oasis (see p.303), with pool and a great view over the desert. Currently closed for renovation and upgrading. Owned by the same firm as the *Maamoun*. **⑦**

Khalfallah, av Taïeb Mehiri ☎06/225624, ⓕ290228. A touch classier than the other budget hotels, but also pricier. All rooms have their own showers, but toilets are on the landing. **③**

Lune ★, rue J Abennaceur ☎06/220218, ⓕ220980. Very good value with pleasant rooms and friendly staff. **③**

Maamoun ★★★, av Taïeb Mehiri ☎06/222433, ⓕ226490. Supposedly the poshest gaff in Gafsa, but the rooms are rather gloomy, and the only thing it's got on the *Gafsa* and the *Lune* (where rooms are half the price) is its swimming pool. **⑤**

Hôtel Moussa, av de la Liberté ☎06/221333. Out on the Tozeur road, about 300m past the post office. Clean, neat and good value. **②**

Hôtel de l'Oasis, 7 rue Ali Belhouane ☎06/222371. Gloomy rooms with windows opening only onto the landing, and communal cold water showers only. **②**

PUTTING THE DEVIL BACK IN HELL

Gafsa has a literary claim to fame in Boccaccio's 1353 classic, the *Decameron*, being the home of Alibech, the innocent virginal heroine of the book's thirtieth and most infamous tale. Setting off into the desert to learn how to serve God, Alibech encounters the pious young hermit Rustico, who agrees to teach her. Rustico, however, soon gets other ideas and persuades her to join him in a rather unorthodox enactment of putting the devil into hell, thus coining a sexual euphemism current in the Italian of the time. When the women of Gafsa find out how Alibech and Rustico have been serving God out in the desert "they burst into such laughter that they are laughing still". English translators, though, found it no laughing matter. Even into the twentieth century, they refused to translate the crucial passages into English, leaving readers to fathom the finer points of Rustico's method from the original Italian text.

Hôtel de la République, 28 rue Ali Belhouane ☎06/221807. Friendly with big rooms, but a bit grubby (especially the loos) and rather noisy, with the street one side and the bus station on the other. ❷

Tunis, 62 av 2 Mars ☎06/221660. The oldest hotel in town, recently renovated, cheap and friendly. Not all rooms have outside windows, but a couple have balconies, and there's a terrace. The communal showers have hot water round the clock, women have their own toilet, and men can pay by the bed (4TD) in a shared room. Best of the ultra-cheapies. ❶

CAMPSITE AND YOUTH HOSTEL

Camping Ghalia, in the oasis ☎06/229135. A new campsite with plots for tents and campervans (not well shaded as yet, but give it time), electricity available, a pool, hot showers and a café that serves pizzas. To get there, follow rue Jema'a el Kebir from behind the Kasbah, across rue Ali Belhouane and into the oasis, taking a right after 700m or so (signposted most of the way).

Maison des Jeunes, rue du Caire ☎06/224468, ⓕ225599. Three- to five-person dorms (5TD) and a 10pm curfew in winter, 11pm or later in summer; camping also possible. To get there, take the Tozeur road past the *Hôtel Moussa*, then the next right and the second left; the reception is on the corner, and the hostel is 100m down on the left. If there's no one at the reception, try the hostel itself.

The Town

Gafsa's centre must have changed very little since Norman Douglas' day. It's still not a town for great sightseeing, and anything of interest is concentrated around the Roman Pools in the corner of the Medina at the bottom end of avenue Bourguiba. The skyline is dominated by the majestic minaret of the spacious **Great Mosque**, overlooking the town from nearby, with the oasis and distant desert beyond it.

Gafsa's focal monument is the **Piscines Romaines** (Roman Pools), which every small boy will automatically assume you've come to see. A left turn at the end of rue Hassouna Ismail (off rue Ali Belhouane by the *Hôtel de l'Oasis*) brings you to two open, rectangular pools in familiar Roman masonry, with inscriptions on the side of the larger, upper pool. The pools were at one time full, and had fish in them, with a hot spring coming up through the bottom of the smaller, lower pool. Lately however, they have been empty due to lack of water, a symptom of the fact that the water table here is receding. The arcaded building overlooking the lower pool is called the **Dar el Bey**, after the ruler who built it. Behind an iron door on the far side steps lead down to what was a hammam using the pools' overflow, now closed because of the lack of water.

On the square by the pools, a small **museum** (Tues–Sun 9.30am–4.30pm; 1.1TD) exhibits stone tools, arrow-heads and shards of decorated ostrich eggshells from the

Capsian culture, and some mosaics from Roman Zammour. The two most impressive mosaics, both from the early fourth century, show the goddess Venus on a fishing trip, and athletes engaged in a series of different pugilistic sports. Some of the Stone Age tools in the museum come from a mound known as **l'Escargotière** which, should you want to find it (though there is little to see), lies up rue Houcine Bouzayen, bearing left at place Pasteur, and then off to the right after 500m or so; a map in the ONTT shows its exact location. The name ("the snailery") comes from the fossils of snails that are found there.

The path behind the large pool and the *Café des Piscines Romaines* leads back to rue Ali Belhouane. As it widens to accommodate cars, check out the large whitewashed mansion on your right, known as **Dar Loungo**. Recently restored, it is worth a look around if you can get somebody to let you in, and the roof offers excellent views over the town – although the best vistas over both the town and oasis are to be had from **Jebel el Meda**, the rocky hillock opposite the *Hôtel Moussa* on the Tozeur road.

A little way up avenue Bourguiba from the Roman Pools stand the pinkly picturesque crenellated walls of the **Kasbah**. It has had a chequered career since it was built by the Hafsids on a Byzantine foundation – it resisted a Turkish corsair's siege in 1551, only to surrender to the same opponent five years later; its worst moment came in 1943, when an Allied ammunition dump blew out most of one wall. This was subsequently replaced, to universal dismay, with new law courts, and the Kasbah remains a rather soulless place until sunset, when the walls glow in harlequin shades of limpid colour. The best view of it is from the back, where the walls remain intact.

On the southern side of the Kasbah, a small egg-domed **marabout** conceals another **hammam** using water from the Roman Pools, but it is currently closed. This one is actually Roman in origin and, when open, admitted women one side and men on the other. Next to the men's hammam, right up by the walls of the Kasbah, is an ancient **Jewish ritual bath**.

The road south from here skirts the oasis and passes the Great Mosque before meeting up with rue Ali Belhouane. At the corner where they meet, if you're here at the right time of year, you can see some vintage technology in action in the form of an electric-powered **olive oil press**, used during the November to January harvest. There is another one some 100m beyond the junction in the oasis, on the way to the *Ghalia* campsite.

Eating and drinking

Most of the **restaurants** around the bus station and cheap hotel area are little more than overpriced greasy spoons. Decent low-priced eats can be found by taking rue Hassouna Ismail off rue Ali Belhouane by the *Hôtel de l'Oasis*, and then the second right, where three restaurants serve basic cheap meals. The *Abid* on the corner of rue Kilanai Metour (daily 10am–11pm) is the best of the three, extremely cheap and very good value, but sometimes gets quite packed. The other two are pretty decent too. Otherwise, you could try the *Restaurant du Paradis*, opposite the *Hôtel Maamoun* on avenue Taïeb Mehiri (daily 7am–9pm), which also offers low-priced dishes, sometimes including couscous, though the choice nowadays is often limited to spit-roast chicken.

More sophisticated eating places, with moderate to high prices, include the *Restaurant Semiramis* (daily noon–2.30pm & 6–10.30pm) on rue Ahmed Snoussi, the neighbouring *Hôtel Gafsa*, whose restaurant is opposite (daily 11am–3pm & 6–11pm), and *Hôtel Maamoun* (daily noon–2.30pm, & 7.30–10pm), down the street, which has a rather expensive à la carte, but a reasonable 9TD set menu.

A good place for members of both sexes to relax with a coffee during the day is the outdoor café at the Maison de Culture, behind the Kasbah on the edge of the Oasis. Alternatively, try the *Café des Piscines Romaines* overlooking the Roman pools.

Listings

Banks There are several banks on av Taïeb Mehiri, including a couple by the cinema. There is a weekend rota, so one bank will be open Saturday and Sunday mornings. Banque de l'Habitat on av Taïeb Mehiri at the corner of rue Houcine Bouziane, and UBCI on av J Abennaceur near the *Hôtel Lune* are among those with ATM machines that accept Visa and Mastercard.

Car rental Achraf Rent-a-Car, c/o Tozeur Voyages, 1 rue Houcine Bouzayen ℡ 06/229182.

Car repairs and spares Mechanics and spare parts suppliers are concentrated in and around rue de la Station. There are a couple of tyre repair shops on av J Abennaceur 50m past the *Hôtel Lune*.

Cinema On av Taïeb Mehiri, opposite the *Tunis Hôtel*, next to the central market. The Maison de Culture behind the Kasbah has a cinema, that screens mainstream films.

Consulates The Algerian consulate is behind 37 rue Houcine Bouzayen ℡ 06/221366 (entrance in rue Abou el Kacem Chabbi), however, see the warning on travel in Algeria on p.185.

Festival The Festival du Borj is a series of theatrical and musical presentations in the Kasbah throughout July.

Hammams Hammam Hassouna Ismail, on rue Hassouna Ismail, one corner from its western end, is new and clean (women 10am–4pm, men 6–10am & 4–8pm). There's an older one at 101 rue Kilani Metoui, with two doors – the right-hand one for men, the left-hand one for women (women 10am–4pm, men 4–10am & 4–8pm).

Hospital The regional hospital is on rue Ibn Sina ℡ 06/225177, up rue Houcine Bouzayen to pl Pasteur, then right.

Internet access Cyber Space, 218 av Taïeb Mehiri, opposite *Hôtel Khalfallah* (daily 8am–3am; 1.8TD/hr); Univers de l'Internet, av Abou el Kacem Chabbi, opposite the Algerian consulate (daily 8.30am–2am; 2TD/hr).

Pharmacy There's a night pharmacy at 16 av Amor Ben Slimane.

Police av Taïeb Mehiri next to the *Hôtel Khalfallah* ℡ 06/225012.

Post office On the corner of av Bourguiba and av de la Liberté, the Tozeur road (city hours). Stamps are also sold at a taxiphone office on av 13 Février at the northern end of pl 7 Novembre.

Supermarket Magasin Général on av Abou el Kacem Chabbi behind the market.

Around Gafsa

Gafsa's position at a transitional point, between the last remnants of the central steppes and mountains to the north and the desert to the south, has always made it an important place. Its significance as a desert "port" can be best appreciated by visiting two of its satellite oases, which can be seen as small islands in the desert, with Gafsa the big port on the shore. Local buses leave regularly from in front of the bus station for the Lalla oasis, 7km east of town. Stay on the bus until it turns around at the end of its route, then walk on a bit further to a small café and two prolific springs. The stark contrast here between shady green and glaring pink hills really brings home the fragility of oasis existence. Sidi Ahmed Zarroug, the other oasis, lies 4km west of town and is now occupied by the luxurious *Hôtel Jugurtha* (see p.300). If you're here in the winter – the only time of year suitable for energetic scrambling – the view out over the desert from the bald ridge which towers over the hotel is little short of magnificent, especially if you climb it in time for sunrise. You can also take a walk into the *hamada*.

There is a **zoo** at **ORBATA** (daily 7am–6.30pm, later in summer; 0.2TD), 5km out on the Tunis road just past the airport. On Wednesdays, there's also a livestock **market** next door. Attached to the zoo is a two-square-kilometre animal park where ostriches and gazelles roam freely, but permission to visit this must be obtained from the Direction des Forêts on the route de Gabès (Mon–Thurs 8.30am–1pm & 3–5.45pm, Fri & Sat 8.30am–1.30pm; ℡ 06/221967), which is just past the train line on the left leaving Gafsa. Orbata can be reached by local bus from in front of the bus station in Gafsa (hourly 7.15am–6.15pm), or by taxi (about 1.5TD).

TRADITIONS IN THE BERBER VILLAGES

Outsiders still cause a stir in Sakket, Sened Jebel or Meich – as you arrive, the women hide in their houses and the men gather into groups to discuss the *hawaja*, or foreigner. Little has changed here in the past two centuries. As in Berber villages in the far south of the country, the villagers retain their distinct ethnic identity (though none has spoken Berber since the nineteenth century), and traditional dress and customs persist. Women wear the *bakhnug*, a shawl embroidered with geometrical patterns to shelter them from the eyes of strangers. Many of the men wear the knee-length trousers that used to be common before World War II. At the centre of each of the villages are marabouts' tombs, with rags and flags hanging from poles: the last place in Tunisia where you can see votive offerings to these village saints. The village oil presses are still animal-powered and women grind their own flour by hand. In winter many people migrate into the pastures with their herds, and the villages are virtually deserted. Today, however, a different type of migration is slowly eroding the community, as many families abandon their villages for an easier life in the city.

Some 20km east of Gafsa on the Gabès road is another oasis, **EL GUETTAR**, reached by bus or louage from Gafsa, an oasis known for its pistachio nuts. The town is nothing much in itself, a ribbon of modern concrete houses along the road, but the huge palmery is rarely visited and farmers here still use old techniques such as the *noria*, a device to draw water from wells by animal power. In ancient times, water was carried down from aquifers on high ground by irrigation tunnels called *foggara* or *khriga*, some of which can still be seen in the region (and also near Douz – see p.339). Teams of workers would dig holes along the course of the *foggara* to excavate the earth and rock, and the holes were used to maintain the system. As you drive along the road these circular pits, some of them 30 to 40 metres deep, are all you can see. Close up, the amount of work that has gone into the kilometres of tunnels below becomes evident. But those here are considered small; in Iran, where the practice originated, the *qanat*, as they term it, can extend for hundreds of kilometres.

At the end of the village, a road to the left leads to the remote Berber mountain villages of **SAKKET** (14km), **SENED JEBEL** (27km) and **MEICH** (42km) – highly worthwhile targets if you're prepared for a moderate adventure and want to meet the locals.

Getting to these villages is difficult. It's possible to catch a bus to El Guettar and from there to walk or, if you're lucky get a lift, to Sakket. To Sened Jebel, you could walk or hitch from Sened Gare, 10km away on the Gafsa–Sfax road. Alternatively, if you catch a louage to El Guettar or Sened Gare, you could negotiate a deal with the driver to take you on. Sened Jebel has a number of disused cave dwellings, some containing old oil presses. East of El Guettar, the main GP15 highway continues across the steppe to **SIDI MANSOUR**, a small village with an important marabout, and thence to Gabès (150km from Gafsa). Buses run regularly both ways.

There are two Roman **mausoleums** at the village of **SIDI AÏCH**, 48km north of Gafsa on a turning off the Sidi Bou Zid road. They stand in splendid isolation just outside the village at the beginning of a piste to Fériana with a lovely backdrop of jagged mountains striped with layers of rock. The original Roman inscriptions are joined by more recent carvings, some as modern as the nineteenth century. Regular *camionettes*, and three buses a day, reach Sidi Aïch from Gafsa.

Meknassy and Bou Hedma National Park المكناسي

The road from Gafsa to Sfax takes you across the barren steppes between the Dorsale mountains to the north and the Chotts to the south. The only town of any size on this

JERID WILDLIFE

The steppes cover a vast area of the centre of the country – from the southern foothills of the Dorsale ridge down to the Chott el Jerid. Most are degraded forests; it's a sobering thought that Hannibal probably got his elephants from this region a few thousand years ago. Over the centuries, the wood has been felled and the land grazed by sheep, goats and camels, resulting in a landscape only barely productive for agriculture.

The steppes, and particularly the low hills and wadies rising up from them, are rich in unusual **small birds**. Worth special mention are crested larks, hoopoe larks (so called because of their long decurved bill and black and white wings), and the even more peculiar Temminck's horned lark, a striking bird with a black and white head pattern and, in breeding plumage, two distinct black "horns". In the rockier parts, look out for the trumpeter finch, a thick-billed pink bird with a weird nasal call. **House buntings** are common in villages and, as they're treated with some reverence by local people, are extremely tame.

Out in the wilder areas, you may see – with some patience and luck – some of the true **desert mammals**. Jerboas and gerbils are reasonably common, as are susliks, a sort of short-tailed ground squirrel with an upright "begging" posture. Most of the larger desert **antelopes** have been hunted out of existence here, but an ambitious reintroduction programme is under way at the Hadaj and Bou Hedma National Parks (see below).

route is **MEKNASSY**, just under 80km east of Gafsa, where you might conceivably need to change louages (they go from here to Sfax, Sened Gare, Sidi Bou Zid and direct to Tunis). It hosts a **Cavalry Festival** of horsemanship every November.

With your own vehicle, you could visit **Bou Hedma National Park** and the adjoining **Hadaj National Park**, just south of Meknassy, where an ambitious programme is in progress to reintroduce gazelle, oryx and addax, as well as ostriches, which only disappeared from the south of the country in the twentieth century. To visit Bou Hedma, you'll first need permission from the Direction Général des Forêts, 30 rue Alain Savary, Tunis (℡01/891497). You may be able to phone them and arrange to pick up your permit at the forestry office (Direction des Forêts/Triq el Ghaba) opposite the train station in **MAZZOUNA**, 25km east of Meknassy. From there, you take the Skhirra road, turning right (no signposting) after 7km and arriving at the park after 10km of tarmac and, currently, 10km of piste due to be surfaced. Even then, much of the park is inaccessible without a 4WD. Hadaj is easier to visit, and you should be able to obtain a permit from the Direction des Forêts in Gafsa, route de Gabès, just past the train station (℡06/221967), but you'd still need your own vehicle.

Metlaoui   المتلوّي

In 1896 a French army vet and amateur geologist, Philippe Thomas, found phosphate deposits around **METLAOUI**. Previously known only for his work on goat diseases, Thomas became a national hero, and his discovery turned an insignificant village into an important mining centre.

The transformation took little over a decade. Thousands of miners were recruited from Algeria and Libya as local people were at first reluctant to work in the mining towns and were later excluded because the mine owners feared they would campaign for better conditions. Conditions were certainly bad; companies provided no accommodation and huge *bidonvilles* grew up without any planning or services. At work there were few safety measures, and one third of employees had to retire – without compensation – because of injury. Unions were discouraged by the companies' policies of maintaining a high turnover of personnel and by pitting ethnic groups against each other, paying Algerians more than Libyans, and Libyans more than Sudanese. So tense were relations that fights used to break out between them, and on one occasion the Algerians burnt down a Libyan shantytown, killing over a hundred people. It was only in the 1930s that the unions managed to unite the workforce and direct their anger against their bosses rather than each other – and conditions then improved radically.

By 1899, phosphate from Metlaoui was being exported to France via the new railway to Sfax, and other mines were being dug in the surrounding hills. The Compagnie des Phosphates de Gafsa was established after independence, and Tunisia is now the fourth largest phosphate producer in the world. Now however, reserves are running low, and the spectre of mass redundancy looms large over a region in which phosphate production is virtually the only industry, and unemployment is already high. The quantity of phosphates mined in Metlaoui and its sister towns of Moulares and Redeyef has already fallen to a fraction of the amount once extracted here, and reserves seem unlikely to last much into the 2010s. Metalaoui is in a slightly better position than its sister towns, since the phosphates are actually processed here. One consequence of the industry's decline is the large-scale migration to the richer towns of the Sahel, in particular Sousse, where there is a suburb called Moulares on account of its domination by immigrants from here.

Metlaoui itself is an odd jumble of French houses dwarfed by overhead phosphate conveyors and heavy mining equipment. The **Musée National des Mines** (Mon–Thurs 8am–noon & 3–5pm, Fri & Sat 8am–1pm; free) was built to house Philippe Thomas's natural history collection about 800m up the Tamerza road, just before the louage station. It's rather a dry and dusty old place and sadly many of the original exhibits, and their labels, were lost in the ten years the museum was closed. The main highlights are two fossilized Eocine turtles in among the old photos and piles of rock, but the museum is worth a look if you're passing through.

Practicalities

The Gafsa road runs through the centre of town until it meets the Tamerza–Tozeur road at a T-junction by a petrol station, bank and cinema. There are two hotels here. The cheap option is the *Ennacim* (☏ & 🖷06/241920; ❸), 300m towards Tozeur on the left, rather dingy and run-down, with en-suite rooms, a bar and a restaurant. Much nicer, if you can afford it, is the two-star *Hôtel Selja* (also spelt *Thelja*), a kilometre towards Gafsa from the main junction (☏06/241570, 🖷241486; ❹), immaculate and comfortable, with air-conditioning and satellite TV in all rooms, and a restaurant that claims to be open round the clock. An alternative place to eat is the *Restaurant Ellafi* (daily except Sun, 11am–4pm & 7–9pm), 100m towards Gafsa from the main junction.

The **post office** (country hours) is off the Gafsa road, about 200m from the main junction, and there's also a Magasin Général **supermarket** about 700m up the Tamerza road, just before the museum. The municipal **swimming pool**, which is off the Gafsa road just 50m from the main junction, is open mid-June to mid-September only.

The **bus station**, about 800m up the Gafsa road from the main junction, just past the level crossing, is served by both SNTRI and SRT Gafsa, with regular daily departures to Gafsa, Tozeur, Nefta, Moulares and Redeyef. Services also run to Tunis, Sfax, Kairouan, Sousse and Gabès (see p.344 for frequency and journey times). **Louages** operate from opposite the bus station and from another station about a kilometre up the Tamerza road by the museum, sometimes cruising from one to the other in search of passengers (apart from that, there is no way of guessing which station your next louage will leave from). They run to Gafsa, Redeyef, Tamerza and Tozeur, but can be a bit sparse, depending on the time of day.

The **train station** is 1.5km from the main junction on the Gafsa road, with an early morning and evening service (Mon–Sat) for Sfax via Gafsa. The evening train connects for Sousse and Tunis, but services are more convenient on Sunday, when the morning train leaves later (8am), and both trains run through to Tunis with no need to change. In the other direction, there is also a daily afternoon service to Redeyef via the Seldja gorge.

There is also a special **tourist train**, the Lézard Rouge, running four times weekly (Tues, Thurs, Fri & Sun) to Seldja and back (20TD return). Originally used by the Bey, the train consists of original nineteenth-century carriages, including the Bey's private car, which is restored in red velvet and leather. The train runs five times weekly, leaving Metlaoui at 10.30am, taking an hour and three-quarters for the round trip. Further information is available from the Galilée Travel/Lézard Rouge office at Metlaoui station (☎ & ℱ 06/241469), through whom reservations can be made, although off season you should be able to turn up at the station just before the train's departure and buy a ticket there and then.

Seldja and around

ثلجة

SELDJA, 16km west of Metlaoui, comprises only a neat white signal box stuck in the middle of nowhere, built by the French along with a remarkable series of bridges and tunnels. Previously, the Romans had diverted water from these ravines by aqueduct to supply nearby agricultural land. Coming from Sbeïtla, their caravans took a short cut through here en route to Ghadames in present-day Libya. From the signal box you can walk back down the tracks to some of the more impressive parts of the gorge, its sheer sides worn completely smooth by the river. Phosphate trains do still pass at regular intervals, so watch your step. As well as the Lézard Rouge (see above), you can get to Seldja from Metlaoui on the afternoon Redeyef train, returning on the same train an hour and a half later. An alternative route to the gorge is by road from Metlaoui, where a track leads out over the flat plain for 5km – too hot to walk – to a rock passage known as the **Coup de Sabre**, or "sword thrust". Legend says that the warrior Al Mansour cut into the rock with one stroke to prepare a bed for Leila, a princess escaping from her husband. There's a four-kilometre path along the foot of the gorge to the signal box – if you walk it, you'll see the wheeling silhouettes of birds of prey overhead.

Moulares and Redeyef

Between Metlaoui and Redeyef, the nondescript mining town of **MOULARES** does not warrant a stop; the only thing of note as you pass through is the little mining train on display by the Metlaoui road on the edge of town.

REDEYEF, the last of the mining towns, is 17km further on from Moulares and, like Metlaoui, has grown up around an old French community, with its bungalows and church. There's nothing much to see here, but you may find yourself passing through on your way to or from Tamerza, and it's a pleasant enough little town. The Gafsa road meets the Tamerza road in front of the **post office** (country hours), and another road off the main junction leads to the square, with a **mosque** and, in front of it, rather resembling a toy train, a mining locomotive and bogeys built by Schötter GmbH of Bremen, Germany. Beyond the main square is the **market**, at its busiest on Sunday, and a **bank**. There is no accommodation in Redeyef.

From the bus station at the beginning of the Gafsa road there are services to Moulares, Metlaoui, Gafsa, Tozeur and Nefta. There are also regular daily services to Tamerza, which can also be picked up at the other end of the market, where you'll also find pick-ups for the same destination. SNTRI buses to Tunis leave from the main square. The train station, with its single late-afternoon departure for Metlaoui (1hr

25min), is 100m up the Tamerza road and off on the left. The service arrives at Metlaoui in good time to catch the Sfax train, though the connection does not work coming the other way. For full details of destinations and journey times, see pp.343–344.

Tamerza and the Chott el Gharsa

West, beyond Redeyef, the towns lose their industrial ugliness and become a series of lovely oases that some consider the most beautiful in the country. Certainly, their remoteness and inaccessibility leaves them unspoilt compared to places like Tozeur and Nefta; but it also means that facilities are few and public transport rare. South of Tamerza, the recently surfaced road to Tozeur crosses the **Chott el Gharsa**, a smaller salt plain giving a taste of the Chott el Jerid itself. Although it is possible to reach Tamerza by bus or louage from Tozeur, sparsity of transport makes a day trip very difficult if you want to take in Chebika, and even more so if you want to see Mides as well. You would need to start off very early in the morning, and be prepared to hitch between Chebika and Tamerza, and to hitch or even walk between Tamerza and Mides. An alternative to take a tour with a company such as LOVA (see p.321) who organize day trips from Tozeur.

Tamerza   تمغزة

TAMERZA (also spelt "Tameghza"), 85km west of Gafsa, with its high cascade and dense cultivation, is one of the least spoiled of all the Jerid oases. The oldest mud-and-stone houses (to the south of the road from Redeyef) were abandoned after torrential floods in 1969, and the new village, a kilometre further on, is built in traditional Arab style with high blank brick walls facing the main street. Three **marabouts** are still maintained in the old village, the most striking being that of Sidi Dar Ben Dhahara with its pointed dome. The very classy four-star *Hôtel Tamerza Palace* (☎06/799634, ℱ799810, ℗www.tamerza-palace.com; ❼), perched on the other side of the *oued*, has excellent views over the oasis and old village from its poolside terrace and each of its cool rooms. A small hotel is under construction on the Chebika road, but in the meantime the only other accommodation is in the rather grotty and overpriced palm-frond bungalows of the *Hôtel des Cascades* (☎& ℱ06/485322; ❸), down a street to the left (avenue de l'Environnement) as you go through the new town. As the name suggests, its just above one of Tamerza's two **waterfalls** – the other is beyond the edge of town, a couple of kilometres towards Chebika. There are panoramic views over the second one from the Chebika road. Avenue de l'Environnement has a few places to **eat**, among them the reasonably priced *Restaurant Chedli* (daily 7am–9pm), which has a set menu at 6.5TD, and excellent couscous, and home-made *harissa* to dip your bread into on request. The *Restaurant Taboulet* up the street (daily 8am–7.30pm) is cheaper, and offers the option of *mechoui*. There's a Syndicat d'Initiative **tourist office** in town too (daily 8am–1pm & 3pm–6pm). The Syndicat keeps a list of local guides and can arrange excursions on foot or by donkey, for example along the gorge to Mides (see opposite). There are buses from here to Redeyef, Tozeur and Tunis (see p.344 for full details). Tamerza hosts an annual **festival** at the end of March, featuring music, dance and equestrian events.

Mides   ميداس

The mountain oasis of **MIDES**, a few kilometres west, is reached by a surfaced road from a junction 4km west of Tamerza towards Redeyef (a piste from the same junction passes a customs post before crossing the border into Algeria). The alternative route is on foot or by donkey along the valley floor from Tamerza, a scenic route through a dramatic narrow **gorge** – the *Hôtel des Cascades* or the Syndicat d'Initiative can arrange donkeys and guides. If you do this trip, take some water with you, and in summer take precautions against heatstroke – it can get roasting hot. The walk takes a couple of hours.

The new Mides settlement and the abandoned **Berber village** stand at opposite ends of the oasis, where the palms provide shade for pomegranates, which in turn shelter lemon and orange trees. Only from the top of the hill, above the ruins and the network of narrow paved streets, can you make out the spectacular position of the old houses, clinging to the sheer rock face of a deep and extremely impressive **gorge**. This stretches for 3km around the village, providing a natural defensive position. The four campsites by the Berber village are currently closed by official order, due to the proximity of the Algerian border, just a kilometre away. Following an incident at Chebika (see below), it appears that the government has cause for concern about fundamentalist incursions across the border. As it is, Mides is full of plain-clothes police keeping a close watch on things. Also by the Berber village is a café with a sign that reads "Buvette + Artisanat", where you can buy fossils and rock crystals. Here you can also find local guide Brahim Eidini, who can take you on a walk to see some of the herbs and medicinal plants that grow wild in the area, though it is best to call him in advance (☎06/460384), preferably after sunset.

From Tamerza to Tozeur

The road **south beyond Tamerza** leads across the Chott el Gharsa to El Hamma du Jerid and Tozeur. The road is now surfaced all the way, and the route is plied by louages, and by two daily buses. The first section of road is rather rough, characterized by sharp bends, sheer drops and breathtaking scenery before it comes down onto the plain for the last 5km before the small oasis of **CHEBIKA**. Behind the new settlement by the road, the old village (abandoned after floods in 1969) perches on a rock platform, bordered by palms and, on the far side, a steep gorge. As at Tamerza, a **cascade** falls from springs high up the cliff, feeding the streams and the agricultural land below. This was the site of the Roman outpost of **Ad Speculum**, from where signals were sent by mirror (*speculum*) tracking the caravans en route to Tozeur. Because of its exposed position, the village was later named Qasr el Shems (Castle of the Sun). The springs are said to have risen up at a point where a wandering camel carrying the body of a holy man, Sidi Sultan, finally came to a halt; the **marabout**, attributed with the usual powers, is buried in the tomb near the ravine.

Chebika is the village described by Jean Duvignaud in his book *Change at Shebika* (see p.487), where he tells of the open rivalry between Chebika and Redeyef since mining began. Wealthy miners bought land here in the oasis, when an annual cathartic ritual stood in for open warfare right up until Independence. The people of Redeyef used to go to a selected spot between the villages, lay out some bread and then hide behind a rock. When the people of Chebika arrived on the scene and pretended to steal the bread, the owners would run out and perform a mock fight before both sides settled down to eat together. Duvignaud describes how similar traditions led to the destruction of the very community they were supposed to sustain. The men from here, for example, often married women from El Hamma, and ceded land from the oasis to the bride's father, depriving the village of its property and increasing the power of the absentee landlord. Agricultural production seldom increased, since the new owners (like the miners) were unskilled, and local families had to borrow to survive.

Chebika was also the scene of an alarming incident in early 1995, when fundamentalist insurgents from Algeria crossed the border and murdered six members of the National Guard as they sat down at sunset to break their Ramadan fast. The BBC's

Arabic service reported the attack, so everyone knew about it, but there was no mention of it in the Tunisian media until a week later, when newspapers carried the story that the National Guard officers had been killed in a car crash.

The Chott el Gharsa and El Hamma du Jerid

Beyond Chebika, the road cuts across the corner of the **Chott el Gharsa**, a salt flat lying in a depression below sea level. Like the Chott el Jerid, it's not a lake – though mirages suggest it might be, maps invariably show it as one; it's only covered in water after a (rare) heavy rainfall. On the other side of the Chott, **EL HAMMA DU JERID**, with its six springs and 110,000 palms, signals the beginning of the large oases around Tozeur. There's a **campsite** here, *Camping Desert Club* (☎06/480133, ☞480300), run by the same proprietor as its namesake in Douz, on a very pleasant little plot among palm trees, with clean toilets and showers and hot water round the clock. El Hamma has a hot spring whose waters, rising at a temperature of 38°C, were much favoured by the Romans, though a later traveller compared the bath to a mustard plaster, and emerged feeling like a boiled lobster. The baths today are in a building just off the road from Chebika, behind the campsite, with pools and showers, and separate facilities for men and women, who can both use the baths daily from 6am to 9pm. There's also an open-air hot spring pool 100m into the oasis (women 6am–6pm, men 6pm–6am).

Tozeur   توزر

TOZEUR has always been the commercial and political centre of the Jerid, and for many years had greater regional power than the central government. This it owed to the date harvest, which made the town an important market and attracted caravans and merchants from the far south. Parts of the old fourteenth-century quarter still survive, but the oasis is the main feature.

In recent years, like so many other parts of the country, Tozeur has been gearing itself up as a major tourist centre. First came the jeep-loads of day-trippers on "safari" from the coast, then the airport with a few charter flights, and finally the Route Touristique, lined with package hotels to make this a fully fledged desert resort. Tozeur still retains much charm, but hustlers abound.

Some history

After the first **Arab invasions**, the Berbers of Tozeur joined the Arab army, which swept west through the Maghreb. By 900, however, Tozeur's radical **Kharijite sect** had begun to resist the rule of the Shiite Fatimids, and in 944 the legendary figure of **Abu Yazid** (or Abu Himara, "the man on the donkey") moved north from Tozeur to lay siege to the Fatimid capital at Mahdia. The rebellion failed and Abu Yazid was killed in 947, but the legend of the unruly southerner became part of Tunisian mythology. Over the next centuries, Tozeur continued to be a centre of revolt; the **Almoravids** found strong support here when they tried to overthrow the **Almohads**, and the town's rebelliousness was only finally suppressed by the **Hafsids** in the fourteenth century.

Thereafter Tozeur lost its military might but developed as the major trading post for southern Tunisia. When Scottish traveller Dr Thomas Shaw arrived in 1757, he noticed the "great traffick" in slaves, brought from as far away as the River Niger; the exchange rate was one slave for two or three quintals of dates (100kg to the quintal). James Bruce, heading for the Nile in 1765, reported that Tozeur was used by merchants from Timbuktu and other Saharan oases, dealing in sufficient wool and dates to load twenty thousand camels each year. But by the middle of the nineteenth century, the Saharan trade had dwindled to one or two small caravans each year, and the oasis was thrown back on its own, still plentiful resources.

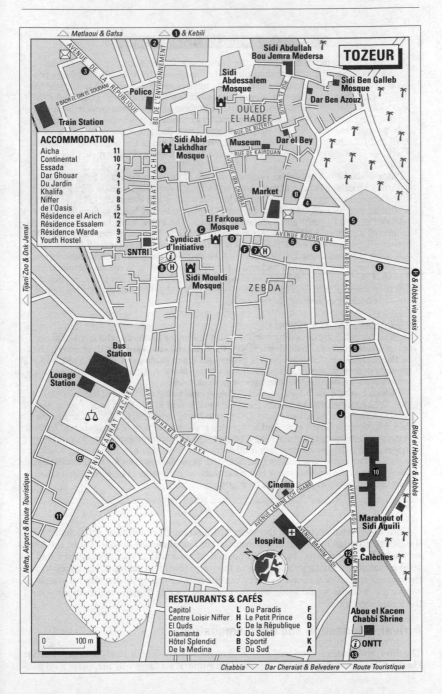

DATES AND DATE FARMERS

Of all the 120 varieties of **date palm**, the finest is the *deglat en nour*, or "finger of light", so called because of the translucent quality of the ripened fruit. Tozeur and Nefta produce 1000 tonnes of these dates every year, most of which is exported to Europe for Christmas. According to legend, a poor village woman died before she could make the pilgrimage to Mecca and was buried with her humble string of beads, made from date stones. The tears the Prophet shed in sympathy germinated the stones and created not only an oasis but also the new variety of date. The palms are artificially pollinated in April and June each year, and the fruit harvested by hand at the beginning of winter. Each tree is expected to yield some fifteen or twenty clusters of dates, each weighing about 10kg.

Palm wine, known as *laghmi*, is simply the sap of the palm, collected from the top of the trunk by cutting off one of the fronds and letting it drip into an earthenware pot tied to the trunk. Tapping the tree for palm wine will weaken and eventually kill it, so palms producing eating-quality dates are not used. *Laghmi* takes 24 hours to ferment, and is available in sweet (fresh) and fermented versions. The latter needs to be treated with caution as it's unpredictably potent and goes off quickly. The wine is generally available between April and October – the *Restaurant de la Medina* in Tozeur serves it fresh in season; otherwise, ask around in the oasis (but be discreet, since sale of fermented *laghmi* is strictly speaking illegal). As for buying the dates themselves, in season the market in Tozeur is as good as any, and you can also get them easily in Gafsa and Douz, but beware that they sometimes have maggots inside (especially if slightly old), and may need opening and checking individually before eating.

THE SHARECROPPERS' TALE

Most of the palms are owned by wealthy (often absentee) landlords, who employ labourers as **sharecroppers**. Instead of a salary, they each receive a share of the harvest. Out on the plains where the main crop is barley, this share is about one-fifth – a share that gives them their name, the *khammes*. In the oases, however, the figure falls to one-tenth, sometimes less, because the date harvest is so valuable.

Without capital of their own, and since they are paid only at the end of the agricultural year, the *khammes* have to borrow from their employers to tide them over. Paying high rates of interest on these loans forces them into heavy debt, which, after a poor harvest, they are often unable to repay. And so they fall into a sort of debt bondage, bound to the employer in perpetuity because they cannot pay off the ever-increasing loans. Since Independence the government has tried to improve their status by introducing a union to combat the employers. Strangely enough the *khammes* have ben far from entusiastic. They see the weather, the cause of poor harvests, as the source of their condition rather than the employers' exploitation of their poverty.

Until the French occupation the town had a strangely ambivalent relationship with the Beys. Although there was a governor, or *caid*, who usually lived in Tunis, the town was actually administered by its own council of elders. Every winter the Bey had to send a *mahalla*, a military expedition to force the town and surrounding tribes to pay their taxes and allow the *caid* to carry out his administrative duties. After a couple of weeks the *mahalla* would leave and the town once again became autonomous – until the following winter.

Arrival, information and accommodation

The **bus** and **louage stations** are on the main Nefta–Kebili road, **avenue Farhat Hached**, at the northern end of avenue Bourguiba. If you arrive by **air**, there's no public transport into town except taxis (around 3TD); Europcar have a desk at the airport (☎06/453388) in case you want to rent a car. Of Tozeur's two **tourist offices**, the friendly and knowledgeable ONTT (Sept–June Mon–Thurs 8.30am–1pm & 3–5.45pm, Fri & Sat 8.30am–1.30pm; July & Aug Mon–Sat 7.30am–1.30pm; ☎06/454503), with some English-speaking staff, is at 89 av Abou el Kacem Chabbi by the *Hôtel el Jerid*. The Syndicat d'Initiative (Mon–Thurs 8am–1pm & 3–6pm, Fri & Sat 8am–1pm; ☎06/462034) is more conveniently located at 143 av Bourguiba by the corner of avenue Farhat Hached. They have lists of bus and plane departures, and can arrange tours of the oasis (15TD/hr by camel, 8TD/hr for up to four people by calèche).

Accommodation

Tozeur has plenty of **hotels**; it's usually possible to find a suitable place for every budget, and there's an excellent campsite. Women on their own need have no worries, except possibly in the very cheapest hotels. The Route Touristique overlooking the Belvedere has a number of three- to five-star tourist hotels, with little to distinguish them, each with swimming pools, nightclubs and money-changing facilities; in fact, the only thing missing is a beach. Prices tend not to vary with the season, but, if they do, high season is often winter not summer.

TOWN-CENTRE HOTELS

Aicha ★, 156 av Farhat Hached ☎06/452788, ⓕ452873. On the Nefta road, towards the airport turn-off. Reasonable for the price, with a choice of room decor, and all rooms en suite, though some can be a bit smelly, so have a sniff before you take the room. Plans for the future include an extension and a pool. ❷

Résidence el Arich, 93 av Abou el Kacem Chabbi ☎06/462644, ⓕ461544, ⓔelarichtozeur @yahoo.fr. A pleasant pension with cool, clean rooms, all en suite, some a/c, and some self-catering family apartments. Breakfast is on the roof terrace. ❸

Continental ★★★, 79 av Abou el Kacem Chabbi ☎06/461411, ⓕ452109. Comfortable if rather impersonal, with a/c rooms and a pool, used mostly by tour groups whisked in from Hammamet and Monastir on whirlwind jeep "safaris" of the south. ❹

Dar Ghouar ★★, rue el Nazriin ☎06/452666, ⓕ461953. Adequate if a little neglected; all rooms are en suite with a/c and TV, but they're rather small and gloomy, some with a tiny token balcony. ❹

Essada, 65 av Bourguiba ☎06/460097, off the street itself, opposite the market. The cheapest place in town, simple but clean and good value. ❶

Résidence Essalem, 21 bd de l'Environnement ☎06/462881. A quiet, family-run place on the Kebili and Degache road, east of town, which is clean, well kept and friendly, with hot water round the clock, and some rooms en suite. ❷

Hôtel du Jardin ★★, bd de l'Environnement ☎06/454196, ⓕ454199,100m east of *Résidence Essalem*. A lovely little place, though a little way out of town, set in a large, pretty garden full of trees and singing birds, with pleasant, tasteful rooms in a choice of yellow, pink or blue decor. ❸

Résidence Karim, 150 av Abou el Kacem Chabbi ☎&ⓕ06/454574. Opposite the calèche stand, a bright clean place, and very friendly, with air-conditioned en-suite rooms and other mod cons that you wouldn't expect for the price, plus a roof terrace with a vista over the oasis. Best value in this price range. ❷

Khalifa, 35 av Bourguiba ☎06/454858. Basic but clean rooms, those upstairs en suite, though some have windows onto the corridor rather than outside. In summer you can sleep on the roof (5TD), but the price per person is the same as a double (or indeed a single), and it is negotiable. ❷

Niffer, 4 rue Général Hussein ☎06/460555, ⓕ461900, at the junction of av Bourguiba with av Farhat Hached. A new place with clean, airy, en-suite rooms reasonably spacious, and bang in the centre of town. ❷

Hôtel de l'Oasis ★★★, 1 av Abou el Kacem Chabbi ☎06/452300, ⓕ461522. Rather a classy joint but friendly with it, and definitely preferable to the three-stars out in the Route Touristique, with comfortable rooms, pleasant gardens, a pool and smart service. ❺

Résidence Warda ★, 29 av Abou el Kacem Chabbi ☎06/452597, ℱ452744. An old favourite, very clean and pleasant, with hot water round the clock, and all bar four rooms en suite, some with a shower, some with a tub, and all a/c. The covered roof terrace has views over town. ❷

ROUTE TOURISTIQUE HOTELS

Abou Nawas Tozeur ★★★★, rte Touristique ☎06/452700, ℱ452686, ℮abounawas.tozeur @abounawas.com.tn. Pleasantly peaceful with tastefully decorated rooms, all with TV, a/c, terrace or balcony, and bathroom with tub. Facilities include a pool, fitness centre and *Star Wars* pinball machine. ❺

Basma ★★★, rte Touristique ☎06/452488, ℱ452294. Friendly and relaxed, with a lot of young French guests, and the usual three-star facilities, including a pool, though the rooms are smallish. Activities include *pétanque*, and there's also a massage service. ❻

Dar Cheraiet ★★★★★, rte Touristique ☎06/454888, ℱ454472, ℮darcherait@tryp.tourism.tn. A very pricey deluxe establishment, adjoining the museum complex, with junior, senior and presidential suites available. ❼

Ksar el Jerid ★★★, 186 av Farhat Hached ☎06/454357, ℱ454515. On the Nefta road, and just off the route touristique, but better value than the three-star hotels that are on it, cool and comfortable with spacious, well-furnished a/c rooms, friendly, efficient staff, and all mod cons, including a pool. ❺

Palm Beach Palace ★★★★★, rte Touristique ☎06/453111, ℱ453911, ℮palmbeach.tozeur @gnet.tn. Tozeur's plushest establishment, purring with understated luxury; facilities include fitness centre, hammam, Jacuzzi, pool and three restaurants. The classiest hotel in town. ❻

Phedra ★★★, rte Touristique ☎06/452185, ℱ452799, ℮hotelphedra.tn@yahoo.fr. A friendly place with great views of the sunset over the Belvedere, even when actually in the pool. Ask for a room with a view. ❺

CAMPSITE AND YOUTH HOSTEL

Campement les Beaux Rêves, av Abou el Kacem Chabbit, 500m beyond the ONTT ☎06/453331, ℱ454208, ⓦbeauxreves.ifrance.com. Sleep in your own tent, in a Bedouin version in a palm-frond hut (6TD), or on a hammock hung between two date palms. It's very pleasant with trees, a stream to bathe in, running water, showers, toilets and café. Camping excursions in jeep and tent are also possible if enough people are interested.

Maison des Jeunes, 29 av de la République ☎06/452335. A couple of hundred metres up the Gafsa road from its junction with av Farhat Hached. A little regimented, as you're up and out by 8.30am and the curfew is at 10pm, but it is friendly. Dorms 4TD.

The Town

Tozeur's backbone is its main street, **avenue Bourguiba**, lined with tourist souvenir shops selling carpets and desert roses. About two-thirds of the way down is the central **place Ibn Chabbat**, flanked by the market and post office. The most interesting part of Tozeur is the ancient **Ouled el Hadef** quarter, between avenue Farhat Hached and avenue Bourguiba, where the architecture, like the lives of its people, is largely traditional. **Avenue Abou el Kacem Chabbi** runs west, parallel to avenue Farhat Hached, alongside the quarters of **Zebda** and **Chabbia**, which have been less zealous about preserving their traditions than Ouled el Hadef. Various turnings from the main road lead into the **oasis**. At the end of avenue Abou el Kacem Chabbi, the road turns a corner by the Dar Cheraiat Museum to become the **Route Touristique**, meeting up with avenue Farhat Hached at the airport turn-off. Straight ahead, off the tarmac, is the road out to the **Belvedere**.

Ouled el Hadef

The oldest part of town, fourteenth-century **Ouled el Hadef**, backs onto the *Hôtel Splendid*, its entrances marked by plans of the quarter. As at Tamerza, its high walls are faced with small rectangular bricks, presenting a blank exterior to the narrow streets. The windowless walls ensure the privacy that is prescribed in the Koran – in fact, the Arabic word for a house, *maskin*, is related to *sakina*, which means "peaceful and holy". A fifteenth-century legal ruling of one Sidi Khalil, brief and to the point, states that "anyone may climb up his date palm but only if he previously informs the neighbour into whose house he might obtain a view". Only traditionally made bricks are used and the brickwork in the quarter is almost unique in Tunisia (see box p.316); the only other place it can be found is in neighbouring Nefta. The bricks themselves are made near the Belvedere.

This is an excellent place to wander around and get lost, despite groups of young boys who sometimes like to bait tourists. Things to look out for, apart from the brickwork, are the palm-trunk ceilings overhead as you pass under archways, and the large doors equipped with three knockers that are still fitted on some houses. Men, women and children each have a different one with its own tone (men left, women right, children underneath the other two), so that any visitor can be greeted by the appropriate member of the household. A door with only two knockers indicates a family without children. Poorer families have doors made of palm-trunks, while richer ones have doors made of true wood. Designs in nails on the doors include horseshoes, for good luck of course, fish to ward off the evil eye, crosses with arrows, and tridents. A green door indicates a religious building rather than a residence.

The main street of the quarter, **rue de Kairouan**, leading from the *Hôtel Splendid* and the *Hôtel de l'Oasis*, runs from one side to the other. On the right is the fourteenth-century **tomb of Sidi Bou Aissa**, now converted into a **Museum of Popular Arts and Traditions** (Tues–Sun 8am–1pm & 3–6pm; 1TD). Among the exhibits are objects from the traditional marriage ceremony – the wooden chests for the bride's clothes, an Egyptian silk dress, and ornamental green and yellow pottery. A collection of manuscripts includes a timetable for the distribution of water through an oasis, devised by Ibn Chabbat in the thirteenth century as a way of ensuring equal supplies for every landowner and only printed by the French. In the courtyard, among miscellaneous statuary, is a traditional three-knocker door, in case you didn't spot any while wandering around the old quarter.

At the far end of rue de Kairouan, two right turns will take you down rue de Bizerte. The rue el Walid, left at the end, leads to the **Medersa of Sidi Abdullah Bou Jemra**. A right, on the other hand, takes you to the main square of the quarter, where a room in the former **Bey's mansion** (no.9) was used for the cave in the film *The English Patient*. The family are usually happy to let visitors in at any reasonable hour, but will expect a gratuity for it. The mosque whose minaret dominates the quarter is that of **Sidi Abdessalem**. Mohammed Said, who runs a shop on rue de Kairouan, 50m southeast of the museum, is a mine of information on the quarter, and is usually happy to explain its quirks to those who are interested.

The mosques on avenue Bourguiba are of limited interest. The **El Farkous Mosque**, with its tall, slender minaret, is attractive and distinctive, but not very ancient, and under major reconstruction. The **Mosque of Sidi Mouldi**, down the road by the Syndicat d'Initiative, has a minaret in a similar style, restored in 1944, but you probably won't be allowed up it to admire the view. The main section of the **Sunday market**, which actually starts on Saturday afternoon, and finishes shortly after lunch on Sunday, takes place in an enclosure by the bus station, but there is also a livestock market, mostly for sheep, goats and horses, on avenue de la République (the El Hamma road), 150m past the post office, where the railway crosses the street.

You may notice that the traditionally dressed women in town and in the oasis wear a distinctive black gown decorated with a single stripe. Originally, a white stripe was worn by women from Tozeur, and a blue one by women from Nefta, but the blue seems to be taking over in Tozeur too. An unmarried girl will have a narrow stripe on her gown, changing it for a broader band when wed.

South of town

Avenue Abou el Kacem Chabbi is named after the great Tozeuri poet (see p.480), whose shrine is tucked away by the ONTT tourist office. With the northern edge of the oasis on one side, it also skirts the quarters of Zebda and Chebbia. **Zebda** borders avenue Bourguiba, across which it glared angrily at Ouled el Hadef, the two in a state of mortal feud until the nineteenth century. **Chabbia**, a little further west along the road, was one of the last places in Tunisia where the bride rode in a camel-borne litter at her marriage ceremony. The camel still joins the procession, but nowadays the bride walks alongside it. If you want to see the real thing, you'll have to go to Jerba. Behind the *Hôtel Continental*, near where the camels and calèches hang out, is the photogenic little **Marabout of Sidi Aguili**, a favourite on postcards of the region.

At the end of avenue Abou el Kacem Chabbi is the **Dar Cheraiet complex** featuring a museum, an Arabian Nights grotto, a restaurant, café and deluxe apartments, with all sorts of additions and extensions in the pipeline. The **museum** (daily 8am–midnight; 3TD) gives an upmarket, sanitized view of Tunisian life, but it's well laid out, with treasures formerly belonging to the Bey, among other fascinating antiques, all with English explanations. If you so desire, attendants dressed up like the Bey's servants will escort you round. The **Arabian Nights Grotto** (same hours as museum; 5TD) is a kind of overblown fairground funhouse complete with mirrors, scary effects and fluorescent decor, based loosely on ideas from the *Thousand and One Nights* (which are mainly set in Egypt and Iraq, and don't actually mention Tunisia). There is little in the way of explanation save a cassette outlining the story as you enter, but you may recognize images such as Ali Baba's cave, Aladdin's genie and Sinbad and the Roc. It definitely has its moments, and is fun in a tacky sort of way, but you should try to avoid getting tangled up with a tour group. The grotto is best visited after dark. There is also now a third exhibition in the complex, **Dar Zamen** (same hours as museum; 5TD), illustrating the history of Tunisia with tableaux and escorts. The complex's café is a handy place to stop for a drink, so long as you don't mind paying well over the odds.

The road and sand track west of Dar Cheraiat follow the main watercourse out to the signposted **Belvedere** – a grandiose name for several large boulders which are, nonetheless, big enough to give a beautiful view over the oasis if you climb them. You

---

BRICKWORK IN TOZEUR AND NEFTA

The **houses** in the old quarters of Nefta and Tozeur are unique in Tunisia. They are constructed of yellowish handmade bricks, some of which protrude in ornate geometrical designs in relief on the walls of the houses, and their shapes and motifs are repeated on local carpets and shawls. The decorative technique was first used in Syria and Iraq during the eighth century and was carried west by the Arab invaders in the tenth century. The only other place it is practised today is in Iran.

Although the old quarters have been extensively restored, the work has largely been carried out in the traditional manner. To make the bricks, local clay and sand are mixed, soaked in water and left to mulch for a day. The mixture is then shaped in a wooden frame and left to dry in the sun. Finally, the bricks are baked in a kiln for three days at temperatures of up to 1000°C. The industry is on something of an upturn at the moment as people are returning to locally made bricks – which provide better insulation against extremes of temperature than breeze blocks. The pattern making protruding bricks also create small patches of shade on the wall, generating convection currents that cool the surface.

For everything you could possibly want to know about the bricks, their manufacture and use in local buildings, a book called *Brick of Tozeur* by Haddan Abdelhamid is available locally (for example at Cheraiet Atef, 31 av Farhat Hached, or at *Résidence Warda*).

can make out the precise boundaries of the cultivated land hemmed in by sand. During the Ottoman period the protective bamboo fences were removed and the oasis went to ruin, battered by the south winds. At night the Belvedere is lit up for the sake of tourists in the *zone touristique* hotels, who have a view onto it.

A hundred metres or so past the Belvedere, south and west, the shards glinting on the ground like broken glass in the sun are in fact **rock crystals**. A little further at the open-air traditional **brick factories**, the workers will be happy to show you how they make the bricks used in Tozeur's distinctive architecture. Two brothers at the first brick factory double up as Tozeur's only potters, and will make pieces to order. The scrub area beyond the Belvedere is an excellent and easily accessible place for spotting desert bird life.

The Oasis

The main attraction of Tozeur, its vast **oasis**, covers around ten square kilometres planted with some 200,000 palms and fed by 200 springs, its water channelled along dykes, or *seguias*, and controlled by a series of sluices. At the time of Ibn Chabbat, in the eleventh century, these streams were blocked with sections of palm trunks, which were opened and closed by orders of the warden. Most tourists visit the oasis on a calèche from the stand opposite the *Résidence Karim* on avenue Abou el Kacem Chabbi, but for those who don't mind a long walk, shanks' pony is an equally pleasant way to wander through the oasis, and one that allows you more flexibility to stop where you fancy.

The main road into the oasis starts in avenue Abou el Kacem Chabbi by the *Hôtel Continental*. Just over 500m along it is the village of **BLED EL HADDAR**, site of Roman **Tusuros**, where a partially restored brickwork **minaret** stands on a course of Roman stonework in an enclosure to the right of the main road. Also in the enclosure is the **Great Mosque**, built around 1190 by the Almoravid Ibn Ghaniya who, like so many others, came to Tozeur to start a rebellion. Its beautiful stone **mihrab**, all the more striking in this plain interior, was the work of craftsmen from the Balearic islands. Like many Islamic buildings, the mosque exploits sunlight, which, during the afternoon, streams through the narrow windows down the central nave to the mihrab. The classic minaret above begins as a circle, develops into an octagon and ends up square; the "crow's nest" is a later addition. On the other side of the tower, a path leads to the reconstructed **tomb of Ibn Chabbat** (first built in 1282), who devised the complex irrigation and cultivation system used in the oasis.

The road continues through some of the oasis's best cultivated land, reaching, after a couple more kilometres, the little village of **ABBÈS**. Just beyond it is the **Marabout of Sidi Bou Lifa**, overshadowed by a venerable old **jujube tree** apparently planted by the saint himself; both are reputed to be over seven hundred years old. Jujube trees, which originated in China, bear fruit which can be eaten fresh or dried, taste a little like dates, and are used in the United States to make large sucking sweets. From here the road meanders lazily a few pleasant kilometres through the oasis, before bringing you back to Tozeur near the top of avenue Bourguiba.

Two hundred metres past the tree and marabout is a garden and zoo, unassumingly called **Paradis** (daily 8am–nightfall; 2TD). The menagerie includes gazelles, several tormented baboons, snakes, and a family of lions, all kept in overcrowded captivity. If you arrive at the same time as a tour group, you can also see such spectacles as performing scorpions and a Coke-drinking camel. More interesting perhaps, though overpriced, are the pistachio, rose, violet and pomegranate syrups made from plants in the garden and sold at the entrance.

Back in town, animal lovers will also want to avoid the **Tijani Zoo** – left from avenue Bourguiba into avenue Farhat Hached, then signposted (right) after some 150m and off to the right a few hundred metres up (daily 8am–nightfall; 1TD). This was once a snake farm, but the reptiles are nowadays a very minor attraction, not even easy to spot beneath their wire gauze.

Eating and drinking

There are a number of budget-oriented and medium-priced **restaurants** along avenue Bourguiba, Abou el Kacem Chabbi and Farhat Hached. For something a little classier, apart from the *Petit Prince*, your best bets are the restaurants of the various starred hotels, most of which do set menus and/or buffet lunch and supper: try the *Continental*, *L'Oasis* and *Dar Ghouar*. Several of the medium-priced places offer local specialities, which usually need to be ordered in advance for at least four people, though some places are flexible. One Tozeur speciality is *metabka*, sometimes referred to as "Berber pizza", which consists of a *harissa* and onion sauce between two chapatti-like griddle-baked unleavened breads, and strictly for onion lovers. Other local dishes include *seffa* and *barkoukech*, both based on something like couscous, though with larger grains; *seffa* is made with vegetables and no meat, while *barkoukech* is served with a sauce that contains two or three different meats such as rabbit, chicken and lamb. There is even a special regional version of couscous: *couscous helba*, made with saltfish. The restaurants on avenue Abou el Kacem Chabbi are not allowed to serve alcohol, so if you want beer or wine with your meal, you'll have to eat elsewhere.

Restaurants

Capitol Restaurant, 158 av Abou el Kacem Chabbi ☎06/462531. A pleasant and very reasonably priced eatery offering *metabka*, *seffa* and *barkoukech* (these usually need to be ordered in advance by a minimum of four people, but ask), and camel steak, as well as the usual staples. Daily 11am–3pm & 6.30–10pm.

Restaurant Diamanta, 94 av Abou el Kacem Chabbi, opposite the road to Bled el Haddar. Moderately priced traditional fare, including a good lamb couscous. Daily noon–3pm & 7–9.30pm.

Restaurant de la Medina, off av Bourguiba at its southern end. A cheap place serving couscous, tajine, *metabka* and, in season, unfermented *laghmi* (palm wine). Daily 11.30am–3pm & 6.30–9.30pm.

Restaurant du Paradis, 75 av Bourguiba, but in fact in a small street off av Bourguiba opposite the market. A small selection of very low-priced Tunisian dishes including either spaghetti or couscous or rice with lamb. Daily noon–3pm & 6–10pm.

Restaurant le Petit Prince, off avenue Abou el Kacem Chabbi near the top of av Bourguiba ☎06/452518. Pricier restaurant offering fine French and Tunisian cooking, including roast rabbit and six different types of coucous. Daily 10am–3pm & 7–11pm.

Restaurant de la République, through the arches between 99 and 101 av Bourguiba. An excellent establishment, popular with tourists and Tunisians alike, with good service, good food and low prices. Daily noon–3pm & 6.30–9.30pm.

Restaurant du Soleil, 58 av Abou Kacem el Chabbi, opposite the *Résidence Warda* ☎06/454220. Good food and pleasant dining at very reasonable prices, with veggie couscous for non-carnivores and, if ordered in advance, *chorba aux herbes du Sahara*, *seffa*, *barkoukech* or camel-meat couscous. Sat–Thurs noon–3pm & 6.30–10pm.

Restaurant Sportif, 163 av Farhat Hached. Cheap and cheerful Tunisian diner. Daily 8am–3pm & 7–9pm.

Restaurant du Sud, 11 av Farhat Hached, opposite the Agil station. Sfaxian specialities at moderate prices, including spaghetti *aux fruits de mer*, plus *metabka*, and four kinds of couscous. Daily 9am–3pm & 6–10pm.

Cafés and bars

The best **patisserie** in town is the *El Quds* at 60 av Bourguiba (daily 6am–10pm), which does fresh fruit milkshakes and several types of baklava. The former *Hôtel Splendid*, opposite the Dar Ghouar, is now a **bar**, though a bit raucous; the bars of the upmarket hotels such as the *Dar Jerid* are your best bet for a quiet drink, especially for women. For a **coffee or tea** in beautiful surroundings, try the *Centre Loisir Niffer* in the oasis (daily 9am–2am, all night in summer), an outdoor café among banana trees and

---

JEDI STOMPING GROUNDS

Few films have such a devoted cult following as *Star Wars*, and Tunisia provided locations for the original 1977 movie, and the first and second prequels, *The Phantom Menace* (1998) and Episode Two. In each film, Tunisia plays the role of the desert planet Tatooine (named after the town of Tataouine), home of Luke Skywalker. As a result, the country has begun to attract quite a number of *Star Wars* fans eager to find themselves a long time ago in a galaxy far, far away. Some locations can be visited with Tunisian travel agencies such as LOVA in Tozeur (see p.321), but it's also possible to visit others under your own steam, especially if you have transport.

Onk Jemal, 30km north of Tozeur (no public transport). The site where Quin-ion and Darth Maul slogged it out in *The Phantom Menace*, and the background for the pod race in the same film, is a popular stop for jeep-borne tour groups. The set is still in place – officially off-limits but due to open with free access on completion of filming of Episode Two. The same site was also used in *The English Patient* – indeed, the piste to get here was made specifically for its film crew. The name Onk Jemal, meaning "Camel's Head", comes from a rock formation resembling the head and hump of a camel.

Shubiel Gorge, by the marabout of Sidi Bou Helal near Kriz (see p.328; no public transport). The location for two ambush scenes in *Star Wars*, of R2-D2 by robotnapping space nomads, and of Luke Skywalker and his robot chums by Sand People. It was christened "Star Wars Canyon" by the film crew, and also used as a location in *Raiders of the Lost Ark* and *The English Patient*, as well as *The Phantom Menace*.

Chott and Dunes west of Nefta, about 10km west of Nefta (no public transport). A piste crossing the main road leads south down onto the Chott to a site used for exterior shots of Luke Skywalker's home, although little remains of the set now. To the north, the same road leads to the dunes where R2-D2 and C-3PO landed in an escape pod at the beginning of *Star Wars*. Neither site is easy to find, and you'd really have to be an enthusiast to go out looking for either of them.

Ajim, Jerba (see pp.378–9; easy access by public transport, though specific sights want searching out). In town, on avenue Abou el Kacem Chabbi, though barely recognizable nowadays, is the entrance to the bar at the space port of Mos Eisley where Luke and Obiwan meet Han Solo in the original *Star Wars*. Obiwan's house in the film is an old mosque 3km up the west coast road towards Borj Jillij, on the seaward side; the entrance to Mos Eisley is another old mosque and domed marabout, 11km further north, again on the seaward side of the road.

Matmata (see pp.354–7; easy access by public transport). The *Hôtel Sidi Driss* was the set for the interior shots of Luke Skywalker's home at the beginning of *Star Wars*. You can sit down to a meal in the exact spot Luke had dinner with his aunt and uncle. The main courtyard also served as a location in the second prequel, and most of the set is still in place.

Ksar Haddada, near Ghoumrassen (see p.401; accessible by public transport): used for the filming of the Mos Espa slave quarters in *The Phantom Menace*.

Ksar Ouled Soltane, 30km south of Tataouine (see p.410; accessible by public transport): used for pick-up shots of the Mos Espa slave quarters in *The Phantom Menace*.

Further details on these locations and their film roles, with photographs and movie stills, can be found at ⓦwww.infomaniak.ch/~lionel/starwars/default.htm and ⓦwww.toysrgus.com/travel/tunisia.html.

bougainvillea-swathed date palms, with a swimming pool and sometimes entertainment in the evenings. To find it, continue for 200m past the *Restaurant le Petit Prince* to the statue of Ibn Chabbat, where you bear left (the right fork leads after 4km to Abbès), then take a right after 100m and it's 150m further on your right.

Listings

Airlines Tunisair, on the Nefta road, opposite Hertz ☎06/452127, also representing Tuninter.

Ballooning Hot-air ballooning is organized by Aeroasis, 138 av Abou el Kacem Chabbi ☎06/454577, with ascents at sunrise or sunset (100TD per person for groups of at least four).

Banks Banque de Tunisie at 13 av Bourguiba and STB at no. 36 both have ATM machines taking Visa and Mastercard. There are two more banks just round the corner in av Farhat Hached (without ATMs). Tozeur's banks maintain a weekend rota, which means that one bank in town will always be open Saturday and Sunday mornings 9am–noon.

Bike rental At a kiosk nearly opposite *Restaurant Diamanta* on av Abou el Kacem Chabbi, you can rent out bicycles (2.5TD/hr), mopeds (5TD/hr), and scooters (10TD/hr). Agence Slim on route Touristique ☎06/461555, almost opposite *Hôtel Hafsi*, also rents bicycles (3TD/hr), mopeds (5TD/hr), and "quads" or beach buggies (25TD/hr).

Car rental Avis, 96 av Farhat Hached ☎06/450543; Europcar, 279 av Farhat Hached ☎06/450119; Hertz, 223 av Farhat Hached ☎06/460214.

Cinema Cine Sahara, 28 av Lamine ech Chábbi, by the junction with rue Mohamed ben Aya.

Festivals Every year around November, a series of camel races and Bedouin spectacles, including camel wrestling (camel versus camel), take place on a site 500m off avenue Abou el Kacem Chabbi. This being Abou el Kacem Chabbi's birthplace (see p.480), there is also a modern poetry festival in February.

Hammams Hammam el Nakhla is at 8 rue Omar Ibn Abdelaziz, behind the Syndicat d'Initiative (daily: men 4–10am, 1.30–6pm & 10pm–1am; women 10am–1pm & 6–10pm). There is also a hammam at 55 av Bourguiba (in fact on a small street off av Bourguiba, three doors away from the *Hôtel Essada*; daily: men 5–9.30am & 3–6pm; women 9.30am–2pm & 6–11pm); you may have to go in the back way, which can be tricky to find.

Horse-riding You can ride a horse, accompanied by a guide, at Ranch Equi-Balade, rte du Belvedere ☎06/452613, just past the *Hôtel Dar Cheraiet* (15TD/hr, 45TD for half a day).

Hospital The regional hospital is on av Brahim Gadi ☎06/453400, off av Abou el Kacem Chabbi, opposite the *Hôtel el Jerid*.

Internet access Palmes Net, off av Farhat Hached, just west of the market enclosure. Not the best nor the cheapest internet office in Tunisia, but the only one in town to date (8am–midnight; 3TD/hr).

Laundry Detersan at 130 av Abou el Kacem Chabbi does machine washes as well as dry cleaning.

Newspapers Some English-language papers and magazines are available at 9 av Bourguiba, between the *Hôtel Khalifa* and avenue Abou el Kacem Chabbi.

Pharmacy There is a night pharmacy at 157 av Farhat Hached, 100m west of the junction with av Mohamed Ben Aya.

Police The regular police are at the junction of bd de l'Environnement with av de la République ☎06/452129; the Garde Nationale are at 180 av Farhat Hached ☎06/454295.

Post office In place Ibn Chabbat, just off av Bourguiba (city hours); changes cash. There's another post office by the Youth Hostel.

Supermarket Magasin Général, 245 av Farhat Hached, out towards the airport turn-off (Tues–Sat 8am–12.30pm & 2.50–7pm, Sun 8am–12.40pm).

Swimming The hotels *Continental* and *Oasis* have pools you can use for a few dinars, as do the hotels on the Route Touristique (the *Phedra*'s has a view). Use of the pool at the *Centre Loisir Niffer* oasis café is free for customers.

Telephones Among the town's numerous Taxiphone offices, one at 60 av Farhat Hached, opposite the end of av Bourguiba, is open 24hr.

MOVING ON FROM TOZEUR

For a rundown of destinations and journey times, see Travel Details on pp.343–344.

There are regular **buses** to Metlaoui, continuing to either Redeyef or Gafsa, and some then to Kairouan and Tunis, Sfax and Sousse (run by SNTRI). There are also buses to Chebika, Tamerza and Kebili (one continuing to Gabès, the other to Douz – you may have to change buses at Kebili). In the other direction, there are regular services to Nefta, and one that continues to the Algerian border at Hazoua.

Louages leave from a yard opposite the bus station. You should have no trouble getting a vehicle from here to Tunis, Nefta, Tamerza, Metlaoui, Gafsa, Kebili, Degache or El Hamma du Jerid; direct louages for Sfax leave mornings only.

Tozeur's **airport** (☎06/453388), 3km out of town, and best reached by taxi (about 1.5TD), has flights to Tunis and Jerba. There are no longer any passenger **train** services to or from Tozeur, though the line (partly washed away by flooding) has been repaired, and the station renovated, a sign of possible reinstatement of passenger services in the future, *insha'Allah*.

Tours LOVA, c/o The Green Travel, rte Touristique ☎09/450484, ⓦwww.lovafrica.com, offer a number of excellent trips, which can be booked at most of the budget hotels, in particular the *Résidence Warda*, who keep fuller details. The most popular outings are half-day excursions to Chebika, Tamerza and Mides (30TD), and to Nefta, the brickworks and the *Star Wars* set at Onk Jemal (30TD), which may also be extended to include a barbeque dinner and starlight desert walk, and a night in a tent out in the desert. A similar trip over two days and a night on camelback (100TD) is also available. Other options include two days and a night to Ksar Ghilaine (120TD), and tailor-made trips to visit film locations, meet nomadic families, observe the stars or look at desert wildlife. Trips to the far south of Tunisia are also possible.

Nefta

نفطة

After travelling the 25km from Tozeur through almost totally barren and dusty land, the oasis at **NEFTA** is quite a shock. You don't notice it immediately – the drab buildings on the edge of the town shield its beginnings – but suddenly its extent becomes clear, as does that of the **Corbeille**, a crater-like depression densely planted with palm trees. The site of Roman Nepte, Nefta, according to the legends, was settled by Kostel, "son of Shem, son of Noah", at the place where water boiled for the first time after the Flood. It is now one of the most important religious centres in Tunisia, traditionally linked with the mystical brotherhoods of **Sufism**; the ridge above the Corbeille is cluttered with simple whitewashed domes and the old quarters somehow manage to pack in 24 mosques and over a hundred shrines.

Arrival, information and accommodation

Avenue Bourguiba, the main road from Tozeur to the Algerian border, splits the town neatly in two. Coming in from Tozeur, it descends into the **Corbeille**, which it bridges at the narrowest point – the area south of here is **Ouled ech Chrif**, one of Nefta's old quarters, and over the bridge is **place de la République**, the centre of town. The main road, boulevard de l'Environnement, swings south from here, skirting the quarter of **Beni Ali** on one side, and the main hotel zone on the other, before continuing on its way towards Algeria. South of the hotels is the **oasis**, and beyond that the silvery gleam of the Chott, which really does look like sea from here. Should you wish to drive around the town, the whole ensemble is now neatly encircled by a belt of tarmac, the northern part of which goes right round the top of the Corbeille.

THE SUFI TRADITION

Sufism, *Tasawwuf* in Arabic, is the Divine Wisdom contained within the *Tariquah*, the spiritual way or path laid down in the Koran. Participants are called faqirs or dervishes, meaning "poor", and strictly speaking the *sufi* is one who has reached the end of the path, which is a direct personal experience of the Unity of God. A *sufi* teacher, variously called a faqir, sheikh or *murshid*, prescribes the chants, recitations and body exercises which have made this sect so famous. Besides the Koran and the *Hadith* (sayings of the Prophet), the *sufi* looks to the *Hadith qudsi*, in which God speaks in the first person through the Prophet. "My slave", reads one typical verse, "comes ever nearer to me through devotion of his free will, until I love him, and when I love him, I am the hearing with which he sees and the hand with which he fights and the foot with which he walks."

Sufism has often had an awkward relationship with orthodox Sunni Islam, threatening to usurp religious law and to substitute mysticism for the knowledge of the truth contained in the Koran, a problem partially resolved as early as the eleventh century by saying that Sufism was a way of "apprehending reality", not of finding out new facts about God. In Tunisia *sufis* have long held considerable power; with the breakdown in the control of central government (from the Almohads in the thirteenth century onwards), the sheikhs had great influence in rural areas, setting up *zaouias* which provided shelter, teaching and administered justice. In the twentieth century, Tunisian liberals as well as the French attacked their autonomy and what they considered an obsolete code of conduct. Many devout Muslims, however, continued to practise the hypnosis, trance-like meditation and saint worship, or maraboutism, with which Sufism had always been linked.

Nefta's **bus station** is on avenue Bourguiba next to the Mobil petrol station, opposite the Syndicat d'Initiative, and **louages** arrive at avenue Bourguiba, halfway between the bridge and the Syndicat d'Initiative **tourist office** (daily 8am–5pm; ✆06/430236), 300m out towards Tozeur on the left. The office is very helpful and rents out camels (5TD/hr), donkeys (3TD/hr) and calèches (6TD/hr for up to four people), each with a compulsory guide (8TD/hr). Alternatively, you can just hire a guide, who may be able able to smooth your way into some of the monuments and direct you on car trips around Nefta (16TD/2hr) or to Chebika, Tamerza and Mides (45TD/day trip).

Accommodation

Nefta doesn't have the widest choice of **accommodation** in Tunisia, but you can find hotels in most categories. Unfortunately, the only really low-budget option, the *Hôtel de la Liberté* – Tunisia's last old-school travellers' hotel, and a leftover from the days when Nefta was a stop on the route from Europe to West and Central Africa – closed following the death of its owner, Mahmoud, and does not look like reopening. Camping is possible at the *Hôtel Marhala*.

HOTELS

Bel Horizon ★★★, rte de la Corbeille ✆06/430088, ℉430500. Up beyond Ez Zaouia. Quiet and comfortable with a nice pool and a/c rooms that all have balconies and a view over the Corbeille. A definite cut above the other three-stars in town. ❹

Caravanserail ★★★, rte Touristique ✆06/430355, ℉430344. Opposite the *Marhala*, and with a choice of three-star or four-star wings – the latter newer, with TV and minibar in all rooms, plus a bathtub as opposed to just a shower. The price in both wings is the same, so ask for the better one. ❻

Habib, pl de la Libération ✆06/430497, ℉430036. The cheapest hotel in town following the demise of the nearby *Liberté*; nicely located, clean and fresh with en-suite rooms, a bar and terrace, and handy for the morning SNTRI bus to Tunis, since the bus parks up outside and the driver spends the night here. ❷

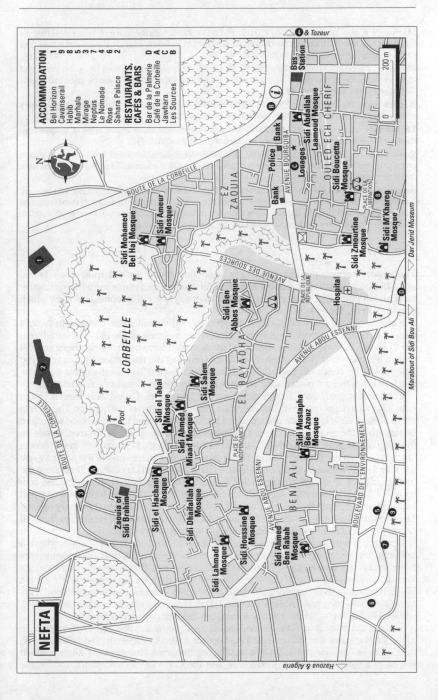

NEFTA

ACCOMMODATION
Bel Horizon   1
Cavanserail   9
Habib   8
Marhala   5
Mirage   3
Neptus   7
Le Nomade   4
Rose   6
Sahara Palace   2

RESTAURANTS,
CAFÉS & BARS
Bar de la Palmerie   D
Café de la Corbeille   A
Jawhara   C
Les Sources   B

Marhala ★★, rte Touristique ☏ 06/430027, Ⓕ 430511, Ⓔ marhala@yahoo.fr. A better deal than its three-star neighbours, though it pretty well equals them in facilities, with a/c rooms and a pool. You can also camp here and use the hotel's facilities. ❹

Mirage ★, rte de la Corbeille ☏ 06/430622, Ⓕ 431182. This place was closed for seven years and looks in places like it was rebuilt in a hurry, but it's not bad value, with a/c and en-suite bathrooms throughout, plus a small pool. ❸

Neptus ★★★, rte Touristique ☏ 06/430698, Ⓕ 430647. Good value with a large pool and nice airy a/c rooms – ask for an upstairs one with a view of the oasis. ❹

Le Nomade, av Bourguiba ☏ 06/430052. On the Tozeur road close to the edge of town. Clean rooms with showers, and a pool, but rather inconveniently located. ❷

Rose ★★★, rte Touristique ☏ 06/430697, Ⓕ 430385. A comfortable tourist hotel with a/c rooms and a pool, but not worth the premium you pay over the *Bel Horizon* and the *Neptus*, which have much the same facilities. ❻

Sahara Palace ★★★★★, rte de la Corbeille ☏ 06/432005, Ⓕ 431444, Ⓔ sangho.nefta@planet.tn. Nefta's most chic hostelry has been patronized by the likes of Catherine Deneuve, Habib Bouguiba, Jacques Chirac and Brigitte Bardot. Closed for renovation for several years, it is now open again, offering the best rooms, the best view and the biggest pool in town. ❼

The Town

The most rewarding pastime in Nefta is wandering round the **old quarters** – Ouled ech Cherif, El Bayadha, Ez Zaouia and Beni Ali – where you can admire the distinctive local architecture and, through the ancient doorways, see the looms and rugs which provide a living for most of the people.

Sadly, torrential rain and flooding in 1990 caused considerable damage to Nefta's ancient buildings – especially in El Bayadha, when a chunk of the old quarter fell into the Corbeille. Although the mosques and many homes have been rebuilt, there are still quite a few gaps in between. Ouled ech Cherif remains the least affected quarter if you fancy a walk to check out the traditional brickwork (see p.316); in the other quarters, much of it has been replaced with cheaper and quicker, but less attractive materials.

Coming into town from Tozeur along avenue Bourguiba, **Ouled ech Cherif** lies to your left. At its heart is place de la Libération, the main square of the quarter. The streets north of place de la Libération are a maze of brick alleyways and tunnels roofed with palm beams, while the quarter's most outstanding mosque, that of **Sidi M'Khareg**, stands on the edge of the oasis, its four-domed minaret restored after severe damage in the floods. On the southern edge of the quarter, a couple of hundred metres east of the palmery bar, the **Dar Jerid Museum** (daily 9am–8pm; 2.5TD) is a collection of items illustrating the traditional lifestyle of local people, including kitchenware, tools for handicrafts, and bedrooms of the late nineteenth and early twentieth centuries. The visit includes a tour and explanation in French by the friendly and enthusiastic staff. Nearby, the newly opened **Dar Houidi** (daily 8.30am–2am; 3TD) houses a similar collection of exhibits in the 17th century home of its proprietor, who is on hand to show visitors around.

Continuing down avenue Bourguiba, you come to place de la République, where a left turn takes you into the heart of the oasis, while a right turn up **avenue des Sources** takes you along the edge of the Corbeille and then crosses it into the **Ez Zaouia** quarter. The edge of the Corbeille offers good views but in general Ez Zaouia is less interesting than the other old quarters and still sustains considerable flood damage. Of its two mosques, **Sidi Mohamed Bel Haj** got away reasonably unscathed, while **Sidi Ameur** was left virtually a ruin, but has since been restored.

Some of the most important monuments in Nefta are along the edge of the Corbeille in the **El Bayadha** area. In the northwest corner of the Corbeille, by the *Hôtel Mirage*, the *Café de la Corbeille*, actually a bar, and the neighbouring *Café Maure el Khazen*, which is a bit of a tourist trap, offer great views over the Corbeille. Just down the road is the

DESERT ROSES

Desert roses, known in French as "sand roses" (*roses de sable*), are ubiquitous throughout the south of Tunisia and you'll see them all over the place, some big, some small, some absolutely enormous, piled high on souvenir stalls, strewn about hotels as part of the decoration, and occasionally mounted at road junctions as part of the street furniture. There is even a daily market dedicated to them ten kilometres west of Nefta. These brown crystalline rock formations that so resemble a petrified flower are in fact made of gypsum, crystals of calcium sulphate. The roses are formed from rising ground water rich in salt, which crystallizes when the water evaporates. Pure gypsum is white and transparent, but desert roses are brown and opaque due to the particles of sand trapped in the crystal. Desert roses are mostly found in the valleys between dunes. The large ones are rarer and can be pretty impressive, but the small ones make cheaper and more practical souvenirs, and you should be able to pick up several for a dinar in places like Tozeur, Nefta, Douz and Kebili. For very serious enthusiasts, it is possible to find your own desert roses, but you'd need transport and a guide. One place to find them is off the road from Kebili to El Fouar – Arafat at the *Camping des Amis* in Kebili may be able to guide you there if he is free. The other place known for desert roses is near Bir Pastor in the very far south (see p.420), but getting there would be a major expedition.

Zaouia of Sidi Brahim, a complex of tombs, courtyards and teaching rooms belonging to the Qadria, the most important of the Sufi orders represented here. Members of the order are often buried here near the saint, who also belonged to it. Beside the *zaouia*, a track leads round a ridge over the Corbeille, past five **mosques**, all small, simple in design and packed closely together. The first you come to is the **Sidi el Hachani Mosque**, then the mosques of **Sidi et Tabaï** and **Sidi Ahmed Miaad**. The oldest is the **Mosque of Sidi Salem**, sometimes called the Great Mosque, approached through an unobtrusive doorway off the narrow street; apart from one strip of carving around the walls, its fifteenth-century courtyard is completely unornamented. Finally comes the **Mosque of Sidi Ben Abbes**, the smallest. The road continues from here across an open space that was until recently the town brickworks. The brickworks have moved 5km out of town along the Hazoua road and the site now hosts Nefta's Thursday **market**. Beyond it, the road leads out onto avenue des Sources near place de la République.

Don't take it personally if the *gardiens* of the *zaouia* and mosques turn you away. Nefta is considered a religious city, and local people generally don't like tourists wandering around their monuments. If you can't get in by yourself, you may be luckier with a Syndicat d'Initiative guide.

The Corbeille

The **Corbeille** is a vast sunken extension of the oasis, like a massive crater full of palm trees gouged out of the middle of Nefta, with steep sides to protect it from the harsh desert wind. North of the bridge, it bends around to the west, spreading into a wedge that takes out a large chunk of town. At its northern extremity, the Corbeille measures almost a kilometre across, and the springs which irrigated it were beneath the defile. Due to the receding water table, these have disappeared and water now has to be pumped from a large pool in the northwestern corner, beneath the *Café de la Corbeille*, to irrigate the crops in the Corbeille and indeed the whole oasis. The best way through the Corbeille from avenue des Sources is to follow the stream from the west to the east end of the valley, which saves trampling on cultivated land. Look out for local eccentric Mohammed, who lives in his garden by the stream, growing henna, tobacco and bananas, and selling *sebsi* pipes, a traditional design made of cane with a clay bowl and formerly used for smoking *takrouri* (marijuana), but now only for the tobacco which he grows. His pipes and tobacco can also be bought at the *Star Wars* shop in place de la Libération.

Norman Douglas (see p.484) liked the Corbeille so much that he wanted it replicated in Tozeur – "all the elements are present," he explained; "it only requires a few thousand years of labour, and what are they in a land like this?" Good views over the Corbeille can be had from the cafés in the northwestern corner, as mentioned on p.324, and from the *Hôtel Sahara Palace*, the town's poshest hostelry, where father of the nation Habib Bourguiba regularly used to stay.

The Nefta Oasis

The **oasis** proper, on the other side of avenue Bourguiba, extends for some ten square kilometres. In addition to over a hundred natural springs, new wells were drilled in the 1960s, which reduced the flow from the springs in both the oasis and the Corbeille. In fact, the natural springs in the oasis have completely dried up, and its date palms were beginning to die from lack of water before the pool in the Corbeille was built to irrigate the oasis artificially.

Numerous tracks lead through the palm groves, all best explored on foot. Set right in the heart of the oasis is the **Marabout of Sidi Bou Ali** – take the road south from place de la République past the hospital and continue for 500m. This is a major place of pilgrimage, particularly on the third day after the Aid el Kebir. For this reason the marabout is closed to non-Muslims, but it's worth the short walk just to get among the surrounding gardens and to see the other, smaller marabouts along the way. Sidi Bou Ali was born in Morocco and came to Tunisia in the thirteenth century, hoping to resolve the religious disagreement which had divided the area. The legend that he planted the first palm trees in the Jerid (bringing the plants from Touggourt in Algeria) doesn't seem very likely, since Ibn Chabbat had already reorganized the oasis at Tozeur.

Eating and drinking

There's a dearth of **restaurants** outside the hotels. Of the cheap hole-in-the wall restaurants on avenue Bourguiba, around the louage station, the *Jawhara* (aka *Chez Laroussi*; daily 5am–3pm & 4–11pm) is by far the best. The *Bar de la Palmerie*, just inside the oasis south of the Sidi M'Khareg mosque (daily except Fri noon–midnight), is good for cheap meals as well as for drinking, and in the party atmosphere in the evenings, everybody makes a great fuss of unexpected guests, though women may find it a little intimidating then. For something more refined, the moderately priced *Restaurant les Sources* by the Syndicat de l'Initiative, where avenue Bourguiba meets the route de la Corbeille (daily 10am–3pm & 5.30–9.30pm) has a limited menu but good food, and the choice of indoor or outdoor terrace eating.

Of the **hotel restaurants**, the *Marhala* is the cheapest (noon–2pm & 7–9.30pm), with a set menu and à la carte. The *Neptus* (12.30–2pm & 8–9.30pm) also offers a set menu, while the *Bel Horizon* and the *Caravanserail* (both 12.30–2pm & 7.30–9.30pm) have rather pricier buffets. The poshest option of course is the *Sahara Palace* (daily noon–2pm & 8–9.30pm), where you have the choice of buffet or à la carte eating.

The most congenial place for a **drink** is the *Bar de la Palmerie* mentioned above, although the *Café de la Corbeille* (serving alcohol; daily 7am–midnight) and the neighbouring *Café Maure el Khazen* (serving tea and coffee; daily 7am–midnight), in the northwestern corner of the Corbeille, have the best views in town.

Listings

Banks Two on av Bourguiba, one opposite the Syndicat d'Initiative, the other between that and the post office (where you can change cash too). When all those are closed, you might be able to persuade the big hotels to change some money for you.

MOVING ON FROM NEFTA

For a rundown of destinations and journey times, see Travel Details on p.343–344.

All **bus services** stop at the bus station on avenue Bourguiba, although the two SNTRI buses to Tunis actually start in place de la Libération, and the morning service parks up there overnight. SNTRI and SRT buses serve Gabès, Gafsa, Kairouan, Metlaoui, Redeyef, Sousse and Sfax, and there are also regular daily local services to Tozeur. The only other services from here are to the Algerian frontier at Hazoua. **Louages** leave from avenue Bourguiba about 100m west of the Syndicat d'Initiative, serving Tozeur and Hazoua, and occasionally (usually early morning) direct to other places such as Gafsa and Sfax.

WEST TO THE ALGERIAN BORDER

The road west from Nefta continues to the Algerian border, 36km away at Hazoua, passing en route the open-air traditional brick factory, 5km out of town, and a market for desert roses (see box p.325), which takes place daily 10km west of town on the south side of the road.

In the past, the **border crossing into Algeria** at Hazoua was on one of the main trans-African overland routes, heading southwest to El Oued and Tamanrasset, and across the desert to Mali or Niger. Travellers still use this route, although the situation in Algeria remains extremely unstable (see p.185). The 5km between the Tunisian and Algerian border posts is plied unreliably by occasional Algerian louages. On the other side, there are frequent buses to El Oued, and from there onward to Toggourt and then Hassi Messaoud, Ouargla and Ghardaia. Algerian dinars can be bought at the border post, but only for cash. While the south of Algeria is less dangerous than its northern coastal area, incidents have occurred as far south as Hassi Messaoud and Ghardaia, and all foreigners remain declared targets of fundamentalist insurgents. In the oil terminals and the far south, foreign workers and tourists have a certain amount of army protection, however, no part of the country can be regarded as completely secure. If you intend to cross southern Algeria despite this danger, be sure to keep track of latest developments, steer well clear of the northern part of the country, and note that the border with Morocco is closed.

Festivals The Festival Populaire de Nefta, held over three days in June or July in pl de la République, features a range of performing arts as well as Sufi chanting and dancing. The Dakhla pilgrimage centred around the Marabout of Sidi Bou Ali on the third day after Aïd el Kebir (see p.40) is a much more religious affair, also featuring *sufi* chanting and dancing, and looks likely to be expanded into an international *sufi* festival with sheikhs and dervishes attending from all over the Muslim world.

Hammams If the baths in the oasis are not what you seek, there's the Hammam el Baraka in pl de la République (daily: men 5am–noon & 5pm–midnight; women 1–5pm).

Hospital The regional hospital ☎ 06/430193 is on rue des Martyrs, south of pl de la République and the Sidi Ben Abbes mosque.

Pharmacy There's one on av Bourguiba between the post office and Syndicat d'Initiative, and another in pl de l'Indépendance.

Police On av Bourguiba, about 100m west of the Syndicat d'Initiative ☎ 06/430134.

Post office On av Bourguiba just by the bridge on the southern side (country hours). International phone calls and currency exchange available.

Swimming pools Most hotels will let non-residents use their pools for a few dinars, while anyone dining at them can normally use the pool without charge.

The Chott and Kebili

The **Chott el Jerid** was once called the "Lake of Marks" – after the palm trunks planted across its normally parched surface to guide trading caravans. Here in 1885, Sir

Lambert Playfair (see p.484) was shown a circular platform in the middle of it, called the "Middle Stone", where camels could pass the night. Although the Chott can be crossed on foot at virtually any point for ten months of the year, tradition has it that leaving the recommended path can be fatal. Tijini, the fourteenth-century Arab historian, recounts the apocryphal story of the death of a thousand camels and their attendants in black mud beneath the thin salt crust. Now the army has built a causeway and road between Tozeur and Kebili, making this once lengthy journey quick and easy.

Villages north of the Chott

DEGACHE sits 10km northeast of Tozeur and claims to have the very best dates in the region. If you find yourself **staying**, the excellent *Bedouina Camping* (☎06/420209) has the usual campsite facilities among date and olive trees, with clean, pleasant en-suite rooms (**③**) and Bedouin-style tents (8TD) for those who don't have their own. The town has basic facilities such as **banks**, a **post office** (country hours) and a municipal **swimming pool** (mid-June to mid-Sept). Apart from a couple of rather unappetizing places in the centre, the campsite is the only place to **eat**; it's a little pricey, but there's cold beer, often a floor show with dinner, reduced rates if you're staying and a cheap and very good breakfast.

A couple of kilometres beyond Degache at **OULED MAJD**, a newly rebuilt but originally ninth-century brick **mosque** stands in the oasis by the remains of the old town – take a track off the main road to the right (south), just east of the date-packing plant. A glance at the base of the minaret reveals that, like the one at Bled el Haddar, it rests on Roman foundations. The minaret with four cupolas is typical of the region, unlike that of the Salaam Mosque on the main road, which bears a striking resemblance to a church tower. From the old mosque, a small road leads east into the oasis, ending after a kilometre at a T-junction, where the **remains** of Roman Gibba can be found just 50m down the right-hand road, mostly lying to the left of it. The ruins, unexcavated and largely overgrown, are all that is left of what was once a palatial mansion.

Continuing east, you cross the village boundary into **ZAOUIET EL ARAB** where, north of the main road, the pretty white **Marabout of Sidi Mohammed Krisanni** sits behind a more recent, and less picturesque, wall of grey breeze blocks. At one time there were seven wells here, in whose memory the village has been rechristened **Saba Abar**, meaning "seven wells", with all the road signs changed accordingly. Local residents however, continue to use the original name.

The next village, **KRIZ**, begins just east of the marabout, and has also been renamed as **El Mahassen**. At the other end of the village, up the hill on the Gafsa road, the hot spring **baths** (daily: men 5am–10pm front entrance; women 6am–6pm side entrance), are clean first thing in the morning, but a bit soupy by lunchtime – those at El Hamma (see p.343) are cleaner. Two kilometres south from Kriz on the Kebili road is a turn-off to the east, signposted "Dghoumes"; two kilometres along this on the left, a road leads up to two **marabouts** perched on the mountainside. The larger, left-hand one is the tomb of Sidi Bou Helal, a thirteenth-century hermit and holy man, the disciple of Sidi Bel Abbes, who lies buried in the other marabout. These marabouts are the site of a large joint *moussem* (saint's day celebration), held on the first Wednesday of the spring school holiday in March. This otherwise desolate spot was used in the filming of *Star Wars* (see box p.319).

Beyond the Dghoumes turn-off, the main road begins to drop down towards sea level as you cross the **Chott**, giving a perfect view of the pale expanse of salt and sand, marked only by a single black tarmac strip. To the east, the mountains gradually march into the distance and the crystal surface is concealed by mirages on every side. The mirage, or *fata morgana*, is caused by the refraction of light from the sky and from objects such as trees as it hits the thin heated air rising from the sun-baked ground.

ROUDAIRE AND PLOUGHSHARE: THE WEST'S PLANS FOR THE CHOTT

In 1876, one Captain Roudaire, working for the French Ministry of War, put forward a plan to dig a canal from the coast at Gabès to the Chott el Fejaj, a finger-like extension of the main Chott pointing eastwards towards the coast. The sea water, he supposed, would flood the entire area of the salt flats, creating a huge inland sea. In part this scheme was prompted by legends from the past: Roudaire thought the Chott was the site of the ancient Bay of Triton, birthplace of Poseidon, crossed by Jason with the Argonauts, and a Roman galley had been found on the northern shores. The Bey would not agree to "so dangerous an experiment", but, once the French had occupied Tunisia, engineers no longer had to worry about his opinion. The project looked set to go ahead and Ferdinand de Lesseps, architect of the Suez Canal, became involved. At that point, to general embarrassment, preliminary surveys revealed that the Chott was, in fact, above sea level.

If Roudaire's project sounds daft, then still worse was to follow. In 1962 the American Atomic Energy Commission set up the benignly named Ploughshare Program to enquire into "the peaceful use of nuclear explosions". In an associated paper, a leading scientist explained how the radiation would be just an "operational nuisance, quickly localized and easily controlled". For some reason, he couldn't put his finger on anywhere in the USA worthy of detonation, but the Bay of Triton seemed like an ideal place. With the mighty atom, the whole of the south and parts of the Sahara could be turned into a lake, open to mineral exploration and tourism. Like the programme itself, the idea was quietly cast aside.

The light is bent upward so that it appears to come from the surface, and is perceived as a reflection, making the sand or tarmac look like water, which always seems to begin a few hundred metres ahead of you. However, it's a shore that constantly recedes, so that in the shimmering heat, the Chott becomes a surreal land of dreamlike optical effects reminiscent of a Tanguy painting. After heavy rain, a rare event in these parts, the Chott is actually covered in water, but only a few inches deep.

The Nefzaoua   النفزوة

The southern side of the Chott, the region called **Nefzaoua**, is an area full of oases, smaller but more frequent than those further north, with lonely clumps of palms standing among the dunes or on the salt flats.

Most of the **oasis villages** are stretched out along the road from Tozeur. They are largely ugly, with little to recommend them, but if you want to see traditional oasis agriculture it's interesting to roam around the palmeries, where villagers will proudly show you their plots and present you with fruit straight from the trees. Just get off the bus or ask the louage to stop at any point; the road is busy, so you should be able to pick up a passing bus or louage to Kebili later.

Just after the road rises out of the Chott proper, a turn-off to the south leads to **FATNASSA** and **DEBEBCHA**, the latter a beautiful site with a marabout, palms, a couple of dunes and some fabulous yardangs (wind-sculpted rocks). It's a great place to watch the sun go down, though not unknown to the jeep "safari" mob. A café provides refreshments. A few kilometres further up the Debebcha road, there's a break in the water channel on your left where, if you wander up to the dunes, you'll be greeted by a brilliant vista over the Chott.

SOUK LAHAD, as its name suggests, hosts a lively Sunday market, as well as a couple of cafés and a bank. Seven kilometres to its north, there's also a three-star **hotel**, the *Les Dunes* (℡05/480711, ℻480563; ❻), complete with swimming pool, restaurant (noon–2.30pm & 7.30–9.30pm) and the usual amenities. It might not be a bad place to stop for lunch if you're passing, since the tour groups who are its main customers tend to arrive in the evening and depart the next morning, leaving it pretty quiet around mid-day. The hotel's outstanding feature is a tower which you can climb to survey the surrounding landscape.

Six kilometres south of Souk Lahad, a road off to the east, just after the village of Tombar (signposted "Rabta"), leads in 4km to **MANSOURA**, where you can bathe in pools originally built by the Romans (daily: men 5–9am & 5–9pm; women 9am–5pm). The village itself is famous for its melons. About a kilometre further on the main road, you reach **TELMINE**, now a compact place whose **oasis** was reputedly planted by conquering Egyptians. It was one of a series of outposts used by the Romans to guard against insurrection, and later became a thriving city – which the Almohads destroyed in 1205. The houses, crowded around narrow streets, still give it a medieval look, and a couple of Roman **reservoir pools** still survive. The **Mosque of Oqba** in the centre, formerly the site of a church, was rededicated by Oqba Ibn Nafi in the seventh century.

Kebili   قبلي

KEBILI, an important market town for slaves until the nineteenth century, is now the administrative centre of the Nefzaoua, 85km southeast of Tozeur. It is not a major centre for tourism, but there are a couple of points of interest, and it is an important interchange, especially going to or from Douz.

The road from Tozeur brings you to a roundabout by a Total petrol station at the bottom of a hill. At the top of the hill, the **bus station** is just to your right, 50m and across the street from a **supermarket**, behind which are the louage stands. One block behind the supermarket is the main street, avenue Bourguiba; to your left (north) is the main road to Gabès and the new road to Gafsa via Seftimi across the Chott el Fejaj and the Jebel Hachichina mountains. To the right (south), avenue Bourguiba passes the town's main square, **place de l'Indépendance**, on the right after 200m. The large hotels are off to the left, just through the oasis, beyond which is the desert, a good place for early birds to watch the sun rise over the mountains. Avenue Bourguiba continues round an S-curve to become boulevard de l'Environnement and the main road to Douz. Four hundred metres after the S-curve, on the left, is a fountain that was used as a bathing pool as long ago as Roman times, and after that a hammam with natural hot water from a three-kilometre-deep borehole. The hammam should be open round the clock, with separate entrances for each sex. Men also have the option of open-air hot water bathing in a pool through the gardens behind the fountain.

THE NEFZAOUA AND THE BEY

Ibn Khaldoun, writing in the fourteenth century, describes the Nefzaoua people as an independent group of Berbers mixed with nomadic Arabs, and in the twelfth and thirteenth centuries they played an important part in the Almoravid rebellion. During the Turkish administration, the Nefzaoua was ruled first from Tripoli and then, in the sixteenth century, from Tunis. Sir Grenville Temple (see p.484) visited in 1835 and found the people quiet after another bout of insurrection. To punish their "rude conduct" the Bey had imposed a fine of 15,000 piastres – much more effective, Temple saw, than the "cutting off of heads: for, as they remark, 'what signify a few heads more or less? We have plenty of them but very few piastres.'" When Kebili became the centre of another revolt twenty years later, the Bey had clearly had enough – he gave orders that the village was to be evacuated and its residents exiled to Cap Bon. Four years later he relented, but only after the villagers had bought back their lands at an extortionate price.

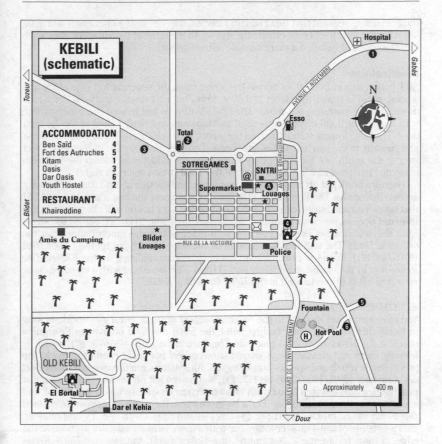

KEBILI (schematic)

Tozeur

Blidet

ACCOMMODATION
Ben Saïd	4
Fort des Autruches	5
Kitam	1
Oasis	3
Dar Oasis	6
Youth Hostel	2

RESTAURANT
Khaireddine	A

Hospital

Gabès

AVENUE 7 NOVEMBRE

N

Esso

Total

SOTREGAMES

AVENUE BOURGUIBA

SNTRI

Supermarket

Louages

Amis du Camping

Blidet Louages

RUE DE LA VICTOIRE

Police

Fountain

Hot Pool

BOULEVARD DE L'ENVIRONNEMENT

OLD KEBILI

El Bortal

Dar el Kehia

0   Approximately   400 m

Douz

Just before you get to the fountain, a road on your right leads down a hill and then 4km through the oasis to **Old Kebili**, the town's original site, complete with four marabouts and a mosque. The old town has been deserted since 1980, though the mosque still blares out the "Allah-o-akbar"s five times daily and an annual date harvest **festival** is held here at the end of November. Also here is a small square called **El Bortal** (the gateway), site of the former slave market, where people from West and Central Africa, after being kidnapped and marched across the desert, were traded as chattel. Though on nothing like the scale of the trans-Atlantic slave trade, the trans-Saharan trade was just as brutal, evil and murderous. On the cross-desert journey, the slaves went on foot, and the many who fell by the wayside were simply left to die. One result of this trade today is the high proportion of Nefzaoua people who are black.

Just before reaching Old Kebili from the modern town, a left turn leads, after 500m, to the ruins of **Dar el Kehia** (the chief's house), named after Ahmed Ben Hamadi, Kebili's first local administrator, appointed by the French in 1882. A cruel opportunist, Ahmed had raced across the Chott to surrender to the French while the elected village sheikh vacillated. His reward was command over his fellow villagers whom he ruled tyrannically for three terrible years. His palace, as he liked to call it, was built from the stones of his neighbours' homes, which he had destroyed. Eventually however, even the colonialists realized that Ben Hamadi's excesses were causing discontent and making it harder to extract taxes efficiently, and so, to the relief of the villagers, they gave him the boot and installed a more capable administrator.

Practicalities

SRT **buses** stop in front of, or across the street from, the supermarket (the office and waiting room is across the street and 50m down, but isn't usually staffed). For a run-down of bus departures, see p.343. The SNTRI office is just behind the supermarket, with louages for local destinations such as Mansoura and Souk Lahad in the lot next door. The main **louage** stand is across the street, with vehicles to Tozeur, Gabès, Gafsa and (usually in the morning) Sfax and Tunis. Louages for Douz are in the next street over to the south, but for Blidet they leave from the Blidet road (down the hill from place de l'Indépendance, or 300m south of the Total station and then right).

There's a **bank** just off place de l'Indépendance, and another about 100m north along avenue Bourguiba. The Banque de l'Habitat, just west near the bus stand, has an ATM that takes Visa and Mastercard, and the **post office** (city hours) will change cash. For **internet access**, the Sameh Publinet (daily 8am–midnight; 2TD/hr), across the street from the supermarket is very efficient with helpful staff and much better than the offices in Douz. The **regional hospital** is on the edge of town out on the Gabès road (℡05/490401). For a low-priced bite to **eat** in clean surroundings, try the *Khaireddine Restaurant* by the louage stand (daily 8am–11pm). For something with a bit more class, your best bet is the restaurant at the *Hôtel Oasis Dar Kebili*.

ACCOMMODATION

You may want to get straight to the Saharan outpost of Douz, but if you decide to **stay** in Kebili there's a very good budget hotel, the *Hôtel Ben Saïd* on avenue Bourguiba opposite the street leading to place de l'Indépendance (℡05/491573; **①**), which is friendly, clean and pleasant, with shared showers and hot water round the clock; the proprietor is young and speaks good English. Alternatives are the two-star *Hôtel Fort des Autruches* (℡05/490933, ℱ491117; **④**), signposted left off avenue Bourguiba, just past the *Ben Saïd* towards Douz, with small but clean en-suite rooms, a small pool, and a sometimes rather raucous bar. For a bit more class, the nearby four-star *Hôtel Oasis Dar Kebili* (℡05/491436, ℱ491295; **⑥**) has pleasant rooms with a/c, TV and minibar, plus a larger pool and a quieter lobby bar with a more intimate upstairs section. At the edge of town on avenue 7 Novembre (the Gabès road), the two-star *Hôtel Kitam* (℡05/491338, ℱ491076; **④**) is also quite comfy, with a pool. At the other end of the scale, the *Hôtel Oasis* (℡05/492432; **②**), 100m down the Tozeur road from the Total station, is marginally cheaper than the *Ben Saïd*, but ramshackle and none too clean, with few outside windows, though some rooms have their own bathroom. The **Maison des Jeunes youth hostel** (℡05/490635), behind the Total station, is not too bad, with small, clean dorms (5TD), refurbished bathrooms and friendly staff; you can come and go as you please during the day, but the curfew is 10pm. There is a low-priced and friendly **campsite**, *Les Amis du Camping* (℡05/492710), on the Blidet road in the oasis, a kilometre and a half out of town, but near to Old Kebili, with space for tents and campervans, plus small Bedouin tents with bedding for those who don't have their own. An on-site café provides drinks and meals, and there are hot water showers.

Douz and around دوز

The road south from Kebili takes you along the edge of the **Great Eastern Erg**, a sea of sand where the dunes reach hundreds of metres in height. Here, at its northerly extent, they are a touch less impressive, but you can at least get the feel of the desert.

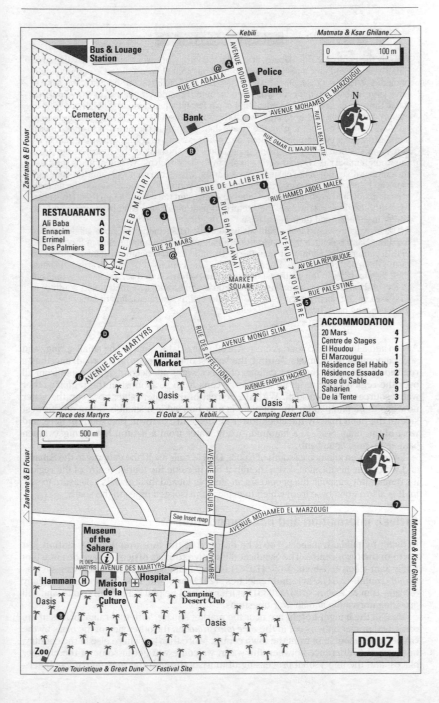

Bus & Louage Station

Kebili

Matmata & Ksar Ghilane

0   100 m

RUE EL ADAALA

AVENUE BOURGUIBA

Police

Bank

Cemetery

Bank

AVENUE MOHAMED EL MARZOUGUI

RUE ALI BEN LATIF

N

RUE OMAR EL MAJOUN

Zaafrane & El Fouar

RUE DE LA LIBERTÉ ①

RUE HAMED ABDEL MALEK

②

AVENUE TAIEB MEHIRI

Ⓒ ③

RUE GHARA JAWAI

④

AVENUE 7 NOVEMBRE

RUE 20 MARS

AV DE LA RÉPUBLIQUE

@

MARKET SQUARE

RUE PALESTINE

RESTAUARANTS

Ali Baba	A
Ennacim	C
Errimel	D
Des Palmiers	B

⑤

ACCOMMODATION

20 Mars	4
Centre de Stages	7
El Houdou	6
El Marzougui	1
Résidence Bel Habib	5
Résidence Essaada	2
Rose du Sable	8
Saharien	9
De la Tente	3

Ⓓ

AVENUE DES MARTYRS

Ⓐ

AVENUE MONGI SLIM

RUE DES AFFECTIONS

Animal Market

AVENUE FARHAT HACHED

Ⓐ ⑥

Oasis

Oasis

▽ *Place des Martyrs*   *El Gola'a* △ *Kebili* △   ▽ *Camping Desert Club*

0   500 m

N

Zaafrane & El Fouar

AVENUE BOURGUIBA

See Inset map

AVENUE MOHAMED EL MARZOUGI

⑦

Matmata & Ksar Ghilane

Museum of the Sahara
ⓘ

PL DES MARTYRS

AVENUE DES MARTYRS

AV 7 NOVEMBRE

Hammam Ⓗ

Maison de la Culture

Hospital

Oasis

⑧

Camping Desert Club

Oasis

⑨

Zoo

DOUZ

▽ *Zone Touristique & Great Dune*   ▽ *Festival Site*

THE MRAZIG

Douz is the centre for the **Mrazig**, originally the family of seventeenth-century patriarch Sidi Merzoug, and now a people numbering about 45,000, whose lifestyle is traditionally nomadic. With the development of schools, medical facilities and housing, the Mrazig have largely abandoned the life which led them to three different areas every year. Even today though, most Douz residents still keep a few sheep and goats, a patch of desert to pasture them and a tent to sleep in when they pop over to tend it, usually during school holidays. For the rest of the year, they leave their animals in the care of a *gardien*. In fact, some Mrazig remain completely nomadic, moving south in spring, when the rains provide good pasture for the sheep and goats. After the shearing of the sheep during April, the women make rugs from the wool to sell in the large towns. Mrazig nomads return to the comparative cool of the oasis for the summer, where the men look after the land and dates and the women prepare food for the coming winter. Two months later, the animals are taken north to fresh lands near Gabès or Gafsa, and the people set up their tents nearby. At the beginning of winter, they return to pick dates or press olives and spend the cooler months around their home base.

The Mrazig are one of four traditionally nomadic tribes in the Nefzaoua, all descended from the Banu Suleim, a tribe from the Arabian peninsula who migrated to Egypt in the eighth century, moved into Libya in the tenth, and settled in southern Tunisia at the end of the thirteenth century (see pp.431 & 432). The land used by the Mrazig to pasture their livestock lies to the southeast of Douz. The **Adhara**, based at Zaafrane, use the land to its south, while the **Ghrib**, based at El Fouar and Sabria, take their flocks southwest. The area to the north, as far as the Chott el Fejaj, belongs to a fourth tribe, the **Beni Yaqoub**, who base themselves in Kebili.

And to add a little local colour, scattered around are date palms fed by small springs and several nondescript hamlets. **Jemna**, the largest of the villages on the road, once had a roadside fountain gushing out gallons of sweet water per second, and people from all over the region came to fill up their jerry cans from it, as most of the region's other water sources were brackish. With the retreat of the water table, however, the water now has to be pumped up; the fountain is now housed in a small building on the west side of the main road by the clock tower in the centre of town. Just south of here, and west of the main road, is a hammam using water from a natural hot spring (women 6am–6pm, men 6pm–6am).

Twenty-seven kilometres south of Kebili, **DOUZ** calls itself "the gateway to the Sahara" and with some justification. Even though it has become the tourist centre of the region, it's remarkably unspoilt: the people are an amiable lot and their town is a pleasure to stay in. It is also a good base from which to explore the isolated oases to the south.

Arrival, information and accommodation

Arriving by public transport, you'll be dropped at the **bus and louage station** just north of the town centre. The Syndicat d'Initiative **tourist office** in place des Martyrs (daily 8am–noon & 3–6pm; ☎05/470341) is very helpful and provides services such as camel rental (2.5TD/hr) and calèches (2TD/hr); the ONTT next door (daily 8.30am–1pm & 3–6pm; ☎05/470351) is friendly and helpful if a little officious, and will provide information and answer questions.

Most of the budget **hotels** are near the market square, with mid-range places in the oasis, and pricier options out in the *zone touristique* on the other side of the oasis by the Great Dune, about 2km from the town centre. More than anywhere else in the country, however, the difference between the warm welcome you get in some of the cheaper places, and the impersonal processing of tourists through the *zone touristique* hotels, means that less is definitely more here. On the other hand, the tourist hotels are usually empty in the daytime, as the tour groups that use them arrive around 4pm and leave in the morning, so you'll have the run of them in between times. Most of them, the *Mouradi* in particular, also claim to be wheelchair-friendly, though of course you should always check that they cater for your particular needs. Finally, if you yearn for the vastness of the open desert, you could opt instead to stay in the nearby oases of Zaafrane or El Faouar (see pp.339 and 341).

Hotels in the town and oasis

Hôtel 20 Mars, 23 rue 20 Mars ☎ & ⓕ05/470269, ⓔbarka5@excite.com. One of the nicest cheapies in the country. It's run by charming people who play music and dance most nights – audience participation expected – and the rooms are clean and pleasant, some with private bathroom. ❷

Résidence Bel Habib, 10 rue Palestine ☎ & ⓕ 05/471115. Very much a fall-back option, basic and neither good value nor especially clean, though it does have a Bedouin tent for tea and a *chicha* on the roof, and an extension under construction for new en-suite rooms. ❷

Résidence Essaada, 18 rue 1 Juin ☎05/470824, ⓕ470378, ⓔessaada1@excite.com. Simple but clean enough, with a roof terrace. ❷

Hôtel el Houdou, av des Martyrs ☎ & ⓕ05/470430. Small, basic rooms but adequate for the price. ❶

El Marzougui, 14 av 7 Novembre ☎05/473030, ⓕ472176. Nice fresh rooms, some with private shower, plus a terrace and pleasant TV lounge. ❷

Rose du Sable, off av des Martyrs in the oasis ☎05/470597, ⓕ470282. Turn left at the very end of av des Martyrs and it's 300m down on the right. Friendly but rather run-down and a bit grubby, with a small pool, private bathrooms, heating in winter and air conditioning in summer. Handy for catching morning SNTRI buses as the drivers usually park up and spend the night here. ❸

Hôtel Saharien ★★★, in the oasis ☎05/471337, ⓕ470339, ⓔhotoasis@gnet.tn. Left off av des Martyrs before the tourist office and it's 500m down on the left, in the oasis. Somewhat better value than its three-star equivalents in the *zone touristique*, with nicely furnished rooms, all with a/c and bathtub, and no less than four pools, including one indoor with hot spring water. ❹

Hôtel de la Tente, 8 rue des Affections ☎05/470468, ⓔnaceur45@atmedica.com. Clean, comfortable, friendly and good value, with English-speaking staff. Some rooms have their own shower, though not all have outside windows, and there's also a garage to keep bicycles and motorbikes. ❷

Hotels in the Zone Touristique

Méhari ★★★, *zone touristique* ☎05/470481, ⓕ471589, ⓔmehari.douz@planet.tn. The first of the *zone touristique* hotels, with a hot-spring pool in addition to the swimming pool, and natural hot spring water in the bathrooms. ❺

Mouradi ★★★★, *zone touristique* ☎05/470303, ⓕ470905, ⓔelmouradi.commercial@planet.tn. The newest and plushest of the *zone touristique* hotels, with spacious rooms some with views of the Great Dune, plus indoor and outdoor pools, and a hammam, sauna and fitness room, but not the most attentive of staff. ❻

Sahara Douz ★★★, *zone touristique* ☎05/470864 or 5, ⓕ 470566, ⓔsaharadouz@planet.tn. There's an indoor hot-spring pool and a hammam, all rooms have a terrace or balcony (some have a bath en suite, others a shower), and the staff even smile. ❹

Sun Palm ★★★, *zone touristique* ☎05/410123, ⓕ470525, ⓔsun.palm@planet.tn. Cool, reasonably spacious a/c rooms, some with showers rather than baths, plus a pool and a hammam. ❺

Touareg ★★★, *zone touristique* ☎05/470057, ⓕ 470313, ⓦwww.hotel-touareg.com. Cosy rooms with balconies but sprayed with rather cloyingly scented air-freshener. Again, specify if you want a bath rather than a shower. ❺

Campsites

Camping Desert Club, rue des Affections ☎ & ⓕ 05/470575. European-style campsite, well-shaded, with a pitch for every tent or vehicle, complete with electric socket. Passports must be surrendered on arrival. Fees are cheap but meals are expensive by local standards.

Centre des Stages et des Vacances campsite, rte de Matmata (no phone). Three kilometres out on the edge of town and rather more rustic than the *Desert Club*, though there's a kitchen and hot running water, with bedding and tents provided if necessary.

The Town

On Thursdays, Douz is transformed by the weekly **market**. Townspeople, nomads, people from nearby villages and tourists pour in to participate in one of Tunisia's most engaging souks, and it says something for Douz that the presence of tourists seems to add to rather than detract from the whole affair. The centre of activity is, of course, the market square itself. Here you can find many of the traditional goods (jackets, leather shoes and slippers) which end up in the cities. You can also buy souvenirs like petrified wood or the inevitable desert roses, or get desert shoes made to measure overnight. In season, you'll find the region's famous *deglat en nour* dates for sale behind the southern side of the square. Don't expect to find many camels nowadays in the livestock section, where most of the animals sold are sheep and goats – if there are any camels, they'll be just to your right as you come down the stairs into the compound, along with horses and donkeys. To find the livestock section, take the western exit (avenue des Martyrs) out of the main market square, then the second left, and follow the throng.

Douz is a place you come to use as a base to head out into the desert, and to meet its hospitable and easy-going people. Its sights, as such, apart from the market, are not particularly spectacular. Top of the list is the **Museum of the Sahara**, on place des Martyrs (Tues–Sun: Sept–May 9.30am–4.30pm; June–Aug 7–11am & 4–7pm; 1.1TD), with a small but interesting collection of exhibits illustrating the traditions of the region's nomadic peoples, with features on camels, the construction and furnishing of bedouin tents, weaving and textiles, and clothing, jewellery and tattoos, all well explained in Arabic and French, but not in English. The road to the right of the museum (as you face it) leads past a natural **hot-spring** bath into the oasis. These are open 6am to noon and 3pm to 7pm for both sexes (separate entrances) and offer the choice of bath or pool but you have to bring your own towel and, for the pool, bathing costume. Further into the oasis past the *Hôtel des Roses des Sables* is the **Borj Shara Zoo** (daily 7am–sunset; 2TD), a sad spectacle of wild desert animals pacing their undersized cages and cowering in fear as visitors approach.

A little further along the same road, you emerge out of the oasis into the *zone touristique*, by the village of Gleissia. Beyond is another popular attraction for tour groups on day-trips, the **Great Dune**. It's a chance to play in the sand for those without the time to get further into the desert – or to go to the beach. The rumour that the dune was built with the aid of bulldozers is untrue, but it probably wouldn't make much difference to most of the people who come here. Still, if you want a quick ride on a camel in

---

THE FESTIVAL OF SAHARA

The wintertime Festival of the Sahara celebrates everything from popular pottery and a traditional marriage to camel fighting (camel versus camel, that is), sand hockey and greyhound racing. It all takes place at a special festival site out beyond the *Hôtel Saharien*. Associated cultural activities such as music, singing and poetry contests take place in the Maison de la Culture in place des Martyrs. Local poet Abdellatif Belgacem Merzoughi, who runs the Museum of the Sahara, is also likely to read samples of his immensely popular verse. Hotels tend to fill up quickly at this time of year, so it's a good idea to arrive early or book ahead. The festival is held at the end of December. The tourist office will have the latest details, and the festival programme should be posted in advance at Ⓦ www.kebili.net.

the desert without spending a day or a week on one, it might fit the bill. About a kilo-metre beyond the *zone touristique* hotels, at the *Café des Dunes*, a firm called Pégase (☎05/470793) runs a track for desert go-karts (7TD a lap, 20TD for four), with the option of guided desert excursions on them, and also offers rides on microlight planes (40TD for 10min), with rides on sand hovercraft and in hot-air balloons possible if booked in advance.

A word of **warning** for women travelling alone in Douz: it is not a good idea to go wandering in the oasis alone, as there have been instances of sexual harassment and even rape.

Eating and drinking

For **eating**, Douz's greatest culinary experience has got to be the *Restaurant Ali Baba* on the Kebili road opposite the bank (daily 8am–11pm), low-priced, with its legendary couscous, fine Mrazig welcome and relaxed atmosphere. You can eat in a Bedouin tent out the back, or go out there for a tea, a chat, and even a hookah after your meal, and all for a good price. Otherwise, most of the cheap hotels double up as eateries, offering the likes of couscous, stew and chicken for a few dinars. The *Bel Habib* and *20 Mars* are safe enough bets, though the latter's restaurant may be closed off-season. There are also a few basic, cheap eateries in town including the *Errimel* on avenue Taïeb Mehiri (daily noon–10pm) and the *Ennucim* at 2 rue de la Liberté (daily 11am–10pm). The *Restaurant des Palmiers* at 13 av Taïeb Mehiri (daily 10am–10pm) is slightly more refined, but there is no upmarket eating in town as such. For something posher and a little pricier, try the Italian restaurant at *Camping Desert Club* (daily 11.30am–2.30pm & in winter 5pm–9.30pm, in summer 7–11pm), or the restaurant at the *Hôtel Saharien* (12.30–2.30pm & 7.30–9.30pm), with a choice of buffet, menu or à la carte.

If you fancy a beer or two, *Camping Desert Club* has a reasonable **bar** (daily noon–midnight).

Listings

Banks Banque du Sud is on av Bourguiba, just north of the junction with av Taïeb Mehiri, and STB in av Taïeb Mehiri 100m to the west. Some of the cheap hotels in town, and some shops, will change money when the banks are closed.

Bike rental Grand Sud, 22 av Taïeb Mehiri by *Café el Amel* ☎05/471777, ✉saharaking@voila.fr, rents out bicycles (2TD/hr).

Car rental Victory Car, 6 av Bourguiba ☎05/471790, ◍www.victorycar.com.tn, with offices nationwide so you do not necessarily have to bring the car back to Douz.

Car repairs Sahara Assistance, off av des Martyrs opposite no.6 ☎05/470901, have a good repu-tation as mechanics for 4WD and two-wheel-drive vehicles. Smaller mechanics' workshops can be found on av Taïeb Mehiri and streets off it near the junction with rue de la Liberté, and there's a puncture repair shop at 15 av Mohamed Merzougui.

Hammams As well as the natural hot-spring baths (see p.336), there's Hammam el Hana, north of the louage station past the cemetery (women 8am–5.30pm, men 6–10pm).

Hospital Just off av des Martyrs, 100m east of the tourist office ☎05/470323.

Internet access There is a Publinet office at 24 rue des Affections (daily 8 or 9am–midnight; 3TD/hr), and a cheaper one in rue el Adaala by *Restaurant Ali Baba* (daily 9am–2am; 1.6TD /hr), though it cannot connect to hotmail.

Laundry A "pressing" shop at 92 av 7 Novembre charges roughly by the kilo for ordinary washing.

Pharmacy The town pharmacies run a rota for night duty, posted in the window.

Police The main police station is on av Bourguiba just north of the junction with av Taïeb Mehiri ☎05/470333. The Garde Nationale are at pl des Martyrs ☎05/470319.

Post office Av Taïeb Mehiri, opposite the end of rue 20 Mars (country hours). Changes cash and has a coin phone.

Supermarkets Magasin B Abdennour on av Taïeb Mehiri, opposite the *Hôtel el Houdou* (daily 7.30am–8pm).

Swimming pools The municipal pool behind the water tower off pl des Martyrs is open in July and August (daily 9am–6pm; 0.2TD). Otherwise, you can use the *Hôtel Saharien*'s pools (including its indoor thermal pool) for a few dinars. Of the *zone touristique* hotels, whose pools you can also use for a few dinars – and which are little used during the day – the best are *Méhari* and the *Sahara Douz*, both of which have a natural hot-spring pool as well as a conventional swimming pool, the one at the *Sahara Douz* is indoor.

Tours The oldest-established operators are Douz Voyages on av Taïeb Mehiri ☎ 05/470178 or 9, opposite the Kebili turn-off. Other firms, less renowned but slightly cheaper, include Les Amis du Sahara ☎ 05/472177, 📧 lads@gnet.tn, and Abdelmoula Voyages ☎ 05/470484, both on av des Martyrs near pl des Martyrs. Each organizes camel tours into the desert and excursions by camel or 4WD to Ksar Ghislaine. Douz Voyages and Les Amis du Sahara also run trips to Jebil. A two-day jeep trip to Ksar Ghilane costs about 350TD for up to seven people, camels around 60TD per person per day. The cheap hotels in town can organize much lower-priced camel trips (around 35TD/day), but check excatly what is included, and make certain you are properly insured. The *Hôtel de la Tente* is one place to ask, and the proprietor of the *Hôtel 20 Mars* runs his own agency, Nefzaoua Voyages, with its office right next to the hotel ☎ 05/472920, 📧 age.nefzaoua@planet.tn. Grand Sud at 22 av Taïeb Mehiri ☎ 05/471777, 📧 saharaking@voila.fr, organizes bicycle trips round the west side of the Chott to Rjim Matouk and Hazoua. You can also get good deals for camel trips in Zaafrane, or try Belgacem Afif at the Petit Prince store in the market square. Some shopkeepers and touts claim to organize cheaper excursions, but these are cheap in every sense of the term, and you risk falling in with dubious operators. Be aware that the desert can get extremely cold at night, so come prepared with warm clothing and if possible, especially in winter, a sleeping bag.

MOVING ON FROM DOUZ

For a rundown of destinations and journey times, see Travel Details on pp.343–344.

Buses and louages all leave from a station north of the cemetery, and a short walk from the town centre. There is no direct public transport to Matmata, although the road is now surfaced.

DOUZ TO KSAR GHILANE

The round trip from Douz takes approximately ten days by camel (see above for operators). By jeep, you can do it in two days for around 350TD for up to seven people. It is sometimes possible to get here from Douz on a supply truck (around 50TD return), for more than the price Tunisians pay, but should entitle you to sit in the driver's cab rather than in the back. This is not a regular form of public transport, and you'll have to arrange it privately; if you are staying at one of the cheap hotels, staff there, or at the *Ali Baba Restaurant*, may help you. You will also be dependent on the supply truck for your return, which usually entails leaving Douz on a Saturday afternoon and coming back on a Sunday morning.

Most jeep tours, the supply truck, and almost everybody with their own transport takes the **pipeline road**, a piste which branches south from the Matmata road (MC104) at the *Café Jelili*, 68km east of Douz (see p.414). It is just about possible to cover this road – with care, and preferably with a local guide – in an ordinary car, but it can be tricky because there are frequent sand drifts and it easy to get stuck (see p.415 for advice about driving in the desert).

Camel treks and a few 4WD tours make a beeline for Ksar Ghilane across open desert. The route passes **Bir el Hag Brahim**, 40km out of Douz and supposedly the gateway to the desert, where the *Café Restaurant du Porte du Désert* is open September to June for travellers passing through. A slight deviation south from the main route passes **Jebil**, an area of high ground 50km west of Ksar Ghilane, where Douz-based travel firms (see above) run campsites for their clients. It's a good area to spot wildlife, with animals such as gazelles attracted by the slightly cooler temperatures, as is **Tembaïn**, another piece of high ground, 20km to the south.

Around Douz

The road out of Douz to the oases of Zaafrane, El Faouar and Sabria is now tarmac all the way. As well as the eight daily buses from Douz, pick-ups do the run cheaply enough, but remember that transport back to Douz dries up around 4pm, so head back by 3.30pm or so if that's where you plan to spend the night. If driving in this region, take the usual precautions for desert driving (see p.415).

Leaving town, a piste turns off to the south, 100m past a school and a sign marking the end of the town limits. After about 4km it passes under a power line which, if you follow it to the right, leads to a *khriga* (see p.304) that once took water from a spring – now dried up due to the falling water table – to the grove of palm trees that lie to your right. The maintenance shafts for the *khriga* are unmarked and unfenced, so if you come here to check out the *khriga*, be careful not to fall down them.

Zaafrane   زعفران

Ten kilometres west of Douz, **ZAAFRANE** is the real gateway to the Grand Erg Oriental. The village lies close to the main through-track and is surrounded on one side by endless dunes, on the other by a cool **oasis**. Zaafrane is the centre for the traditionally nomadic **Adhara** people, whose large black tents, often pitched near to their brick and concrete houses, are made from long strips of wool and goat hair, supported by two wooden poles. Paths lead from the main road to the sand dunes at the far edge of the village. From here the desert stretches into the distance, beyond the remains of old stone houses, washed over by the sand. The Syndicat d'Initiative **tourist office** at the western end of town (daily sunrise–sunset; ☏05/492668) can organize camel rides and treks. Camel drivers and guides hang out just west of the Syndicat, and prices tend to be slightly lower here than in Douz (about 10TD/hr, 35TD/day, plus the same again for a guide and camel for every 2–3 people), but as in Douz, you should avoid ultra-cheap deals from unauthorized operators.

There is a **hotel**, the one-star *Zaafrane*, almost opposite the Syndicat d'Initiative (☏ & ℻05/491720; ❸), which is not a bad old place, with nice, clean, en-suite rooms, all with heating and air-conditioning, and also Bedouin tents between July and September. They usually allow **camping** in the grounds and have a bar if you're in need of a cold beer, a low-priced set menu (daily noon–3pm & 5–9pm), and you can use their pool for a couple of dinars, free if you're eating there. The hotel runs another campsite, 7km into the desert towards El Fouar. There is also a new campsite in Zaafrane, *Campement de Désert* (no phone) where you can stay in your own tent or in a Bedouin tent; it's by the hotel and directly opposite the Syndicat d'Initiative, and rather rustic and without much shade as yet, but with plans for the future.

Whether or not you take the bus to Zaafrane, you'll probably end up hitching back to Douz or on to El Faouar; most passing vehicles will pick up hitchhikers, and louages often stop here to drop off and pick up.

Sabria and El Faouar   الصّابرية

Beyond Zaafrane, louages continue to Sabria and El Faouar, and it's no problem getting a lift. The main attraction is simply the drive through the desert. **SABRIA**, 25km west of Douz and 3km off the El Faouar–Zaafrane road, is the centre for the people of the same name, Arabized Berbers who are part of the larger Ghrib confederation. Spectacular views over the desert greet you when you climb up some of the high dunes around Sabria, with a vast expanse of sand stretching in every direction, dotted with little green oases.

Sabria is one of the few places where the **"Danse de la Chevalure"** is still authentically performed. On the first night of the marriage ceremony, the women remove all

THE SHIP OF THE DESERT

The one-humped **Arabian camel**, or dromedary, is native to North Africa, southwest Asia and the Arabian peninsula, where it was first domesticated some 3000 to 4000 years ago. It is well adapted to the desert, with long double eyelashes to keep sand out of its eyes, nostrils that it can close, and broad, soft, padded feet that are ideal for walking on sand (but not slippery mud or sharp stones). It can eat coarse, thorny vegetation, twigs and dried grass, date stones, even prickly pear cactuses, and thrives on plants with a high salt content that other animals cannot eat. It can also drink salty or brackish water. If really hungry, camels will eat almost anything, but left to their own devices, they'll space themselves out over a wide area to forage, and eat only a small amount from each plant they find, which allows the plants to continue growing, and also lets other animals such as sheep and goats graze in the same area. Most famously, the camel can go for days – a week in summer, two in winter – without water. This is partly because, already well insulated by its thick coat, it can allow its body temperature to rise and fall with the heat of the day, and does not need to keep it down by sweating. The camel's hump stores reserves of fat that can convert into energy, and the hydrogen in the fat can also be oxidized into water when necessary. In fact, a camel can shed up to 40 percent of its body weight through dehydration, and then put it all back by drinking as much as a hundred litres in ten minutes flat. The hump is firm and straight when "full", but becomes soft and leans over as its reserves are depleted.

Camels can cover 160 to 200 kilometres in a day and have been used since the Middle Ages for long-haul **desert travel**, in particular for the pilgrimage to Mecca. They also played a vital role for the Saharan economy in the caravans that traded across the desert. Because the camel moves its left and then right legs together, rather than front and then back legs like a horse, it has a rolling gait that makes for a smoother ride. They are usually docile, good-tempered animals, but the male goes into rut in spring, when it becomes rather grumpy and can kick and bite, and spit its regurgitated stomach contents in anger. Camels have callused pads on their knees and chest to kneel and set down in the hot sand, which they will do on command if trained, but they will usually bellow in protest when being loaded up with goods or passengers to carry.

For many of the nomads in the south of Tunisia, camels represent their worldly wealth, but a camel also has a lot of practical uses. As well as a pack animal and a means of transport, it is a source of meat and also of milk. Its hide can be used for leather, and its hair, which it sheds in huge clumps every spring, is extremely light and durable, providing excellent insulation against extremes of heat and cold – of the traditional North African coat, the *burnous*, the best are made of camel hair rather than cotton or wool – though the fur of the two-humped Bactrian camel is considered superior to that of its Arabian cousin.

Arabic has many different words for camels, depending on their age, sex and breed, just as English does for horses. There are four basic varieties, distinguished by the colour of their coat. The **white camel** (*mehari*) is the fastest, used for hunting and warfare. The **red camel** is used to transport goods, as it can carry the heaviest loads. The **yellow camel** is used, if male, as a stud, and can be bred with females of other varieties to produce both its own breed and its mate's. The **black camel** (*azraq*, meaning "blue") is used for smuggling, since its dark coat makes it hard to spot at night. Finally, camels of mixed breed are considered the best for eating and, if female, milking.

Camels are often left to roam the desert freely, but can be matched to their owner by means of a brand. In the Nefzaoua, the brand is always made on the right back leg, and is based on a shape like the Roman letter "I". Additional markings indicate the tribe, clan and family who own the camel. In fact, many nomads can identify a camel – especially a male camel – simply from its footprints, which are distinctive in the way fingerprints are to humans, except that a male camel's footprint will follow the pattern of its father's.

their jewellery and woollen head coverings and parade before the assembled men and musicians. To the beat of the tambour, and encouragement of the crowd, each dancer whirls her long hair round her head faster and faster. Over several hours the women gradually drop out, and the dance ends when just one is left on the floor.

The old French army fort, **Borj Sabria**, a kilometre beyond the village, is now a **bar, restaurant and campsite** (℡05/494314, ℗495366). Here you can stop for a tea or a beer, eat a moderately priced menu with either couscous or *mechoui*, and stay the night in your own tent or vehicle, or in a Bedouin tent complete with beds and palm-frond fencing to keep out the wind. The roof of the fort offers fabulous views across the desert, and a stroll into the dunes will soon leave you feeling fantastically remote. To get here, bear left at the fork in the road by the patisserie, and follow the sandy track until it ends at the fort.

The road divides after 25km and most traffic goes straight to **EL FAOUAR** (also called Sabria el Faouar), which has a Friday souk. This is the home of the **Ghrib** who, until recently, were a wholly nomadic community, breeding camels, goats and sheep. Like the Mrazig and the Adhara, the Ghrib have partly abandoned their nomadic lifestyle, but many of them continue to live in the traditional way, and the majority still keep livestock, often leaving their animals in the care of a *gardien* and visiting the desert during the school holidays to tend them in person.

The one **hotel** – the three-star *El Faouar* (℡05/460531, ℗460576; **⑤**) – is a reasonable place, especially when not too swamped. Off on the left as you come into the village from Zaafrane, it has a bar and restaurant with a moderately priced buffet (daily 12.30–2pm & 7.30–9pm). The hotel also has a pool, which non-residents can use for a small fee, and rents out sand skis (5TD/hr, free for guests). As well as the rooms, each decorated with its own mural, there is the cheaper option of sleeping in tents (30TD), with breakfast included. Behind the hotel, the dunes begin. While not as huge as the dunes deeper into the erg, the sand mountains round here still stretch immensely to the horizon and satisfy most visitors' desires to be, at last, really in the desert.

El Fouar is connected to Douz by louages, and by six daily buses (1hr), plus three to Kebili (1hr), one SNTRI service to Tunis (7hr), and one SRT service to Gabès (2hr 30min). There are other, smaller oases, unmarked on any of the available maps, between El Faouar and Zaafrane. If you're hitching, you might be dropped off on the way, but there will always be shade and an occasional car later in the afternoon.

North of El Faouar

Paved roads branching off on your right (if coming from Douz) 5km before Zaafrane and 10km after El Fouar (signposted "Dergine") lead back to Kebili via **NOUAIL**, where a *campement* offers **accommodation** in "bungalows" or Bedouin tents (℡05/495584, ℗476584), and allows you to pitch your own tent. Meals are also available.

Between Nouail and Kebili is the picturesque village of **BLIDET**, with a ruined **medina** on a hill topped by a **marabout** and flanked by minor **oases**. There is no direct transport from Zaafrane, Sabria or El Fouar to Blidet or Nouail, but there are louages between Blidet and Kebili, and pick-ups between Nouail and Douz. There are also seven daily buses from Kebili to Blidet, five of which continue to Nouail.

El Gola'a   القلعة

Just north of Douz on the Kebili road, a turn-off to the west leads to **El Gola'a**, a pretty little village and a pleasant day-trip if you are based in Douz. At the highest point, adjoining the Great Mosque, a small park gives views over the whole village, and to the five oases surrounding it. In the past, any force approaching the village could be spied and sized up before they arrived. Nowadays, it's a good spot for watching sunrises and sunsets. Of the mosque itself, the small square minaret is original; the tall octagonal one was added in the 1990s. Down the hill towards the Kebili road, the modern Salaam mosque has an unusual round minaret, which looks particularly funky when lit up at night. You do not have to return to the main road, as there is now a direct surfaced road from El Gola'a straight to Douz.

Towards the coast

For Thomas Shaw in the 1750s, the area east of Kebili to the coast was a "lonesome and uncomfortable desert, the resort of cut-throats and robbers". He recalled, "we saw the recent blood of a Turkish gentleman, who, with three of his servants, had been murdered two days before by these assassins". Nowadays there's no blood and little of interest until El Hamma. At **SAIDANE**, 30km east of Kebili, the old French fort, once a hotel, is now a Garde Nationale post, so resist the temptation to photograph it as you pass. What may pass the time is looking out for the desert birds and mammals that can be spotted along the road.

El Hamma de l'Arad   الحامّة عراد

EL HAMMA DE L'ARAD is 50km east of Saidane and 31km west of Gabès. It is strung out along a single main road that runs through it roughly from north (toward Gabès) to south (toward Kebili), parts of which have been variously named avenue Bourguiba, avenue 7 Novembre and avenue de l'Environnement, according to the political whim of the day, though of course none of the official names are actually used by local residents. In the sixteenth century, unlikely as it may seem, El Hamma was a substantial town and a major **staging post** on the trans-Saharan routes. Then, in the 1630s, the **Matmata** people who lived here refused to pay their taxes to the Bey, who had the town razed to the ground, its citizens expelled, and Arab nomads of the Beni Zid tribe then settled here in place of the recalcitrant Berbers.

El Hamma has quite a history of militancy in modern times too. Its centre is a square called place Daghbaji, with a statue of the man it is named after, **Mohammed Daghbaji**, one of the very first Tunisian fighters for independence from colonial rule. The story goes that in his youth Daghbaji was beaten for no good reason by a French soldier. He later absconded with his weapon after being conscripted to serve in the French army and, taking to the hills with a band of fighters in 1915, began an armed campaign to rid his land of infidel rule. Daghbaji's campaign coincided with the Ouderna rebellion in the south (see p.437), and the Berber rebellion against Italian rule in Libya (see p.416), and years before Bourguiba and the Neo-Destour Party came on the scene, his men proved a major thorn in the side of the colonialists, and killed numerous French soldiers before their leader was finally captured and shot in 1924.

Nor was Daghbaji the only son of El Hamma whose radicalism was ahead of his time. Just 200m further south, near the turn-off for the piste to Matmata, is the bust of local theologian and writer **Tahar Haddad**. A staunch supporter of women's rights, Haddad argued in his 1930 work, *Our Women in Sharia and Society*, that the oppression of women was contrary to the law of Islam, and called on religious grounds for the abolition of polygamy and the veil, and for equal access to education for both sexes. Haddad pointed out that nothing in the Koran or the *hadith* (sayings of the Prophet) supports the imposition of purdah or sexual segregation, arguments that are now gaining greater voice among Muslim women worldwide. A third native of El Hamma whose miltancy predated that of his better-known successors was Haddad's friend **Mohammed Ali el Hammi**, a pioneer of Tunisian trade unionism, who in 1924 founded the CGTT (Confédération Générale Tunisienne des Travailleurs). Even today, El Hamma retains a tradition of militancy, and support for Islamic fundamentalism is strong here, though largely unvoiced in the current political climate.

El Hamma's main point of interest is its natural **hot baths**, which have long attracted visitors from far and wide, and gave it the Roman name Aquae Tacapitanae. There is still a **hammam festival** in March. Leo Africanus was not a fan, noting somewhat irrelevantly, "the hot water tastes like brimstone so that it will in no way quench a man's thirst". Today the **baths** (24hr) are housed in a modern building called Hammam Sidi Abdel Kader, 100m west of place Daghbaji, which is based on Roman foundations; the entrance on the left is for women, men go round the corner to the right. The spring water rises at 47°C, and you can sit in it on submerged seats in a shallow pool, as well as using it for ordinary hammam washing.

El Hamma's other sight is the **Morabi**, the tomb of a local Jewish holy man, Rabbi Sidi Youssef, and scene of an annual Jewish pilgrimage around December. At one time El Hamma had quite a thriving Jewish community, but all of them left for Israel, Tunis or Jerba in the 1950s. To find the tomb, take the street leading east from the main road just south of place Daghbaji, and follow it for some 500m, past a palm grove and a mosque to a little square, where you turn right, and the tomb – a white building with a blue Hebrew inscription – appears on your right after 500m. Apart from the December pilgrimage, the Mòrabi is also visited by Jewish pilgrims who have come to Jerba for *Lag beOmer*, around May (see p.381).

Practicalities

El Hamma has two **hotels**, both simple but clean, the *Hôtel Thermes* on the east side of the main road, 50m north of place Daghbaji (☎05/331120; ❶), and the slightly better and slightly pricier *Hôtel el Hana*, also called *Hôtel de la Quiétude* at 15 rue Abdel Karim el Khatabi, 30m down a side street off the east side of the main road just 30m further north (no phone; ❷). Neither hotel has showers, but the hot baths are close at hand. In the way of **eating**, there are a few small restaurants in town, including the *Restaurant el Adouani*, a cheap diner just 200m north of place Daghbaji on the east side of the main road (daily 7am–6pm), and the slightly less basic *Restaurant Tunisien* on the west side of the main road, just to the north of place Daghbaji (daily 7am–9pm).

There are a couple of **banks** opposite the *Hôtel Thermes*, and a post office (country hours) 50m north of place Daghbaji. On Fridays, an additional attraction is the **market**, centred on the market building just east of place Daghbaji and around the hot baths. The bus and louage station is some 500m north of place Daghbaji, with SRT bus services to Gabès, Jerba, Sfax, Kebili, Douz and Tozeur. There are also SNTRI departures to Tunis via Sfax and Sousse, and in the other direction to Kebili, Douz and El Fouar.

travel details

Trains

Metlaoui to: Gafsa (2 daily; 50min); Mahrès (2 daily; 3hr 30min); Meknassy (2 daily; 2hr 20min); Redeyef (1hr 30min, connecting for Sfax when travelling from Redeyef but not the other way); Sened Gare (2 daily; 1hr 40min); Sfax (2 daily; 4hr).

Metlaoui trains connect once daily Mon–Sat but run direct twice daily Sun – for El Jem (6hr), Sousse (7hr), Bir Bou Regba (8hr) and Tunis (8hr

40min). The Lézard Rouge service runs from Metlaoui to Seldja (4 weekly; 1hr 30min round trip).

Buses

Douz to: El Faouar (6 daily; 1hr); Gabès (4 daily; 2hr 30min); Gafsa (1 daily; 3hr 30min); Kebili (9 daily; 30min); Sabria (6 daily; 40min); Sfax (1 daily; 4hr); Sousse (2 daily; 6hr 30min); Tozeur (3 daily; 2hr); Tunis (2 daily; 9hr); Zaafrane (6 daily; 15min).

El Hamma de l'Arad to: Douz (4 daily; 2hr); El Fouar (1 daily; 2hr); Gabès (18 daily; 40min); Jerba (1 daily; 3hr); Kebili (7 daily; 1hr 30min); Sfax (4 daily; 2hr 30min); Sousse (4 daily; 5hr); Tozeur (1 daily; 3hr); Tunis (4 daily; 7hr–8hr 10min).

Gafsa to: Douz (1 daily; 3hr 30min); Gabès (3 daily; 2hr 30min); El Guettar (14 daily; 30min); Hazoua (1 daily; 3hr 30min); Kairouan (11 daily; 3hr); Kasserine (2 daily; 2hr); Kebili (1 daily; 3hr); Le Kef (1 daily; 4hr); Maknassy (4 daily; 2hr); Metlaoui (22 daily; 1hr); Nefta (8 daily; 3hr); Redeyef (6 daily; 2hr); Sened Gare (8 daily; 1hr); Sfax (5 daily; 3hr); Sidi Aïch (3 daily; 1hr); Sidi Bou Zid (6 daily; 2hr); Sousse (3 daily; 5hr); Tozeur (12 daily; 2hr 30min); Tunis (10 daily; 5hr 30min).

Kebili to: Blidet (7 daily; 30min); Douz (8 daily; 30min); El Fouar (3 daily; 50min); Gabès (7 daily; 2hr); Gafsa (1 daily; 3hr); Kairouan (1 daily; 6hr); Nouail (5 daily; 45min); Sfax (3 daily; 3hr 30min); Sousse (3 daily; 6hr); Tozeur (3 daily; 1hr 30min); Tunis (4 daily; 8hr 30min).

Metlaoui to: Gabès (1 daily; 3hr 30min); Gafsa (22 daily; 1hr); Kairouan (5 daily; 4hr 30min); Moulares (11 daily; 40min); Nefta (10 daily; 2hr); Redeyef (11 daily; 1hr); Sfax (6 daily; 4hr); Sousse (3 daily; 5hr 15min); Tozeur (16 daily; 1hr 30min); Tunis (7 daily; 6hr 30min).

Nefta to: Gabès (1 daily; 4hr), Gafsa (8 daily; 3hr); Hazoua (4 daily; 25min); Kairouan (2 daily; 6hr); Metlaoui (10 daily; 2hr); Redeyef (2 daily; 3hr); Sfax (1 daily; 5hr 30min); Sousse (1 daily; 6hr); Tozeur (14 daily; 30min); Tunis (2 daily; 7hr 30min).

Redeyef to: Moulares (10 daily; 20min); Metlaoui (10 daily; 1hr); Gafsa (6 daily; 2hr); Tozeur (4 daily; 2hr 30min); Nefta (2 daily; 3hr); Tamerza (6 daily; 40min); Tunis (2 daily; 8hr).

Tozeur to: Chebika (2 daily; 1hr); Douz (1 daily; 2hr); Gabès (1 daily; 3hr 30min); Gafsa (12 daily; 2hr 30min); Hazoua (1 daily; 1hr); Kairouan (5 daily; 5hr 30min); Kebili (2 daily; 1hr 30min); Metlaoui (16 daily; 1hr 30min); Nefta (12 daily; 30min); Redeyef (4 daily; 2hr 30min); Sfax (1 daily;

5hr); Sousse (1 daily; 5hr 30min); Tamerza (2 daily; 1hr 15min); Tunis (5 daily; 7hr).

Louages

Louage journey times are roughly three-quarters the time taken by buses on the same route. Frequency depends on demand, but morning is always the best time to get a louage, especially for longer journeys.

Douz to: El Faouar (30min); Gabès (2hr); El Gola'a (10min); Kebili (30min); Sabria (30min); Zaafrane (15min). Pick-ups to Nouail (30min).

Gafsa to: Fériana (1hr); Gabès (2hr); El Guettar (20min); Kasserine (1hr 40min); Metlaoui (40min); Redeyef (1hr 20min); Sened Gare (45min); Sfax (2hr 40min); Sousse (4hr); Tozeur (1hr 30min); Tunis (5hr). Occasional morning services to Nefta (2hr).

Kebili to: Blidet (20min); Gabès (1hr 30min); Gafsa (3hr); Sfax (mornings only; 3hr); Tozeur (1hr 30min); Tunis (7hr).

Meknassy to: Sened Gare (40min); Sfax (1hr 45min); Sidi Bou Zid (1hr); Tunis (4hr 30min).

Metlaoui to: Gafsa (40min); Redeyef (40min); Tamerza (1hr); Tozeur (50min).

Nefta to: Hazoua (25min); Tozeur (30min); occasional morning services to Gafsa (1hr 30min) and Sfax (4hr 30min).

Redeyef to: Gafsa (1hr 20min), Metlaoui (40min).

Tozeur to: Degache (10min); Gafsa (1hr 10min); El Hamma du Jerid (10min); Kebili (1hr 30min); Metlaoui (40min); Nefta (25min); Sfax (mornings only – 4hr); Tamerza (1hr); Tunis (6hr).

Flights

Gafsa to: Tunis (2 weekly; 1hr).

Tozeur to: Frankfurt (1 weekly with Tunisair; 3hr); Jerba (4 weekly with Tunisair; 50min); Paris (2 weekly with Tunisair; 2hr 50min); Tunis (6 weekly with Tuninter; 1hr 15min).

CHAPTER SEVEN

GABÈS AND MATMATA

The towns of Gabès and Matmata lie in a tract of land that swoops below the belly of the Sahel, the fertile terrain stretching south of Sousse. For the most part nondescript, it is punctuated by fecund emerald oases and hemmed by mile upon mile of coast along the gulf. Almost every traveller heading south passes through Gabès, but few take the time to explore its historic quarters and adjacent oasis – both remnants of a turbulent era in Tunisia's past, when the extensive oases were important staging posts for caravans from the other side of the Sahara.

Better known – and decidedly more spectacular – are the weird lunar landscapes and troglodyte villages around Matmata, a town blown to fame by the filming there of

scenes in the *Star Wars* movies. Sometimes the demands of tourism seem disturbingly overbearing in this region, and unless you are with a tour group, it's difficult to make your way around without a car. If you've got one or are willing to hitch, the most genuine experiences are to be found some way off the beaten track – in Berber villages around Matmata like Haddej, where the underground way of life continues unaffected, or others further afield like Tamezret and Taoujou, which are isolated and barely visited, deeply traditional and extremely scenic.

Gabès   قابس

In 1886, a French administrator arrived to take up a post at **GABÈS**, the coastal town billed as the port of the Sahara. "Imagine my surprise", he wrote to his superior, "when I had to disembark onto the beach and walk up the dusty path that is the main street to reach the only building, my office."

Today Gabès has grown in size but is still rather a disappointment. The busy new town, rebuilt after World War II, stretches for kilometres away from the coast and, though the palm groves reach to the sea, they're largely inaccessible at this point, surrounded by the port and industrial complex. On the other hand, Gabès's pivotal position between the sea and the *chotts*, or salt flats, ensures that virtually all traffic between the south and centre of the country passes through here – and there are things worth stopping for. Tucked among the alleys of the old quarters are several fascinating **mosques**; the well-preserved **markets** are as alive with daily commerce as they ever were; and the long, sandy **beach** has the benefit of being almost undeveloped. Most alluringly, away from the main streets, parts of the vast **oasis** really are a haven of peace and shade.

Some history

First occupied by the Phoenicians, Gabès was later a major port of Roman Africa, its name, Tacape, meaning "a wet and irrigated place". In medieval times it was the terminus for many of the trans-Saharan caravans, while the main haj caravan, carrying pilgrims on their obligatory trip to Mecca, passed through on its way to Tripoli and Cairo before reaching the holy city itself, bringing with it thousands of merchants and their goods. Gabès was also famed for its silk, made from silkworms raised on mulberry

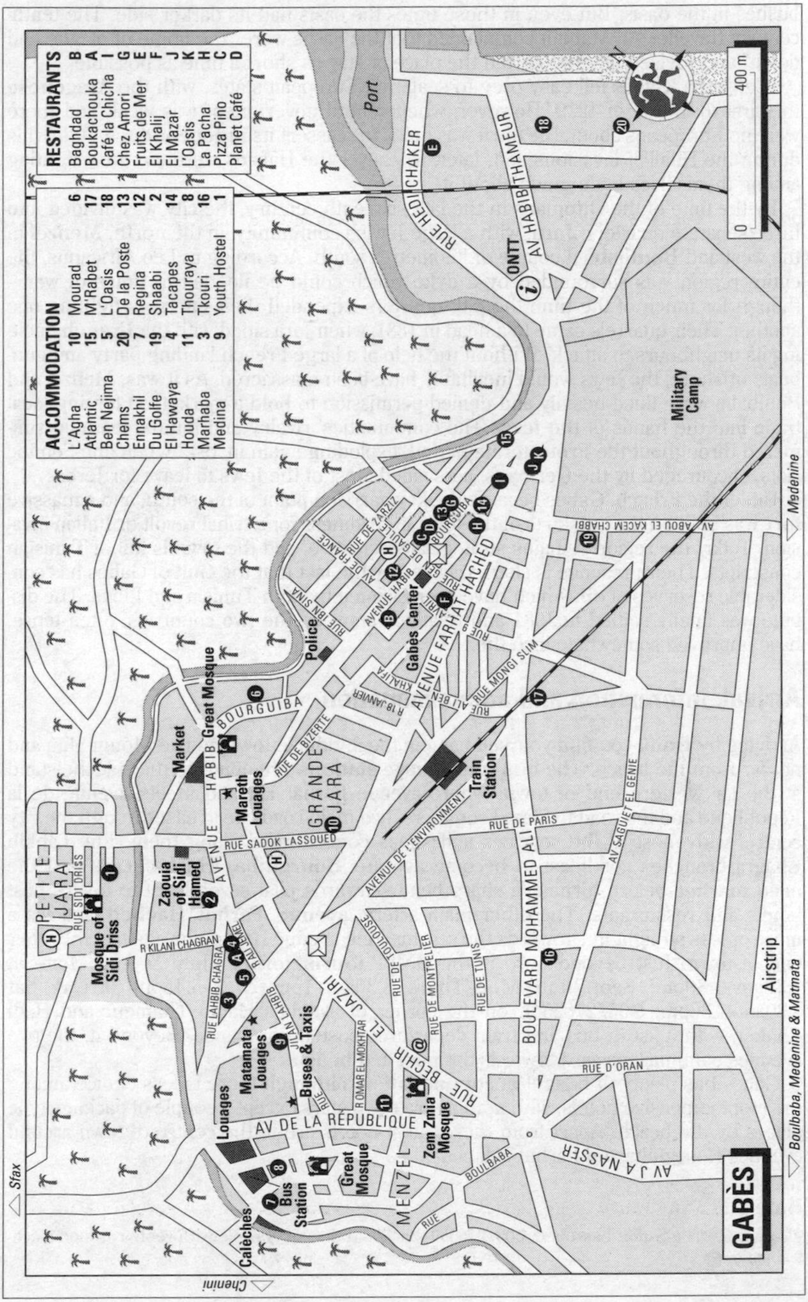

GABÈS

ACCOMMODATION

L'Agha	
Atlantic	
Ben Nejima	
Chems	20
Ennakhil	7
Du Golfe	19
El Hawaya	4
Houda	11
Marhaba	3
Medina	
Mourad	10
M'Rabet	15
L'Oasis	5
De la Poste	13
Regina	12
Shaabi	2
Tacapes	14
Thouraya	8
Tkouri	16
Youth Hostel	9

RESTAURANTS

Baghdad	B
Boukachouka	A
Café la Chicha	I
Chez Amori	G
Fruits de Mer	E
El Khalij	F
El Mazar	J
L'Oasis	K
La Pacha	H
Pizza Pino	C
Planet Café	D

bushes in the oasis. But even in those times the oasis had its darker side. The tenth-century traveller Ali Mahalli complained that the oases were "the home of plague and death" and advised others to avoid the place or stay as short a time as possible.

Like Jerba, Gabès fell easy prey to seafaring European states, with the **Aragonese** the first to invade in 1279. However, when central government was weak and there were no Europeans about, the town was quick to reassert its **independence**. It did this during the Hilalian invasions and, later, whenever the Hafsids were too busy fighting among themselves to do much about it.

By the time of the Ottomans in the late sixteenth century, the city was divided into three separate quarters: **Jara**, with a large Jewish community, in the north, **Menzel** in the west and **Boulbaba** a couple of kilometres south. According to Leo Africanus, the entire region was surrounded by a dyke which could be flooded in times of war – though for much of the time the city quarters expended their energies fighting one another. Their quarrels came to a head in 1881, when Jara sided with the **French**, inciting its neighbours to attack. Without the help of a large French landing party and gunboats offshore, the Jews would inevitably have been massacred. As it was, Menzel and Boulbaba were fined heavily and denied permission to hold a market, so forcing local trade into the hands of the Jews. The communities' rivalry and mutual loathing simmered throughout the Protectorate period, exploding again in 1942 when anti-Semitic riots, encouraged by the Germans, persuaded most of the Jews to leave for Jerba.

Under the French, Gabès became the key garrison point of the south, and a massive **fort** was built on the outskirts of the town in readiness for a tribal revolt or Italian invasion. Today the region remains strategically sensitive, and the town is full of Tunisian conscripts. Their presence is also explained by the fact that the Gulf of Gabès has considerable reserves of **oil**, which have been claimed by both Tunisia and Libya. The dispute was finally settled in 1981 and relations between the two countries, often tense, have improved somewhat since then.

Arrival, information and accommodation

Arriving by **train**, you find yourself bang in the middle of town on rue Mongi Slim and not far from the beach. The **bus and louage stations** are opposite the calèche stand at the far western end of town, where avenue Farhat Hached meets avenue de la République and the road to Sfax. From here, two main roads head east through the city centre, with most of the services and shops concentrated along them. Rue Lahbib Chagra branches northeast to become **avenue Bourguiba**, which curves past the main **market** before turning a sharp bend seawards past several of the town's best hotels and restaurants. The other main artery, **avenue Farhat Hached**, follows a more or less straight line towards the sea, meeting avenue Bourguiba again at the other end of town. Just beyond here is the ONTT **tourist office** (July & Aug Mon–Sat 7.30am–1.30pm; Sept–June Mon–Thurs 8.30am–1pm & 3–5.45pm, Fri & Sat 8.30am–1.30pm; ☎05/270254), on the corner of avenues Habib Thameur and Hedi Chaker, with a list of bus and train departures posted up outside. Beyond it, the two avenues continue seaward towards the **port** and **beach**.

Gabès has plenty of budget **accommodation**, although there is less choice among the more expensive hotels, with nothing over two stars except a couple of package-type places by the beach. Apart from these, most hotels are in the centre of town around avenues Bourguiba and Farhat Hached.

Hotels

L'Agha, 101 rue Sadok Lassoued ☎05/276569. Basic but decent cheapie with rooms around a central patio. ❷

Atlantic ★, 4 av Bourguiba ☏05/220034, 🖷221358. At the junction of av Farhat Hached, this enormous white French colonial building is the oldest hotel in town and creaks with character, but has seen better days. All rooms – some pretty large, others quite small – are en suite with either a bath or shower, and hot water in the mornings and evenings. ❸

Ben Nejima, 68 rue Ali Jemel, on the corner of av Farhat Hached ☏05/271591. Although the rooms are clean and the management friendly, the place is a bit noisy; bathroom facilities are communal. ❷

Chella Club, near Chenini ☏05/227442, 🖷227446. A slightly tacky but pleasant "vacation village" out in the oasis (see p.351), with chalet-style bungalows, all en suite. People come here from Gabès in the evening for the bar, restaurant and live entertainment. ❸

Chems ★★★, on the beach ☏05/270547, 🖷274485. The most modern hotel in town, on the beach, with a nice pool and big spotless rooms, some with a sea view. Wheelchair-friendly. ❺

Ennakhil, behind the bus station ☏05/273598. Hardly luxury, with basic though clean rooms and grim toilets, but it's obviously handy for that early bus. ❷

Hôtel el Hawaya, 36 rue Ali Jemel (no phone). Rock-bottom prices and basic conditions (cold water showers only), and not recommended for women travelling alone, but clean and friendly nonetheless. ❶

Hôtel du Golfe, av Abou el Kacem Chabbi ☏05/271807. Low-priced and rather bleak, but with private showers in all rooms, though you can smell the plumbing in a lot of them. ❷

Houda, av de la République ☏05/220022, 🖷274053. Clean, cool and comfortable, with good views from the top floor and the roof terrace. Most rooms have bathroom and balcony. ❷

Marhaba, av Farhat Hached, opposite the Matmata louage station ☏09/231645. Simple but clean and very cheap with hot water round the clock in shared bathrooms. ❷

Medina, rue Haj Jelani Lahbib ☏05/274271. A good-value little hotel in the Menzel quarter, between av Farhat Hached and av de la République, with shared bathroom facilities, and decent rooms, though the toilets may not be up to scratch by some standards. ❷

Mourad, 300 av Bourguiba, above the UIB bank ☏05/273926. Clean, quiet and very good value, with most of the upstairs rooms being both large and en suite. Best of the cheapies. ❷

M'Rabet, rue Ali Zouaoui ☏05/270260. Off bd Mohamed Ali, near the station. Most of the nice, clean rooms have showers; the others either have a toilet and/or balcony. ❷

L'Oasis ★★★, on the beach ☏05/270781, 🖷271749. A reasonably posh tourist hotel with the usual facilities, including a restaurant and pool, a/c and TV in all rooms, and a sea view from some of them. ❹

Hôtel de la Poste, rue Belgacem el Bazmi ☏05/222182. The second-oldest hotel in town, and a long-time backpackers' favourite that retains a small amount of 1920s charm. Though well run-down, its big rooms come equipped with bidets, apart from which bathroom facilities are shared. ❷

Regina, 138 av Bourguiba ☏05/272095, 🖷221710. Good value budget option, with rooms around an interior patio, all en suite, clean and fresh. ❷

Shaabi, 496 av Bourguiba ☏05/273894. Small hotel with rock-bottom prices, very basic accommodation, and shared bathroom facilities. ❶

Tacapes ★★, 55 av Bourguiba ☏05/270701, 🖷270700. The rooms are clean and comfortable with a/c and TV, but the place is showing its age somewhat. ❸

Thouraya, by the bus station ☏05/274160. The red light above the entrance does mean what you think, but this place also functions as an ordinary low-price hotel, clean and orderly, and fine for spending the night, with shared showers but hot water round the clock. Some beds are better than others, so check before taking a room. ❷

Tkouri, 399 bd Mohamed Ali ☏05/277706. Quiet and clean but not very central; choice of pricier big rooms with bathroom, or cheap small ones without. ❷–❸

Youth hostel

Centre des Stages et des Vacances, rue de l'Oasis, Petite Jara ☏05/270271. Well kept, with dorm accommodation (5TD) and camping; you can come and go as you please till the midnight curfew.

The Town

Gabès is not primarily a seaside resort. The swimming and the long sandy **beach** are reasonable, but no match for Kerkennah and still less for Jerba. Indeed, it almost seems that the beach has been stuck on the eastern end of town as an afterthought. The town itself has all the facilities you would expect from such a pivotal communications centre, but its few places of real interest are concentrated in the **old quarters** of **Jara**, **Menzel** and **Boulbaba**. The **oasis** stretches north and west of the town.

Jara and Menzel

Jara is divided into two parts. The larger chunk of **Grande Jara** extends outwards from the western end of avenue Bourguiba. Its main attraction is the market, open every day except Monday. To the north of the main street, lined with cheap cafés and *gargotes*, a covered passage leads through to the **marketplace**, once crowded with caravans from Ghadames and Algeria. Around its entrance stand bulging panniers, filled with the henna for which Gabès is renowned. This area, being near Jara's Great Mosque, is reserved for "clean" goods – mainly clothes, rugs and spices. Among the adjoining shops are the gold- and silversmiths, while the cobbled street leading down to the river is the territory of the so-called "dirty" crafts of blacksmiths, knife-sharpeners and metalworkers. By the river itself is the unhygienic cattle market, well away from the mosque. The livestock market is held every day except Monday, but market day, when it is busiest, is Sunday.

The **Great Mosque** on avenue Bourguiba, with its huge minaret, still under construction, is recent, as are most of the mosques in Grande Jara, but the **Zaouia of Sidi Hamed**, around the corner at 44 rue Sadok Lassoued, is worth a look for its *koubba* dome and doorways carved in local pink stone, though it is now sadly derelict.

The other part of the quarter, **Petite Jara**, is across the rue de l'Oasis bridge. The **Sidi Driss Mosque** was built here in the eleventh century by an Arab prince of the Banu Jami, descendants of the Banu Hilal invaders. The prayer hall, like much of Jara, has been built using stone from old Roman columns. Many of Jara's other historic mosques, however, have disappeared since World War II, along with its old synagogues and most of its Jewish heritage.

The monuments of **Menzel** – the area around avenue de la République – seem to have survived rather better than Jara's, such as they are. Menzel's Great Mosque, in a square just west of avenue de la République, and the **Zaouia of Sidi Bnei Isa**, down a side street on the other side of the avenue, are both old and attractive buildings, and a stroll down rue Bechir el Jaziri will take you past the **Zem Zmia Mosque**. Even without tracking all these down, however, Menzel is the only quarter of Gabès that really retains its ancient feel, and is definitely the best part of town for an aimless wander. It also has its own **market**, on rue Omar el Mokhtar.

Boulbaba

The third historic quarter, **Boulbaba**, is somewhat removed from the town centre, down at the end of avenue de la République and along avenue J A Nasser, then along rue 6 Octobre, some twenty minutes' walk away – look out for the tall minaret. Buses #3 and #3b run to Boulbaba half-hourly from rue Jilani Lahbib; ask the driver for Sidi Boulbaba. A taxi will cost about 1.5TD. It's worth making the effort to get out here to see Gabès's most important and oldest religious monument.

The **Mosque of Sidi Boulbaba**, on the opposite side of the square from the mosque with the tall minaret, contains the seventh-century tomb of the saint who was Mohammed's barber. Its courtyard is particularly beautiful, surrounded by colonnades and decorated with tiles. Boulbaba arrived here in the seventh century and, like many holy men and marabouts in the south, united warring factions to bring prosperity to the town – of which he is now the patron saint. The surrounding village, which took his name, stood on the site of Roman Tacape and was closed to local Jews and Christians. Non-Muslims may now enter the courtyard of the mosque, but not the prayer hall.

Next to the mosque is an imposing old *medersa*, built in 1692 and now a **Museum of Popular Arts and Traditions** (Tues–Sun: mid-April to mid-Sept 8am–1pm & 4–7pm; mid-Sept to mid-April 9.30am–4.30pm; 1.1TD). The people who run it are welcoming and happy to show you around. The pink stone building itself holds more interest than the exhibits, although these include everyday objects, textiles, a Punic *ossuary* (urn), and a little garden planted with henna, pomegranates, bananas and grapes. Some locally excavated Roman artefacts decorate the grounds.

The Gabès oasis

Part of the **Gabès oasis** starts just behind Petite Jara, leading along to the Sfax road and, in the other direction, to the sea. There are 300,000 palms here, but many are in poor health, spoilt by the damp sea air. The land has changed little since the days when the Roman writer Pliny observed: "Here in the midst of the sand, the soil is well cultivated and fruitful. Here grows a high palm and beneath that palm are olives and under that a fig tree. Under the fig tree grows a pomegranate and beneath that again a vine. Moreover, beneath these there are sown corn, then vegetables or grass." This tiered intercropping continues today, allowing farmers to cultivate an astonishing range of crops, some 400 varieties in total, including henna and spices as well as food produce.

The main oasis villages are on the other side of the Gabès–Sfax road. Most worthwhile – although also most touristed – is **CHENINI**. Bus #7 from Gabès leaves every hour from opposite rue Haj Jelani Lahbib near the junction of avenue de la République, and you can take a place (*plassa*) in a shared taxi from the same spot. Alternatively, you could walk from Gabès – past the louage and calèche stands, then a right turn over the river – but it's a hot trudge of 4km. What most people do is take a calèche tour of the oasis. These all follow much the same route, with obligatory stops to buy souvenirs, but the tours aren't too expensive (15TD for up to four people).

The small direct road winds around the irrigation ditches in a swirl of right-angle bends and ends up at **EL AOUADID**, some 3km away. If you turn left here, the road meanders past the *Café des Cascades*, a pleasant spot for an open-air tea or coffee in the palm trees, eventually arriving at a **crocodile farm** (Tues–Sun 7.30am–6pm, later in summer; 0.5TD). At present this contains a rather unimpressive zoo, but it is due to metamorphose into a **Nature Museum**, with exhibits on wildlife in the oasis, the mountains, the desert and the Gulf of Gabès. Beside it is an open-air café restaurant with a family section, complete with swings and slides for the kids, and in front is a **Roman dam**, made up of several layers of stone holding back a small reservoir. A path behind the dam goes on to the *Chella Club* (see p.349) and finally to some impressive **gorges** at the southwest tip of the oasis. The road along the top leads past the **Marabout of Sidi Ali Bahoul** and on to Chenini itself.

Eating and drinking

Food isn't one of Gabès's high points, but reasonable meals can be found in every price range if you know where to look. If your budget is really tight, there are some *gargotes* on avenue de la République and around the market, and a couple opposite the Matmata louage station on avenue Farhat Hached. Better still, is the unnamed diner (daily 5am–10pm) on avenue Bourguiba by Banque du Sud, two doors from the post office. It's very cheap but clean, and handy for a breakfast of *lablabi* with all the trimmings, or for sandwiches, spit-roast chicken and simple meals.

THE AMAZING DATE PALM

Dates are a big export industry, and bring 52 million dinars' worth of much needed foreign currency into the Tunisian economy. But to the people of the desert, the cultivation of dates is more than just business: it supplies them with a vital source of food, fuel and building materials, to the extent that life would be unimaginable without it.

The date is extremely nutritious – not only high in energy but also rich in niacin, iron, potassium, phosphorus and pantothenic acid. It can be preserved, and when properly stored, will keep for a year or more. On long journeys, when food is scarce, it's possible to survive on dates alone. The stones are also used to feed camels, which happily munch away on them. Dates aren't the only food that can be derived from the palm: palm hearts are a very tasty luxury.

Although the fibrous trunk of the palm is not a true wood, it is sturdy enough to saw into planks to make doors, window shutters and floorboards. In the old quarters of Tozeur and Nefta, where the alleys pass under buildings, the boards overhead are palm wood, just as they are in the entrances to many of the southern ksour. The doors of *ghorfas* in the ksour are also made from palm wood, along with many doors of homes in the old quarters of the desert towns, and the conduits which carry water from spring to cistern.

Palm wood is too valuable to burn, but the fronds of the tree make excellent fuel. Alternatively, they can be used for fencing, to protect crops and gardens from wind and sand – you will often see such fencing installed along the top of roadside dunes to prevent their advance across the road. The fronds are also used to make the huts that nomadic families live in, and to thatch the roofs of houses built with other materials. The spines of the frond can be turned into chairs, beds and other furniture, while the tough green leaves are woven to make anything from baskets to *chicha* fans and floor matting. Even the stalk on which the dates grow can be used as a broom once the dates have been taken from it.

For more on dates, see the box on p.312.

The *Café la Chicha* on rue Ibn Jazar at the junction of avenue Bourguiba and avenue Farhat Hached (daily except Fri 6am–9pm) is a refined if slightly pricey place where women as well as men can relax with a coffee and *chicha*.

Restaurants

Baghdad, 175 av Bourguiba. Low-priced solid Tunisian food. Daily noon–3pm & 5.30–10pm.

Boukachouka, 60 rue Ali Jemel. Tasty food and reasonable prices. Can be good for a breakfast of coffee, bread and an omelette, if they happen to feel like serving it. Daily 9am–10pm.

Restaurant Chez Amori, 84 av Bourguiba. Watch French TV while you eat cheap, copious meals. Daily 10am–11pm.

Restaurant des Fruits de Mer, rue Hedi Chaker by the fishing port. Excellent food including treats like stuffed squid, roast rabbit, and of course barbecued freshly landed fish, all at extremely low prices. Highly recommended. Daily 7am–10pm or later.

Restaurant Pizzeria el Khalij, 142 av Farhat Hached ☎05/221412. One of two recommendable places for pizza or pasta; a little pricier than the *Pino*. Daily except Sun noon–3pm & 6.30–11pm.

Restaurant el Mazar, 39 av Farhat Hached ☎05/272065. Highly regarded, very refined and rather expensive serving French-style food. Daily noon–3pm & 6–11pm.

Restaurant de l'Oasis, 17 av Farhat Hached ☎05/270098. This established place is Gabès's top restaurant, serving excellent food (particularly fish) and with the bonus of a reasonable set menu (7TD). Daily noon–2.45pm & 6.30–9.30pm.

Restaurant la Pacha, 38 av Farhat Hached ☎05/272418. Formerly a posh French restaurant, this place is now rather more populaire, partly because it serves alcohol, and partly because it serves good food in large portions at moderate prices. Daily except Fri noon–3pm & 6–11pm.

Pizza Pino, 114 av Bourguiba. A pleasant and moderately priced little place, doing very passable pizzas. Daily except Sun noon–2.30pm & 5–10pm.

Planet Café, 110 av Bourguiba. This is a good place for breakfast or a snack and also offers pizzas, sandwiches, pasta, or just a coffee and croissant, all at reasonable prices, but no seats so you have to eat standing. Daily 6am–9pm.

Restaurant la Ruche, rte de Sfax, 1km out of town. A popular bar restaurant with a small selection of low-priced, well-cooked, meat dishes such as steak or lamb chops to wash down with beer or wine, though women may not find it a comfortable place to eat in the evening due to the prevailing tavern atmosphere. Daily except Fri 11am–11pm.

Listings

Airlines Tunis Air, 172 av Farhat Hached ☎05/271250.

Banks Several on av Bourguiba, including four near the Gabès Center with ATMs that take Visa and Mastercard. In Menzel, there's the Banque du Sud at the corner of av de la République and rue Omar el Mokhtar.

Bicycle rental 112 av Bourguiba, between the *Pizzeria Pino* and the *Planet Café* (8am–5pm; 5TD/day); but give your chosen mount a good once-over first.

Bookshop Librairie Béchraoui at 75 av Bourguiba has the odd English title among its dusty piles of used books.

Car rental Avis, 4 rue 9 Avril ☎05/270210; Sixt/Express, 154 av Farhat Hached ☎05/274222; Hertz, 30 rue Ibn Jazzar ☎05/270525; Europcar, 6 av Farhat Hached ☎05/274720.

Cinema El Khadra, rue Abou el Kacem Chabbi, near the corner of av Farhat Hached.

Hammams The most central is on rue de Palestine, just off rue Sadok Lassoued – look for the blue and white door (daily men 5am–12.30pm & 6–9pm, women 12.30–6pm). There is also the Hammam el Hana, rue Général de Gaulle, just off av Bourguiba (daily men 7am–noon & 6–9pm, women 1–6pm), and Hammam Sidi Driss in rue Sidi Driss in Petit Jara (men: daily 5am–1pm & 6–10pm, closed Fri; women: daily 1–5pm & Fri 1–10pm).

Internet access The most central Publinet office is at unit 146 upstairs in the Gabès Centre (daily 8am–10pm, 3TD/hr), but there is a better and cheaper one in Gallerie Ben Jaber at 145 rue Bechir Jaziri, opposite the Zem Zmia Mosque (daily 9am–midnight; 2TD/hr).

Medical facilities The regional hospital is in rue Romdhane Ali Dhari ☎05/282700. More central is the Clinique Bon Secours at the eastern end of rue Mongi Slim ☎05/271400, which has an emergency department. There's an all-night pharmacy at 234 rue Mongi Slim, at the corner of rue Ali Ben Khalifa.

Laundry 48 av Bourguiba.

Newspapers Librairie Nefoussi at 16 rue 9 Avril carries *Time* and *Newsweek*, and sometimes British papers or the *Herald Tribune*.

ONA crafts shop Av Farhat Hached, opposite the post office (Mon–Thurs 8.30am–1pm & 3–5.45pm, Fri & Sat 8.30am–1pm).

Police The main police station is on the Medenine road ☎05/270853, but there's a more central one on av Bourguiba near the junction of rue 18 Janvier.

Post offices At the corner of av Farhat Hached and rue Bechir el Jaziri, and on av Bourguiba at the corner of rue General de Gaulle. Both open city hours with money-changing facilities (for cash) and international phones. There are also a few smaller offices around town open country hours.

Supermarkets Magasin Général has two branches: one is in Menzel at the corner of rue Omar el Mokhtar and rue Bechir el Jaziri; the other at the junction of bd Mohammed Ali and rue Mongi Slim. Both are open Sun mornings, but closed Mon.

Swimming pools The *Hôtel Chems* will let you use their pool for a few dinars.

Tours To cover some of the more inaccessible parts of the south with ease, mostly by Land Rover, you might consider a tour run by operators such as Sahara Tours at 11 av Farhat Hached ☎05/270930. A two-day excursion into the desert including a night at Ksar Ghilane (see p.414) will set you back around 100TD.

MOVING ON FROM GABÈS

For a rundown of destinations and journey times, see Travel Details on p.362.

Gabès is the main transport link between the south and the centre of Tunisia, so it's a very good place to pick up connections to anywhere in the country. However, although the town has an airport, there are no passenger flights.

The train station off rue Mongi Slim has three daily departures (one overnight) to Tunis (via Mahrès), Sfax, El Jem and Sousse. You could in theory take the night train and change at Mahrès for Gafsa and Metlaoui, but it would be a very long way round.

In the bus station at the western end of town you'll find services operated by SNTRI, Gabès's own SRT (called SOTREGAMES), and three other SRTs. There are regular buses to Tunis – seven via Kairouan, eleven via Sfax and Sousse, with two continuing to Bizerte. Buses serve major towns all over south and central Tunisia, as well as local destinations such as El Hamma, Matmata, Tamezret, Techine and Toujane. The buses for Mareth and Zarat leave from rue de Bizerte by the Great Mosque.

The main louage station is right in front of the bus station, but louages for Mareth and Zarat leave from rue de Bizerte by the Great Mosque, while those for Nouvelle Matmata depart from avenue Farhat Hached, just west of the junction with rue Haj Jelani Lahbib and rue Ali Jemel. Buses for Matmata stop here too, but louages only go to Nouvelle Matmata, where you have to change for an onward connection to Matmata.

Matmata and around

مطماطة

As the Romans of Bulla Regia once did, the Berbers of **MATMATA**, some 40km due south of Gabès, live underground in **pit dwellings** consisting of a courtyard dug straight down into the soft, crumbly sandstone with rooms excavated into the surrounding walls, and it is these troglodyte dwellings that provide the town's main attraction. In 1959, the government began construction at Nouvelle Matmata, 15km up the road to Gabès, and people started moving in three years later. By the 1970s, when **Star Wars** (see box on p.319) was filmed here and Matmata was discovered by the tourist industry, many Matmatis were already living in more conventional housing, either in Nouvelle Matmata or in the original village. This was not because they preferred the new houses, but rather because these were easier to construct, and there was a housing need for young people. Those who had traditional homes preferred to keep them, except where their location made them prone to flooding.

Tourism proved a mixed blessing for the town, and completely changed the local way of life. Tour groups on "safari" poured in and tramped around the village peering into

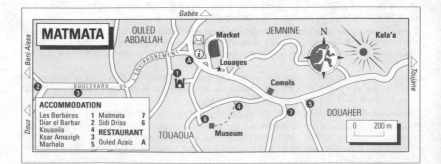

the pits to take photographs of people in their homes. This is tourism at its most voyeuristic, and barbed wire and dogs around many of the pits demonstrate that not everyone in town is happy about it. Others take a more resigned attitude to what is now by far the biggest local industry, and a source of income after all. You'll get repeated invitations into people's houses but you should be prepared to either pay a fee, especially for photographs, or else buy the local handicrafts in exchange for a quick peep. In the evenings, when the tour groups have all gone home, Matmata becomes a much more pleasant, laid-back kind of place, and it's also a useful base for exploring the other villages of this remarkable region.

On the way to Matmata from Gabès, look out for two concrete bunkers, one on each side of the road, half a kilometre past the "Matmata 37km/Gabès 5km" milestone. Dated "le 28.1.36", they were backstops for the wartime **Mareth Line** (see p.361). Buses from Gabès stop briefly on the way at **Nouvelle Matmata**, before beginning the ascent into the Demer mountains; if coming by louage, you will have to change vehicles here. From Nouvelle Matmata, there is also a direct surfaced road to Mareth and Toujane.

The Town

Matmata is spread out around three main roads – to Gabès, Toujane and Douz respectively. Where the three meet – the centre of town – you'll find a Syndicat d'Initiative tourist office (daily 8am–noon & 3–5.30pm, but mostly closed Fri–Sun pm; ☎05/230114), whose staff are very amenable, though you may have to track them down in the *Ouled Azaiz* café opposite. They can organize camels, donkeys and other such rustic means of transport. They will also have information on Matmata's annual tourist festival, held in August.

Coming from Nouvelle Matmata, you climb to the top of the Demer mountains and descend to Matmata in the valley on the other side. At first, with the virtual absence of any buildings above ground, the place looks deserted; in fact, five thousand people still live in the "craters" which come into view as you head further down the road. Nonetheless, spread out as it is across the saddle of the mountain, Matmata seems almost too diffuse to be a village; the structures which have sprung up above the ground now give the lie to its much-heralded "lunar" landscape, while the busloads of snap-happy day-trippers and camel-riding tourists manage at times to completely swamp the place.

Before the bulk of the Matmata tribe moved here in the sixteenth or seventeenth century, a much smaller community lived in ancient Matmata, around the *kala'a*, or **fortress**, just discernible on the heights above today's town. Their homes, built into the mountainside, have been abandoned in favour of the pit dwellings, and trying to climb up there is inadvisable since the *kala'a* overlooks the army camp on the road to Toujane, and your appearance on its ramparts may lead to trouble.

The pit dwellings

The pit dwellings in Matmata follow a regular design some four hundred years old. Most are based around a circular pit with vertical walls, 7m deep and 10m in diameter. Their construction takes advantage of the relative softness of the local sandstone which is easy to dig into. First the pit is excavated, making a central sunken courtyard, equivalent to the patio of a normal Tunisian home, then caves are dug into its sides at the level of the courtyard to serve as rooms. Smaller chambers may be dug out at higher levels, with steps leading up to them. These are usually cisterns or store-rooms, and may have holes in the ceiling to allow grain to be poured into them. A small, covered passageway, sometimes lined with recesses for animals and their fodder, leads from ground level down to the sunken courtyard. In fact, the pit may be dug into a small hillock, so that the tunnel runs horizontally out of the side of it. A simple dwelling takes six to eight months to build, while the largest houses, consisting of two or three pits linked together, take even longer.

THE MATMATA BERBERS

The Berber tribe of the Matmata once lived near the hot springs of El Hamma (see p.342), but were expelled from their original home following a failed rebellion in 1630. While some Berbers did join the Hilalian armies that swept west into Morocco, the Matmata tribe preserved its autonomy until the end of the seventeenth century. The Ottomans always had trouble collecting taxes in this area, and Mohammed Bey was forced to build forts at El Hamma to the north and Bir Soltane in the desert to the west in order to keep the Matmata under control. By the eighteenth century, however, these forts had been abandoned and military expeditions remained the only means of asserting government authority, sometimes with success, sometimes ending in humiliating failure. In 1869, for instance, General Osman led his army into the foothills only to be surprised at night and forced to flee, leaving behind his artillery and richly adorned tent.

Under the French, the Berbers maintained their own tribal court, called the *miad*, which settled questions according to Berber law. In common with all the villages in the south, Matmata was still ruled by a sheikh, or administrator of the community, answerable to a *khalifa* (deputy governor) and the *caid* (governor) at Gabès. The system continued until Independence, and the French officers of the Service des Affaires Indigènes, who supervised tax collection and public works, usually kept out of village affairs. Yet, although they enjoyed some autonomy, the government presence was still strong, as the fort on the outskirts of town – now an army base – testifies.

The rooms in these troglodyte dwellings have the advantage of a **natural temperature control**. In Iraq and Iran people escaped from the intense heat by building wind towers, a primitive kind of air conditioning which forced any breeze down into the living rooms. At Matmata however, this was unnecessary since, as at Bulla Regia, and at Gharian in Libya, the natural insulation of the earth was even more effective in providing cool temperatures during the summer and warmth in the winter, making the rooms comfortable at any time of year.

There are a number of ways to see a pit dwelling while still respecting the privacy of local residents. You can visit or stay in one of three **hotels** originally built as troglodyte homes. Or you can visit the **museum** behind the *Hôtel Sidi Driss* (daily except Sun 8–11am & 1–4pm; 2TD), where a group of local women have set up a display of furniture, utensils and wedding costumes in a former dwelling, with one room now given over to carpet making. The tour is a little bit cursory (most of the women do not speak much French, let alone English) and the exhibits are not really explained, but it's the architecture you've really come to see. Finally, you may be **invited** to visit someone's home. This will either be for money (it's best to agree a price beforehand – the going rate is around 5TD), or for the opportunity to sell you souvenirs. Kids generally wander round the village accosting tourists with invitations, but if no one approaches you, there are houses two to three kilometres along the Douz road and three to four kilometres along the Gabès road with signs outside inviting tourists to view them.

Practicalities

There are **no banks** in Matmata (the nearest are in Gabès and Mareth), but the **post office** (country hours) in the centre of town at the beginning of the Gabès road will change cash, as will the *Kouseila* hotel.

Accommodation

Three of Matmata's **hotels** (the *Sidi Driss*, *Marhala* and *Berbères*) are converted pit dwellings, consisting of several courtyards joined together by underground passages with excavated rooms. A fourth, the *Diar el Barbar*, is a massive – and utterly audacious – modern deluxe version of the same design.

HOTELS

Les Berbères, off the Douz road, near the centre of town ☎05/230024, ☏230097. A friendly hotel in a converted pit dwelling and often booked up by tour groups in summer, when it's best to phone ahead. ❷

Diar el Barbar ★★★★, 1.5km up the Douz road ☎05/230074, ☏230144. An amazing new hotel modelled on a pit dwelling but on a massive scale, incorporating traditional and modern features, with two underground levels of deluxe troglodyte rooms built around several huge courtyards, plus another storey of ordinary rooms on top. All the four-star trappings are here (at a pretty good price), with all rooms en suite, and with a/c and heating in case you are not satisfied with the natural variety. There's also a pool and a large terrace with a panoramic view of the mountains. ❹

Kouseila ★★★, on the Toujane road ☎05/230303, ☏230265. A conventional modern hotel with cool, comfortable a/c rooms. ❹

Marhala, off the Toujane road ☎05/230015, ☏230109. The most popular place in town, especially with tour groups who troop in to eat, but mostly return to Gabès in the evening, leaving it remarkably empty off-season when they've gone. ❸

Matmata ★★, off the Toujane road, just before the *Marhala* ☎05/230066, ☏230177. Spacious, spotless, a/c rooms, and a pool which non-residents can use for a small fee. ❸

Sidi Driss, off the Toujane road nearer the centre of town ☎05/230005, ☏230265. Slightly more basic than the other two pit dwellings, with each room crammed chock-full of beds, though that shouldn't matter off-season. The hotel was used as a location in the original *Star Wars* movie, and much of the set is still in place. ❷

Ksar Amazigh ★★★, 1km up the Douz road ☎05/230088, ☏230173. This is where most upmarket tour groups stay. Its bar, restaurant and "Moorish" café are very peaceful during the day as the groups are all out touring. ❹

Eating and drinking

Your best bet for **food** in Matmata is to try one of the hotels in town. The *Marhala* (daily 11.30am–3pm & 6.30–9pm), *Berbères* (daily 11am–3.30pm & 6–10pm) and *Sidi Driss* (daily 11am–3pm & 6–9pm) all do set menus of salad and couscous. The *Marhala* is the cheapest at 4.5TD, but at the *Sidi Driss*, still moderately priced, you get to eat in the courtyard where Luke Skywalker had dinner with his aunt and uncle in *Star Wars*. Alternatively, you can try the *Ouled Azaiz Café Restaurant* in the very centre of town (daily 8am–midnight), also with a reasonably priced set menu of 5TD. For **drinking**, the obvious place is the *Hôtel Sidi Driss*, the most convivial bar in town.

MOVING ON FROM MATMATA

For a rundown of destinations and journey times, see Travel Details on p.362.

Regular daily buses run to Gabès, one continuing to Jerba, and a summer-only SNTRI bus serves Tunis via Sousse and Sfax. There's also a lunch-time bus to Tamezret that returns three hours later (and an evening one too, but you wouldn't be able to get back), and two daily buses to Techine. Louages only serve Nouvelle Matmata, from where there are connections to Gabès. The road to Douz, 100km east, is now surfaced and easily motorable, but not served by any public transport as yet. The pipeline route to Ksar Ghilane (see p.414), which branches off 32km west of Matmata, is usually passable with care by car, though it is easy to get stuck in sand drifts, and always wise to take along somebody who knows the road. If you do attempt it, check on conditions locally before setting off, and always inform the National Guard of your plans and heed the advice on desert driving on p.415.

Tijma and Haddej

To get some idea of what Matmata must once have been like, it's worth backtracking to the less touristy village of **Haddej**. The Syndicat d'Initiative in Matmata may be able to arrange transport. Failing that, it's a question of walking or hitching 4km along the main road to **Tijma**, where you turn right for Haddej (signposted), about 3km up into the hills. There's a direct footpath between Matmata and Haddej, which you may enjoy if you like hiking (but don't forget precautions against heatstroke and dehydration): follow the Gabès road to the edge of town then take a path to the right just after a café-souvenir shop, following the most trodden route at every junction thereafter. One problem on this path is fierce dogs, especially likely to take umbrage if you stray into someone's garden.

Tijma and jessour terraces   تجمة

The **House of Fatima** in the tiny settlement of **TIJMA**, about 4km north of Matmata, has long been owned by a woman of that name, and presents itself as a typical pit dwelling. Due not least to its unusually sanitized condition, this house is now on the tourist route and the current Fatima, plus daughter, receive the hordes with much aplomb. A bedroom, with its *dukkana* (a sort of bench used as a bed), and a kitchen, with pots and postcards for sale, are both open to view.

Walking through the valleys from Tijma towards Haddej, the luxuriance of the olive, almond and fig trees contrasts with the barrenness of the slopes. The trees flourish on hidden reservoirs of water stored in the thick soil of terraces called **jessour**, made by building stone barriers to hold the soil. Every last drop from the winter downpours on the mountains is channelled into these terraces by shallow ditches and walls and contained for the long dry summer, helping olive and fig trees thrive in the inhospitable desert environment. The *jessour* also protect the plain down below from flooding, but the work involved in building and maintaining them is formidable. Huge quantities of earth need to be piled up behind dry stone walls built across the valley floors, so it's hardly surprising that they're no longer built or even repaired. Most of the local men work in the cities and agriculture has been neglected, with the result that the region's terraces, its agricultural capital, are literally being washed away. Recently however, around the village of Douiret near Tataouine (see p.413), a project has been started to restore the *jessour*, with older people teaching the necessary skills to the young. But whether the project at Douiret marks a trend that will spread to the Matmata region remains uncertain.

Haddej   الهدّاج

Three kilometres northeast of Tijma, **HADDEJ** was formerly the region's most important village and home of the *khalifa*. A primary school among the palm trees marks the centre of town, and the **pit dwellings** lie up ahead. As soon as you arrive, the village children will surround you, asking for pens and offering to show you around (for a little baksheesh, naturally). It's a good idea to take up their offer as the buildings are even better concealed than those at Matmata, and the kids will probably follow you in any case. Many of the pits were abandoned after floods in 1969, when the water covered the courtyards for a week, but an underground **grain store** at the top of the slope is in remarkably good condition. Two tiers of interlocking, arched storerooms have been built into a rock, like the *ghorfas* which dominate the landscape further south.

On the left-hand side of the path leading to the pit dwellings is an **olive press**, one of several in the village, and also subterranean. At the centre of a small domed chamber is a circular stone, connected by a wooden shaft to the ceiling; a stone roller fixed to an axle is pulled around this shaft, crushing the olives spread out on the slab. The skins are taken from the stone and pressed again by a heavy palm trunk fastened at one end to the wall. Oil runs through a series of esparto grass mats into a jar, and the underground location provides the warmth in winter that's needed to separate the waste, which is fed to camels. In a final room, the olives are fermented to give the oil the musty flavour the people of the south appreciate.

Nearby is an underground **marabout** occupied only by its custodian. Another pit house, to the left of the olive press, was used for the village's **marriage ceremonies**. Seven days before the wedding, the bride's family would go into the large underground room to prepare the feast. On the wedding day the bride was brought here on a camel and taken into a small room, reached by the steps leading up from the basement (take a light if you visit). The husband, who was staying in a cell further inside the rock, went through to see the bride and to sign the marriage contract. Taking a back staircase up to ground level, he was led round to the front door to be formally received. When the feast was over, bride and groom would be taken into a cave room at the far end of the house, to remain in conjugal seclusion for several days. Meanwhile, the celebrations went on outside with a company of African comics, jesters and dancers.

Beni Aissa بني عيسى

Neither easy to find nor to get to (there's just one daily minibus from Nouvelle Matmata), **BENI AISSA** is a lovely little village where the people live in the same underground dwellings as in Matmata. About 1.5km west of Matmata, an unpaved road leads off to the right. Some 4.5km along here is another turn-off (left) that takes you after a couple of kilometres to the village. A car will cover the route with no difficulty.

Look out for the group of **marabouts** 100m or so beyond the school, bus stop, shop and postbox that mark Beni Aissa's centre. Beni Aissa is a far cry from tourist-driven Matmata, and people here are not used to curiosity-seekers coming to look at their homes, and may not take kindly to sightseers peering over the edges into their pits. On the other hand, you won't have hordes of kids following you about, nor encounter any tour groups, so a visit here will be quite a different kind of experience, and a rewarding one, so long as you respect the privacy of local residents.

West of Matmata

The main road west from Matmata to Douz skirts the edge of a valley cultivated using the *jessour* system (see opposite). About halfway between Matmata and Tamezret, set 1km back from the road to the right, is the village of **SIDI META**. The first you see of it is a white *koubba* high up on the hillside, all that remains of the old village. At some time in the last two centuries the villagers moved down into the valley below, where, as at Matmata, they dug houses into the soft soil. Like Beni Aissa, Sidi Meta is rarely visited by tourists, and the people, as a result, are very accommodating. There's an **oil press** and an **underground mosque** that are worth seeing, and the village also has a shop where you can buy bottled drinks.

TAMEZRET, built above ground, is packed around several steep slopes, topped by a mosque. One path between the tumbledown houses will take you to the **café** at the summit, where you can get a cup of green tea with almonds and climb onto the roof to see the village of Zeraoua in the distance. There are also some interesting oil presses (*massera*), both ancient and twentieth-century, if you can get somebody to show them to you. Tamezret – and the villages around – is known for its **woollen shawls**, the ceremonial *bakhnoughs*, with striking geometric designs identical to the facial tattoos sometimes seen on older women. The shawls, along with traditional tools, cooking utensils, carpets and costumes, can be seen at the **Berber Museum** (irregular hours; free, but donations appreciated), run by the enthusiastic but knowledgeable Mongi Barras. The museum is a little below the mosque, and also has a recreation of a traditional marriage room, an ancient cave dwelling and a seventh-century Berber home. When wandering around town, be sensitive to the privacy of local residents, especially if you have a camera. Getting to Tamezret may be a problem, however, as there is only one practicable bus that runs the 10km from Matmata, and cars are few and far between.

From Tamezret, there are roads to the villages of **TAOUJOU** and **ZERAOUA**. Both are walkable – 4km and 7km respectively, though the paths are not always easy to follow – but, like Tamezret, neither has accommodation (although someone may take pity on you and put you up). The views across the plateau and into the desert are stupendous, as are the villages – tightly knit communities living in compacted houses that look like a continuous wall from a distance. West of Tamezret, the road, now surfaced, continues across the desert to Douz (see p.332).

Southeast of Matmata

An alternative route from Matmata, heading east out of town past the *kala'a*, leads to Metameur (55km) and Medenine (60km) by way of Toujane. The road from Matmata to Toujane is surfaced, though not well, for part of the way, and can easily be passed, but from Toujane to Metameur it's not surfaced at all, and the state of the piste means slow progress in any car without 4WD. There are no bus or louage services along this route, and it is not a very good prospect for hitching. Most traffic prefers the easier approach to Toujane from Mareth on the Gabès–Medenine road (see opposite), and there's a surfaced road from Nouvelle Matmata too.

The direct road begins to flatten out about 3km out of Matmata, revealing the **Marabout of Sidi Moussa** on a peak to the left. In the early summer this is the scene of an ancient *ziarad*, a tribal pilgrimage attended by thousands of villagers from Matmata, and on the rocks around the tomb you can see the bloodstains from animal sacrifices. Some 8km further along, just off the road, is the village of **TECHINE**, known for its furniture, made from branches covered with clay, plaster and whitewash. It also has a traditional olive press, worked by a donkey, and is served by two daily buses from Gabès and Matmata.

A further, and unsurfaced, 4km on – 15km from Matmata – a turn-off on the other side of the road winds for 8km down an incredibly steep gorge and out onto the plains to reach **BENI ZELTEN**, perched – like Tamezret – on the top of a small hill. Here though, the hilltop village has been deserted in favour of underground dwellings and houses on the valley floor. Nevertheless, it remains a remarkable site, and one that's unknown to most visitors. The road beyond the village continues to Nouvelle Matmata.

Toujane
توجان

Ignoring these detours and continuing along the steadily deteriorating Medenine road, you cross a series of deep gorges and then pass along the escarpment with spectacular views of the plains below. Suddenly the road drops again, this time giving a bird's-eye view of **TOUJANE**, 23km from Gabès. The old town – not to be confused with Nouvelle Toujane (or Dekhila) down below – is one of the most dramatic of the Matmata region villages, spreading across two sides of a deep gorge and built around the foot of a mountain, from whose heights rear two brooding *kala'a* (fortresses). Great views are to be had from the roads coming into Toujane, particularly the one from Mareth, which commands a spectacular panorama of the coastal plain as far as the sea, and a lovely tableau of Toujane itself just before the descent into the village. The direct Matmata road, and the village itself, also offer fine views. The local green tea, made with mountain herbs rather than just mint, is quite refreshing and worth a try.

Once isolated and untouched, Toujane is now sufficiently on the beaten track for five **auberges** to have sprung up, each of which will put you up, and sell such items as locally made carpets, olive oil, and thyme and rosemary honey. None has hot running water or full bathroom facilities, though hot water to wash with can be arranged. The first, and the only officially sanctioned auberge, is *Auberge Hasnawi* at the Matmata end of town (☎05/647955, ☎275730; **❷**), a friendly place in an original troglodyte home where you sleep in cave rooms, basic but nicely done out, and it offers an oil press, a café, and guided walks into the mountains. Spread along the main road towards Mareth, are: *Auberge Troglodyte Dar el Berbère* (☎05/640114; **❶**), the cheapest, with very basic cave accommodation; *Auberge Hamroun* (☎05/640199; **❷**), with rooms in the proprietor's house, but pukka troglodyte-style accommodation being hewn into the rock next to his shop in the near future; *Auberge Shambhala* (no phone; **❷**), with three basic but clean rooms in a former home, consisting of caves at the back extended by building at the front. Finally, at the Mareth end of town, *Dar Touati* (no phone; **❷**) is really a shop, but you can stay with the proprietor's family just up the hill, a bit of a climb, but rewarded with great views.

One bus a day serves Toujane from Gabès and Mareth; otherwise, there are shared yellow cabs from Mareth, which function like louages with four passengers.

Mareth and around مارث

Midway between Gabès and Medenine, **MARETH** has long suffered from its important strategic position, commanding the narrow coastal plain between the Gulf of Gabès and the mountains. In 1936, the French army built a **defensive line** here to withstand a possible attack by the Italians in Libya. The line was first taken by Rommel and, in 1943, it blocked the Allied advance from the east; in the ensuing battle and Allied capture, the line and Mareth itself were virtually destroyed.

Apart from the busy Wednesday **market**, the new town is not wildly interesting, but if you're **staying** the options are the *Hôtel el Iman* (☎ & ☎05/321035; **❷**), on the east side of the main road, just past the louage station, or the cheaper *Hôtel du Golfe* (☎05/236135; **❶**), 100m south on the other side of the main road, which is basic but very friendly. Both hotels have cafés. For changing money, there are also two **banks** in town.

Leaving Mareth, there are **buses** north to Gabès and south to Medenine or Houmt Souk. Further afield, there are buses to Tunis, Sfax, Sousse and Kairouan. Other services reach Tataouine, Zarzis, Ben Gardane and Ras Ajdir. More locally, there are six daily buses to Zarat and one to Toujane. **Louages** go to Gabès and Medenine, but not usually to Houmt Souk. However, it is not difficult to hitch to Jorf, from where you can pick up the ferry to Jerba (see p.366). **Shared yellow taxis** leave from next to the louage station; destinations include Toujane, Zarat and Azaiza.

Zarat

A kilometre north of Mareth, a road branches off east to the town of **ZARAT**. It's a bit of a windblown, dead-end place, but 2km beyond it is a **beach**, marked by a line of roofless white beach huts. Though not the nicest in Tunisia – the sand is hard and the shoreline covered in black seaweed – you won't see another tourist here. Zarat town is connected to Mareth by six daily buses (all continuing to Gabès) and shared yellow cabs.

The Mareth Line

Three kilometres south of Mareth, just before the Jorf turn-off, the main road crosses **Oued Zigazou** on a zigzag bend. It's a seasonal river, dry most of the year, with the main emplacements of the Mareth Line spread out along it. On the *oued*'s north bank is the **Military Museum of the Mareth Line**, run by the Ministry of Defence (Tues–Sun 9am–4pm; 1TD, camera 2TD). Exhibits include maps and reconstructions illustrating Tunisia's role in World War II and the Battle of Mareth (see above), as well as various small arms, and a French gun emplacement that looks remarkably like a dalek from *Dr Who*; the ticket includes a guided tour in English. Outside the museum are **concrete bunkers** that were actually part of the Mareth Line. These have been dug out – they were previously half-buried – and you can go inside them.

Should you wish to see **Rommel's command post** (same hours as the museum, though it may be left open at other times), as illustrated in the museum, it has also been tidied up by the army and is open to the public. To get there, take the Toujane road from Mareth – west off the main road between the two hotels – for 5km to the village of LAZAIZA, just beyond which there's a track to the right that seems to head for an upright rectangle on top of a hill, which is in fact a seismograph. Follow the track for 2km, round the back of the hill with the seismograph, and you will see the command post. The left-hand of the two entrances leads into the sleeping quarters, but you'll need a light of some kind in order to see anything. At the top of the hill by the seismograph are the remains of **trenches**, and a stunning view over the whole plain, which illustrates very clearly indeed how strategic the position was. Rommel set up his HQ here following orders from the Axis high command to strengthen the Mareth Line after their October 1942 defeat at the battle of El Alamein. Fortifications were built up along Oued Zigazou, and the post was chosen for its commanding view over the plain and the whole of the Mareth Line. It was the road to Toujane, then just a path, that allowed Montgomery's eighth army to outflank the German lines by advancing during a single night.

travel details

Trains

Gabès to: Bir Bou Regba (3 daily; 5hr 40min – 1 connecting for Hammamet & Nabeul); El Jem (3 daily; 3hr 40min); Mahrès (3 daily; 1hr 30min); Sfax (3 daily; 2hr 25min); Sousse (3 daily; 4hr 40min); Tunis (3 daily; 6hr 30min).

Buses

Gabès to: Ben Gardane (5 daily; 2hr 15min); Bizerte (2 daily; 8hr); Douz (4 daily; 2hr 30min); Gafsa (3 daily; 2hr 30min); Ghoumrassen (1 daily; 2hr 15min); El Hamma (14 daily; 40min); Jerba (10 daily; 2hr 30min); Kairouan (7 daily; 4hr); Kasserine (4 daily; 4hr); Kebili (7 daily; 2hr); Nefta (1 daily; 4hr); Mareth (roughly hourly; 40min); Matmata (8 daily; 1hr); Medenine (13 daily; 1hr 15min); Ras Ajdir (3 daily; 3hr); Sfax (18 daily; 2hr–2hr 30min); Sidi Bou Zid (3 daily; 3hr 30min); Sousse (13 daily; 4hr 30min); Tamezret (2 daily; 1hr 20min); Tataouine (6 daily; 2hr 15min); Techine (2 daily; 1hr 40min); Toujane (1 daily; 1hr 20min); Tozeur (1 daily; 3hr 30min); Tripoli (3 weekly; 9hr 30min); Tunis (18 daily; 6hr 30min); Zarat (6 daily; 1hr); Zarzis (5 daily; 2hr 30min).

Matmata to: Gabès (8 daily; 1hr); Jerba (1 daily; 4hr); Tamezret (2 daily; 20min); Techine (2 daily; 30min); Tunis (1 daily summer only; 7hr 30min), via Sousse (5hr 30min) and Sfax (3hr).

Mareth to: Ben Gardane (5 daily; 1hr 40min); Bizerte (2 daily; 8hr 30min); Gabès (roughly hourly; 40min); Jerba (10 daily; 2hr); Medenine (13 daily; 40min); Kairouan (5 daily; 4hr 30min); Ras Ajdir (3 daily; 2hr 30min); Sfax (8 daily; 3hr), Sousse (8 daily; 4hr); Tataouine (6 daily; 1hr 40min); Toujane (1 daily; 40min); Tunis (11 daily; 7hr); Zarat (6 daily; 20min); Zarzis (5 daily; 2hr).

Louages

Louage journey times are roughly three-quarters the time taken by buses on the same route. Frequency depends on demand, but morning is always the best time to get a louage, especially for longer journeys.

Gabès to: Ben Gardane (2hr 30min); El Hamma (30min); Gafsa (2hr); Jerba (2hr); Kairouan (3hr 30min); Kebili (1hr 30min); Mareth (30min); Medenine (1hr); Nouvelle Matmata (25min); Sfax (2hr); Sousse (4hr); Tataouine (1hr 45min); Tripoli (7hr); Tunis (6hr 30min); Zarat (30min); Zarzis (2hr 30min).

Mareth to: Gabès (30min); Medenine (30min). Shared taxis to: Azaiza (10min); Toujane (30min); Zarat (10min).

Nouvelle Matmata to: Gabès (25min); Matmata (10min).

CHAPTER EIGHT

JERBA AND THE SOUTHEAST COAST

The island of **Jerba**, joined to the mainland by a causeway since before Roman times, perches at the southern end of the Gulf of Gabès, enclosing the smaller **Gulf of Bou Grara** between island and mainland. Eastwards, the coast dips past the modern town of **Zarzis** and the Bahiret el Biban lagoon before disappearing over the border into Libya.

This sun-soaked corner of Tunisia boasts some of the finest **beaches** in the Mediterranean, arguably *the* finest. Unfortunately, the best of these, in Jerba's north-eastern corner – from **Sidi Mahares** round to **Aghir** – have largely been swamped in recent years by large-scale package tourist developments, and beach hotels are beginning to spread, too, along the mainland coast around Zarzis. In midsummer it's probably a good idea to seek nirvana elsewhere.

However, there are deserted beaches if you have the means to get to them. On the **west coast** of Jerba and **southeast of Zarzis** are strands where you won't see another tourist, and not many Tunisians either. These tend not to be the best beaches, and you should, in any case, check with the local police or National Guard before heading to potentially sensitive areas close to the Libyan border.

Jerban society is quite distinct in many ways from that of mainland Tunisia. Its population forms a patchwork of different **ethnic and religious groups** – Arabs, Berbers and black Africans, Muslims (both Ibadite and Sunni) and Jews – who all differ slightly in their traditions, style of dress, the names they bear and the way they speak. However, all of them share a common Jerban identity: their traditions differ from those of the mainland as much as from each other. One overriding Jerban trait is the business acumen of its people – especially the Ibadites and Jews – and over the centuries this has been of lasting importance to Jerba. Jerban identity is always a problematic idea, as Jerba is not really an island of towns and villages, but of individual homes. The only apparent villages are the two Jewish "ghettos" of Hara Sghira and Hara Kebira. The island's capital **Houmt Souk**, once just a marketplace, only became a town in the twentieth century. Today, however, with the present **tourist influx**, it seems no exaggeration to talk of a **crisis** in Jerba's identity. Nowhere in Tunisia is there such an obvious and direct clash between a still very traditional society and the demands of foreign culture. Services have become strained, prices inflated, and local culture and agriculture

---

MARKET DAYS

Monday – Houmt Souk, Zarzis
Tuesday – Sedghiane, Sedouikech
Wednesday – Guellala, Mouansa
Thursday – Houmt Souk

Friday – Midoun, Mellita, Zarzis
Saturday – Ben Gardane, El May, Souihel
Sunday – Ajim, Hara Sghira, Sidi Chammakh

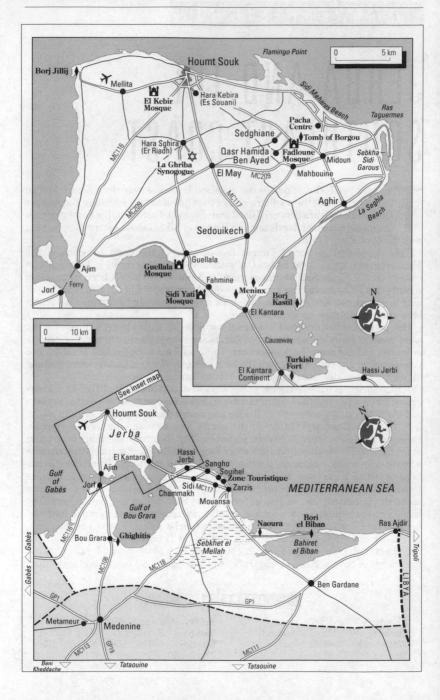

ACCOMMODATION PRICE CODES

The hotels and pensions listed in this book have been price-graded according to the following scale. The prices quoted are for the cheapest available double room in high season. For more on accommodation prices and categories, see Basics, p.29.

❶ Under 10TD
❷ 10–20TD
❸ 20–40TD
❹ 40–70TD

❺ 70–100TD
❻ 100–150TD
❼ 150TD upwards

increasingly ignored. People whose parents worked the land are no longer interested in breaking their backs when easier work and more money is to be had in the tourist industry and its related services. Meanwhile, the demand on water is beginning to threaten the island's drinking water supplies as salinity creeps into the water table, which will also make agriculture more difficult.

Even more serious a threat to the Jerban way of life is **emigration**, with traditional communities disrupted by the departure of Jews to Israel and of young men off to seek their fortunes elsewhere, usually by opening corner shops (known in Tunisia simply as "Jerbans"). People from the island now work as grocers all over Tunisia, and there are Jerban communities throughout Europe and as far away as Brazil.

JERBA   جربة

On the tenth [day] we made the country of the Lotus-Eaters, a race that live on vegetable foods . . . I sent some of my followers inland to find out what sort of human beings might be there, detailing two men for the duty with a third as messenger. Off they went, and it was not long before they were in touch with the Lotus-Eaters. Now it never entered the heads of these natives to kill my friends: what they did was to give them some lotus to taste, and as soon as each had eaten the honeyed fruit of the plant, all thoughts of reporting to us or escaping were banished from his mind. All they now wished for was to stay where they were with the Lotus-Eaters, to browse on the lotus and to forget that they had a home to return to. I had to use force to bring them back to the ships, and they wept on the way, but once on board I dragged them under the benches and left them in irons. I then commanded the rest of my loyal band to embark with all speed on their fast ships, for fear that others of them might eat the lotus and think no more of home. They came on board at once, went to the benches, sat down in their proper places, and struck the white surf with their oars. So we left that country and sailed on sick at heart.

Homer, *The Odyssey* (Book IX)

Jerba, like Gozo and Menorca, claims to be the legendary land of the **Lotus-Eaters** and – low-lying, semi-desert island that it is – it makes good territory for such myth and fantasy. The coast consists largely of beautiful sandy beaches while, inland, unique mosques and houses are scattered among palm groves. Its history and culture are to some extent different from those of the mainland; its architecture is quite distinctive, its ethnic background more diverse. Unfortunately, its seductive packageable charms and easy access through an international airport have brought **tourism** on a big scale. Dozens of hotels line the northern coast, which the government has declared a *zone touristique*, and many of the people who come to stay here see the island as nothing more than a beach in the sun. And indeed Jerba is an excellent **beach resort**: the palm-rustled strands themselves are wonderful, the sea warm and limpid, the mood relaxed and the general scene idyllic. Moreover, the hotels here are some of the country's best and more than adequate by any standard. If all you want is sun and sand, it's just the place to come; on the other hand, if that is all you want, you're missing out.

The island's intimate, farm-divided **interior** exudes a certain magic you won't find anywhere else, a district of country lanes through date and olive groves, with the sea never far away. The beautiful whitewashed, fortified mosques are unique in Tunisia and the island also boasts three historic forts and scattered Roman remains, so far unexcavated. It's a big enough area (around 25km by 22km) to explore, but small enough to do so by bicycle.

Getting to Jerba

Jerba's **airport** is at Mellita (℡05/650233), 6km from Houmt Souk and 12km from the heart of the hotel strip at Sidi Mahares. There is only one daily bus into Houmt Souk, so if you don't have transport laid on by a hotel, and if the bus fails to connect with your arrival, you'll have to take a metered taxi to Houmt Souk (3–5TD) or to the *zone touristique* (6–15TD). Avis, Budget, Hertz, Europcar and Ada all have **car rental** desks at the airport (℡05/650233). Jerba has reasonably inexpensive **flights** with Tuninter to Tunis, as well as international scheduled and charter flights to western Europe.

By road, Jerba can be reached easily enough from the south or north. From the south, most **buses** take you straight through to Houmt Souk, via Zarzis and the causeway. Coming from Gabès and the north, it's faster to use the Jorf–Ajim **ferry**, although one or two buses still go the long way round via Medenine and Zarzis.

For **travelling around** the island, **taxis** are probably your best bet. These are more expensive than buses, but metered and still very reasonable. You may also be able to share with someone and cut costs. **Bicycles, scooters and mopeds** can all be rented easily in both Houmt Souk and the *zone touristique*, where you can also rent **motorbikes**. Failing that, **hitching** is very easy in Jerba, and, depending on the heat, even **walking** is not out of the question for getting around parts of the northwest of the island. If you are **driving**, note that Jerba has a speed limit of 70km/hr, rarely obeyed but sometimes enforced. Jerbans seem to know where the police are waiting to pounce, and tourists are better off keeping within the limit.

Some history

The **Carthaginians** who first settled on Jerba called it Meninx – "land of the receding waters", a reference to the highest tides anywhere in the Mediterranean. With its virtually landlocked gulf, it was an ideal haven for any sheltering fleet, and quickly gained a reputation for trade and commerce. The **Romans** built an extensive city on the southern shores, exporting cloth (dyed imperial purple with the murex shellfish) throughout the Empire.

Under the **Arabs**, Jerba was a centre of almost permanent revolt as it constantly struggled to assert its independence from its overlords. The island strongly supported the **Kharijite rebellion** (see p.431) in 740 and, when the Aghlabids retook the north of Tunisia, Jerba became part of the Rustamids' Kharijite state (based at Tahirt in Algeria), and the island is still one of Kharijism's last strongholds. Later, Jerba supported **Abu Yazid**'s 944 Kharijite rebellion against the **Fatimids**, and also rose unsuccessfully against their successors, the **Zirids** in 1047. In the centuries prior to French domination, it remained a hotbed of defiance, never at peace for long.

JERBA'S TAP WATER

Jerba's tap water is slightly saline and, due to the island's high water table, not as safe to drink as in the rest of the country. You won't catch anything serious, but those with delicate digestive systems should stick to bottled water.

From the twelfth century, Jerba came under serious threat from the Christian kingdoms, especially whichever one had control of Sicily, just across the water. Like Sicily, Jerba was the object of Muslim–Christian rivalry due to its strategic position. In 1135, Sicily's Norman king **Roger II** invaded Jerba, massacring or enslaving much of the population. The island resisted with little success, and remained in Christian hands until retaken by the Almohads in 1159. In 1284, Jerba again suffered a bout of brutal Christian rule under **Roger de Lluria** of Aragon. When the island rose up in 1310, Aragonese troops under **Ramon de Muntaner** murdered or enslaved three-quarters of the island's population and strangled its economy with punitive taxes. In 1333, rebellion by Muslims throughout Aragon's territories in Sicily and North Africa freed Jerba once more, but when the Hafsids attempted to impose their authority on the island, its residents made repeated attempts to regain their autonomy, and for much of the fifteenth century, under the **El Samumni** family, it was virtually independent. The Christians tried to retake it several times, but local resistance rebutted them. During this period, there was also an internal struggle for political and religious domination of the island by two parties representing different strains of Kharijism, the Wahabites and the Nakkarites, the former eventually predominating.

Piratical **merchant-sailors** wrought havoc in Jerba in the sixteenth century. The corsair Aruj **Barbarossa** made his base here in 1510, as did his protégé **Dragut** in 1535. Trapped with his fleet by the flotilla of Charles V of Spain in 1551, Dragut made a famous and daring **naval getaway** (see p.377) from the island. Later putting himself at the disposal of the Turks, he returned with an **Ottoman** fleet to set up shop in 1560, and completely trounced the coalition of European forces under Philip II of Spain that attempted to drive him out.

Under the Ottomans, Jerba became a centre of silk and wool production and its economy thrived. It was also a major terminal for trans-Saharan goods until its main commodity, African **slaves**, was banned in 1846. European merchants preferred to trade here rather than with the unpredictable mainland – if there was an uprising on the mainland, business could go on as usual on the island. This is just what happened in 1881: the islanders, fearing that Jerba would be occupied and sacked by the rebellious tribes on the mainland, welcomed the **French** invaders, gaining for themselves the lasting gratitude of the conquerors.

Houmt Souk

حومة السّوق

Although **HOUMT SOUK** is becoming increasingly commercialized, the Association de Sauvegarde de l'Île de Djerba (ASSIDJE) has made great efforts to preserve its distinctive architecture over the last decade. The island's capital and its one real town, Houmt Souk (meaning "marketplace" – it was originally the site of the island's market, with everything built outwards from the souk) remains a lively and interesting place and, at only 1500m from end to end, a very easy one to find your way around.

Arrival, information and accommodation

If you're not arriving by plane (see opposite), Houmt Souk's **bus station**, run by SRTG Medenine, is in avenue Bourguiba just south of the town centre, with the **louage station** opposite. The ONTT **tourist office** (Sept–June Mon–Thurs 8.30am–1pm & 3–5.45pm, Fri & Sat 8.30am–1pm, July & Aug Mon–Sat 7.30am–1.30pm & 5–7pm; ☏05/650016) is on boulevard de l'Environnement, the coast road to Sidi Mahares, and there's a **Syndicat d'Initiative** (Mon–Thurs 8am–noon & 3–6pm, Fri & Sat 8am–noon; ☏05/650915), on avenue Bourguiba, opposite place Mongi Bali. Most services and

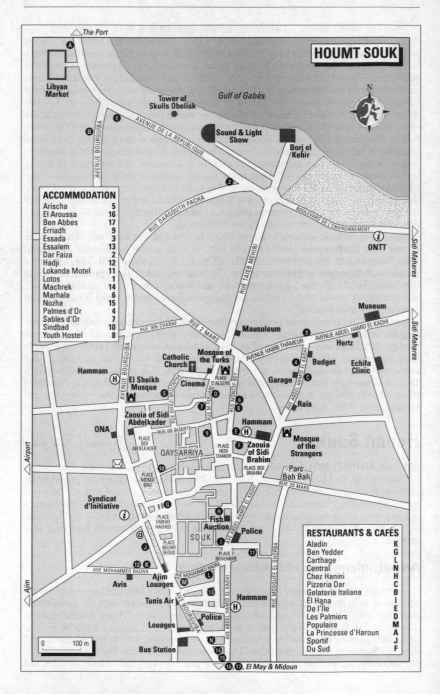

HOUMT SOUK

The Port

Libyan Market

Tower of Skulls Obelisk

Gulf of Gabès

Sound & Light Show

Borj el Kebir

AVENUE DE LA REPUBLIQUE

AVENUE BOURGUIBA

ACCOMMODATION

Arischa	5
El Aroussa	16
Ben Abbes	17
Erriadh	9
Essada	3
Essalem	13
Dar Faiza	2
Hadji	12
Lokanda Motel	11
Lotos	1
Machrek	14
Marhala	6
Nozha	15
Palmes d'Or	4
Sables d'Or	7
Sindbad	10
Youth Hostel	8

RUE DARGOUTH PACHA

BOULEVARD DE L'ENVIRONNEMENT

ONTT

Sidi Mahares

Sidi Mahares

RUE TALEB MEHIRI

RUE IBN CHARAF

RUE 2 MARS

Mausoleum

Museum

AVENUE ABDEL HAMID EL KADHI

Hertz

AVENUE HABIB THAMEUR

Hammam

Catholic Church

Mosque of the Turks

El Sheikh Mosque

Cinema

PLACE D'ALGERIE

Budget

Echifa Clinic

Garage

Raïs

AVE ABDEL HAMID EL KADHI

RUE GHAZI MUSTAPHA

RUE M FERJANI

RUE MONCEF BEY

Zaouia of Sidi Abdelkader

ONA

RUE DE BIZERTE

Hammam

PLACE SIDI ABDELKADER

QAYSARRIYA

PLACE HEDI CHAKER

Zaouia of Sidi Brahim

Mosque of the Strangers

PLACE SIDI BRAHIM

Parc Bah Bah

PLACE MONGI BALI

RUE 20 MARS

Syndicat d'Initiative

PLACE FARHAT HACHED

Fish Auction

Police

PLACE BECHIR SEOUD

SOUK

PLACE 7 NOVEMBRE

AVE ABDEL HAMID EL KADHI

RUE MOSQUEE EL GHORBA

RESTAURANTS & CAFÉS

Aladin	K
Ben Yedder	G
Carthage	L
Central	N
Chez Hanini	H
Pizzeria Dar	C
Gelateria Italiana	B
El Hana	I
De l'Île	E
Les Palmiers	D
Populaire	M
La Princesse d'Haroun	A
Sportif	J
Du Sud	F

AVE MOHAMMED BADRA

Ajim Louages

Avis

AVE MOHAMMED BADRA

Tunis Air

Hammam

AVE BOURGUIBA

Louages

Police

Bus Station

El May & Midoun

0   100 m

Airport

Ajim

shops are on the two main north–south roads, **avenue Bourguiba** to the west and **avenue Abdel Hamid el Kadhi** to the east.

Unless you want to stay by the beach at Sidi Mahares or Aghir, you'll probably end up in one of Houmt Souk's **hotels**. Five of these (including the town's youth hostel) are old converted **fondouks** or *caravanserais*, once offering food and shelter to itinerant merchants and pilgrims. They share a common plan, with a large open courtyard surrounded by arches or colonnades. At the centre, camel trains would be tethered by the well, their goods securely stored on the ground floor. If you're **camping**, Jerba's only two campsites are at Aghir, or you can camp wild at Flamingo Point, Ras Taguermes or on the west coast.

Fondouk hotels

Arischa, 36 rue Ghazi Mustapha, near the catholic church ☏05/650384. The most attractive of the *fondouks*, with vines in the courtyard, a shallow pool of naturally warm spring water, and a nice roof terrace; some rooms have private bathrooms. ❷

Erriadh ★, 10 rue Mohamed Ferjani, off pl Hedi Chaker ☏05/650756, ⓕ650487. Nice, clean rooms with bathrooms, some a/c, others with a ceiling fan, but windows open only onto the central patio. The most expensive of the *fondouks*. ❸

Marhala, 13 rue Moncef Bey ☏05/650416, ⓕ653317. Next door to the youth hostel, and run, like its namesakes in Nefta and Matmata, by the Touring Club of Tunisia. Pleasant basic rooms, some en suite, and the best bar in town. ❸

Sindbad, pl Mongi Bsali ☏05/650047, ⓕ652602. No singles, so you pay for a double if you're on your own. Not as nice as the other *fondouks*, though all rooms have showers. ❷

Other hotels

El Aroussa, av Bourguiba ☏05/650788. A quiet place with a car park, down towards the hospital; a lot of the clientele are holidaymakers from other Arab countries. ❷

Ben Abbes, 158 av Bourguiba ☏05/650128. Out towards the hospital. Clean, modern and quite pleasant self-catering apartments, each with their own kitchen. ❸

Dar Faiza ★, rue de la République ☏05/650083, ⓕ651763. Up near the Borj. A charming and well-run place with en-suite rooms, some a/c, a small pool, family atmosphere and customers who come back year after year. Advance reservation is a good idea, especially in season. ❹

Essada, 6 av Habib Thameur ☏05/651422, ⓕ652520. Cool and quiet, with medium-sized en-suite rooms, all a/c, some with balcony, and a games room with pool tables. ❸

Essalem, rue de Remeda, off pl 7 Novembre ☏ & ☏05/651029. A reasonably comfortable place, tucked away in the backstreets of the town centre; bathroom facilities are shared. ❷

Hadji ★, 44 av Mohamed Badra ☏05/650630, ⓕ652219. Large a/c rooms, some with shower, some with bath; could do with a lick of paint. ❸

Lokanda Motel, passage de la Municipalité ☏05/651513. Not the best hotel in town, but the cheapest, and the rooms and toilets are clean, though there's no hot water. ❶

Lotos, 18 rue de la République ☏05/650026, ⓕ651127. A friendly pension with large, clean, en-suite rooms, associated with the nearby and slightly dearer *Hôtel Dar Faiza*, whose pool and tennis courts are open to *Lotos* guests. ❸

Machrek ★★, av Bourguiba ☏05/653155 or 6, ⓕ653157, ✉arouay.groups@planet.tn. The best hotel in town, with comfortable rooms, a/c and attached bathrooms throughout. There are balconies in some rooms. ❹

Nozha ★, 150 av Bourguiba ☏05/650381, ⓕ620758. Out by the hospital. Friendly, if a little shabby, but all the rooms have balcony, bathroom, a/c and satellite TV. ❸

Les Palmes d'Or ★★, 84 av Abdel Hamid el Kadhi ☏05/653369 or 70, ⓕ653368, ✉palmes.dor @gnet.tn. A cool, clean, quiet place with smallish but pleasant rooms, most with balcony and all with private bathroom, a/c and satellite TV, but a bit pricey. ❹

Hôtel des Sables d'Or, 30 rue Mohamed Ferjani ☏05/650423. Not a *fondouk* but an old palatial house built around a central patio, with immaculate rooms, private showers and shared toilets. ❸

Youth hostel

HI Youth Hostel, 11 rue Moncef Bey, off pl Hedi Chaker ☎ & ☎05/650619. Perhaps a little too basic for some (the bathrooms especially), but very friendly, with double rooms and a distinct lack of rules and regulations, though, in principle at least, there's a midnight curfew. ②

The Town

With a history as stormy and an identity as strong as Jerba's, it is hardly surprising that its capital is full of interest. Houmt Souk's nooks and crannies are gradually being pedestrianized, and its cottage industries are giving way to shops and restaurants that aren't patronized by Jerbans. But in spite of this onslaught, it still has loads of charm and remains one of the country's most pleasant towns. While you can't, unfortunately, enter any of the mosques or *zaouias*, the **fort and museum** are open to the public, and both are worth investigation.

The souk and around

At the very centre of the town is its **souk**, with two *qaysarriya*, arched and covered passageways to the north of place Mongi Bali, where traditionally the most expensive goods were sold, such as prized Egyptian cloth and filigree silver. Coral and jewellery are now the market's pricey mainstays; the leather goods are often pretty shoddy. Be ruthless when you barter – it's often not unreasonable to make an initial offer of a tenth of the quoted price. In the less-tourist-oriented part of the souk, the daily **fish auction** is interesting to visit. Mondays and Thursdays are the souk's busiest days, with traders coming in from around the island. The market is then full of people selling straw baskets and mats, along with musicians from Midoun (see p.379) playing and selling their instruments.

To the east of the *qaysarriya*, in the north-east corner of place Sidi Abdelkader, is the **Zaouia of Sidi Abdelkader**, home of the Association de Sauvegarde de l'Île de Djerba (ASSIDJE), who have restored its pretty, tiled courtyard. Mornings are the best time to pop in for a look, when the sun shines right into it. West of the *qaysarriya*, the **Zaouia of Sidi Brahim**, with its heavily buttressed walls, is typical of the ascetic Ibadite style of architecture (see box on p.383) and looks more military than religious. Building was begun in 1674 but only completed thirty years later under the Bey, Mourad Ben Ali, and it was then used for worship, teaching and as a rest house for travellers. Today it contains the tomb of the saint and his followers and it is still used for prayer, so non-Muslims are not allowed to enter. Across the road is the extravagant **Mosque of the Strangers**, whose contrast with the *zaouia* could hardly be greater – this mosque is covered with domes and topped by an extravagantly carved minaret. Again, it is closed to non-Muslim visitors.

Avenue Moncef Bey, just opposite, leads to the smaller **Mosque of the Turks**, the most interesting of all Houmt Souk's mosques. The unusually shaped minaret was first dubbed "phallic" by the Victorian polymath Sir Harry Johnston – a contentious epithet that has rather stuck. Johnston was convinced of "an unrecognized system of phallic worship throughout the south, and on Jerba all but the most recently built mosques have a phallic emblem on the summit of the minaret".

Just around the corner in a quiet cul-de-sac, the **Catholic church** offers no such mysterious symbols for interpretation: this strange Baroque building was once the centre of a thriving Christian community on Jerba. From the 1840s Greeks, Italians and Maltese came to the island for the sponge-fishing. Some stayed on, and by the 1890s several thousand Europeans were living here. With Independence, however, most left and the church fell into disrepair, eventually to be turned over to more secular uses.

Opposite the *Hôtel Marhala* is another reminder of the island's European links, the **Maltese fondouk** at 30 rue Moncef Bey, where merchants and sponge-collectors once

Sand dunes near Douz

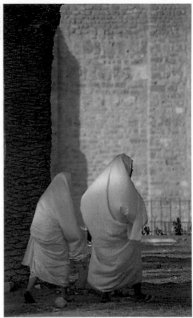
Monastir

Roman ruins at Sbeïtla

Belvedere hot spring, Tozeur

Salt flats

Berber family with pet

A pottery workshop in Guellala

Ksar Ouled Soltane

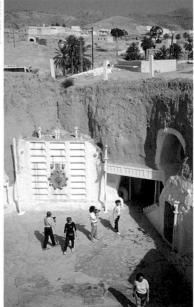

Star Wars set in former troglodyte
home, Matmata

Fadloune Mosque, Jerba

La Ghriba Synagogue, Jerba

Life-size model dinosaurs near Ksar Hadada

stored their goods. In one of the upstairs rooms, a silk weaver (listen for the tell-tale "clack clack" of his loom) makes traditional Jerban wedding dresses: very beautiful, and a snip at around 180TD.

The Borj el Kebir and Libyan market

From the Mosque of the Turks, rue Taïeb Mehiri leads to the fort, variously called the **Borj el Kebir** or **Borj Ghazi Mustapha** (daily except Fri: mid-April to mid-Sept 8am–7pm; mid-Sept to mid-April 9am–5pm; 1.1TD). The site was originally occupied by the Romans, but a fort was first built here by the Aragonese king of Sicily, Roger de Lluria, in 1289. Its history is recounted in a **sound and light show**. The fort's most famous moment came in 1560 when, after Philip II of Spain's armada was wiped out by Dragut's Ottoman fleet, his men retreated inside the fort, only to be massacred by the Turks. The skulls of the Spaniards (by various accounts numbering 500 or 5000) were piled up in a great tower – which stood until European powers prevailed on the Bey, despite strong local opposition, to bury them in 1848. All that remains now of this tower of skulls is a discreet **obelisk** marking the site, 100m over towards the port, behind the viewing stand for the sound and light show. Those of Dragut's forces who died in the fighting are commemorated by a little **mausoleum** on rue Taïeb Mehiri near the corner of rue 2 Mars.

The fort has been excavated but the site is hard to interpret for the untrained eye; for clues, look towards the new bridge over the ditch on the south side, which leads first into a hall (*skifa*) and then into a courtyard between two perimeter walls. On the far side, the tomb of Ghazi Mustapha (who had the fort rebuilt under Ottoman rule) stands on the site of a thirteenth-century mosque. The west wall, with its four massive towers, is original.

A few hundred metres to the west, beyond the new **marina** and behind the *Princesse d'Haroun* restaurant, a "**Libyan market**" takes place on Monday and Thursday mornings, with bargains and goods brought across the border. At one time, most of the traders were Libyan and all sorts of rarities unavailable elsewhere in Tunisia could be found here. Nowadays, the market has become much like any other in Tunisia, though still worth a browse. If you want something approaching the real thing, you'll have to go to Ben Gardane (see p.390).

The Museum of Arts and Popular Traditions

For more concrete historical evidence than that offered by the obscure remnants of the fort, take a look at the concise **Museum of Arts and Popular Traditions**, at the eastern edge of town on avenue Abdel Hamid el Kadhi (daily except Fri: mid-April to mid-Sept 8am–noon & 3–7pm; mid-Sept to mid-April 9.30am–4.30pm; 2.1TD).

The museum's first room, once the *zaouia* of Sidi Ameur, contains **costumes** worn on special occasions and in different parts of the island. Search out in particular the old *fut'a*, a wraparound garment worn by Berber women, and the traditional shawl or *bakhnug*. The long ornamental brooches in the cabinets are worn to indicate tribal allegiance: a Malekite would wear such a brooch on the left, a Berber in the middle and a Bedouin on the right. As in all the regions of the south (much more so than the north), Jerba has its own **marriage rituals**, now threatened by increasing costs and the demand for high dowries from the bride's father. Exhibits illustrate the ceremonies that begin six weeks before the wedding day, when red or yellow eggs are sent as invitations to the guests. During the week before the wedding the bride will receive presents from her husband and his family, including jewellery and ceremonial dress of the kind on display in the museum. She must also apply henna (on two different occasions) to the whole of her palms, fingers and feet; a Berber, though not a Malekite, might use a black paint called *ouchi*. At some stage, both the man and woman will be led in procession around a fertile olive tree, striking their companions with a branch to hasten other marriages in the village. On the Friday before the wedding the bride is formally presented and unveiled to her family, who traditionally throw money at her feet. Finally she is carried to the groom in the privacy of a *palanquin*, a screened canopy placed on the back of a camel.

The museum's second room, the late eighteenth-century former **Zaouia of Sidi Zitouni**, has its original roof of glazed tiles overlaid fish-scale style, with pottery pipes on the inside, but the stuccowork on the walls has been restored. Display cases contain ornamental **jewellery** made by the island's Jewish community. Downstairs is a reconstruction of an old pottery workshop of the sort still used at Guellala (see p.383). A room across the next courtyard was once used as a **kitchen** by pilgrims staying at the sanctuary. The large "Ali-Baba" **jars** are used as marriage chests, since there's little wood on the island. As you leave the museum, have a look at the **weaver's hut**, the *harout*, with its triangular front and sunken external buttressing; like the *houch* (see p.378), these are unique to Jerba.

Eating and drinking

Houmt Souk has a reasonable range of **restaurants**, with plenty of tourist ones (such as the *El Hana* and *de l'Île*) around place Hedi Chaker and place Sidi Brahim, and cheaper places tucked away around town. **Patisseries** and **cafés** are cheap and plentiful, and a couple of hotel bars provide a pleasant enough backdrop for an evening drink.

Restaurants

Aladin, 40 av Mohamed Badra. Next door to the *Hôtel Hadji*. A reasonably priced restaurant, offering *salade Tunisienne*, *brochette*, chicken or couscous. Daily 11am–9pm.

Restaurant Carthage, 11 av Mohamed Badra. Pizza, pasta and grills, all at reasonably low prices. Daily 10am–10pm.

Central, 128 av Bourguiba. Near the bus station. A calm atmosphere with good and reasonably priced couscous, though the other dishes are variable. Daily 8.30am–10.30pm.

Chez Hanini Restaurant Tunisien, in the central souk. Bargain place for a good feed; fish is a particular speciality. Daily except Sunday 11.30am–3pm.

Patisserie Pizzeria Dar,161 av Abdel Hamid el Kadhi. The best pizzas in town, baked in a wood oven and offered at a reasonable price to eat in or take away; also spaghetti and Tunisian dishes. Daily 11.45am–10pm, later in summer.

Hôtel Dar Faiza, rue de la République ☎05/650083. The best of the hotel restaurants, with good fish and a good-value 8.5TD set menu. You'll be joined by the overfed cats that roam about begging for scraps. Daily 12.30–2pm & 7–9.30pm.

El Hana, pl 7 Novembre ☎05/650568. Tucked away by the souk entrance. You can get a meal for around 14TD or order more expensive specialities like "Sole Lord Nelson" or a "Captain's Feast", or even a cheese fondue if you order it a day in advance. Daily 10am–2am.

Restaurant de l'Île, pl Hedi Chaker ☎05/650651. Better than most of the tourist traps, not too pricey and with quite a good 9TD set menu. Daily noon–3pm & 6–10.30pm.

Les Palmiers, pl d'Algérie, at the end of rue Mohamed Ferjani, near the church. Excellent Tunisian food, a pleasant ambience, good service and tables with cloths, all at pretty low prices. The *spaghetti aux fruits de mer* is particularly recommended. Daily noon–3.30pm & 6.30–10pm.

Populaire, 29 av Mohamed Badra. Low-priced diner serving couscous and other Tunisian fare. Daily except Fri 10am–9pm.

La Princesse d'Haroun, at the harbour ☎05/650488. A rather posh and pricey fish restaurant down at the harbour, with a 15TD set menu as well as à la carte. Daily noon–3pm & 6–10pm.

Sportif, 147 av Bourguiba. Moderately priced, moderately good downtown restaurant, serving mostly meat dishes. Daily 11am–9pm.

Restaurant du Sud, pl Sidi Brahim ☎05/650479. One of the better tourist restaurants, with a 9TD ordinary set menu, or a 30TD special seafood menu including wine, and with similar prices à la carte. Daily 9am–10pm.

Cafés and bars

Houmt Souk's **cafés** and **patisseries** are popular places to start the day, with croissants, pastries and sandwiches on sale from early morning onwards. *Café Ben Yedder* in the northeastern corner of place Farhat Hached is a cut above the rest, with a large selection of excellent pastries, as well as sandwiches and of course coffee. The best cakes and ice cream in town however come from *Patisserie Gelateria Italiana* at the port end of avenue Bourguiba (daily 8am–8pm).

As for **drinking**, most places are closed by 8pm. The *Hôtel Marhala* stays open late, with its courtyard serving as a lively saloon bar, but it's sometimes restricted to hotel guests. The *Arischa* is quieter and sometimes stays open late in summer. After closing time, your best bet is to find a restaurant where you can get away with ordering only beer, and perhaps a snack to go with it. Otherwise, you'll have to get a taxi out of town to a hotel such as the *Dar Salem* or the *Strand*, where you can drink till midnight or so. Make sure you can arrange transport back if you do this.

Listings

Airlines Tunis Air, av Bourguiba ☎05/650159; Tuninter, at the airport ☎05/650233, ext 5235.

Banks Mostly in the centre of town on av Bourguiba, with one at least open weekday lunchtime and weekend mornings. There is no shortage of ATMs that will take Visa or Mastercard.

Bike rental The place to rent motorbikes is Holiday Bikes out in the *zone touristique* ☎05/657169, 100m before the Midoun turn-off from the main road; they also do scooters and bicycles. In town, bicycles (10TD/day), scooters (30TD/day) and mopeds (45TD/day) can be rented from Raïs, 155 av Abdel Hamid el Kadhi ☎05/650303.

Boat trips Excursions by boat to Flamingo Point leave from the port most mornings (ask the evening before to find out which boats are going). They usually leave around 8–9am, returning mid-afternoon, and cost around 26TD per person including a barbecued fish lunch. The *Hôtel Lotos* can also arrange a trip.

Car rental Avis, 51 av Mohamed Badra ☎05/650151; Ben Jemaa, 38 av Mohamed Badra ☎05/650340; Budget, 197 av Abdel Hamid el Kadhi ☎05/653444; Hertz, av Habib Thameur ☎05/650196; Europcar, 161 av Abdel Hamid el Kadhi ☎05/657191; Sixt/Express, 167 av Abdel Hamid el Kadhi ☎05/650244; Avis, Hertz, and Europcar all have desks at the airport ☎05/650233. Land Rovers can only be rented with a driver.

Cinema Pl d'Algérie, opposite the Mosque of the Turks.

Festivals There's a summer Ulysses festival in July or August with performances of dancing, music and folklore, and there's a windurfing regatta round the island from Houmt Souk to Ajim at the beginning of September.

Hammams The oldest, friendliest and most central hammam is by the *zaouia* at 17 pl Sidi Brahim (daily: men 5am–noon; women 1–6pm). The Hammam Ziadi at 93 av Bourguiba is cleaner but dearer and less friendly (daily except Tues: men 6am–noon; women 1–6pm). There is another one with similar hours at 117 av Abdel Hamid el Kadhi.

Hospital The regional hospital is at the southern end of av Bourguiba ☎05/650018. There's also a private clinic, the Echifa, near the museum ☎05/652215. One GP used to treating foreigners is Dr Ben Sabah at 164 av Bourguiba ☎05/650238.

Internet access Djerba Cyber Espace, upstairs at 133 av Bourguiba (daily 9am–9pm, 1.5TD/hr).

Kids Parc des Loisirs Bah Bah on rue 20 Mars is a small fairground with rides at 0.5TD a go for kids young and old (Mon–Sat 2–8pm, Sun & school hols 10am–8pm).

Newspapers British papers are usually available at 127 av Bourguiba, near the post office, along with *Time*, *Newsweek* and the *Herald Tribune*, and a very few English books, mostly classics.

ONA crafts shop Av Bourguiba, 100m north of the post office.

Pharmacy There's a night pharmacy at 166 av Bourguiba, and a doctor at 188 av Bourguiba ☎05/620550 on duty 8pm–8am nightly and all day Sun.

Police Av Abdel Hamid el Kadhi, just north of pl 7 Novembre ☎05/650015.

MOVING ON FROM HOUMT SOUK

For a rundown of destinations and journey times, see Travel Details on pp.391–392.

The bus station (☎ 05/650076 for local and SRT services, ☎ 05/652239 for SNTRI services) is off avenue Bourguiba, a couple of hundred metres south of the main market area. Local buses serve the *zone touristique* of Sidi Mahares (#10 & #11; 11 daily), Midoun (#13 and sometimes #10; 6 daily) and Aghir (#10 & #11; 11 daily), with services to Hara Sghira (#14; 4 daily), El May (#16 and sometimes #10; 8 daily), Guellala (#14; 4 daily), Ajim (#12; 3 daily), Sedouikech (#16; 5 daily) and the airport (#15; 1 daily). A map on the bus-station wall shows routes on the island. For transport between Houmt Souk and the *zone touristique* with maximum possible delay, there's a "mini train" twice a day at 3.5TD return (children 2.5TD).

Intercity buses run by regional SRT companies serve Ben Gardane, Medenine, Tataouine and Zarzis, with SNTRI services to Sousse, Kairouan, Tunis and Bizerte. Gabès and Sfax are served by a combination of regional and national buses, with SNTRI services being faster and more comfortable. For destinations north of Gabès, and especially for Tunis, buses are often full and need booking in advance. Louages to Ben Gardane, Gabès, Medenine, Sfax, Tunis, Zarzis and sometimes Tataouine leave from next to the bus station, and those to Ajim, their only destination within Jerba, leave from the traffic island in the middle of avenue Bourguiba, opposite the corner of avenue Mohamed Badra.

Post office Av Bourguiba, opposite pl Mongi Bali, with a special desk just for tourists. In principle, the post office here keeps country hours (July & August also Mon–Thurs 5–9pm & Sun 9–11am).

Supermarkets The best is Bonprix on the airport road 200m west of the post office, but there's also Super at the corner of av Bourguiba with av Mohamed Badra, and Grand Magasin at the corner of rue Tahar Battikh and av Abdel Hamid el Kadhi.

Sidi Mahares beach
سيدي محرس

East of Houmt Souk, before the package tourists' haven of Sidi Mahares, the low sandy peninsula of Ras Rmel – known as **Flamingo Point** – stretches lazily out into the sea. Between November and March, you'll see pink waders here, and often **dolphins** too, just a few metres offshore. Tunisians and Libyans like to **camp** out here in summer, as they do at the other end of the *zone touristique*, and there is no reason why you shouldn't join them.

Bus #11 from Houmt Souk will take you past Flamingo Point and out along **Sidi Mahares beach**, past the tourist complex and the string of hotels along 8km of beach and surf until you reach the lighthouse at Ras Taguermes. The bus stops at most of the hotels en route, and you specify which one you want as you buy the ticket. Prices for staying at these hotels – unless you're pre-booked on a package – are very inflated, especially in summer, though most are good and easily bear comparison with their equivalents in, say, Greece or Spain. Only a few operators – among them Panorama (see p.6) – offer package holidays here from Britain and Ireland. The beach is wide and sandy and stretches for 8km, backed with a virtually unbroken line of hotels. Unfortunately, pollution is a problem on the beach, and most of the hotels provide diesel to wash tar off feet.

As far as facilities go, **beach sports** are available all the way along the beach, and include parascending, water-skiing, jet skiing and windsurfing. You can also rent a pedalo, or be towed behind a speedboat on an inflatable "banana". Most of the hotels also run stables for horse-riding, and rent out bicycles, and there is a **golf course**

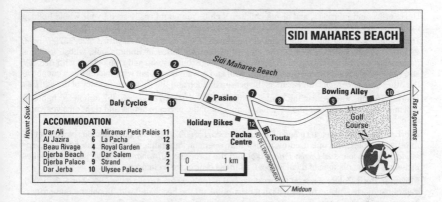

(☎05/745055) with its entrance 1km west of the *Dar Jerba* hotel complex, 500m east of the *Jerba Palace*. A rather snazzy **bowling alley**, Grand Bowling Djerba, can be found just west of the *Dar Jerba* complex (daily 11am–3am, later in summer; ☎05/746806), with a bar and restaurant attached. There's also a hard-currency foreigners-only **casino**, the Pasino (daily 10am–4am; ☎05/757537), on the main road, 1km west of the Midoun turn-off (bd de l'Environnement).

Practicalities

On Sidi Mahares's main road, which runs about 200m inland from the beach road, you can rent a **bicycle**, **scooter** or **motorbike** from Holiday Bikes (☎05/657169), 100m west of the Midoun road (bd de l'Environnement) that starts just by the *Hôtel Djerba Beach*. Daly Cyclos (☎05/657840), 50m east of the turn-off for the *Hôtel al Jazira*, rent out bicycles and **mopeds**. Very near Holiday Bikes, there are two grocery stores calling themselves supermarkets (one just to the west, the other in the Pacha Centre at the junction with bd de l'Environnement). An ordinary Tunisian grocer, selling yoghurt and *leben* among other things, can be found just across boulevard de l'Environnement, from the Pacha centre, and 50m up. English-language **newspapers** are available at hotels used by UK tour operators such as the *Djerba Palace* and the *Djerba Beach*.

Traditional Tunisian **food** at a fair price is available at *Restaurant Touta* on the Midoun road near Holiday Bikes, an oasis of good honest grub in a desert of tourist traps (daily 10am–10pm).

Hotels

Al Jazira ★★, at the western end of the beach ☎05/746420, ☎747403. The first of Jerba's beach hotels when it was originally put up in 1962, but now one of the newest, having been pulled down and rebuilt again from scratch. ❻

Le Beau Rivage, at the western end of the beach ☎05/758230, ☎758123. A friendly, intimate little pension between the *Ulysse Palace* and the *Al Jazira*, 100m from the beach. ❹

Résidence Dar Ali ★★, at the western end of the beach ☎05/758671, ☎758045. A friendly intimate little pension with spotless, comfortable rooms and a pool; the owner's wife is English so the language is spoken. ❹

Dar Jerba, at the eastern end of the beach ☎05/745181, ☎746788, ☎www.darhotels.com. An enormous complex containing three hotels: the four-star *Dahlia*, the three-/four-star *Narjess*, and the three-star *Zahra*, plus the *Appart-Hôtel el Manara* across the street. The complex has all the facilities anyone could want, with six swimming pools (one of them indoor), its own post office, bank,

Hertz office and infirmary, and also a children's club. You could easily spend your whole holiday inside this place, and many guests do. Prices fall by around two-thirds off season. ⑥

Dar Salem ★★★, at the western end of the beach, 300m east of the *Al Jazira* ☎05/757667 or 8, ℻757677. A new hotel opened by the owners of the *Dar Faiza* in Houmt Souk, whose facilities guests may use when in town; the rooms are not huge, but tasteful and comfortable with a/c, TV and some with a sea view, and there's also a pool and private beach, but what makes this a cut above the other *zone touristique* three-stars is the personal touch and the friendly efficiency of the staff. ⑤

Djerba Beach ★★★, near the centre of the beach ☎05/657200, ℻657357, ✉hotel.jerbabeach @planet.tn. Smaller, quieter and friendlier than a lot of the package hotels, and right on a very nice bit of beach. ⑥

Djerba Palace, at the eastern end of the beach ☎05/658600, ℻657635, ✉miramar.djerba@planet.tn. Another complex, this one used by British tour operator Panorama, containing the five-star *Cesar Palace* (⑦) the four-star *Djerba Palace* (⑦) and the three-star *Miramar Park* (⑥), sharing facilities including four pools (one of them indoor), a fitness centre and a children's club.

Miramar Petit Palais ★★★, at the western end of the *zone touristique* ☎05/758233 or 4, ℻758056, ✉miramar.djerba@planet.tn. A smallish tourist hotel, off the beach, but with a pool and quite friendly, now part of the Djerba Palace group, whose facilities guests may use. ⑥

La Pacha, Pacha Centre, junction of main road and bd de l'Environnement ☎05/658827, ℻659171. Officially a pension, this is a small but very comfortable place with biggish rooms, a/c, en-suite bathrooms, and satellite TV, some with a kitchenette, 500m from the beach, but also just about walking distance from Midoun (3km) and some of the sights of inland Jerba mentioned on p.379. ④

Royal Garden ★★★★★, at the eastern end of the beach ☎05/745777, ℻745769; ✉riu.royalgarden@planet.tn. The smartest, most expensive and most luxurious hotel on the island. ⑦

Strand ★, at the western end of the beach, 600m east of the *Al Jazira* ☎05/657430, ℻657014. Cheaper and not as chic as the other beach hotels, without any of their facilities, but clean, comfortable and somewhat cheaper, with its own private beach. Its main interest lies in the fact that its bar is reasonably priced and open till midnight. ④

Ulysse Palace ★★★★, at the western end of the beach, 400m west of the *Al Jazira* ☎05/757422, ℻757850. At one time the best of the beach hotels, and still relatively stylish. ⑥

Ras Taguermes   راس تقرماس

The cape at the end of Sidi Mahares beach, called **Ras Taguermes**, is marked by a red-and-white-striped **lighthouse**. The main local attraction here is the **go-kart track** (daily 9am–6pm; 6TD for 10 laps). Two hundred metres east, at the beginning of the El Kantara road, is a refined and rather pricey **restaurant**, *Le Phare* (daily noon–3pm & 6pm–midnight; ☎05/745382), specializing in seafood, and also serving *gargoulette* (lamb cooked in an earthenware pot) if ordered in advance, with a pleasant terrace for outdoor eating.

Across from the lighthouse begins a **sand spit** enclosing the **Sebkha Sidi Garous** lagoon. In summer, *camping sauvage* is the order of the day, as Tunisian and Libyan families pitch tents or sleep out on the beach. Some 5km down the spit, the two-star *Hôtel Tanit* (☎05/757034, ℻757033; ⑤) offers an alternative for those who don't want to camp out. The spit continues for another 2km beyond the hotel. In winter, look out for **flamingos** and other birds in the lagoon behind.

La Seguia and Aghir

Around the point of Ras Taguermes, on **La Seguia beach**, is a carefully restricted Club Med with three branches – *Jerba la Fidèle, Jerba la Douce* and *Calypso. Jerba la Fidèle* actually has the nicest beach on the island fenced off and monopolized, so you won't be able to use it unless you stay there.

A couple of kilometres beyond, the beach at **AGHIR**, while not quite up to Sidi Mahares's standards in terms of sandiness, is a lot less crowded. After storms, however, the water tends to be infested with jellyfish. At its northern end, the two-star *Hôtel*

Sidi Slim (☎05/750450, ☎750449, ☎htl.sidislim@planet.tn; ❺) has a **campsite**, though the facilities leave much to be desired; the *Centre des Stages et des Vacances* down the road is somewhat preferable (see below). The hotel **restaurant** is open to non-residents, with a 9TD buffet for breakfast, lunch and dinner (daily 6–9.30am, noon–2.30pm & 6.30–9.30pm).

A little further, the pricey but rather jolly and well-managed three-star *Club Palma Djerba* (☎05/750380, ☎750832, ☎palma.djerba@gnet.tn; ❼) has the best bit of Aghir's beach. Next door, near the Midoun–El Kantara junction, the *Centre des Stages et Vacances* **youth hostel** and **campsite** (☎05/750266) offers the choice of four-bed dorms (5TD) cheaper huts or your own tent, and is friendly, if a bit run-down, but only does food (apart from breakfast) in summer, or if there is a group or a substantial number of people staying. Otherwise, you have the choice of eating at neighbouring hotels, going into Midoun or getting in supplies at the grocery store a couple of kilometres up the road by the junction between Aghir and La Seguia. There are eleven daily **buses** from Aghir to Houmt Souk via Sidi Mahares or Midoun, and the journey will cost 5 or 6TD in a taxi.

El Kantara and around   القنطارة

A single twelve-kilometre road leads south from Aghir to **EL KANTARA**, passing some deserted beaches on the way. Halfway along on the left, a track heads 8km over the sand and out along a strip of land to the fort of **Borj Kastil**, built by Alfonso V of Aragon during his brief mid-fifteenth-century tenure of the island. The surrounding rocks are said to be good for underwater fishing.

It was the Carthaginians who created the **causeway** which stretches 7km from El Kantara to the opposite shore. In 1551, Dragut the pirate, trapped with his fleet by the flotilla of Charles V of Spain between the causeway and the fort, made his famously daring naval getaway here. To gain time, he barricaded himself in the fort and held off the Spaniards while his men, under cover of darkness, dug through the causeway, enabling his fleet to escape into the Gulf of Bou Grara. Although it could still be forded at low tide in the intervening period, the causeway was not repaired for over four hundred years, finally reopening in 1953.

The site of ancient **Meninx** is spread around the road junction by El Kantara. Very little now remains of the city established by the Phoenicians and rebuilt by the Romans, but if you want to explore there are two patches of **unexcavated remains** (freely accessible). One area is spread up the Aghir road for 2km or so on both sides, the main area of blocks and fallen columns being about 1km from the causeway on the seaward side of the road, where the forum once stood. A little to the north, on the inland side of the road, a mound marks the site of the former Roman bathhouse, and a kilometre or so further are some Punic catacombs, associated with the Punic port that once stood at the north end of the bay between here and the peninsula where Borj Kastil stands. None of these sites are obvious to the untrained eye however, nor are they easy to find. The other patch of remains is about 100m north of the road to Guellala, less than a kilometre from the causeway (just before the date palms begin), and includes the remains of a basilica whose font is now in the Bardo Museum in Tunis. Again, there is nothing spectacular to be seen, but it is worth a stroll, and a number of nooks and crannies repay closer inspection.

For the intrepid, a small piste leads inland after another 400m, opposite the remains of a Roman cistern (there are also third- and fourth-century catacombs to the north of the road here). About a kilometre and a half up this piste is the ancient and very inter-denominational **Jema'a Haratt Ouirsighen**, originally a Roman temple, then a synagogue for Meninx's Jewish community, which became a church in the fourth century, a Byzantine basilica, and finally a mosque.

The west coast

Long and wild, virtually uninhabited and empty of tourists, the **west coast of Jerba** is not as postcard-pretty as the other coasts, nor as good for swimming, with a rocky shore and shallow water for quite a way out. It is, however, *the* place to really get away from it all – if you can get there, that is. At its northern end is the island's airport; to the south, Ajim, Jerba's main port; and in between no transport at all. If you stay anywhere along this twenty-kilometre shore, you're down to looking after yourself, camping or just sleeping out – no hardship so long as you have adequate supplies of food and water. Two old mosques along this coast appeared in *Star Wars* – see the box on p.319 for further details.

Two roads run out to Jerba's west coast from Houmt Souk. The main road, which is surfaced, passes **MELLITA**, and has some of the oldest *menzels* (parcel of land) on the island. On the way, you pass the **El Kebir Mosque**, 4km out of Houmt Souk to the south of the road; despite the name, "Great Mosque", it's no bigger than any other inland Jerban mosque, and very typical in appearance, with its whitewashed window-less walls and battlement-like mini-minaret looking like a lookout on a mini-fort. It is in fact Jerba's oldest mosque, dating back to the ninth century, when it was considered one of the most important Kharijite mosques in North Africa. If you are Muslim, you can pop in to admire the tenth century mihrab and *minbar*. After Mellita, the road pass-es Jerba's **airport**, and continues to **Borj Jillij**, where a lighthouse was first construct-ed in the sixteenth century on the site of an earlier fort. A new fort was built here in the eighteenth century under Hammouda Bey, but it is now used as a lighthouse once again, running on electricity rather than olive oil lamps. From Borj Jillij you can drive or cycle back along a track by the sea to Houmt Souk, a distance of about 11km.

The main Houmt Souk–Gabès road leads through dull countryside to the fairly drea-ry port of **AJIM**, the most important centre for sponges, which are still taken from the sea floor by divers – now mainly Tunisians, but originally Greeks and Maltese. Ajim is also a centre for the local date harvest, though compared with the *deglat* variety of Tozeur the crop here is poor – three varieties of palm provide nothing edible at all, and are kept only for *laghmi*, or palm wine (see p.312). Be careful, too, if you go swimming here, as the channel swarms with large jellyfish, constantly chewed up in ferry pro-pellers. The channel is also full of octopuses; all along the quay you'll see stacked piles of **octopus traps** in the form of ceramic pots, which are laid on the seabed in the evening. The creatures, looking for hiding places at the end of a night's foraging, crawl into them only to be hauled out in the morning. The raucous and exotic bar in *Star*

JERBAN HOMES

Jerban homes, spread around the countryside, take the form of a *houch* (traditional house) inside a *menzel* (parcel of land), each one belonging to a different family. From the outside, a *houch* looks like a small square fortress, with blank white walls and a tower, called a *ghorfa* or *kouchk*, often crowned with a dome, at each corner. Like the mosques, these houses were designed in response to numerous invasions from the eleventh century onwards, and it's been suggested that the basic plan was taken from the Roman forts, or *limes*, on the mainland. Three large rooms surround the central courtyard, each used by one section of an extended family. The parents in each section sleep in the tower. This is the only part of the house with external windows, tradition-ally placed higher than a man on horseback. The breeze is fed down below through holes in the floor, cooling the entire house. Near the house is a simple guest room (usually facing east) and a threshing floor. The distinctive Jerban well is flanked by two upright supports for a system of pulleys operated by camel or mule; a system you can see all over the island.

Wars, or at least the outside of it, was in fact a house in Ajim, though it is barely recognizable these days, while Obiwan Kenobi's house was an old mosque 3km up the coast – see the box on p.319 for further details.

The Ajim–Jorf **ferry** runs every 30min between 6.30am and 9.30pm, and every hour or two through the night. Foot passengers travel free, cars pay 0.6TD. In a vehicle, try to avoid using the ferry in the evening at weekends, when there can be long queues (at Jorf on Saturdays and at Ajim on Sundays). Between Ajim and Houmt Souk, there are frequent louages. To change money, Ajim has a **bank** on the main road, but no hotels.

Inland to the south

Inland Jerba is a quiet expanse of sleepy homesteads and fortified mosques. People live in homes dotted around the countryside, and places that appear on the map to be villages – **El May**, **Midoun**, **Mahboubine**, **Guellala** – are really little more than markets: people shop and work in them, but few people live there. The only settlements that really qualify for the title of village are the two Jewish "ghettos" of **Hara Sghira** and **Hara Kebira**, whose residents, unlike most of their fellow Jerbans, actually do live in houses grouped closely together.

Midoun ميدون

MIDOUN, the island's second town, is really little more than a bunch of souvenir shops, a trio of banks and a few restaurants, but it's quite a lively place during the Friday souk, when there's also a livestock **market** just out to the southeast. The other event of the week is a "fantasia" of music and dance every Tuesday in the open-air theatre (Jan–June & Sept–Dec 3pm, July & Aug 5pm; 2TD) including a mock Berber wedding, and a performance by a band of *ouled jema'a* musicians, black descendants of slaves who brought their musical traditions with them across the desert.

Midoun's underground **oil press** (*massera*) is worth a look. You'll find it between the mosque on avenue Farhat Hached (the Sidi Mahares road) and the taxiphone office on avenue Salah Ben Youssef – look for the ground-level dome (you can see in through the windows in the dome if the press is closed). As at Haddej and Matmata (see p.354), underground air ensures humidity throughout the winter, necessary to separate the oil. A mule or camel used to turn the stone roller around its base, crushing the olives, but the press is now motor-driven. After pressing, the skins are transferred to a sieve (*chamia*) which is squashed by the weight of a palm trunk, hinged at the wall; the oil and vegetable water drip through into a jar and separate. Around the main room are storage chambers, used by each family for their olives.

Practicalities

Frequent **buses** run from Houmt Souk (#10 via Mahboubine and El May, #13 via Sedghiane), and there are also buses to Aghir and the hotel zone. **Taxis** wait by the main roundabout (around 2.5TD to Aghir or Taguermes, 5TD to Houmt Souk). On Fridays, a **mini-train** runs to Midoun from the beach hotels. There's a Syndicat d'Initiative **tourist office** (Mon–Thurs 9am–noon & 3–5pm, Fri & Sat 9am–1pm), and a **hammam** (Thurs–Sat: men 6am–12.30pm & 6–10pm; women 12.30–5.30pm) in the same street. For medical needs, apart from various **pharmacies** (including a night pharmacy), Midoun has a **hospital** (℡05/657280) and a very reputable **doctor**, Dr El Messabi, Midoun's former mayor, at 20 av Bourguiba (℡05/657305).

For **accommodation**, the budget option is the *Hôtel Jawhara* (℡05/600467; ❷), clean and pleasant with en-suite rooms, though some have no outside window. A more luxurious choice is the spotless *Jerba Midoun* on rue 13 Aôut (℡05/600006, ℻600093; ❹), with

such modern conveniences as air conditioning and a breakfast terrace. The *Restaurant de l'Orient* on the main roundabout (daily 8am–5pm) does cheap and filling Tunisian **food**, as does the *Restaurant Constantine* at 11 av Mohamed Badra (daily 7am–5pm). For more refined eating, there's the good and reasonably priced *Restaurant le Pêcheur* (daily 10am–10pm) on boulevard 7 Novembre (the Houmt Souk road), while the *Restaurant el Guestile* (daily noon–midnight), just off the market square, is pricier and more tourist-oriented and specializes in seafood.

Around Midoun

If you take the direct road from Midoun to Houmt Souk, there are a couple of things en route worth breaking the journey for. Two kilometres out of Midoun, a pyramid-shaped pile of weather-worn sandstone blocks north of the road marks the Punic **Tomb of Borgou** (freely accessible). The sarcophagus was in an underground chamber which is accessible but not very pleasant, since its entrance has been broken open by the drunks who use this as a nocturnal meeting place and toilet. The eleventh century **Fadloune Mosque**, 1km further on the south side of the road, appears anonymously on numerous postcards of the island. It is no longer used for prayers so non-Muslims can go in and look around. It's the classic Jerban Ibadite mosque, with buttressed walls and lantern-style minaret. Also in the compound is an underground cistern and an old flour mill. Another couple of distinctive Jerban **mosques** appear to the north of the road after another 8km or so: the **Ben Yakhlef** with its stumpy minaret is just by the road, with the **Mouzline**, like a sleeker version of the Fadloune, a little way beyond.

A kilometre west of the Fadloune Mosque, a turning southward, signposted "Jema'a el Gueïd", leads after 1km to yet another mosque, not especially outstanding, but turn left in front of the grocery store opposite the mosque, follow the tarmac to a school, and continue around the school on the unsurfaced track. Straight ahead of you at the next junction is **Qasr Hamida Ben Ayed**, a largely ruined eighteenth-century Ottoman palatial mansion built for the local governor. Seven hundred metres to your left is another ruined mansion called Dar Mustapha. The mansions can also be found by taking the Sedghiane turn-off from the Midoun–Houmt Souk road, continuing through **Sedghiane** till the tarmac ends (3km from the main road), and heading off down the track to the left; Qasr Hamida Ben Ahmed is on your right after 1km, and the track to your left leads back to the main road. On a bike, the ride makes a very pleasant excursion into the heart of the Jerban countryside.

A more picturesque route from Midoun to Houmt Souk is by way of Mahboubine and El May, through the vineyards and fruit and olive groves. **MAHBOUBINE**, a couple of kilometres northwest of Midoun, is itself little more than a central square, a couple of cafés and the nineteenth-century **El Kaateb Mosque**, inspired by the Blue Mosque in Istanbul. All along the winding road, behind the high banks (or *tabia*), are the traditional Jerban houses (*houch*), each commanding the *menzel*, or estate, of a different family. The sand tracks to the north of the road here lead past one *menzel* after another – a district best explored by bicycle.

El May and the Jewish villages المي

Right in the centre of Jerba, 8km west of Mahboubine and 9km south of Houmt Souk, **EL MAY** is most notable for its fifteenth-century fortified Kharijite **Mosque of Umm et Turkia**. As in the Zaouia of Sidi Brahim in Houmt Souk, the Mosque's low walls are supported by thick buttresses, and are themselves a metre and a half thick, while the minaret is a squat, rounded stump. The windows however are less typical of classic Jerban mosques. Around its walls a Saturday **market** takes place; other signs of business include two **banks** and a **post office** (country hours). **Buses** pass through here regularly between Houmt Souk and Midoun or Sedouikech.

Hara Sghira (Er Riadh) الحاغة الصغرى (الرياض)

Two kilometres from El May, in the direction of Houmt Souk, the road turns off left for Guellala. On the way is a Jewish settlement called **HARA SGHIRA** (Small Ghetto), now officially **Er Riadh**. Buses pass through seven times a day each way between Houmt Souk and Guellala.

Hara Sghira's **synagogue of El Ghriba** (the miracle) is 1.5km out of the village down a well-signposted road. It is a place of pilgrimage for Jews from all over North Africa on *Lag beOmer*, the 33rd day after the beginning of Passover, and a large new hostel for pilgrims reflects the importance of the site. The present building, dating only from 1920, is covered inside with rather garish tiles. The original synagogue was apparently constructed at the place where a holy stone fell from heaven: an unknown woman arrived, miraculously, at the same time, to direct operations. If the Jews ever leave Jerba, it is said

THE JEWS OF JERBA

Opinion about when **Jews** first came to Jerba is divided: some believe it was in 566 BC, following the fall of Jerusalem to Nebuchadnezzar; others say 71 AD, when the city was taken by Titus. The island community today numbers about 1500, some of whom have returned here after emigrating to Israel. Historically, Jewish **artisans** worked here as jewellers, playing a considerable part in developing the island's commercial reputation. Jerban **Jewish colonies** sprang up over much of the south of mainland Tunisia, often made up of shopkeepers or itinerant blacksmiths. But, while they established small communities in remote villages, they kept their bonds with Jerba, returning to the island during the summer and for important religious festivals.

To begin with Jews were tolerated, but only while they kept to their own community and traditional occupations. **Under the French** their position improved, but they remained second-class citizens relative to the Europeans and European Jews. Their own attitude helped maintain this position, for while other communities took advantage of the educational and financial resources of world Jewish organizations, the Jews of Jerba rejected aid, preferring to keep their strict and distinctive form of Judaism untainted. Consequently they won a reputation as intransigent **traditionalists**, gained far less from the Protectorate than other communities, and became the target of French and Arab anti-Semitism.

The new state of Israel offered an opportunity to make a new life in the Promised Land, and by the early 1950s many Jews were leaving. After Tunisian Independence the trickle of emigrants became a flood and the community shrank, only to revive slightly with the return of some Jews from Israel. Perhaps as a result of Bourguiba's attempts to encourage integration, overt anti-Semitism is rare, and Jerban Jews generally have good relations with their Muslim neighbours. However, anti-Zionism ("We have nothing against Tunisian Jews, it is only the State of Israel we object to") still forms a pretext for occasional outbursts of hatred. As recently as 1985, a policeman, apparently incited by radio broadcasts from Libya, burst into the Ghriba in Hara Sghira and killed three worshippers before he could be restrained.

that the synagogue's silver key will be thrown back to heaven. An inner sanctuary contains several manuscripts, including one of the oldest Torahs in the world. One plaque on the wall offers a benediction for the Supreme Combatant, Bourguiba, and another asks for donations (these are not optional – less than half a dinar and you will promptly be shown the door). The synagogue is closed to tourists on Saturdays.

It is now possible to stay in Hara Sghira, at a small but smart new **hotel** called the *Dar Dhiafa* (☎05/661166, ℻6610793, ✆dardhiafa@gnet.tn; ➏), a tasteful conversion of four houses in the village, with traditional decor but all the modern conveniences of a tourist hotel, including two small swimming pools.

Hara Kebira (Es Souani)   الحاغةا الكبرى (السواني)
The other Jewish village, **HARA KEBIRA** (now officially **Es Souani**), is near Houmt Souk and an easy walk from town (follow avenue Bourguiba south past the hospital and, at the next junction take the road at eleven o'clock, between the Midoun and Kantara turn-offs). Rather more workaday than Hara Sghira, it boasts several synagogues, but none as interesting as El Ghriba, and a small *gargote* at 17 rue des Amandes off the main square (daily 8–11am & 5–8pm, closed Fri pm), which is the only kosher restaurant in the country. The streets are named after fruit and nuts rather than the usual array of politicians, dates and martyrs. One thing to look out for as you wander around the village are the symbols painted in blue on house doorways to ward off the evil eye.

IBADITES AND BERBERS

From the earliest Arab invasions, Jerba became a centre for the **Kharijites**, an ascetic Islamic sect hostile to the Caliphs who ruled the Arab empire, and whose origins go back to the very beginning of the schism between Sunni (orthodox) and Shi'ite Muslims. The Sunnis supported the Ummayad Caliphs and their Abbasid successors, while Shi'ites believed that only the prophet's son-in-law Ali and his descendants had the right to the Caliphate. But in the early days of the dispute, when Ali agreed to arbitration over the question, a group of his followers withdrew their support, declaring that God was the only arbitrator. Taking their name from the Arabic for "to leave" (*kharaja*), they became an ascetic and highly puritan sect, hostile to Sunnis and Shi'ites alike (it was a Kharijite who eventually assassinated Ali), but they had a considerable following among the Berbers, especially since they saw piety rather than (Arab) pedigree as the main criterion for leadership of the Islamic community. With the 909 fall to the Fatimids of their North African states based at Sijilmasa in Morocco and Tahirt in Algeria, Jerba became one of the Kharijites' last refuges, along with the Mzab in Algeria, the Jebel Nafusa in Libya, and the island of Zanzibar in Tanzania.

In fact, for many years the Kharijite population here was divided between two factions, the Wahabites (followers of Tahirt's Rustamid ruler Abdallah Ibn Wahab, whose territory included Jerba) and the Nakkarites (the faction followed by Tozeuri rebel Abu Yazid – see p.431). From the eighth to the fourteenth century, between uniting to fight the common Christian foe, these two factions struggled for political and religious dominance of the island. Eventually, the Wahabites prevailed, and in fact many of the Nakkarite party eventually converted to Sunni Islam. Note that this Wahabite faction of Kharijism has nothing to do with the eighteenth century Wahabite movement from the Arabian peninsula.

Today, Jerba's Kharijites, usually referred to as Wahabites or Ibadites, form nearly half the island's Muslim community and are concentrated in the south and west. They are extremely strict in their religious practice, and follow the dictates of the Koran even more scrupulously than other Muslims. They also differ from Sunni Muslims in certain details of their religious rituals. The austerity of their religion is best expressed in their architecture: they built the most simple and severe of all the 300 mosques and marabouts around the island. In times of war these semi-fortified buildings would serve as a place of refuge for those outside the *houch* or *menzel*, the country houses in the interior (see p.378).

Most of Jerba's dwindling minority of **Berber-speakers** are Ibadites. They live in the south of the island, especially around Ajim, Guellala and Sedouikech. Because they speak a different language, they tend to be at a social disadvantage (getting a job is always a problem, for example), and the low social status of Berber is the main factor behind the decline of the language.

As well as the usual fish and hands, these include a five-armed version of the normally seven- or nine-armed *menorah* (Jewish candelabra).

Guellala قلالة

GUELLALA, on the island's south coast, is the stronghold of Ibadism and the Berber language in Jerba. It also rivals Nabeul in Cap Bon as a centre for handmade **pottery**. The clay is dug out of the hillside on the road to Sedouikech, then bleached and cleaned in the sea. All the products were once exported from a port down the road, and people used to travel around the markets near Tataouine selling their goods. The staple of the industry, the large terracotta vessels used for storing and cooling water and oil, went to markets as far afield as Benghazi and Constantine. Workshops line the main street; though, of the ones operating, only one is still in the original style, partly underground and insulated with stone and soil to protect the drying clay from the heat and wind. The three hundred kilns in the village are constructed with special bricks, made from earth, which has been washed with alluvial deposits. Most of the glazed ware is garish and geared to the market in cheap souvenirs, though the Berber bowls, baked at the lowest temperatures, are more authentic and interesting. A Guellala speciality nowadays is the "magic camel", a water jug in the shape of a camel, with a hole in the base through which it's filled. When placed the right way up, the water miraculously fails to escape from this hole and pours only from the mouth. Guellala has a **bank**, should you need to change any money to invest in a bit of pottery.

One of the shops in town has an underground oil press (the shop with the ceramic map on the door, 50m up the Hara Sghira/Ajim road from the police station and bank), but a more interesting visit can be had half a kilometre up the El Kantara road where, opposite the **post office**, you'll find "**Ali Berber's Cave**". Ali Berber, the indefatigable proprietor, gives a highly entertaining tour of his allegedly Roman and undoubtedly ancient underground pottery and oil press, with a full explanation in French. The **oil press** in use today is on the edge of town (continue past Ali Berber's to the El Kantara turn-off, then 200m down it on the right, before the 7km milestone), is actually much more interesting – a wonderful piece of vintage science-museum technology – but only open in season (Nov & Dec).

Out of town, along the shore, are a couple of interesting mosques and a few bits of Roman masonry. The **Guellala Mosque**, by the beach (1km out of town; take the first surfaced left turn after 100m heading from the police station towards Hara Sghira/Er Riadh, and continue straight ahead when the tarmac veers off to the right), dates back to the fifteenth century and is a favourite on the ubiquitous "Mosquée de Djerba" postcards. It's a lovely place to watch the sun set over the sea between the mosque and the neighbouring palm tree, bathing the seaward-facing walls in a rosy light as it goes down. Half a kilometre west up the beach, you'll find the odd piece of Roman wall; there's more underwater just offshore, and local farmers often turn up pieces of marble and mosaic in their fields. In the other direction, 1.5km east along the coast, the tenth-century **Mosque of Sidi Yati** (another postcard favourite) stands disused and crumbling by the shore.

There are four **buses** a day to Houmt Souk from Guellala, while a **taxi** costs about 6TD, and it's not hard to **hitch** via either Sedouikech or Hara Sghira (Er Riadh).

Sedouikech صدويكش

SEDOUIKECH, 6km east of Guellala, stands on a small plateau, which is the one prominence on the island. The main mosque here is Sunni, but somewhat more interesting is the twelfth- or thirteenth-century Ibadite **Louta Mosque**, which is subterranean, with only its two cupolas above ground, a design that takes the squat windowless form of the typical Jerban mosque to its fullest extreme. Since this is the highest point on the island, the mosque was not only a house of prayer, but also a vantage point from which any approach could be seen. It was restored in the 1990s by the Institut National du Patrimoine. To the east of Sedouikech lies the mausoleum of sixteenth-century hermit **Sidi Satouri**, visited by childless women who hope the saint's *beraka* (blessing in the form of rubbed-off holiness) may help them to conceive. According to legend, Sidi Satouri once turned to stone members of a wedding party who interrupted him at prayer, and perhaps the legend derives from the **megalithic dolmens** that stand to the northwest, of unknown antiquity, but quite probably the oldest artefacts on Jerba.

THE SOUTHEAST COAST

The **mainland behind Jerba** basically consists of the small towns of **Jorf** and **Bou Grara** and, on the country's remote southeast coast, the nascent resort of Zarzis and the route into Libya via Ben Gardane. With most people heading for Jerba's lotus-eating shores, this corner is still a rarely visited part of Tunisia – but it's a region that's likely to become increasingly the subject of tourist development over the next few years, if tourism in Libya continues to develop.

Jorf and Gightis
جرف

JORF, the mainland ferry terminal, is not the most inspiring town in Tunisia. However, the ferry services ensure that you won't be stranded for long, with half-hourly services between 6.30am and 9.30pm, then hourly till 11.30pm, every two hours till 4.30am, and hourly again till 6.30am for the fifteen-minute crossing to Jerba (free for foot-passengers, 0.6TD for cars); try to avoid crossing on weekend evenings when there can be long queues (going to Jerba on Saturdays, coming back on Sundays). There are louages from Jorf to Medenine, but not to Gabès (either change at Medenine, or walk up to the turn-off and hitch). Between Jorf and Gabès the only town is Mareth (see p.361), from where adventurous travellers can strike off to Toujane. En route to Medenine you could stop off to visit the Roman port of **Gightis** – though, as passing louages tend to be full, it can prove difficult to continue on afterwards.

Gightis
جيغيتيس

Established by the Phoenicians, **GIGHTIS** became a trading post under the Carthaginians. The Gulf of Bou Grara could provide shelter for a large fleet and, recognizing its strategic importance, the Romans attacked the city during the first two Punic wars. After the campaign of Julius Caesar from 46 to 40 BC, the Romans assumed control and for the next two hundred years Gightis flourished as a major port of Africa Proconsularis and Byzacenia. The Roman trade route went from Carthage via Hammamet, El Jem and Gabès to Gightis and then on to Oea, Leptis Magna and Ghadames in Tripolitania. The city was later sacked by the Vandals, but the Byzantines thought it worthy of restoration. With the Arab invasion of the seventh century, however, the port was destroyed and the site covered over until excavations in 1906.

The **site** of Gightis (daily except Fri 8am–5pm; 1.1TD) lies next to the main road, 1km south of the village of Bon Grara. In fact, it is not fenced off and you can go in any time, although the *gardien* may come and ask you to pay the entrance fee. The larger central square, the **Forum**, dates from the reign of Emperor Hadrian (117–138 AD) and is overlooked by a **temple** dedicated to Serapis and Isis. A long flight of steps leads up to the top of the red sandstone podium, but little remains of the columns or interior walls. The stone-flagged road down to the port begins by the arch at the other end of the forum and passes, on the left, the **Temple of Bacchus**. Behind the portico, where only the fragments of columns remain, is an underground passage and several small rooms, their purpose unknown. The **port** has long since silted up, but a partly submerged row of stones marks the site of a **jetty**, once 140m long. Stone foundations by the road also give an idea of the town's extent – stretching to the Capitol Temple, at the top of a slight hill, towering above the shops and houses. On the right-hand side of the forum (as you face the sea) are the **baths** and several scraps of mosaic. Walking through the baths, away from the square, the **market** is ahead and just to the right; built in the third century, it consists of a central courtyard surrounded by a walkway, fitted out with shops. Nearby are the remains of villas and a temple of Mercury.

Bou Grara　　　　　　　　　　　　　　　　　　　بو غرارة

The new village of **BOU GRARA** is a kilometre up a sideroad, past the ruins. From the rock, on the right of the site, there's a sweeping view of the inland sea, mud flats and the older fishing port down below. Although French naval architects believed they could build a second Bizerte in this natural harbour, the modern port never quite lived up to the promise of its ancient predecessor: the water was far too shallow to accommodate heavy military vessels and the plans were scrapped.

Jerba to Zarzis and the Libyan frontier

Across the causeway from its namesake in Jerba, **EL KANTARA CONTINENT** has nothing special to commend it except an old **Turkish fort** gazing languidly at Borj Kastil across the water. From here, there are two roads to Zarzis: a coastal road via Hassi Jerbi, passing the tourist hotels and beach zone, and a less scenic but more direct route via Sidi Chammakh.

Some 12km down the coastal road, 9km north of Zarzis at **SANGHO**, two "**hotel clubs**" and a three-star hotel aim to provide everything you need – fortunately, as they're in the middle of nowhere. The three-star *Hôtel Club Oamarit* (☎05/705770, ☏705685; **⑥**) boasts a "semi-Olympic swimming pool with its basin for children" and "various restorative services" intriguingly available from reception. It also has several bars and restaurants, including a pizzeria, and a nightclub. The three-star *Sangho Club* next door (☎05/705124, ☏705715, ⓦwww.sangho.com; **⑦**) is more Club Med in style and altogether more exclusive than the *Oamarit*. On the other side of the *Oamarit*, the *Hôtel Gikitis* (☎05/705800, ☏705002; **⑥**) is quite well appointed for a three-star hotel, with two swimming pools (one indoor, one outdoor) and reasonably spacious rooms. For less than half the price of any of these, you could stay at the smaller but much friendlier two-star *Hôtel Zyen* (☎05/706630, ☏706629; **④**), just opposite the entrance to the *Sangho Club*, comfortable and spotlessly clean, with a/c rooms, a small pool, a large balcony for each room, and an upmarket restaurant (daily noon–3pm & 7–11pm), where you can get a seafood menu for 30TD or a *langouste* menu for 60TD. If none of these are to your taste, just south of the *Sangho Club* is the four-star *Odysée Resort* (☎05/705000, ☏705190, ⓦwww.odyseeresort.com; **⑦**), constructed in a modern adaptation of traditional Berber architecture, with forms reminiscent of Jerban mosques and the southern *ksour* (fortified granaries), with Berber carpets and motifs throughout – even the elevators are made of palm wood and lined with Berber rugs, and the large rooms have balconies overlooking a pool terrace. You can rent bicycles from both the hotel-clubs, and both have **car rental** offices – Hertz at the *Sangho*, Sixt/Express at the *Oamarit* – or you can rent a car from Victory Cars outside (☎05/705275). Sports such as water-skiing, jet skiing and windsurfing are available on the beach, and horse-riding is also possible (there's a ranch opposite the entrance to the *Oamarit*).

Rather more refined than any of these, though in roughly the same price bracket, is the *Sultana Residence* (☎05/705206, ☏705167; **⑥**), less than a kilometre south along the coast. A tranquil, relaxing little place, it's like a classier version of a *pension de famille*, with a pool and a Jacuzzi, nine rooms, each one different, and a pier for sea swimming. A little luxury they also provide – the only place in Tunisia to do so – is mosquito nets.

Zarzis

جرجيس

Halfway down the coast that nearly encloses the Gulf of Bou Grara, **ZARZIS** has a good, long beach with new hotels, though it pales in comparison with Houmt Souk and much of Jerba. Even so, French officers considered it the cushiest posting in the south, a paradise after the parched heat of the interior. It was also the only place south of Gabès that suffered settlement by French colonists. Unfortunately, they didn't get on too well with the military, who feared that if too many colonists arrived they would lose their holiday resort to the civil administration, and did everything they could to make their lives difficult. The colonists, in turn, sent frequent complaints to the government, claiming that the army ruled with "the sword and the bull whip rather than any legal code". In the end, Independence arrived before the military could be persuaded to abandon the town.

The Town

Avenue Mohamed V is the main road in from Jerba. The third exit from **place de la Jeunesse**, the town's central roundabout, is rue Hedi Chaker, which leads to **place 7 Novembre**. From there, avenue Habib Thameur heads off towards the **port** and avenue Bourguiba towards Ben Gardane. The coastal road up to the *zone touristique* leads through a large military camp, so it's probably not the best place for an evening stroll.

Zarzis's **bus station** (☎05/684372 for SRT services, ☎05/681643 for SNTRI services) is down towards the port, beyond the end of avenue Habib Thameur. The *zone touristique* and Sangho can be reached by local bus #1 (10 daily). **Louages** leave just outside (see pp.391–392 for details of bus and louage services).

There isn't much to see around Zarzis. Like Sfax, the town is surrounded by olive plantations, most of which were planted in the twentieth century. Until recently, few travellers ever bothered to go further east, but since Libya has tentatively (though spo-

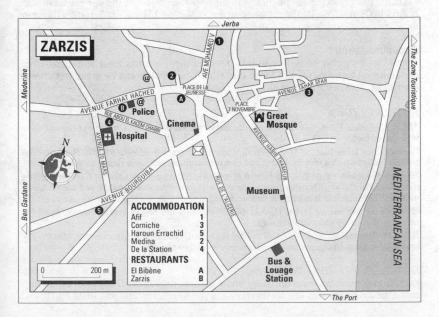

radically) started allowing entry to tourists, Ben Gardane and Ras Ajdir are slightly more on the beaten track. The **beach** at Zarzis's *zone touristique*, 3km north of town, near the village of Souihel, has the best swimming in the area, and the *Zarzis* and *Zita* hotels have decent swimming pools. Barriers at the hotels' entrances prohibit roaming Tunisians, but tourists should be able to get in.

Market days in the souk are Monday and Friday (Saturday in Souihel); there is little of interest in Zarzis otherwise. The main highlight in town is a small **museum** (Tues–Sun: mid-April to mid-Sept 8am–noon & 3–7pm; mid-Sept to mid-April 9.30am–4.30pm; 1.1TD) of locally discovered Roman artefacts in an old church on avenue Habib Thameur. A private **"Museum of Traditions and Costumes"** (variable hours; 2TD) lies between the *zone touristique* and the centre of town; head north on avenue Mohamed V for 1km from place de la Jeunesse, then 700m east on avenue de l'Environnement. It consists of a small collection of old pots, pans and agricultural tools, housed in a hewn-out underground cavern formerly used as an oil press, which is a lot more interesting than any of the exhibits. Its young proprietor is on hand to show you around. The only other thing of interest in Zarzis, other than the beach, is an annual **sponge festival** held in the last week of July.

Practicalities

Place de la Jeunesse has a few **banks** (the Banque du Sud on av Mohamed V has an ATM), as does place 7 November; the **post office** (country hours) is just off the square. There are two **internet offices**: Espace d'Internet on avenue Farhat Hached, about 200m west of place de la Jeunesse (daily 9am–10pm; 2TD/hr), and Publinet (daily 9am–9pm; 2TD/hr), just off avenue Farhat Hached, a block west of the *Hôtel Medina*. There's a Magasin Général **supermarket** at the next roundabout; the **hospital** (℡05/694302) is just around the corner in avenue 20 Mars, with an *infirmerie* opposite at no.43, and a **night pharmacy** at the junction of 20 Mars and avenue Farhat Hached. The **police** station is also on rue 2 Mars (℡05/694745).

On the main road outside the hotels in the *zone touristique* are the **car rental** offices of Avis (℡05/694706), by the entrance to the *Zephir*, and Hertz (℡05/694284), nearer the *Zarzis*.

Accommodation

Zarzis has a number of budget **hotels**, most of them not too great and many often closed for no apparent reason. More upmarket beach hotels can be found in the *zone touristique*, 3km north of town along the coast.

HOTELS IN TOWN

Afif, av Mohamed V ℡05/684639. A very reasonable second best to the *Corniche*: cheap and clean with shared bathrooms. **②**

Corniche, av Tahar Sfar, off pl 7 Novembre towards the sea ℡ & ℡05/692822. The best-value cheapie in Zarzis with a friendly, bright and clean atmosphere, and some rooms en suite. **②**

Haroun Errachid, rte de Ben Gardane ℡ & ℡05/684332. At the beginning of the Ben Gardane road. Reasonable if slightly dingy rooms, some with shower (but shared toilet), and some without windows. The reception is in the café downstairs. **②**

Hôtel de la Station, av Farhat Hached ℡05/684661. By the SNTRI station. Simple, small but decent rooms, many with bathrooms. **②**

Hôtel Medina (aka *Hôtel de Ville*), off av Farhat Hached, near pl de la Jeunesse ℡05/691901. The best hotel in town. Cool, clean rooms with their own bathrooms. **③**

HOTELS IN THE ZONE TOURISTIQUE

Zarzis's *zone touristique* was originally home to three package hotels known as "*les trois zeds*": the *Zarzis* towards the northern end of the beach, the *Zita* just to its north, and the *Zephir*, now closed, to its south, all catering for a mainly German clientele. In recent years, a few smaller hotels have opened up here, plus a number of restaurants.

Amira, on the beach, 300m south of the *Zarzis* ☎ & ℻05/694188. Cheap and friendly, with a beach bar. ❷

Errachid, on the main road about 300m south of the *Zarzis* ☎05/694919. A small, friendly, good-value cheapie, clean and comfortable with a sun terrace and kitchen on the roof. If no one is in reception, ask at the house behind. ❷

Nozha ★★, halfway between the town and the *zone touristique* ☎05/694593, ℻683335. Homely and comfortable, with its own bit of rather exposed rocky beach. ❸

L'Oasis, ☎05/690483. A friendly, quiet little hotel on the main road, across the street and a little to the south of the *Errachid*. All rooms have their own shower. ❸

Zarzis ★★★, northern end of the beach ☎05/684160, ℻694292, ✉zarzis.hotel@planet.tn. Reasonably classy as three-star package hotels go, with a clientele made up mainly of German sun-seekers. Wheelchair-friendly. ❺

Ziha ☎05/684304, ℻694680. A newer, fourth "*zed*", 100m off the beach behind the *Amira*. The rooms are smaller (and slightly cheaper) than in the two surviving original "*zeds*", and the pool is more like a large bathtub. ❹

Zita ★★, north of the *Zarzis* ☎05/694246, ℻684350. Sister hotel to the *Zarzis*, a smaller and lower-key place that closes out of season. ❺

Eating in Zarzis

The best place to **eat** in town is the moderately priced *Restaurant el Bibène*, on avenue Farhat Hached just off place de la Jeunesse (daily 10am–9pm). The *Restaurant de la Station* (daily noon–8.30pm) by the hotel of the same name also offers decent, moderately priced food. Cheaper eats can be had on avenue Farhat Hached at the *Restaurant Zarzis* (daily noon–2.30pm & 6–9pm), by the *Hôtel L'Olivier*.

More upmarket eating can be found in the *zone touristique*. *Le Pirate* (daily 9.30am–midnight; ☎05/684497) is the most prominent restaurant here, with a popular open-air terrace, where you can eat for around 15TD. Slightly pricier but also classier alternatives include *Le Château* just to the south (daily noon–11pm), where dishes include prawn kebabs and octopus provençale, and *La Pacha*, a little way north towards the *Hôtel Zarzis* (daily noon–midnight), specializing in seafood, with live music nightly from 7pm. Across the road from *La Pacha* is a cheap rôtisserie.

SPONGES

Once thought to be a plant, a **sponge** is in fact an animal, but one of the simplest forms of animal life. A sponge has no organs – no heart or brain for example – but consists of cells with different functions. There are over five thousand species in the world; some gather on rocks like moss, while others are free-standing, and only attached at the bottom. They go back a long way in time, indeed, some fossilized sponges from Tunisia date back to the Jurassic period, when the country was underwater. The Mediterranean Sea is very rich in sponges, particularly soft and flexible ones, and people living around the Mediterranean have used them for centuries: the Romans for example used them as toilet paper. A sponge is covered with small holes, or pores, which continually suck in water. Inside the sponge, special cells called choanocytes extract oxygen, and also food in the form of planktonic plants. Waste is expelled through a larger hole in the top called the osculum, or through medium-sized holes called ostia. Sponges are hermaphrodite, but when mating, each sponge takes the role of one sex. The tiny larvae released by the sponge playing the female role drift in the plankton for just a few days before attaching themselves to rocks to start growing. Also, if part of a sponge is broken off it will become an independent animal. Most bathroom "sponges" used nowadays are artificial, made of plastic foam or other chemical products. Tunisia is a good place to find the real thing.

East of Zarzis

The road south towards **Ben Gardane** (there are buses and regular louages) skirts the **Sebkhet el Mellah**, a large salt flat that was the site of a mustard gas factory during World War I and today contains a massive salt mine. Seventeen kilometres south of Zarzis, a road leads to the village of **Biban**, at the end of a long spit. Beyond it (and inaccessible without permission), an old Turkish fort, **Borj el Biban**, sits on a little island of its own. There are a few sandy beaches, mainly on the southern side of the spit – not up to Jerba's standards, but totally deserted if you can get to them. From the east, another spit stretches out towards Borj el Biban, the channel between them once marking the border with Libya. The lagoon enclosed by the two spits, **Bahiret el Biban**, is full of fish and rich in bird life, notably flamingos, spoonbills and other waders. Easily accessible sites for spotting them can be found back on the main road, a few kilometres south of the Biban turn-off, where it crosses the eastern corner of the lagoon.

Ben Gardane   بنڤردين

Off the beaten track for many years, **BEN GARDANE** is the last main town before the Libyan frontier, and a staging post on the route to Libya. The road from Zarzis meets the road to Medenine at a roundabout with a clock in the middle of it, which is where you will be dropped if arriving by SRT bus. Louages and SNTRI buses will leave you 100m from here up the Zarzis road. Also off the roundabout is avenue Habib Thameur, which becomes the road to Ras Ajdir (turn right at the end and then bear left at the next roundabout).

Ben Gardane is also host to no fewer than three markets. The weekly Saturday **souk**, in the centre of town just south of avenue Habib Thameur, is very lively and far more agricultural than others in the south; there is also a **Libyan market**, similar to the one in Houmt Souk, but bigger and less tourist-conscious, in a walled enclosure about a kilometre up the Zarzis road. This operates every day, but especially on Sundays when all the stalls are open. At one time, you could get goods and brands from Egypt and Libya, many not normally seen in Tunisia, and often as not sold from the back of pick-up trucks. Nowadays you will be hard put to find anything here that cannot be bought elsewhere in Tunisia, but the market is still large and lively. Finally, on the road to Mouamarat, 3km south of town (take the road south of the hospital, bear right at the fork after 500m and continue for a couple of kilometres), there is a Thursday-morning **livestock market**.

PRACTICALITIES

Ben Gardane has the usual **banks** (though money-changers at the louage station and on avenue Habib Thameur buy or sell Libyan dinars and sell Tunisian dinars for hard currency). There's also a **post office** (country hours) at the eastern end of avenue Habib Thameur, and a Grand Magasin **supermarket**, about 50m towards Ras Ajdir from the post office.

There are around a dozen **hotels** in Ben Gardane. The biggest and poshest (which isn't saying much) is the *Pavilion Vert* on the Ras Ajdir road (℡05/710103; **③**), with en-suite rooms, but starting to show its age. A good-value alternative is the *Residence Tines*, just next to the SNTRI office (℡05/712378, ℻712658; **②**), with spotless rooms, some en suite, and a garden out back for coffee or pizzas. Other reasonable options include the *El Ouns* (℡05/710920, ℻710258; **②**), a decent enough, dusty city hotel 100m down the Medenine road from its junction with the Zarzis road, also with en-suite rooms. For **food** there are a number of cheap *gargotes* on the main road through town. If you prefer something a little more refined, your only option is the moderately-priced restaurant at the *Pavilion Vert* (open 24hr).

The SRTGM **bus station** (☎05/710026) is on the roundabout where the roads to Zarzis and Ras Ajdir meet. Buses tend to peter out around midday, but there are services to Gabès, Houmt Souk, Medenine, Ras Ajdir and Zarzis. From the SNTRI office, 50m up the Zarzis road (☎05/711400), there are departures to Tunis (via Sfax and Sousse, or by night via Kairouan), all passing through Medenine and Gabès. If you don't coincide with a bus, you'll find **louages** just opposite. Note that for Tripoli, you'll have to change at Ras Ajdir.

Onward to Libya

If you're striking out for **Libya**, the Tunisian frontier post is at **RAS AJDIR**, 33km east of Ben Gardane, but you'll encounter several police checks on the way. Although there is a Libyan embassy in Tunis (see p.105) and a consulate in Sfax (see p.248), it may be easier to arrange a visa from home. At Ras Ajdir, the prevailing atmosphere is one of complete chaos as you get out of your vehicle to go through the various **formalities**, which include filling out a departure card and getting your passport stamped. There are 24-hour **exchange facilities**, but you should avoid using them if possible (apart from the queues, the rates are bad and they may decide on a whim not to change travellers' cheques).

Buying Libyan dinars is quite easy on the road to the frontier. Money-changers line the road all the way from Medenine, waving their wads of bills at passing cars. Ascertain the going rate before you start haggling (it's usually about three times the official rate). If you are coming from Libya, the same money-changers will sell Tunisian currency for dollars, euros, sterling or Libyan dinars. Remember that it is officially illegal to import or export Tunisian currency in or out of Tunisia, or to take Libyan currency into Libya.

There are always plenty of vehicles at the border, and you should have no difficulty finding **transport** to Tripoli, 196km away (4hr). Note that louages in Libya are called *taxi binasser*, or "service taxis". Once over the border, the first thing you notice will probably be the improved state of the roads. The main place of interest between the border and Tripoli is the Roman site at **Sabrata**, with a Punic mausoleum to complement its sisters at Dougga and Maktar among its other well-preserved remains. **Arriving from Libya** at Ras Ajdir, you will find five daily buses plus plenty of louages to Ben Gardane, with onward transport from there, but there are also three direct daily buses from Ras Ajdir to Gabès, and one SNTRI service to Tunis via Kairouan.

travel details

Buses

Ben Gardane to: Gabès (5 daily; 2hr 15min); Houmt Souk (3 daily; 2hr); Kairouan (1 daily; 6hr 30min); Medenine (10 daily; 1hr 20min); Ras Ajdir (5 daily; 40min); Sfax (2 daily; 4hr 30min); Sousse (2 daily; 7hr); Tunis (3 daily; 9hr); Zarzis (5 daily; 1hr).

Houmt Souk (Jerba) to: Ben Gardane (3 daily; 2hr); Bizerte (2 daily; 10hr); Gabès (10 daily; 2hr 30min); Kairouan (3 daily; 7hr); Medenine (6 daily; 2hr); Sousse (2 daily; 6hr 45min); Sfax (4 daily; 4hr 30min); Tataouine (2 daily; 3hr); Tunis (4 daily; 8hr 30min); Zarzis (6 daily; 1hr).

Ras Ajdir to: Ben Gardane (5 daily; 40min); Gabès (3 daily; 3hr); Kairouan (1 daily; 7hr); Tripoli (several daily; 4hr); Tunis (1 daily; 9hr 30min).

Zarzis to: Ben Gardane (5 daily; 1hr); Bizerte (1 daily; 10hr 30min); Gabès (5 daily; 2hr 30min); Houmt Souk (8 daily; 1hr); Kairouan (2 daily; 7hr 30min); Medenine (8 daily; 1hr); Sfax (1 daily; 4hr); Sousse (1 daily; 6hr 30min); Tataouine (1 daily; 2hr); Tunis (2 daily; 9hr).

Louages

Louage journey times are roughly three-quarters the time taken by buses on the same route.

Frequency depends on demand, but morning is always the best time to get a louage, especially for longer journeys.

Ben Gardane to: Gabès (2hr 30min); Houmt Souk (1hr 45min); Medenine (1hr); Ras Ajdir (30min); Tataouine (1hr 20min); Tunis (9hr); Zarzis (45min).

Houmt Souk (Jerba) to: Ajim (20min); Ben Gardane (1hr 45min); Gabès (2hr); Medenine (1hr 20min); Sfax (4hr); Tunis (8hr 30min); Zarzis (1hr); sometimes direct to Tataouine (2hr).

Ras Ajdir to: Ben Gardane (30min); Tripoli (3hr 30min).

Zarzis to: Ben Gardane (45min), Gabès (2hr 30min), Houmt Souk (1hr), Medenine (1hr), Tataouine (1hr 45min); Tunis (9hr).

Ferries

Jorf to: Ajim (every 30min–2hr; 15min).

Flights

Jerba to: Tunis (5 daily with Tuninter; 45min–1hr).

CHAPTER NINE

THE KSOUR

O f all Tunisia, the **south**, the region that dips down towards the border with Libya and Algeria, is the most exciting and remote, and has long been this way. In the Middle Ages, Arab travellers avoided the area because the tribes were notorious for their lawlessness and banditry. It was a reputation that passed onto later generations: during the eighteenth and nineteenth centuries few European travellers entered the region, and only three are known to have visited **Medenine**, still the largest and most important town in the area. Even the intrepid James Bruce, who went on to discover the source of the Nile, preferred to take the boat from Gabès rather than risk his neck with these tribes. When the French invaded in 1881, they too gave the region a wide berth. It was many years before it was fully integrated, and remained under military administration until 1956.

MARKET DAYS

Monday – Tataouine
Thursday – Beni Kheddache, Tataouine

Friday – Ghoumrassen, Ksar Jedid
Sunday – Medenine, Remada

With their steep escarpments, the south's arid mountains are impressive in themselves, but even more striking are the treasures hidden among them: the **ksour** (*ksar* in the singular), which are fortified communal granaries for the region's nomadic tribes, and the ancient Berber villages of **Douiret**, **Chenini**, **Guermessa** and **Ghoumrassen**. Strange and extraordinary as monuments, they are even more remarkable as living settlements in so barren a land.

The people themselves are another reason to visit: there's little of the hassle that you come to expect in the north, and people here are cool and reserved – in part, perhaps, due to the comparative absence of tourists. There are few hotels and facilities to attract visitors, and those who do come tend to be on whistlestop Land Rover tours. If you want to explore in more depth, you'll have to put up with "roughing it in a very moderate way", as Sir Harry Johnston put it in 1892.

Transport is the greatest problem you'll face in travelling independently. The road network is sparse, and joins modern French towns like **Zarzis** (see p.387), **Medenine** and **Tataouine**, rather than the more interesting villages. Buses are few and the louage

---

ACCOMMODATION PRICE CODES

The hotels and pensions listed in this book have been price-graded according to the following scale. The prices quoted are for the **cheapest available double room in high season**. For more on accommodation prices and categories, see Basics, p.29.

① Under 10TD
② 10–20TD
③ 20–40TD
④ 40–70TD

⑤ 70–100TD
⑥ 100–150TD
⑦ 150TD upwards

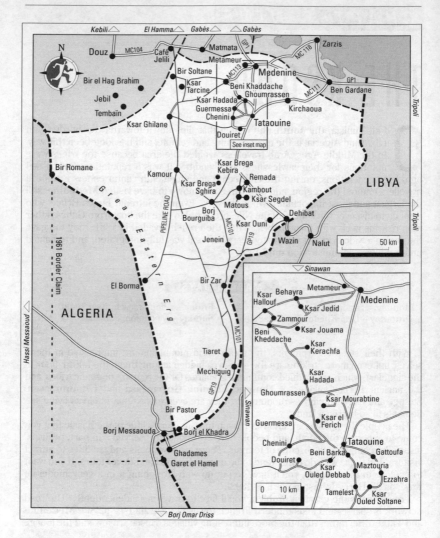

service is less dependable than in the north, so you may have to hire a taxi, arrange a lift or hitch. There is always more transport in the morning and it often dries up completely by the afternoon, so the earlier you set out the better. But there's invariably some way of getting where you want, and the effort is generously rewarded.

Medenine and around مدنين

Before the French occupation, **MEDENINE** was the focus of everything that mattered in the south, with a huge weekly market attracting merchants from as far afield as Tunis, Tripoli, Tebessa in Algeria, and even Bornu in present-day northern Nigeria. It was also the central granary of the **Touazine** and **Khezour**, tribes belonging to the powerful **Ouerghamma confederation** of Berber-speaking tribes (see box p.404), who had moved from Ghoumrassen on the advice of their marabout, Sidi el Assaibi. As a base for the confederation, Medenine grew rapidly from about 1800, and, at its height, the town's *ksar* had some eight thousand *ghorfas*, or cells to store grain. The French established their southern headquarters here and its flimsy appearance hasn't improved much since. Nevertheless the town is the regional centre and you'll have to pass through it at some point, probably even stay the night.

Sadly, Medenine's **ksar** has gradually been demolished since the early twentieth century, when the tribes began to store their grain in silos near the fields rather than carry it all the way into town. One large courtyard remains, right in town on avenue 7 Novembre. With its **ghorfas** converted into curio shops, busloads of holidaymakers are driven in to look at it (nearby cafés double their prices for anyone looking remotely like a tourist). There are some more *ghorfas* behind it, mainly abandoned, but up to three storeys high and giving a much better idea of the original construction. On the whole, the *ksar* is a disappointment, but it forms an introduction to those to the west and further south, which, although originally far smaller, are much better preserved.

The main **market** area is just to the north of the *ksar*. There are stalls out every day, but more so on market day, Sunday, when they take up a large part of the *oued* just south of boulevard 7 Novembre as well.

GHORFAS, KALA'A AND KSOUR

Throughout the south, nomadic Berbers stored their grain in **ghorfas**, small stone cells (the Arabic word means "room" – you can ask for a *ghorfa* in a hotel) a couple of metres high and five to ten metres long. The cells were generally constructed on top of one another and side by side, at times reaching eight storeys. Individual units were always built in the same way, with grain sacks full of earth placed between the two side walls to act as a support during the construction of the roof. A layer of matting was placed over the top of these sacks, in the form of an arch, and then covered with clay, mortar and gypsum. When it had dried, the clay was chipped away, the sacks and net removed, and a palm-wood door fitted at the front. The rough inner walls were covered with plaster, usually with stucco figures such as hands or fish to ward off the evil eye, sometimes with inscriptions or geometric patterns, or spots on the ceiling representing rain.

In the tenth century, the Arab tribes of the Banu Hilal moved west into Tunisia from Egypt at the invitation of the Fatimids and with the promise of rich booty. In the first years of the Arab invasion, the Berbers retreated inland to the high mountaintops, building **forts** (or *kala'a*) near their cave dwellings. Once the Arabs had occupied the fertile land the Berbers were forced into peace treaties and the *kala'a* were replaced by the **ksour** (*ksar* in the singular), fortified granaries belonging to each tribe, where they could store and if need be defend their grain. Ksour were usually built in easily defensible positions, such as at the top of a rocky crag, and consisted of *ghorfas* built one next to the other in several storeys facing into a courtyard. The outer defensive wall of the *ksar* consisted of the back of these *ghorfas*, presenting a blank facade to the would-be assailant. The shape of the perimeter was dictated by the site, whether along a hilltop, as at Ksar Jouama, on a hillside, as at Ksar Ouled Soltane, or down in the more spacious river valley, like Medenine, where the less defensive position of the *ksar* is a mark of its builders' confidence in their military superiority.

But the *ksar* was not just a place to store grain. Often a mosque would be built just outside it, and on Fridays the nomadic farmers would gather here to pray communally, and after prayer, they would spend some time together in the courtyard of the *ksar* drinking tea and exchanging news. Thus the *ksar* became the centre of the community as well as a place to store their food supply and if necessary defend it.

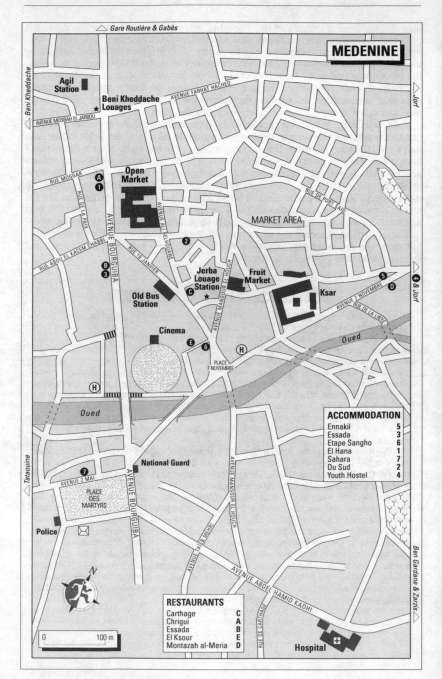

△ *Gare Routière & Gabès*

MEDENINE

Agil
Station

Beni Kheddache
Louages

AVENUE FARHAT HACHED

Beni Kheddache

AVENUE MOSBAH EL JARBOU

RUE MOGGAR

Open
Market

RUE DE LA PAIX

AVENUE BOURGUIBA

RUE ABOUL EL KACEM CHABBI

RUE 18 JANVIER

AVENUE ALI BELHOUANE

RUE DE PORT SAID

MARKET AREA

Jerba
Louage
Station

AVENUE MANSOUR EL HOUCH

Fruit
Market

Ksar

AVENUE 7 NOVEMBRE

RUE DE LA LIBYE

Old Bus
Station

Cinema

PLACE
7 NOVEMBRE

Oued

Oued

ACCOMMODATION
Ennakil   5
Essada   3
Etape Sangho   6
El Hana   1
Sahara   7
Du Sud   2
Youth Hostel   4

National Guard

AVENUE 2 MAI

AVENUE BOURGUIBA

AVENUE MANSOUR EL HOUCH

PLACE
DES
MARTYRS

Police

N

0   100 m

RESTAURANTS
Carthage   C
Chrigui   A
Essada   B
El Ksour   E
Montazah al-Meria D

AVENUE TAIEB MEHRI

AVENUE ABDEL HAMID KADHI

RUE DE CARTHAGE

Hospital

Practicalities

Arriving from most places by bus or louage, you'll probably be dropped at the new *gare routière*, 2km out of town on the Gabès road. Here taxis wait to ferry new arrivals into town. Only if coming from Jerba, Zarzis or Ben Gardane will louages drop you off in the town centre, as will some buses coming from Jerba and Jorf. Buses from Tataouine also stop in the centre of Medenine before continuing up to the *gare routière*.

The town centre is concentrated down by the Oued Medenine el Gueblaoui at **place des Martyrs**, where you'll find the **post office** (city hours). Here **avenue Bourguiba**, the main road in from Gabès, meets the roads to Tataouine (av 2 Mai), Jorf (av 7 Novembre) and Ben Gardane (av Abdel Hamid el Kadhi). The main round-about, **place 7 Novembre**, with a very gaudy tiled sculpture, is 100m up towards Jorf.

Banks are mostly by the main roundabout, place 7 Novembre, or on avenue Bourguiba up above its junction with rue 18 Janvier, with a rota system so that one bank is always open on Saturday and Sunday mornings. The Banque du Sud on avenue Bourguiba at the corner of rue Moggar has an ATM that accepts Visa and Mastercard. There's a **cinema** at the top of a pedestrian area between avenue Bourguiba and place 7 Novembre, and a **hammam** the other side of avenue Bourguiba just by the *oued* (daily: men 5am–noon & 6pm–midnight; women 1–6pm), with another at 24 av 7 Novembre (similar hours). For essential supplies, there's a Grand Magasin **supermarket** at 18 av Bourguiba. The **hospital** (☎05/640830) is on the Ben Gardane road, about 400m up from place des Martyrs, and there's a night pharmacy at 46 av Bourguiba.

Accommodation

Medenine's **hotels** have improved somewhat in recent years and, though there aren't many of them, they offer decent options in both cheap and mid-price ranges. In addition to the hotels in town, there is also accommodation at the nearby *ksar* of Metameur (see p.398).

HOTELS

Ennakil, av 7 Novembre ☎05/640592. The beds are a bit on the soft side but are apparently to be replaced, and the shared toilets and showers could be better, but it's friendly, and the rooms are clean if bare. **②**

Essada, 87 av Bourguiba ☎05/640300. Rather spartan, but clean and with windows opening onto a central terrace, and some rooms with shower. **①**

Hôtel Étape Sangho ★★, pl 7 Novembre ☎05/643878 or 9, ☏640550. The best hotel in town, and not a bad place, with comfortable rooms and a bar, though rather impersonal, and doesn't really have much on the *Sahara*, despite the stars. **④**

El Hana, av Bourguiba ☎05/640690. A simple but clean and respectable hotel, with its own parking space out back, and private showers in some rooms. **①**

Sahara, av 2 Mai ☎05/640007. A pleasant, comfortable place, newly refurbished and good value, with bright clean a/c rooms, all en suite though not huge. Those on the top floor are the cheapest, those on the first floor (with TV) the priciest, and those on the middle floor in between. **②**

Hôtel du Sud, rue Abderrahim Ibn Khaldoun, off av Ali Belhouane ☎05/640354. Basic and not recommended for women. **②**

YOUTH HOSTEL

Maison des Jeunes, rue des Palmiers ☎05/640338. Unsignposted in a group of white buildings about 500m past the *ksar* on the left. A bit of a barracks with the usual rules: curfew at 10pm, up and out at 9am. Dorm beds for 5TD.

MOVING ON FROM MEDENINE

For a rundown of destinations and journey times, see Travel Details on p.421.

Most buses and louages leave from a new *gare routière* 2km up the Gabès road. There are eight daily **buses** to Tunis, five overnight, with two day and two night services going via Sfax and Sousse, the rest via Kairouan, including one that continues to Bizerte.

Eight daily buses (six SRT, two SNTRI) serve Tataouine, five continuing to Ghoumrassen, which also has one direct service. SRT services for Tataouine and Ghoumrassen also stop in the town centre so it is not necessary to go up to the *gare routière* to catch them: stops are on avenue Bourguiba south of *Hôtel Essada*, and avenue 2 Mai west of place des Martyrs, but the bus may well fill up at these stops, leaving standing room only.

Services to Jorf and Jerba use the old bus station on rue 18 Janvier, as do the two morning SRT departures to Zarzis, but the two SNTRI services and two afternoon SRT departures for Zarzis leave from the *gare routière*. The best thing to do is check the latest situation at the old bus station before setting out.

Louages for Gabès, Ghoumrassen, Sfax, Tataouine and Tunis all leave from the *gare routière*, but those for Zarzis, Jerba and Ben Gardane usually leave from the old louage stand off rue 18 Janvier near the old bus station. Louages for Beni Kheddache leave from the beginning of rue Mosbah el Jarbou, next to the Agil station, as do Beni Kheddache buses and *camionettes* for Ksar Hallouf. For a day-trip round some of the *ksour*, a group of four or five may find it economical to negotiate a rate with a louage driver, though officially this may be illegal due to restrictions on the routes that louage drivers are allowed to ply.

Eating and drinking

Medenine is not the place for gourmets, but reasonable **food** can be found here. The best of the cheap eating is the *Restaurant el Ksour* off rue 18 Janvier by the side of the *Hôtel Étape Sangho* (daily 7am–3pm & 6–9pm), with tasty food at low prices, a good sit-down *lablabi* for breakfast, and *shawarma* (Tues–Thurs only). Alternatives in the same price range include the *Restaurant Chrigui* (daily noon–4pm & 6–9pm), on avenue Bourguiba by the *Hôtel el Hana*, the *Restaurant Essada* (daily 7am–midnight), by the hotel of the same name at 91 av Bourguiba, and the *Restaurant Carthage* (daily 6am–11pm), opposite the bus station at rue 18 Janvier. For more refined meals, the *Restaurant Café Patisserie Montazah al-Meria* at 89–93 avenue 7 Novembre (daily 10am–9pm) serves pizzas and grills indoors or in a pleasant back garden overlooking the *oued*, and is also a good place to stop for a coffee. For a beer, your best bet is the bar of the *Hôtel Sahara*.

Metameur   أم التـمـر

The six-hundred-year-old **ksar** of **METAMEUR** has a dramatic silhouette, standing isolated in the plain. Though quite small, with three courtyards and *ghorfas* that reach only three storeys, it's remarkably well preserved and hasn't been converted wholesale to tourist use. It's a short bus ride (6km) along the Medenine–Gabès road, or an easy enough hitch from the top of avenue Bourguiba in Medenine to the turn-off, from where it's a one-kilometre walk to the village.

The village was founded around the thirteenth century by a local marabout, Sidi Ahmed Ben Adjel, who set up shop in a cave, and the local nomads who followed him. Today the village is still occupied by Sidi Ahmed's descendants, the **Temara**, and the descendants of his followers, the Berber **Harraza**. At one time each Harraza family would pay its Arab Temara masters in wheat, barley, oil and the much-prized local wood. In autumn and winter the *ksar* is barely used by the Temara and Harraza tribes-people, as they're out in the plains with their herds; it is at its busiest in summer. On Fridays the **Mosque of Sidi Ahmed Ben Adjel**, housing the saint's tomb, also draws a congregation mainly comprising nomads from the surrounding pastures.

The best preserved of the *ksar*'s courtyards has in the past been used as a hotel, called *Hôtel les Ghorfas* (☎05/640128; ❷), with accommodation in the *ghorfas*. At last check, this was closed, and it remains uncertain whether or not it will reopen. There is however *Café Ghorfa*, which is open until late, and serves snacks as well as tea, coffee and *chicha* pipes.

A piste from Metameur leads west to Toujane and Matmata. It is possible to cover the 56km in a car without 4WD, but progress is slow, and it's faster (and safer) to go the long way round via Gabès.

The Jebel Haouaia   جبل خوية

Although there's a main road south from Medenine straight to Tataouine, with a branch off to Ghoumrassen, it goes through the plain, a route that's uniformly dull. A spectacular alternative is to make a detour to the west via **Ksar Jouama**, **Beni Kheddache** and **Ksar Hadada**, straight through the rugged mountains of **Jebel Haouaia**, where some of the most impressive *ksour* sit perched on mountain spurs.

If you plan on doing this, take note that it's not easy. **Public transport** runs south-west from Medenine as far as Beni Kheddache, and north from Tataouine to Ghoumrassen, and thence to Ksar Hadada; but making the connection without your own car involves hitching the 22km between Beni Kheddache and Ksar Hadada. Otherwise, the easiest route to Ghoumrassen is either by direct bus from Medenine, or from Tataouine in the south (see p.404).

Medenine to Beni Kheddache

Three daily buses, plus regular louages, run west along the road from Medenine to Ksar Jouama and Beni Kheddache. All of them leave from the beginning of avenue Masbah Jarbou (left off av Bourguiba, at the top of the hill by the Agil station). Failing that, you could try hitching from further along the same road.

The bus from Medenine stops briefly after 20km at **KSAR JEDID** (New Ksar), only one-storey high and built in 1916 when the security imposed by the French army allowed the mountain tribes to store their grain safely in the plains. This was the first stage in the process of abandonment: within twenty years, the tribes had stopped using *ksour* altogether, keeping their grain in unprotected silos near the fields. *Camionettes* also connect Ksar Jedid with Medenine and Ksar Hallouf.

From Ksar Jedid the road climbs the escarpment for 8km – where the view from the top is amazing – to **KSAR JOUAMA** and the modern village of the same name. The *ksar*, dramatically perched on the scarp, with sheer drops on three sides, is just visible to the south of the road on the crest of a steep hill. A path from the road, a little walk back from the bus stop and village shop, leads past a deserted **mosque** to the bottleneck of the *ksar* and its entrance **gate**. An inscription gives the date 1177 AH (1763–4 AD), though it may well have been constructed earlier. The Jouama tribe, who founded it, apparently on the ruins of a much older fortified Berber village, were part of the Brega, who moved up here after abandoning their base south of Remada at the end of seventeenth century (see p.418). Decades of disuse have taken their toll – the outer **wall** is now crumbling and some of the **ghorfas** have collapsed – but it still makes a strong impression. If you've taken an early bus, it's possible to stop off at Ksar Jouama and catch the next one – if you can attract the driver's attention. Or try hitching, as it's a busy road.

BENI KHEDDACHE is 8km further on, a large village that used to be another mountain *ksar*. Reginald Rankin (see p.484), who came here in the 1890s, described it as "a sort of Saharan Windsor", with walls 20m high and 90m long and a courtyard covering eighteen thousand square metres. Unfortunately it was demolished by the French just before World War II to make way for a market. However, a few **ghorfas** survive behind the **mosque**, whilst the *ksar* has become a settlement – a village and market centre for the surrounding tribes. Souk day is Thursday.

There are no hotels in Beni Kheddache; the nearest place to sleep is 2km away at Zammour, (see below), and halfway to it, a kilometre up the Zammour road, and right at the top of a hill, is the moderately priced *Restaurant Le Bedouin* (daily 9am–9pm, though best to check in advance; ☎05/637258), with terrace eating and great views. The last bus back to Medenine goes at about 6pm. There are also louages and pick-ups to Medenine and Ksar Hallouf, but none south to Ksar Hadada. You could try **hitching** down there, but start early as the road is very quiet. The piste heading west to Ksar Ghilane (see p.414) is pretty well impassable without 4WD.

Zammour and Ksar Hallouf

Just 2km north of Beni Kheddache (bear right where the road forks) is **ZAMMOUR**, where a track to the right leads up to a **ksar**. Small and largely ruined, it compensates with great views. There is a **"station touristique"** in Zammour (☎ & ℱ05/637196; ❷), where you can sleep in a former cave dwelling, which is cosier than it sounds, with hot showers and hot meals available (though you should phone ahead to arrange these). Two daily buses connect Zammour to Medenine, and there are also louages.

Beyond Zammour, 8km of tarmac and 4km of piste brings you to **KSAR HALLOUF**, a small thirteenth-century *ksar* overlooking a fertile valley. It's worth climbing up for the views of the plain, with Jerba visible in the hazy distance. In the *ksar*, as well as a traditional camel-worked olive press, there's a *Relai* **hotel** (☎05/637148, ℱ637320; ❷), where you can spend the night in a *ghorfa*. It's a bit rustic (there are toilets but no showers), but it's a beautiful spot and even if you don't want to stay there, you could just stop off for a very reasonably priced couscous dinner. Overlooking the *ksar* is a strange curiosity: a circular wall, less than a metre high with a gap facing the rising sun. Opposite the gap is a small altar, where candles are burnt and coins left as offerings. Supposedly this is a marabout, but it's actually pagan in origin (compare the shrine of Lalla Mna in Le Kef mentioned on p.278). Dust from the altar is used as "medicine" against illness, and the shrine is in regular use, though there's a mosque below it, disused and in ruins.

Camionettes run a shuttle service to Beni Kheddache and Medenine. The partly unsurfaced road from Zammour to Hallouf is passable in a regular car, as is the road to Behayra and Ksar Jedid, of which the first 4km is also unsurfaced.

Beni Kheddache to Ksar Hadada

The road south over the plateau from just outside Beni Kheddache heads towards Tataouine via Ksar Hadada and Ghoumrassen, winding across the hillocky plateau of the Jebel Haouaia, through dense plantations of olive and figs that use the same *jessour* technology as in the Matmata (see p.358). General Jamais, commanding a punitive expedition into the region in 1883, called it "a true paradise in the desolation of the south", and the contrast with the desert plains is, indeed, staggering.

The plateau is the home of the **Haouaia** (also spelt Khawaya), intractable enemies of the French. Part of the Ouerghamma confederation, they are one of the few communities who still practise transhumance, the seasonal movement from pastures in the desert to the coastal plain. In the winter months they camp in the plain or in the **Dahar** – the arid plateau to the west of the mountains – returning to their fields in summer for the fig and olive harvests. Since the early twentieth century, however, the Haouaia have abandoned their *ksour* and now live in scattered houses and cave dwellings among their fields.

One of the most impressive of the old *ksour*, **KERACHFA**, dating from the fifteenth or sixteenth century, can be reached along a turning (surfaced) to the east 10km down the road from Beni Kheddache. The **ksar** is a ruin of startlingly Gothic appearance on a spur overlooking the plain. Most of the *ghorfas* have collapsed, but outside the main gate is a fitfully used **underground mosque**. Follow a path around the spur and you come to two abandoned **oil presses**, still in good repair.

Eleven kilometres south of the turn-off to Ksar Kherachfa, and just south of a pillar marking the boundary of the administrative regions of Medenine and Tataouine, life-size mother and baby **iguanadon dinosaurs** by sculptor Abdelaziz Krid overlook the road. Iguanadon was one of the most successful dinosaur species, and also one of the first to be discovered, back in 1825. A herbivore that probably lived in herds, iguanadon was around nine metres from head to tail, and usually moved on all fours, though it could rear up to reach food or defend against predators. Iguanadon remains were discovered a few kilometres north of here, near Beni Kheddache, by French palaeontologist Albert de Lapparent in 1951. There is a parking place below the dinosaur sculpture where you can stop, and a path up to get a closer look. The hill is an outcrop of rock from the Cretaceous period (144–68 million years ago), when dinosaurs roamed these parts, and is to be the site of a dig to find remains for the Memory of the Earth Museum at Tataouine (see p.406). The dig should be open to volunteers – for more details, contact the Association des Amis de la Memoire de la Terre at the museum or on ☎09/438316.

Continuing south on the main road, you pass over the plateau and eventually sight the white minaret and silver dome belonging to the mosque of **KSAR HADADA** (sometimes called Ghoumrassen Hadada). The **ksar** here is no longer used for grain storage and half was used for a time as a hotel, and then as the set for the Mos Espa slave quarters in the *Star Wars* prequel, *The Phantom Menace*. You can usually only visit the part that was used as a hotel and film set, which has been faced with cement and painted, but you can look into the other, abandoned half through an iron gate to see what it was like before being refaced.

When it's time to move on, the only **public transport** is the bus service to Ghoumrassen, where you need in theory to change for points beyond (although the same vehicle may actually continue to Tataouine and Medenine). If you're planning to head north of Ksar Hadada, you really need your own car. From Beni Kheddache, there is transport to Medenine (see p.421).

Ghoumrassen   غمراسن

GHOUMRASSEN, squeezed into a sharp-sided valley, 5km south of Ksar Hadada, is an ancient settlement. French officers found traces of a Roman fort nearby, with inscriptions now lost in a museum somewhere. In the fourteenth century, the historian El Tijani, accompanying the Hafsid ruler of Tunis on the *haj*, stopped at Ghoumrassen for three months. He encountered a community at war with its Arab neighbours, living in caverns within the rock in the shelter of a fortress, the **Kala'a Hamdoun**.

The *kala'a* has now gone, its site marked only by a few pieces of wall at the top of the spur overlooking the main part of the town, next to the white **tomb** of the marabout Sidi Moussa Ben Abdallah (the near-legendary figure who united the Ouerghamma), the texture of its walls reminiscent of melted candle-wax. A path cut into the side of the spur leads up to them. Below, the **cave dwellings**, or *ghar*, remain, cut into the softer strata at the base of the spur. Most consist of a single room, a cooking area near the front and a raised living quarter behind, but some of the larger *ghar* have several rooms separated by massive pillars of stone. A walled courtyard called a *houch* at the front provides a private living area; the outer wall is usually a raised *ghorfa* used for storage.

Each of the five spurs on the northern side of the mountain shelters a separate part of the community, another group living at Ksar Hadada. These have long been at odds and, during the French occupation, when they were brought under the command of a single sheikh, there was frequent fighting. With the construction of the new town in the valley in the 1890s, however, the community was brought together and peace finally achieved. Few families now live in the *ghar*, as they are considered dangerous due to frequent rock falls from the cliff onto courtyards below. As you wander round you can see the devastation these have caused, so do take care. The craggy ridge running eastward from the marabout is marked by natural rock bridges.

A late-nineteenth-century one-storey *ksar*, **Ksar Rosfa**, marked by a huge telecommunications aerial on the hill south of town can be reached from the main Tataouine and Ksar el Ferech road by the "Ghoumrassen 4km/Tataouine 21km" milestone, or from the town centre by taking the street between nos. 277 and 279, and then the fourth right after the *oued*. The main reason for climbing up here is not the *ksar* itself, but the great view it gives over the whole of Ghoumrassen. Immediately below it, houses built against the mountainside are in fact extensions of original cave dwellings which now make up the back room, opening onto the patio of the house.

Ghoumrassen is also the site of the northernmost prehistoric **cave paintings** in Africa, which are between five and ten thousand years old. Unfortunately, most are well worn by weather and vandalism, and hard to find, or even to make out when you do. One site is just at the western end of town, where the road to Ksar Ferech and Tataouine meets the road to Ksar Hadada and Beni Kheddache; the cave paintings are on the south side of the road, just east of the junction, behind a green metal barrier, in reddish-brown paint on the white rock, and very faded. There are some others by a *oued* just south of town, but you would really need a guide to find them – if you are interested, inquire at the Memory of the Earth Museum in Tataouine (℡09/438316), the cave paintings feature in their Memory of the Earth Tour (see p.407).

Ghoumrassen is a market town and very lively during the Friday **souk**, which attracts tribespeople from Nefzaoua seeking the region's esteemed olive oil. Most of the town's shops are on the long main street. There are lots of **cafés** and **patisseries** selling the Ghoumrassen speciality, *ftair* (doughnuts), but no hotels. If you need a **bank**, however, you'll find two, plus a Grand Magasin **supermarket**, and a **post office** (country hours).

A track leading north from the eastern end of town, motorable with care, leads to **Ksar Beni Ghedir**, a one-storey plains *ksar* like Ksar Rosfa and Ksar Jedid. Restored in 2000, this ksar features a traditional oil press, complete with decorations in the plasterwork on the inside of the arches, with a Koranic inscription, spots representing rain, and symbols against the evil eye such as pentagram stars, hands, and fish. The ksar features on the tour run by the Association des Amis de la Memoire de la Terre (see p.407), who plan an agricultural implements museum here.

MOVING ON FROM GHOUMRASSEN

For a rundown of destinations and journey times, see Travel Details on p.421.

If you're driving, the most direct road to Medenine and Tataouine commences at the eastern end of the main street. Roads to Guermessa, Tataouine via Ksar el Ferech, and Beni Kheddache via Ksar Hadada branch off at the other end of town. The **bus station**, a block south of the main street between nos. 41 and 43, has services to Ksar Hadada, Medenine and Tataouine. On schooldays, there are 6am and 6pm buses to Guermessa and Ksar Mourabtine. **Louages** leave from the main street near the bus station (between nos. 45 and 119). **Hitching** to Guermessa shouldn't be too much of a problem: the tarmac road branches off the main Tataouine road just out of town.

Two routes from Ghoumrassen to Tataouine

At the western end of town is the junction where the Ksar Hadada and Guermessa roads meet, and for the more scenic of two routes to Tataouine. This heads southward, passing after 8km the large but unimpressive **Ksar el Ferech**, whose two storeys of *ghorfas*, still in use, lie flat on the plain, another example of the post-colonial *ksour* like Ksar Jedid (see p.399), and far less imposing than the traditional mountain-top *ksour* of yore. There's a pretty marabout and oil press just outside the entrance, and inside the *ksar*, a café and moderately priced restaurant (advance orders only; ☎05/832210), where you can stop for a break, and even take a ride around the *ksar* on a camel. It is possible to camp here and even stay in a *ghorfa* – contact the café for details. The *ksar* lies a kilometre and a half north of the modern village of Ferech.

Half a kilometre south of the "Ghoumrassen 10km/Tataouine 15km" milestone, the unexcavated remains of **Dakyanus**, a Roman fort, lie 200m east of the road, but all that can be seen are few blocks of stone, and a mound showing the fort's outline. Holes in the ground here are the burrows of jerboas, hunted by the jackals and foxes which, like their prey, tend to come out only at night. A little way south, and a couple of kilometres before the Chenini turn-off, the three-star *Hôtel Dakyanus* (☎05/832232, ☎832198; ⑤), with cool rooms and a 25-metre pool, offers a cheaper but less stylish alternative to the *Sangho*, 7km further down the road (see p.406). Overlooking the road at the Chenini turn-off are two **bunkers** in the hillside, dating from the 1930s and built at the same time as the Mareth Line (see p.361) to defend the route north against a possible Italian invasion. The road to Tataouine continues past the Memory of the Earth Museum (see p.406) to meet the Remada road at place de la Memoire de la Terre, 2km south of town.

Heading east out of Ghoumrassen on the more direct route to Tataouine, a turn-off after 8km leads to the twelfth-century **Ksar Mourabtine**, 4km off the main road and accessible by bus (twice) on school days only. The old *ksar* here, small, abandoned in 1973, but still largely intact, with up to four storeys of *ghorfas*, stands on a crag over-looking the village. Outside the entrance is the mosque, with a number of abandoned oil presses round to its left. The path up to the *ksar* climbs through the village burial ground and past a number of abandoned *ghar* in the crag, and many of the stones here include fossils of sea animals from the Jurassic period, when this area was underwater. From the top, you can see as far as Guermessa and Chenini to the southwest. Though well off the beaten track, this *ksar* is definitely worth a visit if you have the means to get here, and also features on the Memory of the Earth Tour (see p.407).

Guermessa
قرماسة

The traditional Berber village of **GUERMESSA**, 8km southwest of Ghoumrassen, sees far fewer tourists than its sister villages of Chenini and Douiret to the south (see pp.411 and 413), perhaps because it was rather difficult to reach until recently. Even now, despite surfaced roads from Tataouine and Ghoumrassen, and the two daily school **buses** to Ghoumrassen, it's not exactly well connected and has few facilities.

According to legend, Guermessa was founded following the arrival in the region of two holy men, Sidi Ibrahim, son of a marabout from Kairouan, and Sidi Bando, his slave. When they asked for water to wash before praying, the local residents had to shame-facedly admit that they didn't have enough, whereupon the heavens opened up and a downpour ensued, a sign that led Ibrahim and Bando to remain here preaching the Koran. Sidi Ibrahim's *zaouia* (tomb) stands below the original village, long abandoned and now just a ruin. The village that superseded it grew up around the *zaouia* of Ibrahim's son, Sidi Hamza. It is built around a spur with a ruined **kala'a** on its peak, up to which leads a distinctive paved **pathway** from the valley below, no mean engineering achievement considering the size of the slabs. Although it's still inhabited, the con-

THE OUERGHAMMA CONFEDERATION

The Hilalian invasion by Arab tribes from Egypt in the mid-eleventh century displaced the Berber nomads who had occupied the fertile Jefara plain south of Gabès until that time. Driven westwards into the hills, they had to be content with mounting raids on their former territory. In the sixteenth century, a marabout by the name of **Sidi Moussa Ben Abdallah** established a *zaouia* at Ghoumrassen, and managed to unite the local feuding tribes, both Arab and Berber, into a confederation called the **Ouerghamma**, which became a formidable military force, controlling both the mountains and the plain. The security created by the confederation, enabled the Ouerghamma, a century later, and on the advice of another marabout, **Sidi el Assaibi**, to build a new capital in the middle of the plain at Medenine.

Of all the Ouerghamma tribes, the most feared were the **Ouderna**, based in the Jebel Abiadh south of Tataouine. A 1916 report by British military intelligence claimed that the Bey's army "dreaded" the Ouderna and, indeed, as late as 1875, the Ouderna had defeated a Beylical army and seized two cannons from it. By 1883, however, along with most of the Ouerghamma, they had submitted to **French rule**. Nonetheless, a number of rebels from the Khezzour and Touazin tribes fled to Libya, from where they launched raids for some time before the French were able to secure the border.

During World War I, when both France and Italy were ranged against the Ottoman empire, the Ouderna again attempted an uprising against French rule, hoping to join with Berber rebels who had all but ousted the Italians from northwestern Libya, and to return both Libya and Tunisia to Ottoman rule. The Allied victory however, and the destruction of the Ottoman empire, put paid to those plans for good.

struction of a new village in the plains is gradually drawing families away, and within a decade or so it too will most likely face abandonment.

The flat-topped hill above the village, Ras el Metmana, is the scene of a unique ritual in the wedding celebrations of Guermessi men. Before the wedding itself, the groom comes up here with his friends to stamp his footprint into the ground as a mark of farewell to bachelorhood.

Tataouine (Foum Tataouine)   تطاوين

FOUM TATAOUINE – meaning "the mouth of the springs" – evokes an image of the desert outpost, a palm oasis surrounded by drifting sand. *Star Wars* fans on the other hand may remember it as Luke Skywalker's home planet, the film having been largely shot in the south of Tunisia (see box, p.319). Either way, the reality is rather different, for the town is new, busy and drab, built by the French administrators on a site some 50km south of Medenine that had previously been just a caravan halt with a spring. The French decided it was a good site for a military base, administrative centre and souk, and moved their government offices here from Douiret in 1890, beginning construction in the same year of the marketplace, which opened for business in 1892. Within a few years, market traders were building homes here, and the town's first mosque (on the Medenine road, next to the *Hôtel Jawhara*) was opened to meet their spiritual needs in 1898.

Though Tataouine has little of historic interest in itself, within a radius of 25km are some of the most impressive sites in Tunisia. With Tunisia's southernmost hotels and banks, Tataouine is a better base for exploration than Medenine, with enough accessible goals to its north and west – like Ghoumrassen, Guermessa, Ksar Hadada, Chenini and Douiret – to fill a week or more, while to the southeast of the town there are interesting *ksour* within walking distance (see p.407), and further south the well-preserved *ksour* of the Jebel Abiadh, which can now be explored as a loop starting and finishing

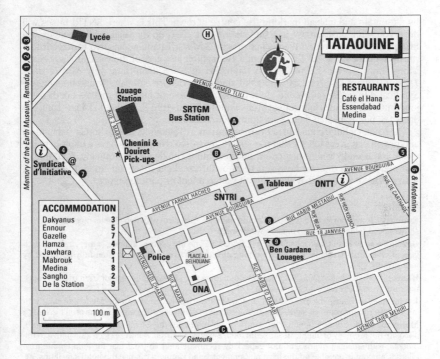

at Tataouine. Public transport to these places is sparse, but scooters and bicycles can now be rented in town. Tataouine itself, despite its lack of any historic depth, has a certain inexplicable charm – don't be surprised if you find yourself making excuses to delay leaving. In March the **Festival of the Ksour** enlivens the town in pale imitation of Douz's Saharan Festival, with mock traditional marriages and a rather tame pop concert. More information can be obtained from the festival committee (☎ & ℱ05/851833).

Tataouine was built as the far south's administrative centre and **garrison town** and the military presence is still strong – be careful not to incur the wrath of army personnel by climbing the rocks behind the military camps along the Remada road for the view. As late as 1950 the soldiers outnumbered the civilians by three to one. Most of them were members of a penal battalion of the French army and French Foreign Legion, and many were German. Indeed, in the 1930s, German was the town's third language.

The town's other function was as a **market centre**. At the beginning of the twentieth century, the French had great expectations of this market as a focus of Saharan trade. It was not to be, as trade had already dwindled and what was left passed through Tripoli, where ivory and gold could be sold openly.

Arrival, information and accommodation

Tataouine's main street, **avenue Bourguiba**, is a continuation of the main road from Medenine. **Avenue Ahmed Tlili** splits off from it near the centre of town and heads out toward Remada and most of the *ksour*. Avenue Bourguiba continues through the town centre to meet **avenue Hedi Chaker**, which is the road out to Ezzahra. About halfway between these two junctions stood a statue of Habib Bourguiba, now replaced by a fountain and tableau marking the centre of town. This is where SNTRI buses will drop you; SRT buses arrive at a bus station just 100m up the road, while louages will bring you to a yard round the corner off rue 2 Mars. Tataouine has two **tourist information offices**: the ONTT, on avenue Bourguiba just east of the tableau (Sept–June Mon–Thurs 8.30am–1.30pm & 3–5.45pm, Fri & Sat 8.30am–1pm; July & Aug daily 7.30am–1.30pm & 5–7pm; ☎05/850686), and a much more enthusiastic and informative Syndicat d'Initiative on avenue Hedi Chaker, a couple of hundred metres north of its junction with avenue Bourguiba (Mon–Thurs 8.30am–1pm & 3–6pm, Fri 8am–1pm, Sat 8am–1.30pm, Ramadan daily 8am–2pm; ☎05/850850).

There isn't a huge choice of **accommodation** in Tataouine. Cheap hotels are in town and not all that great (check that the sheets are fresh). New hotels have a habit of being clean and friendly when they open, but becoming run-down very quickly. A couple of kilometres south of town however, there is an excellent three-star hotel, the *Sangho*, with a place next door that allows you to pitch a tent or park a camper.

Hotels

Ennour, 107 av Bourguiba ☎05/860131. Adequate for the price, with two nice terraces and shared showers and toilets; ask for an outside window. ❶

Gazelle ★★, av Hedi Chaker ☎05/860009, ☎862860. The top address in town, rather drab but with decent en-suite, a/c rooms. It's best to phone ahead or arrive early, as it's often fully occupied by tour groups. ❸

Hamza, av Hedi Chaker ☎05/863506. Very popular, with a shower and toilet for each trio of rooms, but not the spotless place it once was. ❷

Jawhara, 82 av Bourguiba ☎05/860621. A good-value, friendly cheapie on the Medenine road with large clean rooms, some en suite, though the communal toilets for the other rooms aren't great. ❷

Mabrouk ★★★, rte de Chenini, 2km south of town, just up the Chenini/Ghoumrassen turn-off, opposite the Memory of the Earth Museum ☎05/862805, ☎850100. A lower-priced alternative to the *Sangho*, with smallish rooms, and not especially recommended, in particular for lone female travellers. Camping is possible on the bare plot opposite, and campers can use the hotel's facilities. ❹

Medina, rue Habib Mestaoui ☎05/860999. Rather run-down, though still not bad for the price, with communal bathroom facilities and a great view from the roof terrace. ❷

Sangho ★★★, rte de Chenini ☎05/860102, ☎862177, ☎sangho.tataouine@planet.tn. Just up the Chenini/Ghoumrassen turn-off, 2km south of town. A cut above the usual three-star traps, very classy with tasteful bungalow rooms and full facilities including a pool. Public areas have interesting displays of historic photographs, World War II artillery cases, and fossils, and there's even a herb garden. ❺

Hôtel de la Station, rue 18 Janvier ☎05/860104. A ramshackle but cheap and friendly longstanding backpacker's favourite, where charming staff make up for the slightly rudimentary rooms (though some have their own shower) and sporadic hot water. ❶

In and around town

Tataouine's modern **marketplace**, off avenue Bourguiba in place Ali Belhouane, is very lively, and it's worth trying to coincide with the souk held on Mondays and Thursdays. The square fills with merchants from all over the south buying sheep in the early summer, olives in the autumn and locally made blankets year-round. Other merchants, mainly from Jerba, sell groceries and plastic knick-knacks. It's always very colourful, with tribespeople coming in from distant villages and nomadic encampments, and pedlars stocking up with the goods they then sell from their camels' backs to people in the remotest communities.

The Memory of the Earth Museum

Tataouine's main place of interest is the **Museum of the Memory of the Earth** (Tues–Sun 9.30am–4.30pm; 1.5TD), 2km south of town on the Chenini/Ghoumrassen turn-off. The junction for the turn-off, has been rechristened place de la Memoire de la Terre, and is graced with a large sculpture of the globe. Petrified tree trunks stand in among the date palms at the junction's north-west corner, and 200m down the turn-off, a life-size model of a **Spinosaurus dinosaur** by sculptor Abdelaziz Krid looms ferociously on the hillside overlooking the road. Spinosaurus was a carnivore of the Cretaceous period whose remains have been discovered in the region. The museum itself, a silver-roofed building, has displays of fossils, half-size sculptures of an iguanadon and a pterodactyl, and explanations about the local fossil beds. Tataouine itself is on an outcrop of rock from the Jurassic period (144–208 million years ago), when it was submerged, and so fossils from that period are of sea animals. The Dahar mountain range to the west however, is made of rock dating from the Cretaceous period (68–144 million years ago), when it was above water. The museum is run by a local association called Les Amis de la Memoire de la Terre, who run a **Memory of the Earth Tour** of the area, visiting sites where fossils have been found, as well as local cave paintings and *ksour*, and a dig site for fossilized dinosaur bones. For further details, ask at the museum or call the association's president Dr Habib Belhedi on ☏05/860540.

The association also have a **show house** titled "Le Monde des Ksours Tataouine" in Cité 7 Novembre, 6km north of Tataouine proper, built using indigenous methods and materials, with original doors and locks. The aim of the house was to show that buildings could be created using traditional methods and local materials in a style that did not have to be foreign to be modern. Originally intended as a residence, it now houses a collection of tools, utensils, textiles and looms. It was not yet officially open to the public at the time of writing, but you may be able to arrange a visit by contacting the association at the museum or the number given above.

Ksour within walking distance of town

Ksar Megabla is the easiest *ksar* to reach from Tataouine. Just head down the Remada road for about 1km and then turn right (alongside a little park), cross the *oued* and continue along the surfaced road towards the mosque straight ahead. The *ksar*, originally put up in 1408 or 1409, is well preserved, with three-storey *ghorfas* and the remains of storage racks and broken pottery, but children here may harass visiting tourists with demands for money or pens, and have been known to turn nasty if refused.

There's another *ksar* on a hill to the left of the Remada road, opposite the turn-off – one of a number called **Ksar Deghaghora** – but it overlooks a military camp and you're not welcome up there, especially with a camera. A third *ksar* within walking distance of town is **Ksar Gurga** (see p.409).

Eating and drinking

When it comes to **food** in Tataouine, you are not exactly spoilt for choice. The best place in town is the low-priced *Restaurant Essendabad*, just across rue 1 Juin from the bus station (Mon–Sat noon–3pm & 5.30–8.30pm). Another good, cheap place is the *Restaurant Medina* (Mon–Thurs & Sun 8am–8pm), in a little square behind the louage station, off avenue Farhat Hached and rue 1 Juin, where you can eat outside. The *Hôtel Gazelle*'s moderately priced restaurant (daily noon–3pm & 5.30–8.30pm) is slightly more upmarket and serves beer. For anything posher than that, you'll have to trek down to the *Sangho*, 3km south of town, where you have the choice of a rather pricier buffet or à la carte restaurant, with more moderately priced wood oven pizzas in summer.

A Tataouine speciality, now common all over the country, is the **kab el ghezal**, or *corne de gazelle*, a sweet pastry horn filled with honey and nuts. *Cornes de gazelle* are available at any patisserie in town, but were in fact invented by Tayef Dounisi whose patisserie is on avenue Bourguiba by the SNTRI office, although better ones can be had at La Gazelle opposite the *Hôtel de la Station*. That hotel's café serves freshly squeezed orange and carrot juice, and the *Hôtel Gazelle* is the only place where you can get a beer.

Listings

Banks There are several banks in town, mostly on av Farhat Hached and av Bourguiba, but only the Banque du Sud at the western end of av Bourguiba has an ATM.

Bike rental Bikes (1.5TD/hr) and motor-scooters (5TD/hr) can be rented at Motos Plus next to the *Hôtel Hamza* on avenue Hedi Chaker.

Hammam The most convenient hammam is down a side street by the Mobil garage, opposite the bus station – bear left after 20m and it's at the end of the street (daily 4am–8pm men, 6am–5pm women).

Hospital The hospital (☎05/860114) is 9km north of town at the Ghoumrassen turn-off from the Medenine road, and there's an emergency medical service (☎05/860902) behind the Garde Nationale office, opposite the *Hôtel Gazelle*. Dr Habib Belhedi in rue Habib Ghandour (☎05/860540) is the local dentist and is also a qualified GP.

Internet access The best office is LM Net Service (24hr; 2TD/hr), between the hotels *Gazelle* and *Hamza* on av Hedi Chaker, or there's Tataouinet just west of the bus station on av Ahmed Tlili (daily 8am–midnight; 2TD/hr).

ONA crafts shop In the southwest corner of pl Ali Belhouane.

Pharmacy There's a night pharmacy on the corner of rue Habib Mestaoui and rue de Carthage.

Police The main station is at pl des Martyrs ☎05/860814.

Post office On avenue Hedi Chaker opposite the western end of av Bourguiba (city hours).

MOVING ON FROM TATAOUINE

For a rundown of destinations and journey times, see Travel Details on p.421.

The SNTRI office is at 67 av Bourguiba (☎05/862138), with three daily **buses** for Tunis: two – one morning, one evening – taking the slower route, via Gabès, Sfax and Sousse; and an evening service taking the faster route, via Kairouan. All leave from across the road by the tableau. Buses operated by SRTG Medenine run from the bus station at avenue Ahmed Tlili with rue 1 Juin (☎05/860031), which is just a couple of blocks away from the tableau in avenue Bourguiba.

Local bus services are not frequent, but reach Chenini, Ezzahra, Ksar Ouled Debbab and Ksar Ouled Soltane, and are best picked up at the *lycée*, 100m west and across the street, as the driver usually turns the bus there without taking it into the terminal; however, check first.

Most **louages** operate out of a yard on rue 2 Mars (☎05/862874), except for those travelling to Ben Gardane, which leave from just by the *Hôtel de la Station*.

There are also **camionettes** and Peugeots to villages around the region that function like louages (but eight passengers instead of five) and cost very little (less than a dinar a place). They are most plentiful before midday, so set out early. For Chenini, Douiret, Maztouria and Ksar Ouled Soltane, they leave from rue 2 Mars, just north of avenue Farhat Hached. For Gattoufa and Ezzahra, they leave from in front of the *Café el Hana*, three blocks south of the market.

As in Medenine, a group of up to four people may be able to negotiate a deal with a **taxi** to one or more of the local *ksour* and Berber villages (try a louage if there are five in your group), so long as the driver is licensed to operate in the area you want to visit, and is otherwise prepared to risk problems with the police for taking you there. Taxis can usually be found in place 18 Janvier or on rue 1 Juin. Expect to pay around 5–8TD each way to places such as Chenini, Douiret and Guermessa (plus around 5TD/hr for the driver to wait while you look around).

Supermarket For supplies, the Grand Magasin is by the market in pl Ali Belhouane.

Swimming pool The municipal pool is some way from the centre, 500m up the Ben Gardane road on the northeastern edge of town, but is clean and well-run (open daily except Mon, 10am–noon & 1–6pm).

The Maztouria loop

To the east and south of Tataouine stretches the mountain range of **Jebel Abiadh**, home of the **Ouderna** tribe – the most powerful in the south and part of the Ouerghamma confederation – and of several smaller Berber communities. Though *ksour* and villages litter the mountains, the sites aren't as dramatic as Douiret and Chenini, to the west of Tataouine (see pp.411 and 413); even so, they're still pretty impressive, and have the great advantage of being free of tourist parties.

The Berbers living in these mountains lacked the independence enjoyed by the larger communities at Douiret, Chenini and Guermessa, and most shared their village with semi-nomadic groups who claimed Arab origins, or else the village was closely linked to a neighbouring nomadic tribe's *ksar*. Some French anthropologists – ever eager to find and stir up differences between Arab and Berber – maintained that the Ouderna, the dominant tribe, had Berber serfs who paid them olives, figs and wool in return for "protection". It was, they claimed, "a veritable slavery such that the Ouderna can spill the blood of his Berber client without fear of the law". In reality there were bonds between the supposedly Arab nomads and the sedentary Berber villagers, but these represented an exchange of services: in return for agricultural produce the nomads guarded the herds of their sedentary neighbours, who thus gained access to widely dispersed pastures without the trouble of a lifestyle on the move.

Tarmac now reaches all the way round from Tataouine through the villages of Maztouria, Tamelest, Gattoufa and back, and the *ksour* here can be visited in a loop from Tataouine, so long as you have **transport**. With your own wheels, this can easily be done in a day, visiting, if you've a mind to, every single *ksar* en route. You may also be able to negotiate a deal with a taxi, especially if there's a group of you. Otherwise, the problem is that, though *camionettes* and even buses get as far as Ksar Ouled Soltane in one direction (three daily), and Ezzahra in the other (two daily), they don't as yet link, with 10km in between that you would have to hitch or walk.

The Maztouria loop is described here from Tataouine to Ksar Ouled Soltane, then to Ezzahra and back to Tataouine, but you may of course wish to do all or part of it the other way round, and you'd be hard pressed to visit all the main *ksour* in a single day.

Beni Barka بني بركة

A kilometre south of Tataouine, where the *oued* crosses the Remada road just south of Ksar Deghaghora (see p.407), a paved road to the east, signposted "Beni Barka", takes you up into the Jebel Abiadh – "White Mountains" – proper. This road passes a large number of *ksour* in varying states of repair, though you'd need to be a serious enthusiast to want to visit all of them. The first is the deserted **Ksar Gurga**, on your right after 1km and still within walking distance of Tataouine.

After another 4km, you'll be able to see the village of **BENI BARKA**, also on your right, pitched atop the escarpment as you approach along the valley floor. You'll have to ask the bus to stop, and walk up the steep track to the top. Formerly an important market, the centre of a thriving Berber community linked to the Arabs of Ksar Ouled Debbab, most of it is now in ruins. Even so, the **entrance gate**, dating from the fourteenth century or earlier, is spectacular, standing on the edge of the cliff and offering good views across the plain. The village has been deserted in favour of the many new cave dwellings in the surrounding slopes, some of them excavated 8m into the rock. As you walk up to the old village, look out for ripple marks in the rocks and fossils of ammonites and sea molluscs, proof that this area has not always been desert.

Maztouria and Tamelest

South of Beni Barka, the road passes a number of desolate *ksour*. **Ksar Zoltane** is up on the west side of the road, about 1km south of Beni Barka. A couple of kilometres further south, a road branching off eastward brings you after 5km to the small, circular **Ksar Tounket**. Meanwhile, 7km south of Beni Barka is the new village of **MAZTOURIA**, around 20km southeast of Tataouine, where many of the surrounding people have settled near a spring.

As you enter Maztouria town, you pass more abandoned *ksour* up to the west of the road – a rough but passable track leads up to them from just south of the Ksar Tounket turn-off. The first, round and compact, is **Ksar Ouled Aoun**. It is followed by three rectangular *ksour*, starting with **Ksar Aouadid**, now largely restored, whose massive stone walls are highly impressive, giving it the look of a fortress. Large iron-clad doors guard the entrance, whose archway still bears part of its original eleventh-century inscription. Next is **Ksar Kedim** (or Ksar Zenetes), also on the right overlooking Maztouria. Rather more ruined than Ksar Aouadad, its huge gateway has been restored and, according to the inscription inside the arch, was built in 1091 AD, shortly after the Hilalian invasion. Indeed, this is the great-granddaddy of all the *ksour*, and the first built, hence its name – *kedim* meaning "old". It is usually ascribed to the Zenetes, the ancestors of the region's Berber tribes. Inside, part of the decoration is still intact on some of the *ghorfas'* doorways and there is an underground **well** reached by a tunnel. Beyond it, the next *ksar* is called **Ksar Dahar** (also known as Ksar Deghaghora), entered through a strange tunnel-like gateway, and accessible via a track leading up from the main road in the middle of the village.

Six kilometres south of Maztouria is the village of **TAMELEST**, also built to settle the region's nomads. Overlooking the village is the *ksar* of the same name, the thirteenth-century granary of the **Ouled Chehida**, the Ouderna's most powerful group. In 1915 their sheikh led the only full-scale tribal revolt against the French. Although the Ouderna managed to overwhelm the telegraph stations in the south, the French garrisons held out, and within a month the tribespeople were defeated by a column from the north and forced into Libya as refugees. Much of the damage done to this *ksar*, and others in the Jebel Abiadh, dates from this period.

Ksar Ouled Soltane

قصر أولاد سلطان

The road splits 2km beyond Tamelest. **Ksar Sedra**, with a number of cave dwellings in the rock beneath it, overlooks the right fork; the left leads to **Ksar Ouled Soltane**, 3km away and (along with Ezzahra) one of the best-preserved *ksour* in the south, its *ghorfas* now refaced to their original state, though with cement rather than the original materials. Ksar Ouled Soltane was built by the Ouled Chehida (of whom the Ouled Soltane are descendants) on low land where it can be seen for miles around, a tribute to their confidence in troubled times. To get to the entrance, walk around the top of the hill, past the mosque and next to the shops and **café**. The two courtyards inside date from the fifteenth and the nineteenth centuries respectively and are connected by a passage made from palm wood. *Ghorfas* rise four storeys high and are still used to store grain and olives. On Friday afternoons the courtyards function as meeting places for the community, the majority of whom spend most of the year in the pastures with their herds of sheep, goats and camels. Thus, not only is the *ksar* intact but so is the way of life that goes with it. The explanation for this, unique in the south, lies in the Ouled Chehida's reluctance to migrate to the cities, along with the *ksar's* continued isolation from tourism. It's a community with a strong identity and a traditional lifestyle, one of the few left in Tunisia.

Beyond Ouled Soltane, the tarmac road is new, and at the time of writing there is no public transport. To get to Ezzahra, 10km away, you could either walk or hitch. In between, there is little to see in any case. Two and a half kilometres beyond Ouled Soltane, at **Mghit**, the road forks: bear right for Ezzahra. Three kilometres further, or 5km from Ezzahra, a track branches off southward to **Ksar Grimissa**.

Ezzahra الزّهراء

The *ksar* at **Ezzahra**, 21km south of Tataouine via Gattoufa, is almost a twin to Ksar Ouled Soltane. Like Ouled Soltane, it consists of two courtyards, both very well preserved, and it is still a meeting place where the community come on Fridays to pray. Thus Friday afternoons here, as at Ouled Soltane, have the feel of a sabbath (though the Muslim Friday is not really a sabbath in the Christian sense). The first and more recent of the *ksar's* two courtyards is the one that is used as a meeting place, and one of the *ghorfas* functions as a grocery store, but the second, older courtyard is much more impressive, with up to four storeys of *ghorfas*.

Four kilometres north of Ezzahra, a track to the east of the road leads 3km (the last part very rocky, but still motorable with care) to **Ksar Beni Yakzer**. Tall, imposing and built partly into the side of a rocky crag next to two small marabouts, Beni Yazker looks like the setting for a ghost story, and is actually a lot more impressive from the outside than within, being largely ruined. Beneath it, more *ghorfas* are built into the rock.

Gattoufa and Beni Blel

The villages of Gattoufa and Beni Blel stand next to each other, 10km south of Tataouine and 11km north of Ezzahra. Between them, a road branches off to **Beni Mhira**, 23km distant and host to an annual festival of traditional games in early March; Beni Mhira is also where signposts from Tataouine point to when leaving town in this direction. **Beni Blel**'s *ksar*, adjoining the village mosque, is not in a marvellous state of repair, though it does reach up to four storeys high, but **Gattoufa**, less than 1km north, has two *ksour*, both rather more interesting. The smaller and more recent of the two, **Ksar Gattoufa**, stands at the southern end of the village and, though only two storeys high, is in a good state and still partly in use, with a water cistern in the centre. The older of the two *ksour*, **Ksar Jellidet**, at the northern end of the village by the post office and the mosque, is derelict but not too ruined, with *ghorfas* up to three storeys high. *Camionettes* stop in front of Ksar Gattoufa, and there is a café opposite in case you need a drink before continuing on your way. Gattoufa is linked to Tataouine by a road that twists and writhes, with lovely scenery all the way.

The Berber villages

The region's most famous attractions, the three troglodyte Berber villages of **Chenini**, **Douiret** and **Guermessa** (the latter covered on p.403) are all startlingly alike, each with its *kala'a* and ruined village atop a craggy hill, counterbalanced by a white mosque, with a new village beneath. Where they differ chiefly is in their accessibility, and the number of visitors they receive, but they do also have slightly different sights to offer. Although Chenini is the village that receives the most visitors (eager would-be guides wait to greet you), Douiret is the only one with accommodation, and will undoubtedly be the most rewarding to visit when its museum opens.

Chenini شنـنـي

Most people approach the ruggedly scenic **CHENINI** along the paved road directly from Tataouine, 20km east. You can squeeze into a *camionette* from rue 2 Mars in

THE BERBER VILLAGES: A LIFESTYLE UNDER THREAT

Life in the Berber villages of Ghoumrassen, Guermessa, Chenini and Douiret has traditionally revolved around **agriculture**. Considerable effort has been put into the construction of *jessour* (agricultural terraces) and cisterns so that trees can be planted in the arid landscape. Although sheep and goats were once raised here, too, they were a small part of the economy and the villagers never participated in the transhumance of their nomad neighbours. One solution to the poverty of the region was emigration. Young men would go to work in the city for a few years and then return to their village, spending the money they had saved on the bride price to give to a bride's family, or a new *jessour*. Emigrants from each village had a specialist profession: the Douiri and Guermessi worked as vegetable market porters, the Ghoumrassini sold doughnuts, and the Chenini newspapers. Today, however, the young men go further afield, often to France and Libya, stay away longer and marry outside the community. Many do not return. As you look round the villages, you'll notice that women vastly outnumber men, most of whom are old – evidence that migration is killing the community. This is doubly sad, since these villages represent the last of the region's Berber culture.

Berber was the predominant **language** in Tunisia under the Romans, but after the Arab conquest it was quickly overtaken by Arabic – the language of the new religion, of law and government. Berber only survived in the communities of the south, and here too it was in gradual decline. By the end of the nineteenth century Berber was only spoken as a first language in Douiret, Chenini and Guermessa and, with the French occupation, the extension of government to the south and the imposition of Islamic law, Arabic finally made inroads here, too. However, migration and the consequent dispersal of the Berber population was the deathblow. Now, only older people in Chenini and Douiret speak the language. Young people can understand it, but their children probably won't. In Guermessa, nobody now speaks Berber.

This process of Arabization continued during the **colonial period** despite the efforts of the French to separate the Berbers from their Arab neighbours. French anthropologists claimed that they were in fact Europeans who had migrated to North Africa at an early date. While the Arabs were caricatured as lazy, sly and tyrannical, the Berbers were supposedly industrious, honest and democratic (all considered evidence of their purported European origins), and for these reasons worthy of a privileged place in Tunisian society. In reality of course, the French were attempting to divide and rule, and the Berbers, on the whole, refused to play the game. While accepting many of the privileges offered by the government, including an independent administration and large tracts of Arab land, they remained just as hostile to the French as their Arab neighbours.

Tataouine, take a taxi (around 20TD return including waiting time, but you may have to haggle) or hitch, which is easiest on market days (Mon & Thurs) when trucks return to Chenini at noon.

Chenini is best seen from a distance. This Berber village is built around a peak surmounted by a ruined **kala'a**, with a white **mosque** resting on a crook of the spur, the whole ensemble intensely dramatic in its size and desolation. From the distance each row of dwellings fronted by their *ghorfa* cling to the steep mountainside. Reginald Rankin, travelling in the 1890s, was mightily impressed: "I have seen nearly all the so-called wonders of the world and unhesitatingly say that the cave dwellings of the Saharan troglodytes seem to me the most wonderful thing of all." An inscription in one of the *ghorfas* gives the date 590 AH (1194–5 AD), but the village is certainly older than that.

As at Ghoumrassen, the mostly inhabited **ghar** are dug into soft strata on the slopes below the fortress, and several levels of cave dwellings form bands around the spur that are joined by steep walkways. You can visit a working camel-drawn **oil press**, an underground communal bakery, and even enter some of the houses, but you'll usually be charged, so fix a price before you enter. This is increasingly a problem, as Chenini has suffered from overexposure to parties of tourists, most of whom arrive in the morning. If you want the place more to yourself, go later.

While Chenini itself is something special, the **views** from here are also quite outstanding. For a leisurely **walk** with brilliant vistas, follow the path up from the mosque in the village, along the hillside above the underground mosque (see below), down to a spring where the villagers collect water.

Even older than the village around the *kala'a* is an abandoned village a kilometre along the escarpment. Here only the **Jemaa Kedima** (the "old mosque"), an underground mosque, survives. Below the leaning minaret are two interconnected rooms, one housing the **tomb** of a marabout, the other those of the **Seven Sleepers**. According to folk legend – quite a common one in the region – seven Christians were imprisoned in this underground hiding place during the Roman occupation. Four centuries later, when their cell was opened, they awoke as if they had been asleep. All that time, however, their bodies had continued to grow, so that they were now just under 4m tall. Only when they had been converted to Islam did they die, their bodies buried here in these long tombs.

Chenini has a **post office** and a **restaurant** called the *Relai de Chenini* (☎05/850601), with a reasonably priced set menu, and even beer. At a pinch, if there are only one or two of you, they may allow you to sleep here, but don't count on it. The very rough back route to Guermessa leaves the Tataouine road 6km back from Chenini, and is just about passable in a car if you go slowly, though a 4WD vehicle is preferable. The direct road to Douiret is now surfaced, but for the intrepid, there's an eight-kilometre footpath over the mountain, although it's not easy to follow, and enlisting the help of a guide might be a wise idea.

Douiret   دويرات

The paved road turns off the Remada road 8km south of Tataouine at **Ksar Ouled Debbab**. Now abandoned, though used for a time as a hotel, Ouled Debbab is the largest *ksar* of the tribe of the same name. Although some claim an exotic Arab Hilalian line of descent, they probably share the indigenous Berber origins of neighbouring **DOUIRET**, 11km down the paved road, utterly Berber and immediately impressive.

Douiret is much less visited by tourists, and in particular by tourist buses, than its sister village of Chenini, and is consequently much more laid-back. It also has the advantage of having a place to stay the night. Like Chenini, it can be reached by *camionette* from rue 2 Mars in Tatouine, or you could negotiate a deal with a taxi driver to bring you up here.

The village is currently undergoing **restoration** by the Association pour la Sauvegarde de la Nature et la Protection de l'Environnement de Douiret (ASNAPED), which is restoring not only the village itself (with EU funding), but also the surrounding *jessour* (terraces – see p.358). The *jessour* allow desert cultivation of trees such as olive and fig by capturing and storing water that runs off the mountains after rain, which is rare but usually heavy. The terracing also protects the plain below from floods, but emigation has left a dearth of farmers to build and maintain the *jessour*, and traditional skills are being forgotten – ASNAPED has gone as far afield as Beni Kheddache to find older people who can pass on the techniques.

ASNAPED's main project in the village is the construction of a **museum of traditional life** in what used to be a troglodyte family home. It is now being restored to show how people lived here, illustrated with the items they used in their everyday home life. Next door, the association are setting up a **study centre** in a small building that was briefly an office of administration in the late nineteenth century before the French base moved to Tataouine.

Above the museum and study centre is the white **Nakhla Mosque**, setting off the soft colour of the mountainside. The mosque is currently under restoration, and will be open to visitors. The façade is modern, but the inner prayer hall at the back, built into the rock, is as old as the village itself, dating back to the thirteenth century. In fact it may be even older, as Donatist Christians in the region under the Romans and Byzantines used to gather in underground churches to pray, and this could have been one of them.

Indeed, Roman coins have been found in the ruined **kala'a** perched on a peak at the very top of the village, some 700m high. If you climb up onto the precarious rubble of the *kala'a*, the panoramic views over the surrounding desert are stunning. Douiret is much like Chenini in appearance, though the **ghar**, inhabited by 3500 people in 1850, are now mostly unoccupied. A new village was built on the plain in the 1960s, offering modern conveniences like electricity and running water, and most villagers have set up home there, or moved further afield to Tunis or even France. Fewer than twenty residents now remain in the old village.

Wandering around Douiret, you can find **oil presses** (three of them in use), **bakeries** and **inscriptions** in remarkably good condition. On the plain below is an old **graveyard** with the whitewashed tombs of revered marabouts, and there is another ancient subterranean mosque, the **Kerma Mosque**, by an ancient fig tree to the west of the village. A **café** in the village serves mint tea and Turkish coffee, and currently houses a small collection of utensils and implements destined for eventual display in the museum. Down below the old village, in what used to be a school, **accommodation** is available in the *HI Centre de Camping et de Vacances* (℡05/860530, ℻862659), with nice clean dorms (5TD), bathroom facilities and a campsite.

Camionettes back to Tataouine are most easily located in the new village. Other vehicles will usually give people lifts, too.

Ksar Ghilane   قصر غيلان

If you have a 4WD, there are routes out to **KSAR GHILANE**, 75km west of Tataouine, from the road between Chenini and Douiret, and from Beni Kheddache, Douz and Matmata. The safest and easiest is the **pipeline road** which branches off from the surfaced Douz–Matmata road at the *Café Jelili*, 32km west of Matmata, 68km east of Douz. The piste is nowadays well maintained, and can even be passed in a normal car, although it's a juddery 84km, and you are very likely to get stuck in sand drifts, so 4WD is preferable. The best thing is to travel in convoy with other vehicles that can help you if need be. However you travel, always carry enough water, take the appropriate precautions (see box opposite), and inform the National Guard before you set out and when you arrive. Thirty-seven kilometres south of the *Café Jelili*, there's another pitstop at **Bir Soltane**, a well whose sweet water is renowned throughout the region, and often taken by the tankerful to places like Douz, where it is much preferred to the rather brackish tapwater. The *Café les Deux Frères* here serves beverages to thirsty travellers. A detour from here, for those with 4WD and an insatiable appetite for ruins, follows a piste to the east, just 300m south of Bir Soltane, turning south after 8km towards **Ksar Tarcine**, the remains of what was originally the Roman *limes* fort of Tibubuci. After another 11km, you'll see it on top of a hillock lying 4km to the west of the piste. Back on the pipeline road, the last 17km before Ksar Ghilane is surfaced.

An oasis situated where the *hamada* (stony desert) meets the *erg* (sand desert), Ksar Ghilane used to be a frighteningly desolate place. Such was its importance that the Romans built a **fort** to defend it, one of a chain, the *limes* (pronounced "lee-mess", not like the fruit), that extended the full length of the colonial frontier. Ksar Ghilane is linked traditionally with the Nefzaoua area south of the Chott el Jerid, and in particular

DRIVING IN THE DESERT

Driving in the desert is potentially hazardous and claims victims every year. You should not drive in desert regions – let alone think of leaving the main surfaced roads – without taking all the necessary precautions. Don't assume everything will be fine; consider what could happen if you were to break down in the middle of nowhere with little chance of anyone passing for hours, or even days.

First, make sure your vehicle is up to the terrain. Do all the usual fuel, oil and water checks and make sure you're carrying tools and a jack and spare tyre, preferably two. Take spare fuel if possible, and carry at least **five litres of water** per person at all times. Don't forget, either, to take high-factor suntan lotion, a sunhat and sunglasses, and appropriate clothing, including warm clothes for night-time, when the desert can get bitterly cold, especially in winter. A shovel is invaluable, as even a tarmac road can get covered in drifts, and steel sand ladders or mats will help you get unstuck too. A compass is a very good idea.

Always inform the National Guard of your arrival and departure at every post on your journey. Tell them where you're going and when you expect to arrive (occasionally you may be refused permission). If you can't find the Guard, tell the police instead. Keep to well-defined pistes as much as possible, and in open desert always travel in convoy, never alone. Mobile phone coverage does not extend far into the desert – Ksar Ghilane is out of range for example.

Some pistes may become partially covered by sand drifts, and it is easy to get stuck if you are in a two-wheel-drive car, although you can sometimes get through by going full-throttle in third gear while waving the steering wheel sharply back and forth. If you do get stuck in sand, you will probably need help to dig yourself out, although digging the wheels out and putting stones and branches under the tyres may work.

If you get stuck in a sandstorm, stop. Point your vehicle downwind and wait until the storm abates. This will avoid damage to your engine. And if you break down or get lost, there's one fundamental rule that's more likely to save your life than any other: **stay with your vehicle**. Don't go wandering off into the desert alone, as dehydration, sunstroke and heat exhaustion can strike amazingly quickly, and a car is a lot easier to find than a person wandering around.

The *Sahara Handbook*, by Simon and Jan Glen (Lascelles), contains much timeless good advice on preparing and driving a vehicle in the desert.

with Douz, since it is part of the area used traditionally by that town's Mrazig people to pasture their flocks. Entering Ksar Ghilane, the first thing you come across is the village, built to house people working in the oasis and servicing the growing tourist industry here. Just south of the village is a **monument** to the column of African and French troops under General Leclerc, who passed through here in 1943 on their way from Lake Chad – over 2000km across the desert on foot – to join Montgomery's Commonwealth forces in an assault on the Mareth Line (see p.361).

The oasis lies to the north of the village. The **spring**, a tepid 25°C, is in the oasis just past the campsites, and emerges in a pool that you can bathe in. The only other sight as such is the **Roman Fort**, 3km north-west in the desert. Since motor vehicles are prohibited from driving over the dunes to it, the only way to reach it is by foot (take water and sun protection) or camel.

Practicalities

There are three places to **stay** in Ksar Ghilane, all in the oasis. The first that you come to is *Campement le Paradis* (☎05/470255, ☎470515), run by Douz-based tour firm Mrazig Voyages, which offers the choice of a traditional Bedouin tent (15TD, 20TD full board) or a deluxe tent that sleeps eight, though a smaller group or even a couple may be lucky and get one to themselves off-season. You can also pitch your own tent, though few people do. Bathroom facilities are nice and clean, and the tents are situated away from the generator. Cheaper, but also rougher and readier, is the *Campement Ghislane* right next to the spring (☎05/460100, ☏460110), with full-board accommodation in Bedouin tents (8TD) and decent bathroom facilities. Both campsites have restaurants and bars, and serve moderately priced meals in principle at any time of the day or night. The other place to stay is the four-star *Relais Pansea* (☎05/900506, ☏05/621872; **❻**), with a pool, an observation tower to survey the oasis and watch the sunset, and deluxe en-suite tents for those who want to experience the wilderness without having to rough it. It is also possible to camp *sauvage* in the dunes.

If you are going to Ksar Ghilane under your own steam, it is wise to bring supplies, as there are no grocery stores in Ksar Ghilane, and everything costs that little bit more here. The only way to get here without your own 4WD is with a tour from Douz, Zaafrane or Tozeur, or from places further afield such as Jerba or Gabès. Supply trucks follow the pipeline road there, but many tourist excursions by camel or 4WD take the scenic route, in more or less a straight line from Douz (see p.338). One feature of this journey, largely off-piste across open desert, is that the sand gradually reddens in colour, from light beige around Douz to a deep orange by the time you reach Ksar Ghilane.

Remada and the extreme south ر مَـادة

REMADA, 70km south of Tataouine, is yet another garrison town imposed on the south by the French and has nothing of great interest. When the French arrived, there was a small oasis and the remains of a **Roman fort** nearby, part of the *limes* (see p.414), now incorporated into the army base. In the 1970s and 1980s, when relations with Libya were tense, this area was considered a first line in the defence of Tunisia against possible Libyan incursions, especially after seven "terrorists" were caught crossing the border in 1986, with the 1980 Gafsa incident (see p.299) still fresh in people's minds. Since then, relations between the two countries have improved, and it is the border with Algeria, and the threat of incursion by that country's fundamentalist rebels, that now preoccupies the Tunisian authorities.

There's nowhere to stay in Remada, and your best bet is to return to Tataouine by bus or louage before they dry up around 3pm. If you get stuck, you'll just have to throw yourself on the mercy of the local police, who may have a spare cell for the night. The only **restaurant** in town is very basic, and you're just as well off buying food from one of the shops. Bring enough dinars with you as there's no bank either. **Market day** is Sunday.

Dehibat and around ذهيـبـة

There are two buses a day from Remada to **DEHIBAT** and it's a fairly regular run by louage. The village has again been taken over by the army but the old **ksar**, now a barracks, is still there. There's nowhere to stay in Dehibat, though you're only likely to be here if you're self-sufficient and equipped for desert travel.

From the 1880s until 1911, sovereignty over this tiny village was disputed between the French and the Turkish administration of Libya. The Dehibi had deserted the village to live in Matmata and Douiret a century earlier, but the French paid them to return and substantiate their claim. Eventually, when the Italians invaded Libya, the French persuaded them to concede the village and its lands, but when Italy entered World War I on the side of the Allies in 1915, Libyan rebels in Tripolitania (northwestern Libya) had a golden opportunity to return Islamic rule with Turkish and German backing. Having driven the Italians from most of northwestern Libya, they crossed the border and laid seige to Dehibat, hoping that a military victory here would provoke a rebellion against the French in Tunisia. They would probably have gained the support of several southern Tunisian tribes, and the Ouderna did in fact rise up in rebellion, but the French sent in 30,000 troops to relieve Dehibat. The Libyans continued to hold out against Italian rule until the Allied victory in Europe cut off their support. Today's military presence here indicates Tunisia's continued insecurity over the district, although smuggling is another possible reason for it.

Dehibat used to be a point of entry into Libya, but the border crossing here was closed at last check (by Libya), though it may reopen in the future. In the meantime, the only authorized crossing is at Ras Ajdir on the coast (see p.391). Even when the border at Dehibat was open, passport and customs checks were much more stringent down here, and took somewhat longer than at Ras Ajdir. From Wazin, on the Libyan side, there is transport to Nalut, 47km away, where there are connections to Ghadames, Tripoli and the rest of Libya.

West of Dehibat are the ruins of **Ksar Ouni**, which was at one time an important regional centre, and the first Berber village built in the area. It is reached via a piste that turns off the Remada road about 10km north-west of Dehibat, passing the modern village of Ouni Jedid (New Ouni). Ksar Ouni contains a number of troglodyte dwellings, a handful of oil presses, and a mosque with an inscription dating it to 549 AH (1154–5 AD), but its most intriguing feature is the remains of a lookout tower, unique in the region, which has led to the suggestion that this was originally a ribat.

The far south

Travelling south from Remada and Dehibat, or beyond Kamour on the pipeline road south of Ksar Ghilane, requires a pass from the Gouvernorat in Tataouine. At one time, these were very difficult to obtain, but nowadays are pretty routine, so long as you have transport; a guide is also strongly advisable. Apart from the road to Dehibat, none of the roads south of Remada are surfaced, and there is no public transport, so if you don't have a 4WD, you'll have to go on an organized tour. Either way, the person to contact is Ali Béchir at the **Syndicat d'Initiative** in Tataouine (BP 108, 3200 Tataouine; ☎05/850850, ℻05/850999), who can arrange the permit, the guide and the transport.

To obtain a **permit** to travel in the far south, it is best to apply in advance by faxing Mr Béchir at the Syndicat, stating the names, birth dates and passport numbers of all the people in your party, plus the number of vehicles you are taking, a rough itinerary, and your dates of entry and departure. It's best to include all the places you might visit, even if you change your mind later. You can apply in person at the Syndicat d'Initiative, and the permit can usually be issued on the same working day if you arrive early enough, though this cannot be guaranteed. The Syndicat forwards your application to the Governorat, who issue the permit, but it's much easier to apply via the Syndicat than go directly to the Governorat yourself.

As well as working at the Syndicat, Mr Béchir also runs a firm called Sahara Atlas, which organizes 4WD **tours** in the far south (around 100TD per person per day for a group of four or more). As well as the vehicle, he can organize tents, sleeping bags, food and a guide. For further details, he can be contacted through the Syndicat d'Initiative, or directly on ☎09/438333.

There aren't many sights as such in the remote areas of the far south. What most people come for is the scenery, especially the massive sand dunes of the Great Eastern Erg, along with the remoteness few tourists get to see, plus the chance to spot wildlife such as the elusive gazelle.

West of Remada

The Demmer mountains to the south and west of Remada contain a number of **abandoned villages**, whose collapsed ruins, plus the eroded landscape of their terraced *jessour*, are all that remains of what was once a flourishing economy. Between the sixteenth and eighteenth centuries, the tribes abandoned a total of 25 villages between Douiret and Dehibat. Why they left remains a mystery: the French colonialists blamed the expansion of the Ouderna into the region, though climatic change and plague epidemics may also have played a part. More recently, it has been suggested that the Berbers supported the expansion of Ottoman power into this region in the early seventeenth century, an expansion opposed by local nomadic Arab tribes such as the Traïfa. When the Traïfa rebelled against Turkish rule in the 1670s, Ottoman troops stationed in the region called on the Berber villagers for support, and this marked the end of the villagers' relationship with the Traïfa, who had allowed them to pasture animals in their lands and offered military protection against brigands in return for annual tribute. The Traïfa may even have responded by expelling the Berbers from their villages, and although the Traïfa rebellion was quashed by the Ottomans in 1696, the Berbers' precarious position in this remote area was largely dependent on a relationship with the nomads that had now ended, and it was probably this which forced them to leave.

Ksar Brega Kebira and Ksar Brega Sghira

That may well be the reality reflected in the legend of **Ksar Brega Kebira** and **Ksar Brega Sghira**, two abandoned villages situated some 15km north-west of Remada, and accessible from the piste to Borj Bourguiba that leaves the Tataouine–Remada road around 29km north of Remada, 42km south of Tataouine. Brega Kebira, the larger of the two villages (*kebira* meaning large, *sghira* small) is also the more spectacular, especially at sunset.

The story goes that every year the Brega paid annual tribute to the Traïfa for pasturage and protection, but the demands became more onerous until one year a woollen shawl was required from every Brega family in addition. Reluctantly, the Brega came up with the goods, but the Traïfa claimed there was a deficit, which they made up by seizing the shawl from the daughter of the Brega's sheikh (holy man). In the face of this humiliation, the sheikh left the village that night and took the road north. In the morning, his neighbours found two pigeons under an uptuned wooden bowl outside his house. One, in full plumage, flew away when the bowl was lifted. The other, completely plucked, was unable to fly, but had this message in verse attached to its leg: "The one that takes off will regain a land of security and comfort; the one that remains will be left without shirt or plumage." Seeing this, the remaining villagers set off after him, burning their homes behind them. When the Traïfa chief heard of this, he realized he had gone too far, and sent messengers asking the Brega to return, but their chief responded with a curse: "May your men be consigned to flames. May the women of your tribe be taken by your Black slaves. May your soldiers be turned into dead meat." The curse did not take long to be realized: when the Turks put down the Traïfa rebellion, it was with great brutality: the men were massacred, and the women taken as camp concubines by the Ottoman troops, many of whom had the status of slaves.

Apart from its legend, Ksar Brega Kebira has a **subterranean mosque**, similar to those at Douiret (see p.413). It is said to have been founded by Oqba Ibn Nafi on his way north to bring Islam to Tunisia, and inscriptions found here have been attributed to a companion of the Prophet Mohammed, although the use of Maghrebi as opposed to Middle Eastern script makes this unlikely. Like the mosques at Douiret however, this one may originally have been a clandestine Donatist church in the period before Islam.

Ksar Segdel قصر سقدل

An easier trip out from Remada is to the villages in the **Jebel Segdel** mountain range to the south and southwest. It's possible to reach the village of **Ksar Segdel** on foot, an eight-hour hike southward over a flat plain – you may be able to find a guide at the Maison du Peuple (a sort of cultural centre), beyond the marketplace on the Borj Bourguiba road. Otherwise you will need a 4WD and follow a less direct route. Heading west out of Remada towards Borj Bourguiba, you pass a checkpoint some 9km from Remada at **Kambout**, after which you take a turn-off to the left towards the abandoned village of **Matous**. Beyond Matous, the road turns eastward to reach Ksar Segdel, perched high on an escarpment above a canyon with great views, but is a tough climb. The village, topped by a *kala'a*, consists of three levels of troglodyte dwellings driven horizontally into the rock. Some are more sophisticated than others, fronted with walls that are faced and decorated, one with pictures of boats. This may have been the residence of a Traïfa chief, since the Segdel, who lived here, were big allies of the Traïfa, and allowed them to move into the village and set up a command centre for their war against the Turks. The biggest battle took place in the *oued* below the escarpment, and resulted in a victory for the Traïfa, which gave them control of the region. The victory proved short-lived however, and Segdel were abandoned when the Ottomans finally crushed the Traïfa revolt. Today the only residents of the village are said to be jackals.

Borj Bourguiba to Borj el Khadra

Southwest of Kambout, the main piste continues to **BORJ BOURGUIBA**, 40km southwest of Remada. This military prison and settlement takes its name from the ex-president, who was interned here under the Protectorate (when it was called Borj le Boeuf). Ironically enough, the prison held many of Bourguiba's own political enemies in the 1970s and 1980s.

South of Borj Bourguiba, there is little in the way of settlements, ancient or modern, bar a handful of military posts and oil terminals, yet the main piste south, MC101, was once a major trading route, plied for centuries by caravans travelling between Ghadames and the coast. South of Tataouine, the only sources of water were wells, and the caravan route followed a trail between them. Borj Bourguiba was originally just a well in the desert – called Bir Kecira – as was **JENEIN**, 62km to its south, which isn't much more today. As a source of water however, it was an important stop on the road, and the French set up a military base here in 1898 to maintain control over it. The next well was 33km further south at **BIR ZAR**.

To the west of the caravan trail lies the Great Eastern Erg, a vast sand desert of massive dunes, which stretches all the way down the west side of the southernmost tip of Tunisia. About halfway between Jenein and Bir Zar, where route GP19 joins from the east, a very rough piste leads west into the erg, finally reaching the oil terminal at **EL BORMA**, which is also at the southern end of the pipeline road from El Hamma via Ksar Ghilane. Here you will probably have to show your travel permit several times. Although it is an oil terminal, you can't just pull into the petrol station and buy fuel; first you have to go to the administration building of the oil company SITEP, who will issue you with a coupon that you exchange for fuel, and which will cost about a third more than usual. SITEP also have accommodation here (no phone; ❺), mainly for the benefit of their workers – you may be able to take a room if there's one free, but prices are steep.

The area south of El Borma is dominated by huge dunes, and El Borma is a possible base for exploring them via a difficult piste that leads southeast from El Borma deep into the erg. This is **gazelle** country, so keep your eyes peeled – you are only likely to see them at a distance. The piste eventually rejoins the main road at **TIARET**, another well on the caravan trail, 56km south of Bir Zar. Tiaret is also an oil terminal, and this piste linking it with El Borma was once much used by oil tankers, but it is often well sanded up, and parts of it can be very difficult to get through. The oil company TRAP-SA have a guesthouse at Tiaret (no phone; ❺), mainly for their workers, but travellers may use it, though again prices are steep.

Seventeen kilometres south-east of Tiaret, on a parallel piste, is another ancient well at **MECHIGUIG**. A monument here commemorates the 1896 death of nutty rightwing French aristocrat, the Marquis de Morès, who advocated a French–Islamic front

DESERT WILDLIFE

Predictably, the **stony desert** or *hamada* that covers much of the southeast of Tunisia has a sparse wildlife population, but the sand desert in the southwest has even less. Neither habitat owes very much to Mediterranean influence, with the huge Sahara to the south dominating the ecosystem. **Plants** are thin on the ground, but the wonder is that they can survive at all. They do this by special adaptation, their leaves often reduced to thin strips to reduce water loss to a minimum. Another strategy evolved by some plants is to have swollen leaves which can store water; cacti are best known for this, but many other plants do it too.

The small **desert mammals** are almost entirely nocturnal, feeding on plants and seeds in the cool of the night. The big ears of the **jerboas** are not just for acute hearing – they may also serve a temperature control function in the same way as an elephant's ears do. On the other hand, **lizards** are mostly active by day – though hard to see easily since they have a surprising turn of speed.

Birds fall into two groups – those that concentrate around the oases, and the true desert dwellers that live out in the inhospitable wastes. In the oases themselves **palm doves** have their "home" habitat, and they've spread to the rest of Tunisia's towns in much the same way as the collared dove has done in northern Europe. If you're truly devoted, rubbish tips are worth exploring for scavenging ravens. Out in the desert and away from the villages and oases, you'll come across many of the steppe birds – larks, wheatears, cream-coloured coursers, shrikes and so on. Lurk around any area of oasis water in the early morning and the reward may be a flock of fast-flying **sandgrouse** coming in to drink. Tataouine is a good base for seeing desert wildlife, with the full range of species. This was the last region in Tunisia where ostriches were found, though any sighting today of a large long-legged bird with a black and white neck is likely to be the **Houbara bustard** – a little-studied rarity.

against what he believed was a conspiracy of Jews and Anglo-Saxons to rule the world at the expense of France and the Latin race. While on an ill-conceived expedition to give support, and possibly arms, to the Mahdists holding out against British rule in Sudan, Morès was killed by his Chaamba camel drivers and Tuareg supply brokers following a row over payment. When his camel refused to turn and flee, Morès rather foolishly shot the beast, which keeled over on top of his rifle, sealing his fate. To ensure the inclusion of Mechiguig in their territory, the French stationed a garrison here and christened it Fort Pervinquière. In 1915, when the tribes of western Libya rebelled against colonial rule (see p.416), the Italian garrison at Sinawan were forced to flee across the border here to ask the French for protection.

Ninety kilometres south of Mechiguig, **BIR PISTOR** was one of five new wells sunk along the old caravan route by the French. The main point of interest here is an area 6km to the southeast which is known for its profusion of desert roses.

Borj el Khadra   برج الخضراء

Beyond Bir Pistor, the piste continues for 19km to **BORJ EL KHADRA** (also called Borj el Hattaba, formerly Fort Saint), at the southernmost tip of Tunisia, where the borders of Libya and Algeria meet. The fort was built by the French in the 1920s to mark the extent of Tunisian territory. During World War II it was taken by Italian troops numbering 200, despite a brave attempt by its twelve French and Tunisian defenders, but was retaken for Free France four months later by General Leclerc's column of mainly West African troops on their epic march from Chad to support the Allied assault on Mareth (see p.361). Nor was this the fort's last taste of action. During the Bizerte crisis of 1961 (see p.440), when France still controlled Algeria, Tunisian troops based here laid siege to two French forts across the border in pursuit of a territorial claim. Before independence, the Tunisia–Algeria border south of Bir Romane had been considered "provisional", and a 1910 treaty mentioned Garet el Hamel, 30km south of Borj el Khadra, as the southernmost point on Tunisia's border with Libya; as a result, Tunisian president Habib Bourguiba now claimed a border that ran due south from Bir Romane and due west from Garet el Hamel. The French sent in their air force to relieve the siege, and a cemetery near the fort here is the last resting place of more than 200 Tunisian soldiers who were killed. A ceasefire came into effect at the same time here as in Bizerte, and the two issues were settled together. Today, you cannot legally cross the border at Borj el Khadra, and even if you could, there's nothing very exciting on the Algerian side (the nearest important town being the oil terminal at Hassi Messaoud, 500km northwest), though there is a route south to Borj Omar Driss, over pistes to Tamanrasset and into West Africa. On the Libyan side, the ancient and fascinating former caravan terminus of Ghadames beckons – indeed, you can see it – but the only way to reach it is to go all the way up to Ras Ajdir and come back down on the other side of the frontier.

travel details

Buses

Ghoumrassen to: Gabès (3 daily; 2hr 15min); Guermessa (2 daily schooldays only; 20min); Ksar Hadada (5 daily; 10min); Ksar Mourabtine (2 daily schooldays only; 20min); Medenine (6 daily; 1hr); Tataouine (6 daily; 45min); Tunis (3 daily; 9hr).

Medenine to: Ben Gardane (5 daily; 1hr 20min); Beni Kheddache (3 daily; 45min); Bizerte (1 daily; 9hr); Gabès (12 daily; 1hr); Ghoumrassen (6 daily; 1hr 30min); Jerba (6 daily; 2hr); Kairouan (4 daily; 4hr 30min); Ras Ajdir (2 daily; 2hr 15min); Sfax (5 daily; 3hr); Sousse (5 daily; 5hr 30min); Tataouine (8 daily; 1hr); Tunis (8 daily; 8hr); Zammour (2 daily; 1hr); Zarzis (6 daily; 1hr).

Tataouine to: Chenini (2 daily; 40min); Ezzahra (2 daily; 40min); Gabès (4 daily; 2hr 15min); Ghoumrassen (7 daily; 45min); Jerba (3 daily; 3hr); Kairouan (1 daily; 5hr 30min); Ksar Ouled Debbab (4 daily; 30min); Ksar Ouled Soltane (3 daily; 40min); Maztouria (3 daily; 20min); Medenine (9 daily; 1hr); Remada (1 daily; 2hr); Sfax (2 daily; 4hr); Sousse (2 daily; 6hr 30min); Tunis (3 daily; 8–9hr); Zarzis (1 daily; 2hr).

Louages and camionettes

Louage journey times are roughly three-quarters the time taken by buses on the same route. Frequency depends on demand, but morning is always the best time to get a louage, especially for longer journeys. Journeys served by camionette rather than louage are indicated.

Ghoumrassen to: Medenine (1hr); Tunis (8hr 30min).

Medenine to: Ben Gardane (1hr); Beni Kheddache (30min); Gabès (1hr); Ghoumrassen (1hr); Jerba (1hr 20min); Ksar Hallouf (*camionette*, 1hr); Sfax (3hr); Tataouine (45min); Tunis (7hr 30min); Zammour (40min); Zarzis (1hr).

Tataouine to: Ben Gardane (1hr 20min); Chenini (*camionette*, 40min); Douiret (*camionette*, 40min); Ezzahra (*camionette*, 40min); Gabès (1hr 45min); Gattoufa (*camionette*, 20min); Jerba (2hr); Ksar Ouled Soltane (*camionette*, 40min); Maztouria (*camionette*, 15min); Medenine (40min); Remada (1hr 20min); Tunis (8hr); Zarzis (1hr 45min).

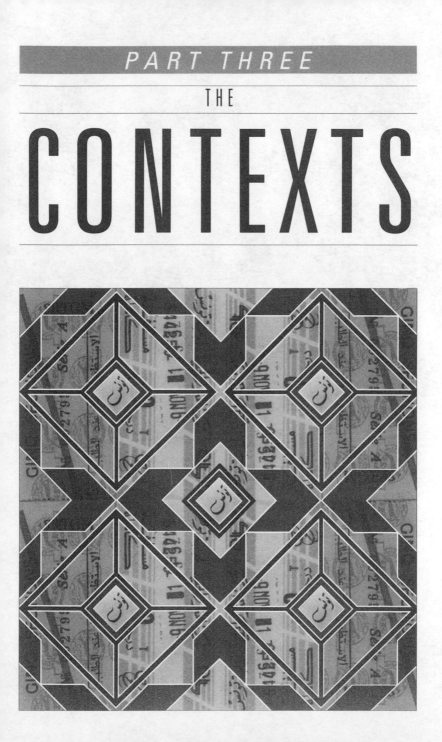

THE HISTORICAL FRAMEWORK

Tunisia has a long, dense and complicated history. The region was host to some of the earliest tool-making human cultures and centre of the still dimly understood Carthaginian Empire. The Romans left a clear mark and Islam arrived early in the faith's history at the end of the seventh century. Modern Tunisia is a comparatively recent creation, but the roots of the country in its present shape go back to the eighth century.

PREHISTORY

Around a million years ago, **early hominids** were living in North Africa's tropical climate, hunting with the primitive tools known as "pebble culture". These gradually gave way to heavy hand-axes, until, about 50,000 years ago, the discovery of fire encouraged what was by now almost *Homo sapiens* to live in fixed settlements. A culture known as **Aterian** began to make smaller, more specialized tools, and the next step forward was the arrival about 10,000 years ago of Caucasoid Proto-Hamites from western Asia. These people were probably fair-skinned, buried some of their dead, spoke a language related to ancient Egyptian, and made the most sophisticated tools yet: barbed arrows and long, thin blades, which have been found near Gafsa and have given their name to the influential culture (Capsian Man) found as far away as Kenya.

The blades found at Gafsa have been dated to around 6000 BC, and for the next 4000 years **Capsian people**, perhaps with some infiltration from further east, continued to live in caves and survive by hunting and gathering. About 2000 BC the introduction of metals from Sicily brought Tunisia into the Bronze Age, but it was still a relatively small-scale society of nomadic hunters that the Phoenicians encountered when they arrived at the beginning of the first millennium BC. Contemporary Greek accounts consistently distinguish "Libyans" from "Ethiopians" in North Africa, and the Libyans were descended from the Proto-Hamites, fair-skinned in contrast to the Ethiopians, and still speaking their remote Libyc language. The Greeks called them *barbaroi*, a name originally attached to any people who did not speak Greek and which found its final form as **Berbers**. Today's pure Berbers, of whom there are very few in Tunisia (most live in Algeria and Morocco), are the descendants of these Proto-Hamites.

THE CARTHAGINIAN EMPIRE 814–146 BC

The **Phoenicians** were originally drawn to North Africa from their home in the region of modern Lebanon because they needed staging posts for the long haul across the Mediterranean. Traders supreme of the ancient world, they were already heavily involved in exploiting the resources of Spain and beyond (principally metals), and the towns they founded (such as Sousse, Utica and Bizerte) were important transit points.

Traditionally, the earliest of these ports was founded around 1100 BC, **Carthage** itself in 814. Part of this ancient tradition was the myth of the foundation of Carthage (*Qart Hadasht*: New City) by Queen Dido (or Elissa) and a band of exiled nobles from the Phoenician homeland. The myth may reflect a genuine influx of the Phoenician ruling class, caused by Assyrian pressure at home in the ninth century BC; but it may just be a later rationalization of Carthage's supremacy among the cities in North Africa. There is little archeological evidence to support the gap between the foundations, and ninth-century dates all round may be more accurate.

At first, the Phoenician trading posts were more or less isolated enclaves on the coast. Links with the homeland were strong, and there was no reason to use the hinterland for more than immediate needs. Towards the end of the seventh century BC, however, a rival for Punic (Phoenician) trade domination appeared as **Greeks**, based in southern Italy and Sicily, began to extend their reach through southern France and eastern Spain. Conflict was inevitable, and the Phoenician cities amalgamated for security under Carthage – though the relationship was never to be easy. Fighting through the sixth century went Carthage's way, but in 480 BC the Battle of Himera in Sicily resulted in a decisive Greek victory. Forced from now on to fight its own battle for survival in the western Mediterranean, Carthage became increasingly independent of the homeland and simultaneously extended its control over the Tunisian hinterland: the Carthagian Empire was born. The year 396 BC saw another bad defeat in Sicily followed by domestic upheavals; then in 310 BC the Greek king of Syracuse, Agathocles, boldly eluding a Carthaginian army which had landed in Sicily, descended on Cap Bon, and for three years devastated North Africa.

This episode was the last to involve Greeks against Carthage. **Rome** had been gradually superseding the Greeks in Italy and Sicily, and henceforth Carthage's struggle for domination of the Mediterranean basin and Europe was with this formidable opponent. The first of three famous **Punic Wars** (263–241) consisted mainly of naval skirmishes around Sicily, but also included one episode of war on land which became enshrined in Roman national legend. The Roman general **Regulus** landed with an army in Africa and had some success before being defeated and captured along with his force. He was allowed to return on parole to Rome to plead before the Senate for acceptance of Carthaginian terms, but when this was refused he kept his word as a man of honour and returned to certain death and a place in the pantheon of Roman national heroes. Roman versions of the story dwell with loving detail on the grief of his family and the brutality of his death at Carthaginian hands.

Carthage finally lost the war and had to accept Roman terms, surrendering its fleet and agreeing on spheres of influence in Spain. It was to Spain, however, that the Carthaginians soon turned their attention. After preliminary manoeuvring by both sides, the Carthaginian general **Hannibal** deliberately moved over the agreed border in 218 BC and proceeded to make his legendary march (with elephants) through France and over the Alps. Although he won initial victories at Trasimene and Cannae, he remained isolated in Italy for several years with no support, either locally or from home, which would enable him to take Rome. This was in part because the Roman Scipio had been tying down Carthaginian forces at home, and in 202 Hannibal was finally compelled to return. Scipio defeated him at the **Battle of Zama** in central Tunisia, winning the official title "Africanus". Hannibal fled to Asia Minor – and to his own place in Roman legend as a dreaded but respected opponent.

Carthage had to surrender its fleet again, and to refrain from training elephants. Although Carthaginian power had now been effectively nullified, for many Romans a threat remained as long as the city physically existed. The arch-conservative Cato used to end every speech in the Senate, whatever the subject, with the phrase "Carthage must be destroyed." A story goes that one day he came into the Senate and deliberately spilt some ripe figs onto the floor. Questioned, he replied that these were Carthaginian figs – the implication being that a Carthage this healthy was one Carthage too many.

The hawks won the day, and in 150 BC a third war was provoked, culminating in the final, apocalyptic **sack of Carthage** in 146 BC. Descriptions of this are predictably lurid, and the ruins were ploughed over with the proverbial salt to ensure that they remained barren. The Carthaginian Empire was well and truly obliterated, and the Romans set up the province of Africa in northern Tunisia.

CARTHAGINIAN CIVILIZATION

The **Carthaginians** always aroused hostility; by the seventh century BC Homer was describing a typical Phoenician as "grasping and well versed in deceit". Unfortunately, so little has survived of their civilization that we are forced to rely almost entirely on Greek and Roman accounts, which deserve the same caution as modern Western descriptions of, say, Libya. "Phoenician faith" was a proverbial Roman term for dishonesty, and Roman mothers used to tell their children "Hannibal's coming" to make them quiet.

But the Carthaginians seem to have succeeded in antagonizing many of the people they came across. Hannibal crucially failed to secure any local support during his long stay in Italy, and the Romans later claimed to have had little difficulty in persuading North Africa's Berbers to transfer their allegiance. A simplistic explanation for this might be found in the Carthaginian **commercial vocation**. Their exploits in pursuit of profit were legendary. Two of these – fifth-century BC voyages west round the coast of Africa and north as far as Brittany – may be apocryphal, but at the very least they reflect Carthaginian interest in distant markets.

The competitiveness which made them such successful traders left them ill-equipped to get on with others, or even among themselves. The **Truceless War** (241–237 BC) is a graphic example. Carthage had always relied on its naval strength, recruiting mercenaries whenever a land army became necessary. When peace was made at the end of the First Punic War, there were no funds to pay the mercenaries. The authorities tried to solve the problem by sending the mercenaries off to Sicca (Le Kef), but with the support of the oppressed Berbers they turned on their erstwhile masters and a four-year struggle of unrelieved brutality ensued. After hiring yet more mercenaries, the Carthaginians finally won – but the episode indicates a reliance on wealth rather than loyalty, manifestly an unsuitable policy for a country aspiring to Great Power status.

From what can be gathered of **Carthaginian society**, it was oligarchical and conservative and permanently divided into jealous factions, which prevented any unified policy from being carried out. Power was concentrated in the hands of the ruling aristocratic families (or whichever one had the support of the army) and, although many of the native Berbers were technically free, in practice the tribute demanded made them resentful of their effective subjection.

Characteristically for such a society, **religion** and **art** remained essentially anti-humanistic. The most important gods were **Baal** and his consort **Tanit**, and their worship included child-sacrifice – a practice which, somewhat hypocritically, made the Romans throw up their hands in horror. But details of the less lurid aspects of their religion are barely known. At first the gods were worshipped at *tophets* (holy places), just a sacred area with perhaps a small shrine to hold a divine effigy, but gradually, under Greek influence, these became more substantial, with a monumental porch and a courtyard attached. By the fourth century BC some Greek cults were even introduced, though in modified form.

Carthaginian art was almost all derived from foreign sources – Egyptian, then Greek – and much of what little there is consists of uneasy attempts to reproduce what had been seen elsewhere. There are few original characteristics, and the most distinctive Carthaginian image – the symbol of the goddess Tanit, a bare circle balanced on a triangle – only proves the anti-humanist trend.

So few archeological remains have been found that it is difficult to imagine what Carthaginian **towns** looked like. Only domestic housing has so far been uncovered, at Kerkouane and Carthage, with none of the great public buildings which characterized Greco-Roman civilization. Under Greek influence, though, more regular civic planning may have come in. Outside their cities the Carthaginians eventually adapted very successfully after their early disinterest. Their expansion into the Sahel and the Medjerda Valley after the fifth century BC was successful enough to be mentioned by Agathocles's expedition of 310 BC, and the theoretician Mago wrote a treatise on farming that was so highly regarded that the Roman Senate ordered its translation in 146 BC.

ROMAN AFRICA 112 BC–439 AD

The immediate attitude of the **Romans** to their acquisition in Africa was less than positive. The destruction of Carthage had been a preventive measure designed to protect the Straits of Sicily and ensure the safety of Italy: there were no plans for colonization, and the province of Africa consisted of no more than the Carthaginians had controlled, roughly everything east of a line from Thabraca (Tabarka) to Thaenae (Sfax).

Even so, Romans seem to have moved to Africa on their own initiative. In 112 BC, it was the native king **Jugurtha**'s misguided slaughter of Romans living at Cirta (Constantine in Algeria) which forced the Senate to intervene in

Africa against his rampaging; presumably these were traders who had moved in to exploit the new territory. Jugurtha was king of Numidia, the native kingdom that stretched west from the Roman border through Algeria. He was the grandson of Massinissa, a Numidian king who had provided invaluable support for the Romans against Carthage in the second century BC; now that the Carthaginian threat had gone, however, there was no more incentive to support the Romans than there had been to support Carthage previously. The Romans had created a power vacuum in their province which they were eventually going to have to fill.

Jugurtha was finally defeated in 105 BC, and a few veterans were settled in the north of the province. It was only in 46 BC, however, when Julius Caesar finally won the Roman Civil War against Pompeii at the Battle of Thapsus (near Mahdia), that **colonization** really took off. The existing province was extended to the west by a line running south from Hippo Regius (Annaba in Algeria), and to the east by the addition of Tripolitania (western Libya), and renamed Africa Proconsularis. As a symbol of the Roman presence, **Carthage** was refounded in 44 BC.

Under the Empire (from 30 BC), growth in Africa was phenomenal, made possible by a combination of political and economic factors. Politically, Africa was for two centuries one of the most stable provinces of the Empire. Where a small part of France required four Roman legions (of 6000 men each) to maintain its defences, the whole of Africa needed only one. Its base moved steadily further west during the first century AD, from Haïdra on the Tunisian border to Tebessa in Algeria, and Lambaesis near Batna; and a line of frontier forts was established, running westwards from the Chott el Jerid, and east from Ghadames at the southern tip of Tunisia. Within the province, the characteristic network of Roman roads grew, but they were designed to facilitate trade rather than defence.

The **agricultural trade** in question was the basis of Africa's economy. In the first century AD, Africa provided two-thirds of Rome's grain requirements, to Egypt's one-third. As Rome's population swelled, the supply of grain grew to supreme importance – this in the era Juvenal coined the phrase "bread and circuses". When bad weather one year kept grain ships from sailing there was widespread panic in Rome.

Accordingly, the Romans invested a great deal of time and expertise in developing the province's infrastructure, maximizing the potential which the Carthaginians had barely touched on – they only had themselves to feed, after all. In the second century AD, olive oil production began to be encouraged in the Sahel, and other products included: a gaudy yellow marble (from Chemtou); purple dye; wild animals for amphitheatre displays; coral; wood; and plain domestic pottery; which by the second century was being exported all over the Empire.

Throughout the first two centuries AD there was hardly an interruption in Africa's steady increase in prosperity and importance. By about 200 AD as many as one-sixth of Roman senators were of African origin and, in the Severans from Tripolitania, Africa provided a dynasty of emperors. In 180, however, there was a portent of things to come. The proconsul of Africa tried twelve Christians and executed them when they refused to recant their faith. The rise of **Christianity** in Africa, signalled also by the polemical writings of Tertullian, was a symptom of the problems threatening the Empire throughout its unwieldy expanse.

In 238 Thysdrus (El Jem) was the scene of a revolt which spread over the Empire and ushered in half a century of great unrest. The golden age was over and, while commitment to the Imperial way of life steadily dropped, Christianity became more widespread. In 312 Emperor Constantine was converted and the Empire became officially Christian. Constantine was trying in effect to restore the Empire to the hearts of its people, but in Africa he was foiled by the **Donatist** schism in the local Church. This was caused by Christians unwilling to accept priests who had renounced their faith in the face of persecution; to avoid being "tainted" by such priests, they formed their own communion. One famous supporter of the official Church, who spent his life trying to heal the rift, was St Augustine of Hippo.

Throughout the fourth and fifth centuries the Empire gradually crumbled in the face of internal tyranny and external aggression. One such tyranny in Africa, under Gildo (386–98), put Rome in a quandary: whether to put the upstart down, risking disruption of the all-important grain supply, or just to cut their losses. In the end, Gildo and his 70,000 men were suppressed. The external problem, raiding by local tribes, was equally serious. One theory holds that the tribes had a secret weapon which decisively increased their combat strength – the camel; more likely, internal dissension was too great for organized resistance on any scale. Donatist supporters probably aided the **Vandals**, a Germanic tribe which invaded North Africa from Spain in the 420s. Their capture of Carthage in 439 put an end to the Roman era, and effectively cut the area off from western Europe. From now on, the region's loyalties would lie in a different direction.

IMPERIAL ROME

African society under the **Roman Empire** settled to two levels: a wealthy, urban, Romanized people, and a poorer, rural native culture. A good deal is known about the rich, because they left behind material remains that can be seen everywhere in Tunisia today, but the life of the rural Berber population remains obscure. Although limited opportunities for social advancement did exist, the essential gap between the two groups was never eradicated, and the alienation of less privileged Berbers was an important factor in the eventual disintegration of Imperial culture. To be fair to the Romans, most of those better off were of local origin: when one speaks of "Romans", this is usually a reference to Romanized Africans. There was opportunity for Imperial citizens to make good – as never under Carthage – and many made the most of it, as the number of African senators and emperors shows.

The most striking fact about the **towns** is that there were so many: literally hundreds. These smallish settlements of 5000 to 15,000 inhabitants provided homes for farming landlords, markets for their produce – and a perfect environment for one-upmanship. In the absence of any external pressures, wealth was diverted into civic and private rivalry: local plutocrats put money into buildings and facilities on which their names would be prominently displayed. The ensuing prestige translated without too much difficulty into political office.

The basic aim was **Romanization**, and this meant building institutions which fostered Roman values. The spiritual heart of any self-respecting town was the **Forum**, a regular paved space enclosed by colonnades and surrounded by administrative and religious buildings. The most important of the town's religious buildings, the **Capitol**, was almost always in the Forum: it was dedicated to the Capitoline trio of Jupiter, Juno and Minerva, patrons of the Empire. Other temples and shrines served cults which were a curious mixture of Roman and local influences; the Carthaginian goddess Tanit, for instance, was given a Roman name, Caelestis (Heavenly One), and worshipped all over Africa Proconsularis. Priesthood was a temporal matter, open only to those of a certain social status and thus closely tied to political authority.

Baths may not seem like an obvious Imperial building type, but they became almost synonymous with Roman civilization. They were magnificent buildings, their soaring vaulted ceilings impressive products of Roman engineering, but the activity they housed made them central to Imperial life. Surrounded by mosaics and statuary, citizens of all ranks could pay a small fee and spend hours there. Bathing was only a small part of the ritual, which also included exercising in gymnasia, reading in libraries or just sitting around. Other public facilities such as theatres and amphitheatres were usually set on the outskirts of town, not far from the vast cemeteries of ostentatious mausoleums which lined approach roads. By 250 AD, the countryside was crisscrossed by 20,000km of roads, aqueducts and bridges.

In material terms Roman Africa was a great success, though historians have tended to exaggerate Rome's achievement. Culturally Roman Africa, best known for its lawyers, was less spectacular. Nevertheless the **mosaics**, used to decorate private homes and public buildings, reached heights in Africa almost without equal – perhaps partly because there was so little other artistic activity. The greatest name in **literature** was Apuleius, author of *The Golden Ass*, who was born in modern Algeria; others were Tertullian and St Augustine, the Christian writers. But these Christian names are a reminder of how briefly the Empire flourished. Once its citizens lost faith in the Imperial dream, from the third century onwards, the physical fabric also began to crumble. No great Roman buildings were erected after 250 AD, and those already standing went unrepaired. The only new constructions were churches, often built in the ruins of older temples and baths, and the **Vandals** that came later inherited a way of life that was only a shadow of its former incarnation.

THE VANDALS 439–533

One of the northern tribes which harassed the Roman Empire to its end, the **Vandals** were a Germanic tribe of Arian Christians who worked their way through Spain into Africa. If the Donatist Berbers hoped that they would be rewarded for their support against the Romans, they were sadly mistaken. Religious persecution continued – including destruction of religious and other images, the Vandals' most famous characteristic. If half the Roman statues in the Bardo Museum, for example, seem to have had their noses and penises knocked off, that is down to the Vandals.

Religion apart, the conquerors found what remained of Roman luxury fatally congenial – there are reports of a great pleasure palace south of Carthage. They never got any further than northern Tunisia and, after the death of **King Genseric** in 477, a succession of weak rulers tried unsuccessfully to levy extortionate taxes from the ever-rebellious Berbers.

THE BYZANTINES 533–646

After little more than a century, the Vandals offered a tempting target to the resurgent eastern half of the Roman Empire, now established in Byzantium (modern Istanbul). The great Emperor Justinian had grandiose plans for recovering the lost realms of the western Empire, and to this end dispatched **Belisarius**, his general, in 533. Belisarius sailed with his army to Sicily, now held by the Ostrogoths, hoping to exploit their differences with the Vandals. In the event, the landing and conquest were so easy that this was unnecessary.

The same cannot be said for the next century of **Byzantine rule**. As virtual absentee landlords, hoping to exploit the territory, the Byzantines found themselves no more able than the Vandals to control the insurgent Berbers of the west and south. They made a more concerted effort, building massive fortresses whose ruins are almost the only reminder of their presence, but the Berbers were gradually proving that they could not be ruled by force alone, and Tunisia was too remote from Byzantium to be a prime concern. In 646 the Prefect Gregory declared the province independent of Byzantium, but his new state lasted only a year before falling to the **Arabs**.

THE FIRST ARAB RULERS 647–800

When the first wave of **Arab invaders** hit North Africa from the east and defeated and killed the Byzantine Prefect Gregory at Sbeïtla in 647, their new religion of Islam was less than fifty years old. After victory at Sbeïtla, the first invaders stayed long enough only to collect their share of the rich booty distributed. It was the third Islamic wave, led by **Oqba Ibn Nafi**, which finally put down roots, after advancing northward through the country from Ghadames in Libya to make Tunisia part of a vast Arab empire ruled by the **Ummayad Caliphs** from Damascus. Ibn Nafi founded Kairouan as regional capital in 670. The rest of the seventh century was taken up with quelling the last of the Berber resistance, led most famously by a legendary Jewish queen, Kahina; but in the eighth century it was with Berber converts in their army that the Arabs advanced to Spain (and ultimately as far as Poitiers in central France).

However, as with Donatism 400 years earlier, the Berbers turned to heresy as a way of asserting their independence. It took the form of **Kharijism**, a movement hostile to central government, which denied any need for the Caliph to be an Arab, and advocated his election from among all true believers (see p.383). This idea became very popular among the Berbers, who rose in rebellion under its banner. First defeated outside Kairouan in 742, they went on to conquer the city in 757 but were driven out four years later and their movement pushed into the south of the country, which remained part of a Kharijite state until 909. The Ibadites of Jerba are all that remains of it today but, paradoxically, it was Kharijism which brought Islam to almost all Berbers, making Islamicization of North Africa far more lasting than Romanization had ever been. Disaffection continued, but the Berbers now broadly shared a faith with their rulers.

THE AGHLABIDS 800–909

By the end of the eighth century, the **Abassid Caliphs** – who had usurped the Ummayads in 749 and moved their capital to Baghdad – were finding it ever harder to hold onto Spain and North Africa. When Ibrahim Ibn Aghlab put down a military rebellion and declared himself governor in 800, Tunisia became independent in all but name. The Caliph who accepted this situation, incidentally, was Haroun al-Rashid of *Arabian Nights* fame. For a century, Ibn Aghlab's descendants, the **Aghlabids**, controlled the whole country bar the Kharijite south. Unpopular in religious circles because of their dissolute lifestyle, the Aghlabids tried to make up for it by constructing and embellishing religious buildings throughout their domain. They also built a series of walled cities and ribats, most importantly Sousse, from where, in 827, they launched a successful invasion of Sicily. The island remained in Islamic hands until the eleventh century, and in 846 an Arab raiding party even managed to attack Rome and sack St Peter's.

The Aghlabids' building programme, their conquest of Sicily and raids on Italy, and their concern for irrigation and agriculture, made their reign something of a **golden age** for Tunisia. Their effect on culture was also strong: by the time their emirate fell, more people in Tunisia spoke Arabic than Berber.

FATIMIDS AND ZIRIDS 909–1148

Meanwhile, yet another heresy was finding fertile ground in North Africa. The **Ismailis**, a Shi'ite faction, sent one **Abu Abdullah** to Algeria as a missionary for their cause. He soon converted a number of formerly Kharijite Berbers, who joined him to invade the Aghlabid state in 903. When they took Kairouan six years later, the Syrian Ismaili leader **Obaidallah Said** decided to come to Tunisia and take over, but was imprisoned en route by Kharijites in Sijilmasa (Morocco). Abu Abdullah struck west and attacked the Kharijites, destroying their Tahirt-based state, which controlled Jerba and the south of Tunisia. On his liberation, Obaidallah declared himself Mahdi (see p.233) and took political power. Claiming descent from the Prophet's daughter Fatima, he began the **Fatimid dynasty** and built a new capital at Mahdia. He showed his gratitude to Abu Abdullah by having him assassinated.

Obaidallah and his successors made themselves highly unpopular through their attacks on the orthodox Sunni faith of most of their subjects – they had a distinguished lawyer flogged in the Great Mosque at Kairouan and various prominent Sunni theologians assassinated – and the extortionate taxes they levied to finance overseas military exploits. It was the Kharijites, however, who rose up against them. Led by **Abu Yazid** from Tozeur, they besieged Mahdia in 944 and Kairouan the following year. The revolt was not crushed until 947.

In fact, the Fatimids were never primarily interested in Tunisia: they had their eyes on Egypt, and then the Caliphate itself. Obaidallah launched an abortive **campaign against Egypt** in 914–15 but, driven out by an army from Baghdad, had to be content with consolidating his power base and establishing control of Morocco and Sicily. In 961, however, his great-grandson El Muizz seized an opportune moment and finally achieved the long-desired conquest of Egypt, founding the forerunner of modern Cairo. The Fatimids ruled Egypt until overthrown by Saladin in 1171. They left Tunisia in the charge of their nominees, the **Zirids**.

This arrangement lasted until 984, when the Zirids, under pressure from their subjects, withdrew allegiance to the heretical Fatimids, later transferring it to the Sunni Caliphs in Baghdad. The Fatimids responded by unleashing against their former representatives the **Banu Hilal**, a restive nomadic tribe who had been causing them trouble in Egypt. The Fatimids persuaded the Hilalians and another tribe, the Banu Suleim, to migrate westward with the promise of free land and rich booty. The Banu Suleim, for the time being, stopped in Libya, but the Banu Hilal descended on Tunisia in an orgy of destruction – Ibn Khaldoun compared them to a swarm of locusts – which may in reality have been merely the culmination of an already advanced process of disintegration. At any rate, they were more than a match for the Zirids, who abandoned Kairouan (sacked by the Banu Hilal in 1057) and holed up in Mahdia, leaving cities such as Tunis, Sfax, Gabès and Gafsa virtually independent, and the countryside under the control of **nomads** who had little understanding of sedentary agriculture and little use for the **infrastructure** in place. This infrastructure, which had since Roman times helped to keep the region unified, fell into disuse. The country reverted to the fragmented condition of early Phoenician times – a few isolated coastal centres, and an unproductive stateless interior.

ALMOHADS AND ALMORAVIDS 1159–1229

This disarray was exploited by maritime Europeans: the **Normans** recaptured Sicily in 1072, then took Jerba and ports on the east coast, and finally Mahdia in 1148, thus ending the last remnants of the Zirid state.

They were evicted by the **Almohads**, a religious movement from Morocco which followed the teachings of a revolutionary preacher named Ibn Tumart, whom they had declared Mahdi. After driving the ruling **Almoravids** out of Morocco and Spain into final refuge on the Balearic Islands, the Almohads turned their attention eastwards to Tunisia. They took Tunis in 1159 and Mahdia the following year, and came to control an area stretching from Spain to Libya, uniting the Maghreb under a regime based in Marrakesh.

The Almohads' rule saw a massive growth in **Sufism** and an atmosphere of religious turmoil, but their biggest threat in Tunisia came in 1184 when they tried to subjugate the Balearic Islands. Pre-empting attack, the Almoravids under **Ibn Ghaniya** launched an invasion of Tunisia and set up a base in the Jerid. From there, they went on to conquer most of the country; but just as Tunis fell to them in 1203, an Almohad force captured their home base of Majorca and cut off their armies.

THE HAFSIDS 1207–1574

Having regained Tunisia, the Almohads left it in the hands of a governor whose family, the **Hafsids**, ruled it from then on, declaring independence in 1229 when the Marrakesh regime repudiated Ibn Tumart's teachings. Many saw the Hafsids as the Almohads' legitimate heirs.

The Hafsids made **Tunis** their capital and gave the country the new orientation it needed. Contact with Europe was re-established after a gap of several centuries, and the trading state created by the Hafsids is recognizably the direct ancestor of modern Tunisia.

Mediterranean relations were both friendly and hostile, mutually threatening and beneficial. The Hafsids sent ships to Valencia in 1238 to help the Muslim citizens defend themselves against the Christian kingdom of Aragon; but, with Valencia's fall, they opened trading relations with Aragon. These grew to such an extent that eventually a large number of

Christians lived in Tunisia under Aragonese protection, and were even allowed to preach their religion.

This did not prevent a **crusade** (the eighth crusade) being led against Tunisia by Louis IX of France. Louis's expedition was prompted by a desire to convert the Hafsid Sultan el Mustansir and by debts owed to French traders in Tunis; but after taking Carthage, the French king died suddenly of plague (he was later canonized).

Trade was now booming in the Mediterranean, and Tunis was exploiting it more successfully than anyone. Complex agreements were signed with European states such as Venice, Pisa and Genoa. There was also trade across the desert with West Africa, and in 1262 an embassy even arrived from Norway.

Hand in hand with trade went piracy – the two were often indistinguishable – and the **corsairs of Barbary** (as North Africa was now known in Europe) became the legendary scourge of Christian merchants, plundering their goods on the high seas and selling their crews into slavery. Christian corsairs were just as efficient as their Muslim counterparts, and Genoa and Pisa had their own **slave markets**. Credit arrangements between Barbary and Europe included provisions for ransoming captured merchants and sailors.

With the proceeds of these activities, **El Mustansir** (1249–77) created a kingdom in Tunis that was recognized as the leading monarchy in the Islamic world. Cultural life flourished and building programmes established what became Tunisia's classic style of architecture, influenced by the Andalusian artisans who were encouraged to immigrate from Spain.

After El Mustansir's death, however, the Hafsid state was riven with internal strife and became so weak that Tunisia began to disintegrate into small **city-states** once again – Gabès, Gafsa and Tozeur being the main ones. Christians from Sicily occupied Jerba in 1284 and the Kerkennah Islands in 1286, and the region was twice split with rival sultans in Tunis and Bougie (Algeria). One result of this split was the arrival of the Arab tribe from which most of southern Tunisia's nomads claim descent, the **Banu Suleim**, who had been invited to migrate westward with the Banu Hilal by Egypt's Fatimid rulers back in the tenth century (see p.431), and who had settled in Libya. In attempting to wrest control of Hafsid territory from his Bougie-based

THE HISTORICAL FRAMEWORK/433

EARLY ISLAMIC SOCIETY

Although **Islam** reached virtually all the Berbers, largely through the medium of rural marabouts, society was little more homogeneous than under the Romans. The rulers – whether Aghlabid, Fatimid or Zirid – had little in common with most of their subjects. The resentment of the ever-oppressed Berbers was felt even in the most apparently stable periods – hence, for example, the secluded palaces built by the Aghlabids outside Kairouan. Occasionally this found focus in a leader such as Abu Yazid from Tozeur and the rulers were forced to defend themselves.

Urban society, however, flourished. Scholarship, law and education centred on mosques and the religious tradition (see p.456), and, in the first centuries Arab culture here (as elsewhere) was able to absorb and disperse the knowledge it acquired during its rapid expansion. A specific example in Tunisia was the introduction around Gabès of silk culture, which had first been encountered in China. **Ibn Khaldoun**, a truly original thinker, was born in Tunis in 1332 and lived through an eventful 74 years, which took in scholarship, exile and high political office. His best-known work, *Al Muqaddimah* (see p.485), set out historical principles way ahead of its time. He saw history as a cycle reflecting the relative power of desert tribes and an urban state. The tribes were strong because life in the desert was harsh, they were constantly at war with their neighbours, and shared *assabiya*, the solidarity that derived from common descent and interests. The cities (and the states they supported) were, by contrast, weak, because the luxury of urban life corrupted people's bodies and their society. Tribes that were greedy for the wealth that control of a city offered, could defeat and take over a state that was internally weak. But, as the new rulers settled into the same mould, they also succumbed ultimately to another tribe. And so history unfolded in a cycle of dynastic rise and fall, but not progress.

The physical breadth of Arab culture played a large part in spreading knowledge. The geographer **Ibn Battuta**, born in Tangier in 1304, is estimated to have travelled 120,000km in his life.

Even in early centuries, before the advent of the Ottoman Turks, it was a surprisingly cosmopolitan society – much more so than the bloodthirsty and intolerant image fostered by its Christian opponents. The Fatimid general Jawhar (Pearl), who captured Egypt in 970, had been a Christian eunuch slave in Sicily, which was itself a remarkable example of its period: when the Normans recaptured Sicily for Christendom in the eleventh century, they found the Arab culture so congenial that they happily made the most of it while at the same time raiding the Tunisian coast. In 1270 Louis IX's expeditionary force at Carthage found itself fighting against the army of Frederick of Castile, who had been engaged by the sultan.

Islamic art, however, took a very different form from that of Europe. The ban on human and animal images removed at a stroke the narrative core of representative art, leaving an emphasis on disembodied form that came to be seen in **architecture** as well as in the **decorative arts**. For all their surface brilliance, Islamic buildings are distinguished most by their manipulation of space, whether in a courtyard or a dome. In a Christian cathedral, large spaces are intended to be filled; but while spaces in mosques – whether courtyards or prayer halls – are also filled, it is when empty that they have most significance, symbolizing the all-embracing nature of Islam. Early architecture in Tunisia – the Great Mosques at Kairouan, Sousse, Tunis and Sfax – illustrates this aspect particularly well.

Later buildings from the Hafsid period onwards became locked into a more conservative and provincial style, with an emphasis on decoration rather than space. The classic elements of Tunisian architecture are the horseshoe arch (a more restrained version than elsewhere in the Maghreb) and internal stucco decoration, a skill first brought by Andalusian artisans. Along with other features – tiles, doorways, relief patterns on minarets – these make for a tradition that is at its best extremely elegant; at its worst, trivially pretty – a sort of classical Rococo. Certainly the majesty of the early buildings was lost when the Fatimids took their skills to Cairo in the tenth century.

rival, Tunis's sultan **Abu Hafs** (1284–95) called on the Banu Suleim for support, promising them feudal overlordship in much of the countryside, the Banu Hilal having largely moved further west to pastures new in the meantime. As nomads, the Banu Suleim had no experience in managing agriculture, and their domination of the Sahel devas-

tated the olive industry, but in the south their descendants eventually worked out a stable system in which the sedentary Berbers supplied them with a tribute of agricultural products in return for military protection and pasturage rights. The split in the Hafsid sultanate meanwhile was healed again in 1370, when the Bougie sultan, **Abul-**

Abbas, captured Tunis, took control of all the city-states and islands, and reunited the country, beginning a Hafsid revival that lasted another century. In 1390, he even saw off a joint European expedition against Mahdia.

The Hafsids continued to rule until 1574 although their state was in decline, losing any real power after 1534. Even so, they had presided over a settled and prosperous era lasting more than three hundred years, one to which Tunisians still look back with some pride.

SPANISH–TURKISH RIVALRY 1534–1574

The sixteenth century in the western Mediterranean was glamorous but violent. Moorish civilization in Spain was being toppled by the resurgent Christians and, encouraged by the capture of Granada in 1492, the Spanish launched naval raids on the ports of the Maghreb with some success. Opposition to these Christian corsairs came from the **Barbarossa** brothers, Aruj and Khair ed Din, who based themselves on Jerba and set about winning back the Maghreb for Islam. After Aruj died in 1518, Khair ed Din petitioned the **Ottoman Turks** for support: still exhilarated by their capture of Constantinople in 1453, they needed no second invitation to contest such a vital region with the infidels, and Tunisia became the front line of an east–west confrontation.

In 1529 Barbarossa took Algiers, then in 1534 he expelled the now abject Hafsids from Tunis, at the same time taking control of the east coast and Kairouan. This was too much for the Spanish, who sent a massive army in 1535 and restored the Hafsid **Moulay Hassan** as a puppet ruler. Events continued at this sort of pace for the next half-century, with Spain, France, Turkey, Naples and other powers all disputing the North African coast. In 1536 Francis I of France allied himself secretly with the Ottoman sultan against their common enemy, Charles V of Spain. Fully supporting the pope's denunciation of this unholy pact, Charles tried to make his own arrangement with the real regional power, Barbarossa, under which Barbarossa would become Spanish viceroy of the North African coast in return for helping to crush France and Turkey. This eventually fell through, however, and in 1544 Charles and Francis managed to resolve their differences in another treaty which nullified the previous two at a stroke.

Fighting in the field was fierce – the pyramid of skulls which stood on Jerba until 1849 was the result of one clash between Turks and Spanish – but the Turks gradually gained the upper hand. **Dragut**, a pirate who had been enslaved by the Spanish and ransomed by Barbarossa, had extended his control from Jerba as far as Kairouan by 1557, and a flurry of activity at Tunis brought the war to a close. Taken from the Spanish in 1569 by an Algerian Turk, it fell to Don John of Austria in 1573, and then for the last time in 1574 to the combined Ottoman forces of Algiers, Tripoli and Turkey itself.

EARLY OTTOMAN RULE 1574–1704

Tunis (like Algiers) was made a **Regency** of the Ottoman Empire, governed by a complex system which only helped to intensify internal strife. Power was divided between the **Bey**, a civil administrator in charge of the taxes levied from every town; the **Dey**, a military commander with access to the proceeds of foreign trade and piracy; and the **Pasha**, the Ottoman sultan's representative. At first it was the Deys who controlled the country: Othman Dey (1598–1610) and Youssef Dey (1610–37) were two commanders who left their mark on the architecture of Tunis, and by building up the fleet to renew its activities in the Mediterranean. In 1604 Jerba was brought back under Tunis's control. But while the Deys were busy with foreign and military affairs, Murad Bey and his son Hammouda Pasha (who combined the offices of Bey and Pasha), were strengthening their grip on domestic power, starting the first line of hereditary Beys, known as the **Muradids**. Firearms and the professional Turkish army allowed them to hold power far more effectively than any previous government and, unlike the Hafsids before them, they faced no threat of a tribal coup.

As the century wore on **European traders** were allowed back into the country. The first permanent French consulate was built in the Tunis Medina in 1659, and an agreement was signed with Britain in 1662. Not that trade was any more tranquil than it had been before – in 1654 the British Admiral Blake bombarded and destroyed the pirate base of Porto Farina (Ghar el Melkh). But contact with the outside world boosted the opportunities for trade and began a short period of relative prosperity.

REFUGEES

One by-product of the Muslim–Christian struggles of the sixteenth century had a lasting impact on all the countries of the central Maghreb: the immigration of **Spanish Muslims** following their expulsion by the triumphant Christians in 1609.

Relations between the Muslims of the Maghreb and Spain had always been close, especially after the fall of Seville in 1248 and ensuing Christian advances. The Hafsid rulers of Tunis, who had previously held high command in Spain, were particularly welcoming and perhaps 100,000 immigrants arrived during the three centuries of their rule. Beginning in 1609, though, pressure on Muslims and Jews to leave Spain unless they converted to Christianity became a formal expulsion: in the provinces of Valencia, Andalusia and Murcia in 1609, Aragon in 1610, and finally in Catalonia, Castile and Extremadura.

In 1609 alone, 80,000 refugees arrived in Tunisia at a time when the entire population of Tunis was probably around the same figure. The wealthy urban elite were encouraged to settle in prestigious streets set aside for them: Rue des Andalous in the southwest of the Tunis Medina is the most obvious example. Smaller-scale artisans went to existing smaller towns in the north such as Jedeida and Tebourba. And the majority, rural farmers, founded small communities in three main areas: the northeast corner of the country, between Tunis and Bizerte, the fertile base of Cap Bon, in towns like Soliman and Grombalia; and the Medjerda Valley, from Medjez el Bab westwards.

Religion apart, these immigrants were more Spanish than North African and spoke Spanish rather than Arabic. When their writers composed satires against the Spanish Inquisition, they wrote in Castilian verse. More than a hundred years after their arrival, in the early eighteenth century, the French traveller Peyssonel found the inhabitants of Soliman and Tebourba still speaking Spanish. Their food and clothing were different and, with their eyes always on their abandoned homeland, they were reluctant to dilute their culture by marrying outside their community.

Eventually they became assimilated, but the Andalusian immigrants have left a lasting imprint on Tunisian culture. The single most visible and concentrated remnant of Andalusian immigration is Testour (see pp.267–9), a small farming town in the Medjerda Valley with a recognizably Spanish flavour.

THE HUSAYNIDS 1704–1883

The Muradid line of Beys came to an end at the beginning of the eighteenth century, when an Algerian invasion had to be repulsed. The successful commander was **Husayn Bin Ali**, a Turkish soldier of Greek origin based in Le Kef, who took control of the country on the basis of his success. Despite his Ottoman ties, he came to identify more and more with internal Tunisian interests, and from this time on the Ottoman connection, never very strong, was little more than nominal.

Such problems as Husayn had were closer to home. Having groomed a nephew, Ali Pasha, to succeed him, Husayn produced a son who naturally replaced Ali as heir. Ali responded by rebelling against his uncle, enlisting the support of the ever-hopeful Algerian Turks. Husayn was defeated once near the border at Le Kef in 1735, then killed at a battle near Kairouan in 1740. Now Husayn's sons in turn obtained Algerian support against the usurper: they too were defeated near Le Kef (1746), but ten years later succeeded in expelling Ali Pasha from Tunis. After seeing off (with some difficulty) their over-enthusiastic Algerian supporters, **Ali Bey** (1759–81) and **Hammouda Bey** (1781–1813) made Tunis once again a secure, prosperous and independent power in the Mediterranean.

But whatever their success in international politics, the Beys failed to bring Tunisia fully under their control. Even at its apogee under Hammouda Bey, the Husaynid state only governed the cities, the Sahel and the Tell. In the steppes of central Tunisia and in the far south the **tribes** were virtually autonomous. They paid their taxes irregularly, when forced to by a *mahalla* (military expedition), and though they might admit the Bey's sovereignty as commander of the faithful, they would not allow him to intervene in their affairs.

The **early years of the nineteenth century** were the turning point of modern Tunisia. Under Hammouda Bey the economy and the state had been strong, but in following years both collapsed under assault from Europe. Co-operation between European navies after the

Treaty of Aix-la-Chapelle in 1816 effectively put an end to Mediterranean piracy, an important source of revenue for the Beys. To make up the loss they increased taxes on trade and agriculture, which placed a heavy burden on the economy. At the same time industrialization gave European manufacturers a competitive edge that enabled them to subvert Tunisian products, first in the Mediterranean and then in the domestic market. By the 1840s Tunisia's balance of trade surplus had become a deficit.

Tunisia was also beleaguered politically. In 1830 France had seized the Beylik of Algiers on the feeblest of excuses, and in 1836 it signalled its interest in Tunisia by sending a fleet to discourage a Turkish invasion. To secure foreign protection without falling under the control of any one power, the Beys had to offer trading concessions to each of the European governments in turn, thereby aggravating the country's economic decline.

Ahmed Bey (1837–55) attempted to strengthen the state through internal reform, extending his control of local government and founding a **European-style army**. But this failed. The government could not afford these expenses and had to increase taxes and borrow from abroad. Furthermore, by employing French military advisers and going on a state visit to France in 1846, Ahmed Bey brought Tunisia firmly into the French camp, and once they had a grip they would not let go. Ahmed's successors, Mohammed Bey (1855–59) and Mohammed es-Sadok Bey (1869–82), were less dedicated to government reform than to a life of luxury. Their reckless expenditure on palaces and neglect of the administration brought the country to the brink of collapse. Not only did they contract debts at disadvantageous rates but, in 1864, the doubling of the **poll tax** led to a widespread revolt. At one point the European consuls, fearing that the capital would be overrun, packed their bags and were ready to leave. In the end the revolt fizzled out when the government backed down and the tribes fell out with each other. But by then the government's weakness was clear to all inside and outside Tunisia.

THE SCRAMBLE FOR TUNISIA

Unable to increase taxes, the Tunisian government was virtually bankrupt. Trying to keep itself afloat, the country borrowed at ever-increasing rates from European (mainly French) banks in a spiral encouraged by the European powers. By 1869 Tunisia's main creditors – France, Britain and Italy – feared the Tunisian government would be unable to service these debts and that this might serve as a pretext for one of the powers to invade. In a rare moment of international co-operation they set up an **International Financial Commission** that effectively supervised every act of the Tunisian administration. Behind the scenes, however, the powers were jockeying for position. They fought among themselves to secure the contracts awarded by the Bey – the TGM railway in Tunis, for instance – and influence at court.

The only Tunisian who came close to arresting this decline was **Kherredin**. As a minister in Mustapha Khaznader's government (1857–64) he had masterminded a form of constitutional monarchy that guaranteed the **civil rights** of Tunisian and foreign citizens (the name of which, *destour*, meaning "constitution" in Arabic, eventually gave its name to the pro-Independence Destour Party). But jealousy at court and his unpopular pro-Turkish policies had led to his dismissal in 1862. When he returned from retirement in 1869, to head first the International Financial Commission and then the Bey's government, he realized that Tunisia's only hope was to play one power against another while strengthening from within. He reformed the administration, local government and the legal system, and seemed set to restore government control over the tribes and their finances. A rapprochement with Turkey enabled him to set the British and Germans, who did not want the ailing Turkish Empire broken up, against the French and Italians, who did, and so postpone the threatened French invasion.

Kherredin's government was short-lived (1870–77). Despite his reforms, the economy was still weak, and when he tried to embroil Tunisia in Turkey's war with Russia, as a loyal country of the Ottoman Empire, the French consul, **Theodore Roustan**, was able to galvanize opposition at court and have him overthrown. Without his directing hand the administration foundered. Worse still, the French were able to secure an agreement on the division of the Ottoman Empire with Britain and Germany at the Congress of Berlin in 1878. In return for Cyprus, Britain gave France a free hand in Tunisia. And so Tunisia's fate was sealed.

France's only rival in Tunisia was now Italy – a new nation eager to join the colonial powers – and when the Italians appeared to be getting the upper hand at court the French decided to act.

In **1881** France announced that 9000 Khroumir tribesmen had raided Algeria, an action they had actually encouraged, and that it was compelled to defend its territory. A force of 30,000 men was sent across the border, occupying first Le Kef and then Tunis, where the Bey signed the **Treaty of Ksar Said**, ceding to the French all control over foreign affairs.

The Bey had given in without a fight, ordering his garrisons to surrender; in the words of a Tunisian song, "he sold his people like vegetables". Even so, resistance continued piecemeal among the tribes, led by a former *caid* (provincial governor), **Ali ben Khalifa en-Naffati**. But when **Sfax** fell in July 1882, bombarded into submission by nine ironclads and four gunboats, and then **Kairouan** in October, many of the tribespeople submitted. The remainder (100,000 people, a tenth of the population) fled to Libya as dissident refugees. There, disappointed by the sultan's indifference and starving in squalid camps, they gradually gave in. By 1885 there were probably fewer than 1000 dissidents left.

Having defeated all opposition, the French secured their control of Tunisia. In 1883 the **Treaty of the Bardo** recognized the Bey as the nominal ruler but forced him to comply with any "suggestions" made by the French Resident General. Thus, while Tunisian administrators retained executive powers, the French alone made policy.

THE FRENCH PROTECTORATE 1881–1956

Colonial policy in Tunisia was less aggressive than in Algeria where the French exerted direct control, and evicted Algerians to make way for colonists after repeated rebellions. In Tunisia they were more clandestine, advancing similar policies through law reform, usually with spurious claims to Islamic legitimacy. But the results were very much the same.

Large colonial estates were established in the Tell and Sahel by dispossessing Tunisians who lacked titles to their land. Tens of thousands of independent farmers were reduced to landless day-labourers. Iron, lead and phosphate mining concessions were granted to French companies. Taxation increased markedly but government expenditure only met the needs of the colonists. A Tunisian-sponsored colonization fund was established in 1897 to encourage **French immigration**. Roads, wells and dams were built to facilitate colonization, not local development. Railways and ports were provided for the export of Tunisian resources to the metropole. Markets and advantageous tariffs allowed French goods to flood Tunisia, swamping local industry and draining precious local capital. In short, colonization upturned the local economy.

Within less than twenty years European settlers made up almost five percent of the population: 25,000 were French, but they were outnumbered by some 70,000 Italians. Most of the French colonists were government officials. They monopolized the higher echelons of the administration; few Tunisians achieved higher rank than a clerk. The **Italians**, fleeing impoverishment in southern Italy, set up small farms and businesses. Competition between the two communities was rife, occasionally violent. Eventually the French, fearing that their colonists would be overwhelmed by the militant Italians, many of whom were fervent supporters of Mussolini, had to restrict their immigration to redress the imbalance.

During World War I, the Ouderna in southern Tunisia launched a revolt against French rule in support of the Ottoman Empire, which had lined up against France. But there was little Tunisian **resistance**, at first, because its urban elite, always cosmopolitan, was not over-resentful of the French presence. Life for them, particularly those around the Bey, was still very comfortable, and the resentment of the poorer classes had no outlet beyond sporadic outbreaks of violence. Those who sought reform, moreover, were admirers of France's material and economic power. These **Young Tunisians** wanted co-operation with "mother France", not confrontation: they wanted to learn before seeking full Independence.

Unfortunately, the French were by no means as conciliatory. Led by the newspaper publisher de Carnières, a strong colonial lobby opposed every reform. They saw **education** as a particular threat because it would make Tunisians unsuitable for the role they were born to fill, that of servant and labourer. Their efforts were rewarded by cuts in the education budget and restriction of primary education to fewer than ten percent of the population.

Elitist and intellectual, the Young Tunisian movement could not rally popular support. Nor, despite demands for a wide range of constitutional rights, could its successor, the **Destour Party**, formed in 1920. Dominated by members of Tunisia's small professional and entrepreneurial middle class, they too were out of touch with the grass roots of Tunisian society. Their nationalism came across in a blend of nostalgia and legal hair-splitting rather than an active and broad-based campaign for independence.

Throughout the 1920s, however, growing resentment was fuelled by the economic depression. Violent demonstrations against French containing measures gave it some expression, but there was little organization. Ever more reactionary, Destour had nothing to offer, and a new organ was needed to channel popular nationalism. It was to meet this need that a group of rebels formed the breakaway **Neo-Destour Party** in March 1934 in Ksar Essaf. Their secretary-general was **Habib Bourguiba**, whose background epitomized the ideals of the new party. Born in 1903 into a lower-middle-class Monastir family, Bourguiba grasped the few opportunities that were allowed to him. He won a scholarship to the Sadiki College in Tunis, then another to study in Paris, where he became a lawyer and married a French woman, returning to Tunis in 1927. His political activism did not actually begin until 1932, when he founded a newspaper, *L'Action Tunisienne*; two years later the new party was formed.

Bourguiba was able to identify and give voice to popular aspirations in a way that the old Destour Party never had, and – for the first time ordinary people acquired some (albeit outlawed) political muscle. Bourguiba was a formidable populist, and Neo-Destour immediately drew massive support for its aims of **self-determination and a return to Islam**. Ever the pragmatist, Bourguiba could be heard in these years advocating a return to the veil for women.

The French were quick to spot the threat posed by this new opponent. Six months after its foundation, they declared the party illegal and, for the first of many times over the next two decades, arrested Bourguiba. But their insecurity, and popular unrest, continued through the 1930s, fuelled by the situation in Europe and the growing ambition of **Mussolini**'s Fascist Italy. Having helped themselves to Libya in 1912, and Ethiopia in 1936 – to the horror of the ineffectual League of Nations – the Italians' hopes of a new African empire were rampant, and they had always felt cheated of Tunisia. The French built the **Mareth Line** – an African Maginot Line – south of Gabès, and when Bourguiba was arrested after another violent demonstration in 1938 he was quietly interned in France to avoid any suggestion of weakness in Tunisia.

WORLD WAR II IN TUNISIA

Ironically, when France fell in **World War II**, the **Italians** took Bourguiba to Rome, hoping for his support in their claim. Since, however, he trusted Italy and Germany's puppet Vichy regime in France even less than the Free French, he consistently supported the Allies, even when the **Germans** landed in Tunisia in November 1942.

The Germans had invaded in response to a double Allied advance: British and Commonwealth forces across the desert from Egypt (after El Alamein), and the Americans from Algeria following the **Operation Torch** landings of November 1942. The Allies needed Tunisia as a base to invade Italy, "the soft underbelly of Europe"; the Nazis needed it to control the Sicilian Channel and thereby cut off Allied shipping from Egypt and India. By the end of the month the Allies had the west of the country, but as winter set in they found the going harder than anticipated and, in February, **Rommel**'s retreating forces found a weak spot in the Americans' defences at **Kasserine** and inflicted a serious defeat. In spite of this setback, American forces held the line before the Algerian border as Commonwealth troops streamed into Tunisia from the east. By this time too, the Allies were able to decode Rommel's most secret messages, learn his plans in advance, and identify and sink German supply ships.

The Germans held the **Mareth Line**. By stealth, however, and using routes thought impassable by the Germans, **Montgomery**'s Eighth Army managed to get round the line, and control it by the end of March 1943, linking up with the Americans to the west. They were also joined by General Leclerc's column of mainly African Free French troops, who had marched across the desert from Chad to support them. Over the next month, the Allies advanced through the country, their toughest battle was at **Takrouna**, which fell to New Zealand troops on April 19. On May 7, the Allies took Tunis and Bizerte, leaving the Germans only Cap Bon, for which a fierce battle was expected. In the event, however, German forces in Cap Bon surrendered only two days later.

The campaign fought in Tunisia is little known compared with the "glamour" of Tobruk and El Alamein, but the Allies alone left **15,000 dead**. Without Tunisia, moreover, the invasion of Europe would not have been possible.

THE STRUGGLE FOR INDEPENDENCE 1945–1956

After the war, the French took up much where they had left off. To all appearances, Bourguiba's political support for the Allies, and the military support of many Tunisians who had fought for them, had very little effect on relations – but French intransigence would almost certainly have been hardened still further had the Tunisians supported the Axis. Even so, **Bourguiba** had to make a hurried exit from Tunis in 1945 to avoid arrest. He went to Cairo, and spent the next few years travelling world capitals to drum up support for his country's cause, with considerable success. A born showman, he took to the stage of world politics with some panache.

Back at home, popular nationalism was growing steadily. The **UGTT**, a Tunisian-only trade union federation formed in 1946, became an important vehicle of resistance in Bourguiba's absence. A strike in Sfax in 1947 was put down violently. By 1950 the French were ready to talk, and even accepted Bourguiba as a negotiator. After he put forward proposals in Paris, which included safeguards for French interests in Tunisia, a government was installed in 1951, headed by **Mohammed Chenik**, who had led a nationalist administration against the Axis occupation. But, in a pattern that was repeated later in Algeria, the first signs of concession from the French home government produced a sudden hardening in the resistance of the Tunisian French. Under pressure from them, the French government reversed its policy. Bourguiba was exiled to Tabarka, then France, and **violence** escalated. In December 1952, **Farhat Hached**, secretary-general of the UGTT and a close friend and ally of Bourguiba, was gunned down in Tunis by the **Red Hand**, a group of French settler terrorists.

This only attracted international sympathy for the Tunisians: the Latin American countries had succeeded in getting their problems onto the UN agenda, and a resolution was passed calling for the resumption of **French–Tunisian talks**. There were those in France and Tunisia who thought the issue could be squashed, including a repressive French resident-general immortalized for stating: "there can be no question of putting Monsieur Bourguiba on trial. Tunisians, who are apt to forget easily, have already almost forgotten his name." But if there was no legal outlet for nationalism, the guerrilla gangs who began to appear in the hills showed that it could not be simply ignored. In 1954 France suddenly reversed its policy, worried by recent disasters in Indo-China and fearing that, if they did not come to an agreement with Bourguiba, more radical politicians might gain the upper hand. Pierre Mendès-France came to Tunis with plans for internal self-government. After many months of talks, agreement was reached in June 1955, and Bourguiba returned to Tunis to an ecstatic welcome.

The agreement, however, only gave Tunisia limited internal autonomy – foreign policy and some aspects of the economy were still to be controlled by France – and this gave Bourguiba's traditional opponents an angle of attack. They claimed that he had compromised and betrayed the Tunisian nation – this was the time in the 1950s when pan-Arabism, inspired by Nasser in Egypt, was running strong. Bourguiba's leading opponent, **Salah Ben Youssef**, defeated politically in December 1955, took to guerrilla warfare with Egyptian and Algerian support. By 1956, though, his revolt had been suppressed; Ben Youssef escaped to Cairo, and five years later was murdered in Frankfurt.

Bourguiba had always retained the support of the people, and he was well aware that full independence was within his grasp; on **March 20, 1956**, soon after Morocco, Tunisia became an Independent state.

TUNISIA UNDER HABIB BOURGUIBA 1956–1987

In the years following **Independence** Bourguiba set up the political and legal framework for the kind of state he had envisaged. Almost immediately **elections** were held for the national assembly, the result virtually a clean sweep for Bourguiba's **Front National**. By 1959 the constitution had been passed in the assembly. It gave Bourguiba wide powers as president, including nomination of government and civil service personnel, and initiation of legislation. Since all members of the assembly were nominees of the party (restyled the Parti Socialiste Destourien or **PSD**), the government became Bourguiba's personal fiefdom. The small Communist Party was banned in 1963, to leave what was in theory a one-party state – in practice, a benevolent dictatorship under the Supreme Combatant. With the political framework in place, Bourguiba immediately set about bringing in the sweeping **social reforms** he had long sought. While in opposition, circumstances dictated his call for a return to the Muslim veil for women, but new marriage laws gave women a more powerful voice, and outlawed polygamy (though never very widespread). Women were given the franchise, equal pay was made statutory, family planning introduced on a wide scale, and education for women strongly encouraged (see p.464).

Another area of planned reform was more narrowly **religious**, and here Bourguiba had to tread very carefully to avoid alienating the religious establishment. He downgraded the great Zitouna University in Tunis to a theological faculty of the modern university, and even more daringly, attempted to end the tradition of Ramadan (see p.457). Working from within Islamic tradition, he obtained official support with an ingenious argument: to be engaged in a *jihad* (holy war) excuses you from observing Ramadan, so the Tunisian *"jihad"* against underdevelopment extends to all of its people. What is remarkable is not the ingeniousness of the argument nor that it ultimately failed, but Bourguiba's audacity in challenging such a basic thread of Tunisian life, and in getting official support from the Mufti of Tunis. The main centre of resistance to change was the holy city of **Kairouan**, which had previously also opposed the enforcement of monogamy; the citizens

pointedly observed Ramadan a day early, simultaneously with Cairo, in a gesture of Arab solidarity.

The first decade of independence was a period of mixed success. It took several years to hive off the last remnants of the **colonial presence**, occasionally at some cost. The first of the problems was the naval arsenal at Bizerte, where the French had stayed on after Independence because of NATO's decision that it was a vital link. To begin with there was no antagonism, but then in 1958 French planes from Algeria bombed the border village of **Sakiet Sidi Youssef**. This incident, at the beginning of the Algerian War of Independence, was denounced as "a new Guernica". Tunisia demanded the evacuation of Bizerte, the French refused, and the Tunisian army saw action for the first time. Some 1300 Tunisian lives were lost in a symbolic and drawn-out action before the French agreed to leave. Another moment of colonial tension came in 1964, when Bourguiba, under the influence of the young left wing of his party, suddenly **nationalized** the land of remaining settlers. Given his determination to maintain close relations with France, relations were soon back to normal, helped by Bourguiba's unusually repentant tone in conceding a lack of experience.

During this decade Bourguiba set his pragmatic style in **foreign policy** – a pragmatism that could at times seem paradoxically radical. In 1965, during a visit to the Middle East, he referred to the existence of Israel as a "colonial fact", implying that the Arabs should negotiate over the Palestinian question. At a time two years before the June War, when Arab rhetoric, led by Nasser, was more concerned with driving the Israelis into the sea, this was not a move calculated to improve solidarity. Indeed, Bourguiba's relations with Nasser remained explosive, partly because Bourguiba felt that he had been upstaged by Nasser as the leading man of the Arab world. Bourguiba's Western orientation – in 1966 he voiced approval of US bombing in Vietnam – was another stumbling block, and in 1968 Tunisia boycotted the Arab League because of what it felt were pro-Soviet tendencies.

At home Bourguiba had other problems, caused largely by the rise of **Ahmed Ben Salah**. Once a leader of the UGTT trades union organization, Ben Salah had been forced out after daring to claim an equal role for the unions in government. However, in 1961 the president switched course, appointing Ben Salah as Minister of Planning, and began to direct the country along an increasingly leftist course. Collectivization was introduced, particularly in agriculture, with co-operatives being formed out of the old peasant smallholdings. Bourguiba went around the country on well-publicized outings where he was shown riding through prickly-pear fences, a traditional symbol of the smallholder's pride. But in 1969 Bourguiba decided that collectivization was a failure. Ben Salah and his policies were purged, and the country was given a violent twist to the right.

The Ben Salah affair was typical of Bourguiba's avowedly autocratic **style of government**: guided by the demands of the moment rather than by any long-term overriding principles, yet somehow still carrying the vast majority of the population. By appointing a **prime minister** to deal with executive matters – from 1969 – and so putting himself somewhere above everyday politics, he made himself a figure of almost royal detachment. When mistakes were made he could sacrifice a subordinate, such as Ben Salah, and enhance his own reputation by appearing to correct misjudgements that were ultimately his own responsibility. Ever a master of political infighting, as well as the wider stage, Bourguiba resisted an attempt at the beginning of the 1970s to reduce his influence within the party, and in 1974 he was elected president for life.

As the 1970s wore on, however, Tunisia's international reputation for political stability in the developing world was being threatened. Early in the decade the government began to legislate against strikes, and the country's **human rights** record brought it to the attention of Amnesty International. Deteriorating relations between the government and unions eventually came to a head when a strike in the mining industry was followed in January 1978 with the first **general strike** since Independence, called by the UGTT. The strike was violently suppressed by government forces and arrests were made, and then in June the Socialist Democratic Movement was (illegally) formed. On the second anniversary of the general strike the mysterious **"Gafsa incident"** (see p.299), possibly a Libyan-backed coup attempt, was clearly an attempt at destabilization, however badly calculated.

By now, though, the government promised **political liberalization**. In 1981 other political parties were legalized – providing, that is, they were representative, constitutional, "preserved national gains", and rejected fanaticism, violence and foreign dependence. This, in effect, meant that the government could choose and manacle the opposition by rejecting the applications for legalization made by parties they considered too popular. As it was, the PSD/UGTT federation won all 136 seats in the 1981 **election**, the first free election since 1956, prompting complaints of electoral malpractice from the recently formed Socialist Democrats and Popular Unity Movement.

Even more serious was the question of **Islamic fundamentalism**. Like every moderate Arab state, Tunisia was worried by the prospect of the Iranian Revolution spreading to its own shores and, as early as 1979, the government had banned the fundamentalists. In 1981 two religious movements appeared, the Mouvement de la Tendence Islamique (**MTI**) and the Rassemblement Nationale Arabe (**RNA**), only to be banned just before the elections. Soon after, over 100 of their leaders were summarily arrested and sentenced to long prison terms – arrests that presaged a new era of repression.

Meanwhile, discontent was fuelled by high **unemployment** (14 percent according to government statistics, but 20 to 40 percent among the young), by **poverty** (average income was only $2 per day), and **repression** administered by the police and the Destour Party's unofficial militia. There was little chance of an organized popular opposition because of the crackdown on dissidents. Consequently, when Tunisia's youth exploded in January 1984, following the government's announcement that it would remove the **subsidy on bread** (Tunisia has one of the world's highest bread consumptions), **rioting** was spontaneous. It began in the south and west, the poorest regions, and quickly spread to Tunis. After ugly street battles with the police, in which at least eighty people were killed, Bourguiba announced on television that the subsidy had been restored, and the riots ended almost as suddenly as they had begun.

At a government level there was some doubt as to who would be sacrificed – there being no question that Bourguiba, though head of state, would relinquish responsibility. After a brief period of uncertainty the prime minister, **Mohammed Mzali**, survived, and **Driss Guiga**, the interior minister, was made scapegoat. Yet although the government soon settled down to its austerity programme and raised the price of bread again within a couple of months, everyone knew that the riots had shaken the leadership. This tacit understanding in turn hardened government attitudes towards the opposition – and encouraged the regime's opponents to redouble their efforts.

The UGTT under **Habib Achour** quickly dissociated itself from their electoral alliance and began to campaign rigorously on the government's economic and human rights records. Achour, a rival of Bourguiba's since the 1950s, set himself up as the unofficial leader of the opposition, in the hope that he could rally the young behind a socialist flag and overthrow the government. He had little chance, and in January 1986, was arrested and imprisoned with twenty other union leaders on trumped-up charges.

BOURGUIBA'S DECLINE

With the unions now under the government's thumb it was the **fundamentalists** who represented the greatest threat. For a short time the government appeared conciliatory and accorded the banned MTI's emir, **Abd el Fateh Morou**, a sort of semi-recognition. But after continued student unrest and a series of bomb attacks on ministry buildings it clamped down harder than ever. **General Zine el Abidine Ben Ali**, the officer who commanded the riot troops in 1984, was appointed Minister of the Interior. Police soon appeared on the campuses, 1500 students were arrested, a publishing house with fundamentalist sympathies was closed down, and a purge of the civil service and armed forces began.

Bourguiba, who had virtually retired in the early 1980s, feared he was losing control and began to reassert his authority. Early in 1986 he divorced and expelled his wife, Wassila, a formidable woman with her own political aspirations, and, under the guise of an anti-corruption campaign, arrested her relatives and minions. He appointed the ninety-strong Central Committee of the Destour Party, a body usually elected by party members. Then he dismissed Mzali, whom he had only just publically named as his successor, and replaced him with the economist **Rachib Sfar**.

Mzali, a liberal with dreams of opening up the electoral process, was a threat to Bourguiba's power. It was no surprise, then, that the **elections of November 1986** were a sham, even boycotted by the recognized opposition parties. As for the fundamentalists, Bourguiba became even more determined that they should be eliminated. They were, he stated in private, a menace to the very nature of the secular state he had created, and to destroy them would be the last great service he could render his country.

Early in 1987 the police began arresting suspects on the streets and soon more than 2000 people had been jailed, among them **Rachid Ghannuchi**, the new leader of MTI. The Tunisian League of Human Rights complained about torture and detention without charge, only to find its offices closed and its leader under arrest. Men shaved off their beards to avoid suspicion and women took off their *chadors*. The government broke off relations with Iran, claiming that Iranian diplomats were inciting political unrest and providing fundamentalists with arms. Shortly afterwards Rachid Ghannuchi and ninety other fundamentalists were charged with promoting terrorism and conspiring with Iran to overthrow the state.

Far from frightening them into submission, the campaign of repression sparked off a series of retaliatory **demonstrations and bombings**. And in August the fundamentalists showed that they were willing to strike at the government's Achilles heel – the economy. Bombs planted at four hotels near Monastir injured twelve tourists and threatened to mar Tunisia's reputation as a safe holiday resort. With **tourism** the country's most important source of foreign exchange and an employer of ten percent of the population, this would be a severe blow.

Fortunately, the government backed down from further confrontation. At the end of September, only nine of the fundamentalists on trial were sentenced to death and five were sentenced *in absentia*. Amid rumours of Bourguiba's ill health, Rachid Sfar then resigned as prime minister, to be replaced by General Ben Ali. Within a week (on November 7, 1987, a date commemorated in the names of many streets), Ben Ali had seized power in a **palace coup**. Bourguiba was diagnosed as senile, not surprisingly given his decrepit appearance in the previous months, and forced to retire. Ben

Ali's opponents and rivals were meanwhile placed under house arrest and a new administration was formed. Bourguiba died in April 2000.

TUNISIA SINCE BOURGUIBA

Most Tunisians sighed with relief at the change of regime. Despite continuing affection for Bourguiba, particularly among older people who remembered the French occupation, he was considered too old and out of touch to govern effectively. The question of succession had, moreover, created a great deal of uncertainty over the previous decade and its settlement was seen as a sign of returning stability.

Once in power, Ben Ali pursued a policy of **national reconciliation**, releasing 5000 political prisoners over the next six months, including MTI leader Rachid Ghannuchi. He reduced government interference in the internal politics of the UGTT and began to introduce **political reforms**, banning imprisonment without trial, relaxing political censorship and putting the presidency up for election every five years.

In 1988, Ben Ali announced that the ruling PSD was to change its name again, henceforth known as the Rassemblement Constitutionnel Démocratique (**RCD**). Limited freedom of political activity was also introduced, with opposition parties allowed to operate, and recognized by the State, so long as they were not anti-constitutional, religious, ethnic nor regional. A number of opposition parties were legalized – though not the fundamentalist MTI.

At the RCD's first conference in 1988, Ben Ali promised free expression and free **elections**. The latter materialized the following year, and resulted in the RCD taking all the seats and, apparently, eighty percent of the vote. Their main challengers were Islamic fundamentalists who, banned from fighting the election as a party, fought as independents and obtained up to a quarter of the vote in some areas and some 14 percent overall. The MTI, now called **Hizb en Nahdha** ("Renewal Party"), dismissed the elections as fraudulent, and Rachid Ghannuchi moved to Paris where he felt freer to speak out.

Political **liberalization** continued, with more amnesties and talk of legalizing Hizb en Nahdha, but when this proved to be little more than talk Hizb en Nahdha began to step up its activities. In December 1989, a group of fundamentalist students began a hunger strike in protest at government attempts to close the faculty of theology at Zitouna University in Tunis. Allegations of government inaction following the **January 1990 floods**, which killed thirty people and left thousands homeless, added fuel to the movement, together with a strike by municipal workers, riots in Nefta and Sidi Bou Zid, and clashes in Sfax and Kairouan between police and students associated with Hizb en Nahdha. The alarm bells really started ringing when fundamentalists scored a massive victory in **Algerian municipal elections** in June 1990. Arrests began in September as **repression** set in. Twelve opposition publications were closed and Hizb en Nahdha's student organization banned. Meanwhile, moves were made to bring the legal opposition into the establishment fold. Legal opposition parties were given free seats in 1991 by-elections, and guaranteed **handouts** from the pork barrel. The illegal opposition were portrayed as "terrorists", with allegations of bomb-making and coup attempts, and groups such as **Amnesty International** began to express concern over **human rights**. In October 1991, three fundamentalists were executed for the murder of a security guard in a raid on RCD offices.

Tensions reached a climax in 1992. While the government in neighbouring Algeria cancelled general elections that were about to be won by the FIS Islamist party, the Tunisian government held mass trials of the 300 principally **Islamist dissidents** who had been arrested a year earlier. Most were sentenced to lengthy terms in prison, and **Rachid Ghannuchi**, the Hizb en Nahdha leader, tried *in absentia*, received a life sentence, although he was subsequently granted political asylum in Britain.

The trials attracted criticism in the West from human rights observers such as Amnesty, which reported the alleged torture and harassment of Islamists and their women relatives. Amnesty's allegations were strenuously denied by the government, as well as by several opposition parties and prominent Tunisian women activists, but they were followed in 1994 by a critical human rights assessment from the US State Department. The government's response was to protest its innocence on the one hand, while at the same time to protest and crack down on what it perceived as unfair coverage. Meanwhile, the regime continued to consolidate its position. In 1994, **Ben Ali** was re-elected president, officially winning 99.9 percent of the vote. The ruling RCD gained 97.7 percent, but four legal opposition parties were guaranteed a share of parliamentary seats somewhat larger than their tiny percentage of the poll would normally warrant.

Since 1994, Ben Ali has continued to consolidate his position. The threat from Islamic fundamentalism has if anything faded, with most Tunisians far too horrified by the situation in Algeria to contemplate anything similar in Tunisia. In February 1995, however, Algerian-based fundamentalist guerrillas attacked a frontier post at Chebika, killing National Guard Officers. This was interpreted by some as a warning from Algerian Islamists to the Tunisian government not to support the Algerian regime. In July 1995, meanwhile, the government attempted to clamp down on media freedom by imposing strict controls on the use of TV satellite dishes, and later that year banned broadcasts to Tunisia by Italian TV station RAI Uno. In October 1995, Mohammed Mouada, leader of one of the legal opposition parties, the MDS, was arrested on what were widely seen as trumped-up charges of working for Libya after he had publicly attacked the government for establishing a one-party state. He was sentenced to eleven years' imprisonment along with a party colleague, but later released conditionally, while the government extended opposition representation at national and municipal levels. Nonetheless, criticism of human rights violations by Tunisia continues, with regular arrests of activists and allegations of a "widening circle of repression" by Amnesty. September 1997 saw the arrest of human rights activist Khémais Ksila after his declaration of a hunger strike in protest at harassment of legitimate opposition parties. Despite such harassment, Ben Ali declared on a visit to France that there were no political prisoners in Tunisia, and the official opposition were allowed to field token candidates at the 1999 presidential elections, which did not prevent Ben Ali from securing 99.45 percent of the declared vote.

TUNISIA'S FOREIGN RELATIONS

Ben Ali's problems don't stop at home. **Relations between Tunisia and its neighbours**, especially Libya, have had their ups and downs. In the late 1970s Tunisia accused Libya of interfering in its internal affairs, and it was

generally believed that Libya had backed the "Gafsa coup" in 1980. After Tunisia lost a border dispute settled at the International Court of Justice, tension increased. In 1985 the Libyan Voice of Vengeance radio station called on Tunisians to massacre their Jewish community and police shortly after arrested seven suspected "terrorists" crossing the border. Libya then expelled 31,000 Tunisian workers, most of them illegal immigrants. Libyan troops began to mobilize on the border and Habib Bourguiba said privately that he was ready for war. Arbitration by Kuwait managed to avert such drastic measures, but relations between the two leaders remained sour.

Since Ben Ali took power, however, there has been a dramatic improvement. The **Great Arab Maghreb**, based on a 1983 treaty between Tunisia and Algeria, has gradually widened to include Morocco, Mauritania and Libya. Libya compensated the workers expelled in 1985 and opened its frontier with Tunisia, while the two countries have agreed freedom of movement between them, the right of their citizens to live and work in both countries, and there has been amicable settlement of a dispute over Mediterranean oil-fields. The establishment of the **Arab Maghreb Union** (UMA), an EEC-like organization of the five Maghreb states, has helped to normalize relations further, although it has not lived up to the dreams of Maghrebian unity that greeted its foundation.

Ben Ali has also been successful in maintaining good **relations with the West**, in particular France and the USA. America was the first country to recognize Tunisia's independence and bonds between the two countries have since been solid. Tunisia has **Peace Corps** workers and American military advisers, and in 1986 the Tunisian and American armies carried out a joint exercise. Many Tunisians believe that Ben Ali, who was trained in the USA, came to power with America's tacit support if not positive blessing. Certainly Tunisia makes a valuable United States ally: not only does it lie between Algeria and Libya, but the naval base at Bizerte is among the most strategic in the Mediterranean.

Relations with the West, however, came under great strain during the **Gulf War**. In Tunisia, public opinion was massively behind Iraq's leader, Saddam Hussein, seen as a champion of the Arab nation against Western inter-

TUNISIAN STREET NAMES

Throughout Tunisia, you will come across **street names** commemorating key dates and personalities from the country's recent history; the following is a brief rundown.

Bechir Sfar (1856–1917) and **Ali Bach Hamba** (1876–1918) were two early nationalists who co-founded the Young Tunisians movement in 1907. A famous speech by Sfar in 1906 is considered one of the key events in the development of Tunisian nationalism, and he was known as the "second father of the reawakening", the first being the Turkish official **Kherredin** (see p.436). Next in the sequence of nationalist movements was the Destour Party, founded in 1920 by **Abdelaziz Thaalbi** (1874–1944), but soon to be overtaken by the Neo-Destour Party, founded on March 2, 1934, at the Congress of Ksar Hellal by the young French-educated lawyer **Habib Bourguiba** (1903–2000).

Among Bourguiba's colleagues in the movement were **Hedi Nouira**, **Habib Thameur** (1909–49) and **Ali Belhouane** (1909–58), a teacher at Sadiki College. On **April 9, 1938**, Belhouane led an anti-French demonstration in Tunis that ended in violence, with as many as a hundred people killed; the result of the demonstration was the banning by the French authorities of Neo-Destour and the arrest of Bourguiba and other leaders. Bourguiba moved from jail in France to Rome before returning to Tunisia in 1942, but he found himself as unwelcome as before by the authorities. On March 25, 1945, he made a dramatic escape by fishing boat from Kerkennah (see p.436) and spent the next few years abroad. In his absence a reconstituted Neo-Destour received valuable support from the UGTT national union movement (*Union Générale Tunisienne de Travail*), among whose leaders were **Habib Achour** and **Farhat Hached** (assassinated in 1952). Negotiations for independence proceeded with Bourguiba in exile on the island of La Galite off Tabarka (see p.173–174), but on **June 1, 1955** he made a triumphant return to Tunis to supervise the final stages, and on **March 20, 1956** the final protocol was signed in Paris. Following Independence, Bourguiba served as president until **November 7, 1987**, when he was peacefully deposed by the current incumbent Ben Ali.

ests. The fundamentalist opposition, funded largely from Saudi Arabia, was unable to capitalize on this feeling and Ben Ali successfully outflanked them, opposing American intervention, but not strongly enough to alienate his Western friends. Since then, he has been eager to increase links with Europe, particularly France.

One undercurrent of tension between Tunisia and the EU lies in the number of Tunisian and other Maghrebian nationals eager to **migrate** to Europe in search of a better life. Although demographically the EU actually needs young immigrants, European governments pander to racist sentiment by bringing in stricter and stricter immigration controls. The result has been a huge increase in the number of Maghrebians attempting to evade border controls and enter the EU illegally. Most illegal Tunisian immigrants end up in France and Italy, where they play a vital role in the informal economy, but where they are also the victims of racism and exploitation, and where many drift into petty crime. Italy in particular has an alarming number of young Tunisians in its jails, and in 1998 signed a treaty with Tunisia to allow for the repatriation of illegal Tunisian immigrants.

Another possible source of friction between Tunisia and the EU lies in the field of **human rights**. In 1995, the EU signed an Association Agreement with Tunisia, which binds the parties to respect human rights and democratic principles. Since then however, government harassment of human rights organizations, arrests of activists, and attacks on press freedom have prompted European parliamentarians to pass a series of resolutions expressing concern at the situation and call for "a joint evaluation of respect for human rights in Tunisia". Meanwhile, and despite his 1997 declaration that there were no political prisoners in the country, Ben Ali released 500 in November 1999, but Amnesty estimate there are still about another thousand in Tunisian jails.

PROSPECTS FOR THE 21ST CENTURY

The **economy** is still shaky after the ravages of high inflation in the 1970s, but an IMF-imposed austerity programme stemmed Tunisia's huge national debt and kept inflation at manageable levels – officially, at least, less than ten percent. Inevitably, this has involved unpopular measures such as an **earnings freeze** for public employees (the state is Tunisia's biggest employer), **devaluation of the dinar** and **abolition of food subsidies** – only this time gradually, to avoid serious repercussions like those of 1984.

The future is, however, far from certain for Ben Ali and Tunisia. As Bourguiba's heir, Ben Ali has a hard act to follow in many ways. When future generations look back they will judge Bourguiba as the father of his country. Following Independence, he provided Tunisia with the framework for a constitutional and secular democracy, even if the reality did not quite live up to the ideal. His self-identification with the country's destiny gave Tunisians a national cohesion lacking in many developing countries.

Tunisia's standard of living is one of the highest in the developing world, with little of the extreme poverty experienced in Morocco and Egypt. All Tunisians have access to education as far as university level and to health services. Actual social progress may have lagged behind the radical legal framework introduced nearly forty years ago, but it is a mark of just how far Tunisia has come that it tends to be judged – not least by Tunisians themselves – by Western standards rather than those of Africa.

The tradition of secularism and development seems safe enough in Ben Ali's hands, and yet, as the country returns to **political repression and fundamentalist unrest**, the question remains: how many of Bourguiba's vices may Ben Ali have inherited along with his virtues?

ARCHITECTURE

Seeing the ancient sites in Tunisia inevitably takes you to mosques – which usually follow the same basic plan, whatever their size, style and age, the most important model in Tunisia being the Great Mosque of Kairouan. Besides this religious architecture Tunisia has a wealth of domestic architecture which, unadvertised and often hidden, can reveal just as much about Tunisia as any mosque or beylical palace. The best way to view domestic architecture is just to wander the medinas and the villages. Although you can walk into many of the semi-public outer courtyards, you should be sensitive – like most people, Tunisians get upset if strangers walk uninvited into their homes.

This brief account is an attempt to introduce and explain the design, development and function of Tunisian buildings.

MOSQUES

All mosques face **Mecca**, the birthplace of Islam, the site of the *Ka'aba*, the place of pilgrimage, and, most important of all, the direction of prayer. In the mosque this direction is shown by the **mihrab**, a shallow alcove in the *qibla* (literally, "the facing") wall. This is not an altar. The direction, not the niche, is sacred and representations of the *Ka'aba* are often placed there to emphasize this point. The mosque is built around the axis passing through the mihrab and at right angles to the *qibla* wall, so

that the whole building faces Mecca. (Incidentally, toilets and beds are usually aligned at right angles to the axis so as not to profane.)

The mosque is a place of worship and a sanctuary, its separation from the world outside guaranteed by high, often windowless walls and strong gates. Inside, large mosques usually have a courtyard like houses do. The parallel is important, for Islam considers its adherents a family. At the *qibla* end of this courtyard, nearest Mecca, is the **prayer hall** – broad rather than long because the front row of worshippers receives greater *baraka*, or blessing from Allah, than those behind. What restricts their breadth is the ability of worshippers at either end to hear the calls to prayer and so act in unison with the rest of the congregation.

The prayer hall has to be ritually pure, so it is usually separated from the rest of the mosque by a step or balustrade – before entering, worshippers must take off their shoes so that no dirt is carried in. The worshipper must also wash before prayer – either partially or totally depending on their state of ritual impurity – and a **washing fountain**, a well leading to the cistern below, is often provided in the centre of the courtyard (as at Kairouan's Great Mosque) or in a washing room to the side (as at the Jema'a Zitouna in Tunis).

There are few interior features inside the prayer hall. The **imam** leads the prayer and preaches from a **minbar** – a pulpit, usually just a flight of steps in ornately carved wood, occasionally a permanent structure in stone. The imam sits on the second step from the top, the highest step being reserved for the Prophet. In the days before loudspeakers the imam's voice was amplified by the **muezzin** sitting on a raised wooden platform, or **dikka**, and then relayed through the congregation by strategically placed respondents, the *muballighun*. Today the only other piece of furniture is the **kursi essura**, the wooden lectern, usually placed next to the *minbar*. This is important because recitation (*tawliq*), considered a great art in Islamic society, is the basis of the service. Otherwise the prayer hall is bare. There are no pews (the congregation sit on a floor covered with carpets in richer establishments and alfa matting in poorer), no elaborate screens, and no paintings, though mosques are usually decorated with geometric designs and calligraphic quotes from the Koran.

Other rooms or buildings may be added to this basic design according to the size and function of the mosque. There is usually a **minaret**, the most distinctive feature of the mosque on the skyline, from where the muezzin calls the faithful to prayer. In Tunisia, most minarets are square, a mark of mosques that follow the Malekite rite, conforming to the strictest school of Islamic legal interpretation (see p.460). In Ottoman times, the Hanefite school of jurisprudence, strong in Turkey, gained influence here, and mosques following the Hanefite rite were built with octagonal minarets. Some mosques have **tombs**, often crowded against the *qibla* wall, sometimes the centrepiece and *raison d'être* of the building. Others have **dormitories** for pilgrims or students, or a school room and library. But all these are appendices to the basic plan, for, in essence, the mosque is simply the mihrab and the prayer hall. Most of the **masjid** – mosques used for daily prayer – are just that. It is only the larger congregational mosques used for Friday prayer, the **jema'a**, that have all these features.

Stylistically, a gradual move can be traced towards lighter construction and more ornate decoration over time. The first mosques, those of the **Aghlabids**, used heavy columns, frequently of Roman origin, massive construction, and little or no decoration. The prayer halls were, consequently, dark, and much more impressive in their sheer size than in their architecture. Later the Zirids introduced the first domes which gave prayer halls extra light and a sense of space. With brighter interiors artists were able to develop finer and more sophisticated decoration. Under the **Hafsids** these trends continued, with domes becoming larger and covering more and more of the prayer hall, and decoration becoming more detailed and sumptuous. Then, during the **seventeenth century**, Turkish architects revolutionized styles. The dome was extended to cover the whole prayer hall, the superstructure was reduced to a minimum, allowing for more windows, and **Ottoman** and **Italian** decorative features – the keel arch, painted tiles and stucco plasterwork – were adopted. Prohibitive construction costs prevented the architects of smaller-scale mosques from adopting the massive domes seen at the Jema'a Sidi Mehrez in Tunis, but more modest Ottoman ornamental features spread throughout the country. Since then, styles of construction have changed little, except that modern mosques are built in reinforced concrete and their tiles and arches are more likely to be mass-produced than hand-crafted.

OTHER RELIGIOUS BUILDINGS

In addition to simple mosques, two other types of religious building are common in Tunisia. The **medersa** (often pronounced, and sometimes spelt, "madrassa") is a religious school where theology is taught, and often by extension, Islamic law and science. Traditionally, students generally would lodge as well as study here, so there are boarding rooms, usually small, as well as classrooms. Nonetheless, the *medersa* is centred on a mosque, so it will have a courtyard beyond the main entrance, typically with a fountain, and a prayer hall beyond that. Classrooms are also situated off the main courtyard, usually to the sides, while students' sleeping quarters are normally arranged around the upper floor. *Medersas* are generally to be found in the medina areas of large towns and cities – Tunis in particular has a large number.

More common in the countryside are **zaouias**, also called **marabouts**, though strictly speaking the marabout is the person buried inside. If renowned, he will attract pilgrims, especially on a specific day of the year known as a *moussem*, when a local festival is celebrated. The holiness of the marabout building is such that it is believed to bestow *beraka*, a blessing, on those who come to pray. A *zaouia* is the tomb of a holy man, usually a *sufi* hermit, and is typically a small whitewashed building with a small dome or **koubba**, often found among the ordinary tombs in a graveyard. A larger *zaouia* may have a prayer hall attached, and function like a mosque. It will certainly have a mihrab, though not usually a minaret. Since one of the best ways to attract *beraka* is by giving alms, *zaouias* often function as centres for distribution of funds to the needy.

WALLED CITIES AND FORTIFICATIONS

As in Europe and the Middle East, cities in Tunisia were traditionally surrounded by a **wall**, and many, including Sousse, Sfax, Kairouan and

Le Kef, are still largely intact. The purpose of the wall was defensive and at many times in Tunisia's history cities were left to fend for themselves with central government unable to provide an army to fend off Christian invaders, rebel forces or marauding nomadic tribes. The top of the wall was always accessible from the inside, with a protected **rampart** from which defenders could aim missiles at an attacking force.

The wall would have **gates** (*bab*), usually two, to allow access, and these might be staggered so that an invader would have to turn two corners when passing through them, thus slowing down an invading force. Alternatively, as at Mahdia, the gate might be a *skifa*, or passageway, which defenders could control from above, closing it off with iron grilles, or pouring hot oil onto those below. As times became more settled, new gates would be opened in the wall to allow freer access, and these would open directly into the city.

A walled city would have a **kasbah** or citadel, usually at the highest point, as a fortress to defend the entire city, and a last fallback should the walls be penetrated. The main **mosque** on the other hand would usually be right at the heart of the city, surrounded by market areas, with the cleanest trades nearest the mosque and the dirtier ones further away from it. Near the gates, there would be **fondouks** – merchants' "hotels", known in the Middle East as caravanserais – where visiting traders could stable their animals downstairs and themselves board upstairs. A *fondouk* therefore consists of two floors of rooms surrounding a large central courtyard; one of the best places to see this kind of building is Houmt Souk in Jerba, where several have been converted into tourist hotels. The other vital public building is of course the public bath, or **hammam** (see pp.48–49). This follows a design that has barely changed since Roman times, with a changing room, then a succession of bathing rooms from a cool to a hot room, heated by a wood oven fed from outside. The hot room is usually surmounted by a dome with small glass windows in it, allowing light to enter, but preventing the heat from escaping.

Aside from walled cities, rulers have sometimes felt it necessary to construct fortifications in the countryside, or along the coast. In particular the Aghlabids felt it necessary in the ninth century to construct **ribats** along the coast to protect the country from Christian invaders, and these can still be seen today at Sousse and Monastir. Because the purpose of the ribat was to defend the faithful against the infidel, military service was seen as a religious activity and those who served there were seen as holy warriors. The ribat would be their home, and would therefore have sleeping quarters for those serving in its defence. Square and surrounded by thick walls, it also has a lookout tower on each corner. The Byzantines, and later the Ottomans, used a more European style of fort, usually called a **borj** or sometimes **ksar**, to defend or control strategic points in the country.

In the far south, from the tenth century, the Berbers were forced to build fortified villages to defend themselves against the invading Banu Hilal. These were topped with a fort called a **kala'a**. Nomadic tribes in the same region built fortified granaries called **ksour** (the plural of *ksar*) to defend their food supplies against their enemies. For more on these, see p.395.

DOMESTIC ARCHITECTURE

For Tunisians the **home** should be genuinely private. Walking around the medina in any city you are immediately struck by the lack of windows looking out onto the narrow streets. Those that exist have heavy bars or ironwork grilles, and doors leading into the houses are made of thick wood reinforced with iron studs. Tunisian houses look in towards the family, not out towards the wider world.

The traditional Tunisian home, as elsewhere in North Africa and the Middle East, is centred around a **courtyard** or **patio**, *wust al-dar* in Arabic. This is usually open to the sky, though it may be partially covered, and rooms are arranged around it. The courtyard provides fresh air and light, while its walls prevent the sun from shining directly into it, thus keeping it cool. Traditionally, the courtyard had a well or fountain, in the centre or in the wall to one side. Otherwise, it might have a a a cistern, or *madjus*, under the floor, to collect and contain the rainwater that fell on the marble floors and the roofs of storage cellars. Wells and cisterns have of course become rather obsolete nowadays, replaced by a sink with taps in the kitchen. In courtyards where the fountain was not in the centre of the courtyard, its place there might be taken by a tree, typically an orange tree. In large mansions, the patio might even contain a whole garden.

The entrance from the street does not lead directly into the courtyard, but into a vestibule called a **skifa**. In a larger home, and especially in the medinas of northern cities such as Tunis, Bizerte, Sousse and Kairouan, this would be a **hall**, with benches built against the wall, where the man of the house could receive guests without taking them into the family quarters. The reason for doing this was so that within the home, the women could go about unveiled, protected from the sight of strangers. Even smaller houses without a *skifa*, typically in the old quarters of the Jerid towns such as Tozeur and Nefta, have a chicane-like passage that protects the courtyard from street view. A very large house might have been built with an outer courtyard, the *wust el-dwiriya*, where the men of the family could entertain visitors while the women were safe in the privacy of the inner patio. There might even be further courtyards so that a single building could accommodate numerous related families.

The living quarters, including bedrooms and kitchen, are arranged around the courtyard. Often, a gallery surrounds the courtyard on the upper floor, with bedrooms and living quarters off that. Rather than have separate bedrooms and living rooms, a traditional Tunisian home has rooms for the family to relax during the day, and where close friends are admitted, which then double as sleeping quarters at night. The lower floors, readily accessible through the courtyard, are often used for storage space.

In contrast to the plain and anonymous outside walls of Tunisian houses, the courtyards and the living rooms behind them displayed extravagant **decoration**. Since the Middle Ages floors have been made of tessellated slabs termed *keddal*, with designs of black and white marble (from the Jebel Ichkeul) in the wealthiest houses. In the seventeenth century hand-painted **tiles** from Qellaline and Nabeul became popular (to be replaced by cheap Italian factory-made copies in the nineteenth century), and most houses have tiles up to shoulder-height on the walls. A fashion for ornate geometric **stuccowork** also developed in the seventeenth century, and in the houses of wealthier Tunisians this delicate tracery begins above the tiles and continues over the vaults. During the nineteenth century, **paintwork**, abandoned

in the fifteenth century, regained favour, particularly on the wooden ceilings and rafters of upper floors. Consequently the houses of wealthy families were full of colour and ornamentation.

Architectural features changed with fashion. During the seventeenth century, when North Africa was opened up to Mediterranean (particularly Italian) influences, a **loggia** was often added to the courtyard, usually three "Moorish" arches on classical columns. More substantial houses had peristyle courtyards, a balcony supported on vaults with ornate wooden balustrades. Twin windows were yet another Italian import.

Urban houses were crammed into the limited space inside the city walls, making housing densities very high. For this reason the city streets were narrow, convoluted and seemingly chaotic. Yet chaotic they certainly were not. Within the city each ethnic group occupied its own **fariq**, or quarter. In Tunis, for instance, the Jews were segregated in the Hafsia and surrounded by a wall, the Europeans down near the Bab el Bahr. Early on in the indigenous quarters there was no segregation by class or wealth; instead, the households were clustered in loose ethnic or family groups. Many of the streets were impasses, sometimes called **darb**, hidden from major thoroughfares by sharp bends. Family groups lived around these *darb*, which still bear their names. The street provided a sort of outer courtyard used by the wider family group.

This urban structure and building style began to change when the **French** arrived. The new grid cities they built – the **Villes Nouvelles** – became the favoured quarters of wealthy Tunisians, who gradually abandoned the medinas. Their new houses or, more often, apartments, reflected their aspirations to French culture and the assimilation of a new individualism. Boulevards and segregation by wealth replaced the equality of the **medina**'s narrow streets; isolated houses replaced the intimacy of the *darb*; and the smaller house of the nuclear family replaced the huge segmented house of the extended family.

Independence accelerated rather than reversed the process of Westernization. The new Tunisian middle class soon assimilated the social values and tastes of their European predecessors and, with them, their architecture.

Expensive **suburbs**, much like those around any southern European city, gradually surrounded the larger towns. Today some of the architects are returning to the details of traditional housing, using arches, painted (though factory-produced) tiles, and even stucco plaster, but the inspiration and the design remain fundamentally European.

The departure of the wealthy inhabitants has inevitably led to the **decline of the medinas**. Houses have been divided up into one-room apartments, *oukala*, where families live in appalling conditions of overcrowding. Without an influential political lobby, some of the medinas' residents go without electricity, water or mains drainage. The fabric of the buildings has also suffered from lack of repair, unsympathetic modifications and dangerous extensions on roofs and walls. Faced with deteriorating conditions and soaring rents, many of the original residents preferred to move out, if only to a dilapidated suburb on the outskirts of the city, leaving the medina to recent immigrants.

Rural domestic architecture has undergone the same transformation as urban architecture in the last century. Houses, usually of reinforced concrete, that follow the same pseudo-European design, are squeezing out traditional styles. Tunisia's architectural diversity is being replaced by a rather tacky and depressing homogeneity, though in recent years there have been moves against this. The Jerid for example has seen a revival of traditional brick-making (see p.316), and also making a comeback are domed and rounded roofs, which cool the interior of a room due to the convection currents they create.

A CHRONOLOGY:
MONUMENTS AND EVENTS

Tunisian buildings often bear a plaque stating the date of construction, or sometimes of restoration or additions to the building. Although the calendar and the old Arabic numerals are unfamiliar, if you treat this as a puzzle to solve it's not difficult to translate.

1	2	3	4	5	6	7	8	9	0

The 1 and the 9 are easy enough and the others don't take long to become familiar with. As for the years, the Islamic calendar began with the Hegira, Mohammed's flight to Medina in 622 AD (which was thus 1 AH). Moreover, the Muslim year is a little shorter than the Western. To convert AH to AD, you add 622, then subtract the original AH year multiplied by 3/100, ignore anything after the decimal point and you have the AD year in which that AH year began. Thus, for example, 1421 AH = 1421 + 622 − [3/100 x 1421], and therefore began in 2000 AD.

10,000–6000 BC	**Capsian Man** appears throughout North Africa	Implements found near Gafsa give name to this culture
2000	Introduction of metals from Sicily begins Bronze Age	
1100	Earliest Phoenician settlements	
c. 800	**Carthage** and other major Phoenician ports founded	
600–300	Increasing conflict in western Mediterranean between **Carthaginians** and **Greeks**	
310	Expedition of Agathocles from Syracuse into Carthaginian territory	**Carthaginian civilization** almost completely lost, thanks to Romans and overbuilding. Some houses at Carthage and Kerkouane; many funerary artefacts; occasional monuments (Maktar, Dougga, etc)
263–241	First Punic War between Carthage and Rome, including Regulus expedition	
218–202	Second Punic War – Hannibal crosses Alps from Spain with elephants	
150–146	Third Punic War – Carthage sacked in 146	First informal Roman settlements in new province
112–105	Jugurthine War in province of Africa	
46 BC	Caesar defeats Pompeii at Battle of Thapsus: Roman Civil War won, Carthage refounded	
1–200 AD	Almost uninterrupted growth in prosperity of Africa as rich province of **Roman Empire**; control gradually extended west to Morocco, south to Chott	**Roman** town plans and buildings imposed throughout province: theatres, baths, temples, forums, amphitheatres, bridges, aqueducts

193	**Severan** dynasty of African Emperors from Libya	
235	Uprising at Thysdrus makes Gordian briefly emperor – end of the Empire's golden era	El Jem amphitheatre possibly built now, but after 250 AD fewer and fewer Roman monuments. **Churches** built in ruins of old Roman buildings
312	Empire becomes officially Christian, but Donatist schism in Africa is vehicle for disaffection with Imperial rule	
429–535	Carthage falls to **Vandal** invaders from Germany (429), who rule province for a century	Vandals leave minor monumental marks: Basilica of Hildeguns at Maktar and chapel at Haïdra
535	**Byzantine** invasion, inspired by Justinian and led by Belisarius, drives out Vandals	Many **fortresses** (Ksar Lemsa, Biar el Aouani, Borj Younga) indicate fragility of Byzantine control
647	**Arab invaders** defeat Byzantine Prefect **Gregory** at Sbeïtla	
670	Third wave of invasion under **Oqba Iba Nafi** settles and founds Kairouan as capital	First **mosque** built at Kairouan on site of present Great Mosque
800–900	Prosperous **Aghlabid** dynasty rules Tunisia from Kairouan; Sicily captured 835	Aghlabids build **Great Mosques** at Kairouan, Tunis, Sousse, Sfax, and **ribats** along the coast
909–970	Heretical **Fatimids** rule from Mahdia, resisting **Kharijite** revolt led by Abu Yazid (940), then move to Egypt, from where they unleash destructive Banu Hilal invasion	Fatimids build Great Mosque at Mahdia, make additions to Great Mosque at Sfax
1059–1159	**Khourassanid** dynasty rules principality of Tunis during Hilalian invasions – **Normans** and other Christians raid east coast	Hilalians destroy much vital infrastructure throughout the country; Ksar Mosque built in Tunis
1236–1534	**Hafsid** dynasty establishes Tunis as capital; a century of great prosperity and prestige, followed by gradual decline	Tunis **Kasbah** and **medersas** built; influx of **Andalusian** artisans brings Moorish techniques such as stuccowork; Hafsid architecture becomes the "classic" style of the country; first great souks in Tunis
1270	Abortive invasion (Crusade) by Louis IX (St Louis) of France	
1300–1400	Mediterranean trade and Christian attacks; domestic insecurity	
1534–81	**Hispano-Turkish** struggles for control of Tunisia and North African coast: Tunis taken by Turks (1534), Spanish (1535), Algerian Turks (1569), Don John of Austria (1573), combined Turks (1574)	Many Spanish and Turkish **forts** along the coast (La Goulette, Bizerte, Kélibia)

1580–1705	Regency of Tunis part of Turkish **Ottoman Empire**, ruled by Deys and Beys; Othman Dey (1598–1610) and Murad Bey (1610–37) secure power	**Hanefite** mosques built (octagonal minarets) in Tunis: Youssef Dey (1616) and Hammouda Pasha (1655); increasing use of Italianate elements, but also pure Turkish Sidi Mehrez mosque in Tunis (1675)
1600–1700	**Trade** and **piracy** at their height; French Consulate established in Tunis 1659, agreement with Britain 1662; Porto Farina bombarded by British Admiral Blake (1654)	
1705	**Husaynid** dynasty established; Turkish connection increasingly nominal, internal struggles aggravated by Algerian Turks	Security and prosperity bring lavish building programmes: **Mosque of the Dyers** (1716) and **Mosque of Sahib at Tabaa** (1780s); **medersas** throughout Tunis Medina; **palaces** (Dar Ben Abdallah, Dar Husayn)
1700–1800	Tunisia's last great era before independence under Ali Bey (1759–81) and Hammouda Bey (1781–1813)	
1741	Expeditions against coral establishments at Tabarka and Cap Negre	
1784	French and Venetian fleets bombard Tunisian ports	
1830	**French** takeover in Algeria; slave trade ends, leaving Tunisia in increasing economic straits; England, France and Italy all manoeuvring for position	Last luxurious buildings help to bankrupt the country; **palaces** at Bardo, Mohammedia; **arsenal** at Ghar el Melkh
1860–64	**Kherredin**'s constitutional reform	Kherredin's Sadiki College built in Tunis
1869	International Financial Commission takes over bankrupt country's finances	Pseudo-Oriental **cathedrals** built at Carthage and Tunis
1869–77	Kherredin prime minister; administrative and judicial reform, diplomatic measures to prevent colonization	
1881	**French invasion**, on spurious excuse of Khroumiri raids, and colonization	**French quarters**, founded outside old medinas, become city centres; vast estates created and farmhouses built in the countryside; naval arsenal founded at Bizerte. Art Nouveau, mock-Moorish and Art Deco buildings in Tunis, Sousse, Sfax
1920	Nationalist Destour Party founded	

1930	Catholic Congress at Carthage helps inspire Bourguiba's nationalism	
1934	**Neo-Destour Party** founded and soon banned by French	
1942–43	Tunisian Campaign (WWII)	Mareth Line emplacements; Commonwealth, French, US and German cemeteries stand as reminders
1952	Farhat Hached murdered by Red Hand terrorists; Tunisia problem discussed at UN	
1955	Bourguiba returns to Tunis with internal autonomy	
1956	**Independence**, March 20	
1957	Declaration of **Republic**	
1963		Bourguiba Mausoleum at Monastir
1976	The first major strike, and demonstrations	
1978	The first general strike since Independence sparks off a wave of government repression	
1980	Gafsa "coup" attempt	
1981	First free elections; parties restricted; accusations of vote-rigging	
1984	Bread riots start in the south and spread to Tunis	
1985	Conflict with Libya comes to the brink of war	
1987	Bourguiba overthrown by Prime Minister Zine el Abidine Ben Ali	

ISLAM: THE BACKGROUND

Since many visitors to Tunisia will be new to Islam, a very basic background is given here to give a sense of Tunisia's place in the modern Islamic world.

A NEW FAITH

Islam is Arabic "submission", meaning submission to God, and a Muslim is one who submits to God and His laws. The founder of Islam was the **Prophet Mohammed** (sometimes spelt Muhammad), an Arab from the rich trading city of Mecca, now in Saudi Arabia, which was also a centre for poetry, an important art form in Arab culture. In about 610 AD Mohammed received the first revelation of the Koran, the word of God, dictated in verse via the archangel Gabriel (the first verse he received was almost certainly 96:1: "Recite in the name of your Lord who creates: creates man from a clot of blood"). Although God had sent messages for humanity to other prophets – the Torah to Moses, the Psalms to David and the Gospel to Jesus, who is recognized in Islam as a prophet but not as divine – these messages had become corrupted. The Koran, written in verse, was unchangeable, and Mohammed was therefore the final prophet, the "seal of the prophets," after whom no further revelations were needed.

The main characteristic of the new religion Mohammed founded was its directness, a reaction to the increasing complexity of the established faiths, and its essential tenet was simply: "there is no God but God, and Mohammed is His Prophet." There is no intermediary between people and God in the form of an institutionalized priesthood or complicated liturgy, and worship in the form of prayer is a direct and personal communication with God. As well as the central article of faith, the four other **basic requirements** in Islam are five-times-daily prayers, the pilgrimage (*haj*) to Mecca, the Ramadan fast and the giving of alms: together these form the five pillars of Islam.

The five times for **prayer** (bearing in mind that the Islamic day begins at sunset) are sunset, after dark, dawn, noon and afternoon. Prayer can be performed pretty much anywhere, but preferably in a mosque. In the past and even

today in some places, a **muezzin** would climb his minaret each time and call the faithful. Nowadays the **call to prayer** is likely to be less frequent, and prerecorded; even so, this most distinctive of Islamic sounds has a beauty all its own, especially when neighbouring *muezzins* are audible simultaneously. The message itself is equally moving: "God is most great. I testify that there is no god but Allah. I testify that Mohammed is His Prophet. Come to prayer, come to security. God is most great." In the morning another phrase is added: "prayer is better than sleep." The most easily recognizable phrase is *"Allah-o-Akbar"* (God is most great).

Prayer is preceded by **ritual washing** and is performed with the feet bare. Facing towards Mecca (the direction indicated in a mosque by the mihrab – though prayer can be uttered anywhere), the worshipper recites the *Fatiha*, the first chapter of the Koran: "Praise be to God, Lord of the Worlds, the Compassionate, the Merciful, King of the Day of Judgment. We worship You and seek Your aid. Guide us on the straight path, the path of those on whom You have bestowed Your grace, not the path of those who incur Your anger nor of those who go astray." The same words are then repeated twice in the prostrate position, with some interjections of *"Allah Akbar"*. It is a highly ritualized procedure, with the prostrate position symbolic of the worshipper's role as servant, and the sight of thousands of people going through the same motions simultaneously in a mosque (in a *jema'a*, rather than a *masjid*, or "local mosque") is a powerful one. Here the whole community comes together for prayer, led by an **imam**, who may also deliver the *Khutba*, or sermon.

The **pilgrimage**, or *haj*, to Mecca is an annual event, when millions come from all over the world to Mohammed's birthplace. Here they go through several days of rituals, the central one a sevenfold circumambulation of the *Ka'aba*, before kissing a black stone set in its wall. Islam requires that Muslims should go on *haj* as often as is practically possible, although for the poor it may well be a once-in-a-lifetime occasion. In Tunisia, from the earliest times to the French occupation, pilgrims assembled at towns along a well-established route, passing through Kairouan and Gabès, to join the *rakeb*, a caravan numbering thousands of people. They would then make the journey to Mecca by foot or camel. The French made it a lot easier. They

THE EVIL EYE

The superstition that envious looks bring **bad luck**, though disapproved of by strict Muslims, is ingrained in Arab culture. Even when admiring something belonging to a friend, formulas are uttered to ward off this **"evil eye"**. More unlucky than the remarks of friends, however, are the jealous glances of strangers.

For this reason, various charms are used against the evil eye. One of the most common is the so-called **"Hand of Fatima"**. The Fatima referred to is the Prophet's daughter, although what connection there is between her and the symbol of the hand remains obscure. It may be that the five fingers of the hand, like the five points of the pentagram star, represent the five daily prayers or the **five pillars of Islam** (declaration of faith, prayer, pilgrimage, charity and observation of Ramadan). Certainly, the symbol is often combined with a Koranic quotation, or with the names of Allah and Mohammed written in Arabic script. Then again, the pentagram and the significance of the number five predate Islam and are often associated with Jewish mysticism. It is interesting to note that Jerban Jews share this belief in the evil eye, and use similar symbols to ward it off, even more than do their Muslim neighbours.

Another charm against the evil eye is the **fish**. Again, its origins are obscure, though it's believed that it was originally a phallic fertility symbol. Whatever the truth, you'll see charms against the evil eye all over the place, in the form of car stickers, hands and fish painted on houses, and cards pinned up on the walls of shops.

didn't want just anyone going on the *haj*, where they might pick up bad political habits like nationalism, so they restricted pilgrims to several hundred a year and laid on transport in the form of a special pilgrim boat. Now the government still helps many of the poor to make their *haj* by air, and the month when all the pilgrims leave for Mecca is still a great time of celebration in Tunisia. The apocryphal story that seven visits to Kairouan equal one *haj* to Mecca expresses the unusual reverence in which the city is held.

Ramadan is the name of the ninth month in the Islamic calendar, the month in which the Koran was revealed to Mohammed. The custom of fasting is modelled directly on Jewish and Christian practice, and for the whole of the month believers must forgo all forms of consumption – food, drink, cigarettes, sex – between sunrise and sunset. A few categories of people are exempted: travellers, children, pregnant women and warriors engaged in a *jihad*, or holy war. Given the climates in which most Muslims live, the fast is a formidable undertaking, but in practice it becomes a time of some intense celebration, as the abstinence of the day is more than compensated for by huge consumption during the night.

The tenets of the Muslim faith are based solidly on the text of the **Koran** (more correctly spelt "Qur'an"). More than just a holy book, the Koran is the literal word of God: Mohammed wrote it down, but it was God who dictated it. What the Koran says therefore cannot be chal-

lenged, and it is not open to interpretation; one who submits to God's will must accept it, lock, stock and barrel, and obedience to the laws of the Koran lies at the heart of Islam. Dictated in verse, the Koran could be learnt even by those who did not read, and shortly after Mohammed's death it was codified and its 114 **suras** (chapters) put in order – not the order in which Mohammed had received them, but (apart from the first) starting with the longest and finishing with the shortest. Less authoritative than the Koran are the **hadith**, or sayings of the Prophet. Because there is less certainty about which were genuine – a "safe" *hadith* comes complete with an account of who exactly heard Mohammed say it – and because they emanated from Mohammed rather than God, the *hadith* do not carry the same authority as the Koran, although they are also used as a guide to the faithful.

Based on the five "pillars of faith" and firmly underwritten by the Koran and to a lesser extent the *hadith*, Islam was an inspirational faith for the Arab people, but it was far from being exclusively Arab. All who convert to Islam are accepted as members of the community, regardless of their ethnic origin, a principle that gained the new religion wide acceptance in the course of the Arab advance, among Turks, Iranians and, in North Africa, the Berbers.

When Mohammed first preached his new creed in Mecca however, it did not gain immediate acceptance, especially as it threatened powerful interest groups, and Mohammed and his followers were persecuted and eventually in 622 they fled to Medina, the city whose name has come to stand for all walled cities in the Arab world. This flight, called the Hegira or Hijra, marks the beginning of a new era, symbolized by the adoption of a new calendar starting in 622 AD. The year 2000 saw the start of the year 1421 in the Islamic calendar, 1421 AH (see p.452 for more on Islamic dates).

THE OLD BELIEFS

Whatever success Islam had during its early period of rapid expansion, it did not entirely eradicate **pre-existing religion**. Animistic beliefs in the powers of stones and trees (as at Fernana) and rites of ancestor worship were incorporated into the new faith, as was a belief in *baraka*, the power to work miracles given by God to some men. These "saints", or **marabouts**, formed a pantheon of intermediaries between the people and God. Some had particular powers, to cure disease or generate rain, and prayers and sacrifices were made to them at their tombs for these services. Others acquired reverence as founder-guardians of a tribe.

Baraka was not only embodied in tomb, it was also transmitted through blood, and the descendants of these holy men enjoyed a particular respect – the *sharifs*, descendants of the Prophet, more than any other. Some of them could even perform miracles. Ascetics and preachers might also acquire the status of a marabout, at least during their lifetime. In the fifteenth and sixteenth centuries, Tunisia was flooded with these holy men, most of them coming from Morocco. During a later time of crisis, in the nineteenth century, another wave arose, warning of the approaching Armageddon.

The dualism of the older faith was also retained as a belief in **bori**, or evil spirits, and the evil eye. These led to rituals of exorcism, many of which were performed by Black Africans who were believed to be particularly powerful against the *bori*. You still see little bags of herbs around the necks of children to protect them against any harm, and the "hand of Fatima" is a widespread symbol, but today these beliefs are on the way out. They persist in remote rural areas where religious life still focuses on the marabout's tomb rather than the mosque.

ISLAM'S DEVELOPMENT

By **800 AD**, the new religion was dominant over an area stretching from Afghanistan in the east to Spain in the west. Given the rapidity of this expansion, it was inevitable that Islam would acquire some of the trappings of the older religions to which it had been a reaction, in the form of hierarchical and doctrinal disputes.

Like most religions, Islam soon developed its own institutions and, with them, particular interest groups. In the early years there was an understanding that consensus legitimized authority, the law and religion. By the ninth century, however, the **ulema** (the learned ones) – that is, the *imam* and the sheikhs of the religious colleges – had come to monopolize the interpretation of the Koran and the Prophet's sayings. They became a religious establishment, wielding considerable power and controlling great wealth. Under their control the religion itself became increasingly intellectual and dogmatic. And so the scene was set for the division of the faithful.

The **first dispute** arose soon after the death of Mohammed, and has remained the biggest single split in the faith – equivalent to the Catholic–Protestant schism in Christianity. When the Prophet died, the spiritual leadership of the faith was the object of fierce contention among several Caliphs (rulers). A substantial minority felt that the new Caliph should be in direct descent from the Prophet, and their candidate was Ali, a cousin of the Prophet married to his daughter, Fatima. Eventually, Ali's supporters broke away from the **Sunni** mainstream to form the **Shi'a** branch of Islam.

Although the two groups agreed broadly in their respect for the Koran and its tradition (the *hadith*), the Shi'ites were forced into a more allegorical interpretation of the Koran in order to support their claims for a divinely inspired leader. Even the orthodox Sunnis found themselves increasingly unable to agree on points of legal detail (all law was taken from the Koran), and by the twelfth century, four **madhabs**, or schools of legal thought, had been established within the Sunni community: Hanefite, Shafite, Malekite and Hanbalite. Together with two Shi'a *madhabs*, these still account for the great majority of Muslims.

But there were also smaller and more radical sects. The **Kharijites**, or "Secessionists", were one of the earliest (see p.383). Puritanical in the extreme, they held that anyone guilty of serious sin deserved death. The rigour of this sect appealed particularly to subject peoples such as the Berbers in North Africa, alienated by the excesses of their new rulers, the more so because the Kharijites denied any necessity for Arab leadership – the Caliph, they said, should be elected for his piety from among all true believers.

Sufism, which remains a force in southern Tunisia, is not so much a breakaway sect as the name for a different emphasis within Islam, focusing on the ecstatic and the mystical rather than the intellectual niceties of Koranic interpretation. It is a blanket term for the many different brotherhoods, often spread widely over the Islamic world, who evolved various practices in the attempt to attain some sort of mystic communion with God. The name *sufi* derives from the word for "wool", after the simple woollen clothes worn by early ascetics. During the eighteenth and nineteenth centuries, many of these Sufi brotherhoods spread throughout the Islamic world, with lodges as far apart as Yemen and Morocco linked by allegiance to their founder's teachings and, in some cases, a well-structured administrative hierarchy. They became institutions – and, in the case of the Senoussi of Cyrenaica, a government with a state.

The secret of the Sufi groups' success lay in their ability to meet the **religious needs** of the community ignored by orthodox Islam. Some, such as the intellectual Rahamania, placed great emphasis on learning, whereas others adopted more colourful practices in order to reach a state of **religious ecstasy**. The Aissouia, better known as the "whirling dervishes", used self-flagellation and music to induce a trance. Many of these brotherhoods are still active in Tunisia, though their secrecy, unorthodox practices, wealth and ability to mobilize a large part of the population arouse great suspicion among the religious establishment and in the government.

With these basic institutions, Islam came to exert a profound influence over every aspect of life in one of the great civilizations of the world. Unlike Christianity – at least Protestant Christianity, which has to some extent accepted the separation of Church and State – Islam sees no such distinction. The **sharia**, or religious

law, *is* civil law, and in a process of gradual accretion numerous layers have been added to the original code, the *Sunna* entrusted to the Prophet. Many controversial practices, such as *purdah* (the seclusion of women), polygamy and slavery, have been declared not to be part of the original code – but remain very much a question of interpretation.

Perhaps Islam's most fundamental role was in **education**, which was based almost entirely on the Koran. Young children (mainly boys) whose parents could afford it were sent to the *kouttab*, or primary school, where they learned to read and write by learning the Koran (often all 6200 verses) by heart. If they continued their studies, it would still be under religious auspices because the great universities, such as al-Azhar in Cairo (founded by Fatimids from Tunisia in the tenth century) and the Zitouna in Tunis, were attached to mosques. Students might live and do some of their study in *medersas*, or residential colleges, but teaching was based at the mosque, and the syllabus remained religious. Law, grammar, science, logic – all were subsidiary to the Koranic tradition as handed down from generation to generation. For several centuries Arab philosophers and scientists produced work that built on the Greco-Roman achievements they inherited, and was hundreds of years ahead of contemporary Europe – their role in transmitting this culture to the European Renaissance has gone generally unappreciated.

DECLINE AND CRISIS

Despite its vigour, there was also a very static element in Islam and, as it developed, Arab culture became oppressed by the weight of a **religious tradition** increasingly hostile to free enquiry. Anything that threatened the authority of the religious establishment was gradually suppressed, and the dynamism which had taken the Arabs so far in so short a time was replaced by a society unable to make the innovations that would keep them ahead of the fast-rising Europeans. The Arabs learned how to make paper from the Chinese when they captured Samarkand in 704, but refused for centuries to manufacture books mechanically because it was an invention unsanctioned by God and tradition.

At first this stagnation was relatively unimportant because the Arab world was so far ahead of Europe in every field. But as the pendulum began to swing in the other direction there was no facility for adapting to match the Europeans. Napoleon's expedition to Egypt in 1798 was the beginning of a century in which almost every Islamic country came under the control of one or other of the European powers. Under **colonial rule**, Islam became the focus of opposition. In Algeria and Libya, *sufi* brotherhoods led the resistance movement, drawing the support of the masses with a call to war, the *jihad*, a war to protect their faith as much as their country. But by the time it came to fight the battles, the wars had already been lost to the factories of Manchester and Lille.

In the nineteenth and twentieth centuries, colonization inevitably led to something of a **crisis** in religious confidence. Islam had once been the basis of a great civilization and was now dominated by infidel foreigners.

There were two alternatives: either Islam could try to adapt itself in some way to the essentially secular ways which had brought prosperity to the West, or it could reject Western influence entirely; by purifying itself, it might rediscover its former strength. In practical terms, few Islamic countries under Western control were in a position at first to adopt either alternative – but these were the poles between which Islamic thought was operating.

Following World War II, the **decolonization** process, accelerated in many countries by the contribution of Islamic consciousness to the nationalist movements, brought political autonomy. More importantly, **oil** brought economic self-sufficiency and the possibility of true independence from the West. The result was that many Islamic countries could now afford to reject Western values.

Some countries, notoriously to Western perceptions, have chosen to return to or maintain a more or less **traditional form of fundamentalist Islam**. To see this course, as many do in the West, as a deliberate return to barbarism is a failure to understand the context. A return to the totality of Islam is to choose one consistent spiritual identity, one that is deeply embedded in the consciousness of a culture unusually aware of tradition.

Conflict with the West is another aspect of the return to Islam. Adoption of Islamic values signals a rejection of Western society's values – which are perceived as being based on greed and exploitation. Traditional Islam offers a pos-

itivist brand of freedom, with substantial historical backing, which is clearly opposed to Western secularism. The most extreme Islamic fundamentalists are not passive reactionaries thinking of the past, but young radicals, often students, keen to assert new-found independence. Islam has in a sense become the anti-imperialist religion and there is frequent confusion and even conflict between secular, left-wing ideals and more purely religious ones.

But the rejection of all Western values does involve missing out on liberal trends from the West, notably sexuality equality – trends which many people, not least in Tunisia, see as both desirable and also completely reconcilable with Islam (see "Women in Tunisia", p.464). The hope is that the supremacy of Islam, a vital part of national identities, can be maintained while shedding what are seen as its less desirable elements. Most Islamic countries have now embarked on this formidable balancing act in their social and political lives.

ISLAM IN MODERN TUNISIA

For a country now so advanced in its secularization, **Tunisia** has always had a strong religious tradition. After Mecca, Medina and Jerusalem, Kairouan is the most holy city for Muslims, still visited at the Mouled every year by visitors from all over the Islamic world. The university at Tunis's Great Mosque was long respected, and Tunisia's Malekite teachers still enjoy a high reputation. Yet at the same time there is a greatly revered Jewish shrine on Jerba (the Ghriba), and although the Jewish population has diminished over the last thirty years tolerance is still unusually high.

The majority of Tunisians have always belonged to the **Malekite** school of the Sunni orthodoxy (their mosques easily recognizable by square minarets). The Turks brought with them the teaching of the **Hanefite** school (these mosques have octagonal minarets), which still survives among Turkish-descended families; but there is little (if any) conflict between the schools, and since both are Sunni the two groups can use each others' mosques. Between them, these groups account for the vast majority of Muslims in Tunisia; for the **Kharijites** of Jerba, and the **Sufis** of Nefta, see p.383 and p.322 respectively.

Despite these long traditions, though, Tunisia – or at least Tunis itself – has always had a **cosmopolitan** element and therefore remained more open to innovation. Kherredin's attempt to introduce constitutional government in 1860 was a failure, but it was a move that several Islamic states have still to make. Since Independence, Bourguiba had to tread a narrow path between secularization and loyalty to Islamic tradition. With evidence of willingness to adopt Western values, vital Western aid and co-operation have always been abundant. At the same time the Islamic tradition has to be respected enough for the country to remain in favour with wealthier Arab countries, for both political and economic reasons.

After Independence, Bourguiba, broadly speaking, tried to **secularize** the country – as far as possible with the religious establishment's support – and with some success. During the 1950s and 1960s, religious observance dropped steadily, particularly in Tunis and among the younger generation. At the end of the twentieth century the trend reversed. Local and foreign funding boosted the number of mosques more than three-fold. What is more, the mosques are now full, with predominantly youthful congregations.

Today Islam gives the young a sense of identity and solidarity in a world they see as hostile. It has also given them hope. The *imams'* calls for a **return to Islamic values** are interpreted by many as an indirect criticism of a government that has done so much to Westernize Tunisia, and of the middle classes who live affluently amid poverty. Political fundamentalists, such as those in the illegal opposition party, Hizb en Nadha, have gone further, demanding that Islamic values and principles are applied in law and government to create an Islamic Republic along Iranian lines.

It is difficult to tell how many Tunisians would support such a radical constitutional change. Most have some sympathy with the

fundamentalists' point of view but cling to their Westernized and materialist lifestyle. Fundamentalism's most fervent supporters are among the **very poor** or the frustrated **lower middle class**, who have gained little from Bourguibism. But to what extent their fundamentalism is a reaction to and expression of poverty and oppression or a genuine ideological commitment is unclear.

The government has tried to deflect criticism and return moderate fundamentalists to the fold of legitimate politics. It has proclaimed its Islamic credentials, stressing the pre-eminence of Islam as the official religion rather than the secular nature of the state. Ministers now make great show of their religious observance. Affronts to Islam, such as the sale of alcohol on Fridays, have been stopped, and the outward trappings of **Islamicization** have been adopted. Arabic, for instance, is more and more important as the language of instruction at all levels of education.

These gestures may have appeased the moderates, but the **radicals** remain unmoved. As their opposition became more vocal, Bourguiba, who feared fundamentalism as a threat to both the Destour Party and the secular nature of the state he had created, grew determined to root out what he saw as a danger. Confrontation escalated into violence from 1985 to 1987, and Tunisia seemed set to fall into a downward spiral of repression, dissidence and terrorism. Executions of fundamentalists during General Ben Ali's first years in office indicate his similar determination to keep State and religion apart. It would be a great achievement if, like Hussein in Jordan, he could divert the radicals into parliamentary politics and thus institutionalize a revolutionary movement. The price the middle classes would have to pay for political stability – further, inevitable Islamicization – might be worth paying.

TRADITIONAL SOCIETY

Traditionally, the family was the foundation of Tunisian society. Now, however, that society is changing and new allegiances and values are emerging that conflict with the old.

THE OLD TRADITIONS

In traditional society (which today means in rural areas and the poorer parts of the cities), the **extended family** was the fundamental social group. Tunisians spent much of their social life with close relatives and also tended to marry within the family network (for a man, marriage to his father's brother's daughter was the ideal), and mutual obligations meant that families were tied economically. Land in rural areas, for instance, was usually co-owned with brothers or cousins. If a man wanted to build a house or clear some land he would call on his relatives to help, on the understanding that he would reciprocate later. In the same way, if he had financial difficulties, or needed money to celebrate his daughter's wedding in proper style, he could rely on support from his close relatives.

Wider social groups were defined in the same family terms by means of descent from a common ancestor. In this way traditional Tunisian society was composed of a series of ever larger families: the nuclear family, the extended family, a lineage, a village or tribe. The frequency and intensity of social interaction declined as the size of the social group increased but, even at the scale of village or tribe, there were still communal rights and reciprocal obligations that unified the group.

Individuals were identified by their **genealogy**: Ahmed Ben (son of) Mohammed Ben Ahmed Ben Slim, along a chain of names. A distant ancestor usually identified the individual's lineage inside his community, but if he travelled to another village he would adopt the village name; and if he went to a city, his tribe's name. There were no surnames that identified the individual definitively or transcended social context. People were always a member of such and such a family.

The family also created **honour** in the sense that reputation and good name derived from the achievements of ancestors and the length of an identifiable genealogy. People whose ancestors were sheikhs, marabouts, or even *hajis* (those who have made the pilgrimage to Mecca) are always identified as such. The more esteemed the ancestor, the more detailed the genealogy. A *sharif*, for instance, will trace his ancestry right back to the Prophet Mohammed.

Because honour was derived from descent and was shared by an extended group, attacks on individuals could escalate into a **vendetta**. A family shamed had to take appropriate revenge (an eye for an eye, a tooth for a tooth) if honour was to be saved, and reciprocal attacks could build up into long-lasting feuds. Most of these vendettas began with verbal or sexual attacks on women, for in this patriarchal society it was here that honour was most sensitive. Murder might be resolved by the payment of *dia*, blood money, but never an attack on a woman.

BREAKDOWN OF TRADITIONAL VALUES

Now that Tunisians are moving to the **cities**, this traditional society is breaking down. Migrants leaving the rural areas try to find accommodation near relatives or members of the same village community. The poorer suburbs of Tunis and Sousse, and the *oukala* in Tunis Medina are full of these transplanted rural communities. Many of the migrants also return to their home for the summer marriage season, the highlight of communal life, when social bonds are reaffirmed by complex webs of visiting and hospitality. But they're no longer temporary residents in the city, returning to their village when they have earned enough to get married and set up their own farm; they are now committed to an urban lifestyle and look at the village as their origin – not their goal.

After a couple of years in the city the migrant's visits home become, typically, less frequent, and social life begins to cross communal barriers, with **marriages** often taking place outside the community. Most important of all, income differentials among urban workers discourage the mutual aid that formerly united members of the same family. Gradually the **individual**, with personal identity and interests, emerges, and distant family and community fade into the background.

Among these dislocated urban dwellers new allegiances and identities develop – those of

income and class. A new ethos of personal advancement takes the place of the redundant ideals of the community and mutual aid and, with this, new conflicts emerge between rich and poor. It is this struggle, expressed in the battle between the governing party and the secular middle class on the one side, and the aspiring poor, newly educated and fundamentalist on the other, that characterizes Tunisian politics today.

CUSTOMS AND CELEBRATIONS

As traditional society has been subverted by new social structures, so **customs** have been replaced by more "refined" mores. Tunisians still love celebrations, marriages in particular, but in the cities they have lost much of their social significance and zest. If you want to see Tunisian customs at their liveliest, you have to go to the small towns and villages.

Every stage of the **life cycle** is associated with its own celebration and customs: birth, circumcision (in the far south, this includes some girls), marriage and death. It is only at **marriage**, however, that strangers are welcome. Paradoxically enough in this patrilineal society, marriage – the social relationship that crosses patrilineages – is the most public of all social events. It is a matter of honour that the celebration is as splendid and well attended as possible. Most of the village turns out, and unexpected guests, even foreigners, are always welcomed.

Marriage ceremonies differ from region to region, but they are always lengthy affairs taking several days, usually in the summer when migrants return home. The first days are spent in preparation. The bride has henna applied to her feet and hands and has all her body hair removed, before being taken to the groom's house where separate receptions are held, accompanied by much music, usually performed by hired singers, drummers and pipe-players, and ritual praise-singing. The ceremony and the communal celebration follow, usually a massive feast with more music and dancing. The consummation of the marriage is, however, the climax, and in rural areas sometimes a semi-public event, with the groom's mother present to

confirm her daughter-in-law's virginity. More often the bedsheet is produced as evidence and, at this news, guns go off and the music starts all over again.

The other major celebration in village and tribal life is the **ziara** or **moussem**, a communal pilgrimage to the tomb of a marabout, usually the community's "patron saint" or eponymous ancestor, again a summer event. In the past everybody participated, even in nomadic communities, where it was the only occasion in the year when everyone would camp together. As a communal – as much as a religious – activity it was important in re-affirming the bonds between members of the community. With everyone gathered around the tomb, visiting would take place, deals would be clinched and marriages arranged.

Pilgrims walked barefoot to the tomb, usually accompanied by music and singing, waving flags bearing religious slogans. There they made a communal prayer and then sacrificed an animal, sometimes a sheep but more often a bull. The **meat** was divided into scrupulously equal portions (symbolic equality being important in tribal life) and distributed to each of the families. The real celebration came afterwards, with feasting and dancing.

Today, sadly, these festivals are becoming less and less common. The disintegration of village and tribal life, sapped by emigration and assaulted by affluence, is partly to blame, but the real cause is the expansion of **religious orthodoxy**. Tunisia's *imams* have no place for the marabouts next to God and so they lambast the old faith. As new mosques have penetrated the remotest villages, the marabouts' hegemony has been broken and their legitimacy undermined by the attacks of the educated religious establishment. The government encourages the trend. It doesn't want the people's religious allegiance scattered among a series of local saints, but wants it centralized instead, where it is easier to control and manipulate. Consequently, schools throughout the country promote orthodox Islam and dismiss its local forms. As attendance at the mosques and schools increases, that at the *ziara* declines.

WOMEN IN TUNISIA

When still a young child, I told myself that if one day I had the power to do so, I would make haste to redress the wrong done to women.

Habib Bourguiba

Before Independence, Tunisian women shared the oppression experienced in most Arab countries. That their position has changed as much as it has is due largely to ex-president Bourguiba's personal vision and his ability to institute far-reaching reforms. Almost the first thing he did after Independence was to introduce the Personal Status Code, an attempt to improve the social position and treatment of women. Hitherto such issues had been controlled by the *sharia*, the Holy Law based on the Koran and *hadith*.

This discussion of the position of Tunisian women is followed by personal accounts of women travellers in the country.

WOMEN'S TRADITIONAL STATUS

In the eighth century the **Islamic code** had in fact improved women's status: the dowry (*mahr*) was paid to the bride instead of to her guardian; rights of inheritance and control of income were restored, albeit in a very limited sense. Divorce, though solely a man's right, was to be effective only after a three-month waiting period, the '*idda*, and the husband was supposed to maintain his wife (though the responsibility fell mainly on her brothers) and offer some explanation for his conduct. These limited reforms were, however, later ignored, and Mohammed's own conciliatory attitude (and that of Aysha, one of his wives) disappeared under the stern injunctions of the Koran itself.

Women were henceforth **veiled and segregated** to protect their virginity and reputation; **polygamy** remained common, **marriages** were contracted when the girl was young, and **divorce** proceedings became quite arbitrary. A man could repudiate his wife simply by pronouncing the *talaq* three times in three months – but the three were often all pronounced at once, with no recourse for the woman and no '*idda*. Although it was possible to guard against

polygamy by inserting a prohibition in the marriage contract, and to receive a portion of the *mahr* on divorce, such measures were seldom taken. A married woman lived in a patriarchal family and was expected to produce sons at regular intervals. Likewise the institution of **habous**, a legal entail excluding women, meant that they rarely received property through inheritance as was their right; and in the courts, a woman's word was worth less than that of a man.

Women, on the whole, enjoyed greater freedom in **rural areas** than in the cities. They were able to walk about within the village without the veil, and enjoyed considerable influence over their husbands, and power over their dependants, within the home. Most women drew an independent income from the sale of artefacts or animal produce. Divorce was rare, partly because parents consulted their children over the choice of spouse, and partly because of the social stigma attached. Moreover, the proximity of their own family afforded wives a certain protection and shelter. Nevertheless, their status was a far cry from Mohammed's concept of equality.

REFORM

It is against this background that the radicalism of the **1956 Code** must be measured. In Turkey another great reformer, Mustafa Kemal (Ataturk), had simply abolished the *sharia* and introduced the Swiss Civil Code. Bourguiba, influenced by early twentieth-century women's rights campaigner **Tahar Haddad** (see p.342), and helped in certain areas by the more egalitarian personal laws of Tunisia's Malekite school, justified his own reforms from within the original Koranic texts and thus secured the support of Tunisia's spiritual head, the sheikh of Zitouna. The marriage age was raised – to 19 for women, 20 for men – and informed consent made necessary. Polygamy was outlawed completely: Mohammed had stipulated that each wife should be treated equally and this was held to be impossible. *Sharia* and civil courts were merged together, divorce became a civil matter, and the formulaic *talaq* was abolished. The Koran itself states that arbitration is needed when there is marital discord: **divorce**, reasonably enough, is felt to be evidence of this. But although a woman can now sue for divorce on grounds of "mental incompatibility", alimony is not always granted. Bourguiba also encouraged people to think of the *mahr* as purely symbolic and gave his second wife a token one dinar. Custody of children has been restored to the woman at divorce, though only until the boy is 7 or the girl is 9. **Abortion** rights were introduced over the next fifteen years, along with an extensive and effective family-planning campaign. Legislation was passed on equal pay and, as the French left, opportunities for work were created. Women obtained **the vote** in two stages during 1956 and 1957.

Actual **social change** has been slow to follow these comparatively radical laws. A telling indication of the staying power of traditional attitudes is the assertion, frequently heard among young and otherwise liberal men, that women now have "too much power". Despite the efforts of the Union Nationale des Femmes Tunisiennes (UNFT), formed in 1956 to introduce the reforms to the country, female **illiteracy** is higher than male, far fewer women than men have attended secondary school and university, and many of the rural poor, especially the Berbers, are unaware of their legal rights. Opinion polls among the lower classes in the ever-expanding cities, heavily affected by unemployment, show a decline in support for a woman's **right to work**. Much of the independence that a job might otherwise bring can also be frustrated by the difficulty of finding somewhere to live, because women living alone can be regarded as immoral, though it is becoming more acceptable nowadays for women to rent flats alone, a change largely due to the need for unmarried students to rent when attending university away from home. Nonetheless, a job in itself does not necessarily bring emancipation. In fact, it has been argued that male authority may actually have increased inside the family as a result of women entering the labour market, because money earned is often paid directly to a husband or male relative, or used for the dowry – the goods which the bride herself brings to a marriage.

The economic recession, combined with the upsurge of fundamentalism, may lie behind this reaction. Following the 1979 Iranian revolution, a number of women, particularly in the cities, took to wearing the Iranian headscarf-like veil, or **chador**, instead of the traditional Tunisian *sifsari* – the white veil-cum-cloak often gripped between the teeth to hide the face. Most have stopped wearing it since such a badge of support for Islamic fundamentalism invites unwelcome attention from the authorities. If support for fundamentalism continues to grow however, Tunisian women may find themselves caught between the break-up of the extended family on the one hand – already causing problems of isolation in the cities – and new reactionary pressures on the other.

WOMEN VISITORS TO TUNISIA

As briefly outlined on pp.49–50, a woman traveller in Tunisia (either alone or with a female or male companion) faces certain unavoidable difficulties. With the right approach, skill and luck, some of these can be overcome, but, as the following personal and very different accounts show, the problems are enduring ones and (though originally written several years ago) they still hold true. Further feedback and comments from women travellers – and from Tunisian women and men – would be much appreciated for the next edition.

A SURFACE LIBERALISM

Linda Cooley taught in Tunisia for six years. The original version of this article first appeared in *Women Travel* (Rough Guides, 1990).

Tunisian women enjoy a measure of **freedom and equality under the law** unknown in many other Arab countries. Polygamy was abolished in the mid-1950s when Tunisia became independent. Divorce laws have been altered in women's favour. Most girls attend school. A reasonably large percentage of women are in higher education. Many women work outside the home. There are women in the professions and two women ministers in the government. An established feminist group exists, which holds regular meetings in the *Club Tahar Haddad* in the capital's Medina, and there is even a feminist magazine, *El Mar'aa*.

But the presence of so many women in public can be misleading. It may lull you into a false sense of security when you first arrive and lead to false expectations of what you can and cannot do. If you walk around the capital (and remember, this is very unrepresentative of the rest of the country), you will see women in jeans and the latest fashions, sometimes sitting in cafés, even girls walking along holding hands with their boyfriends. But what you cannot see and should know is that these same fashionably dressed girls have fathers who expect them to be home by eight o'clock at the latest, who expect them to be virgins at their wedding and who often expect them to marry a relative chosen by the parents. The clothes may have changed in recent years, the number of women at work may have changed, but, deep down, **social attitudes** remain unaltered. The Tunisian women you see in the streets are most often going to work or going home. The idea of a woman travelling abroad on her own, in this traditional Arab society, is understandably considered strange.

It is important to realize this before setting off on solo (or even two-women) travels. And to realize, too, how superficial are many of the Europeanized images – even in Tunis. **Bars** are not like those in France, but exclusively male domains, and if you wander in for a rest and a beer you will be stared at. Similarly, you can't expect to be able to chat to the man at the next table in the café about the best place to have lunch or the best time to visit the mosque, without your conversation being taken as an invitation to get more closely acquainted. **Western movies** have done an excellent job of persuading Tunisian men that all Western women spend their lives jumping in and out of bed with any willing male.

All this may sound somewhat offputting. Yet in six years living in Tunis, I often travelled alone, I travelled with my son and I travelled with another woman. Perhaps I was lucky, but apart from the unwanted attentions of a few men nothing happened to me. There is no part of the country that it is unsafe to visit – you can see everything.

But **travelling alone**, it is incredibly hard to get to know the people, and it is hard to relax, never being sure about how your behaviour will be interpreted if you do. I learnt to cope by avoiding direct eye contact with men, and above all never smiling at strangers. I once found myself being followed home because I inadvertently smiled at a man as we reached for the same tin of tomato sauce in the supermarket. It may irk you to keep your silence; not to answer like with like; not to show occasional disdain; but in the long run it will make your life more pleasant. After a while, the ignoring game becomes a reality; you really don't notice that anyone has spoken to you! If you cannot learn to ignore the hassle from men you will probably find yourself impatient to leave Tunisia after a very short time – it is an easy country for a woman on her own to dislike.

Travelling with a man makes it all much simpler. The stereotyped images on both sides (yours of pushy Arab men; theirs of loose foreign women) can be dispensed with and everyone can act naturally. Men will talk to you both as you're sitting in a café or waiting for a bus – and generally just for the pleasure of talking with someone different, nothing more. You may well get invited home to meet their families, where you'll be able to talk to the women in the home too, as, unlike in many other Arab countries, Tunisian women and men eat together.

You can also go to the **hammam** (public baths) with the women of the house. This is very worthwhile, as it is the one place where women can meet traditionally as a group, away from all the pressures of a male-dominated society. Unless you speak Arabic, it is difficult to talk to the older women there, who rarely speak French, but they are more than willing to show you how to remove the hairs from your body, to henna your hair, to use *tfal* (a kind of shampoo made from mud) and to give you a thorough scrub with a sort of loofah mitten. You could, of course, go on your own to the hammam, but it's much better to go with a Tunisian woman, and introductions are almost exclusively made through men.

Another possibility is that, if you express curiosity, you may well find yourself invited to a **wedding** (you don't have to know the bride or groom – hundreds of people attend Arab weddings who hardly know the couple), or some other traditional event. Total strangers can be very hospitable when it comes to sharing their customs and food with you. I once had the most beautiful couscous brought out to the field where I was eating my picnic of cheese sandwiches; but then, I was with my son and a male companion.

Alone or with another woman it is all possible. But you do miss a great deal of what is, essentially, Tunisian life. Hopefully through more contact between foreign women and Tunisians a greater understanding will ensue on both sides, and the lone woman traveller will become more easily accepted. Meanwhile, ideas are changing – but very slowly.

FROM BOTH SIDES OF THE FENCE
Dee Eltaïef is an English woman married to a Tunisian man and lives in Sousse.

Tunisia is one of the most **progressive** Muslim countries in the world as regards its treatment of women, who have equal opportunities in education and work, are allowed to drive, to travel abroad, to have private bank accounts, wear European clothes and watch European television, go to the cinema, choose their own husband and inherit according to the law. All of this may sound very mundane to a Westerner, but by comparison to other Arab or Muslim countries it is very enlightened.

But, despite these progressive laws which protect women's rights, **tradition** also plays an important role in their lives. Girls are brought up to be homemakers and mothers, and are schooled from an early age for their wedding day (considered to be the highlight of their life), the gathering of a trousseau and the very real possibility that their marriage will be arranged by their family. To be unmarried by the late 20s is definitely considered to be "on the shelf", regardless of a career. So by being a wife and then a mother, a girl's status in society is assured and recognized.

Traditional roles originate from economic practicalities as much as anything else. The man provides for his wife and children, and a woman's day-to-day duties involve a lot of **domestic work**, with stone floors that need daily washing, and extensive food preparation (cleaning fish, plucking chickens, shelling peas, grinding spices, as well as annual tasks like preparing couscous and sun-drying tomatoes). There are no frozen foods here and only limited tinned goods, and because many families do not have a refrigerator, food has to be bought and prepared on a daily basis. Few people have vacuum cleaners or washing machines, and rugs must be beaten and clothes washed by hand. If the house has no running water, this has to be collected from the well or pump. Bearing the chores in mind, it is understandable that women's work in the home can be considered full-time, especially if you add several children as well. There are few New Age Tunisian men so the bulk of these jobs are left to the women, although men still often do the shopping. Following this scenario, the children will be trained to help and invariably follow the parental roles, with girls bearing the brunt of domestic jobs, and boys encouraged in the education stakes in order to get a good job so they can support their future wives and children, as well as their parents in old age. The girls of the family are often married, do not have an income, and therefore cannot help out financially. So from an early age the roles are set.

There is tremendous **social pressure** for marriage. Even if a girl goes on to further education, this is still often seen as a secondary status to that of a married woman, and having a job and income does not give her the same level of independence as in Europe. Until she is married she lives in the family home, helps with domestic duties and pools any income for the benefit of the whole family. But there is always a background encouragement for her to find a husband and clean her own floors instead of her parents'. **Virginity** is still a desirable commodity, even in so-called sophisticated circles, and single parents and unmarried mothers are a rarity, there being considerable social stigma attached to pregnancy outside marriage. Tunisian society is interdependent on a vast network of family members and friends, meaning that there are very few places that a single woman could go to seek privacy. Even cities operate as large villages and there are few secrets in a country with only eight million inhabitants. The arranging of marriages still goes on today, although it tends to be more of a tacit approval of the couple's intentions rather than the go-between couplings of strangers.

From the **male point of view**, a husband wants his home well looked after; if his new wife is pretty, as well as a good homemaker, he considers it a bonus. The average Tunisian man will continue to socialize with his male friends after marriage, and is therefore not necessarily looking for intellectual compatibility in his wife; in fact, many believe that wives should be "moulded" by their husbands and a brilliant intellect in a woman is not a desirable characteristic. A man wants a wife to be the mother of his children and provide regular sex; he would expect to marry a virgin, probably several years his junior. Her parents will vet the prospective husband to make sure he is able to support a wife and children, and has a firm financial basis in order to buy the basic essentials for a home. He would also be expected to buy gifts for his prospective bride, usually in the form of expensive gold jewellery. This can be a costly invest-ment from a man's point of view, so he's looking for value for money apart from anything else. He does not necessarily expect to be "in love", and if they are compatible in other areas it is assumed love will follow. The groom is not expected to be a virgin; in fact, he is expected to have sown his wild oats and be ready to set-tle down. As all married Tunisian girls are sup-posed to be virgins, and all prospective hus-bands expected to be men of the world, one can only presume that a certain amount of conve-nient temporary homosexuality can serve a pur-pose, as can the local prostitutes, the discreet wife of someone else or the nubile tourists who come on holiday.

With such a complex background, the stage is set for **tourists** to provide a very attractive alternative, which leads to many misunder-standings. Firstly, many female European tourists are not inhibited in consummating a relationship with an attractive Tunisian male. The Tunisian is happy to oblige, thus being pro-vided with sex and a certain kudos among his friends in having "pulled" a European; if he plays his cards right he might get invited to Europe, be given gifts and have his beers paid for locally. It also does not spoil his chances of a good marriage later to a Tunisian girl when he's ready to settle down.

As Tunisian girls are simply not available for this type of relationship, one can perhaps understand the gravitation of Tunisian males to European tourists. The sexual licence shown in current films also creates an image of freedom and willingness. Many female tourists encour-age the myth by not considering they have had a good holiday unless they have had several boyfriends. If the liaison gets as far as a mixed marriage, there may still be ulterior motives involved. As many of the boys who chase after tourists are not in a financial position to provide the gold dowry for a Tunisian bride, it is one way round a celibate life. Also many may use the marriage as an entrée into a European country, for which they would have no hope of getting a visa without the foreign wife.

Many Tunisian males with little personal experience of European cultures may be more influenced by what they see on television or what their own fertile imaginations can provide, so it's largely a question of clearly giving out the right signals. If you bathe topless, don't expect a lot of respect from any man who has seen your breasts. If you behave circumspectly and immediately reprove any advances, double meanings or hint of familiarity, you will earn the respect of both Tunisian men and women as you travel through their country. You will also be setting a standard which other female travellers will be happy to follow, and, just as all Tunisians cannot be grouped in the same category, so they will understand that not all female tourists can be the same either.

In **recent years**, attitudes have been chang-ing, not so much in rural areas, but in more cos-mopolitan towns like the capital, or those with a heavy tourist influence like Sousse. One con-tributory factor is the continuation of mixed-sex education. Friendships are formed between boys and girls which don't necessarily end at the school gate. Another factor is the emer-gence of suitable venues where friends can meet casually, often places designed for tourists. In Sousse, for example, the tourist ghetto of Port el Kantaoui has always served this purpose, joined now by shopping malls, tourist cafés and an ice-cream parlour, to say nothing of discotheques. Tunisian couples are now actually walking and holding hands in pub-lic. Even five years ago, this would have been considered very forward, except for newly mar-ried couples, identifiable by the bride's newly hennaed feet. Couples can also be seen on the beach together and in mixed groups during the summer season, with bikinis and swimming costumes on show.

Nonetheless, the attention given to female tourists by Tunisian men remains more or less constant. The best plan is to completely ignore the whistles, questions or comments. Replying only fuels men's interest – they see it as "the green light," and move in for more serious chat-ting up. In Tunisia it is not considered rude to ignore a "hello" or equivalent in the street, however strange it may feel to you, and it is the only way to get the message across that you are not interested. Chatting up tourists is the national pastime and lies second only to foot-ball as a sport. All European countries now require visas for Tunisians wishing to visit, so interest in European girls from the EU – those from Eastern Europe are far less likely to be tar-geted – can often have a hidden agenda. In any case, and regardless of ulterior motives, avail-able sex will never go out of fashion.

SURVIVAL SKILLS

Dr Carol Higham travelled around northern Africa and lived in Tunis for eight months.

As a fair-skinned Caucasian, I turn pink when exposed to the sun, and during my travels it was obvious everywhere I went that I was not Tunisian. Repeated advances from men taught me some basic urban survival skills that most Western women already possess to some degree.

1. Dress modestly. You will see Tunisian women in miniskirts and tank tops, but you must remember that most of them, too, are harassed on a daily basis, and also that they have connections with Tunisia. When they are in their own neighbourhood, everyone knows their family, which gives them some degree of protection, an advantage that foreign women do not have. Dressing in a long skirt and modest blouse or T-shirt will give a certain amount of immunity, although you should still expect occasional unwanted advances. My neighbours and several women I knew taught me defence skills because they felt I dressed in a way that was respectful towards their society.

2. Wear sunglasses. I found this cut down on unwanted eye contact as well as allowing me to watch out for potential trouble on public transport.

3. Make contact with Tunisian women and older men. I found that Tunisians are very observant people. The men on the front desk of the hotel we booked into became protective of me within a week, and I found I could sit in the lobby without being hassled. In our second week, I had a bad allergy reaction to some food and remained in our room for several days. The maid, Hedia, took it upon herself to check on me, and in faltering French we talked. She was very helpful and just as curious about me as I was about her. In the market, I always bought from the older men as they tended to be polite and very helpful. One day, a young man walked up and kissed me; the stall owner went after him with a broom and apologized to me about his behaviour. From that time on, he called me *binte*, or "daughter", as did some of the other men – older Tunisian men do not approve of most of this licence and, if they consider you a friend or valued customer, they will use their influence to stave off young men.

Because I lived in a neighbourhood for eight months, I met and befriended several Tunisian women. I also found that being friendly to Tunisian women in shops sometimes led to friendships. Women who work outside the home are not only sympathetic to your problems but they also have solutions – they know where the largely hidden restaurants are that are patronized by women.

On the street, it is best to act like you're in a large, anonymous city, but, when dealing with people in shops and souks, behave as if it is a small town, always asking how people and their families are and what they recommend you buy. They will initially be suspicious but will soon become equally friendly. Remember, Tunisia is still a very family-oriented society: family connections are important, and the more connections you make, the more included you feel.

4. Be open to questions and curiosity. Often when I became friendly with women, they would ask me embarrassing questions. One woman wanted to know why I did not shave the hair on my arms and offered to remove it with hot sugar water. Several times on the TGM, *hajas* (older women) would look through my shopping basket and ask me what a non-Tunisian was going to do with various products, then give me some good cooking tips. I always figured that if they were interested enough to ask the question and felt comfortable doing it, it was up to me to answer it.

5. Establish a pattern. I tried to patronize the same stores again and again and played on my one advantage: I was distinctive. Within a month or so of arriving, I felt perfectly comfortable exploring the souks by myself even though I spoke no Arabic, as the hawkers had come to recognize me and ignored me unless I entered their store. Then I found they were happy to answer questions and very helpful. The same was true of people in the corner stores and restaurants. We often ate at a little *gargote* on Ibn Khaldoun that served wonderful *keftagi*. One day I asked the cook what was in it. From that point on, I got special service and she would always give me *keftagi* no matter what I ordered. She would also send her son to clear a spot and wipe down the table for me. My husband found this both funny and irritating because he ended up eating standing up most of the time.

6. Overtip waiters. When I did not want to wait in the hotel lobby, I sometimes went to the *Café Africa*. Here, I applied big-city techniques, spreading the newspaper all over my table and avoiding eye contact. I also overtipped the waiters, and by the second week a newspaper was unnecessary. I could read a book, while the waiters intercepted men headed for my table. I had another advantage in my own neighbourhood: as my husband not only spoke some Tunisian Arabic but also looked somewhat Tunisian, I became an accepted member of my neighbourhood community, and was able to go into local cafés alone, with the waiters always asking about him and staving off unwanted advances.

7. Don't be afraid to confront. Early in our stay, two young men began to follow me and call out comments. I initially ignored them, but when one of them grabbed my skirt I turned around and hit him with my market basket. They instantly scattered. It was then that I became aware of the café across the street, where the men were clapping at the show I had put on.

Later, I related this story to a Tunisian friend of ours who has a daughter. He felt that once young men cross the line of touching, they deserve what they get, and had taught his daughter where to kick and how to punch. I can count on one hand the times I had to get physical or even threaten to get physical with men. I found simply turning on someone who follows you and heading towards them screaming "Izzy" does wonders. If you feel threatened, create a scene. The aggressor will usually back off, or other people will intervene.

Tunisia is like anywhere else in the world, in that strangers are more open to problems. When I saw tourists wearing halter tops and tight shorts in the souks, yelling because someone had touched them, I used to wonder what would happen if they dressed like that and walked around at a street fair in New York or Chicago. As I look back on my nine months there, I realize that I spent most of the time alone, exploring the souks, markets and museums, and I really had very few problems. Once you establish relationships with people in Tunisia, you will see a whole other part of the country that is wonderful and delightful.

WILDLIFE

For a country a mere 800km long by 250km wide, Tunisia packs in an amazing variety of habitats. Although northern Tunisia will be familiar to anyone who knows the Mediterranean – a combination of limestone and sandstone hills, pine and cork oak forest, and agricultural land – as soon as you get south of the great Dorsale ridge of mountains that splits the country, you're into something totally different: steppe deserts north of the Chott el Jerid, and true rolling sand dunes to the south, with fertile oases punctuating both.

It takes some practice to identify promising wildlife sites. Look for sites with a variety of different **habitats**, such as a hillside with woodland, scrub and rocky gorges. **Fresh water** is invariably a magnet and always worth checking out. **Deciduous woodland** is terrific, but give the monotonous olive groves a miss. For flowers, look for **colour**, which often indicates richness, especially on hillsides. A site with a **wide variety of plants** will tend to be richer in insects, and hence small birds and reptiles, too.

The **time of day** is important, too. While flowers, insects and reptiles can be watched right through the day and are best when it's hot, birds are most active at dawn and dusk. A walk through the woods at dawn or within the two hours afterwards can yield ten times as many birds as the same walk at midday.

CLIMATE AND HABITAT DESTRUCTIONS

Climate, as always, plays a major role in determining the distribution of plants and animals. Any visitor from wetter climes has to keep the lack of water firmly in mind – it's the dominant factor. Although Tunisia includes the wettest place in North Africa (the cork oak forests around Aïn Draham on the Algerian border), large areas of the south have an annual average rainfall of less than 50mm. And average rainfall totals are highly misleading: what actually happens is that there is no rain at all for years, and then a sudden deluge. This patchiness is common in the north as well.

This is confusing for the average naturalist. It means that animals and plants have adapted to become highly flexible and unpredictable in their appearances. While in Britain you can go to a wood and see the same orchids flowering year after year, you can't always do that in Tunisia. After a very wet year, parts of the desert will bloom in a blaze of colour, the *sebkhas* will flood and suddenly support huge populations of wintering birds. After a very dry winter, annual plants may simply not germinate, some perennials will retreat into their bulbs or roots and not even flower, and the desert will remain devoid of vegetation.

Along with climate, **agriculture** is the other hugely important factor. The fertile north of the country has been used as an intensive agricultural belt from the first century BC right through to the French occupation, and agricultural pressures are no less intense now, with Tunisia's population growing at 2.5 percent annually. This has meant that the original forests have long since been cleared, and many of the scrubby Mediterranean hillside regions have been converted to arable land or greatly modified by the pressure of grazing.

Grazing accounts for changes to the desert, too, with the familiar pattern of desertification being caused by a combination of overgrazing and climatic change. Many people who live in the south depend on wood for their cooking and heating; combine this with over seven million grazing animals and you can see why forests have degraded to scrubland and desert.

FIELD GUIDES AND TIMES TO VISIT

Despite the loss of habitats, Tunisia still has abundant **plant and animal life**, and much of it can easily be seen. One problem is the lack of **identification** books. Birds are fine – many of the standard field guides include North Africa – but **plants** are a problem since the only comprehensive guides to flora in Tunisia are highly technical, out of print, unillustrated, and in French. The following accounts therefore concentrate on species that can also be found in the northern Mediterranean, or which are covered in Oleg Polunin and Anthony Huxley's standard field guide, *Flowers of the Mediterranean* (Chatto, 1990). For general coverage of the wildlife sites of Tunisia and a detailed rundown of the species, Pete Raine's *Mediterranean Wildlife* (Rough Guides, o/p, 1990) is an invaluable companion.

Spring is a good time to visit. Not only are the hillsides in full flower, but April and May are also the best times for migrating birds passing through Tunisia on their way to breeding grounds further north. By **high summer** much of the country is burnt out, but good flowers are still to be found in the mountains and on the coast, and breeding is in full swing for summer migrant birds from further south. **Autumn** sees the return migration of European breeding birds, as well as a late flowering of many species of bulbs. **Winter** is the best time to visit the deserts of the south, with many of the desert plants choosing this time to flower (water permitting), and the winter season also sees the build-up of birds from Europe and Russia with huge concentrations of wildfowl and waders.

BIRDS

Tunisia's **bird** population varies widely depending on the time of the year – it's more obviously affected by migration than countries further north. During spring migration, the country can seem like the avian equivalent of Piccadilly Circus in the rush hour, when summer visitors like **bee-eaters** arrive to breed from their winter quarters south of the Sahara; winter visitors, mostly **waders and wildfowl**, leave to migrate the thousands of kilometres to their breeding grounds in northern Europe; spring migrants such as **honey buzzards** pass through, sometimes in huge numbers; and the

resident birds just stay where they are. In autumn, the same happens but in reverse. The best book on Tunisian bird-spotting, if you can get hold of it, is the Danish-published *The Birds of Tunisia* by Peter Thomsen and Peder Jacobsen (Jelling Bey Frykheri, 1979).

FARMLAND

Farmland can be rewarding, especially where the fields are small and broken up by trees or patches of scrub. Finches are much in evidence here – familiar goldfinches, linnets and chaffinches are joined by the yellow serin, a distant relative of the canary. Nightingales are a common summer visitor and the colourful and exotic hoopoe can be found wherever there are suitable old trees for nesting. Another abundant farmland species is the resident corn bunting, a heavy, brown bird with a monotonous song usually described as like the jangling of a bunch of keys. The song of the small resident fan-tailed warbler is no less monotonous, a repetitive "tsip" delivered in its undulating flight. Farmland attracts migrating quails and is often hunted over by black kites – long-tailed, with level wings – and marsh harriers, with equally long tails but wings tilted upwards. Black and white great grey shrikes are also found here, often perching on telegraph wires; they're joined in summer by their smaller, red-headed relative, the woodchat shrike.

WOODLAND AND MOUNTAINS

Deciduous **woodlands** are really only found in the Khroumerie region in the northwest of the country, and are home to many birds which, though common in Europe, are rare in Africa. Look for **woodpeckers**, **jays**, **wrens** and **tits** all year round, with **warblers**, **nightingales** and **wrynecks** in summer. Coniferous woodlands are less exciting, although **finches**, tits and some warblers are common.

The scrubby hillsides of the north are rewarding for small species. **Sardinian warblers**, with their glossy black caps, red eyes and scratchy song, are abundant. One species found only in North Africa is **Moussier's redstart**, an extremely beautiful small bird, with a striking plumage of orange, black and white. **Stonechats** are resident in this type of habitat, and the same zones are widely used as feeding stations by migrating **wheatears**, **warblers** and **wagtails**. **Barbary partridges**, another

North African species, breed on these hillsides too.

Mountains, whether the forested hills around Aïn Draham, the limestone ridge of the Dorsale, or the barren massifs of the south, are the best place to see resident **birds of prey**. **Buzzards**, **eagles**, **vultures**, **kites** and **falcons** all use the rocks as breeding sites, gliding out over the surrounding plains in search of food. **Blue rock thrushes**, very like blackbirds but a superb powder-blue colour, are also found in mountains, as are **black wheatears** and **rock buntings**.

THE COAST

Tunisia's **coastline** varies from the rocky shore of the north, around Bizerte, to flat mud flats in the southeast. Predictably, this is the place for **sea birds**: a wide variety of gulls and terns spend the winter here, including the **slender-billed gull** and the **Caspian tern**. The latter is the largest of the terns of the region, almost gull-sized and with a very stout red bill. The islands off the north coast have colonies of two species of **shearwater**. But it's the tidal mud flats of the Gulf of Gabès that hold the most exciting birds, with huge wintering populations of **waders** (primarily **dunlin**, **sandpipers**, **stints** and **redshank**), along with large numbers of more exotic species such as **flamingos**, **spoonbills** and **avocets**.

DESERT BIRDS

Finally, the hills, *oueds* (dry stream beds) and oases of the **deserts** hold their own specialities. There is a truly bewildering variety of **larks** and **wheatears** around here, enough to tax the keenest ornithologist. One especially strange lark is the **hoopoe lark**, so called because of its long, decurved bill and black and white wings. Its song starts on the ground with a series of repeated notes, slowly ascending in pitch until the bird culminates with a final flurry of notes as it takes off vertically and then spirals down to start all over again. Another desert bird with an extraordinary call is the **trumpeter finch**, locally quite common.

MAMMALS

Although the top-of-the-food-chain predators such as lion and leopard were finally shot out early last century, there are still exciting species such as **jackal**, **wild boar**, **porcupine**, **mon-**

goose and **genet**, a beautiful tree-climbing carnivore with a spotted coat and a long ringed tail. The cats are still represented by **wild cats** and (it is said) **lynx**. But ignore anyone who says it's easy to see mammals: they're shy and often nocturnal, with good reason considering the long history of hunting. But the wooded mountains of the Khroumerie hold a good range of species, as do some of the limestone mountains like Djebel Ichkeul.

Further south, small desert rodents are of interest. **Desert rats**, **gerbils** and **jerboas** lope around the desert at night, and a species of **suslik**, *Psamnomys* (a sort of short-tailed ground squirrel with a characteristic upright "begging" posture), is common on the salt marshes and *sebkhas* of the south. Most of the larger desert antelopes have been reduced to the point of extinction by disturbance and hunting, but a programme to reintroduce **gazelle**, **oryx** and **addax** (as well as **ostrich**, which has only been exterminated this century south of Medenine) is in progress at the national park of Bou Hedma, in the steppes near Maknassy. **Fennec foxes** (a beautiful desert fox with huge ears) certainly used to occur on Chott el Jerid but may have disappeared by now.

One final **mammal** that may still exist on the shores of Tunisia is the **Mediterranean monk seal**, which is down to its last few hundred, mostly in Greece and Turkey. Perhaps a few still hang on around some of the islands off the north coast.

REPTILES AND AMPHIBIANS

Throughout the country, reptiles and amphibians are much in evidence. **Lizards** and **skinks** are everywhere on the dry hillsides, small **geckos** come out in the evenings to pursue their useful insect-eating lifestyle on the walls and ceilings of older buildings, and **frogs** and **toads** croak a deafening spring chorus wherever there is fresh water. The handsome **painted frog** is widespread, blotched in brown and green. In the desert, you sometimes see **desert lizards** running like the wind on their hind legs from bush to bush. **Tortoises** and **pond terrapins** are both (locally) quite abundant. A dozen species of **snakes** also occur; although only some are poisonous, they do include several species of **viper**, and you should be cautious when out walking on rocky hillsides – shorts and sandals are perhaps not a good idea.

BUTTERFLIES AND INVERTEBRATES

Butterflies are the most obvious insects. In spring, huge numbers of the migrant **painted lady** cross Tunisia from further south, bound for Europe. It's a pretty extraordinary phenomenon, for although they breed in northern Europe the young insects are doomed, as they can only very rarely survive the northern winters in hibernation. **Clouded yellows**, a deep yellow with black wing-edges, undertake a similar migration but in smaller numbers. A small yellow butterfly with orange wingtips is likely to be the **Moroccan orangetip**, very common in early spring. Three striking species are the **Cleopatra** (*Gonepteryx*), like a huge **brimstone** but with orange patches on its yellow wings, and two species of **swallowtail**. Early summer is probably the time when butterflies on the wing are at their peak. Other striking animals of the lower orders include **praying mantises**, harmless but unnerving assassins of the undergrowth and, of course, **scorpions** (see p.19), which you are most unlikely to come across unless you go looking under rocks or bark.

MARINE LIFE

Finally, the **marine life** of the rocky northern coast is well worth mentioning. Some of the best snorkelling and diving in the Mediterranean is here around the **coral reefs** off Tabarka, Cap Serrat and especially off the marine national park of the Zembra isles. The coral is long dead, a memory of a time when the Mediterranean was a much warmer sea, but it holds extensive seaweed beds and numerous fish. Sadly, spearfishing is much promoted as a tourist activity.

On the other hand, the Tunisian **fishing** industry is one of the best regulated in the Mediterranean, with the National Fisheries Board (ONP) doing a superb job in ensuring that offshore fishing remains at a sustainable level. Apparently the weight of fish per area in Tunisian waters is some twenty times the weight in areas around Sicily, where trawling is notoriously exploitative. A trip round any fish market, and especially the big one in rue d'Allemagne in Tunis, gives some idea of the range and quality of what can be caught.

FLORA

The **flora of Tunisia** stands at the crossroads between the Mediterranean flora of the north and the desert plants of the south. The forests of the Khroumerie have an almost northern European feel, with cork oak, flowering ash and even hawthorn growing above bracken, while only a few finely tuned species survive in the waterless desert conditions.

FARMLAND

Farmland hosts a colourful mass of plants in spring and early summer, especially around the field margins. Characteristic plants include **scarlet pimpernel** (confusingly, bright blue in much of the Mediterranean region), **poppies**, **marigolds**, **daisies** and **campions**. The borage family is well represented; most plants of this family have hairy stems and leaves, and five-petalled flowers which are often pink in bud but blue in bloom. The **common borage** has nodding star-shaped bright blue flowers (which you can eat in salads, incidentally), the **forget-me-nots** are in the same family and so are the **buglosses**. There are a number of different bugloss species (*Echium*) in Tunisia, but they all have blue or purple trumpet-shaped flowers with protruding pink stamens. One common species in this family that breaks the blue-flowered rule is **honeywort** (*Cerinthe major*), which has unusual chocolate-tipped yellow flowers hanging in a fused tube.

Various **convolvulus** species are common: there are pink varieties in early summer and, in spring, a colourful species is the aptly named *Convolvulus tricolor* – blue around the edge, yellow in the middle, and white in between.

Although the uncultivated field margins have most of the farmland species, an occasional field will have escaped the attentions of the herbicide spray, and here you can see a blaze of colour from miles off, including the bright yellow of *Chrysanthemum coronanum*, the scarlet of poppies, and sometimes the nodding pink of **wild gladioli**.

A plant to watch out for on grazed agricultural land is the **asphodel** (*Asphodelus microcarpus*). It grows up to 1m in height, with flowering spikes flung up from a narrow-leaved basal bulb; the flowers are pink with darker veins. It's the classic indicator species of **overgrazed land**, since livestock won't touch it, and it slowly takes over as other, more nutritious species are eaten away. In some parts of Tunisia the asphodel forms a virtual monoculture over large stretches of impoverished land.

One final group consists of introduced species. **Mimosa** or wattle is widespread, with long pendant strings of yellow flowers in spring. It's an Australian species, and well adapted to a hot dry climate. So are the **eucalyptus** (gum) trees, which have been widely planted both in forests and for roadside shade; it's hot enough for them to flower here, often very strikingly in a mass of yellow or red blossom.

On farms and around villages you're bound to see the **prickly pear**, a large cactus introduced to this side of the Atlantic, it is said, by Christopher Columbus. The **century plant** (*Agave americana*) is another American species, brought over from Mexico in the eighteenth century; it produces a huge flowering spike up to 10m high when it's ten to twenty years old, and then dies, although suckers around its edge may live on. Much smaller, but equally noticeable, is the **Bermuda buttercup**. A very common wayside plant, it flowers in spring in a sheet of absolutely brilliant yellow among bright-green, trefoliate leaves. Despite its name, it was introduced from South Africa, as was the **Hottentot fig** (*Carpobrotus*). This last species now dominates sandy cliffs and banks by the sea, with its mat of fleshy leaves and psychedelic pink or yellow flowers.

THE COAST

The **coastal areas** also hold many of these farmland plants, and were in fact their original habitat in many cases. Field margins are continually being disturbed, and the plough creates an ecological niche similar to the effect of the sea and shifting sand. Three common plants around the Tunisian coast are all familiar to British gardeners. **White alyssum** (*Lobularia manbma*), beloved as an edging plant by bedding-plant enthusiasts, grows sprawlingly with clusters of white flowers; **Virginia stock** (*Malcolmia mantima*) has tiny pink, red or purple four-petalled flowers; and the everlasting **sea lavender** (still known as *Statice*, although botanists have renamed it *Limonium*) has papery blue and white flowers.

Salt marshes are a common feature of the east coast, and inland there are vast dry salt lakes (*sebkkas*). These are often dominated by plants of the **glasswort** family – low shrubs with fleshy cylindrical stems and minute flowers. Only real plant freaks will want to sort them out down to species level, as they're a very difficult group.

HILLSIDES AND MOUNTAINS

The scrub-covered **hillsides** of the north, and the slopes of the wetter limestone mountains of the centre, form perhaps the classic Mediterranean botanical habitat, equivalent to the *garigue* of France or the *matorral* of the Iberian peninsula. Here you can find the aromatic shrubs of **rosemary**, **sage** and **thyme**, together with the **rockroses** (*Cistus*), with their profusion of flat white or pink flowers. Limestone hills tend to have a wider variety of ground flowers than the sandstone ones; peer under the bushes for many **orchid** species, as well as **irises**, including the delightful, tiny *Iris sisyrinchium*, which only flowers in the afternoon after the heat of the sun has warmed it. A noticeable spring species here, also common on farmland, is a small **valerian**, *Fedia cornucopiae* – low-growing with clusters of pink tubed flowers. It seems to be unpalatable to goats: you see it flowering profusely where everything else has been grazed out. One plant which is heavily grazed is the **dwarf fan palm** (*Chaemerops humilis*), a low-growing relation of the ubiquitous date palm; on ungrazed hillsides (if you can find any) it can sometimes be dominant.

DESERT SPECIES

The **sand and stone deserts** south of the Dorsale mountains have a quite different flora. Plants are sparse, except in the oases, where many of the farmland and hillside species mentioned above can be found, and they are highly adapted to the dry conditions. They survive in two ways. Sunlight is so abundant that they don't need big leaves to gather energy, so their leaves are reduced to **narrow stems** in order to reduce water loss by transpiration. The other technique is to try to store water, and some desert plants have fleshy, swollen leaves for this purpose. Many desert plants and shrubs have ferocious **spines**, too, as protection against grazing animals, although there's not much that can protect against the camel, which will even feed on prickly pear.

LEGENDARY TUNISIA

Long before acquiring its present name, when it still belonged primarily to early Mediterranean civilization, the land of Tunisia featured in two of the greatest poems of European literature: Homer's *Odyssey* and Virgil's *Aeneid*. More than two thousand years later, this remote past drew many travellers to what was now a French colony, among them the writer Gustave Flaubert, whose novel *Salammbô* revisited one spectacular episode of the Carthaginian era.

In **Homer**'s epic of wandering and survival, the hero Odysseus, on his way home from Troy with a group of faithful but often foolish companions, must overcome a series of tests set by hostile gods and goddesses before finally being allowed to return to the island of Ithaca. Many of the episodes, such as the encounter with the one-eyed Cyclops, are part of European mythology, and the **Land of the Lotus-Eaters** (see passage on p.365) is among them.

There is an obvious and enduring fascination in the idea of a lifestyle emptied of cares by a mysterious substance, and it is not surprising that different places claim identity with Homer's idyllic land. Jerba's claim, however, is supported by ancient tradition. While describing the peoples of North Africa, the fifth-century BC historian Herodotus comes to the Gindanes. "Within their territory," he continues, "a headland runs out into the sea, and it is here that the Lotus-Eaters dwell, a tribe which lives exclusively on the fruit of the lotus. It is about the size of a mastic-berry, and as sweet as a date. The Lotus-Eaters also make wine from it." The geographical similarity with Jerba is unmistakable, though the lotus (a type of waterlily, depicted on ancient Egyptian tomb paintings) is apparently now extinct in Tunisia.

VIRGIL: THE AENEID

Like Odysseus, Virgil's hero Aeneas has difficulty escaping the seductive charms of this part of Africa, but the episode is much more emotionally and politically involved. Aeneas and Dido represent Rome and Carthage respectively, but Aeneas' choice between his love for Dido and his commitment to found a new Troy – that is, Rome – also represents the conflict between personal desires and public duty. Dido has given everything for Aeneas, alienating both the neighbouring Numidians, by rejecting marriage with one of their kings, and her own people, through her infidelity to her dead husband. Aeneas knows therefore that to abandon Dido will be to destroy her. At first he plans to leave secretly, but Dido realizes his intentions and, here, confronts him. Dido's eventual suicide on a funeral pyre symbolizes the inevitable destruction of Carthage by Imperial Rome.

THE END OF THE AFFAIR

At last Dido accosted Aeneas, speaking first, and denounced him:

"Traitor, did you actually believe that you could disguise so wicked a deed and leave my country without a word? And can nothing hold you, not our love, nor our once plighted hands, nor even the cruel death that must await your Dido? Are you so unfeeling that you labour at your fleet under a wintry sky, in haste to traverse the high seas in the teeth of the northerly gales? Why, had you not now been searching for a home which you have never seen in some alien land, and had ancient Troy itself been still standing, would you have been planning to sail even there over such tempestuous seas? Is it from me that you are trying to escape? Oh, by the tears which I shed, by your own plighted hand, for I have left myself, poor fool, no other appeal, and by our union, by the true marriage which it was to be, oh, if I was ever kind to you, or if anything about me made you happy, please,

please, if it is not too late to beg you, have pity for the ruin of a home, and change your mind. It was because of you that I earned the hate of Africa's tribes and the lords of the Numidians, and the hostility of my Tyrians also; and it was because of you that I let my honour die, the fair fame which used to be mine and my only hope of immortality. In whose hands are you leaving me to face my death, my Guest? I used to call you Husband, but the word has shrunk to Guest. What does the future hold for me now? My brother Pygmalion coming to demolish my walls, or this Gaetulian Iarbas, marrying me by capture? At least, if I had a son of yours conceived before you left, some tiny Aeneas to play about my hall and bring you back to me if only in his likeness, I might not then have felt so utterly entrapped and forsaken."

She finished. He, remembering Jupiter's warning, held his eyes steady and strained to master the agony within him. At last he spoke shortly:

"Your Majesty, I shall never deny that I am in your debt for all those many acts of kindness which you may well recount to me. And for long as I have consciousness and breath of life controls my movement, I shall never tire, Elissa, of your memory. Now I shall speak briefly of the facts. I had no thought of hiding my present departure under any deceit. Do not imagine that. Nor have I ever made any marriage-rite my pretext, for I never had such a compact with you. If my destiny had allowed me to guide my life as I myself would have chosen, and solve my problems according to my own preference, I should have made the city of Troy, with its loved remembrances of my own folk, my first care; and, with Priam's tall citadel still standing, I should have refounded Troy's fortress to be strong once more after her defeat. But in fact Apollo at Grynium, where he gives his divination in Lycia by the lots, has insistently commanded me to make my way to Italy's noble land. Italy must be my love and my homeland now. If you, a Phoenician, are faithful to your Carthaginian fortress here, content to look on no other city but this city in far-away Africa, what is the objection if Trojans settle in Italy? It is no sin, if we, like you, look for a kingdom in a foreign country. Each time the night shrouds the earth in its moist shadows, each time the fiery stars arise, the anxious wraith of my father Anchises warns me in sleep, and I am afraid. My son Ascanius also serves as a warning to me; I think of his dear self, and of the wrong which I do

him in defrauding him of his Italian kingdom, where Fate has given him his lands. And now Jove himself has sent the Spokesman of the Gods – this I swear to you by my son's life and by my father – who flew swiftly through the air, and delivered the command to me. With my own eyes I saw the divine messenger in clearest light entering the city gate, and heard his voice with my own ears. Cease, therefore, to upset yourself, and me also, with these protests. It is not by my own choice that I voyage onward to Italy."

Throughout this declaration Dido had remained standing, turned away from Aeneas but glaring at him over her shoulder with eyes which roved about his whole figure in a voiceless stare. Then her fury broke:

"Traitor, no goddess was ever your mother nor was it Dardanus who founded your line. No, your parent was Mount Caucasus, rugged, rocky, and hard, and tigers of Hyrcania nursed you ... For what need have I of concealment now? Why hold myself in check any longer as if there could be anything worse to come?... Has he spared a sigh or a look in response to my weeping, or has he once softened, or shed a tear of pity for one who loved him? Depth beyond depth of iniquity! Neither Supreme Juno, nor the Father who is Saturn's son, can possibly look with the impartial eyes of justice on what is happening now. No faith is left sure in the wide world. I welcomed him, a shipwrecked beggar, and like a fool I allowed him to share my royal place. I saved his comrades from death and gave him back his lost fleet ... The Furies have me now, they burn, they drive ...! So, now, it seems, he has his orders from Apollo's own Lycian oracle, and next even the Spokesman of the Gods is sent by Jove himself to deliver through the air to him the same ghastly command! So I am to believe that the High Powers exercise their minds about such a matter and let concern for it disturb their calm! Oh, I am not holding you. I do not dispute your words. Go, quest for Italy before the winds; sail over the waves in search of your kingdom. But I still believe that, if there is any power for righteousness in Heaven, you will drink to the dregs the cup of punishment amid sea-rocks, and as you suffer cry 'Dido' again and again. Though far, yet I shall be near, haunting you with flames of blackest pitch. And when death's chill has parted my body from its breath, wherever you go my spectre will be there. You will have your punishment, you villain. And I shall hear; the news will reach me deep in the world of death."

She did not finish, but at these words broke off sharply. She hurried in her misery away and hid from sight, leaving Aeneas anxious and hesitant, and longing to say much more to her. Dido fainted, and fell; and her maids took her up, carried her to her marble bedroom and laid her on her bed.

Taken from Book IV of the Penguin Classics edition, translated by W. F. Jackson Knight

GUSTAVE FLAUBERT: SALAMMBÔ

In the nineteenth century, Carthage's abrupt and tragic end captured the imaginations of many Europeans, among them Gustave Flaubert. His impulse to write about ancient Carthage owed as much to the present as the past; on his first trip to the East in 1851, Flaubert had become obsessed with "the Orient", that mythical land created by feverish post-Romantic sensibilities. The plot, such as it is, follows the War of the Mercenaries (241–237 BC) – though with significant additions from the author, including the character of Salammbô, sex symbol supreme. For the bulk of the novel, Flaubert attempts to recreate the atmosphere of Carthage as an ancient Orient, something of a cross between a Cecil B. De Mille epic and a video nasty. It is also, however, highly imaginative, not to say fantastic, and a whole generation saw the Orient in terms quite as excessive as Flaubert's.

In this episode, Hanno, one of the Carthaginian generals, is in Utica snatching in typical style a brief respite from the rigours of campaigning against the Mercenaries, or Barbarians.

HANNO TAKES A BATH

Three hours later he was still plunged in the cinnamon oil with which the bath had been filled; and as he bathed, he ate on a stretched out ox hide, flamingo tongues with poppy seed seasoned with honey. Beside him, his doctor, standing motionless in a long yellow robe, had the bath heated up from time to time and two boys leaning on the steps of the pool rubbed his legs. But the care of his body did not interrupt his concern for the welfare of the state, and he was dictating a letter to the Grand Council and, as some prisoners had just been taken, wondering what terrible punishment to invent.

"Stop!" he said to a slave who stood writing in the hollow of his hand. "Have them brought in! I want to see them."

And from the back of the room filled with white steam where torches cast spots of red three Barbarians were pushed in: a Samnite, a Spartan, and a Cappadocian.

"Continue!" said Hanno.

"Rejoice light of the Baals! Your Suffete has exterminated the greedy dogs! Blessings on the Republic! Order prayers to be offered!" He noticed the captives, and then roaring with laughter: "Ha ha! My brave men from Sicca! You are not shouting so loudly today! Here I am! Do you recognize me? Where are your swords then? What terrible men, really!" And he pretended to try and hide, as if he were afraid. "You demanded horses, women, land, judicial office, no doubt, and priesthood! Why not? All right, I will give you land, and land you will never leave! You will be married to brand new gallows! Your pay? It will be melted in your mouths in the form of lead ingots! And I will set you in good positions, very high, among the clouds, so that you can be near the eagles!"

The three Barbarians, hairy and covered in rags, looked at him without understanding what he was saying. Wounded in the knees, they had been seized and bound with ropes, and the ends of the heavy chains on their hands dragged along the floor. Hanno was angry at their impassivity.

"On your knees! On your knees! Jackals! Dirt! Vermin! Excrement! So they do not answer! Enough! Silence! Have them flayed alive! No! In a moment!"

He was puffing like a hippopotamus, rolling his eyes. The scented oil ran out beneath the bulk of his body, and sticking to his scaly skin made it look pink in the torchlight.

He went on:

"For four days we have greatly suffered from the sun. Crossing the Macar some mules were lost. Despite their position, the extraordinary courage … Ah! Demonades how I am suffering! Heat up the bricks and make them red hot!"

There was a clattering of rakes and furnaces. The incense smoked more fiercely in its large burners, and the naked masseurs, sweating like sponges, squeezed over his joints a paste composed of corn, sulphur, black wine, bitches' milk, myrrh, galbanum, and styrax. He was tormented by constant thirst: the man in yellow did not give in to this craving and, holding out a golden cup in which steamed a viper's brew:

"Drink!" he said, "so that the strength of the serpents, children of the sun, may penetrate the marrow of your bones, and take courage, reflection of the Gods! Besides, you know that a priest of Eschmoûn is watching the cruel stars around the Dog from which your illness derives. They are growing paler, like the spots on your skin, and you are not to die of it."

"Oh, yes, that is right," repeated the Suffete, "I am not to die of it!" And from his purplish lips escaped a breath more noisome than the stench of a corpse. Two coals seemed to burn in place of his eyes which had no eyebrows left; a mass of wrinkled skin hung down over his forehead; his two ears, standing out from his head, were beginning to swell, and the deep creases which made semi-circles around his nostrils gave him a strange and frightening look, like that of a wild beast. His distorted voice sounded like a roar; he said:

"Perhaps you are right, Demonades? In fact a lot of the ulcers have closed up. I feel quite robust. Just look how I eat!"

Then less out of greed than for show, and to prove to himself that he was well, he attacked cheese and tarragon stuffing, filleted fish, pumpkins, oysters, with eggs, horseradish, truffles and kebabs of little birds. As he looked at the prisoners he revelled in imagining their punishment. However he remembered Sicca, and fury at all his pains burst out in insults at these three men.

"Ah! Traitors! Wretches! Infamous cursed creatures! And you exposed me to your outrages, me! Me! The Suffete! Their services, the price of their blood, as they call it! Oh yes! Their blood! Their blood!" Then talking to himself: "They will all perish! Not one will be sold! It would be better to take them to Carthage! I should be seen … but I have probably not brought enough chains? Write: send me … How many of them are there? Go and ask Muthumbal! Go! No mercy! Cut off all their hands, and bring them to me in baskets!"

But strange cries, at once hoarse and shrill, could be heard in the room, above Hanno's voice and the clattering of the dishes being set round him. The noise increased, and suddenly the furious trumpeting of the elephants broke out as if battle was starting again. A great tumult surrounded the town.

The Carthaginians had not tried to pursue the Barbarians. They had settled at the foot of the walls, with their baggage, their servants, their whole satrap retinue and they were making merry in their handsome pearl-edged tents, while all that remained of the Mercenary camp was a heap of ruins on the plain. Spendius had recovered his courage. He sent out Zarxas to Mâtho, went through the woods, rallied his men (losses had not been heavy) – and furious at having been beaten in battle, they reformed their lines, when someone discovered a vat of paraffin, no doubt abandoned by the Carthaginians. Then Spendius had pigs collected from the farms, smeared them with pitch, set light to it and drove them towards Utica.

The elephants, frightened by these flames, took flight. The ground sloped upwards, they were assailed by javelins, and turned back – and with mighty blows of their tusks and hooves they ripped, smothered, flattened the Carthaginians. Behind them, the Barbarians were coming down the hill; the Punic camp, with no defences, was sacked at the first charge, and the Carthaginians were crushed against the gates, for no one would open them for fear of the Mercenaries.

Dawn was breaking; from the west appeared Mâtho's infantrymen. At the same time horsemen came in sight; it was Narr'Havas with his Numidians. Jumping over the ravines and bushes, they drove the fugitives like hounds hunting hares. This reversal of fortune interrupted the Suffete. He cried out to be helped out of the bath. The three captives were still before him. Then a Negro (the same one who carried his parasol in battle) leaned over to his ear.

"Well now …?" the Suffete slowly replied. "Oh! kill them!" he added brusquely.

The Ethiopian drew a long dagger from his belt and the three heads fell. One of them, bouncing amid the debris of the feast, jumped into the pool, and floated there for a while, with open mouth and staring eyes. The morning light was filtering in through cracks in the wall; the three bodies, lying on their chests, were streaming blood like three fountains, and a sheet of blood covered the mosaics, which had been sprinkled with blue powder. The Suffete soaked his hand in this still warm slime, and rubbed his knees with it: it had remedial powers.

Taken from the Penguin Classics edition, translated by A. J. Krailsheimer

TUNISIAN LITERATURE

Modern literature right across the Maghreb is tied up with questions of national and linguistic identity. Traditional local Arabic forms and language have wrestled with the language of their colonizers, and the internationally best-known works have mostly been written in French. Tunisia has yet to produce a writer as widely known as Morocco's Tahar Ben Jelloun or Algeria's Rachid Mimouni, nor does it have a resident foreign sage and interpreter to play the role that Paul Bowles did in Morocco. In the first half of the twentieth century, though, two extraordinary writers – both fated to die young – emerged from colonial Tunisia.

ABOU EL KACEM CHABBI

Abou el Kacem Chabbi *(1909–34), a native of Tozeur, was the son of a judge who sent him at the age of 12 to study at the Zitouna mosque in Tunis. He subsequently studied law, but was more interested in poetry, which he read widely. Goethe, Lamartine and the Syrian-American Gibran Kahlil Gibran were particular influences.*

By the age of 18 his own poetry was being published and in 1929 he delivered a famous and influential lecture in Tunis on "The Poetic Imagination of the Arabs". Rejecting the stifling weight of the past as represented by classical Arabic poetry, he made a plea for the poet's "freedom to imagine". His own work, while retaining the essentials of classical form and language, expresses a distinctly Romantic sensibility. The poems are full of solitary individu-

als yearning for self-expression, frequently in settings of mountains covered with rushing streams and leafy forests. Neither Tunis nor Tozeur has many of these, but Chabbi spent his summers in Aïn Draham and would have drawn inspiration from the scenery there. He died of a cardiac problem at 25, but not before achieving an extraordinary reputation. His poem "The Will of Life" has been taught to schoolchildren across the Arab world. Like several of his poems, it hints at the frustrations of the colonized state in which Chabbi found himself and his country.

THE WILL OF LIFE

If one day the people should choose life
Fate is certain to respond.
The night will surely retreat,
and fetters be broken!
He who is not embraced by the longing for life
will evaporate in vacancy and be forgotten –
Grief to anyone not aroused by the breathing desire for life!
Let him beware the slap of oblivion!
This is what life said to me,
this is how its spirit spoke.

The wind muttered between the ravines;
"When I aspire to a goal,
I ride my wishes, forgetting caution,
face the wilderness, the rugged trails
and flaming days –
He who does not like scaling mountains
will live eternally in potholes."

So the sap of youth churned in my heart
as other winds raged within my breast.
I bent my head, listening to
the clap of thunder,
the chime of the draft,
the cadence of the rain.

When I asked the earth,
"Mother, do you hate mankind?"
She replied, "I bless those with ambition,
those who brave danger –
I curse the ones not keeping step with time,
who are content to live a fossil life.
The vibrating universe loves what moves
and despises the dead, forgetting their greatness.
The horizon hugs no stiffened bird,
nor does the bee kiss a withered flower.
Not even graves would hold the dead,

save for the tenderness in my motherly heart!
Woe to one not longing for life!
Let him beware the curse of extinction!"

On an autumn night laden with boredom,
I was so drunk on starlight my sadness drank too.
I asked the dark
"Does life return the spring of youth
once it is withered?"
The lips of darkness did not move,
nor did the virginal dawn.
Then the forest gently spoke
like the quiver of a chord:
"Winter comes, winter of mist,
winter of snow, winter of rain,
and magic dissolves.
What budded and ripened,
the gleaming angles of fields
and quiet magic of the sky –
gone like branches
that fall with their leaves.
Now the wind tosses dead petals,
the flood buries them haphazardly.
All perish like a lovely dream
which shimmered in some heart then
disappeared.
Only the seeds remain, kernels of memory,
still embracing, even under the fog, the
snows,
the heaps of earth –
the shadow of life that never palls,
the green germ of spring
dreaming of birdcall,
the musk of flowers, the tang of fruit."

✳✳✳

The diaphanous night revealed a Beauty
that kindled the mind.
A strange magic was flung across the skies
as a giant wizard lit the glittering stars.
Incense drifted from flowers on the moon's
quiet wings ...
a holy hymn ringing out in a temple!
Across the universe it was proclaimed:
Endeavour is the flame of life,
the heart of victory.
If the spirit chooses life,
Fate is certain to respond!

From Songs of Life, *translated by Lena
Jayyusi and Naomi Shihab Nye
(Beit al-Hikma, Carthage, 1987)*

ALI DU'AJI

*Another member of the same Tunis literary circle, **Ali Du'aji** (1909–49) wrote plays, stories and songs, and edited literary journals. Like al-Shabbi, he wrote in Arabic but read much foreign literature: Chekhov, Flaubert, Jack London and Mark Twain. Twain's influence in particular is detectable in the ironic modern tone of Du'aji's observations of contemporary urban life. One of his most striking works, "Bar-Hopping Along the Mediterranean", a series of sketches describing a Mediterranean cruise in 1933, offers a rare glimpse of the dominant European culture through Tunisian eyes.*

"At the Beach at Hammam-Lif", the short sketch reprinted here, is typical of Du'aji's portraits of everyday Tunisian life. Deceptively casual, it carries more weight than might at first appear. Its narrator, rootless and anonymous in the crowd, shares the dreamy alienation of Albert Camus' Outsider, while the switches in cultural reference – from Romeo and Juliet to the palace of the Alhambra in Granada – betray a Western and Arab duality. In just a few elegant paragraphs, Du'aji conveys the complex texture of Tunis's new urban culture: simultaneously old and new, Arab and Western.

AT THE BEACH AT HAMMAM-LIF

The car on the train was packed with a very heavy woman, and heavy she was! Added to her weight, she wore a red cape, the same colour as her lips and fingernails. Just as she filled the car with her flesh, she filled it with her movements, and with her son too. Wouldn't you know, her son had a big fat head and he too was wearing red. I imagined that wearing red and being fat ran in the family. The kid was screaming like he was crying, but he wasn't crying at all. Everyone in the car was bothered by the screaming. They just wanted to keep him happy by giving him what he wanted. The questions kept coming. One person asked him what he wanted; another bounced him on his knee; a third patted him on the nose. But the kid got angrier and screamed all the more, as though he were screaming just for the sake of screaming. He didn't want a sandwich, he didn't want a toy horn. To tell the truth, twenty minutes was all I could take of this little brat, and I decided to move to another car.

I didn't see anyone at first, and I went in thinking the coast was clear. That is, until I walked past the second compartment where I found a young couple whom we would classically refer to as "Romeo and Juliet". Romeo was over six feet tall, gaunt and very pale, with a long nose. He looked like a poet. Juliet was Sicilian, medium height, and wearing bright yellow, the way a king would wear an ermine robe. They were speaking in whispers and moving their hands a lot to overcome the loud noise around them. Romeo would put up his hands, then pull his left hand forward as though he were saying: "I love you and I'll kill your father with a dagger if ..." Juliet was rolling her fingers around as though she were answering: "I'll embroider you a scarf that you'll be proud to wear in front of the vice-consul."

It was unbearable, sitting next to a pair of lovers, seeing and hearing only gestures ... And for this I took the train? Yes, I took it to go to Hammam-Lif. What was important was that I get there. So I decided to leave all the cars altogether, sit out the journey on one of the car steps watching the telegraph poles and counting them where I could.

From the station to the beach, I walked quickly so I could get to see the bathers. What's nice is that it's not just the "nose" beach, but every-other-part-of-the-body beach as well, the thigh beach and the breast beach and ... and ... and ...

The beach was full of peanut and lemonade vendors, and of bathers too, and wonderful white sheets.

The peanut and lemonade vendors are notorious for their filthiness and arrogance. As for the bathers, men and women alike, stripped of their clothes and their modesty, they feel the heat at times and throw themselves into the water. When they get cold in the water, they stretch out exposing their bodies, catching the rays of the sun. And there they were, all day long, between hot and cold.

Tradition has it that a person who bathes all day long is considered one of the "in-crowd", while the person who gives up and gets dressed after half an hour is considered an outsider.

The white sheets are something else. Those wrapped up in them are creatures who follow the tradition of their grandmothers, covering their soft bodies. Keeping up with the times, they come out to the beach mocking this one's hair-do and that one's wrinkled trousers. There's

one who forgets that she's veiled and shows you her pretty face. Then she remembers and disappears under her veil after electrically charging up four young men on the beach who had been watching her all the while.

Walking along that road I was imagining all those bodies dressed in Andalusian clothes with wide pantaloons, belly dancing in a courtyard at al-Hambra. Then, all of a sudden, a bird drilling in air manoeuvres dropped a bomb on my fez that I didn't notice. If it weren't for the passers-by laughing and pointing at my venerable head, I wouldn't have realized that there was something there that was arousing the curiosity of all these distinguished people. I took off the fez and found it decorated from that damned bird's bomb. Who was it who described the bird as an angel? If I found him, I'd show him a devil.

It was better that I not stay at Hammam-Lif nor at "the pool" after it got out that I was wearing the target for bird manoeuvres on my head. So I headed back. By the grace of God I found the train empty except for an old man who knew every single villa along the tracks that ran from Hammam-Lif to Tunis.

From Sleepless Nights, *translated by William Granara (Beit al-Hikma, Carthage, 1991)*

MUSTAPHA TLILI

Educated in Paris and the US and a resident of New York, **Mustapha Tlili** *(born 1937) writes – unlike al-Shabbi and Du'aji – in French. Lion Mountain, first published in 1988, was his fourth novel. Set in an anonymous village, it is a stark exploration of national identity in post-colonial North Africa. Represented by the narrator's mother Horia and her Nubian steward Saad, who lost a leg at the Battle of Monte Cassino in World War II, the villagers share a strong sense of local identity and history. Though barely affected by the French, after Independence their community is threatened by the new State's demand for central control, and the story's violent ending has a sense of tragic inevitability.*

In the extract that follows, the village receives its first representative of the new Independent government.

LION MOUNTAIN

The delegate, the new authorities' very first representative in Lion Mountain, wanted to enrol all adult males in the Party. The portrait Saad draws of him is hardly flattering. A short, slightly built young man, it seems. His forehead is low and narrow. He has a thin moustache. Like one of those circumflex accents Little Brother used to pen so neatly but with too much ink when he was still at school, the moustache sits upon a dry and bony face deeply pitted by smallpox. Petty malevolence made flesh and blood.

And the man appears to be very full of himself. Always sprucely turned out, with a perpetually dashing air. He invariably wears a three-piece suit of shiny black material. It seems that from the first day, nobody was left in any doubt at all about the man's colossal self-importance, arrogance and conceit, which he shows off at the wheel of a luxurious black Citroën, driving with ostentation and contempt through the narrow, stony streets of our poor little village at breakneck speed, making an incredible racket and leaving behind great clouds of dust.

As soon as he took charge of the Delegation, which had remained unoccupied for more than a year, our little village tyrant, who thirsted for influence and authority, selected – out of all the possible candidates to fill the office of public crier – Horia's retarded farmhand. Who would ever have imagined it?

And so from dawn to dusk for three days running, the Simpleton shouted his lungs out in every corner of Lion Mountain: in the Spring, our former French quarter; in the old village, from house to house and in front of every street stall; even at the doors of the mosque, as well as for the benefit of the ruminating camels in the livestock market, the exhausted mules and donkeys brutalized by the heat and human stupidity, assorted skeletal stray dogs, and the cackling chickens roaming freely over Highway 15 as it lay dreaming in the spring sunshine.

And what tidings did this inspired messenger bring? That the Party was the Motherland. That everyone should prove his great worth by acquiring a Party card – upon payment of a certain sum, of course. And no holdouts, or else! Recalcitrants risked losing their share of irrigation water. Close scrutiny would unmask the guilty ones.

Since what was at stake was the life or death of their crops and tiny plots of land, the source of all wellbeing for them and theirs, all male adults had felt they had no other choice but to accept their fate and trudge off, one by one, heads bowed in resignation, to the former police station now serving as headquarters for the new authorities.

Horia's property was upstream, however, and too close to the spring to risk being deprived of its fair share of water. Following the example of the other villagers, and just to be on the safe side, Saad had nevertheless thought it wise to ask Imam Sadek for his advice. The latter, after careful consideration, had confirmed the Nubian's original opinion. No, Horia and Saad weren't at risk, that was quite true. Still, it was better to be practical, after all, and cooperate with the authorities. In a word, to avoid unnecessary complications, the imam had advised against causing any trouble, because he, too, was beginning to be apprehensive about the future.

As always, however, Saad will end up doing exactly as he pleases. As always, he'll insist on seeing things only in their simplest, most essential light. And to get to the heart of a problem, he had decided there was only one way to go.

His reasoning was crystal clear. The house isn't on fire, he told himself. The village is in no danger, right? Now, he, Saad, learned all he needs to know about danger at Monte Cassino. No one, and certainly not that scarecrow of a petty tyrant at the Delegation, has to cry danger while waving a Party card under his nose. If Horia, if Imam Sadek, or the Ouled El-Gharib clan were threatened, then, yes, it would be understandable. In which case, plenty of people can vouch for the Corporal's courage. Everyone knows what he can do. Even though he has only one leg left, through the fault of the Infidels, nobody doubts that if he had to, he would not hesitate to take up a weapon. Even … to take the machine gun from its hiding place under the ancient mulberry tree, the same gun the Simpleton discovered one day while chasing around after partridges, and which has been kept in perfect shape, unbeknownst to anyone, not even Horia, thanks to his secret but constant attention. No, really, decided the Nubian, the house is not on fire. Thank the Party anyway for having thought of him. And thanks also to Monsieur the Delegate and Madame the Motherland. It's very nice, all that, but really, no thanks.

From Lion Mountain, *translated by Linda Coverdale (Little Brown, 1990)*

BOOKS

Publishing details below give the British, then US publisher, where both exist. Books designated o/p are currently out of print, but still worth tracking down secondhand or in libraries, and some will occasionally be reprinted or published in a new edition.

One firm specializing in reprinting original editions of early travellers' books on North Africa is Darf (227 West End Lane, London NW6 1QS; ☎020/7431 7009, ℱ7431 7655). The Maghreb Bookshop (45 Burton St, London WC1H 9AL, ☎020/7388 1840), the English-speaking world's main specialist on the Maghreb, has a wide range of titles, including many out of print, and also publishes the *Maghreb Review*, the most important journal on the Maghrebian countries in English.

TWENTIETH-CENTURY TRAVEL WRITERS

Norman Douglas, *Fountains in the Sand* (OUP, UK, o/p). A bigot, who saw the Chott, like just about everything else in Tunisia, as a symbol for the "sterility of the Arab soul," Douglas nonetheless writes in a compelling style about his travels around the Jerid.

Katy Hounsell-Robert, *Katy in Tunisia* (Nigel Day). A chatty and readable modern account of an Englishwoman's jolly jaunts in Tunisia. At times not very well informed, but easy to identify with when travelling in the country.

Aldous Huxley, "In a Tunisia Oasis" (in *The Olive Tree*; Ayer US). By far the best of a largely barren English tradition of travel writing on Tunisia, despite the snide and rather racist tone. The oasis in question is Nefta.

Reginald Rankin, *Tunisia* (o/p). Wholly eccentric and spiced with prejudice, arrogance and sheer stupidity, but still a good read in spite, or because of, all that.

Sacheverell Sitwell, *Mauretania* (o/p). Written by the aristocratic brother of the more famous Osbert and Edith, a member of the pre-war international glamour set, who played a prolific but insignificant part in the era's travel-writing boom.

EARLY TRAVELLERS

Leo Africanus, *History and Description of Africa* (translated by J. Pory, 1896, o/p). Written by a Spanish Moor who converted to Christianity after being captured at sea by Christian corsairs. He got his nickname from the pope, who encouraged him to write about the Arabs of Barbary. Not surprisingly, there's more than a whiff of propaganda in some of the accounts.

James Bruce, *Travels to Discover the Source of the Nile in the Years 1768–73* (Gregg International, UK). Deleted after the first edition, the Tunisia section is but a small part of this six-volume account of Bruce's journey from Algiers to Ethiopia. His fascination with people's behaviour, brilliantly conveyed in blunt and lively style, makes this some of the most entertaining travel writing ever published.

D. Bruun, *Cave-Dwellers of Southern Tunisia* (Darf, UK). Bruun was one of the first Europeans to live with the people of Matmata and Haddej, and his sympathetic 1898 account retains its interest.

Olfert Dapper, *Africa* (translated by J. Ogilby, 1670, o/p). An encyclopedic compendium of reports culled from many different sources, full of fascinating nuggets.

Alexandre Dumas, *Tangier to Tunis* (Peter Owen, UK, o/p). Dumas is not at his best here, and the editing has shortened the chapters on Tunisia, but there are some amusing vignettes in this rare translation of one of the many French travellers – Dumas visited in 1846.

Sir Harry Johnston, "A Journey Through the Tunisian Sahara" (1898, *Geographic Magazine*, vol. 9). Johnston, though handicapped by a lack of basic knowledge, was one of the first Englishmen to make an effort, during his travels from Jerba to Matmata, to understand the Tunisian people and their way of life.

Lt Col Sir R. Lambert Playfair, *Murray's Handbook for Travellers in Algeria and Tunis* (1891, Murray, o/p). Written by a British consul at Algiers whose unimaginative outlook is redeemed only slightly by his erudition.

Sir Grenville Temple, *Excursions in the Mediterranean* (1835, o/p). An early imperialist view of Tunisia. The author, something of a Romantic artist, produced some unlikely versions of the monuments and scenery he encountered.

ANCIENT HISTORY AND LITERATURE

Saint Augustine, *Confessions* (Penguin, UK/US). The saint's most accessible work, a spiritual auto-biography; **Peter Brown**, *Augustine of Hippo: A Biography* (Penguin, UK/US). Brown's classic biography contains much interesting background material on the Africa of Augustine's time.

Serge Lancel, *Carthage* (Blackwell, UK/US). An authoritative history of Carthage, translated from the French.

Livy, *The War with Hannibal* (Penguin Classic, UK/Viking Press US). One of Flaubert's sources and the classic Roman account of the Carthaginian general whose attempt to take Rome was foiled by the inability of his elephants to negotiate the Alps.

Susan Raven, *Rome in Africa* (Longman, UK/US). A well-illustrated survey of Roman (and Carthaginian) North Africa.

Sallust, *The Jugurthine War* (Penguin, UK/Viking Press US). Concise but entertaining and at times rather melodramatic account by a Roman histori-an of the war between the Numidian king Jugurtha and the Roman Army under Marius.

David Soren et al., *Carthage* (Norton, o/p/, Touchstone, o/p). Written by Carthage archeolo-gists to accompany a museum exhibition that toured North America, this is a very readable introduction to the Carthaginian and Roman cul-tures of ancient Tunisia.

Virgil, *The Aeneid* (Penguin, UK/US). Books I and IV of the great Roman epic poem tell the tragic love story of Queen Dido (founder of Carthage) and Aeneas (founder of Rome), an inspiration to artists of every age since.

TUNISIAN AND ARAB HISTORY

Jamil M. Abun-Nasr, *A History of the Maghreb in the Islamic Period* (CUP, UK). An authoritative history of the region by a distinguished Lebanese historian, but not exactly light reading.

Lisa Anderson, *The State and Social Transfor-mation in Tunisia and Libya, 1830–1980* (Princeton University Press, UK/US, o/p). Don't be put off by the academic title, as this is a good review of Tunisian and Libyan political and social history.

Ernle Bradford, *The Sultan's Admiral* (Hodder and Stoughton, UK, o/p). A very readable biog-

raphy of Khair ed Din Barbarossa, giving an excellent taste of the corsair rivalries of the six-teenth century.

Leon Carl Brown, *The Tunisia of Ahmed Bey, 1837–1856* (Princeton University Press, US, o/p). A fascinating insight into nineteenth-century Tunisia and the problems faced by an Arab gov-ernment struggling to keep itself out of European clutches.

Julia A. Clancy-Smith, *Rebel and Saint* (California UP, UK/US). Subtitled "Muslim Notables, Popular Protest, Colonial Encounters (Algeria and Tunisia 1900–4)", this book looks at local community leaders and their reaction to colonial rule at the beginning of the twentieth century.

Albert Hourani, *A History of the Arab Peoples* (Faber/Harvard UP). If you have the time to read it, this expansive and panoramic view of Arab history is the best available.

Charles-André Julien, *History of North Africa from the Arab Conquest to 1830* (Routledge o/p). An easier read than Abun Nasr, which it compli-ments well, although the last English version was in 1970 (updated editions are available in French).

Ibn Khaldoun, *The Muqaddimah* (Routledge, UK/US). A translation, by N.J. Dawood, of the masterpiece by Tunisia's great fourteenth-cen-tury historian, whose fascinating mix of sociolo-gy, history and anthropology was centuries ahead of its time.

Wifrid Knapp, *Tunisia* (Thames & Hudson, UK, o/p). The most worthwhile of several introduc-tory history-background books that came out in the 1960s and 1970s.

Peter Mansfield, *The Arabs* (Penguin, UK/US). By far the best introduction to the Arab world available. A general history of the region, from Islam's beginnings to the late 1970s, followed by a short section on each country and two excellent concluding chapters: "Through European Eyes" and "Through Arab Eyes".

Arthur Marsden, *British Diplomacy and Tunis, 1875–1902* (Scottish Academic Press, UK, o/p). If you want to see how devious and calculating the foreign powers were in dividing up the Mediterranean, then this is the book to read – very scholarly but never dry.

Charles Messenger, *The Tunisian Campaign* (Ian Allan, UK, o/p). A pictorial history of World War II in Tunisia.

Magali Morsy, *North Africa 1800–1900: A Survey from the Nile Valley to the Atlantic* (Longman, UK/US, o/p). An excellent history of North Africa in a period of crisis, placing Tunisia in the context of North Africa as a whole.

Richard Pean, *Islamic Tunisia, Tunisia under the Beys, Saharan Tunisia, Tunisia's Berber Heritage, Roman and Punic Tunisia, Ancient Tunisia* (Regie 3, Tunisia only). A series of six highly informative souvenir booklets for tourists in Tunisia, published in English and other languages by the National Heritage Agency, illustrating the country's rich architectural and cultural heritage from different periods in the country's history, with colour plates throughout.

Kenneth J. Perkins, *Historical Dictionary of Tunisia* (Scarecrow, US). A concise but comprehensive reference book on the history of Tunisia, mainly since the Arab invasion, but also covering earlier periods.

W. Perkins, *Tunisia: Crossroads of the Islamic and European Worlds* (Scarecrow, UK/US). The best pocket history of Tunisia available. Authoritative and a good read.

Samir Radwan, Vali Jamal and Ajit Ghose, *Tunisia: Rural Labour and Social Transformation* (Routledge, UK). Lots of graphs and statistics in this analytical appraisal of the Tunisian economy and its development since the 1960s. Very detailed, and not a light read.

Barnaby Rogerson, *A Traveller's History of North Africa: Morocco, Tunisia, Libya, Algeria* (Windrush Press, UK). A welcoming key to unlock the complexities of this area's culture and way of life.

MODERN LITERATURE

If you read French, look out for the publications of Éditions Sindbad and Éditions Salammbô in Tunisia. They publish contemporary writers in their original language and in translation. Tunisian literature in English is rare.

Abou el Kacem Chabbi, *Songs of Life* (Beit Al-Hikma, Carthage). Poetry doesn't translate any better from Arabic than from other languages, but this does at least provide a sense of the Romantic sensibility of Tunisia's national poet (see p.480).

Hedi Bouraoui, *Return to Thyna* (York University Bookstore, Canada). Bouraoui, who writes in French, is one of Tunisia's most well-known novelists, but this is his only work that has been published in English.

Ali Du'aji, *Sleepless Nights* (Beit Al-Hikma, Carthage). Short sketches by the mid-century writer, translated – unusually – into English (see p.481).

Gustave Flaubert, *Salammbô* (Penguin, UK/US). Sex, violence and more violence in Flaubert's "historical" account of Carthage's brutal civil war with its Mercenaries (241–237 BC), which really owes less to history than to its author's obsession with the fabulous Orient. An extraordinarily bad novel, but a very enjoyable read – see pp.478–479 for an excerpt.

André Gide, *Amyntas* (J. Lane, o/p/Ecco Press). An early work by the French writer whose experiences in the North African colonies (including meeting Oscar Wilde) were a lasting influence.

Gisèle Halimi, *Milk for the Orange Tree* (Quartet, UK/US). Halimi is a Jewish civil rights lawyer in France, part of whose autobiographical account paints a picture of her childhood in Tunisia.

Monia Hejaiej, *Behind Closed Doors* (Quartet, UK/Rutgers US). A compilation by a Tunisian-American researcher of traditional women's oral literature in the form of tales by three expert storytellers from Tunis, reflecting their very different attitudes to life, love, sex and social norms.

Patricia Highsmith, *The Tremor of Forgery* (Penguin/Grove Atlantic). Set in 1960s Hammamet, this is a characteristically creepy piece of work by the author of the Ripley books. Although Graham Greene described it as her finest novel, it is only intermittently available.

Sabiha Khemir, *Waiting in the Future for the Past to Come* (Quartet, UK/US). A novel written – unusually – in English by a Tunisian author, consisting of a series of interconnected stories about an imaginary coastal town called Korba during the decades following Independence.

Amin Maalouf, *Leo the African* (Abacus/New Amsterdam). An interesting attempt by a Lebanese writer at the fictional autobiography of Leo Africanus, the Christian convert whose career mirrors the to-and-fro of the sixteenth-century Mediterranean (see p.484).

Albert Memmi, *Colonizer and the Colonized* (Earthscan/Beacon); *The Pillar of Salt* (Elek, o/p/Beacon). Tunisia's most distinguished novelist, whose main theme is the problem of identity for North African Jews such as himself. Other books of his available in English include *The Scorpion* (O'Hara, US) and *Jews and Arabs* (O'Hara, US).

Mustapha Tlili, *Lion Mountain* (Arcade, UK/US). Excellent characterization in this short novel about the tragic effects of progress, tourism and dictatorship on a remote Tell village (see pp.482–483).

ISLAM AND SOCIETY

The Koran (Penguin, UK/US; OUP, o/p). The word of God as handed down to the Prophet Mohammed is the basis of all Islam, and notoriously untranslatable. The OUP translation is better than N. J. Dawood's stultifyingly prosaic Penguin version. Other popular translations are by Marmaduke Pickthal (Kitab Bhavan) and by Abdallah Yusuf Ali (Wordsworth).

Nadia Abu Zahra, *Sidi Ameur: a Tunisian Village* (Ithaca Press, UK). Account by an Egyptian anthropologist of a village near Monastir in 1965–8, examining social change and village traditions. Especially good on the lifestyle of local women.

François Burgat, *The Islamists in North Africa* (Texas UP, US). Slightly dated but still highly relevant examination of Islamic fundamentalism as a political movement in the region.

Jean Duvignaud, *Change at Shebika* (Allen Lane, o/p/ Texas UP, o/p). An account by one of a group of French and Tunisian sociologists who spent a year in Chebika in the 1960s when it was an isolated village, describing the position of women, families, religion and work, but most of all the impact of social change on local tradition.

Jacques Jomier, *How to Understand Islam* (Crossroads, UK/US). A comprehensive, readable introduction to Islam and what it's about.

N. Minai, *Women in Islam* (John Murray, o/p/Putnam, o/p). A historical survey and an analysis of contemporary Arab society, looking at the changing status of women from the time of Mohammed, plus the customs and traditions at each stage of a woman's life in different Muslim countries.

Samir Radman, Vali Jamal and Ajit Ghose, *Tunisia – Rural Labour and Structural Transformation* (Routledge, 1991). A study of the Tunisian economy in the 1970s and 1980s, analysing the causes of its boom and decline.

Edward Said, *Orientalism: Western Concepts of the Orient* (Penguin/Random House). An analysis of Western attitudes to the Arab world, attacking the endemic racism of Western "experts" and showing how the myth of "The Orient" was created and fostered by colonialism.

Lucette Valensi and Abraham Udovitch, *The Last Arab Jews* (Gordon and Breach, US). The definitive study of the Jerban community, its history, sociology and prospects. Good illustrations too. Lucette Valensi has also written *Tunisian Peasants in the Eighteenth and Nineteenth Centuries* (CUP, UK).

Mia Zussman, *Development and Disenchantment in Rural Tunisia – The Bourguiba Years* (Westview Press, UK/US). A detailed ethnographic study of the north Tunisian town of Mejerda during the Bourguiba era.

ART AND ARCHITECTURE

Michael Brett, *The Moors* (Orbis, o/p/Salem House, o/p). A glossy picture book on the western Arabs, with an unusually well-informed text by an expert in the field. A good investment.

T. Burkhardt, *Art of Islam* (World of Islam Festival Publishing, UK, o/p). A highly conceptual and impressionistic account of the relationship between Islamic doctrine and its art. Some of the best illustrations around, even if the text is at times hard to grasp.

R. Dunbabih, *The Mosaics of Roman North Africa* (Clarendon Press, US, o/p). Dry and academic, this is unfortunately the only work in English on Tunisia's Roman mosaics.

Georges Fradier and André Martin, *Mosaiques Romaines de Tunisie* (Cérès editions, Tunisia). A coffee-table book of all those wonderful mosaics, and a great souvenir. The text is in French, but it's the pictures you really want.

Derek Hill and Lucien Golvin, *Islamic Architecture of North Africa* (Faber, o/p/Shoe String Press, o/p). It's a sad comment that this is the best available introduction to Tunisian architecture. Intended originally as an artists' guide to Islamic patterns, the pictures are numerous but of variable quality; the fuller historical introduction and notes on individual buildings are useful.

Anthony Hutt, *Islamic Architecture – North Africa* (Scorpion, UK, o/p). Little more than a picture book, but almost unique in its focus on the region.

LANGUAGE

Arabic is a notoriously difficult language for Westerners to learn, and further complicated by its variation from country to country within the Arab world, not only in pronunciation but in vocabulary. Fortunately, however, Tunisia is virtually bilingual, and even in the remotest of places you will find someone who can also speak French. With even basic school-knowledge French you'll find you can get by quite well.

For all this, though, French was the language of colonialism and any attempt at Arabic – even the most stumbling – will be well received. Included here are some very basic words and phrases; if you want to learn seriously, the Bourguiba School in Tunis (see p.104) is highly recommended and exceptional value.

TUNISIAN ARABIC

The transliteration is highly approximate, and intended to function phonetically. "Kh" represents a sound like the "ch" in loch, while "gh" represents a sort of gargling sound like a French "r".

BASICS

Yes	*Ayi, Aiwa*	We	*Ihna*
No	*La*	You (plural)	*Intoo*
Please	*Minfadlik**	They	*Hoom*
Thank you	*BarkAllahufik*,*	There's, Is there?,	*Famma(?)*
	Shukran	There are, Are there?	
Excuse me	*Samahanee*	There isn't, There aren't	*Famma aysh*
I	*Ana*	Good	*Behi*
You	*Inti, Inta**	Not good	*Mish behi, Khayeb*
She	*Hiya*	A lot	*Barsha, Yasser*
He	*Huwa*	A little	*Shwaya*

DIRECTIONS AND TRAVELLING

Is there a … near here?	*Fee … qareb min hina?*	Right	*Limin*
Where is the …?	*Fayn el …?*	Near	*Qareb*
Hotel	*Nezel*	Far	*Bayeed*
Restaurant	*Mataam*	Here	*Hina*
Bank	*Bunk*	There	*Radi, Hinik**
Train (station)	*(Mahata el) tran*	When?	*Waqtesh?*
Bus (station)	*(Mahata el) car*	First	*El uwel*
Museum	*Methab*	Next	*El jai*
Ruin	*Athar*	Last	*El akher*
Toilet	*Mihath*	Could you write it please?	*Yoomkintnajim tek*
Straight on	*Tul*		*tabah minfadlik?**
Left	*Lisaar*		

*In theory, there are two singular forms of "you": inti when addressing a woman and inta when addressing a man. In most of Tunisia, however, inti is used for everyone (to the shocked surprise of non-Tunisian Arab men). A lot of words referring to "you" end in -ik; strictly speaking, when addressing a man this should be -ak.

ARABIC NUMBERS

1	Wahad	10	Ashara	100	Mia
2	Zous, Etneen	20	Ashreen	200	Miateen
3	Tlaata	30	Talaateen	300	Tlaata mia
4	Arbaa	40	Arabaeen	400	Arba mia
5	Khamsa	50	Khamseen	1000	Alf
6	Sitta	60	Sitteen	2000	Alfayn
7	Sabaa	70	Sabaeen	5000	Khams alef
8	Tmaania	80	Temaaneen		
9	Tissa	90	Tissaeen		

GREETINGS AND FAREWELLS

Hello	Assalama	Goodbye	Bisalama, Filaman
Good morning	Sabah el khir	My name's ...	Ismi ...
(response)	(Sabah en nour)	What's your name?	Sismik?*
Good evening	Missa el khir	Where are you from?	Mineen inti?, Mineen inta?*
(response)	(Missa en nour)		
How are you?	Ashnooa ahwalik*	I'm from ...	Ana min ...
Fine, thanks	Labes elhamdulillah	Bon voyage	Treq salama
And you?	Winti?, Winta?*	See you later	N'shoofik* minbad
Good night	Tisbah ala khir		

SHOPPING AND ACCOMMODATION

Have you got ...?	Andik*...?	(Too) expensive	Ghalee (barsha)
A room	Bit, Ghorfa	Still expensive	Mazal ghalee
A shower	Doosh	Have you got anything ...?	'Andik*haja...?
Hot	Skhoon	better	...khir
Cold	Biird	... cheaper	...arkhis
Can I have a ...?	Yoomkin wahad ...?	... bigger	...akbar
Can I buy ...?	Yoomkin ashtiri ...?	... smaller	... asghar
Can I see ...?	Yoomkin ashoofa ...?	I haven't got any	Ma'andish
How much is ...?	Kaddesh ...?	Open	Mahloul
This	Hada	Closed	Msaker
That	Hadik*		

OTHER COMMON OR USEFUL EXPRESSIONS

Slowly	Shwaya shwaya		the future, repeated in response)
Go away	Imshi, Barra		
Later	Minbad	In the name of God	Bismillah (used when starting a meal or journey)
Never mind	Maalesh		
The same	Kif kif		
Praise be to God	El Hamdulillah (used whenever mentioning any kind of good fortune, repeated in response)	Money	Floos
		Let's go!	Yalla, Nimshi!
		Chill out	Wasa balek (lit: "lengthen your mind")
		Shame on you!	Shooma!
		I don't know	Ma'arfsh, Mish 'arif
God willing	Insh'Allah (used in any reference to hopes or	I don't understand	Mefehemsh, Mish fehem

TIME AND DAYS

What time is it?	*Kaddesh loweqet?*	Now	*El an*
One o'clock	*El wahad*	Later	*Minbad*
Five past one	*El wahad wa draj*	Today	*El yoom*
Ten past one	*El wahad wa darjeen*	Tomorrow	*Ghudwa*
Quarter past one	*El wahad warbo'o*	Yesterday	*El barah*
Twenty past one	*El wahad warba'a*	Sunday	*El had*
Twenty-five past one	*El wahad wa khamsa*	Monday	*El tneen*
Half-past one	*El wahad wa nuss*	Tuesday	*El tlata*
Twenty-five to two	*El wahad wa sabaa*	Wednesday	*El arba*
Twenty to two	*El etneen ghir arba'a*	Thursday	*El khemis*
Quarter to two	*El etneen ghir arbo'o*	Friday	*Ej jemaa*
Ten to two	*El etneen ghir darjeen*	Saturday	*Es sebt*
Five to two	*El etneen ghir draj*		

FRENCH ESSENTIALS

BASICS AND GREETINGS

Yes, No	*Oui, Non*	Thank you	*Merci*
Good morning	*Bonjour*	Could you?	*Pourriez-vous?*
Good evening	*Bonsoir*	Why?	*Pourquoi?*
Good night	*Bonne nuit*	What?	*Quoi?*
Sorry, Excuse me	*Pardon*	Open	*Ouvert*
How are you?	*Ça va?*	Closed	*Fermé*
Goodbye	*Au revoir*	Go away!	*Va-t-en!*
Please	*S'il vous plaît*	Stop messing me about!	*Arrête de m'emmerder!*

DIRECTIONS

Where is the road for ...?	*Quelle est la route pour ...?*	Far	*Loin*
Where is ...?	*Où est ...?*	When?	*Quand?*
Do you have ...?	*Avez vous ...?*	At what time?	*À quelle heure?*
... a room?	*...une chambre?*	Write it down, please	*Écrivez-le, s'il vous plaît*
Here, There	*Ici, Là*	Now	*Maintenant*
Right	*À droite*	Later	*Plus tard*
Left	*À gauche*	Never	*Jamais*
Straight on	*Tout droit*	Today	*Aujourd'hui*
Near	*Proche, Près*	Tomorrow	*Demain*
		Yesterday	*Hier*

BUYING

How much/many?	*Combien?*	Like this/that	*Comme ceci/cela*
How much does that cost?	*Combien ça coute?*	What is it?	*Qu'est-ce que c'est?*
Too expensive	*Trop cher*	Enough	*Assez*
More, Less	*Plus, Moins*	Big	*Grand*
Cheap	*Bon marché*	Little	*Petit*

TRAVEL ESSENTIALS

Passport	*Passeport*	Train station	*Gare*
Currency exchange	*Change*	Ferry	*Bac*
Post office	*Poste, PTT*	Lorry	*Camion*
Stamps	*Timbres-postes*	Ticket (return)	*Billet (de retour)*
Left luggage	*Consigne*	Bank	*Banque*
Bus	*Car, Autobus*	Key	*Clé*
Bus station	*Gare routière*	Roof	*Terrasse d'équipage*
Railway	*Chemin de fer*	Visa	*Visa*
Airport	*Aéroport*	Money	*Argent*

GESTURES

Tunisians are great **gesticulators**. The classic motion involves joining thumb and fingertips and holding the hand upwards; thoroughly infectious, this sign can mean almost anything, depending on the circumstances. Waved fiercely it conveys impatience; held quietly it means wait, patience; and shaken deliberately in conversation it claims ultimate authority for what's being said. As elsewhere in the Middle East, and round much of the Mediterranean, the word "no" is accompanied by a click of the tongue and toss of the head – flourishes which can at first seem contemptuously dismissive, but aren't intended that way. Also apt to be confusing is "come this way": the beckoning hand pointing downward, it often looks as though you're being told to go away. Sex in general is indicated by cutting one hand against the other.

GLOSSARY

ABBASIDS Dynasty of Caliphs who ruled the Arab Empire from Baghdad 749–1258.

AGHLABIDS Arab dynasty, ruled northern and central Tunisia from Kairouan 800–909.

AH *Anno Hegirae* (after the Hegira), Islamic date, the equivalent of AD, dated from Mohammed's flight to Medina (see p.458).

AÏN Spring.

ALMOHADS Religious movement from Morocco, which came to control the whole Maghreb, from Marrakesh to Tunisia, in the twelfth century.

ALMORAVIDS Dynasty which ruled Morocco in the eleventh century and invaded Tunisia in the twelfth.

ARIANISM Christian heresy followed by the Vandals, based on an attempt to reconcile Christianity with Germanic pagan religions.

ASM Association de Sauvegarde de la Medina, an organization dedicated to preserving the architectural heritage of old Arab towns.

AUTOGARE Bus and louage station.

BAB Door or gate.

BAKSHEESH Alms or tips.

BARBARY European term for North Africa in the sixteenth to nineteenth centuries.

BASILICA Roman building type with aisles, later used for churches.

BERBERS The non-Arab native inhabitants of North Africa since about 4000 BC, speaking their own language. Very few pure Berbers survive in Tunisia, though they form the majority in Morocco and Algeria.

BEY Ottoman official, in practice the ruler of Tunisia in the eighteenth and nineteenth centuries (the adjective is "beylical").

BIR Hole in the ground.

BORJ Fort.

BOURNOUSE Long woollen or camel-hair men's outer garment, often with hood.

BYZANTINE The continuation of the Roman Empire in the East, ruled from Byzantium (now Istanbul), which controlled Tunisia 533–646 AD.

CAMIONETTE Pick-up truck, often used as a form of transport in remote rural areas.

CALDARIUM Hot room in a Roman bath.

CALÈCHE Horse-drawn tourist carriage.

CAPITAL Stone "cushion" at the top of a column or pillar.

CAPITOL Central temple of a Roman town equivalent to a cathedral.

CARTHAGE Phoenician colony founded around the ninth century BC, which became capital of the Carthaginian Empire finally defeated by Rome and destroyed in 146BC, but later refounded as a Roman city.

CELLA Inner sanctuary of a temple.

CHÉCHIA Red felt hat, like a soft fez.

CHICHA (sheesha) Café water pipe.

CHOTT Flat dry area; refers to salt lakes and occasionally beaches.

CORSAIRS Muslim and Christian pirates who operated in the Mediterranean from the thirteenth to the nineteenth centuries.

CROISEMENT Road junction, turn-off.

DAR House or palace.

DEY Ottoman military officer of junior rank. Their control of troops meant they effectively ruled Tunisia in the early seventeenth century.

DONATISM Fourth- or fifth-century dissident Christian church set up to avoid "contamination" by insincere Catholic priests.

DRIBA Entrance hall.

EL QUDS (El Qods, El Quods, El Kuds) Jerusalem, the third holy city of Islam.

ERG Sand desert.

ENNAHDHA Hizb en Nahdha – illegal fundamentalist political party.

FATIMIDS Dynasty of Ismaili Shi'ite Muslims who ruled Tunisia from Mahdia 909–984, and Egypt 961–1171.

FORUM Enclosed open space at the centre of a Roman town.

FONDOUK Inn, storehouse and sometimes trading base, known as a caravanserai in the eastern part of the Arab world.

FRIGIDARIUM Cold room in Roman bath.

GARGOTE Cheap restaurant or café.

GHAR Cave.

GHORFA Room – refers in particular to the cells used to store grain inside a *ksar*.

GHRIBA Ancient Jewish synagogue.

HADITH Statements of the Prophet Mohammed as reported by his Companions

HAFSIDS Dynasty that ruled Tunisia from Tunis 1207–1574. Originally governors for the Almohads, they declared independence in 1236 when the Marrakesh regime ditched Ibn Tumart's teachings, and were widely seen as the Almohads' true heirs.

HAJ (hadj) Pilgrimage to Mecca, or someone who has made this journey (older people are politely assumed to have done it, and so are addressed as *haj*).

HAMADA Stony desert.

HAMMAM (Turkish) bath.

HANEFITE One of the four schools of orthodox Sunni Islam, founded in the eighth century. Widespread in Anatolia and brought by the Turks to North Africa, the school's mosques are distinguished by octagonal minarets. The school is less austere than the native Malekite school, laying some stress on commercial success.

HILALIANS (Banu Hilal) Nomadic Arabs who invaded Tunisia in the eleventh century, were outside the control of its Zirid rulers, and severely disrupted its infrastructure.

HIZB EN NAHDHA (Renewal Party) Illegal fundamentalist political party, formerly the MTI.

HOUCH Jerban house, which looks like a small fortress (see p.378).

HUSAYNIDS Dynasty of Beys who ruled Tunisia from 1705 until (nominally) 1956.

HYPOSTYLE Hall supported by pillars, as in many prayer halls of mosques.

IBADITE Member of the main branch of Kharijism.

IMAM Roughly the Islamic equivalent of a Protestant pastor; leads the congregation of a mosque in prayer.

IMPASSE Blind alley.

INFIRMERIE Clinic staffed by nurses for dealing with general medical complaints.

ISMAILI Shi'a splinter formed on the death of the sixth Shi'ite Imam (equivalent to the Sunni Caliph), which claimed that only descendants of his son Ismail could be given the title of Imam.

JEBEL (djebel) Mountain.

JEMA'A (Djema'a) Great Mosque, or Friday Mosque (*Grande Mosquée*), the central place of worship in any town. During the week citizens may worship at *masjids*, smaller local mosques, but on Fridays they worship together at the *jemaa*, to hear the imam's homily.

KALA'A Stone hillfort.

KASBAH Administrative centre and/or fort of an Arab town.

KEF Rock.

KHARIJITES The "Secessionists", an early heretical sect, still surviving in Jerba, which found eager adherents among the Berbers in the first years of the Arab conquest (see p.383).

KHOURASSINIDS Dynasty of princes who ruled the Tunis region during the eleventh century.

KOUBBA Dome, the correct name for the tomb of a marabout.

KOUTTAB Koranic primary school.

KSAR/KSOUR (plural). Communal fortified granary built mainly in the south.

LALLA Female saint.

LIMES (pronounced "lee-mess") Chain of forts built along the frontier of the Roman Empire.

LOUAGE Service taxi (see p.24).

LTDH Ligue Tunisienne des Droits de l'Homme, Tunisian human rights group, barely tolerated by the government.

MAGHREB "West" in Arabic, used of the countries of the Maghrebine confederation (Morocco, Algeria, Tunisia, Libya and Mauritania), especially the first three.

MAHDI The "divinely guided one", Islam's equivalent of the second coming (see p.233). Various people have claimed to be the Mahdi. Three are referred to in this book: Obaidallah, founder of Mahdia and the Fatimid dynasty; Ibn Tumart, founder of the Almohads; and Mohammed Ahmed, who liberated Sudan from the British in 1886.

MALEKITE School of orthodox Sunni Islam, founded at Medina (Arabia) in the eighth century and dominant in North Africa for many centuries, with mosques distinguished by square minarets. More rigorous than the Hanefite, many people consider it the purest school.

MALOUF Andalusian-based traditional folk music.

MAMELUKES Caste of soldiers, originally slaves, who ruled Egypt for 250 years and retained high office in the Ottoman empire.

MARABOUT Holy man, and by extension his place of burial. These tombs, dotted all over the North African countryside, are often centres of cult worship. Marabouts played a vital role in spreading Islam among the Berbers.

MASJID Small local mosque, for everyday (rather than Friday) prayer.

MDS Mouvement des Démocrates Socialistes, legal opposition political party.

MEDERSA (medressa, madrassa) Residential college of Islamic education, usually in the form of a courtyard surrounded by students' cells. These colleges spread throughout the Islamic world from the thirteenth century onwards, generally as state foundations teaching the local orthodoxy.

MENZEL Dwelling place – in Jerba refers to the family *houch* and the enclosure around it.

MIDHA Ritual washing and latrine facility attached to mosque.

MIHRAB Niche indicating the direction of Mecca (and of prayer).

MINARET Tower attached to a mosque from which the *muezzin* gives the call to prayer.

MINBAR Pulpit from which the *imam* delivers homily at Friday prayers in a *jemaa*.

MOUSSEM Annual local celebration held in honour of a marabout.

MR Mouvement de la Rénovation, legal opposition political party.

MTI Mouvement de la Tendance Islamique, illegal fundamentalist political party, renamed Hizb en Nahdaha in 1989.

MUEZZIN Singer who gives the call to prayer.

MURADIDS The first hereditary line of Beys who ruled during the seventeenth century, nominally under the Ottoman sultan.

NADOR Watchtower.

ONA (also ONAT) Organisation Nationale de l'Artisanat (Tunisien*)*. The national crafts organi-

zation: their shops are expensive but useful for pre-bargaining guidelines.

ONTT Office Nationale de Tourisme et Thermalisme (National Office of Tourism and Spas).

OTTOMAN Empire, based in Constantinople (Istanbul) from the fifteenth century to World War I, to which Tunisia belonged as a regency.

OUED (wadi) Creek or seasonal river – may only carry water for a few days a year.

OUERGHAMMA Tribal confederation, based at Ghoumrassen and later Medenine, which dominated the far south of Tunisia from the sixteenth to the nineteenth century (see p.404).

PALAESTRA Roman gymnasium.

PCOT Parti Communiste des Ouvriers Tunisiens, illegal Tunisian Communist party.

PERISTYLE Court enclosed by columns.

PHOENICIANS First great trading nation of Mediterranean history. Originally from what is now Lebanon, they founded trading posts (some of which became the Carthaginian Empire) along the southern Mediterranean coast from around the eleventh century BC.

PRESSING Dry cleaner.

PROTECTORATE The period of French control (1881–1956). The Beys stayed, and French rule was largely indirect and less repressive than in neighbouring Algeria.

PSD Parti Socialiste Destourien, the title of the ruling political party from 1964 (before that it was called the Neo-Destour Party) until 1988, when it was renamed the RCD.

PTT Postes, Télécommunications et Télédiffusion. Post office.

PUBLINET Public internet office.

PUNIC Of Carthaginians and their culture.

PUP Parti de l'Unité Populaire, legal opposition political party.

QIBLA Direction of prayer, physically indicated by the mihrab.

RAS Headland or cape (literally: "head").

RCD Rassemblement Constitutionnel Démocratique, ruling political party, formerly the PSD.

RIBAT Monastic fortress, a building type which sprang up on the North African coast in the ninth century. Marabout originally meant "an inhabitant of a ribat".

RUSTAMIDS Kharijite dynasty who ruled the south of Tunisia from Tahirt (modern Tagdemt in Algeria) 761–909 (see p.217).

SABAT Room built in vault over narrow street.

SAHEL Coast (see p.189).

SCHOLA Institutional Roman building.

SEBKHA Salt-encrusted mud flat.

SHI'A Schismatic Islamic sect whose split from the Sunni majority in the seventh century remains the biggest sectarian division in the faith. Shi'ites emphasized the spiritual side of Islam in reaction to the power of the Umayyad Caliphs (see p.458).

SIDI Lord, saint – title of holy men.

SIFSARI Light women's outer garment wrapped around the body, which can also be used as a veil if held between the teeth. Tunisia's answer to the sari.

SKIFA Narrow passage, entrance, vestibule.

SRT Societé Régionale des Transports (Regional bus company).

SOUK Originally a covered urban market, now used of any kind of market, but especially a weekly one.

STELA Tombstone (plural "stelae").

SUFI Unorthodox sects in Islam which take their teachings, often with mystical associations, from one originating teacher. Some cults spread throughout the Islamic world, transmitted by *zaouias*.

SUNNI Islamic orthodoxy; the vast majority of Muslims are Sunni, though they belong to a particular school, such as the Malekite or Hanefite.

TAXIPHONE Public telephone for national and international calls.

TOPHET Phoenician burial place.

TOURBET Islamic mausoleum.

TRICLINIUM Roman dining room.

TUAREGS Nomadic Saharan Berbers.

UDU Union Démocratique Unioniste, legal opposition political party.

UMA Union du Maghreb Arabe, union of Maghrebian countries (Tunisia, Algeria, Libya, Mauretania and Morocco).

UMAYYADS Dynasty of Caliphs who ruled the Arab Empire from Damascus 661–749. The same family ruled Spain 756–1031.

VANDALS Germanic tribe who sacked Carthage in 439 AD and ruled in Tunisia until 535 (see p.430).

WHITE FATHERS Order of monks cloaked in white *bournouse*-style habits founded in 1870 and based originally in Carthage, later in Thibar.

ZAOUIA A sanctuary around a marabout's tomb, a seminary-type base for his followers, and by extension his followers as a group or cult.

ZIARA Annual local celebration held in honour of a marabout.

ZIRIDS Dynasty that ruled Tunisia in the eleventh century. Originally governors for the Fatimids, they declared independence in 984, but by 1057 ruled not much more than Mahdia.

ZITOUNA Olive tree.

INDEX

The ideas expressed in this code were developed by and for independent travellers.

Learn About The Country You're Visiting
Start enjoying your travels before you leave by tapping into as many sources of information as you can.

The Cost Of Your Holiday
Think about where your money goes - be fair and realistic about how cheaply you travel. Try and put money into local peoples' hands; drink local beer or fruit juice rather than imported brands and stay in locally owned accommodation. Haggle with humour and not aggressively. Pay what something is worth to you and remember how wealthy you are compared to local people.

Embrace The Local Culture
Open your mind to new cultures and traditions. Think carefully about what's appropriate in terms of your clothes and the way you behave. You'll earn respect and be more readily welcomed by local people. Respect local laws and attitudes towards drugs and alcohol that vary in different countries and communities. Think about the impact you could have on them.

Exploring The World – The Travellers' Code
Being sensitive to these ideas means getting more out of your travels - and giving more back to the people you meet and the places you visit.

Minimise Your Environmental Impact
Think about what happens to your rubbish - take biodegradable products and a water filter bottle. Be sensitive to limited resources like water, fuel and electricity. Help preserve local wildlife and habitats by respecting rules and regulations, such as sticking to footpaths and not standing on coral.

Don't Rely On Guidebooks
Use your guidebook as a starting point, not the only source of information. Talk to locals, then discover your own adventure!

Be Discreet With Photography
Don't treat people as part of the landscape, they may not want their picture taken. Ask first and respect their wishes.

Tourism Concern works with people the world over to promote tourism that benefits their communities, but we can only carry on our work with the support of people like you. For membership details or to find out how to make your travels work for local people and the environment, visit our website

www.tourismconcern.org.uk

Tourism Concern
Campaigning for Ethical and Fairly Traded Tourism